ECONOMIC ORGANIZATION
IN CHINESE SOCIETY

Contributors

Lawrence W. Crissman

Donald R. DeGlopper

Craig Dietrich

Mark Elvin

Susan Mann Jones

Thomas A. Metzger

Ramon H. Myers

Stephen M. Olsen

Burton Pasternak

John C. Pelzel

Robert H. Silin

E-tu Zen Sun

Barbara E. Ward

ECONOMIC ORGANIZATION IN CHINESE SOCIETY

Edited by W. E. WILLMOTT

Stanford University Press, Stanford, California 1972

330.951
Ec7
81311
Dec.1972

Stanford University Press, Stanford, California
© 1972 by the Board of Trustees of the Leland Stanford Junior University
Printed in the United States of America
ISBN 0-8047-0794-4   LC 72-153822

Preface

The papers in this volume were presented in their preliminary form to a conference on economic organization in Chinese society that took place at Sainte-Adèle-en-haut, Quebec, in August 1969 under the auspices of the Subcommittee on Research on Chinese Society of the Joint Committee on Contemporary China of the Social Science Research Council (New York) and the American Council of Learned Societies. This conference was one of a series that has become the basis of a Stanford University Press series, Studies in Chinese Society. The present volume is the third in this Stanford series, on which particulars are given opposite.

Apart from the papers published together here, four others were read and discussed at the conference. Christopher Howe, of the School of Oriental and African Studies in London University, read a paper on the employment structure and the sources of labor in Shanghai, 1949–1957, which appears in *The City in Communist China*, edited by John Lewis, in the Stanford series referred to above. Carl Riskin's excellent paper on small-scale local industry in contemporary China appears in *China Quarterly* 46 (April–June, 1971), and Barry Richman's interesting summary of management ideology and organization in large-scale industry in contemporary China will appear in modified form elsewhere. Myron Cohen's comparative study of corporation and contract in Taiwan, mainland China, and overseas, was unfortunately not available for publication here.

In addition to these authors, the conference was enriched by the participation of four discussants, Robert F. Dernberger, Albert Feuerwerker, Ralph Heunemann, and G. William Skinner. The diversity of disciplines represented at the conference—history, economics, anthropology, and sociology—led to a fruitful interchange of points of view, ably recorded by Clive Ansley and J. Bruce Jacobs. After the conference the record of the entire proceedings was made available to the writers of all the papers, and copies have been deposited at a score of the major centers of Asian studies in the English-speaking world. The conference record was also available to me in writing the introduction, many of the ideas in which are therefore the products of discussion, although I must bear full responsibility for the interpretation they reflect. Kay Ryland and Bryce Wood of the SSRC (New York) looked after the administration of the conference and distributed the materials; Mrs. Ryland also attended the conference. I wish to record my thanks to all these individuals, whose work has contributed substantially to the preparation of this volume.

There are serious gaps in this book. For instance, there is only one paper on economic organization in the People's Republic of China. My original plans, which called for others, had to be abandoned because the kind of fieldwork necessary to solid anthropological research was still virtually impossible when this conference was being organized. Another serious omission is the whole subject of handicraft industry, knowledge of which is of course crucial to an understanding of economic organization in traditional China and thus to the transformation of that organization in the twentieth century. Here is a fruitful area of investigation that awaits the student, whether he be anthropologist, historian, or economist.

The central aim of the series of conferences from which this volume emerged is to encourage sociological and anthropological research on Chinese society. This book therefore represents a beginning in the study of Chinese economic anthropology, not a definitive or general statement on it. It is our collective hope that the papers will inspire other social scientists to follow the lines here pursued, to design and carry out more definitive research on our topics, to test our propositions in the light of this further research, and to fill out those areas in which our knowledge of Chinese economic organization is as yet so rudimentary.

W.E.W.

Vancouver, Canada, October 1971

Contents

Contributors

LAWRENCE W. CRISSMAN received a B.A. (honors) in Chinese language and civilization from the State University of Iowa in 1964, and is currently completing a Ph.D. in anthropology from Cornell University. After studying at the London School of Economics he conducted field research in Changhua Hsien, Taiwan, in 1967–68. He has published an article entitled "The Segmentary Structure of Urban Overseas Chinese Communities" in *Man*, 2, 2 (1967), and is currently an Instructor of Anthropology at the University of Illinois, Urbana-Champaign.

DONALD R. DEGLOPPER received his M.A. from the University of London in 1965, and his Ph.D. from Cornell University in 1971. From 1966 to 1968 he did field research on Taiwan, supported by the Foreign Area Fellowship Program. He is now Assistant Professor of Anthropology and Asian Studies at Cornell University. At present he is interested in Taiwanese local history and in models of social relations in Chinese culture.

CRAIG DIETRICH, who received his Ph.D. from the University of Chicago in 1970, holds a joint appointment from Bowdoin College and the University of Maine at Portland as Assistant Professor of History. He is currently studying the relationship of values, technology, and economic organization in late traditional China and other premodern societies.

MARK ELVIN received his Ph.D. from the Faculty of Oriental Studies of the University of Cambridge, and has taught there and in the Department of Economic History at Glasgow University, where he now holds the position of Lecturer. He has published articles on the legal history of early modern China, local self-government in late Ch'ing Shanghai, land tenure in China from Sung to Republican times, and Sung science and technology. He has translated Japanese works on the Ming tribute grain system and on commerce and society in the Sung for *Michigan Abstracts,* of which he is the editor. His book *The Pattern of the Chinese Past* is now in press at Eyre Methuen, scheduled to appear in late 1972.

SUSAN MANN JONES is a doctoral candidate in the Department of Asian Languages, Stanford University. She is currently teaching Chinese history at Northwestern University, The Evening Divisions, and pursuing research in the Far Eastern Library of the University of Chicago. She has been affiliated with the Stanford Program on East Asian Local Systems since its inception, as a participant in the Ning-Shao project.

THOMAS A. METZGER received his Ph.D. from Harvard University and is now Assistant Professor of History at the University of California, San Diego. His research has been mainly in the field of Ch'ing bureaucracy and its relation to commerce. He is the author of *The Internal Organization of Ch'ing Bureaucracy,* now in press at Harvard University Press.

RAMON H. MYERS received his Ph.D. from the University of Washington, Seattle, in 1960 and is now Professor of Economics and History at the University of Miami, Coral Gables, Florida. His research has focused on Asian agriculture and economic development. He is the author of *The Chinese Peasant Economy: Agricultural Development in Hopei and Shantung, 1890–1949* and numerous articles on Chinese economic history.

STEPHEN M. OLSEN received his Ph.D. from Cornell University. He spent 1966–68 in Taiwan doing Chinese-language training and fieldwork for his dissertation on social class, values, and family socialization in Taipei. He is presently Assistant Professor of Sociology at Stanford University.

BURTON PASTERNAK received his Ph.D. from Columbia University. He is now Assistant Professor of Anthropology at Hunter College, City University of New York. His research has been concerned primarily with social organization in rural China, and he is the author of several articles on this subject.

JOHN C. PELZEL is Director of the Harvard-Yenching Institute and Professor of Anthropology at Harvard University. From 1947 to 1949 he was associated with the Civil Information and Education Section, SCAP, Tokyo, working on a project to revise the romanization system for Japanese, supervising a national sample survey of literacy, and doing fieldwork on the social organization of a community of small iron factories. In 1949 he received his Ph.D. from Harvard. In accord with his interest in the comparative social organization of China and Japan, he has done fieldwork in Hong Kong and taught at the University of Tokyo. He has edited *Nihonjin no yomi-kaki nōryoku* (Japanese literacy; 1951) and co-edited *A Selected List of Books and Articles on Japan* (1954).

ROBERT H. SILIN received his Ph.D. in 1971 from Harvard University. He is now Assistant Professor of Anthropology at New York University. His research interests have been primarily in the fields of Chinese economic institutions and the analysis of Chinese formal organizations. A book reflecting these interests is now in preparation.

E-TU ZEN SUN received her M.A. and Ph.D. degrees in history from Radcliffe College, and is now Professor of Chinese History at the Pennsylvania State University. She has published widely in professional journals on Chinese economic and institutional history. Among her books are *Chinese Railways and British Interests, 1898–1911; Ch'ing Administrative Terms*; and (cotranslator and editor) *T'ien-kung k'ai-wu: Chinese Technology in the Seventeenth Century*. She is currently working on an interpretative history of China.

BARBARA E. WARD taught school in West Africa during World War II. After the war, she studied social anthropology under Raymond Firth at the London School of Economics. Her main research interests have been in Hong Kong and among overseas Chinese. She was scientific director and editor of the UNESCO publication *Women in the New Asia*, and is the author of "Cash or Credit Crops?" in *Economic Development and Cultural Change* (January 1960), "Chinese Fishermen: Their Post-Peasant Economy" in Maurice Freedman, ed., *Social Organization: Essays Presented to Raymond Firth* (1968), and other articles. She has held posts at Birkbeck College and at the School of Oriental and African Studies, University of London, and is at present Research Fellow at Clare Hall and Director of Studies in Anthropology at Newnham College, Cambridge.

W. E. WILLMOTT, Professor of Anthropology and Lecturer in Asian Studies at the University of British Columbia, was born in Chengtu, China. He did undergraduate work at Oberlin College and McGill University, and received an M.A. from McGill for his research in the Canadian Arctic among the Eskimos. A doctoral dissertation on the political structure of the Chinese community in Cambodia earned him the Ph.D. from the London School of Economics, University of London. He has published on the Eskimos and on the overseas Chinese in Cambodia and in Canada.

ECONOMIC ORGANIZATION
IN CHINESE SOCIETY

Introduction

W. E. WILLMOTT

Each of the papers in this volume can stand alone. When they are brought together between two covers, it is valid to ask what unites them, for the reader will immediately appreciate that the topics range widely, including such diverse areas as North China, Hong Kong, and Taiwan, such diverse times as the eighteenth and twentieth centuries, and such diverse societies as contemporary mainland China, Hong Kong, prewar Taiwan, and late Imperial China. However, they are united by more than having benefitted from discussion in a single conference: each deals with some aspect of Chinese economic organization. It might be well to explain at the outset what we mean by that term.

As we have tried to indicate in the title, this is not a book on Chinese economics, for it does not attempt a purely economic analysis of the movement of goods, factors in production, or monetary systems. Rather, it examines the system of social relationships that underlie and surround the economic processes. We are interested in the kinds of groups involved in the production and distribution of goods, in the quality of the relationships that unite individuals and groups in the process, in the cultural values that shape the motivations of people entering into economic transactions. In brief, we are interested in examining the nature of Chinese society and culture as it is manifest in economic activity.

For such an undertaking the kind of questions asked of the material is dictated by considerations quite different from those of formal economic analysis. Our approach is that of economic anthropology, which in this context includes economic sociology. Neil Smelser has put it succinctly (1963: 32):

Economic sociology is the application of the general frame of reference, variables, and explanatory models of sociology to that complex of activities concerned with the production, distribution, exchange, and consumption of scarce goods and services.

Smelser goes on to point out that economic sociology examines social relationships in two "settings": within "concrete economic units," and "between economic units and their social environment" (*ibid.*: 33). A paper with the first kind of setting is Professor Pelzel's unique description of the internal organization of a single production brigade in a commune in southern China. Some of the papers, like Susan Jones's study of the *ch'ien chuang*, or native banks, of Ningpo, operate in both settings. This paper analyzes both the internal structure of these banks and their relationships with Ningpo trade, government officials and institutions, guilds, family loyalties, and other financial institutions both Chinese and foreign.

In Smelser's second setting, the social environment of economic units, the expectations of anthropology are somewhat wider than those of sociology. For an anthropologist, the "environment" of any social institution includes not only the society in which it functions but also its physical surroundings and the technological connection between the two: in brief, the cultural ecology. When, therefore, Professor Pasternak, an anthropologist working in history, analyzes the relationship between irrigation systems and the structure of family groupings in central Taiwan, he is looking at the ecological determinants of social forms. When Professor Elvin, an historian doing excellent anthropology, analyzes the relationship between the technology of cotton production and the social institutions surrounding it, he is looking at the social determinants of technology. Both of these approaches are those of economic anthropology.

In economic anthropology today there is a strong emphasis on exchange, based on the assumption that every economic relationship involves exchange between the parties. In a formal sense this is true by definition, for there is no relationship unless something—goods, money, words, women, respect, terror—is transacted. The shortcoming of exchange theory lies in its facile assumption of the reciprocal nature of all relationships and its consequent neglect of the phenomenon of exploitation. Our understanding of the landlord-tenant relationship, for instance, is obscured rather than clarified if we think of that relationship as a reciprocal transaction in which the rice and deference moving in one direction somehow equal the tenancy and contempt moving in the other. Exploitation involves non-reciprocal economic relationships in which the more advantaged party uses political means to maintain his advantage. The importance of recognizing exploitation can be seen here in the papers by Myers, Metzger, Elvin, and Jones. Indeed, the Chinese methods of handling exploitative relationships are of particular interest in the comparative study of culture, as I shall point out later.

What, then, is meant by Chinese economic organization? It should be apparent now that by economic organization we mean the system of social relationships involved in the production and distribution of scarce goods and services, whether the system involves equal exchange or exploitation. But what is meant by *Chinese* economic organization? The production brigade on the mainland of China and the rice village on Taiwan, the factory in Hong Kong today and the silk manufactory in eighteenth-century Canton, the government salt monopoly in Ch'ing China and the government-sponsored irrigation project on Taiwan today—all these we recognize as "Chinese" forms of economic organization simply because they are all products of Chinese minds tackling different environments at different times. One could say that this book attempts to provide some preliminary and partial answers to the question, for out of the comparison and sociological analysis of these different economic units in their different historical contexts should come some indications of what specifically is meant by "Chinese" in the context of economic organization.

Because we are still only at the beginning of the study, it would be grossly premature to attempt any general statement on the nature of Chinese economic organization. Nevertheless, taken individually and together, the papers here presented afford us useful insights into some aspects of it.

One of these aspects is the role of the state in Chinese economic enterprise. Professor Metzger's paper sheds new light, not only upon the salt monopoly *per se*, but also upon the rationality and organizational ability of the state in handling an immense enterprise two centuries ago. Even in times of crisis, the state was able, through its various agencies, to ensure the steady flow of vast quantities of salt from the coastal pans throughout the Yangtze Valley, constantly adjusting its relationships with private enterprise as the exigencies of the situation demanded. It is in the nature of these relationships that one may search for the "Chineseness" of state enterprise, for they appear to involve a measure of mutual adaptation that is not found, for instance, either in the state domination of the economic system of Meiji Japan or in the struggle between city and state in eighteenth-century Western Europe. Metzger calls this relationship "co-optation." It may also be found in the relationship between state and financial institutions, notably the Shansi banks described by Susan Jones, and in the relationship between the Imperial Silkworks and private contractors outlined by Professor Sun. An echo of it is heard even in the commune described by Professor Pelzel, where an administration is able to benefit from the talents of a local entrepreneur, despite his ideologically dubious motives, by offering him some recompense in power and prestige within the brigade. The relationship is one that serves the state while at the same time permitting private gain, and it involves a compromise between public and private interests at every point.

Another aspect of Chinese economic organization, obviously impinging on co-optation, is the compartmentalized nature of all enterprise, a structure that Professor Audrey Donnithorne in a private communication to me has aptly characterized as "cellular." This cellular form is most clearly demonstrated in the papers on the cotton and silk industries, but it is also apparent in the paper on the so-called salt monopoly. Professor Dietrich shows that during the Ch'ing dynasty the production and distribution of cotton textiles were divided into various stages, each of which was undertaken by separate small units. Professor Elvin has developed this picture to demonstrate how such extreme compartmentalization inhibited technological development in cotton manufacture once the basic technology had been established during the early Ming dynasty. A similarly compartmentalized process of production was to be found in silk manufacture, as Professor Sun ably shows. Even in salt, where the government monopoly was of immense proportions, production and distribution were carried out by many small units, in partial competition with each other, all of which were coordinated by the salt commissioner by means of varied and complicated techniques. Chinese economic organization reveals little vertical integration.

In agriculture, too, local units are relatively self-sufficient, whether they be the manors of Sung agriculture, the households and standard market communities of Ming-Ch'ing rural China, or the group-team-brigade-commune-*hsien* system of today. For more than two millennia, the Chinese have emphasized local economic autonomy, the integration provided by state and market being based solidly upon local responsibility rather than upon central control or forced redistribution.

A conclusion that might be drawn from the cellular nature of Chinese economic organization is that there is no overall Chinese economic system and that future research should therefore focus primarily on local systems or on the internal organization of small units. Although such an approach would undoubtedly prove fruitful, there are grounds for arguing that these units are pervaded by a common set of values, a common Chinese economic culture that molds individual motivations in economic relationships. This culture is examined most directly here by Olsen, DeGlopper, Silin, and Ward. Co-optation and responsibility are aspects of this culture that I have already mentioned. Another is the strongly positive valuation of work itself. Whether it be in a small glass factory in Hong Kong, in the rice fields of Taiwan, or in the tangerine orchards of Kwangtung, the Chinese believe that hard work is good. The value placed on work is examined briefly here by Professor Olsen, who refers to Ryan's earlier and more detailed analysis of the values of overseas Chinese in Java (Ryan 1961), but it is so fundamental to Chinese economic enterprise that it has been taken for granted by most social scientists represented in this volume. Here is an area of Chinese ideology that could benefit from research in various disciplines.

Several of the papers here deal with the question of particularism in Chinese economic relationships. Professor Silin finds that in a situation of sharp competition in a Hong Kong vegetable market the relationships between individuals involve non-economic strands that he summarizes in the term *kan-ch'ing*, "rapport."* Even in an unusually stable business community like that of Lukang, Taiwan, Professor DeGlopper demonstrates that, despite an emphasis upon individual entrepreneurial freedom of action, businessmen base decisions about buying goods and extending credit upon the particularistic relations they have developed. The same phenomenon is described by Professor Ward in the hiring policy and organization of work in a glass factory in Hong Kong, and one can also see it in the historical studies of the salt monopoly and the Ningpo banks by Professor Metzger and Susan Jones. Indeed, the "co-optation" of entrepreneurs by the state, discussed above, operates through the development of particularistic relationships betwen individual agents and businessmen.

Of course the coincidence of economic relationships with particularistic relationships based on kinship or locality is a worldwide phenomenon, particularly evident in societies not yet pervaded by the bureaucratic values of advanced industrialism. What seems to be uniquely Chinese is the *conscious particularization* of economic relationships, the attempt to develop a multiplicity of ties between individuals associated by economic transactions. Professor Ward has described this as "the strong preference for multiplex rather than single-stranded relationships." To point out the difference by hyperbole, one might say that economic transactions occur along particularistic lines in all pre-industrial societies, but the Chinese develop particularistic links between those involved in economic transactions. Even in contemporary China, if the River Brigade studied by Professor Pelzel is typical, planners try to bring brigade membership into correspondence with the particularistic loyalties of previous village communities.

Each of these aspects of Chinese economic culture can be placed in

* All Chinese words appearing in the text are rendered in Wade-Giles romanization. All but the most familiar words appearing in italics and the less familiar proper names as well may be found in the Character List, pp. 441–46.

the context of Chinese culture by examining its consistency with Chinese values governing other kinds of relationships. I have already suggested that the four values mentioned here are interrelated. Explaining them, however, involves going beyond a mere integration with other values, and seeking their historical roots in earlier patterns of relationships, for culture can be seen as an adaptation to previously existing social and ecological systems. Using this cultural-ecological approach, Professor Elvin provides a clue to understanding perhaps far more than the technology of cotton in his concept of a "high-level equilibrium trap." The evolution of traditional Chinese society from the manor to the standard market community produced a large measure of stability in the face of rising population and increasing productivity throughout the Ch'ing period.

This process, called "agricultural involution" by Geertz (1966), involves the absorption of increasing population into an existing social structure through elaboration rather than basic modification of social forms and cultural values. A scarcity of labor, which would have favored technological innovation on all fronts, did not develop in China because increasingly intensive cultivation was able to support a rapidly expanding population. Professor Elvin demonstrates that labor was in greater supply than cotton, which competed with wet rice for land, so that there was no impetus to increase labor's productivity in the industry. Unlike eighteenth-century England, where the rise in population followed technological advances (Childe 1951), China experienced a rapid increase in population during the Ming and Ch'ing dynasties (Ho 1959) that was supported by unchanging agricultural techniques operating within unchanging social forms. The standard market community was thus a social "high-level equilibrium trap," somewhat different from the "folk society" usually associated with peasant agriculture (Steward 1959: 53).

In Java, Geertz argues that involution resulted from the intervention of Dutch colonialism, in particular from the economic isolation of the exploitative Dutch capitalists from subsistence agriculture despite their social integration in the rural village. In China, this same process came about without colonial intervention because the cellular nature of rural society isolated agriculture from the emergent capitalist forms in cotton production and distribution. Chinese rural society became "relatively egalitarian, competitive, and fragmented," as Professor Elvin has said in another context (1970: 108).

Professor Myers provides a sort of "proof" of my interpretation in his paper. He demonstrates that the increasing commercialization of agriculture on the Mainland in the early decades of this century did not produce new forms of agricultural production, but merely lowered the standard of living by increasing the ratio of people to land on the farm. In contrast, Myers shows that on Taiwan, where a Japanese government intervened decisively on the rural scene, commercialization was accompanied by advances in the technology of agriculture and a marked rise in standards of living.

In my mind, this contrast is borne out in the findings of Professor Crissman on the nature of marketing in central Taiwan. Crissman's study indicates, among other things, that instead of the traditional Chinese pattern of discrete market communities (Skinner 1964) a far more complex pattern of marketing has emerged involving the specialization of markets and the patronage of multiple markets by farmers ("post-peasants") who are not satisfied with doing all their marketing in one town. Perhaps one can predict that in such circumstances the values underlying economic relationships will become more universalistic than traditional Chinese culture could allow. In contrast, the persistence of cellular economic organization on the Mainland, in the form of brigades and communes, may have preserved traditional values even in a socialist society—values considered so undesirable in that society that massive intervention on a cultural level has been undertaken against them in the form of successive "anti" campaigns and, more recently, the Great Proletarian Cultural Revolution.

I would be wrong to imply that the foregoing speculations represent the aims of the scholars whose painstaking and judicious research has produced this book. I have included them simply to indicate that this volume provides a wealth of material on which anthropologists, historians, sociologists, and institutional economists may work, and that they will find this wealth, not only in the papers themselves, but in the comparisons that will inevitably be made between them.

The Organizational Capabilities of the Ch'ing State in the Field of Commerce: The Liang-huai Salt Monopoly, 1740–1840

THOMAS A. METZGER

Mainland China in the last century has witnessed a great expansion of the state's role in economic organization.* This expansion has involved an increase in the state's organizational capabilities,† notably an improvement in its capacity to organize large-scale, complex commercial operations.

What continuities and discontinuities has this change involved? Did the Ch'ing heritage of organizational capabilities shape the character of modern developments, or was it swept aside in favor of a totally new scheme of things?

This question cannot be answered unless we understand the nature of the Ch'ing state's commercial capabilities. Yet the literature on this question mainly contains two inadequate views: the view that the Ch'ing state had "overriding" or "total" power in the field of commerce, and the view that in its relations with commerce the Ch'ing state suffered from various dysfunctional characteristics, such as administrative rigidity, lack of professional specialization on the part of its officials, and corruption. Apart from the fact that these two views tend to contradict each other, the former view fails to conform to obvious facts, and the latter is one-sided.

* I am greatly indebted to several members of the Conference, but particularly Mark Elvin, for stimulating criticism that helped me clarify my interpretation, and to W. E. Willmott for valuable editorial guidance. I am also most grateful to Ramon W. Myers, Dwight Perkins, and Yeh-chien Wang for advice on various points. My work on the salt monopoly has from the start been inspired by John K. Fairbank's conception of the subject and involves a great intellectual debt to him. It also involves one to Robert N. Bellah, Kwang-Ching Liu, and Lien-sheng Yang. This article is based on a longer study in progress, and not all documentation used in the latter can be referred to here.

† On the "capabilities" of political systems in various fields, see Almond and Powell 1966.

A better understanding of Ch'ing commercial capabilities can be gained if we look at them as a mix of functional and dysfunctional characteristics, even though a shortage of statistical information inhibits our efforts to weight these various characteristics relative to each other. Although lacking "total power," the Ch'ing state still had impressive commercial capabilities, a fact which can be explained only if we put its dysfunctional tendencies in perspective and examine its positive organizational resources as well.

In this paper I shall try to describe the mix of functional and dysfunctional factors found in the Ch'ing administration of the Liang-huai zone of its salt monopoly. Because of its large size, this zone was one of the severest tests of the state's organizational capabilities: Liang-huai shipped salt from the coast of northern Kiangsu into seven provinces, Kiangsu, Anhwei, Honan, Kiangsi, Hunan, Hupeh, and Kweichow. Some of the data I use go back to the seventeenth century, but most of them refer to the period 1740–1840, which subdivides into periods of prosperity (1740–1805), increasing difficulty (1805–30), and partial recovery (1831–40).

P. T. Ho's study (P. T. Ho 1954) sheds great light on the conditions of the Liang-huai salt merchants, but little work has been done on governmental activities at Liang-huai. Moreover, what work has been done has focused only on the dysfunctional aspects of these activities. Distinguished experts on the salt administration, such as Tso Shu-chen, Ho Wei-ning, Chou Wei-liang, and Tseng Yang-feng, have deplored the Liang-huai merchants' great power, saying it was used to corrupt the whole administration of the monopoly (Chou Wei-liang 1963, 142: 9; Tseng 1966: 115; Ho Wei-ning 1966, 1: 219–20). Indeed, since at least Ming times the monopoly has had the reputation of being *hu-t'u* (in a mess) (Ho Wei-ning 1966, 1: 213, Tseng 1966: 113), and officials often contemptuously lumped together as *pi* (corrupt practices) both complicated fiscal adjustments and dishonest practices. This hyperbolic outlook has been largely due to the normative, policy-oriented approach of scholars and officials within the Chinese tradition, who rightfully were more interested in doing away with bad practices than in nicely weighing functional against dysfunctional factors. Saeki Tomi's valuable book (1962) similarly stresses dysfunctional factors and ignores much data in the Liang-huai salt gazetteers concerning the various routine adjustments through which the state tried to counter dysfunctional tendencies.*

---

* Saeki's neglect of the question of the temporal and locational shifts of shipments in the face of economic vicissitudes and his problematic notion of the irrational "freezing" of zonal boundaries are examples of his one-sided stress on dys-

In this paper I shall begin by discussing three major factors that inhibited the development of strong, economically rational executive leadership in Liang-huai: first, the vast size of Liang-huai and the prevalence both inside and outside the monopoly's organization of various elements indifferent or hostile to its goals; second, the connected fact that the Liang-huai organization had had to "co-opt" (Selznick 1949) rich merchants who limited the power of salt officials; and third, the particular kind of bureaucratic structure that had evolved over the centuries, largely without reference to the monopoly *per se*, and that tended to inhibit strong, flexible executive leadership.

Seeking under these circumstances to mobilize its human resources and deal with occasionally great situational difficulties, the Liang-huai leadership still had the capability to manipulate a complex spectrum of coercive and economic sanctions in order to enforce and facilitate its procedures.* It could also change its procedures in order to make them more easily enforceable, or it could change its leadership structure in order to obtain more effective manipulation of its sanctions.

However, there were downhill changes and there were uphill changes. Manipulating economic sanctions by shifting or postponing economic obligations was relatively easy and downhill, but basically changing economic obligations at the expense of powerful interests, as with reducing the tax rate or canceling major tax debts, was an uphill change requiring strong-nerved executive leadership. This leadership could emerge in moments of crisis, but political support for the necessary follow-through measures was hard to obtain.

The themes of my discussion, therefore, are the awkwardness of the Liang-huai organizational structure; the skill with which the Liang-huai leadership, despite this awkwardness, usually kept the monopoly running by manipulating a variety of sanctions; and the factors making for partial success in times of particularly great stress.

The Problem of Size

Liang-huai was large in terms of physical space, number of organizational members, number of clients, amount of salt, and amount of revenue. Therefore it faced the problem of eliciting complex organizational

---

functional tendencies (see below). I should emphasize that my discussion of functional aspects is not based on any factors unique to the period of "partial recovery" (1831–40), when T'ao Chu (1779–1839), head of Liang-huai in 1831–39, carried out some impressive reforms (Hummel 1944, 2: 710–11). My understanding of Liang-huai is based to a large extent on the 1806 edition of the Liang-huai salt gazetteer, an administrative manual consisting of laws and other administrative communications going back to the beginning of the dynasty.

* In my concept of sanctions, I basically follow Etzioni 1961.

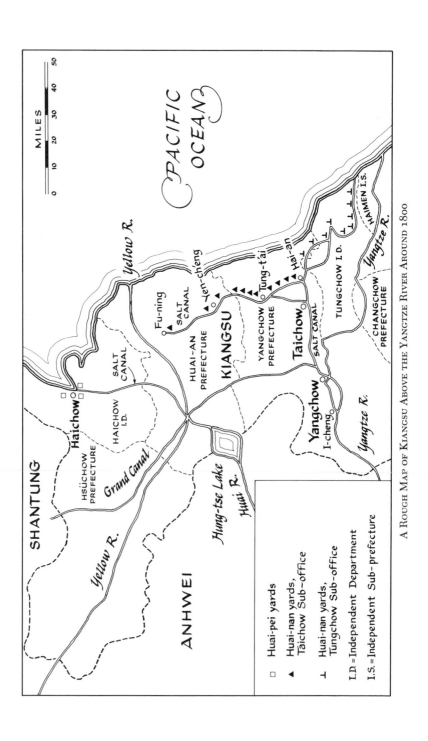

A Rough Map of Kiangsu Above the Yangtze River Around 1800

Legend:

□ Huai-pei yards

▲ Huai-nan yards, Taichow Sub-office

⊥ Huai-nan yards, Tungchow Sub-office

I.D. = Independent Department

I.S. = Independent Sub-prefecture

behavior from a large number of persons who frequently had deviant inclinations and who, spread out over a vast area, were linked through relatively slow, pre-modern methods of communication.

The zone of Liang-huai was divided into two sub-zones, Huai-nan and Huai-pei, each of which had its own *ch'ang* (yards, salt-production yards) and its own markets. The accompanying map shows the locations of the three Huai-pei and the twenty Huai-nan yards. These yards were territorial-administrative units in which most economic facilities were privately owned. The yards were under the jurisdiction partly of the district or other local government unit in which they were located, and partly of the Liang-huai salt officials stationed in them. Their large size is seen most clearly from the geography of the eight Huai-nan yards in Yangchow Prefecture. These were situated side by side along some forty miles of the salt canal and stretched east toward the ocean, which was some fifteen to twenty-five miles away from the salt canal. Conservatively, therefore, the average yard was some fifty square miles in area, and the Liang-huai yards altogether must have occupied a thousand square miles or more.

There were some civilians (*min*) in the yards, but probably most of the people there were involved in salt production. Salt workers bought some food from traders coming to the yards (LHYFC 806, ch. 9: 29a, ch. 41: 39a), but salt workers themselves farmed a good deal, often growing the typical Yangtze delta mixture of cotton and beans. Therefore, floods hurting yard crops were a serious worry for salt officials (TYT, ch. 44: 25a, ch. 45: 25a, ch. 50: 10-a; LHYFC 1806, ch. 41: 13a, 36a–37b, 39a). Similarly, in Ming times salt workers had been issued *tsao-ti* (farming land for salt workers) (Ho Wei-ning 1966, 1: 317–18). For those salt workers inclined toward legal behavior, farming must have been an economic cushion allowing some conformity even to monopoly regulations that were economically disadvantageous.

The large size of the yards was due to the presence not only of farmland but also of *t'ing* or *t'ing-ch'ang* (salt plots) and *ts'ao-tang* (reedgrowing marshes). Salt plots were needed to prepare a salty earth used in filters through which sea water was passed to make brine. This technique, probably developed in T'ang times, reduced fuel costs (Ho Weining 1966, 1: 307). The land for each salt plot was chosen according to the richness of the salt vapors that rose from it mainly during the five or six hottest months of the year and during appropriate short-term weather. Partly because of these temporal factors, Liang-huai production was limited to roughly four months a year (LHYFC 1806, ch. 30: 6a–b). It is clear that these plots of land were located above under-

ground salt lagoons, the salt in which had been left behind by the re-
treating ocean many years before. In warm weather, salty vapors rose
to the surface of the salt plots on account of a capillary effect.* To facilitate this effect, the surface of the plot had to be made hard and smooth.
A plot could be in production after one year, but rich production could
require up to five years of gradual development (LHYFC 1806, ch.
4: 10b, ch. 30: 12a). It should be noted that the social visibility of the
salt plots facilitated policing.

Earth taken from these salt plots had to be thoroughly impregnated
with salt and kept dry. At the right time, the plot was broken up; sea
water was lightly sprinkled on it; it had to be raked over and over again,
absorbing the salt vapors; and the raked earth had to be kept out of the
rain (Salt: Production and Taxation 1906: 17–18; LHYFC 1806, ch.
4: 10b). When the salty earth was ready, it was placed with other ingredients in a container, and sea water was then dripped through this
filter. The resulting brine was judged ready when a plant called shih-lien
floated properly on it. In the Huai-pei yards, the brine was poured into
evaporating ponds. In Huai-nan, the brine was boiled in pots placed on
stoves, which burned the reeds from the ts'ao-tang (reed-growing
marshes). Final crystallization of the salt in the pots required adding
to the brine a plant called tsao-chia or tsao-chiao (Gleditschia chinensis).

The Huai-pei and Huai-nan subzones each had their own salt markets, which were divided into three areas: a peddlers' area, with no
formalized tax levy; shih-an (ports where salt is made available for consumption), which had light tax rates; and kang-an (distant ports), which
produced nearly all the Liang-huai revenue. The principle behind this
division was that of segregating markets according to the ease with
which they could be policed and thereby made to absorb legal salt.
Consumers in shih-an had the legal alternative of buying no salt at all
during the Ch'ing dynasty, but the term shih-an connoted a policy of
issuing or selling salt to consumers on a directly coercive basis going
back to the shih-yen (salt issued directly for consumption) system of
the Later T'ang dynasty (A.D. 923–36) and the shih-yen-ti (areas where
salt is issued directly for consumption) of the Yuan dynasty (Ho Wei-
ning 1966, I: 157; Tseng 1966: 108). Thus in the case of the most trou-
blesome markets, the state at various times wavered between the policy
of direct coercion and that of partial or complete abandonment of the
market to smugglers.

* For this explanation, I am greatly indebted to Professor Yüan-hui Li of the
Department of Geological Sciences, Harvard University, who is not, of course, responsible for any mistakes I may have made.

The peddler areas and the *shih-an* receiving salt from the Huai-pei yards were all in Kiangsu above the Yangtze, as were all those peddler areas and nearly all those *shih-an* receiving salt from the Huai-nan yards. (A few Huai-nan *shih-an* were on the southern shore of the Yangtze and in Anhwei.) Northern Kiangsu, in other words, was devoted to these two types of markets, except for a few places outside the Liang-huai zone, notably the five westernmost districts of Hsüchow Prefecture, which were in the Shantung zone. Generally the peddler areas were near the yards in the east, while the *shih-an* were in the vicinity of the Grand Canal. The main exception was the district of I-cheng, where the central Huai-nan salt depot was located, the I-cheng Station. This district was largely supplied by persons sweeping up spilled salt at the I-cheng Station. As of about 1800, Liang-huai peddler areas in northern Kiangsu totaled nine districts or similar units, and Liang-huai *shih-an* in northern Kiangsu totaled thirteen districts or similar units (LHYFC 1806, ch. 8).

Much peddler and *shih-an* salt was picked up by peddlers and traders directly at the yards, but some salt for *shih-an* was conveniently siphoned off the mainstream of shipments as the latter proceeded through canals from the yards to either of the two main depots, the I-cheng Station for Huai-nan, and the Huai Station for Huai-pei (the latter was near the intersection of the Grand Canal and the Yellow River).

All *kang-an* (distant ports) shipments passed through one of these two stations. All in Anhwei and Honan, the Huai-pei *kang* markets were reached mostly via the Huai River. Huai-nan *kang* shipments went via the Yangtze River to markets in Anhwei, Kweichow, and, by far the most important, Hunan, Hupeh, and Kiangsi.

Even though a depth of some five feet was adequate for the salt boats, silting in the southern canals connecting the Tungchow yards and leading to I-cheng was a serious problem (LHYFC 1806, ch. 9: 4a). In about 1785, because canals had silted up, salt from two Tungchow yards was taken overland directly south to the Yangtze and then shipped by boat to the I-cheng Station (LHYFC 1806, ch. 12: 17b). Probably problems of policing precluded permanent use of the Yangtze. In other cases, changes in transport routes could flexibly be made on a permanent basis. For instance, around 1790, expensive, partly overland routes to some Huai-pei markets in Anhwei were abandoned in favor of a cheaper route via the Grand Canal and the Yangtze (LHYFC 1806, ch. 12: 18a–20a). Before 1736, the four yards just below Fu-ning shipped directly west to the Grand Canal; after 1736, they shipped south via Yen-ch'eng (LHYFC 1806, ch. 9: 15b).

Besides peddler, *shih-an*, and *kang-an* salt, there were four main ways in which salt legally entered the Liang-huai markets. First, fishing boats obtained salt from the Liang-huai yards. Peddlers' and fishermen's salt together were said to total about a hundred million catties annually in the 1830's, about 17 percent of the regular Huai-nan quota (TWI, ch. 18: 35b–36b). Second, grain tribute boats returning from the Peking area could each bring in forty catties for the needs of their crews (LHYFC 1806, ch. 13: 40b–41a). Third, in nine Liang-huai districts and other local government units of Hupeh and Hunan, the residents were allowed to buy small quantities of salt in immediately adjacent parts of the Szechwan and Kwangtung zones respectively (LHYFC 1806, ch. 6: 12a–15b); these Liang-huai markets were thus formally recognized buffers. Fourth, salt seized from smugglers was sometimes sold in Liang-huai markets. (Salt could also be shipped in from other zones and often was around 1900.)

Besides these seven main channels of legal salt, Liang-huai markets illegally received salt originating either in Liang-huai yards or in other zones. Smuggling was carried out both by people legally involved in Liang-huai affairs and by persons without any legal connection to Liang-huai. From a spatial point of view, therefore, Liang-huai officials were confronted with a multifocal system spread out over a vast area.

The population of this area was great, too. Taking the provinces of Kiangsi, Hunan, and Hupeh, which absorbed somewhere between half and two-thirds of the Liang-huai production, we have plausible figures indicating an increase of 420 percent from 13.6 million persons in 1393 to 71.1 million persons in 1812 (P. T. Ho 1959: 10, 56).

The total official amount of Liang-huai salt production over just about the same period increased by some 340 percent or more. Figures referring to about 1370 give us about 140 million catties as the total Liang-huai quota (Ho Wei-ning 1966, I: 240). By 1645 the total Liang-huai quota was 280 million catties. By 1726 it was about 450 million catties. By about 1800, officially recognized shipments had reached about 610 million catties, resulting in the 340 percent increase noted above, but this figure of 610 million excludes some 100 million catties of fishermen's and peddlers' salt, as well as the controversial hundred catties or so per bag added by about 1820 (see below). These Ch'ing increases in the quota were attained partly by increasing the annual quota of *yin* (fiscal weight unit) from 1.41 to 1.68 million but mostly by increasing the weight of the *yin* from 227 to 364 catties, plus certain extra, partly controversial amounts. For instance, in about 1725, explicitly because the current supply of salt was not enough for the markets of Hunan, Hupeh, Kiangsi, and the districts around Nanking, the weight of the *yin* bound for these areas was increased by 13 percent (from 294 catties to 334 catties) (TCHTSL, 10: 8062 [ch. 223: 5a]; LHYFC 1806, ch. 11: 20a–b). These increases did not just absorb already-existing illegal production but required deliberate government efforts to *kuang yen-ch'an* (expand salt production), which were slowed especially by the problem of developing new salt plots (LHYFC 1806, ch. 30: 11b–12a, ch. 24: 5b). To a large extent, therefore, production kept up with population increases, a fact illustrating the flexibility of the salt administration.

When we relate these figures on salt shipments to data on taxes and price changes, we also can show that the eighteenth-century increase in Liang-huai taxes was reasonable if not unduly light. We have seen that those annual salt shipments bearing virtually all Liang-huai taxes rose from 450 million catties around 1726 to 610 million catties by 1800. During this time the Hankow wholesale price, at which about half the Liang-huai shipments were sold, rose about 120 percent from some .13 taels per packet of 8.25 catties around 1723 to at least .29 taels in 1788 (LHYFC 1806, ch. 23: 2a; ch. 24: 27a).* This price rise was linked to a general trend of rising prices in this period studied by Professor Han-sheng Chuan. This trend centered on the rising price of grain, which directly increased labor costs for the salt monopoly. (Workers were often paid in money, which they used to buy grain.) At the same time, the effective demand for salt was high in the grain-exporting and essentially salt-free provinces of Hunan, Hupeh, and Kiangsi.

If we conservatively assume that there was an 80 percent rise in the wholesale price of Liang-huai salt between 1726 and 1800, and if we keep in mind the increasing size of the salt shipments, then we can conclude that the money value of Liang-huai shipments rose about 140 percent during this same period. Yet taxes rose only 100 percent, from about two million taels in 1730 to about four million taels by about 1795 (TYT, ch. 42: 5a–b, ch. 38: 30b–31a; LHYFC 1693, 2: 835, 1070).

---

* The Hankow wholesale price, i.e., the price paid by local wholesalers for salt brought by the shipping merchants from the Liang-huai depot at I-cheng, was carefully observed, and official reports of it were basically reliable. As we know from an official investigation of 1740 and from Pao Shih-ch'en's remarks some ninety years later, this price was officially reported in *k'u-p'ing wen-yin*, i.e. silver regarded as pure by local standards and weighed according to the local version of the standard *liang* (ounce) of the Board of Revenue. While Hankow sales were actually made using a local ounce and silver of varying fineness, the local wholesalers had to pay the shippers an amount of local silver equivalent in value to the price of the salt in *k'u-p'ing wen-yin*, and consumers in turn were made to pay retailers an amount of local copper cash equivalent in value to the price of the salt in *k'u-p'ing wen-yin* (LHYFC 1806, ch. 23: 18b–19a; Pao, ch. 5: 18a–b, 21b).

Admittedly in the next decades the Liang-huai tax policy was problematic. There were many tax increases that clearly were not matched by any increase in the money value of the shipments. This increasingly dysfunctional tax policy helped produce a great decline in Liang-huai sales (see below). The annual tax quotas reached some seven million taels or more by 1820 and were lowered to about five million taels in 1831. These quotas were correlated to high tax rates, putting a heavy tax burden on merchants, but as sales declined, these quotas were not met. Thus T'ao Chu claimed that in the period 1807–27 inclusive, the annual amount of revenue actually collected averaged about one and a half million taels. However, his critics claimed that in this period more than four million taels were collected annually on the average, more than the roughly three million taels that, all parties agreed, was the amount collected by T'ao annually on the average in the years 1831–38 inclusive (TWI, ch. 16: 3a–b, ch. 18: 64b–66a; LHYFC, 1904, ch. 4: 13b–15a, ch. 138: 4a). The nature of the fiscal accounting system allowed this lack of clarity about the total quotas and the total amounts actually collected (see below). Be that as it may, tax policy as a whole was more functional than has usually been supposed and yielded significant revenues. Judging from Professor Yeh-chien Wang's current research, we can say that the four million taels collected around 1800 were some 6 percent of the Ch'ing state's total annual revenue.

Besides spatial area, number of consumers, quantity of salt shipped, and amount of tax revenue, the large size of Liang-huai involved the great number of members of the Liang-huai organizational complex. First of all, the working force at the Liang-huai yards increased along with the other increases mentioned above. According to quotas referring to about 1370, the Liang-huai yards had a total of 15,516 salt-worker households, including 38,050 salt workers and 1,210 men occupying positions of local leadership in the yards (Fujii 1952, 1: 75, 89). By 1645, Liang-huai was officially said to have more than 66,000 *tsao-ting* (salt workers), and by 1806 the official figure was more than 672,000 (LHYFC 1806, ch. 29: 1b–7b).*

---

* The early Ming figures may be accurate, since the state then directly financed production and so required reliable figures. The Ch'ing figures are for *ting*, a term usually denoting only a fiscal unit in Ch'ing times (P. T. Ho 1959) but here probably referring to adult males: yard taxes were levied on a land-unit basis (mostly on the reed-growing marshes), not on a per-head basis (CTHPTL 1851, ch. 29: 8, 19b). Population registration in the yards was carried out by Liang-huai officials and was administratively distinct from the regular provincial population registry. In 1776 the Liang-huai head stated that statistics on numbers of salt workers in the yards had hitherto been entered in the annual Liang-huai fiscal evaluations for salt shipments and revenue (*k'ao-ch'eng*) and not into the provincial population records. The head

Besides salt workers, the Liang-huai organizational complex had thousands of members, such as packers, porters, peddlers, local traders, boatmen handling junks with crews of up to thirty hands, business firms with many employees, officials, clerks, policing personnel, and other non-officials working as employees of the state. According to Pao Shih-ch'en (1775–1855), there were about 130 yard merchants (*ch'ang-shang*) handling the wholesaling at the biggest Huai-pei yard around 1834 (Yamamura 1942: 856; Pao, ch. 7: 23a). Around 1906 the salt trade in Hunan alone was estimated to involve about 1,000 traders, 6,000 to 9,000 junkmen, and about 1,000 officials and other state employees, including policing personnel (*Salt Production and Taxation* 1906: 65–67). The latter source also estimates that Liang-huai salt operations as a whole around 1906 involved a total of 369,000 people, of whom "230,000 were workers at the *ch'ang*, 24,090 were official personnel, and 115,000 were engaged in commerce," including 80,000 persons constituting the "crews of the 2,000 salt junks" (Adshead 1970: 148; *Salt Production and Taxation* 1906: viii, 147–48, 223). These 1906 figures are suggestive, but taking into account the large figure for salt workers given in 1806, we may estimate that by 1800 the Liang-huai organizational complex had 400,000 members.

The Problem of Co-optation

Instead of directly incorporating these 400,000 members into its bureaucracy, the Ch'ing state allowed nearly all of them to retain a private or semiprivate status and also found itself involved in a complex web of cooperation with powerful merchants whose interests sometimes conflicted with its own. The essence of this conflict was the age-old question of *chung-pao*, the corrupt absorption of profits by the middle rungs of society at the expense of both the state and the common people. The state often sought to advance legal sales and tax collection by promoting a balanced pattern of economic incentives favoring those low-status groups directly engaged in the production, distribution, and consumption of salt, while powerful, high-status merchants often acted to upset such a pattern of incentives by seeking to increase their own immediate profits at the expense of these lower-status groups, whether by cheating salt makers when measuring salt, fleecing the poorer traders financially dependent on them, or raising prices for consumers.

Why did the legally all-powerful state co-opt such powerful merchants,

wanted to continue this practice, and clearly he had his way (LHYFC 1806, 29: 1a–b). However, not all persons registered as salt workers actually produced salt (*ibid.*, 27: 9b).

tolerating such divergent interests? Certainly some basically structural factors were involved. If the merchants had been replaced by officials, the salaries of the latter would have absorbed many of the profits of the monopoly, while the officials themselves would have had similar corrupt tendencies toward *chung-pao*. Moreover, officials tended to be unskillful in commercial affairs, as Su Tung-p'o (1036–1101) already had noted (Sa 1965–66, IV: 38). Admittedly in the 1830's the state itself managed some salt shipments at a profit (TWI, ch. 17: 1a–b), but on the whole, the increasing size of the monopoly must have called for increasing inputs of managerial skill which the officials would have been hard-pressed to supply.

But in having to rely on merchants, the state still had a choice between dealing with a few powerful, large-scale merchants and with many low-status, small-scale merchants. It is hard to argue that from a purely technical standpoint there was an obvious case to be made for the superiority of either group. Large-scale merchants were used in the Huai-pei sub-zone for more than two centuries, but when T'ao Chu switched to small-scale traders in the 1830's, he was enormously successful. In about 1839, his knowledgeable friend and adviser Wei Yüan (1794–1856) was convinced that the same switch could successfully be made even in the Huai-nan sub-zone, the huge quotas of which in the 1830's were moved mainly by some fifteen large-scale merchants (Wei Yüan: 724; TYT, ch. 37: 47a, ch. 42: 3a–b).

From an ideological standpoint, there similarly were well-founded prejudices on both sides of the question. Generally speaking, the officials' attitude toward rich merchants fluctuated between two poles: they could be regarded either as trustworthy, respectable, and able persons with the capital necessary to move goods as the state wished, or as corrupt schemers using financial manipulations to divert profits from both the state and the poorer, honest traders. Conversely, small-scale traders could be regarded as either the foundation of honest, efficient commerce or untrustworthy riffraff and former smugglers who put immediate profits above long-range considerations of cooperation with the state.

Given the uncertainty in the factors listed above, we must stress situational political factors as basic in the state's decision to work with powerful Liang-huai merchants. In the seventeenth century, the financial rise of these merchants coincided with a period when state policies at Liang-huai were marked by weakness and timidity, or at least by a tendency to put primacy on immediate fiscal needs rather than the maintenance of old organizational patterns. The combination of new commercial forces and state financial shortages seems to have been conducive to the institutionalization of organizational innovations. The polity then was economically too pressed to object to new kinds of institutional arrangements. At the same time, when financially indebted to merchants, the state was vulnerable to the expanding moral claims made by merchants on the basis of these obligations.

Such was the situation underlying the establishment of the *kang-fa* (system of hereditary licenses) in 1617 at Liang-huai by Yüan Shih-chen, then head of Liang-huai. The *kang-fa* provided a stable, legal foundation for powerful merchant interests previously denounced by Yüan as criminally corrupt. Thus formally ensconced, rich merchants increasingly shared the Liang-huai leadership with Liang-huai officials. This case of co-optation is one of the most striking instances in Chinese history of a major, formalized increase in merchant political power achieved through a struggle against powerful officials in the state bureaucracy. Therefore it deserves detailed examination.*

The problem at Liang-huai in 1616 was due in part to a great flow of totally illegal salt coming out of the Liang-huai yards and undermining legal sales in the Liang-huai markets (HMCSWP 29: 269–70). Despite this flow, however, it was clear that legal sales could flourish again if the legal price could be brought down and if the flow of merchant investment in legal salt could be revived.

The main obstacle here was that the state for years had been making merchants pay taxes on future shipments as a condition for making current shipments, and by 1616 merchants were largely unwilling or unable to pay new taxes until the state let them ship the salt due on their old tax receipts.

Investment at that time operated according to a revised version of the *k'ai chung fa* (system of deliveries according to listed regulations) (Fujii

---

* *Kang* was a generic term, going back at least to T'ang times, denoting "a shipment of goods," often a group of boats organized to make a shipment counted as one unit in a series of such shipments. In the 1617 *kang-fa*, Liang-huai shipments were divided into *kang* (groups), but the term *kang-fa* referred not only to this division but also to *all* the new Liang-huai regulations of 1617, among which the granting of hereditary privileges was crucial.

The following discussion of the *kang-fa* is based on the ten-point reform memorial presented by the Board of Revenue in the winter of 1616–17 and written up by Yüan Shih-chen, then on the staff of the Board (HMCSWP 29: 185–346); on Yüan's subsequent bitter attack on the *t'un-hu* (speculators) (HMCSWP 29: 346–53); on the summary of the regulations of the *kang-fa*, designed by Yüan (HMCSWP 29: 355–64); and on eight other documents about the *kang-fa* written within some years of its establishment (HMCSWP 29: 364–403). Establishment of the *kang-fa* is described in Fujii Hiroshi 1943, 54, 7: 718–27. Fujii's account pays less attention than mine to the first reform proposal and so fails to bring out clearly the reversal of Ming policy in the face of merchant pressure. Anyone discussing the Ming salt monopoly is enormously indebted to Fujii's truly masterly articles.

1941; Ho Wei-ning 1966, 1: 220–21). This system, when originally set up in the beginning of the Ming, called for the delivery of supplies by merchants to various areas, mostly frontier areas, in return for the right to make salt shipments. Well before 1500, merchants had begun delivering silver instead of supplies, and these silver deliveries were being made in the early 1600's. While the economic rationality of these silver deliveries is not clear, they did permit the belief, important to Ming officials, that salt monopoly procedures still accorded with the *tsu-chih* (institutions of the imperial ancestors).

Around 1600, a *pien-shang* (frontier merchant) delivered about .2 taels to a frontier station in return for a *ts'ang-k'an* (granary receipt), which he could sell at Yangchow to a *nei-shang* (interior merchant) for some .25 taels (LHYFC 1693, 2: 713; HMCSWP 29: 277). The interior merchant handed in this granary receipt to the Liang-huai salt office, which issued him a *yin* (master license) in return. However, before using this master license, the interior merchant also had to pay the other major tax, the *yü-yin* (silver for extra salt), for which he received a *hsiao-p'iao* (little receipt).*

Well before 1600, the state began requiring that interior merchants also pay the *yü-yin* on future shipments as a condition for making their current shipments. This practice was called *t'ao-ta yü-cheng* (making shipments interconnected and collecting taxes in advance). It not only increased the interior merchants' costs but also meant that current shipments were increasingly reserved for merchants who had paid taxes in advance. Eventually an interior merchant who purchased a granary receipt had to wait some ten years before he could use it (HMCSWP 29: 204, 276). As a result, the effective demand for granary receipts declined to the point that frontier merchants lacked incentive to ship silver to frontier stations, creating deficits in the quotas of revenue due to be collected there (HMCSWP 29: 277). This was the notorious problem of *chi-yin* (accumulated granary receipts and little receipts), which by 1617 were held by interior merchants for salt shipments totaling the Huai-nan quotas for some three years (HMCSWP 29: 358).

---

*The "extra salt" in the term *yü-yin* (extra-salt silver) obviously referred to the salt added to the "regular" weight of the *yin* (fiscal weight unit). The 200 catties fixed as the weight of the *yin* in 1390 (Ho Wei-ning 1966, I: 240) were regarded as "regular salt," while the 200 catties eventually added were regarded as "extra salt" (LHYFC 1693, 2: 750). In 1616, the *yin* at Liang-huai was about 570 catties, and Yüan Shih-chen reduced it to about 450 catties (HMCSWP 29: 399). Besides *ts'ang-k'an*, names for the border receipt were *pien-ch'ao*, *k'an-ho*, *pien-yin*, and *yin-ch'ao*. The price of the border receipt at Yangchow was variously called *cheng-chia*, *cheng-yin chih chia*, and *yin-chia*. Besides *yü-yin*, "silver for extra salt" was called *yü-k'o*, *yü-yen chia-yin*, *yü-yen chih yin*, and *yü-yen chih chia* (HMCSWP, 29: 211, 214, 215, 225, 227, 230, 289, 293, 356).

The state therefore had to be willing to forgo some current tax revenue by reserving a greater share of current shipments for holders of old tax receipts. It had to make some sort of package deal inducing the latter to pay new taxes by convincing them that their old tax receipts would be more promptly honored.

This led to another major problem, at least in the eyes of the Board of Revenue. Many granary receipts had been bought up by a small number of rich interior merchants called *t'un-hu* (speculators who buy up much of an item) (HMCSWP 29: 218, 365, 381, 261). *T'un-hu* would hold granary receipts for some years until shipments became available for them and then sell them at a high price to other interior merchants. They also had bought up many of the "little receipts" issued for advance payment of *yü-yin* (silver for extra salt) (HMCSWP 29: 218, 365, 381, 261, 278).

The Board of Revenue blamed the *t'un-hu* for the high price of granary receipts. If holders of old tax receipts were now to be offered attractive terms for making their shipments more promptly, would not this procedure favor exactly these evil speculators whose "monopolization of profits" had caused the salt administration so much trouble? The Board of Revenue, in its original plan, was determined that the speculators would not be so favored. Far from being offered hereditary rights as an inducement to invest, the speculators were to be forced to sell their old granary receipts at a government-controlled price to other interior merchants and were not to be allowed to buy any of the new granary receipts for purposes of speculation (HMCSWP 29: 284, 257–58, 262–63, 252–53, 281–82).

When the speculators vehemently opposed this plan, Yüan Shih-chen denounced them as "corrupt" criminals who by their machinations had "seized . . . the empire's foremost source of authority over the flow of wealth"; he charged that their profits exceeded Liang-huai tax revenue. Simultaneously, though, he stressed that he did not want to "destroy" them and was open-minded regarding any new proposals (HMCSWP 29: 348–49, 352).

Shortly thereafter, Yüan Shih-chen devised his second plan, the *kang-fa* (system of hereditary licenses), which was an immediate and great success. The crux of the *kang-fa* was that it allowed the speculators (*t'un-hu*) to use their old tax receipts by investing in the new shipments with almost no restrictions (HMCSWP 29: 381); rewarded the *t'un-hu* (and others) with hereditary rights to ship; and established an arrangement more satisfactory to the merchants for annually mixing shipments for old and new tax receipts.

Thus the speculators, having refused to cooperate in terms of the original reform plan, obtained another plan entirely favorable to them. Subsequently Liang-huai sales were brisk, and the shipments for all the old accumulated tax receipts were carried out by about 1630 (LHYFC 1693, 2: 745). Explaining why he had changed the Board of Revenue's original plan, Yüan Shih-chen pointed out that although the speculators deserved to be criminally prosecuted for "cheating" the state, it had been necessary to cooperate with them because they were the only merchants available with any capital (HMCSWP 29: 381–82). Their co-optation was accompanied by a great improvement in the social relations between the merchant community and the officials. Previously salt merchants had not even visited the Liang-huai offices, afraid of being imprisoned and coerced into making more tax payments (HMCSWP 29: 287).

As the Ch'ing came to power in 1644, their policy at Liang-huai was a flexible mixture of innovations and respect for Ming regulations, especially those in the Ming book *Yen-fa-k'ao* (Study of salt laws), which was frequently referred to and regarded as authoritative by the Board of Revenue in those early years (LHYFC 1806, ch. 7: 4a–6a). Reordering and somewhat rationalizing the Liang-huai monopoly,* the Ch'ing officials sought to create an atmosphere of stability encouraging merchant investments. They felt dependent on the shippers as "men who produce wealth for the court" and explicitly concluded that the flow of revenue depended on satisfying the interests of these men (LHYFC 1693, 2: 877, 880, 692–93).

However, at the same time they were confronted with a merchant community that was in a state of confusing flux. It was no longer clear to the officials who the merchants were and what they were doing. About half of the merchants listed in the register of hereditary rights were no longer active by 1660 (LHYFC 1693, 2: 877; LHYFC 1806, ch. 11: 6a). In Ming times, interior merchants with hereditary rights sold their salt at the I-chen (i.e. I-cheng) Station to *shui-shang* (water merchants), who then shipped the salt up the Yangtze to wholesaling centers like Hankow. However in 1661 the Liang-huai head stated that despite this distinction between interior and water merchants, merchants actually were dealing with one another as they wished in an uncontrolled manner

---

* For instance, the Ch'ing abolished the awkward *k'ai-chung-fa*, which called for deliveries of silver to the frontier, leading one official in 1693 to say that the Ch'ing Liang-huai system was "the reverse" of the Ming (LHYFC 1693, 1: 22). The Ch'ing also eliminated an expensive interruption in the movement by canal of Huai-nan salt to the major station at I-chen (later called I-cheng). Just outside the city of Yangchow, at the "Yangchow Depot," the Ming had had the salt bags unloaded and regrouped to form one of the large sets of shipments into which Huai-nan salt was divided. After such a set (*tan*) was formed, the salt was reloaded and went to the I-chen Station (LHYFC 1904, ch. 93: 11b–12b).

(LHYFC 1693, 2: 877). The Ch'ing system whereby a *single* merchant shipped salt from the yards to wholesaling centers like Hankow was thus gradually taking shape.

The Ch'ing therefore had to fashion a new leadership structure that would both satisfy rich merchants and realistically assign responsibility to merchants actually engaged in shipping. Their solution, devised in 1677, was to appoint twenty-four wealthy merchants as leaders of the shippers (LHYFC 1693, 2: 1007; LHYFC 1806, 18: 41b–42a). This was the origin of the famous *tsung-shang* (head merchants), whose numbers varied from time to time. Anyone wanting to ship had to be "placed under" one of these head merchants. Specifically, this meant (at least in later times) that anyone who had obtained a license (*chu-tan*) to ship in a particular year could not do so until he had been registered in a tax register at the Liang-huai headquarters under the name of the head merchant guaranteeing him. (Holders of hereditary rights annually obtained these *chu-tan* and could sell them if they wished.)

Co-optation therefore took the form of not only granting hereditary rights to merchants but also appointing powerful merchants to act as intermediaries between the state and the other shippers. As intermediaries, the head merchants had broad administrative responsibilities, including, eventually, disposal of the some of the Liang-huai revenue. They developed extraordinary power, not only over other shippers, but also within the network of officialdom, as has been made clear elsewhere (P. T. Ho 1954; Saeki 1962). The idea that the leading Liang-huai shippers had "seized" "authority" or "power" rightfully belonging to the state, voiced at first by Yüan Shih-chen, was echoed in Ch'ing criticism.

There was a similar but less striking increase of merchant power in the field of wholesaling at the yards, and again this increase was realized against significant official opposition. In this case, the rise of powerful merchants was perhaps more clearly due solely to economically technical reasons.

The problem here was based on the structural need for some intermediaries between the shippers and the salt workers. First, large batches of salt had to be collected in advance from the thousands of small producers in order to be available for quick, convenient delivery to large-scale shippers. The shippers themselves could not do this, both because dealing with the workers required a local person familiar with yard conditions, and because the government wanted to minimize the time spent at the yards by shippers in order to minimize illegal buying (Pao, ch. 7: 9b; LHYFC 1806, ch. 10: 8b–9a, 1b–3a). Second, someone had to finance production costs and help the producers by buying up their production when shippers were not immediately available and by tiding them over bad times. Third, local leadership was useful for collecting taxes, policing, handling relief, and administering sales.

At the beginning of the Ming, these functions had been largely filled by the state, but they had become increasingly privatized. A central factor here was the gradual switch, going back to around 1500, from the collection of salt as a tax (*yen-k'o*) from the salt workers to the collection of the *che-chia* (money tax paid in lieu of the value of the salt previously collected as a tax) (Ho Wei-ning 1966, 1: 240–41).* To the extent that the state failed to collect salt, the shippers had to obtain salt privately.

Those rich salt makers owning many stoves and obviously using hired labor—a phenomenon dating back at least to 1517 (Hatano 1950: 22)— were in a good position to become middlemen. In Ming times, supposedly even before the switch to the *che-chia*, there were private persons handling the storing and shipping out of salt (LHYFC 1806, ch. 10: 8a). Possibly some middlemen were recruited from the families of those salt merchants squeezed out of their previous distributive roles by the troubles and reorganization of the late Ming and early Ch'ing periods. "Local bullies" and "corrupt salt makers" also played a role in yard wholesaling (LHYFC 1806, ch. 10: 2a–b). Obviously a major role was played by agents of shippers using the latters' capital. One account states that such agents set up *yüan* (depots) in the yards to handle transactions, and that some agents later became independent wholesalers known as either "depot merchants" or "yard merchants" (LHYFC 1806, ch. 10: 11a–b; Saeki 1962: 81). It should be added that even in Ch'ing times, state capital played a role in the yards at times.

Even though *ch'ang-shang* (yard merchants) were said to go back to the Shun-chih period (1644–61) and were clearly on the scene by 1745 (Saeki 1962: 60), a detailed report by the Liang-huai salt controller in that year iterated the government's opposition to the rise of such fully established brokers, denouncing some middlemen who had obtained licenses from the Soochow provincial treasurer and set themselves up as *mai-pu yen-hang* (salt wholesalers). At this time there was a variety of yard middlemen, and the salt controller wanted to avoid the rise of powerful, price-manipulating dealers (LHYFC 1806, ch. 10: 7b–10a). However, only ten years later, yard merchants owning salt plots and

---

*Originally the price paid for the *yin* (master license) included the purchase price of the salt. Therefore when the state collected salt, it simply issued salt to the *yin*-holder, and when it collected money from the salt workers, it issued this money to the *yin*-holder for him to buy salt with (see LHYFC 1693, 2: 709, 713–14). By 1616, however, the cost of yard salt was entirely outside the cost of the *yin* (master license).

boiling facilities were given shares proportionate to their property, just as salt workers were, in the distribution of newly formed reed-growing marshes. True, at this time yard merchants owned virtually no salt plots in seven of the eleven Taichow yards (LHYFC 1806, 27: 9b–10; Hatano 1950: 27). Their property, however, grew in the next decades. They and other merchants owned 80 percent of the Huai-nan salt plots and boiling facilities by 1839, according to Wei Yüan (1839: 717).

This rise of yard merchants can be connected to the apparent fact that they delivered salt at a lower and more stable price than independent salt workers did (Wei Yüan 1839: 716–17). Yard merchants were also more likely to have the financial ability to store salt for a year or more before selling, a procedure that improved quality (Saeki 1962: 117; TYT, ch. 31: 18b). Therefore the state had to weigh any hostility it felt toward powerful merchants against its acute interest in low prices and high quality.

The Problem of Bureaucratic Structure

Trying to control this complicated, partly powerful mixture of numerous private and semiprivate persons, Liang-huai officials also had to contend with a complex, constricting governmental framework around and above them.

Whether in the economic or some other field, any organizational complex of the Ch'ing bureaucracy can usually be seen as involving five kinds of offices: executive offices (along with the emperor); supervisory offices; advisory offices; coordinating offices; and client offices. The Liang-huai bureaucratic complex was an open-ended network made up of these five kinds of offices rather than a clearly delimited corporate structure with a "charter." Indeed there was not even a generic name for the kind of thing Liang-huai was, what we call a "zone" of the monopoly; Liang-huai was usually referred to merely by its proper name. Although it was thought of as *t'ung-hsia* (exercising jurisdiction) over market and production areas, it largely lacked territorial jurisdiction (LHYFC 1806, 32: ch. 11b–13a; TYT, ch. 31: 3a).

Executive offices were those carrying out a task or issuing orders about it. The Ch'ing distinguished between lower offices that *ch'eng* (received responsibility to carry out a task) and superior offices that *tu* (supervised) them, but *tu* generally involved sending orders to subordinate offices and so was an "executive" activity in our sense. Also a high office was sometimes given executive authority to direct (*kuan-li*) those offices normally in charge of a task.

The executive responsibilities at Liang-huai consisted of carrying out bureaucratically internal tasks like discipline, personnel management, and management of treasuries; collecting taxes; and controlling production and distribution to some extent.

Also, largely because of the spatial arrangement of monopoly work, Liang-huai salt officials had to assume some of the executive responsibilities of regular provincial administration. Although largely a specialized organization, Liang-huai was also a politically organized territorial community, especially relative to its 350,000 or more salt workers living in yards totaling 1,000 square miles or more.

By 1742, yard supervisors could adjudicate routine cases involving salt matters and salt personnel, but in non-salt matters, not to mention matters also involving civilians, they could not even make arrests. Because salt workers consequently thieved and gambled with impunity, the yard supervisor in 1746 was given broad authority in arresting them, although adjudication of more serious crimes still was handled by the local magistrate (LHYFC 1806, ch. 33: 12b–15b). Tax, relief, population registration, and *pao-chia* matters all were independently handled by the yards (LHYFC 1806, ch. 29: 1a–b, 13a–14a).

Liang-huai executive responsibilities were divided between a specialized, hierarchically unified staff of some thirty-seven Liang-huai salt officials under the Liang-huai head and in charge of production and shipping off, and the regular provincial administration in the market provinces, including five taotais with monopoly responsibilities, which handled the last stages of distribution.

As was typical in Ch'ing administration, the regular Liang-huai staff of thirty-seven or so officials was supplemented by friends giving advice, like Wei Yüan, who advised T'ao Chu; private secretaries (*mu-yu*) (LHYFC 1904, ch. 3: 12a); and officials between posts or candidates for offices rather freely commissioned (*wei-yüan*) by the Liang-huai head to help or even direct the regular Liang-huai officials. For instance, because Haichow, the Huai-pei administrative center, was so far from Yangchow, T'ao said, he had to have an experienced man in charge there. In 1832 he "commissioned" Tsou Hsi-ch'un, a former taotai once stationed near Haichow and thus well informed on Huai-pei salt affairs, to "direct" the regular Huai-pei officials (TYT, ch. 31: 13b, ch. 33: 24a–b, ch. 37: 26a–27b, ch. 38: 15a–17a, ch. 40: 16b). Tsou's contribution to the success of the ticket reform was considerable (Metzger 1962).

The Liang-huai head could effectively control this staff not only because he had executive authority over it but also because he played a major role in appointing it and was in frequent, routine communication with it relative to the movement of Liang-huai shipments and the collection of taxes. There was a problem, however, in defining the office of the Liang-huai head, a problem that led to a succession of different arrangements.

First, there was a contradiction between a rank low enough so that regular conferences with merchants would be socially comfortable (TWI, ch. 17: 24a) and a rank high enough to elicit cooperation from high regional officials, especially those with distributive responsibilities. Second, there was a contradiction between the need to concentrate on salt affairs and the advantage of combining in one person authority over both provincial and salt affairs. To seize this advantage, the office of Nanking governor-general, previously just *kuan-li* (directing) Liang-huai affairs in a general way, was given the immediate leadership of Liang-huai in 1831. But this led to the problem that the Nanking governor-general could not adequately budget his time between his provincial headquarters in Nanking and his salt headquarters in Yangchow (TYT, ch. 31: 8b, ch. 42: 7b; TWI, ch. 17: 34a).

By "supervision," I mean regularly checking to see that executive responsibilities were properly carried out and on this basis advising the emperor. The Ch'ing referred to offices that routinely *chi-ch'a* (examined) other offices, but they did not apply this term to the six boards, even though the six boards essentially were "staff" offices supervising the performance of executive responsibilities by other offices. One should also keep in mind offices supervising offices that supervised, especially the Six Sections of the Censorate, which respectively *chi-ch'a* (examined) the six boards. All six boards supervised Liang-huai, but the Board of Revenue was the most important.

The emperor, the Liang-huai head, and the Board of Revenue formed Liang-huai's triangle of supreme leadership. Executive initiative was largely with the Liang-huai head, since the emperor mainly responded to suggestions rather than exercising leadership in an active way. The Liang-huai head could usually count on imperial support for his proposals, but he had to frame them prudently, since the Board of Revenue, wary of tendencies to evade centrally imposed responsibilities, usually felt obliged to snipe at him whenever possible. The Board particularly tended to oppose any growth in the head's fiscal discretion and often tried to insist on the fulfillment of tax obligations in cases where the head was interested in lightening taxes in order to facilitate sales. The degree of conflict with the Board allowed the head to make many routine decisions but often put him on the defensive when difficult decisions were required.

This triangular relation contrasted with the system realized in parts of the Han and T'ang periods, according to which a high capital official, sometimes one participating in or even dominating the *Tsai-hsiang* (Prime Office), apparently had executive responsibility for the empire's salt monopoly and even other fiscal affairs as well. Liu Yen's (716–80) position in 779 is an example (Ho Wei-ning 1966, 1: 35–38, 94–98, 133–34, 143–48).

The decline of the latter system was not due to the development of the salt monopoly *per se* but to a more general change in the structure of the imperial bureaucracy. Early Han bureaucracy was based on the principle of concentrating great power in the hands of individual offices. The Early Han Prime Office, for instance, was usually filled by only one man, was not checked by any office of comparable stature, had great executive initiative, and within a fluctuating scope determined by the emperor, had executive discretion in sending orders to other offices. In later times, particularly by the Sung period, the principle of mutual checks between offices, both at the capital and regionally, became far more important. Whatever executive authority capital offices had had tended to decrease, and by Ch'ing times the emperor's centralized power to a large extent turned on scattering power among many offices and on maintaining a competitive check between regional offices with executive authority and capital offices with "staff" authority.*

The Liang-huai head also had to be on guard against the wide, almost indefinite variety of offices with the right to advise on Liang-huai affairs. For instance, in about 1723, a vice-president of the Board of Civil Officials joined in a memorial about fluctuations in the price of salt (LHYFC 1806, ch. 23: 1a). About the same time, a reader of the Han-lin Academy memorialized asking to switch a port from Liang-huai to another zone (LHYFC 1806, ch. 6: 5a–b). In about 1737 a vice-president of the Board of War asked in a memorial that the salt price be lowered in certain Liang-huai markets (LHYFC 1806, 6: 10a–b). T'ao Chu's critics included censors, a member of the Banqueting Court, and one of the Court of the Imperial Stud (TYT, ch. 37: 46a, ch. 40: 16a, ch. 35: 47b). The emperor's seeking of advice (*i*) from a broad circle of officials, often convened at the capital to hold a conference, was a major feature of Ch'ing bureaucracy, especially in early times (Fu 1967: 93).

Besides executive, supervisory, and advisory offices, coordination was required with a variety of offices not dealing directly with Liang-huai salt affairs. For instance, the Liang-huai officials stationed at the yards

---

* The nature of Han, T'ang, and Sung bureaucracies is made clear to a considerable extent in Yen Keng-wang 1961, in the writings of Chou Tao-chi, particularly Chou Tao-chi 1964, and in Sa 1965–66.

in Yangchow Prefecture had to coordinate with local officials in matters of water control. These yards were low-lying and subject to flooding from either the sea or the lakes in the west, and there sometimes were conflicts between yard and local government interests over the disposal of flooding waters. Salt boats had to coordinate with grain tribute boats over the use of the Grand Canal. Actions regarding both legal and illegal salt shipments between Liang-huai and other monopoly zones had to be coordinated.

Finally, client offices were essentially those receiving money taken out of Liang-huai revenue.

Apart from informal or illegal levies, most Liang-huai revenue was collected from the shippers at the Liang-huai headquarters in Yangchow according to a publicly displayed schedule of rates per *yin* (fiscal weight unit) (TYT, ch. 35: 46b). However, only about half (about two million taels) of the resulting revenue was reported to the Board of Revenue in the regular annual fiscal report (*tsou-hsiao-ts'e*), although the Board sometimes sought more systematic reports about the remaining amounts (Saeki 1962: 15). These remaining amounts, many of which were regarded as *wai-chih wai-hsiao* (fiscal items paid out and closed as correct by regional offices), were spent either for Liang-huai administrative needs or for those of many other offices, which could memorialize the emperor in order to put pressure on Liang-huai to meet its fiscal obligations (TWI, ch. 18: 22a–b, ch. 16: 22b, ch. 18: 26, 39b).

The fact that pressure from the emperor was used to hurry Liang-huai into meeting its *wai-chih wai-hsiao* obligations shows how the latter still involved some central control even though they were not included in the regular annual report to the Board of Revenue. Yet there obviously were difficulties in centralizing the flow of fiscal information. There is every reason to believe that information was readily available to officials at Peking about the total number of *yin* (fiscal weight units) annually sold in Liang-huai markets and about nearly all the legal levies paid per *yin*. But deriving a figure for total Liang-huai revenue from this information would have required complicated calculations, because different classes of *yin* had different tax schedules. Moreover, there seems to have been no felt administrative need for exact knowledge about total Liang-huai revenue. Therefore it is not surprising that our statistics for the latter are only the rough estimates given above.

We also have to note the fact that officials could not agree even on such rough estimates in the case of Liang-huai revenue in the years 1807–27 (see above). This situation stemmed partly from confusing fiscal arrangements made during those years. For instance, according to T'ao, some of the money delivered as tax revenue by Liang-huai in those years actually consisted of capital that various offices had deposited at Liang-huai to be used by Liang-huai merchants to produce interest (after the capital was used for taxes, the interest payments due to be paid to these offices were met by levying another tax on the Liang-huai merchants) (TWI, ch. 16: 3a–b, ch. 18: 64b–66a). All such complications in the flow of fiscal information, reflecting the complex relations between Liang-huai and its client offices, inhibited the rational weighing of conflicting fiscal claims when tax policy had to be adjusted to deal with economic vicissitudes.

Success and Failure in Meeting Problems

The Liang-huai bureaucracy, particularly the leadership triangle of emperor, Board of Revenue, and Liang-huai head, countered tendencies toward deviancy mainly by manipulating normative, coercive, and remunerative sanctions. It could also change its procedures to make them more easily enforceable and change its leadership structure in order to obtain more efficient manipulation of its sanctions.

Normative sanctions were important but require only brief discussion. Obviously grounded in attitudes developed through the processes of socialization in the family, a diffuse respect for authority among millions of Liang-huai members and clients often tipped the scales in favor of conforming behavior when, but only when, roughly adequate coercive and remunerative sanctions also were present. Accordingly, the officials sought to devise a situation where the potential deviant had the prospect of *li-shao fa-yen* (few profits and a severe law). Officials repeatedly said that, unless pressed economically, many people could be counted on to act legally. In the eyes of officials, such people, often those in the more urban localities, *shao chih wei fa* (understood to a slight extent that the law should be feared). On the other hand, there were places notorious for the unruliness of the local population, and smugglers, especially in rural areas, were sometimes popular with the common people, who helped them escape arrest (Saeki 1962: 203). After all, there was an old tradition, going back at least to Huang Ch'ao of the T'ang, for salt smugglers to lead popular rebellions (*ibid.*: 5). Yet rural areas were not necessarily more lawless than urban ones. There seems to have been an ideal density of population: both large, deserted areas and highly congested centers of transport were hard to control.

Two major points should be noted about Liang-huai coercive sanctions, i.e. application of the various criminal laws against smuggling. First, coercive measures could greatly reduce the illegal flow from the Liang-huai yards and from the returning grain tribute boats illegally bringing salt from the Tientsin area through the Grand Canal into the Yangtze Valley. T'ao Chu estimated that altogether these boats could annually carry about 100 million catties into the best markets of Hunan, Hupeh, and Kiangsi (TYT, ch. 50: 5a; LHYFC 1904, ch. 4: 10b). Because priority was put on speeding these boats along, officials were afraid to inspect them and thus lay themselves open to the charge of delaying the grain tribute (TYT, ch. 50: 21b). When the breakdown of Lianghuai in 1830 convinced the court that smuggling by these boats had to stop, policing efforts on the Grand Canal obtained full political backing and were so successful that in late 1833 T'ao Chu was faced by a protest from the director-general of the grain tribute. His men having lost a major source of income, he charged that T'ao Chu's inspections were delaying the grain tribute and requested that shipments of Tientsin salt into the Yangtze Valley be legalized. (T'ao Chu's refutation of this protest was accepted by the emperor.) This protest allows us to accept T'ao's claim of success in controlling this smuggling (TYT, ch. 32: 31a–35b, ch. 40: 9a–12b, ch. 44: 28a, ch. 50: 1a–8a, 16a–24b, ch. 51: 5a–7b).

The reliability of all such claims seems considerable also when we remember that T'ao was surrounded by hostile critics, such as well-connected merchants whom he had removed from the position of head merchant. For instance, one head merchant whom T'ao had ousted in 1831 had a close relative who was a censor and who, apparently on this merchant's advice, memorialized criticizing T'ao (TYT, ch. 42: 31b). Such opponents were eagerly waiting to take advantage of any shortcoming of T'ao, and smuggling by grain tribute boats was a socially visible matter that could not be hidden from them. This visibility is reflected in T'ao's statement that previously the large extent of smuggling by grain tribute boats was "common knowledge" (Saeki 1962: 136).

Policing the Yangtze also seems to have been technically practical to some extent. In the 1820's the bandit Huang Yü-lin had considerable naval power on the Yangtze, and his armed fleet, including boats carrying 100 tons or more, shipped salt from the Liang-huai yards to Hupeh and Kiangsi (Saeki 1962: 162–65). However, there is no mention of such a powerful illegal organization on the Yangtze during T'ao's years.

At the same time, control could also be effective in limiting the amount of salt illegally leaving the Liang-huai yards in the legal shipments that passed through the I-cheng Station. These shipments proceeded under detailed locational and temporal imperatives regarding the buying, moving, packing, and inspecting of the salt, while the officials supervising these actions issued the merchants various licenses and receipts and kept records, some of which were then cross-checked against each other.

The familiar criticism was made against this system that complex procedures generate corruption, but the great uproar in the 1820's about *shang-ssu* (illegal salt carried by legal merchants) involved considerable semantic confusion. It was common in the 1820's to say that any salt found in a bag above the *cheng* (regular) quota of 364 catties was "illegal." However, much of these allegedly illegal amounts were in fact legally added wastage. This wastage was denounced as "illegal" because to officials it connoted merchant corruption. Charges were made in the 1820's that with illegally added salt, the legal bags were reaching 500 to 600 catties (Pao, ch. 3: 5b). T'ao Chu himself at times denounced these added amounts. However, he revealingly said that they were "*the same as* [emphasis added] illegal salt carried in the midst of legal salt" (Saeki 1962: 180–82; TYT, ch. 30: 2a–b, 48a). Moreover, T'ao also stated unequivocally that in 1830 or earlier, 530 catties or more per bag was officially allowed. According to him, yard merchants at this time were financially pressed to sell their salt quickly. Because it thus was not stored long enough, the salt lacked firmness, and so more than the usual amount of it was spilled in transit. The large bags were allowed partly to make up for this extra loss (TYT, ch. 31: 18b–19a, 35: 45b–46b).

There is also other evidence that Liang-huai officials could effectively control the size of the bags passing through I-cheng. A major part of T'ao's 1831 reform at Huai-nan was the adoption of a 500-catty bag. This was advantageous to the merchants not only because 36 catties were untaxed and 100 catties were taxed at a reduced rate, but because these large, 500-catty bags annually saved the merchants "at least several hundred thousand taels." Although these larger bags were awkward to weigh for inspection, all packing and transport charges were figured on a per-bag basis (LHYFC 1806, ch. 7: 10b–11a, 8a–b; TYT, ch. 31: 18a–24b; TWI, ch. 17: 4a–7a). If T'ao Chu had not been able to control the weight of the bags going through the I-cheng Station, why should the question of the size of the bags have been so important to him?

With vigorous leadership, therefore, illegal salt from Tientsin and the Liang-huai yards could be kept off the Yangtze to a large extent. Admittedly, less could be done about the illegal flow from the yards into northern Kiangsu, but this area had anyway been largely written off as peddler markets and *shih-an*.

The second major point about coercive sanctions is their low efficacy in dealing with the flow of *lin-ssu* (illegal salt from neighboring zones) into the lucrative markets of Hunan, Hupeh, and Kiangsi. In the winter of 1833–34, an anonymous person reported to the emperor, and T'ao did not deny, that in these three provinces the price of legal salt ranged from 60 to more than 70 cash per catty, while the price of illegal salt ranged only up to a little more than 30 cash per catty (TYT, ch. 52: 29a; Saeki 1962: 117–20). Although the best-quality Liang-huai salt was sent to Hunan and Hupeh (Wei Yüan: 717), Liang-huai salt often had worse quality and sold on worse terms than smuggled salt. The latter was often more easily obtainable in smaller amounts, for credit, on barter terms, and in villages (Saeki 1962: 196; TYT, 52: 31b).

In the early seventeenth century, *lin-ssu* was a considerably lesser problem in Hunan and Hupeh than in Kiangsi, although Hunan and Hupeh already then were the richest Liang-huai markets (HMCSWP, 29: 324–25, 400). A late-eighteenth-century report is similar (LHYFC 1806, ch. 15: 16b). However, all three provinces tended to have a similarly serious problem in T'ao Chu's time.

The question of *lin-ssu* brings us to the major issue of remunerative sanctions, i.e. material incentives. A lumbering bureaucracy like Liang-huai was bound always to involve many economically unnatural procedures easily leading to deviancy, but there was also a margin within which economic incentives could be either raised or lowered through a variety of factors.

On the one hand, economic incentives were lowered as bureaucratic and merchant interests or mistakes led to bad or rigid salt policies, corruption, expensive financing, and failures to repair facilities. They could also be lowered by situational factors such as organizational snarls, short-term variations in supply or demand, more general price and monetary fluctuations, population trends influencing effective demand, natural disasters, and political disruption.

Such factors could also lead to vicious circles. For instance, reduction of economic incentives on the side of either distribution or production eventually undermined the other side as well. As legal sales failed, monopoly personnel were under increasing pressure to smuggle, hurting legal sales still more. Especially at Liang-huai, where shippers usually had to pay most taxes before leaving the main depot, many merchants had to borrow funds, and interest costs rose when sales declined, thus again pushing up prices. Finally, as the legal trade declined, the illegal trade gained its own momentum.

On the other hand, to raise economic incentives in the face of these tendencies, Liang-huai officials took often effective measures to stabilize or, occasionally, lower prices; to control and facilitate shipments; to shift or change economic obligations; to invest in facilities like canals; and, somewhat more rarely, to change procedures and the leadership structure. Some of the highlights and problems of this impressive program of positive economic sanctions can be outlined here.

Price control is best illustrated by the Hankow wholesale price per *pao* (packet) in the period between 1831 and 1839. Mainly by lowering taxes, T'ao reduced this price in 1831 from roughly .331 taels to roughly .265 taels, with brisk sales ensuing (TYT, ch. 52: 31a–32b). In another statement, he said that in 1831 he lowered the shippers' total outlay per *yin* (fiscal weight unit) shipped to Hankow from about 12.3 to about 10.2 taels (TYT, ch. 31: 18b). The Hankow price shortly rose to about .285 taels, where it generally stayed through the 1830's, despite the fact that the costs of shippers gradually rose again to about 12 taels per *yin*. Wei Yüan's view in about 1839 was that if the Hankow price in 1831 had stayed at .265 taels, all *lin-ssu* (illegal salt from neighboring zones) would have stopped (Wei Yüan: 712, 715, 718, 726; TYT, ch. 52: 31a–33b, ch. 37: 26b).

Attempts to control the Hankow price were complicated and energetic, going back to governmental discussions of 1740–41. These discussions in a sense used the "adversary" method, with the Hupeh governor arguing on behalf of consumers for a low price, the Liang-huai head arguing on behalf of merchants for a higher one, and the emperor expressing concern that the price be fair to both merchants and consumers. The state tried to take into account the merchants' profit margin, the length and difficulty of the local wholesalers' routes, and variations in price due to the quality of the salt, market conditions, units of measure for silver and salt, and the quality of the silver. In about 1751 the emperor noted that while the state could adjust prices somewhat, it had to follow general price trends (LHYFC 1806, ch. 23: 6b–22a, ch. 24: 9b–12b). A 1788 official investigation listed some twenty categories of expenses totaling 12.049 taels per *yin* of 344 catties, which the merchants were allowed to sell at the rate of about .29 taels per packet, supposedly realizing a profit of about 3 per cent, i.e. .3 taels per *yin* (LHYFC 1806, ch. 24: 25b–27a, 29a).

Actually, one could argue that profits were either higher or lower. On the one hand, for more than thirty years the *yin* had weighed 364 catties (LHYFC 1806, ch. 11: 20a–b). Therefore, the terms outlined above suggest that the merchants had some two extra packets in each *yin*. Moreover, while the government calculated their costs in high-quality silver, the merchants were said to use cheaper silver in meeting most of their expenses, except taxes (Pao, ch. 5: 18a–b). On the other hand, some expenses like interest charges were not included in the official figures, which represented not so much the shippers' total expenses as those expenses that the government felt could be legitimate reasons for raising the price.

I believe that these various considerations tended to cancel each other out. If so, two interesting conclusions follow. First, the margin of profit generally was small, perhaps only twice what the government intended, say 6 percent. Second, caught between a partly controlled price at Hankow and heavy expenses of a legitimate nature, the shippers had little left over for the illegal levies and "squeeze" that of course were not included by the government in calculating their costs. In other words, informal and illegal levies would seem to have been much less than the formal ones, and accounts of the corruption of salt officials must have involved considerable hyperbole. Be that as it may, armed with some knowledge about expenses and with a law demanding respect for the officially set prices, officials played a significant role in price stabilization.

Price control was backed up by procedures to control and facilitate shipments. There were four crucial ligatures where economic incentives were particularly endangered. First there was the problem of absorbing the production of all the yards when merchants were attracted to those yards with better-quality salt and lower transport costs. Second, there was the problem of coordinating tax-collection with sales in the case of the shippers. Occasionally shippers were allowed to pay some of their main taxes after selling at Hankow or Nanchang, but the state usually insisted on tax-collection prior to leaving I-cheng. Third, there was the problem of paying the boatmen enough to dissuade them from smuggling. The need to keep the salt price down made it difficult to raise boatmen's fees, and obtaining return cargoes such as grain at Hankow was a major problem. Fourth, there was the problem of devising a wholesaling procedure at Hankow fair to both the Yangchow shippers and the local traders.

Various efforts were made, often unsuccessfully, to solve these four problems, and the interconnection of these problems and others led to a basic emphasis on speed. Various time-limits were in effect. Officials continually urged distributive personnel to hurry, and officials themselves had to meet fiscal deadlines. If boats from I-cheng arrived late at Hankow, Hankow prices tended to rise, and shippers usually lacked capital to make new investments until the old shipments had been sold. Moreover, dawdling boats had more opportunities to sell illegally; shippers dawdling at the yards could buy illegally; and if shippers did not continuously make purchases at the yards, yard personnel suffered. The official emphasis on speed inhibited the officials' ability to extort illegal fees by delaying shipments, but the need repeatedly to inspect shipments reduced speed.

Huai-nan shipments took place throughout the year (LHYFC 1806, ch. 12: 11b), but the summer and early fall were the time of peak sales. It took some four months for the salt to go from the yards to Hankow, of which two months or more were spent bringing the salt to I-cheng and repacking it there (LHYFC 1806, ch. 15: 17a–b, ch. 18: 44b, ch. 24: 6a). Around 1746 there were many Yangtze salt boats carrying 400 tons or more, but officials ordered merchants to put precedence on hiring the faster, smaller boats, and by 1820 few boats, if any, carried more than 200 tons (LHYFC 1806, ch. 12: 10b–12b; Pao, ch. 3: 7a).

While the emphasis on speed often raised economic incentives to co-operate with the monopoly, so did the officials' practice of shifting or changing economic obligations in order to adjust to economic vicissitudes. Adjustments in the amount of salt were various. We have seen that salt quotas to a considerable extent did increase with population. This increase was facilitated by the explicit Ch'ing idea that briskness of sales, not just the often unreliable population figures, should be a criterion for adjusting the quotas of particular localities. However, *reducing* quotas was a difficult change, risking the opposition of the Board of Revenue. Therefore in the period between 1746 and 1781, when sales were very good, the successive Liang-huai heads, fearing future embarrassment, were wary of increasing the annual quota of *yin* (fiscal weight unit). They preferred to increase the size of the *yin* and repeatedly to ship in advance quotas due in future years (*t'i-yin*). As an emergency device, salt could also be shipped between zones.

Even if the total amount of salt remained unchanged, locational adjustments were common. When a place had bad sales, part or all of its quota would be shipped to another place within the same zone that had good sales. This simultaneously was a way of meeting rising demand in the good area while avoiding any rigid increase in its salt quota. Called *jung-hsiao* (selling salt by shifting shipments), this technique went back to a precedent of 1523 (LHYFC 1806, ch. 15: 1a).

There was a pattern of largely unsuccessful opposition to these switches on the part of the Board of Revenue. It often felt that switches violated "regular" (*cheng*) procedure, led to excessively frequent changes in the law, promoted confusion and thus increased smuggling, and were a way of evading the hard task of policing bad markets and the obligation of raising quotas in good markets. Yet by the late eighteenth century, the head of Liang-huai on his own discretion at the beginning of the year's shipments ordered many shifts on the basis of the previous year's experience, including major ones from Kiangsi to Hu-kwang (LHYFC 1806, ch. 15: 16b–18a). Within Hu-kwang (Hunan and

Hupeh), local traders could routinely shift shipments almost anywhere depending on market conditions, according to a law originating in about 1710 (TCHTSL 10: 8062 [ch. 223: 4b]). The situation in Kiangsi was similar.

A less usual form of locational adjustment was changing economically irrational zonal boundaries, which were a major cause of *lin-ssu* (illegal salt from neighboring zones). Along with various Ch'ing officials, Saeki recognizes that economically irrational boundaries were often retained because they were strategically rational, but he also emphasizes their irrational "freezing" on account of various vested interests (Saeki 1962: 89–103). I do not agree with him on this latter point for two reasons.

First, I am impressed by the Ch'ing arguments for buffer areas with geographically strategic features facilitating policing. For instance, Saeki (p. 92) cites Chu Shih's (1665–1736) view on the economic irrationality of keeping Chinkiang in the Liang-che zone while it was flooded with the cheaper Liang-huai salt. He does not cite the counter-argument made in about 1724 that allowing Liang-huai salt legally to cross the Yangtze into Chinkiang would turn Chinkiang into a smugglers' base endangering the really valuable Liang-che markets like Soochow (LHYFC 1806, ch. 6: 3b–5a).

Second, Saeki's argument that the interests of officials favored "freezing" zonal boundaries is perhaps one-sided. Some boundary problems were inherently dilemmas; officials were not necessarily eager to try on pain of disciplinary sanctions to meet the quotas of bad markets; and a few boundary changes were in fact made.

For instance, at the beginning of the Ch'ing period the three Kiangsi prefectures of Nan-an, Kan-chou, and Chi-an all belonged to the Kwangtung zone. In about 1663, they all went to Liang-huai. In about 1666, Nan-an and Kan-chou went back to Kwangtung; in about 1678 they went back to Liang-huai; and in about 1686 they finally went back to Kwangtung. All these changes were made on various plausible grounds of economic rationality partly reflecting the turbulent political conditions of the day and including the need of the Kwangtung governor in 1685 for more markets to absorb increasing production (LHYFC 1693, 2: 1093–95).

Saeki notes (p. 111) the problem of the illegal flow of Kwangtung salt into the three southern Hunan prefectures of Heng-chou, Pao-ch'ing, and Yung-chou. These three prefectures had been switched back from the Kwangtung zone to the Liang-huai zone in 1667 on grounds of economic rationality (LHYFC 1693, 2: 947–49). Liang-huai lost these markets in 1675 because the rebellion of Wu San-kuei disrupted shipments.

As Hunan sales gradually resumed in 1678, the Liang-huai head argued unsuccessfully that these markets did not belong in the Liang-huai zone (LHYFC 1806, ch. 19: 26b), and they were returned to it. This example shows that the interests of salt officials were not necessarily in the direction of maximizing the number of markets under them; problematic markets were unwelcome responsibilities.

Saeki states (p. 99) that economically irrational boundaries existed also because powerful Yangchow shippers had vested interests in retaining markets individually assigned to them on a hereditary basis. However, markets like these three Hunan prefectures were not assigned to individual Yangchow shippers. On the contrary, the latter generally made their profits solely from selling at Nanchang and Hankow and, with only a few exceptions, lacked specific connections to the localities receiving salt from these two cities. Even those few who did have such connections had little interest in retaining unprofitable markets. After all, whether or not they made a profit, they had to meet the tax quotas due on such markets. For instance, Chi-an Prefecture in Kiangsi, vulnerable to illegal salt from the Kwangtung zone, was sometimes specifically assigned to a Yangchow shipper. In about 1744, the merchant assigned to it went bankrupt and asked the Liang-huai officials to find a substitute for him (LHYFC 1806, ch. 15: 7a–8a).

Apart from locational adjustments, shipments and taxes were very often temporally shifted. They were often staggered, along with their taxes, over future years, a practice called *tai-yün* (shipping an old quota along with a current one). Occasionally shipments could be canceled with only part of their taxes remaining as debts (*ch'ung-hsiao*). Frequently in bad years the deadline for the annual fiscal report was moved further into the future with the understanding that future sales would be hurried in order gradually to move the deadline back to its proper time.

Maintaining economic incentives also involved the problem of adjusting the tax rate to economic vicissitudes. We have seen that, in the eighteenth century, tax increases relative to the money value of the shipments were reasonable if not unduly light, and that T'ao Chu in 1831 was able to reduce tax rates, thus lowering prices and stimulating sales. However, aside from lack of centralized fiscal accounting and the pressures of vested interests, tax policy was limited in two ways.

First, Ch'ing officials were aware of changes in the salt price and the weight of the *yin* (fiscal weight unit), but never to my knowledge did they draw these factors into any discussion of taxes: they discussed taxes only in terms of the tax rate per *yin*. The thought of justified tax increases was somewhat alien to them, and they felt rhetorically comfortable complaining about the increasingly crushing burden of Liang-huai taxes, a complaint they would have had to qualify if they had taken into account the rising money value of Liang-huai shipments. This attitude limited their systematic understanding of the tax question.

Second, there was a law greatly limiting the cancellation of salt-tax debts. It was a precedent that was said to have arisen out of a complicated episode beginning in 1675 (Metzger in press, chap. 3). Because of this precedent, adjustment of the salt tax to economic vicissitudes was more difficult than in the case of the land tax. In the period of "increasing difficulty" (1805–30), many tax obligations attached to unsold shipments were not canceled but rather shifted to shipments that could be sold. This increased the expenses connected to these latter shipments, raising prices, and so lowering sales still more. However, even though T'ao Chu hyperbolically denied it (TYT, ch. 42: 4b), salt taxes could to some extent be postponed or canceled, at least in a *de facto* manner, as one can see from the arrangements made in 1822, 1828, 1829, and 1831 regarding some 50 million taels of tax debts Liang-huai had accumulated (TYT, ch. 30: 54a–b, ch. 31: 40b–41a, ch. 32: 54a–55a; TWI, ch. 16: 3a; Pao, ch. 5: 10b; LHYFC 1904, ch. 3: 4a–b, 23b–25b).

During our period of "increasing difficulty" (1805–30), economic incentives gradually decreased to the point that the mix of sanctions manipulated by officials became less effective and deviancy increased. From 1821 through 1830, close to half the quotas were not sold (Saeki 1962: 318; TWI, ch. 17: 11b–15a). Two major reasons for this decline in sales seem clear. First, prices were pushed up by major increases in the tax rate after 1800. Second, the rising price of silver relative to copper cash during much of this period (King 1965: 140–43) played havoc with retail prices, as traders had to ask for more copper cash from consumers in order to make wholesale purchases, which were paid for in silver. Wei Yüan said in about 1839 that although costs in silver had not greatly changed for Liang-huai merchants since the late eighteenth century, the price of silver relative to copper had doubled (Wei Yüan: 712). According to Professor Yeh-chien Wang (private communication), the price of silver began to rise steeply in about 1825. These two factors, combined with rigidity in tax policy, stimulated the vicious circles noted above.

Yet we should not exaggerate the decline of the monopoly. In early 1832 T'ao Chu presented the annual disciplinary *k'ao-ch'eng* (examination of administrative results) for salt taotais and local magistrates during the year of Tao-kuang 10 (essentially 1830), one of the worst. Referring to Liang-huai markets in Kiangsi, Anhwei, Honan, and Kiangsu with a total annual quota of 912,566 *yin*, T'ao reported that 499,125 *yin* had been sold; 256,253 *yin* had not been sold; and reports accounting for 157,188 *yin* either had not yet come in or required rechecking. All sales in 1830, however, were from shipments belonging to pre-1830 quotas. Sales of salt from the 1830 quotas did not begin until the winter of 1831–32 (TYT, ch. 38: 12a–14b, ch. 30: 4a, 53b).

Suggestions for reform fell essentially into four groups. First, some officials believed that the leadership structure was the key, particularly the corruption stemming from the co-optation of powerful merchants (Pao, ch. 5: 11a–b). Second, some officials were greatly attracted by the idea of intensifying coercive sanctions, i.e. in *ch'i-ssu* (arresting smugglers), or otherwise forcing people to buy legally (TYT, ch. 49: 32a–39a). Third, some like Wei Yüan strongly doubted the effectiveness of coercion and focused on remunerative sanctions, especially lowering prices. Wei Yüan adduced the old monopoly idea of *chien-chia ti-ssu* (lower the price of legal salt in order to fight off illegal salt) (Wei Yüan: 711). Fourth, some believed that changing procedures was the key. Here, a prominent and appealing idea, ascribed to both Wang Yang-ming (1472–1528) and Liu Yen, was that payment of all taxes at the yards was the solution to all difficulties (TYT, ch. 30: 45a–47a, ch. 37: 46a–50a; Adshead 1970, 75–76).

T'ao Chu's reforms in 1831 and 1832 combined some aspects of all four approaches. In Huai-pei, his failure in 1831 was followed by the spectacular and continued success of the ticket system initiated in 1832. This success was based on "un-co-opting" hereditary merchants in favor of small-scale traders and greatly reducing costs (Metzger 1962). In Huai-nan, T'ao's success was great but problematic. Compared with the previous twenty years, he probably increased the average annual amount of revenue and definitely increased that of sales, shipping off the equivalent of more than five years of quotas in 1831–35 inclusive (TWI, ch. 17: 8b–9a). The crux of his Huai-nan success was his reduction of costs and prices and of smuggling from the Liang-huai yards and by the grain tribute boats. His success was limited, however, by the interrelated factors of an insufficiently reduced price and the continuing influx of *lin-ssu* (illegal salt from neighboring zones) into Hunan, Hupeh, and Kiangsi. Wei Yüan urged reducing costs and prices still more in order to increase sales and revenue. However, the most obvious way to do this, eliminating more levies, involved opposing the interests of powerful offices like the Imperial Household (TYT, ch. 33: 25a–29b, ch. 38: 29a–38b).

T'ao Chu lacked the political capital required to overcome such opposition. This was partly because he had made a mistake in his calculations that prevented him from meeting his commitments and so made him vulnerable to criticism. When in 1831 he had made his original commitments on shipment deadlines, he had been over-optimistic in thinking that he could both ship his current quotas on time and dispose of some two million *yin* of salt belonging to pre-1831 quotas.

T'ao's sales in 1831 were excellent but mostly absorbed only this old salt. T'ao had committed himself to ship the 1831 quota on time, beginning to move it in early 1831 (TYT, ch. 30: 53b–54a). However, he was many months late, beginning to ship it only in the winter of 1831–32 (TYT, ch. 37: 49a, ch. 35: 42a–b). Thus set behind, he never caught up, and in the winter of 1835–36 he had to arrange to ship the 1835 quota in installments over ten years (TWI, 17: 8a–21a).

Therefore, although his annual sales were rather good, he failed to meet the commitments he had made when obtaining the court's consent to his financially painful reforms. He vigorously defended himself in memorials by citing the large amount of salt he had sold and blaming his problems on either his predecessors or weak policing efforts in provinces outside his jurisdiction. The court appreciated his position to the extent that it did not finally condemn him for the basic shortcoming of *t'ui-hsieh* (trying to escape blame by shifting one's responsibilities onto others). Indeed, he retired honorably.

Still, however understandable, his lateness was not passed over as a forgivable slip and put him repeatedly on the political defensive. Thus, he had to be satisfied with partial success and tried to persuade the court that slow, gradual improvement was a more reasonable goal than a quick return to the prosperity of the eighteenth century.

Conclusion

More attention has usually been paid to the ingenuity and energy with which deviants violated Ch'ing laws on commerce than to the strenuous efforts made by the state to elicit conformist behavior. There seems to have been a tendency to assume that the Ch'ing state inevitably was able to elicit a minimum of conformist behavior but that any efforts on its part greatly to stretch its power were likely to fail because of its officials' lethargy, corruption, particularism, contempt for commerce, lack of specialization, administrative inflexibility, Confucian-Legalist ideology, and rigid notions of hierarchy and authority precluding flexible cooperation with private groups.

Students of the Ch'ing period, however, are becoming increasingly convinced that all the items in this catalogue require serious qualification. For instance, "lethargy," emphasized by Pye (Pye 1968: 129), was not only a behavioral trait but also a behavioral problem vigorously attacked by a system of disciplinary law and an ethic of public duty, both of which stressed the value of *li* (fully exerting oneself). The officials' basic attitude toward commerce was not that it was a necessary evil but that it was a necessary good likely to turn evil unless properly controlled. The phrase *li-shang pien-min* (make conditions materially advantageous for the merchants and the common people) (LHYFC 1904, ch. 1: 7b) expressed a common official attitude with roots going back at least to Mencius and Hsün-tzu. True, there were often vested interests and special snags inhibiting flexibility, such as the Ch'ing law limiting salt-tax cancellations. However, flexibility is abundantly illustrated by the Liang-huai officials' manipulation of remunerative sanctions. Moreover, this flexibility had deep ideological roots. For instance, the principle of "drawing from surpluses to make up deficits," going back to the *Classic of Poetry* and the *Classic of Changes*, was used to legitimate the spatial shifting of salt shipments according to economic vicissitudes in the face of the Board of Revenue's insistence on *cheng* (regular) procedure (TWI, ch. 18: 59a, 63b).

This stress on remunerative sanctions contrasted with both the Legalist stress on coercive sanctions and the Confucian stress on normative ones. Eclectically playing on the whole spectrum of sanctions, Ch'ing officials often were aware that governing is difficult and requires compromises between the state and other groups, a view similarly contrasting with a favorite idea of Chou Confucians and Legalists that governing is easy if only one adopts the right principles. Although Lucian Pye has spoken of their "extreme stress on hierarchy and ideology" as precluding "any explicitly acknowledged and legitimately accepted linkage between the realm of government and that of private interests" (Pye 1968: 16), Ch'ing officials typically advocated policies that would *ling kung ssu liang pien* (bring about a situation that would be convenient from the standpoint of public and private needs) (CSL, Yung-cheng, ch. 69: 5a; LCYFC 1729, 1: 65). Indeed, to a large extent they perceived the problem of governing as one of balancing the interests of the state and the people. Rather than insisting on a "pure and uncompromised concept of authority" (Pye 1968: 17), they perceived the flow of authority as inherently impure and as involving adjustments to the interests of private groups.* Thus in the seventeenth century Liang-huai officials formally co-opted merchants who had previously been regarded as criminally violating the proper order of the state.

At the same time, however, such factors promoting the ability of offi-

---

* On these various points, see Metzger 1970 and my book *The Internal Organization of Ch'ing Bureaucracy*, now in press at Harvard University Press.

cials to organize commerce were combined with inhibiting factors. Ch'ing ideology and education precluded the mature combination in one interest group of both political dedication and economically technical skills. Officials were often interested in actively promoting commerce but not in directly engaging in it themselves. Because they therefore often had to recruit persons economically more skillful but politically less dedicated than they, leadership in state commercial organizations tended to lack coherence.

Moreover, the political dedication of the officials themselves was problematic. Lack of trust within the bureaucracy was reflected in the design of the bureaucratic structure, which tended to stress constricting control at the expense of vigorous executive initiative. At the same time, exceedingly uncertain political support in the society at large meant that officials in large and complex undertakings had to elicit cooperation from many persons with frequently deviant inclinations. Relative to the strength of these inclinations, the state tended to suffer from a shortage of sanctions, however efficiently it could manipulate what sanctions it had. For instance, without the support of specific physical or geographical advantages, coercive sanctions were often ineffective.

Clearly, much the same repertoire of organizational skills—particularly flexible manipulation of sanctions—was available for most of the economic undertakings of the Ch'ing state, whether in the productive, distributive, or contextual areas (e.g. the monetary system). However, the persisting problem of coherent economic leadership and political support in Ch'ing times precluded state attempts extensively to control many profitable sectors of commerce such as the domestic trade in cotton, grain, tea, and alcoholic beverages.

Certainly in Ch'ing times such a contest between functional and dysfunctional factors can be seen not only in the realm of state economic organization but also in that of the private market sector and that of the partly undifferentiated peasant economy. Each sector had its own repertoire of capabilities and its own syndrome of problems. With the ideological, political, and economic changes of modern times, this repertoire changed in each sector, but so did the technological and organizational level of the economic tasks that had to be performed. With partly new capabilities, the state in modern China also has to be evaluated in terms of partly new standards and goals.

Finance in Ningpo: The 'Ch'ien Chuang,' 1750–1880

The earliest form of the *ch'ien chuang** banking system appeared in the
commercial center of Ningpo during the last half of the eighteenth century. The growth and fortunes of the system were bound up with the
economy of the trade and marketing area within which it functioned.†
The period described, 1750 to about 1880, is one of almost continuous
expansion of that economy. Between 1750 and 1842, prior to the opening
of Ningpo as a treaty port, most of the influential *ch'ien chuang* in the
city were founded or developed. They were formal banking institutions
that issued notes and used a clearinghouse. From 1842 until about 1865,
the expansion of *ch'ien chuang* in Ningpo and Shanghai quickened as the
locus of foreign (primarily Western) trade shifted from Canton northward to Shanghai, and the clientele of the *ch'ien chuang* became increasingly involved in the import-export and transshipping trade with the
West. The years between 1865 and 1875 or 1880 are considered the high
point in the development of the *ch'ien chuang*. By this later period, the
center of the *ch'ien chuang* system had long been Shanghai, not Ningpo.
Institutional growth had far outstripped the confines of local and even

---

* Frank Tamagna defines a *ch'ien chuang* or "native bank" as "a financial firm
established in the form of a single proprietorship or partnership by members of a
family, a clan, or a closed circle of friends, for the purpose of handling deposits,
lending, remittances, and exchange of money, with unlimited responsibility guaranteed by all resources of the proprietor or of the partners" (Tamagna 1942: 57).

† The development of banking has been described as a "progressive centraliza-
tion of clearance" in the course of which the geographical area encompassed, the
number of social and economic activities embraced, and the duration of credit
periods all increase (Usher 1943: 4). The growth of the *ch'ien chuang* system is an
excellent illustration of this developmental process. I am indebted to Ramon Myers
for calling my attention to the similarities between the *ch'ien chuang* and the early
deposit banks in Europe that are the subject of Usher's study.

regional systems, as Chinese investors sought the profits of far-flung markets. The development of this institution is here explored on several levels: the individual financier, the bank itself, and the guild organization that linked them.*

Banking in traditional China was viewed by contemporaries and is widely characterized in the literature as a regional phenomenon (Tamagna 1942: 19; Wagel 1915: 158; King 1965: 46; SHCCSL: 770–71; Nishizato 1967a: 2). Chinese and Japanese economic historians use the terms *pei pang* or *pei p'ai* (northern clique) and *nan páng* or *nan p'ai* (southern clique) to refer to the two major Chinese banking systems, the Shansi banks and the *ch'ien chuang* or "native banks" (Hirohata 1933: 312–13; G. H. Chang 1938b: 310). In this paper I shall use the terms "Shansi bank" and *ch'ien chuang* to refer to them.

The Shansi banks and the *ch'ien chuang* differed in several crucial ways, and there has been much speculation as to the probable causes of these differences. The Shansi banks dealt in interregional remittance transactions and functioned (in the absence of a central national bank) as a quasi-governmental institution. They were bankers' banks, granting individual merchant loans only in the south, where their range of functions was more restricted. They were functionally divided into central and branch organs, controlled by three major local groups (Kagawa 1948: 75). Their sphere of influence was centered north of the Yangtze, in particular in Peking and Tientsin.

The *ch'ien chuang*, by contrast, were independent, small-scale institutions, specific to various local systems (Hirohata 1933: 314–15). With a few exceptions, interregional ties were limited to the Yangtze Valley trade network. Such ties were informal, typically ownership by a single person of several *ch'ien chuang*.† They were relatively free from central

* The preparation of the initial version of this paper owes much to the guidance of professors G. William Skinner and Yoshinobu Shiba. In revising it I have benefitted from the astute criticisms of participants in the research conference on economic organization in Chinese society, in particular those of Ralph Heunemann, Albert Feuerwerker, and Mark Elvin. The paper was revised during a year's fellowship granted by the American Association of University Women.

† In practice the domains of the Shansi banks and the *ch'ien chuang* were not altogether mutually exclusive. For example, the Shansi banks maintained branches in Amoy and Canton through the nineteenth century, although they were outnumbered by the "local banks" or *ch'ien chuang* (IMC 1882–91: 517–18, 572). In Foochow it was reported in 1890 that of the six "large" banks in the city, five were Shansi banks (*ibid.*: 425). The key centers for *ch'ien chuang* late in the nineteenth century were Shanghai and Hangchow (Wang Hsiao-t'ung 1933: 221–22). By the early 1900's, two large *ch'ien chuang* had established Shansi-type remittance banks with branches in Tientsin, Peking, and Shanghai (SKZS 3: 562–64; C. L. Chang

governmental control and received no governmental support: during the pre-Republican period as their status improved they became repositories for circuit and district funds, but they neither held deposits for, nor issued direct loans to, the central government (L. S. Yang 1952: 85; IMC 1882–91: 427). They were merchant banks, whose capital was lent to local traders against the security of goods in transit or, more often, on the personal guarantee of the borrower (IMC 1882–91: 379). This capital, in the early stages of development, was supplied by the owners themselves; later, substantial amounts were obtained from individual depositors (King 1965: 96). These *ch'ien chuang* controlled local financial transactions in the Yangtze ports and in the central and southern coastal areas of China, acting as centers for monetary exchange as well as for the issue of credit notes for trade and tax purposes.

Various explanations have been given for the development of these two distinct banking systems (Tamagna 1942: 16–18; King 1965: 92–97; Ch'en 1937: 20–22; C. L. Chang 1962: 174–80). From these, several conclusions may be drawn. The interregional spread of the Shansi banking organization was fostered at the earliest stages by (a) an economic base in Shansi that was conducive to the rise of domestic interregional trade in silk, salt, and iron, and the consequent development of a trade organization to tap this potential source of wealth; (b) a location that kept trade primarily landlocked; and (c) proximity to the capital, which allowed the government to oversee the financial operations that evolved from this trade network and to co-opt them to serve its own fiscal needs.

Trade in the South, by contrast, was oriented to coastal and foreign ports. By the late eighteenth century, foreign coins had come into general use as a medium of exchange for this trade. Already protected from direct governmental controls by the miles that separated it from the capital, the southern trade won a further measure of autonomy in its use of a foreign currency.*

1962: 178). Although generally a *ch'ien chuang* was confined to one city and had no branches, it maintained diffuse ties with other *ch'ien chuang* in the form of loose associations called *lien* or *pang*. The former were native banks recognizable by a common character in their names, the capital for which was supplied by a single investor. The latter groups tended to be more broadly distributed, linked by *t'ung-hsiang* ties (Kagawa, 1948: 12–13). Kagawa points out that the unlimited liability assumed by the *ch'ien chuang* created a need for broadening and strengthening ties of mutual responsibility.

* The first foreign currency accepted as standard coinage in China was the Carolus dollar of Spain; after the mid-1850's, the Mexican dollar also came into widespread use. Throughout the nineteenth century, the Canton merchants and the East India Company assigned the dollar a nominal value of .72 taels. However, the dollar was used both as a coin and as a unit of account, the value of which varied in different places and at different times. For a detailed discussion of the various roles

Thus the Shansi banks and the *ch'ien chuang*, although both originated in trade and mercantile organization, were destined for divergent courses of development. The early interest shown by the government in supporting and then using the evolving network of interregional remittances controlled by the Shansi merchants was important to the success of the Shansi banking system. Originating, by popular account, in the early eighteenth century, the Shansi banking network was beginning to be co-opted by the government by the mid-nineteenth century.* Co-optation did not necessarily imply exploitation, for the Shansi banks flourished under relatively light central government control. They accepted government funds for deposit at no interest and lent the money at usurious rates to other banks (Stanley 1961: 28; SKZS 3: 556–58). Other loans went to bright young candidates in the civil service examinations at the capital. Later the earnings of these same men were collected in the form of deposits and investments as they moved from post to lucrative post throughout the empire (Stanley 1961: 28).† In its zeal to insure the solvency of this repository of official funds, the government bolstered the established hegemony of the three Shansi banking cliques by requiring that individuals or companies desiring to found similar institutions be endorsed by members of the established group (C. L. Chang 1962: 175). The Shansi banks, for their part, took pains to make sure that their employees were of such caliber and rank as befitted brokers for the elite (*ibid.*: 177; Ch'en 1937: 155).

With government funds to finance an interregional banking system, and with an expanding role as the intermediary in financial transactions between imperial and provincial treasuries, the Shansi banks were assured of success, and the 1870's and 1880's saw the zenith of their development.

The development of the southern group of financial institutions, the *ch'ien chuang*, proceeded with the growth of commerce in their area and

---

played by the dollar in the Chinese monetary system, see King 1965: 81–90. In the city of Ningpo, silver dollars came into use as early as the Chia-ch'ing period (1796–1821) (YHTC 1936: 256a).

* Stanley, citing a memorial of 1864 that warned against connivance between Shansi bankers and underlings in the treasury, describes the Shansi banking system as "firmly entrenched" in government finance by the early T'ung-chih reign (Stanley 1961: 28). Like the *ch'ien chuang*, the Shansi banks flourished during the Taiping Rebellion, when their facilities were employed to ensure the safe transport of government funds through the countryside, and their resources were tapped to make up provincial quotas for military levies. See below, pp. 67–71.

† "As officials were liable to frequent transfers, Shansi banks were an ideal place to deposit spoils. Officials did not have to take their cash when transferred. Shansi bankers had also proven very trustworthy to the officials in not revealing the amount of their deposits during government probes of corruption" (C. L. Chang 1962: 175 [n82]). See also Ch'en 1937: 154.

the corresponding increase in the size and complexity of existing monetary institutions. Commerce in the South was distinguished from that in the North by a greater volume of foreign and coastal trade; by the widespread use of foreign silver coins as the medium of exchange in major commercial centers; by a high degree of local variation in currency and units of account, reinforced by dialect differences; and finally, by the efficient water-transport system centered on the Yangtze River Valley, which carried the expanding trade in silk, tea, cotton, and (after 1842) opium (Ho 1959: 196). A sophisticated local banking system well suited to this area grew up in and around Ningpo, first tied to Shanghai, then expanding from there throughout South and central China. Each major commercial center in which *ch'ien chuang* were formed retained its own peculiar exchange system based on a local unit of account; each issued its own kind of credit in the form of notes or passbooks. *Ch'ien chuang* remained independent, small-scale organizations whose activities were coordinated by local guilds and bankers' associations.

Contrary to certain popular accounts, the *ch'ien chuang* were not organized overnight, an instant response to a specific crisis, but economic historians can at best speculate on their precise origins and immediate predecessors. Katō Shigeshi views the money-changing shops (*ch'ien p'u* and *tui fang*) of the Southern Sung as the ancestors of the *ch'ien chuang* of the Ch'ing period. These primitive monetary institutions performed various functions, such as buying and selling bullion, working in precious metals, and assaying coinage (Katō 1952: 463–65). Katō suggests that such *ch'ien p'u* began to assume true banking functions as early as the Ch'ien-lung period (1736–96). According to him, during this time of long-term relative stability, the expansion of trade necessitated the development of a convenient and portable medium of exchange, with the result that drafts were issued that were redeemable either for copper cash or for silver taels. At the same time, people looking for a place to invest their surplus capital turned to the *ch'ien p'u* and *ch'ien chuang*, which became in time virtual merchant banks (*ibid.*: 476). Most scholars agree with Katō that the *ch'ien chuang* had become true banks at least by the Chia-ch'ing period (1796–1821) (Stanley 1961: 22–23; P'eng 1954: 608–10; SHCCSL: 7; G. H. Chang 1938a: 25–26).

Katō's hypothesis points up two factors in the Chinese economy of the eighteenth century that were conducive to the development of a banking system: parallel bimetallism (requiring money-changing institutions and specialists)* and the growth of trade (creating a need both for credit

---

* A clear discussion of the nature of a parallel bimetallic system may be found in King 1965: 40–42. It is important to note that the two Chinese currencies of this era served two separate markets—copper was used in retail trade and for daily

and for a convenient, portable medium of exchange. Evidence for the
growth of domestic trade during the eighteenth century can be found
in the rise of merchant guilds in urban centers, the expansion of the rural
marketing system, and in numerous accounts of a rising standard of living
and of unprecedented levels of affluence and conspicuous consumption
among the elite.* The increased demand for silver and copper engen-
dered by expanding trade created its own strains. In traditional China
the silver used in wholesale transactions was not coined, but had to be
weighed and assayed for fineness. This not only made it cumbersome
and impossible to transport for any distance without elaborate security
and impedimenta, but further increased the complexity of interregional
exchanges because weights, measures, and assaying techniques varied
with each local system. The supply of copper cash (used in retail transactions) was limited by the production capacity of the Yunnan copper
mines and by recurrent difficulties in transporting copper bullion to
provincial mints. In addition, the government never successfully controlled the debasement of its copper currency by defacement and coun-
terfeiting of coins. Finally, seasonal demands for cash when taxes fell
due, and at the New Year (when debts were repaid), regularly outstripped the capacity of the provincial mints (King 1965: 58).

These are some of the reasons why banking began in China. As in
many other cultures, it began in the hands of that social group most often
involved in monetary transactions, the merchants (Ch'en 1937: 26–28;
Ashton 1955: 180; Hammond 1957: 75–76; Cameron 1967: 159–60).
Among them, the Ningpo traders were early innovators. The credit system they created to serve their needs went with them as they traded,
and outgrew the local system of Ningpo as they did.

Ningpo had a long history as a commercial center.† The city was first
designated an official port of trade during the Northern Sung, when an

wages, silver in the wholesale market and for larger salaries—and hence two separate sectors of the population. See below, pp. 63–64.

* The degree or rate of growth in the empire as a whole is impossible to quantify.
A good sense of the quality as well as the quantity of trade and affluence is provided in the various writings of Ho Ping-ti, whose conclusions are based on an exceptionally comprehensive investigation of local gazetteers. See in particular Ho
1959; 197–204; Ho 1967: 194–95; Ho 1954: 155–57. Katō's sampling of data on
rural markets indicates a general growth in rural marketing beginning in the K'ang-
hsi period (Katō 1936: 170). Suzuki Chūsei's study of the mid-Ch'ing period points
to the easing of external pressures in the north and the growth of foreign trade in
the south beginning in the eighteenth century as primary factors underlying the century of what Ho has called *pax sinica* (Suzuki 1952: 1–17).

† An article on the role of Ningpo in the history of foreign trade in China has
been published in *Kuo feng* vol. 3, no. 9, by Chang Tao-yüan; but has come to my
attention too late for use in the preparation of this paper.

Office of Overseas Trade (Shih Po Ssu) was established there at the end of the tenth century (Fujita 1917: 183–92). During the Southern Sung, with the court at Hangchow, Ningpo (then called Ming-chou) served as the major port of entry for goods sent by sea to the capital, and was guarded by military stations on Ting-hai in the outlying Chusan archipelago (Arimoto 1931b: 26–27; 1931a, 111–12; Lo 1955: 490–91). A large population increase, the rise of a shipbuilding industry, and improvements in water control systems accompanied this growth of trade at the port (Lo 1955: 498–500; Shiba, in press; Negishi 1951: 31).

From the eighth century until the Ch'ing period, Ningpo remained a major port of entry for the Japan trade, and for official emissaries sent by the Japanese government (Kimiya 1931; Reischauer 1940: 145–46). Centrally located on the China coast, with a sheltered and relatively unsilted natural harbor and inland connections with Hangchow leading to Nanking and Peking via the Grand Canal, Ningpo became the logical entrepôt when the Japanese could no longer use their Korean route.* At the beginning of the Ming, Ningpo was designated the official port of entry for trade with Japan, and the experience her merchants gained in that trade can be regarded as a preparation for her later trade with the West.†

In the eighteenth century, Western traders seeking a way out of the Canton system turned to Ningpo, where the Chekiang silk they wanted could be bought without transshipment and without the intervention of

---

* The Japanese prior to 702 had used a shorter northern route via Korea and the Shantung peninsula, but were forced in that year (apparently by Silla's blockade of the sea) to master the longer and more hazardous route from western Japan to the southern coast of China (Reischauer 1940: 145–46; Tsunoda 1951: 41). Foreign trade at Ningpo was by no means limited to the Japan trade, but as early as the Sung included Korea, Java, Champa, Sumatra, and the Philippines (Fujita 1917: 191–92).

† "Official" trade between China and Japan flourished during the fifteenth and sixteenth centuries, during which time it fell increasingly into the hands of private merchants. When China severed all relations with Japan and terminated official Sino-Japanese trade in 1598, both Chinese and Japanese merchants continued private business as usual. When in 1635 Japan began to impose trade restrictions of her own, a virtual monopoly of the private trade was handed to the Chinese (Hall 1949: 447–48). Under the protection and patronage of the Cheng clan, Fukienese traders first seized control of Sino-Japanese trade out of Nagasaki, the only Japanese port that was still open to foreign trade after 1635. But after Ningpo was reopened to official trade in 1695, Ningpo merchants set themselves the task of wresting control from the Fukienese. In 1715 Ningpo shippers were awarded twenty-two of the fifty-one permits issued for trade at Nagasaki. Nanking merchants got twenty, and the Fukienese got none. (Yamawaki 1960: 23–24). Thus at the beginning of the eighteenth century Ningpo was a logical choice for Westerners looking for alternative outlets for the foreign trade centered then at Canton. Initial liaisons formed by British traders in Ningpo were *sub rosa* and were strictly forbidden when called to the attention of the throne (Fu 1966, 1: 200–204, 215, 218–20).

the Cohong monopoly. In 1756, 1757, and 1759 the Ch'ien-lung Emperor tried to halt British incursions into the trade at Ningpo, issuing warnings and raising tariffs. He may have sensed the futility of his efforts from the beginning, for his edict of August 4, 1756, notes that the "barbarians" were probably invited into Ningpo by native brokers and interpreters who hoped to profit from trading with them (Fu 1966, 1: 200–201). And indeed neither higher tariffs nor imperial injunctions appear to have stood in the way of the new trade, although since it never became legal its volume cannot be estimated.

During the course of the eighteenth century, Fukienese interests continued to be strong in the silk trade at Ningpo,* and the Ningpo merchants began to feel inhibited in their profit-taking by the ties of kinship, friendship, and neighborliness that were an unavoidable consequence of doing business in their home city. At the same time, Shanghai was emerging as the major entrepôt of the Chinese coastal trade, and was well on its way to becoming the major trade center for all China.† Not surprisingly, then, by the end of the century many Ningpo merchants had been drawn out of their local system northward to Shanghai and the mouth of the Yangtze.

By the beginning of the nineteenth century, Ningpo merchants were thus experienced in both foreign and domestic trade. They had business interests as distant as Nagasaki and as near as Shanghai; their city con-

---

* Fukienese merchants were already engaged in domestic trade at Ningpo during the Ming period, exchanging sugar for silk and textiles. Until 1863, Fukienese sugar bound for Shantung and points north was shipped via Ningpo (GBSP vol. 71, 1866). In the course of this time, Ningpo had become the port used by Fukienese merchants for their silk trade with Japan, and they monopolized the licensed shipping trade at Nagasaki until a growth of the shipping industry in Ningpo and Nanking in the late seventeenth century began to threaten their control (Yamawaki 1960: 24–25, 31–32). Fukienese trade guilds dealing in sugar, together with Shantung merchant guilds, maintained a strong foothold in domestic trade at Ningpo through the nineteenth century. As late as 1891 the Customs Inspectorate reported that the three most powerful merchant guilds in Ningpo remained the Fukien *hui kuan* (IMC 1882–91: 384; cf. GBSP vol. 91, 1881). Trade in peas and bean cake from the north was controlled by the Shantung guild (GBSP vol. 80, 1884–85).

† On the growth of Shanghai as a trade center prior to 1842, see Murphey 1953: 66–67; Murphey 1970: 34–35. He finds that "by the beginning of the nineteenth century Shanghai was the principal port for the trade of the Yangtze basin, and the center of coastal trade between north and south China." Although Shanghai was handicapped by problems with silting that Ningpo did not face, Shanghai enjoyed direct access to navigable inland water transport on the Yangtze, whereas Ningpo encountered persistent difficulties with crude haulovers on its inland canal system. Ningpo financiers enjoyed a uniquely advantageous position precisely because they became bankers in Shanghai, outside of their own local system and one step higher in the hierarchy of local systems nodes (G. W. Skinner, in press).

trolled the northeastern market for Chekiang and was the node of a growing local trading system that sprawled westward into the Shao-hsing area. It seems clear that the impetus for the Ningpo credit system lay in the demands for credit and exchange media posed by this established and now expanding trade network.* But the origins of the particular form of credit that developed in Ningpo, the *kuo-chang* (transfer-tael) system, are as uncertain as those of the Shansi banks.

Mark Elvin suggests the strong possibility that credit institutions of the Ningpo type were borrowed from Japan. In fact there is a great similarity between the *daifukuchō* (passbook) system instituted at Osaka during the late seventeenth century, and the *kuo-chang* system at Ningpo (see Crawcour 1961; Soyeda 1896: 412–13; Matsuyoshi 1932: 20). The case of the Ningpo emigré Sung Su-ch'ing, who represented the Hoso-kawa family, suggests the existence of as yet undocumented private liaisons between Ningpo and Japanese traders (see also Tsunoda 1951: 119, 128, *et passim*). Although the Japan trade originated in Nagasaki after 1635, and the *daifukuchō* were in use primarily in remittances between Edo and Osaka, the Osaka region was the original domain of the Hoso-kawa, and Ningpo merchants had links there at least through the mid-sixteenth century (Y. T. Wang 1964: 4; Ishihara 1964: 122).†

According to one popular notion, the system began when the Taiping Rebellion disrupted trade routes from Yunnan and copper cash grew scarce on the market (YHTC 1936: 73b–73a):‡

* The relationship between the development of the credit system and the growth of trade is clearly reciprocal. Arimoto lists several ways in which he finds that the transfer-tael system stimulated trade by Ningpo merchants outside Ningpo itself. The system provided both borrower and lender with a permanent, objective record of debts and loans so that these obligations could not be "forgotten" or evaded, even by friends or relatives. Ningpo capital was freed for investment outside the local system, since credit obviated the need for capital accumulation at home. Merchants had a ready source of credit to meet unexpected demands for money, which enabled them to take advantage of low prices no matter where they were (Arimoto 1931a: 126–28; 1931b: 586–88).

† I do not know whether the *daifukuchō* system was in use at Nagasaki, nor have I investigated the nature of remittances between Nagasaki and Ningpo. I am indebted to Mr. Elvin for directing me to Japanese sources on the Hosokawa-Ōuchi rivalry and the trade between Ningpo and Nagasaki.

‡ It should be noted that this "popular notion" is correct in ascribing important changes in the financial system to the Hsien-feng period; they are simply the wrong changes (see below, pp. 67–68). The nature of the data makes it impossible to determine when banks actually began to create credit. The evidence of commentaries such as this, where bank notes or passbook transactions are seen as compensating for a currency shortage, leaves little doubt that credit was being created (see Usher 1943: 24–25). It has further been noted that in medieval Europe, "in many periods when coins were badly clipped and worn, the denomination of account in

During the Hsien-feng reign (1851–62) the copper route from Yunnan was blocked, and the southeast suffered a shortage of cash that was especially severe in Ningpo, where the amount of cash in circulation dropped precipitously. Life grew steadily more difficult, panic set in, there was talk of rebellion. Some people with an eye to the future instituted a certain number of *ch'ien chuang*. These *ch'ien chuang* together pooled a sum of money for lending. Every merchant kept an account of withdrawals from and payments to a given *ch'ien chuang*, and went to the *ch'ien chuang* to have these recorded. The following day each *chuang* published a paper that was exchanged with the others and audited, after which the accounts were settled. Like relatives they gave and took, sharing profits and losses alike, availing themselves of one another's help. Within several months the crisis had passed, and from that time on, trade on the market was conducted without ready cash. Once an amount was entered in an account, it was considered good credit.

There is, however, ample evidence that a credit and banking system existed in Ningpo before the opening of the treaty ports, and certainly well before the Taiping Rebellion. In 1838 a memorial from the governor of Chekiang, Wu-erh-kung-e, refers to the large number of *ch'ien p'u* in Ningpo, a phenomenon he ascribes to the city's prominence as a seaport and trade center. He goes on to say that although these banks insist that they do not issue bank drafts or promissory notes, they do in fact make use of a so-called *ch'ien p'iao*, a note circulated with the backing of a monetary reserve, to avoid the inconvenience of circulating money (Nishizato 1967a: 10).

Private writings are more revealing. One such source is the autobiography of Tuan Kuang-ch'ing, a bureaucrat who held various local offices in the Ningpo region, ultimately rising to the post of circuit intendant for Shao-hsing and Ningpo Prefectures during the 1850's and 1860's. Tuan was acutely interested in the political and economic workings of the local system over which he presided. His notes of 1858 describe a well-established and efficiently functioning system of banking and credit originating at some time in the vague past. Note that, according to him, pass-

---

bank books was a more significant symbol of value than mere coin" (*ibid.*: 12). The state of copper currency during the latter half of the nineteenth century in China suggests that this situation was also present in the Chinese case. In his description of the early banking system at Osaka, Crawcour states that credit could theoretically be created up to three times the amount of original deposits, and that "Towards the end of the Tokugawa period, notes issued for sixty to seventy thousand *ryō* were often backed by no more than ten thousand *ryō*" (Crawcour 1961: 356). At the same time, the coin shortage in the Chinese case introduced a note of instability that resulted in periodic discounting of bank notes. The failure of one bank to redeem its notes for full cash value could and did cause runs on other banks and occasionally a full-scale crash (King 1965: 103).

books and drafts were both used as credit instruments, and that notes of reputable banks were negotiable by any bearer (Tuan 1968: 122–23):

The port of Ningpo has long had a reputation for money-lending. . . . This has been true since the time when the wealthy families of Ningpo opened *ch'ien chuang*, and everyone who had any money wanted to deposit it in these shops, receiving a certain rate of interest on the sum from the manager. In turn, merchants in every line of business have borrowed money from these *ch'ien chuang*, likewise paying interest on it. They simply record their transactions in a passbook, eliminating the need for an exchange of cash. The people, too, in supplying their daily needs, merely draw a draft on a money house (*ch'ien tien*) for the amount they need and use the draft as payment. This is more convenient than using cash, and it spares having to compute the rate of exchange. In time people have become willing to pay a discount on silver when they exchange cash for notes because notes are more convenient to use; since the *ch'ien chuang* have the backing of wealthy families, no one cares that the notes are not personal ones. Thus the Ningpo merchants need only their word, not money, when they trade. When they make a purchase, they simply transfer taels through the *ch'ien tien*; the *ch'ien chuang* will in turn directly credit any amount from 10,000 silver dollars to several times that sum to the seller's account. Dollars and taels need never change hands. The continual growth of the port at Ningpo, and the preeminence of the name and wealth of Ningpo in the whole province, is due to this. Ningpo subscriptions since the Rebellion have been the largest in the province, yet they are still regarded as small because of the enormous wealth of the Ningpo people.

In May of 1852, beginning his term as magistrate of Yin Hsien, Tuan issued a proclamation announcing that "The total *ting* tax, reckoned in *Yung chiang* transfer taels (*kuo-chang*), is to be 2,600 coppers on each tael of silver, and 4,600 coppers on each *shih* of autumn rice" (YHTC 1936: 72b–73a; Tomita n.d.: 21–23).

Further evidence of the early development of finance and credit in Ningpo is provided by its human export to Shanghai—those individuals and families who, both independently and as guild members, were primarily responsible for Ningpo's reputation for commercial acumen.

By 1796, Ningpo merchants had congregated in Shanghai in sufficient numbers to sponsor the construction of a *t'ung-hsiang* guild hall, the Ssuming Kung So. Within this body, members gravitated into smaller occupational groupings (*t'ung-yeh t'uan-t'i*) (Negishi 1951: 32–34). The financial or bankers' group seems to have been a dominant faction within the guild, but its early organization and activities are obscure. There is little doubt of the power of this group beyond the guild and in the city

of Shanghai as a whole, for the Shanghai Native Bankers' Guild was
virtually run throughout its history by members of a Ningpo–Shao-hsing
clique.* Ningpo bankers retained their control over an ever larger and
more corporate bankers' organization by initiating a series of affiliations,
first with Shao-hsing bankers, then with other bankers' groups in Shanghai, taking care to preserve their own hegemony all the while (*ibid.*: 63).

The Shanghai Native Bankers' Guild (Shang-hai Ch'ien Yeh T'ung
Yeh Kung Hui) is said to have been formed as early as the Ch'ien-lung
period (1736–96); it is known that their guild hall in the Nei Yüan, or
eastern courtyard, of the Ch'eng Huang Miao, was built during that
period. Negishi pushes the origin of the guild back still further, because
the capacity to finance construction of a guild hall comes only after a
period of organization during which temporary quarters are generally
used (*ibid.*: 97). It seems most likely that, although financial guilds
composed of money-changers and silver- or goldsmiths had been in
existence for some time in the Shanghai area (perhaps as early as the
Sung period), guilds formed under the leadership of true native bankers
came into existence only in the early nineteenth century (*ibid.*: 101).
The large, Ningpo-based merchant families who were to retain control of
banking and guild organization in the financial market of Shanghai for
over a century began to emerge at this time.

Members of Ningpo merchant families are first specifically said to be
engaged in banking activity in Shanghai between 1796 and 1821. However, these men cannot be viewed as true bankers, but rather as merchants diversifying their interests and investments. Among the earliest
were Li Yeh-t'ing and Fang Chieh-t'ang of Chen-hai. The rags-to-riches
success stories of these two men may or may not be exaggerated. Even
after the Ningpo banking families were well established in Shanghai and
elsewhere in the second half of the century, they retained generous reserves of funds and clan support in the Ningpo region.†

---

* The "natural local system" that constitutes the hinterland of Ningpo is defined
in this paper as the surrounding *hsien* of Yin, Chen-hai, Tz'u-ch'i, Feng-hua, and
Ting-hai (all a part of Ningpo Prefecture during most of the Ch'ing period), as well
as two *hsien* to the west that are historically associated with Shao-hsing Prefecture:
Yü-yao and Shang-yü. References to "Shao-hsing" bankers or members of the "Shao-
hsing clique" in banking always refer to people from these two districts.

† The investments from home were well repaid. The Customs Inspectorate at
Ningpo reported in 1891 that "The constant excess of exportations over importa-
tions of treasure . . . would, if not made up for in some way, drain the port of its
silver and leave it without a circulating medium. There are no signs of any want of
currency, loans on good security being easily negotiable at fair rates of interest. It
is certain, therefore, that money is constantly coming into the port through channels
of which the Customs Returns take no cognizance. The large passenger traffic would
account for the bringing in of large sums each year in excess of what goes away

Li Yeh-t'ing came to Shanghai from his home in 1822, during his fifteenth year. His first job was with a wine shop, where he worked carrying warm wine to the crews of the sampans in port.* About five years later he got a job working on a sampan. It was customary for sampan owners to permit their employees to carry small amounts of produce to sell for their own profit, and in this manner the thrifty Li accumulated enough money, together with funds furnished by his elder brother back in Chen-hai, to acquire a fleet of ten boats. The new Chiu Ta Sampan Company transported raw cotton and other products of the southeast to northern ports, where they were exchanged for oil, beans, and wood products. To finance this trade, Li relied on loans from a *ch'ien chuang* in Shanghai. Since such loans were paid off only when the northern goods were sold back in Shanghai, and since piracy and accidents were frequent in that trade, a considerable risk was involved. To avoid damaging the credit of the *ch'ien chuang* with which he dealt, Li was forced to contract his loans in secret and to rely on personal ties with a *ch'ien chuang* employee, one Chao P'u-chai, in order to get the loans at all. Li's profits eventually enabled him to found three *ch'ien chuang* of his own in Shanghai. On Li's death the three *ch'ien chuang* he owned were divided between his own branch of the family and that of his elder brother, each taking charge of one bank and sharing joint ownership of the third. The Li *ch'ien chuang* continued to function in Shanghai until the Revolution of 1911 (SHCCSL: 734–36; Nishizato 1967a: 6–9; Shiba, in press).

The foundations for the rise of another prominent Ningpo merchant-banking family were also being laid in this early period. These were the descendants of Fang Chieh-t'ang, who had earlier made a small fortune in merchandising grain and foodstuffs, and whose nephews had come with him early in 1800 when his business expanded from Ch'i-ch'iao, Chen-hai, to Shanghai. One of these nephews, Fang Jun-chai, opened a *ch'ien chuang* in the south market in Shanghai, where he also traded in raw cotton and other miscellaneous goods. His capital is said to have totalled sixty to seventy thousand taels. The Fang lineage soon had *ch'ien*

---

through the same channel; for the passengers are chiefly Ningpo men who go abroad for employment, and on revisiting their home at intervals bring with them their savings and leave them here. . . ." (IMC 1882–91: 366–67).

* Li probably got even this menial job through a *t'ung-hsiang* tie, although my source does not say so. Yeh Ch'eng-chung's career began similarly (Ho 1964, 308–10). G. W. Skinner observes (personal communication) that sending young boys to make their own way in the big city is an excellent means of socializing entrepreneurs of the future. That is, young men like Li are not necessarily off to make money (which they do not need) but to build character and initiative (which their families feel they will not acquire in the comfort of home).

chuang and other enterprises in Ningpo, Hangchow, and Hankow, and business ties in Shao-hsing, Nanking, Shasi, I-ch'ang, and Huchow (SHCCSL: 730–32; Nishizato 1967a: 8–9; Shiba, in press).

Before the travels of Ningpo's enterprising envoys carry this story too far afield, I shall return to Ningpo and reconstruct the emerging system of finance and credit that underlay the proliferation of her trade network in south China and in the coastal trade.

It can be assumed that the Ningpo credit system, the transfer-tael system, was well established by 1850. This is clear from the testimony of Tuan Kuang-ch'ing and from the 1838 memorial. Further evidence is supplied by expressions of social unrest during the 1850's. These protests, discussed in a later section, were directed against an emerging financial elite in the Ningpo region. A description of the developed credit system itself at that time will help to explain why it became a target for protestors.

The system in its simplest form worked through the *ch'ien chuang*, which acted as clearing houses for individual exchange transactions. Traders, merchants, and gentry or officials who kept accounts with these *ch'ien chuang* were issued passbooks in which they recorded the date and amount of and the parties to each transaction. No cash passed from hand to hand. Passbooks were handed in for auditing at the end of every day, at which time representatives of the various *ch'ien chuang* met and settled up their accounts with such cash payments as might be necessary. Accounts were reckoned in terms of the *Chiang p'ing* tael, an imaginary unit of account unique to Ningpo. Its value fluctuated with that of the dollar until 1856, and of the Shanghai tael thereafter. A number of variations on the standard passbook transaction evolved as the institution grew in complexity. The Yin Hsien gazetteer of 1936 describes nine optional versions of the transfer tael available during the Republican period, although presumably these options date back at least to the beginning of the century (YHTC 1936: 73a–76b; Arimoto 1931a: 116–20).

The first was the standard transfer-tael procedure (*chang pu kuochang*), used primarily by merchants because of the volume of their financial transactions, although other people also had passbooks. Individual passbooks were issued annually by the various *ch'ien chuang* to each depositor. Suppose, for example, merchant A, who keeps his account with Bank X, buys 1,000 taels' worth of goods from merchant B who has an account with Bank Y. A agrees to pay B in transfer taels, and they exchange the names of their respective banks. A then notes in his passbook the date and the bank (Y) to which the amount must be paid. He then sends this to Bank X, his own bank. At the same time, B makes an entry in his own passbook recording the same information, and sends it to Bank Y. The two passbooks are audited that evening by the respective banks, and the following morning the collecting Bank Y sends a notice of the transaction to X for verification, after which the funds are in fact transferred.

Individuals who had accounts with *ch'ien chuang* for purposes other than trade were more likely to keep an account book with the bank. In this system, called the *ching che kuo-chang*, A could, upon presentation of an account book, transfer a sum from his own Bank X to the account of Party B who deposited with Bank Y. The bank would record the transaction for him in his account book and then pay out the sum on his behalf. The sum would be credited to B's account only after the two banks had verified the transaction.

The transfer-tael system also had a mail service to accommodate people in rural areas, towns, or other ports outside Ningpo who could not use the two systems just described.* If, for example, Party A in Chen-hai had an account with Bank X in Ningpo but wished to pay a sum to Party B in Ningpo, he could inform his bank of his wishes in a letter. The bank would first verify his seal on the letter, then do as he had asked, notifying him that they had done so. Or if Party A wanted to pay a sum to Party B of Feng-hua, B having an account with Bank Y in Ningpo, the same procedure would be followed, Bank X simply paying Bank Y instead of Party B. The 1936 gazetteer comments on this transfer system: "A sum of money is thus transported over land and sea between two places a hundred *li* apart, with no more effort than the lifting of a hand" (YHTC 1936: 74a).

An alternative method of exchange was the use of a bank draft (*chuang p'iao*). A number of drafts were issued annually to each depositor by his native bank. Each draft was divided into three sections. The left was kept by the bank, the right was kept by the depositor, and the center was used as the certificate of payment. The minimum sum in which drafts could be issued was five *yüan* in 1936. These drafts were not negotiable for cash, but only for transfer taels (credit); furthermore, they were not negotiable until ten to fifteen days after issue unless the payee specified otherwise.

If a depositor wished a speedier payment of funds than the transfer-

---

* Ningpo people pioneered in the development of private post offices (*min hsin chü*), which date unofficially from the Ming period, but were known to be spreading rapidly (there were "several thousand all over the empire") during the years 1851–74 (Lou 1958: 54–55). Initially created to serve the interests of merchants and to carry mail for the Shao-hsing *mu-yu*, these postal services were probably put to early use by Ningpo bankers, but I have not investigated the chronology further (*ibid.*: 53–57). I am grateful to Preston Torbert for directing me to Lou's study.

tael system permitted—i.e., if he could not wait overnight to complete the transaction—he could employ the "stamp transfer-tael system" (*kai yin kuo-chang*). For instance, if A were buying a house from B and wanted possession of the deed immediately, while B insisted on collecting his money at once, their respective banks would, on request, make the exchange and stamp it that same day. Naturally, transfer of taels by clients within the same bank involved no delay and no exchange of statements between banks.

The banks also made available a special precautionary measure, the "verification system" (*ya tzu kuo-chang*), for cases in which a payee's credit was in doubt. For example, A and B are mutually in debt: A owes B 700 taels, and B owes A 800. However, A is reluctant to pay B until he is certain that B can pay him. In order to avoid having to cancel a transfer-tael transaction, A instead can request a stamp of verification on both transfer statements before they are paid. This brings to the attention of the bank the questionable standing of B's credit and enables the bank to halt the transaction, if necessary, before it is completed.

Provision was also made for merchants, especially salt merchants and those engaged in northern and southern coastal trade, who wished to collect transfer-tael payments before they were due. In the ordinary transfer-tael system, this was not possible.

Prior to 1933, there also existed a so-called "official transfer-tael system" (*kuei yin kuo-chang*) in which the unit of account was the official silver unit employed by the Shanghai banks rather than the local unit. This system was employed by Shanghai merchants who had accounts with Ningpo banks. All transactions arranged in Ningpo under this system had to be stamped and verified by a Shanghai *ch'ien chuang* before they became final.

The internal organization of the Ningpo *ch'ien chuang* through which the transfer-tael system operated was the prototype for *ch'ien chuang* elsewhere in China. The partner-owners, who generally numbered from four to six, did not involve themselves directly in the operation of the bank. Instead they employed a salaried manager (*ching shou*), whose authority was unchecked even by a supervisory board. The manager and his appointed staff tended to be from the same native place. The manager was assisted by one or two assistant managers (*fu shou*) who concerned themselves with the actual business management of the bank, the manager frequently being involved in matters of public relations (with the owner-partners as well as with clients). Ningpo *ch'ien chuang* also reserved one or more positions in the administration of the bank for relatives of owner-partners or influential clients. These individuals were called *san chien*, a title possibly suggestive of a brokerage function.

There were two accounting staffs, an inner office (*nei chang fang*) and an outer office (*wai chang fang*). Of the two, the former was regarded as the more important branch of banking activity. It consisted of the secretarial office (*hsin fang*), which was responsible for all clerical work, including letters and (later) telegrams calling for a transfer of funds; and the offices of the chief accountant (*fang chang chu jen*) and the treasurer or cashier (*fang chang fang k'uan yüan*). There was also a silver office, or shroff (*yin fang*), in charge of the assay of bullion reserves.

The outer office operated a bureau of public relations. It was headed by a street runner or customer's man (*p'ao chieh*) who solicited business by personally canvassing for deposits and negotiating loans. He was also responsible for investigating the credit rating of prospective clients, and for checking on the use made of bank loans. He served as the middleman between the bank and its clients. The market representative (*chang t'ou*) represented the bank in the guild discussions that established the official local interest rate and set the official exchange rate between local currency and other currencies or units of account.

This staff was assisted by apprentices who served for two to five years, during which time they progressed from running errands to delivering passbooks to keeping accounts. The bank also employed a watchman (*chan ssu*) who was responsible for guarding the reserves of the bank and for transporting currency or bullion from one bank to another.

A man who had served many years as manager might also be given an honorary title and salary by the partner-owners upon his retirement. This "chairman of the board" was called the *t'ai shang huang* (YHTC 1936: 71b–72a; G. H. Chang 1938a: 27–28; Arimoto 1931b: 582–84).

Individual banking institutions were ordered hierarchically according to the nature and size of the transactions they handled. These in turn were a reflection of the clientele to whom they catered. At the lowest level were the money-changing shops, the *ch'ien p'u* or *ch'ien tien*, establishments that accommodated the needs of the peasant, the petty trader, or the artisan, who conducted most of his transactions in copper cash but occasionally found it necessary to obtain silver for taxes or other purposes. Money-changing shops assayed, weighed, and exchanged silver, but did not issue loans or extend credit. The consumer could obtain small loans from pawnshops, or from small private loan offices, which are known to have existed as early as the Yung-cheng period (1723–36), although it is unclear whether these latter credit institutions were widespread or widely used (Miyazaki 1950: 7).

At the next level were the *ch'ien chuang*, which issued credit but possessed less than a specified amount of liquid capital (as of 1858, 30,000 taels). Members of this group of banks were not permitted to participate directly in the transfer-tael system, but were required to have their loans underwritten by a member of the *ta t'ung hang* group (banks with a capitalization of 30,000 to 50,000 taels) (King 1965: 195; YHTC 1936: 71b). The *ch'ien chuang* themselves, at least prior to 1911, catered primarily to members of the elite—merchants, gentry, or bureaucrats—who were regularly involved in transactions requiring the deposit or loan of large sums of silver.

The credit system outlined above not only facilitated trade and market transactions between individuals and firms in Ningpo, but helped to integrate the economy of the city with that of the prefecture as a whole, and served as one of the key institutions linking the trade of Ningpo to higher-level interregional and foreign trade through Shanghai and other commercial centers. This integration is expressed at the lowest level in the cyclic nature of the ties that bound the banks and their creditors. There was, first of all, a daily cycle of meetings at nine A.M. and four P.M. At the first meeting, exchange and interest rates (based, after about 1860, on silver prices in Shanghai) were set for the day, and at the second all accounts were cleared and the differences settled in cash. This daily cycle involved negotiations among representatives from each *ch'ien chuang* (not to mention daily communication with the Shanghai market), who met at the local bankers' guild hall for this purpose (SSZ 13: 824–26). Ningpo was one of the few cities in the southeast in which the volume of trade and the pervasiveness of the credit system necessitated a daily reckoning of the local interest rate on loans; in most inland areas, interest and exchange rates were adjusted on a monthly or even an annual basis (YHTC 1936: 256a).

There was also a monthly cycle according to which money orders drawn on Ningpo native banks by banks or merchants in other cities were paid up, with interest. Most of these payments were made to Shanghai concerns.

All loans were classified as either long-term or short-term, and fell due on a regular schedule. Long-term loans ran for six months, with half the payment due after three months. Short-term loans, called *chin lung chi*, were issued at a higher rate of interest on the twentieth day of the twelfth month, just when debts fell due but money was scarce. These loans were issued for one, two, or at most three months, and were payable on the twentieth day of the month (*ibid.*: 72a).

At the beginning of each lunar year, usually between the fifth and the twentieth day of the first month, ties between depositors and *ch'ien chuang* were renewed with the traditional delivery of a new passbook to the customer. When he delivered the passbook, the *p'ao chieh* could not only reaffirm the existing credit relationship with the client and solicit additional deposits, but also reevaluate the financial standing of his client for the coming year through subtle inquiries and observation (G. H. Chang 1939: 139).

The temporal patterns of interaction fostered by the *ch'ien chuang* banking system thus assumed both personal and institutional forms. At the lowest level, they bound the staff of a small financial organization under the close personal supervision of a manager who was solely responsible for the solvency of the enterprise. He reported annually to the partner-owners on the operations of the bank; he and certain members of his staff annually solicited accounts from merchants, gentry, and officials, and assumed in return unlimited liability for their clients' financial commitments.

At higher levels, individual banks were linked by the necessity of cooperative arrangements for clearing funds and by their mutual interest in maintaining exchange and interest rates at a profitable level in relation to rates outside of Ningpo. It was this need for negotiation and mutual accommodation, as well as the traditional impetus for creating occupational guilds, that gave rise to the larger banking guilds and associations.* The organizational solidarity of Ningpo-based financial groups was increased by the sense of community based on *t'ung-hsiang* ties when such groups came into being outside of Ningpo.

Because the most is known of the Ningpo financial guild that formed in Shanghai, the following description of guild structure and function is based on its operations (SSZ 13: 824–27). Cooperation between banks in Shanghai was institutionalized at two levels: that of an organization based on occupational ties, the Shang-hai Ch'ien Yeh Kung So, or Shanghai Native Bankers' Guild: and that of the Shang-hai Hui Hua Tsung Hui, or Shanghai Native Bankers' Clearing Association, an arm of the former.† These groups acted both to control their membership from within and to serve as a buffer against competition and control by organizations outside the guild—foreign banks, rival financial institutions (in particular the Shansi banks), and of course the government. Membership in the guild was determined by vote of the member banks and re-

---

* Ch'en believes that one cause of the decline of the Shansi banks was the failure of the three Shansi banking groups (*pang*) to establish an overarching guild organization through which they could have aided one another in crises (1937: 44).

† "It is not clear whether the clearinghouse arrangement was a Chinese innovation. The earliest example was the *kuo-chang* 'offset accounts' system in Ningpo, which might have been used already in the 18th century. . . ." (L. S. Yang 1952: 86). Professor Yang is the first economic historian to point to formal, institutional similarities between the Ningpo credit system and the banking system at Shanghai, in addition to the linkages in the person of Ningpo financiers at Shanghai.

quired a minimum capitalization specified by the guild. Annually the guild members elected a president and an executive committee (Tamagna 1942: 79–80. Each member bank was charged an equal monthly fee to cover guild expenses (Morse 1909: 12, 15).

The guild organization supplied the channels through which representatives of individual banks settled their mutual debts, determined daily interest rates, and presided over the liquidation of member banks. Clearing and rate-fixing functions were the concern of the smaller clearing association within the guild. The guild could and often did extend loans to member banks to tide them over a crisis, since it served the interests of all banks to maintain the confidence of depositors. The guild assumed responsibility for setting rules for apprenticeships, standards of fair practice, and uniform assaying procedures. It also acted as a court of law to which members were required to submit grievances. For violating the rules of the guild, a bank might be fined (according to the size of its capital), suspended, expelled, or boycotted by other member banks (Tamagna 1942: 79–80).

The pervasiveness of guild controls and of the influence of Ningpo bankers within the Shanghai banking guild itself did not come about overnight. As previously noted, the Ningpo bankers in Shanghai were first organized informally as a small trade body within the larger *t'ung-hsiang* organization, the Shang-hai Ssu-ming Kung So. This group of financiers quickly became known as the *Ning-po ch'ien yeh pang*, which continued into the Republican period to control financial and commercial transactions in Shanghai. They first allied themselves with Shao-hsing bankers, together organizing all the native bankers in the Shang-hai Ch'ien Yeh T'ung Yeh Kung Hui. Their control of this body was perpetuated by financial support from prominent clans in Ningpo—Shih, Fang, Yeh, Yen, Hsü, and others—and by the success of the powerful Ningpo financiers themselves, who were resourceful and intelligent bank managers (Negishi 1951: 63; SHCCSL: 770–71).

The written history of the Shanghai Bankers' Guild begins in 1842, when the guild hall constructed during the eighteenth century was restored after being damaged in a fire that year. Fires struck again in 1853 and in 1860–61, when the Taiping rebels entered the city and demolished the hall completely (Negishi 1951: 102–3; Kuo 1933: 832–33).

The decade of the rebellion marks a significant turning point in the rise of the Ningpo banking system and its purveyors.* In the city of

---

* The discussion that follows adds a new dimension to Erh-min Wang's thesis that the rebellion, by forcing men of wealth and influence to seek refuge in the foreign settlements in Shanghai, played a crucial role in stimulating economic growth

Ningpo itself, the rebellion appears to have affected commercial development in a paradoxical way. The growth of foreign trade in the city just after it was opened as a treaty port in 1842 was unexpectedly slow, and it is clear from British consular reports and other sources that for a time Ningpo was little more than an intermediary port for the transshipment of goods imported and exported through Shanghai (Shiba, in press; GBSP vol. 71, 1866; Chang Kuo-hui 1963: 93–94; Fairbank 1953: 329–31).

But in the 1850's and 1860's, financial institutions and trade in Ningpo were subjected to a number of stresses that stimulated trade at the same time that they were economically and socially disruptive. Private and official writings of this period reveal the level of sophistication already achieved in the Ningpo banking system by 1850 and the complexity with which it interacted with other social and political institutions in the area.

Charles Stanley, Albert Feuerwerker, and others have pointed to the significance of the Taiping Rebellion as a turning point in the development of commerce in China. Stanley notes that whereas the pre-Taiping merchant world was dominated by the Canton trade and the salt merchants, the opening of the treaty ports in 1842 diminished the first, and the disruption of the southeast between 1861 and 1864 ended the already waning power of the second. After 1864, trade passed decisively into the hands of individual merchants and financial institutions (Stanley 1961: 2). Feuerwerker further stresses the increasing political and fiscal independence of the provinces that came with the development of regional power centers during the rebellion. When the provincial treasurer could neither collect nor disperse the funds of the central government, provincial governors and military leaders turned to the private financier and to a local source of income, the likin tax on goods in transit (Feuerwerker 1958: 41–43).

The decade of the Taiping Rebellion saw a complex of economic strains with conflicting effects on social unrest in Ningpo. During the 1850's the fiscal structure of the empire as a whole was foundering under the abortive currency reforms of the Hsien-feng reign (1851–62). Instead of halting the debasement of copper coins and standardizing the issue of a national treasury bank note, the reform effort collapsed when the new "big-cash" currency issues were devalued and the government could not back its notes with an adequate cash reserve (King 1965: 144–63). In addition, a crucial reversal in the rate of exchange between

---

in that city and its commercial hinterland. See Erh-min Wang, "The History and Impact of the Practice of Borrowing Foreign Troops in the Yangtze Valley, 1860–1864: The Key to the Critical Changes in the Early Stages of the Opening of Shanghai as a Trade Port" (unpublished paper, 1969).

copper and silver occurred in the course of the 1850's. Beginning in about 1808, the rate had moved steadily against copper, from an average of twelve or thirteen hundred cash per tael to twenty-two or twenty-three hundred cash per tael by the middle of the century, double and in the extreme instance triple the previous base rates. After 1856, however, the value of copper rallied as the Moslem rebellion in Yunnan made copper scarce; exchange rates dropped to fifteen or sixteen hundred and even as low as eleven hundred cash per tael (Yang Tuan-liu 1962: 191–95).

In Ningpo two local disturbances resulted directly from these changes.* In both cases, the losses incurred by bankers, officials, and merchants were being passed on to the lower-level producer. And in both cases the peasant was neither ignorant of nor passively resigned to the burden.† In April of 1852 when a farmer sold his rice in Ningpo, he received only 3,000 cash per *shih*, or just half its wholesale value in silver, because the exchange value of copper had been cut in half (the exchange rate having risen in the south from 1,000 to 2,000 cash per tael). At the same time, and for the same reason, the local magistrate had begun to collect the land tax, assessed in taels but paid in cash, according to the new rate of exchange, increasing the peasants' tax liability from 2,600 to 3,600 cash per tael. The peasant producer thus found the income from his rice crop cut in half and his taxes simultaneously increased by nearly forty percent (Tomita n.d.: 13–16, 39–41; Wright 1966: 152–53). The peasants rioted, destroying the prefectural offices and burning the houses of the local tax collector and the treasurer to the ground (Tomita n.d.: 21–23). The tax was subsequently adjusted.

The Ningpo fishermen's riot six years later involved not only the manipulation of exchange rates, but the credit system as a whole. The cuttlefish or squid had traditionally provided the coastal people of Ningpo with a stable if seasonal livelihood, supplemented by farm work in the off-season. Like most other Ningpo businesses, the fishing industry

---

* The British consul reported in 1865 that whereas "up to 1860" Ningpo had been a relatively "cheap" place to live, with an abundance of copper cash, between 1860 and 1864 prices rose with the cash shortage until it was the "most expensive" of all the ports (GBSP vol. 53, 1865).

† A life of labor on the land was no guarantee that the peasant in traditional China would be naïve, or even hesitant, in the pursuit of profit. Maurice Freedman writes of the Chinese peasants and artisans who migrated overseas, for example, that their financial shrewdness rested "above all on three characteristics of the society in which they were raised: the respectability of the pursuit of riches, the relative immunity of surplus wealth from confiscation by political superiors, and the legitimacy of careful and interested financial dealings between neighbors and even close kinsmen" (1959: 65).

had begun to use a credit system by the mid-nineteenth century. The system involved people at all levels of the industry as well as the banks, for even the fishermen who brought in the catch accepted payment in credit notes rather than money.* Incoming boats were met at sea by brokers in boats sent out by wholesalers in Ningpo. A fisherman identified the broker with whom he customarily dealt by the wholesaler's company flag displayed on the broker's boat. The brokers assessed the size and value of the catches and bought them on the wholesaler's behalf. They paid the fishermen on the spot, not in money but in notes (*hang p'iao*) issued by the wholesaling firm. The fishermen had to take the company notes to a *ch'ien chuang* to be exchanged for cash. The riot was touched off in 1858 when the local banks rediscounted the notes so steeply that the fishermen received only half their face value (Himeda 1967: 86–88).† The banks had reacted to the currency shortage by over-extending credit in response to the demands of a hard-pressed clientele. But since they had assumed unlimited liability for their clients, they faced enormous losses and were inclined to shift some of the burden to the producers. Wrote Tuan Kuang-ch'ing in 1858:‡

I observed once that although the city of Ningpo is a great one, the port of trade itself is actually hollow. One sees only account books and never real money. I compared it to a very old tree which, though its leaves and branches are flourishing, is hollow inside—when a strong wind comes along, it will immediately crash to the ground. My friends found this metaphor very amusing. Later on, the credit system became even more pervasive in trade, at the very time that the cash reserves of the native banks were shrinking. When you traded notes for cash, the premium that initially was no more than fifty coppers per thousand grew to one hundred and even four or five hundred coppers.

Paradoxically, at this very time trade and banking began to flourish in Ningpo as never before. The British consul at Ningpo in 1865 describes an enormous upswing in trade during the years 1859 to 1864, for reasons all related to the rebellion. Rebel forces occupied Soochow, cutting off trade routes through Shanghai and forcing silk, tea, and other exports to find outlets at Ningpo. From December 9, 1861, to June of

---

* Himeda alleges that the fishermen actually preferred credit to cash because of the threat of piracy. Although piracy was an important factor, Barbara E. Ward has pointed out that personal credit relationships between peasant producers and middlemen also served the mutual interests of both parties involved by providing a reliable source of credit for the peasant and a reliable source of income for the dealer (Ward 1967: 140, 142).

† I am grateful to Professor Shiba for providing me with this article.

‡ Tuan 1968: 122–23. For a similar observation by a Westerner living in Ningpo, see Morse 1890: 80–81.

1862, Ningpo was virtually a free port because the occupying rebels had closed the Imperial Customs House. Rice had to be imported during the occupation, since rice cultivation had been halted in the hinterland, and Ningpo was the natural alternative port of entry for the embattled area. Finally, Shanghai tea merchants fled to Ningpo for refuge when the rebels disrupted their trade routes, bringing with them their trade in green tea (GBSP, vol. 71, 1865).

Prices rose steadily, and copper cash grew scarcer and scarcer, especially in the five years after 1860. The drain on copper currency in Ningpo, part of a nation-wide shortage of copper, was increased by a number of factors. Imports of rice through the port of Ningpo not only continued, but increased during the 1860's. Although the farmers of the hinterland were now free to plant rice again, many of them turned to cotton instead, hoping to benefit from the disruption of cotton cultivation in the United States during the Civil War. When copper cash ran out, the imported rice had to be paid for in silver dollars. As long as any copper was available, however, foreign merchants demanded payment in copper, which they then sold for a profit in cities such as Hankow, where the supply was shorter still (GBSP, vol. 71, 1866).

There can be no doubt that the lucrative nature of banking activity during this period caused many people to found or speculate in banking enterprises whose principal assets were large stores of enthusiasm. However, the owners of established *ch'ien chuang* in Ningpo remained among the wealthiest men in the country. It was to their vast store of funds that the central government and its official representatives turned for aid in financing the war against the Taipings. In doing so, they created a relationship that was an important factor in the subsequent proliferation of the *ch'ien chuang* in the south, and the gradual displacement of the once-powerful Shansi banking empire. Into the Republican period, the coordination and control of such interests was vested primarily in the native bankers themselves through their guilds, subject to the peculiar limitations of the Chinese case—e.g. the absence of a stable currency.

What follows is an examination of the collision and collusion of these interest groups—the guilds and the banking families who dominated them, officials, and, later, foreign banking institutions. The era of the Taiping Rebellion appears to have brought about a significant change in the nature and extent of guild controls in trade and banking, as the pattern of marketing activity in Shanghai during the rebellion will illustrate. In the eighth month of 1860, the Taiping rebels entered Shanghai. Up until that time, the majority of marketing activity had been conducted in the south market (*nan shih*) of the city, rather than the north market (*pei shih*) where the foreign settlements were located. By the time peace was restored in 1862, most of the trade had shifted to the relative security of the north market and the foreign community (Kuo 1933: 809–10). Specialization of trade functions grew out of the physical separation, the south market dealing in grains during the latter half of the year, the north market in tea and silk during the first half of the year (Ch'in 1926: 22–23). Until 1883 the financial guild at Shanghai remained in the original Nei Yüan hall, but within that period it became apparent that separate guild halls were needed to accommodate the specialized needs of the now divergent market areas (Ferguson 1906: 60). In 1883 the Nan Shih Ch'ien Yeh Kung So was constructed, followed in 1889–91 by the erection of the Pei Shih Ch'ien Yeh Hui Kuan. The latter was, by Negishi's account, much the more elaborate and prosperous of the two (1951: 103–5). Annual meetings of the entire guild continued to be held at the parent hall. The memorial record of 1925 for the Pei Shih Hui Kuan, written by Feng Ping of Tz'u-ch'i, notes that the building project was headed by Ch'en Kan of Yü-yao; sponsors included two others from Yü-yao, one from Shang-yü, one from Yin Hsien, and two from Tz'u-ch'i (Kuo 1933: 834–35).

These guilds, like the trade guilds in Ningpo, came into their own during the Taiping period with the rise of speculation and the proliferation of wildcat banks under the impetus of burgeoning trade. Between 1858 and 1860, promissory notes (*chuang p'iao*) became widely negotiable in foreign trade, particularly in the opium trade. Banks were organized for the sole purpose of issuing such notes. Established banks at Shanghai, finding it necessary to protect their reputation and credit in the face of the newcomers, issued a plea in 1863 through the Shanghai Bankers' Guild that guild members refuse to honor bank drafts drawn on non-member banks (Negishi 1951: 12; Chang Kuo-hui 1963: 89).

Still another factor in the unprecedented growth of banking during this period was the foreign bank, which began during this time to extend long-term and short-term ("chop") loans to Chinese banks (Nishizato 1967a: 16). Such loans were negotiated through agents (compradores), hired by the foreign banks. The agents employed their own staffs of accountants and assayers, or shroffs, and exercised considerable influence in their role as brokers. Owners and managers of *ch'ien chuang* themselves are also known to have acted as compradores (Chang Kuo-hui 1963: 88–89). An observer in Shanghai in 1906 wrote (Ferguson 1906: 56–57):

The compradore with his accountants and shroffs is an *imperium in imperio*: he decides upon the value of gold bar, silver bar, and coins, placing his own value upon their fineness. . . . When native banks wish to negotiate a loan from a foreign bank, the compradore decides upon the security and is held responsible if the security fails. He also attends to the transfer of money to and from inland places where there are no foreign banks. In short, he is the medium through whom all transactions are carried on between a foreign bank and Chinese banks or merchants.

Foreign bankers did not take this interest in the financial solvency of Chinese banks purely out of altruism; their speculations in local currency were extremely profitable.* Moreover, *chuang p'iao* were so widely used in trade at this time that foreign banks could not refuse to accept them as negotiable tender,† but the native bankers' guild controlled the clearinghouse at which all such drafts were exchanged and paid off in money. Since the use of the clearinghouse was restricted to guild members, a foreign bank had to keep an account with at least one native bank that belonged to the guild in order to gain access to the clearing process. In exchange for maintaining a deposit with such a bank, the foreign bank received a token interest payment and the privilege of cashing bank drafts through it ("Why Chinese native banks are more powerful . . .": 134–35). I suspect that compradores arranged and manipulated this liaison as well. It has been suggested that the *ch'ien chuang* entirely recouped their losses from government levies by serving as brokers between the Western and Chinese financial spheres (Kagawa 1948: 120–22). The power of compradores and of native banking guilds over the relations between native and foreign banks belies the popular notion that foreign banks manipulated and controlled native money markets through the chop loan (G. H. Chang 1939: 136–37).

The bankers' guilds were well aware of the crucial nature of the role they played in both foreign and domestic trade, and of the consequent need to preserve harmony and solidarity among guild members (Kuo 1933: 832–34):

If the administration of commerce is not in order, and currency is in a state of flux, the business transactions of the entire port suffer the consequences. But as long as the bankers can maintain order and discipline through their control of prices and exchange rates in both sections of the market, then this hall can truly serve to consolidate the interests of its members for the maximal benefit of all, and to provide a hearing for complaints and grievances.

---

* Tamagna 1942: 15–16. Even foreign merchant houses found speculation in the Chinese money market more lucrative than trade, where costs were multiplied by the necessity of dealing through middlemen, and where profits were uncertain precisely because of the volatile money market (Murphey 1970: 19–20).

† Nishizato attributes the wide negotiability of these notes to the far-flung business interests and influence of the Ningpo and Shao-hsing banking families (1967a: 15).

But Chinese banking was pervaded by local and family ties that made this ideal difficult to achieve.* The leaders of the guild were well aware of the problem, as the following extract from an address by one of its presidents will show (Negishi 1951: 109):

Banking in Shanghai has always been divided into cliques (*pang p'ai*). These are the Ningpo, the Shao-hsing, and the Soochow groups. Another large one is the Chinkiang group. Whenever a large organization is formed, the members naturally split into such groupings. After the opening of foreign trade, knowledge and experience in China changed radically from what they had been in ancient times, but the problem of native ties remained difficult to resolve. Within the same profession there is much jealousy, and within the same clique much covert manipulating. People compete with one another, opinions differ widely, no one walks in step as a body. From this time forward, I am hopeful that we will all be of one mind and one heart.

The President spoke, of course, out of a long tradition in which his fellow inhabitants of the Ningpo region had dominated the Ningpo and Shanghai markets through the very particularistic ties he condemned. Fathers who intended their sons to go into business in Ningpo, for example, arranged for the sons to serve at least one apprenticeship in a *ch'ien chuang* before they came of age, to acquaint themselves with the personnel and practices of local banking operations (Arimoto 1931b: 588). The central government recognized the hegemony of financial barons like the Hsieh and Hu clans of Yü-yao, and Ch'in, Yen, Feng, Tung, and Yüan clans of Tz'u-ch'i, the Lou clan of Yin, and the Fang, Yeh, and Li clans of Chen-hai, and began to make use of it during the Taiping Rebellion. As the drain on the central treasury continued with the protracted struggle against the rebels, local officials were directed to visit the homes of the wealthy people of their districts and personally solicit contributions for the military effort. Tuan Kuang-ch'ing was one such official whose description of the canvass survives. In the sixth month of 1863, Tuan traveled to Tz'u-ch'i to the home of the banker Feng Wang-ch'ing. Feng was not just the first wealthy man on Tuan's list, but the head of a banking family that owned many of the other banks in the area. When pressed, he estimated that Tuan could collect about seven hundred thousand taels if all the banks contributed. However, he suggested that Tuan himself pay a call on all the bank managers he expected to contribute, since they had already been under heavy pressure for donations and he did not wish to be responsible for bothering them again. Tuan countered by proposing that Feng set an example for

---

* For an insightful statement of the advantages of particularism in banking practices, see G. H. Chang 1938a: 29–32.

the other banks by agreeing to give a certain sum and specifying the manner of payment. In the end, Feng did more than this. He called a meeting of all the local bank managers, at which he set a quota for each of them and arranged for payments to begin at the end of the month, all sums to be paid in full by year's end. Responsibility for collecting the payments would be rotated among the contributors. Whether Feng did all this as a favor to Tuan, who was well liked in the area, or because he preferred to have a say in the final agreement, is not clear. Whatever his motivation was, his influence was effective. Tuan writes that he got at least a hundred thousand strings of cash from each bank by appealing personally to the contributors. After canvassing the banks, he turned to other businesses. Tuan also mentions that banks refusing to contribute were required to submit their books for an audit, and were then docked accordingly (Tuan 1968: 174–75).

Although the imperial government repeatedly solicited such large donations from the *chien chuang*, there was evidently no fear that they would be ruined or even greatly set back as a result. During the height of the Rebellion, imperial officials like Tuan deposited their private incomes as well as the tax revenues of their districts in local *ch'ien chuang*. Tuan wrote in 1860 that he had deposited all of his earnings as an official, some 40,000 taels, in the Yu Ch'ang Ch'ien Chuang in Ningpo (*ibid.*: 187–79). Very close relationships sometimes developed between these officials and their bankers, as the case of Hu Kuang-yung indicates.* In Chekiang in 1862, no tax levies were accepted as legally paid unless they were deposited with one of Hu's banks (*ibid.*: 192–93). Stanley suggests that Governor Wang Yu-ling issued this order either to reward Hu for his services in procuring military supplies or "perhaps in the interest of efficiency and the protection of funds in transit during the prevailing disturbances" (Stanley 1961: 9–10). Of course, if Wang's earnings were

---

* See Stanley (1961) for an examination of the relationship between Hu Kuang-yung, the Yangtze Valley financier, and Tso Tsung-t'ang. See also Toyama (1945) and Spence (1969: 63–70) on the relationship between Frederick Townsend Ward and Yang Fang, a financier from Yin Hsien. Recent scholarship has begun, belatedly, to correct the stereotype of the Chinese merchant as wealthy but lacking prestige, his riches ever prey to a rapacious central government. Rhoads Murphey supplies a brief summary of literature reflecting this more realistic appraisal in his monograph on the treaty ports, concluding that "Ch'ing official and actual policy toward merchants and commerce, often characterized as ruinously oppressive, is probably better seen as reflecting the close mutuality of merchant and bureaucratic interests. . . ." (Murphey 1970: 13). The growth and functions of the local system of credit and banking in Ningpo indicate that relations between officials, merchant-financiers, and peasant producers were indeed characterized by antagonisms, but also by a high degree of mutual accommodation and profit.

deposited in Hu's bank, his interest in ensuring Hu's financial success would be still clearer.

The financial empire of the Ningpo merchant bankers, bolstered by official patronage and foreign investment, reached its highest development in the last quarter of the nineteenth century. The banks served as middlemen for the foreign banks and traders in Shanghai and for the domestic traders in the Yangtze Valley. Linked together by clan ties based in the Ningpo region, the *ch'ien chuang* in the Valley provided a safe and relatively stable medium of credit and exchange to support the flourishing trade in foreign goods in the inland areas (Chang Kuohui 1963: 97–98). The city of Ningpo, a transshipping center for Shanghai, maintained direct financial ties with that port and with inland trade centers in Shao-hsing, Hangchow, and elsewhere, through her twenty-two *ch'ien chuang*. One scholar believes that it was the Ningpo credit system alone that enabled goods from Ningpo to be traded as far into the interior as Yü-shan Hsien in Kiangsi and Hui-chou, Anhwei (*ibid.*: 93–94). The *ch'ien chuang* served as "brokers" between the city and countryside in China—middlemen who made possible the flow of capital between the city and rural areas by regulating exchange rates and by supplying capital to urban merchants and brokers who purchased the produce of rural areas, or who sold foreign goods there. They also lent money to small rural money shops that provided credit for the villagers (Kagawa 1948: 126–28).

In summary, several factors can be cited that were conducive to the rise of the Ningpo banking system. Ningpo was a historical entrepôt in which both foreign and domestic trade seem to have grown in volume steadily from 1715 to the end of the eighteenth century. In the foreign sector, Ningpo traders captured the Japan trade from their Fukienese rivals and, especially after 1757, Ningpo began to attract the attention of European merchants seeking a direct port of entry to the Chekiang silk market. The Yangtze Valley remained, however, the key to the South China trading area, and Ningpo merchants by the end of the century were firmly entrenched at the mouth of the delta in Shanghai. Because money had to be sent so regularly between Ningpo and Shanghai, and because Ningpo merchants trading out of Shanghai in the coastal trade always needed credit, a passbook system or the issue of bills of trade was a natural and much-needed development. Verbal agreements between members of the same trade association sufficed for small transactions between individuals. As the volume of trade grew, however, wealthy merchants began to provide rudimentary banking services to brokers in their employ, or to trusted clients. As noted above, there were other characteristics of the Chinese economy as a whole—in particular, parallel bimetallism with locally varying exchange rates—that had given rise to a group of specialists in currency exchange. Some of these money-changers became full-time specialists in banking, providing centralized exchange and credit services and employing pre-existing channels of negotiation to serve clearinghouse functions as well.

In this regard it is again worth noting how well this early Chinese banking system was adapted to the absence of a stable currency supply and a standardized coinage. Not only were the origins of traditional banking houses intimately connected with earlier exchange functions, but fluctuating exchange rates and interest rates ensured both profits and a continued monopoly to specialists with access to the unique channels of communication and the specialized techniques for determining rates that had been developed in the course of performing these functions.* Local officials and customs personnel were understandably loath to press for the uniform currency desired by foreign traders, since they themselves made profits on the conversion of taxes or duties into the official unit of collection, the *k'u p'ing* or the Haikwan tael, respectively (Ferguson 1906: 73; Hirohata 1933: 312–13).

Although it worked very well in its own context, the *ch'ien chuang* system was ultimately vulnerable to forces outside the control of its guilds, such as shortages in the native currency supply, the increasing dependence on foreign capital in the form of chop loans, and the growth of speculative investment in the foreign stock market by bankers and depositors (Nishizato 1967a: 12). This vulnerability was closely tied to a tendency toward speculation within the banking system itself: credit was extended to the point where there were insufficient reserves to meet runs on the banks. The guild organization could carry the native banks through major crises such as the strains caused during the 1860's by the Taiping Rebellion and the crash of Hu Kuang-yung's banks in 1883 (GBSP, vol. 80, 1884–5; vol. 82, 1884). But it was unable to prevent the growing use of foreign capital by member banks, although it was able

---

* "It must be stated that the present inaccuracy of valuation [of the fineness of silver], while leaving a good margin for profit to bankers, can only maintain in a market where there is a [common consent in commercial circles that it is] profitable to local interests. . . . One fixed principle obtains in all places, and this principle is to hold the local value of silver somewhat different from that of any other place, so that the banks can charge not only for transfer expenses but also make a small profit themselves on the different rates of exchange" (Ferguson 1906: 66–67). For an example of the different units of account used in Ningpo alone in 1889, see Morse 1890: 60.

to control this relationship for some time. The chop loans, at first used only occasionally, began to be used habitually when the time neared for the quarterly settling of accounts. Their easy availability tempted many a *ch'ien chuang* manager to overextend his resources as long as no supervisory office called him to account (Nishizato 1967a: 16).

The central government did not control domestic currency supplies or banking policies through a central agency, nor did it act to check the growing influence of the external money market in the Chinese economy.* In the absence of regulation by the central government and of municipal institutions that might have provided a legal framework for banking operations, the Ningpo banking system created its own regulatory agencies—the guild and the clearinghouse. Although these agencies proved ultimately vulnerable to alien forces, until that time their members enjoyed considerable autonomy.† The *ch'ien chuang* in traditional China were remarkably free of the governmental controls that served to protect and sustain comparably sophisticated banking systems in other cultures. They can thus be viewed as examples of the self-regulating, autonomous, segmentary organizations—based on ties of locality, occupation, and surname—typical of the city in late traditional China (Crissman 1967: 200, 202).

---

* This stands in marked contrast to the Japanese case, where the Meiji government assumed the task of amassing and dispensing capital for industry, thereby keeping opportunities for investment at home under internal control. See Smith 1955, especially pp. 36–41, on the reasons for the failure of initial government efforts to induce private financing of the industrialization effort. Once guild controls in China were circumvented, as in the rubber crisis of 1910, the Chinese investor had neither legal standards to regulate nor guarantees to insure his heavy speculation in foreign markets. See Elvin 1969: 57; Bergère 1964: 2–3.

† Tamagna in fact concludes that, until 1910, foreign trade and capital were crucial underpinnings of the success of the *ch'ien chuang*, which developed "under the impulse of foreign trade." The *ch'ien chuang* grew precisely because of "their growing independence . . . from any national banking system, while Shansi bankers were losing their government connection and their influence over local banks" (Tamagna 1942: 20–21).

Sericulture and Silk Textile Production in Ch'ing China

This paper seeks to reconstruct the characteristics of the silk industry in China from the early seventeenth to the late nineteenth century: from its heyday under the traditional system to the beginnings of limited modernization. The treatment is largely descriptive and qualitative, and the emphasis will be on traditional methods of conducting the various aspects of the industry, including the production of raw silk in the country and the avenues of trade in silk goods. The period before the beginning of modernization saw the handicraft technology remaining on its pre-industrial plateau; and in terms of the economic organization of the industry the traditional forms with their intricate interrelationships had not changed much for centuries. By looking at the way in which the industry functioned, one gains a view of the baseline from which modernization was to start.

Silk in the Traditional Scene

When the Ch'ing dynasty established its rule in China, it inherited from the Ming an agrarian economy in which sericulture was well established both as a source of primary goods and as an item of fiscal reckoning in the administration of the empire. The lower Yangtze region was already an outstanding producer of silk. The summer tax (*hsia shui*) of the Ming was levied in a specific silk fabric known as *chüan*. The importance of silk was reemphasized in the early Ch'ing when the practice of levies in silk fabrics was reinforced. In 1686 the amounts of silk fabrics and raw silk due from Kiangsu, Anhwei, Chekiang, and Shansi were specified in an order concerning taxes in kind. The order distinguished among various types of silk textiles produced in localities where a proficiency in certain weaving techniques was well known. One of the silk cloths specifically required of the provinces, for example, was the fabric woven in Lu-chou, Shansi, which was used for certain court functions. This particular fabric was considered indispensable to the Grand Sacrifices (*ta chi*) at the Imperial Court. Thus as late as 1884 it was singled out to remain on the "in kind" list and not allowed to be commuted to money payment as several other local products of Shansi had been on account of the large arrears in kind that had accumulated.*

The importance of silk in imperial finances was a reflection of its established place in the economy of pre-modern China. In this regard, one must first of all realize that the label of "luxury˙ goods" customarily bestowed on silk fabrics of all sorts, is misleading when applied to China. Instead, silk textiles made up a kind of "prestige" commodity. Its varieties were numerous and its price range wide, but the raw material was in all cases silk, and its use was not confined to the members of the elite at the tip of the economic and social pyramid. Silk fabrics were used at many levels of society for a variety of things in addition to clothing. It has been estimated that in the nineteenth century, in spite of a progressive increase in the amount of silk exported, some fifty-five percent of the raw silk produced in China went into the domestic market.

Before the Taiping wars (1850–65) devastated the silk regions of eastern China, the inhabitants of Hangchow, one of the main centers for silk, were reported by an English traveler as being uninhibited consumers of silk stuffs (Fortune 1852: 37):

The people of Hang-chow dress gaily, and are remarkable among the Chinese for their dandyism. All except the lowest labourers and coolies strutted about in dresses composed of silk, satin, and crepe. . . . The natives of Hangchow, both rich and poor, were never contented unless gaily dressed in silks and satins.

Although this was an extreme example of the extent to which silk was used for clothing, it is nonetheless revealing. There were no sumptuary laws concerning the main categories of dress materials, so that, as soon or as long as the financial means of the consumer allowed, he could use silk fabrics in any way he wished.

Tucked away in many of the vernacular novels written during the Ming and Ch'ing periods are bits of concrete information on the people's

---

* KCTSCC, "Shih huo tien" (Section on economics), ch. 249; *Ta Ch'ing hui tien shih li* (Precedents of the statutes of the Ch'ing dynasty), 1886 edition, ch. 940: 17b–18a. Since 1667 two types of Lu silk cloth had been woven in Shansi Province according to government specifications, known by their measurements as "large Lu" and "small Lu" silk cloths. See also *Tung hua lu: Kuang-hsü*, Shanghai reprint ed., 1958, 2: 1639, memorial of Chang Chih-tung, Jan. 4, 1884.

general modes of life. From these one learns that silk fabrics of varying quality were not at all unusual clothing materials for what one might call the middle gentry and the middle and lower-middle levels of the urban commercial classes. Furthermore, silk also figured in a large variety of social functions at various class levels: bolts of silk material were used as personal gifts between individuals, as religious offerings at temples and shrines by people even of modest means, and as decorations on buildings during festive occasions in town and village. Even the foot soldier was a consumer of silk, for a properly outfitted infantryman was supposed to decorate his lance, at least on dress occasions, with a piece of red silk stuff tied to its tip.*

Such diverse uses of silk made the silk industry an important factor in Chinese society and culture. Sericulture as a supplementary source of income for the peasantry of many provinces had become entrenched even before the Manchu conquest, and the Ch'ing authorities fully recognized the significance of this activity for the maintenance of the agrarian economy. When overall economic administrative policies were discussed, the promotion of sericulture was in the great majority of cases included as an integral part of them. To those trying to find ways to integrate Yunnan more closely into the nation in the eighteenth century, for example, sericulture seemed a necessary part of the scheme (KCTSCC, "Chih fang tien," ch. 1454).

The adoption of the Chekiang-Kiangsu type of silk culture by other parts of the country could be traced to a much earlier date,† but during the Ch'ing period the spread of the mulberry—and in a few cases the use of silk-oak leaves for producing the tussore silk as well—had been consistently noted in nearly all provinces. From Kwangtung and Fukien on the coast to Hupeh and Szechwan along the middle and upper Yangtze, from Shensi in the north to Kweichow and Kwangsi in the southwest, many localities began to practice sericulture for the first time, or

---

* Examples may be cited from many novels. The few instances given here come from *Chin p'ing mei, Shui hu chuan, Hsing shih yin yuan*, and, for the late Ch'ing, *Kuan ch'ang hsien hsing chi*. It is essential to be aware of the great diversity of silk fabrics, and the specialized consumer markets they served. For example, a silk piece-goods shop in Soochow specialized in making and selling the black silk crepe headkerchiefs widely used by women (presumably from the Ming to early or middle Ch'ing times). This shop had been famous for the quality of its wares since its founding during the Ming. Obviously a shop could not have prospered for many generations had its special commodity not had a broad purchasing public (Ch'ü Tui-chih 1945: 31).

† An example can be seen in *Hsü Kuang-ch'i chi* (Collected writings of Hsü Kuang-ch'i), ed. by Wang Chung-min, 2: 490. In a letter written in 1616 from Peking, Hsü urged his son to send him mulberry seeds from their family estate near Shanghai, so that he could start an experimental mulberry grove in Tientsin.

substantially improved their techniques. Some of these new areas soon
began to produce very high-quality silk. The silk fabrics produced at
Changchow, Fukien, for instance, were considered in the eighteenth
century nearly to rival the products of Soochow, which had served as the
model.* Sericulture and its related handicraft industries constituted one
of the main forms of diversification in the agrarian economy of traditional China, and as such provided the system with a necessary degree
of resilience, thereby contributing to the prolonged institutional "stability" of that economy. This was the underlying cause that prompted so
many local administrators to promote sericulture so assiduously wherever
silk could be produced at a reasonable profit. One might conclude that,
with the passage of time, the promotion of sericulture had worked itself
into the administrative ethos of the traditional culture, and had come
to be regarded as a part of the government's duties in the realm of public
administration. As a part of their striving for recognition as meritorious
public servants, local officials took it upon themselves to urge the people
of their district to adopt silk as a cash crop, where the natural conditions
allowed, or to devise improvements in their techniques of silk production. The following are but a few examples out of a vast number showing local officials in their role as guardians of the economic well-being
of the areas under their jurisdiction.

In the early Ch'ien-lung period (1736–96) the government promulgated an agricultural handbook entitled *Shou shih t'ung k'ao.* One of
the book's eight sections was devoted to instructions for cultivating mulberry trees and raising silkworms; these were activities to be undertaken
by the general farming population on an individual household basis,
but with the encouragement of the local authorities (Sung 1947: 78).
In 1737–42, a prefect introduced the making of Shantung tussore silk
and silk fabrics into Tsun-i, Kweichow, where he found silk-oak trees
growing in abundance, thus laying the foundation for a local industry
that flourished into the late nineteenth century. Sericulture in Kweichow
was further developed when in 1840 Governor Ho Ch'ang-ling reported
the successful planting in that province of mulberry trees, of which 140,-
000 were already on the road to maturity. From this beginning the production of regular silk was expected to be established in the province.
In 1751 the governor of Shensi promulgated the procedures whereby
government silk-production centers were established in the provincial

---

* KCTSCC, "Chih fang tien" (Section on geography), ch. 1104, on Chang-chow;
for some examples of chapters on other provinces listing local products that include
silk and silk fabrics, see chs. 1167, 1178 (Hupeh); 202, 230 (Shantung); 324
(Shansi); 435 (Honan); 509 (Shensi); 592 (Szechwan); see also NYS 1: 432 on
Kwangsi in the 1870's.

capital and nearby prefectural cities. These centers not only raised silk-worms, but also encouraged sericulture among the populace by buying mulberry leaves and cocoons from them and by teaching weaving to those who wished to learn. The provincial authorities of Fukien reported in 1740 on the importing of Chekiang sericulturists at government expense in an effort to introduce silk culture into certain areas in Fukien, a project that was apparently successful. A similar project was undertaken in Hunan in 1755, where a government textile workshop was established that employed artisans brought in from Kiangsu and Chekiang; it was hoped that private silk firms would follow this lead and thus in time create a silk industry for Hunan, where the natural environment was favorable to the raising of mulberry trees and silkworms.

As late as the 1890's this traditional pattern of government activity continued in evidence: Governor-general Chang Chih-tung reported in 1893 on a Hupeh project that had been launched in 1890, in which the provincial government dispatched agents to Chekiang to buy large quantities of mulberry seedlings. These were distributed to a number of districts for transplanting and further growth. The young trees were then given to the local people free of charge, along with copies of a handbook on sericulture. From 1890 to 1893 10,000,000 mulberry saplings were reported to have been distributed this way, of which the survival rate differed from place to place, ranging from 60 to 100 percent. In 1893 the trees had matured and the plan then was to establish a government textile center at the provincial capital, where Chekiang weavers would be employed to teach the local people. In the remote and inaccessible districts, where the inhabitants might find it difficult to sell their silk on the commercial market, local officials were asked to purchase the silk with government funds and send it to the textile center for use there (HCCTLT, ch. 24: 4–8, 12; CCTL: 141, 223).

The geographical distribution of sericulture during the Ch'ing, therefore, was not static, but continued to widen throughout most of China proper. However, by late Ch'ing times the important silk-producing centers were located primarily in four areas of the country: (1) Chekiang and Kiangsu in the lower Yangtze–Lake T'ai region, with main centers in and around Hangchow, Hu-chou, Soochow, and Nanking; (2) Kwang-tung, with centers at Shun-te and Canton; (3) Szechwan, with main centers at Chengtu, Chia-ting, and Chungking; (4) Shantung, where the product was chiefly the oak-fed "wild" silk used for weaving the pongee or tussore type of cloth (LSTL, 3: 28). Of these four areas, Shantung was the leading producer of mulberry silk until the southward migrations at the end of the Northern Sung promoted the growth of a flourishing silk industry south of the Yangtze. Szechwan had long been a silk producer, but was a relative newcomer to large-scale production, although long before the mid-nineteenth century its brocade (*Shu chin*) was a famous article in domestic trade. The most important areas in the total historical context, therefore, were the other two on our list: the lower Yangtze–Lake T'ai region, and southern Kwangtung near Canton, the former on account of its long dominance of the Chinese silk industry in skill, variety, quantity, and quality of production, and the latter because of the role of foreign trade in the development of its silk industry. The following discussion will be focused largely on these two areas.

The Production of Raw Silk

From the planting and cultivation of mulberry trees to the raising and care of silkworms through the period of cocoon-making, until the silk fibers had been reeled and wound into hanks of specific weights, sericulture was—as it continues to be—an extremely laborious process.* In the silk districts of Hu-chou and Soochow, for example, many activities were customarily suspended during "silkworm month," the fourth month of the lunar calendar: "The doors of the houses were closed, the government temporarily stopped the collection of taxes, and the people in the neighborhood stopped all social visitings, celebrations, and wakes; these were known as 'silkworm taboos.'"† This seasonal aspect of sericulture exerted a basic influence on the rhythm of the rural economy. Even within the season there were variations in rhythm. Unwinding the cocoon and winding the silk into hanks had to begin at a certain very critical stage of development, and to be completed before the moth hatched. The pace of work during these few days was invariably frantic. In this connection there exists an unsolved technological puzzle that awaits further investigation. Had the methods for preserving cocoons that were described in Yuan and Ming books of agriculture been in practice,‡

---

* This refers to the raising of silkworms on the leaves of various strains of the mulberry tree, which accounted for the bulk of Chinese silk. Much less labor was demanded of those who produced tussore or pongee silk, made by a different silkworm "pastured" on silk-oak trees. This variant of sericulture was first practiced in Shantung and later spread to some southern provinces such as Kwangtung, Kwangsi, and Kweichow.

† KCTSCC, "Chih fang tien," ch. 676, 974: the item on Soochow refers specifically to the lake-side town of Chen-tse, a famous silk mart from the early eighteenth century on.

‡ The three methods of preserving the cocoon mentioned in Wang Chen's *Nung shu* (Book of Agriculture) and in *Nung sang chi yao*, an agricultural handbook compiled by the Yuan Bureau of Agriculture, were steaming, drying in sunlight, and soaking in brine. The first, considered the most effective, is described in detail in both works. The steaming utensil is also described in a mid-sixteenth-century edition of Wang Chen's book. See *Nung sang chi yao*, ch. 4: 14a–15b. Amano Gennosuke, "Gen no Oshin Nosho no kenkyu" (in Yabuuchi 1967: 445–46), reproduces a

the crucial reeling operation might have been spread over a longer period of time, as the danger that the chrysalis might hatch and thereby destroy the cocoon would have been considerably lessened. Losses would have been reduced, and the traditional trading pattern of raw silk might have been different. However, no record has turned up of the use by Ch'ing sericulturists of any of the three methods mentioned in earlier works, and it was only in the late nineteenth century that heat-killing the chrysalis was introduced from abroad to improve the silk-reeling step in the process of making silk.

In Hu-chou and Soochow, sericulture, the mainstay of the local economy since the mid-Ming, found its fullest expression as the basis of a way of life. According to Chang Lü-hsiang's treatise on agriculture, which was based on contemporary conditions in the countryside around Hu-chou and dated 1658, it was very much to the cultivator's advantage to plant his land in mulberry rather than rice, terrain and soil permitting. Chang maintains that one *mou* of mulberry trees would provide enough leaves to raise from two or three to ten trays of silkworms. In a year when the price of silk was high and that of rice low, one tray of silkworms alone would yield as much income as one *mou* of rice. Even when the price situation was reversed, the income from mulberry trees could still be comparable, *mou* for *mou*, to that from rice.* As the early Ch'ing encyclopedist put it: "The people of Hu-chou depend on the silkworms as [others] on farming the land; therefore a successful silk crop means an increase in wealth, and an unsuccessful one spells hardship" (KCTSCC, "Chih fang tien," ch. 972, 974).

Although the production of silk was quite decentralized, and was largely a peasant household activity, some phases of it were sometimes commercialized even before the Ch'ing period. Hsü Kuang-ch'i, who owned a large estate near Shanghai, wrote in 1611 to his son, "Judging from the size of our current crop of mulberry leaves, we can probably raise thirty or forty baskets [of silkworms] this year. If we do not have enough hands to care for such a large quantity of worms, how about selling a part of the leaves?" (Wang Chung-min 1963 2: 482).

---

picture of a "cocoon steamer" from the Chia-ching edition of Wang's *Nung shu*. The Ch'ing imperially commissioned pictorial depiction of agricultural and sericultural techniques: the *Yü chih keng chih t'u* 2: 12 refers to "crystals of salt" and well-water, and to keeping the cocoons in a sealed earthen jar for ten days. This may be a reference to the brine-soaking method, but the statement is vague, and sounds almost as if an earlier technique were now imperfectly understood.

* Ch'en Heng-li, 1958: 252. Chang Lü-hsiang wrote the *Pu Nung shu* in the late 1650's as an addendum to the well-known earlier work *Shen shih nung shu*; both he and Shen were natives of the Lake T'ai area and well acquainted with the local economic conditions as well as with contemporary agricultural techniques.

That selling mulberry leaves was not a practice restricted to the disposal of surplus leaves from relatively large estates is indicated by the account given by Chu Kuo-chen, a scholar-official active in the early seventeenth century and therefore Hsü's contemporary. He specifically recognized a "quite numerous" class of the farming population of Huchou as "those who depend on mulberry crops for a living (*yeh sang che*)." Although the majority of sericulturists grew their own mulberry trees, there were many who did not have enough leaves, and it was the practice for these people to place orders for mulberry leaves ahead of the season with growers who had them to sell. This procedure was known as "taking the tip of the leaves" (*miao yeh*). In Chu's time, for 160 catties of leaves (the amount needed to feed one catty of silkworms), the price was a little over half a tael, or slightly less if the order was prepaid. One catty of silkworms would produce enough raw silk to sell for a little over one tael in silver (Chu, ch. 2: 15). When the sellers of mulberry leaves could not meet their orders, they imported additional leaves from neighboring districts, an expedient that subjected them to the ups and downs of the market price. Our Ming author concludes that the safest procedure would be either to plant enough mulberry trees for one's own use or to sell, or both, or for the keeper of silkworms to place advance orders on leaves.*

The trade in mulberry leaves continued under the Ch'ing. The number of references to the trade in surviving documents indicates that it became more widely prevalent from the eighteenth century onward, when internal peace and increased domestic and foreign demand stimulated silk production. Mulberry leaves are reported for sale in Shensi in 1751, and in the Ch'ing-yang district of Anhwei in 1893. In Ch'ing-yang the price of mulberry leaves was a highly variable factor in the local economy.† In the lower Yangtze region, where the leaves could be harvested twice a year, one *mou* of top-grade land planted in mulberry trees could yield up to 2,000 catties of leaves.‡ There, the trade in leaves was already flourishing by the mid-eighteenth century. One of the chief sources of supply was East Tung-t'ing Island in Lake T'ai, where mulberry-leaf markets were busy places at silkworm time in the spring. Leaves from this island supplied the silk producers on the south shore of the lake (Chin, ch. 6: 34). In the mid-nineteenth century the leaf trade had become an established part of the economy of Hu-chou,

---

* Chu Kuo-chen, ch. 2: 15a. "Even an omniscient Immortal," runs a late-Ming proverb, "is unable to foretell the price of [mulberry] leaves."
† Entry no. 1275, *I wen lu* (Periodical of general knowledge), 1893, in NYS 1: 429.
‡ *Wu-ch'ing wen hsien*, ch. 9, quoted in TPCIMY, 2: 1040.

where the leaves were sold in units of *ko* (20 catties) or of *tan* (100 catties). The market prices ranged widely, so that in a depressed year the leaf-producers were faced with financial disaster. The practice of advance orders also continued to prevail. Furthermore, at this time leaves were sometimes bought on credit—presumably to be paid for when the season's new silk was sold.* The producer who used credit in this way was of course under pressure to convert his output into cash at once, but the fact that he was able to get credit in the first place indicates that there was an active silk market in the area where he would find a ready demand for his silk. Brokers in mulberry leaves, known as *ch'ing yeh hang* (green-leaf firms), had made their appearance in this locality, and were operating as middlemen between the producers of leaves and the raisers of silkworms.

The commercialization of mulberry leaves did not automatically lead the way to large-scale production of raw silk. From local histories we learn that sericulture was still primarily carried out in peasant households, whose supply of leaves was usually inadequate. For such small-scale individual producers, short-term loans were often the answer. There is evidence that the need for these loans—at 10 percent interest—was a perennial problem faced by the small peasant, as a couplet in one of the poems describing the rural situation indicates: "Wishing only that our debt may be repaid soon this year, so that [our] request to borrow will not be refused next spring" (P'eng Tse-i 1957: 457).

As sericulture spread it became regionally specialized, as again Hu-chou may illustrate. In 1611 Hsü Kuang-ch'i instructed his son in a matter-of-fact tone to "hire some Hu-chou natives to tend the [cocoon room] fires and make silk. First hire a Hu-chou man who lives in Shanghai, on a trial basis; if he does not work out, go to Hu-chou next year to hire the truly skilled. . . ." (Wang Chung-min 1963, 2: 482). Indeed, if the procedures considered proper for the care of mulberry trees in the late eighteenth and early nineteenth centuries are indicative, every step of mulberry culture required a vast amount of careful labor and a great degree of skill. For example, the best leaf-producing trees were all grafted stock. The ordinary or "wild" stock produced many berries and relatively few leaves, "unfit for feeding silkworms" (Chang Hsing-fu: 5). It is perhaps not surprising, then, that the ordinary peasant seldom had a sufficient supply of mulberry leaves from his own farm yard.

Although there are no clear data on the distribution of mulberry groves, the tree was certainly impressively widespread in the Lake T'ai

---

* *Hu-chou fu chih* (Gazetteer of Hu-chou Prefecture), T'ung-chih edition, ch. 30, quoted in TPCIMY, 1: 353.

region and in the level areas of western Chekiang. From the accounts of alert travelers it is evident that sericulture in Chekiang flourished steadily through the eighteenth century and well into the nineteenth, before the Taiping wars devastated a goodly portion of these areas. Lord Macartney, passing through central Chekiang in 1794, remarked on the "charming fruitful country" west of Hangchow, where tea and mulberry trees flourished (Cranmer-Byng 1962: 182). Half a century later Robert Fortune had this to report while traveling toward Hangchow (Fortune 1852: 28):

During the space of two days—and in that time I must have travelled upwards of a hundred miles—I saw little else than mulberry trees. They were evidently carefully cultivated, and in the highest state of health, producing fine, large and glossy leaves. When it is remembered that I was going in a straight direction through the country, some idea may be formed of the extent of this enormous silk district, which probably occupies a circle of at least a hundred miles in diameter. And this, it must be remembered, is only one of the silk districts of China, but it is the principal and the best one.

By the 1840's, Hu-chou apparently had silk plantations that were able to specialize in large-scale production of this single crop. Thomas Allom described the "silk farm" as a large establishment of many buildings, owned by an old family of Hu-chou named Lou and conveniently situated on a tributary to the Grand Canal. The finished raw silk was brought in hanks from the reeling sheds to be stored in buildings next to the main house. When a sufficient amount had been accumulated, the silk was piled on flat-bottomed boats with bamboo canopies and transported to the Canal. There it might be bought by a single buyer "as speculation" or transferred to some "home manufacturer," or it might be sent further to the urban markets of Hangchow or Chusan. The producer was not concerned with the ultimate use of the silk (CR 16, 5: 235).

In such a large-scale operation the producer was able to furnish the necessary raw materials and specialized labor. He was also able, should the current price of silk be unsatisfactory, to withhold his goods and await a better price. The small peasant producers, by contrast, had no choice but to sell their silk as fast as possible: "A farmer today depends on selling his silk to pay taxes and debts. Should the silk production meet with a mishap he would be under the dual pressure of public and private indebtedness. Who can afford to speculate on the future and await better prices?"*

Thus, the local silk market was the meeting point of several different

---

* Ch'ang-hsin hsien chih (Gazetteer of Ch'ang-hsin District), T'ung-chih, ed., ch. 8: 40, in P'eng Tse-i 1957: 219; Tung Li-chou's poem "Selling Silk," printed

TABLE 1. MAIN TYPES OF SILK DEALERS IN NAN-HSÜN, CHEKIANG, *ca.* 1850

Type of firm	Nature of silk business
Kuang-hang (*Kwangtung* firms), also known as *k'o hang* or visitors' firms	Acting as brokers to merchants from Kwangtung and export merchants from Shanghai
Hsiang ssu hang (country silk firms)	Buying exclusively from individual peasant producers
Ching hang (warp-silk firms)	Buying the appropriate fibers and making warp-silk yarns
Hua chuang (brokerage firms)	Small establishments specializing in buying from producers and selling to larger firms
Hsiao ling t'ou (small producers' agencies)	Selling the output of small peasant producers for a commission
Ching chuang (Nanking firms)	Buying for the Imperial Silkworks at Nanking

types of producers. The small town of Nan-hsün outside Hu-chou was one such spot. It was a major entrepôt of raw silk, and the peak of business activity was reached when the buyers, both local and long-distance, had gathered at the end of each spring for the trading in silk. The trade was carried out in a special section in the southern part of town, where a variety of silk firms set up shop during the season, creating a great deal of traffic and hubbub in the crowded streets. Several local sources give the breakdown shown in Table 1 of the types of firms and their specialties as they function soon after the Treaty of Nanking (P'eng Tse-i 1957: 475).

Across the vast Lake T'ai on its eastern shore, lay Soochow, where sericulture and the manufacture of silk textiles were important industries that rivaled even those of Hu-chou. Its natives were wont to boast that "the silk from Soochow clothes the entire empire" (*ibid.*: 209). Silk production and sales generally took place in the towns surrounding Soochow, such as Chen-tse and Shuang-lin, where silk had been a mainstay of the economy since the Ch'ien-lung period, and where wholesale buyers congregated each year to purchase the new silk. "Thus, even though the taxes are heavy and the populace in financial straits, still

---

in the Hsien-feng edition of *Gazetteer of Nan-hsün* (in P'eng Tse-i, 1957: 475), contains this explicit passage:

> I met my southern neighbor the rich old man
> who came to town also to sell his silk;
> waving his hand at me, he cautioned:
> "No, no—wait for a higher price
> next year before you sell!"
> His honest concern touches me,
> but how can I ignore
> the [tax] notices from the district government?

they have managed to avoid destitution; here the houses are more numerous and the boat traffic heavier than in other places: all these are the great benefits of sericulture."* The small producers of both Hu-chou and Soochow found sericulture the surest means of earning enough to meet the tax rates as well as the demands of daily living, if not to keep themselves out of debt (ibid.: 210).

It is clear, then, that the lot of most silk producers was determined directly by the immediate cash value of the commodity they created. Ever since the Ming period, the market price of silk had been advancing at a steady though moderate rate. Over a period of approximately two and a half centuries, from the second half of the fourteenth to the late sixteenth century, the price of chüan per bolt rose from 0.50 to 0.70 tael, an increase of 40 percent (P'eng Hsin-wei 1958: 499–502). Considering the time span involved, the influx of silver from abroad that began in the sixteenth century, and the increased importance of the money sector in the total economy in late Ming times, such an increase can only be regarded as mild.

Available figures on export prices of raw silk and official Ch'ing documents from the eighteenth century show a moderate trend of rising prices during the first third of the century, and a steep climb of silk prices from the early Ch'ien-lung reign onward. More specifically, one can divide the trends into three distinct segments between 1699 and 1799 (see Table 2).

1. 1699–1702: The price of raw silk hovered around 130 taels per picul (100 catties) the average being 132 taels, which was also the prevailing price for 1702. This price, representing quite a stable level over several years, is used as the base figure in calculating the price indexes in the following paragraphs. Thus 132 taels is 100 on the index.

2. 1703–ca. 1740: After a sharp (and as yet unexplained) dip in 1704 to 100 taels (index = 76+), the export prices fluctuated. The general trend was still a moderate increase, with a high point of 155 to 159 taels per picul in 1731. The average of these highs, 157 taels per picul, is 118 on the index.

3. ca. 1740–1799: In 1750 the price stood at 175 taels per picul (index = 131.8), and from then on it never went below that level. Instead, it continued to shoot upward, reaching 300 taels per picul in 1770 (index = 227+), and peaking at 310 taels in 1784 (index = 234+). In the 1790's the price index leveled off closer to the 200 mark, with the index for 1793 at 193, and for 1799 at 204.

---

* Ibid.: 209; also Wu-chiang hsien chih (Gazetteer of Wu-chiang District), Ch'ien-lung edition, ch. 5: 13–14; Wu-chiang was a district just south of the prefectural city of Soochow.

TABLE 2. PRICE INDEXES FOR RAW SILK IN THE EIGHTEENTH CENTURY,
BASED ON EXPORT PRICES

Year	Price per picul (taels)	Index	Average price (taels)
1702	132	100	
1703	140	106+	
1704	100	76+	
1722	150	113+	
1723	142–144	100.8	143
1724	155	117+	
1731	155–159	118+	157
1750	175	131.8+	
1755	190–195	145.4+	192.5
1757	225–250	180+	238
1763	245	185+	
1765	269	203.7+	
1770	300	227+	
1775	275–277.5	209+	276
1783	275	207+	
1784	310	234+	
1792	312	236+	
1793	255	193+	
1799	270	204+	

SOURCE: Adapted from Ch'üan Han-sheng 1957: 534; Morse 1925, 2: 8, 203, 204.
NOTE: The 1792 price is for Chekiang silk only.

Thus, during the century from 1699 to 1799, which coincided with the high-Ch'ing period of domestic peace and economic growth, the export price of silk had more than doubled. More than 80 percent of this increase occurred between 1750 and 1799. What this meant to the silk producer and the weaver was clear. Until the end of the 1730's the prices followed a path of gradual advance, so that the producer could be relatively certain of the rate of return for his labor. From mid-century on, however, the combined cumulative effects of the influx of silver and rising demands in foreign trade* had produced a much more drastic inflationary process that led to the series of sharp rises in price, as seen above. Moreover, within the overall trend of steep price rises there were short-term cycles resulting from such local factors as inclement weather, damage to the silkworm crops, and hoarding by the large speculators (Shih 1968: 3, 21–22; Spence 1966: 101 and Appendix A). For the small producer, therefore, higher prices did not always imply better material benefits; in fact, for the cottage weaver who had to buy his raw material, higher silk prices usually meant financial hardship.

* In 1750 the British Parliament reduced the import duty on Chinese silk to the same level as that on Italian silk, a move that led directly to the East India Company's decision to "venture on a quantity" (Morse 1925 1: 288).

TABLE 3. RAW SILK EXPORTS IN EIGHTEENTH-CENTURY CANTON
(ENGLISH SHIPS ONLY)

Year	Raw silk transacted (piculs)		Price per picul (taels)
1723	100		145
1731	145		155–159
1750	1,192		175
1755	1,000		275–277.5[a]
1792	3,263	{1,500 in Company ships {1,763 in Country ships[b]	312 200

SOURCE: Morse 1925, 1: 177, 200, 291; 2: 8, 203, 204.
[a] In 1775 half the total was sold at each price.
[b] Free traders operating with the permission of the East India Company.

A portion of the silk from the Hu-chou and Soochow regions found its way to the foreign trade at Canton, where it was called "Nankeen silk" by some Western merchants. The increase in the amount exported, and the relationship of that increase to the price trends just described can be gauged from the sample data in Table 3 pertaining to the largest foreign trader, the British East India Company.

The last item in Column 2 of Table 3 shows a significant new feature in the Canton trade: over half (1,763 piculs) of the large total figure for 1792 is "Canton" silk as distinguished from Nankeen silk. The bulk of this "Canton" silk was actually produced in the nearby district of Shun-te, where sericulture had a long history. At the beginning of the Ch'ing, the noted scholar-official Ch'ü Ta-chün, writing of the economy of Kwangtung, observed that ten *mou* of land planted in mulberry would adequately support a family of eight (NYS, 2: 432). Smaller communities in the vicinity of Shun-te—such as Chiu-chiang—had been known since early Ch'ing times for their farmers' ability to make the most of limited acreages by engaging in fish farming and sericulture.[*] Sericulture in Shun-te increased gradually in economic importance from its beginnings in the late eighteenth century, to the Hsien-feng period (1851–62) when some ten thousand bales (1 bale = 71 or 72 catties) of silk were exported per year. The main varieties of silkworms used were at first those introduced from the Hu-chou region of Chekiang, but toward the second half of the nineteenth century these were superseded by a variety called "silver cocoons," which produced more silk per worm and were raised largely for export silk (*Shun-te hsien chih*, ch. 1: 24–26).

[*] *Kuang-chou fu chih* (Gazetteer of Canton Prefecture), ch. 15: 20b: "Chiu-chiang is a small place where fish ponds occupy half the land area. Fish are raised in the ponds, and mulberry trees are planted on the dykes; the men sell fish, and the women tend silkworms."

Silk production at Shun-te was encouraged by a combination of several factors. First, the numerous natural waterways that cut through the land made extensive rice culture difficult. By building earthen embankments at the water's edge, however, the local people found that they could enclose enough land to survive economically if they raised a high-value cash crop. These polder lands were enclosed by dykes called *wei* and known as *wei* preceded by a place name, or as *chi t'ien* (filled land). Mulberry was so often planted there that these areas were locally termed *sang chi* or "mulberry polders" (*ibid.*, ch. 4). A second factor was the warm climate and long growing season, which enabled the Shun-te sericulturist to reap up to six crops of mulberry leaves per year and thus as many of silkworms. A reasonably good year saw one *mou* of mulberry groves yield approximately 3,400 catties of leaves, with the largest yields (700–800 catties) in the second and third crops (*ibid.*, ch. 1: 23–24). In other words, unlike his Yangtze or Lake T'ai counterpart, whose brief silk-making season lasted only to the end of spring, the silk producer in the Shun-te area was gainfully engaged in his work each year from April to November or December.

A third and very important factor in the growth of sericulture in the Shun-te region was the stimulus provided by the export trade, concentrated at Canton until after the Treaty of Nanking. With the sharp increase in both export demand and export prices in the second half of the eighteenth century, Shun-te, in the immediate hinterland of Canton, began to develop as a silk center, so that toward the end of the century it was supplying the exporters at the port city with local raw silk in considerable quantities. Unlike the lower Yangtze–Lake T'ai region, Shun-te had the export trade from the beginning as a major outlet for its silk, and by the nineteenth century it had become a major center for the silk trade. Export merchants from Canton established agencies in Shun-te to buy the raw silk and silk textiles they needed for the foreign trade. In 1848 a Western observer reported that the total amount of silk produced in the Shun-te area was some four hundred thousand pounds in a good year, but as little as fifty thousand pounds in a bad year. Shun-te's silk was at that time known in the trade as *t'u ssu*, "local silk," a term that had customarily been used to designate all silk other than that from Chekiang (Hedde 1848: 427–28). The close tie between Shun-te sericulture and the export trade undoubtedly made the local producers more responsive to the requirements of foreign markets. This would partially explain why modern reeling techniques appeared earlier here than in the lower Yangtze region.

Besides Kiangsu-Chekiang and southern Kwangtung, other areas also practiced sericulture more or less extensively. The portion of the output that was not used locally in these areas was channelled into the considerable domestic trade of China. To give one example, Lu-an Prefecture in Shansi was required to deliver a certain quota of silk fabrics to Peking every year. Since Lu-an produced little raw silk, the fabrics were woven from silk bought from such silk-producing provinces as Szechwan and Chekiang. In the Tao-kuang period (1821–50) the total value of silk bought at the "silk market" of Ch'i-chiang, Szechwan, by merchants of the provinces of Shansi and Shensi was reported to be in the "neighborhood of a million taels."* It may be recalled that it was the enormous scale of the Chinese domestic consumption of silk that most impressed Robert Fortune when he described the sudden great increase in the export of raw silk at Shanghai: within two or three years after the opening of this port the amount of silk exported had jumped from 3,000 to 20,000 bales (from 2,160 to 15,400 piculs) per year. Fortune concluded, lacking evidence to the contrary, that this showed "the enormous quantity which must have been in the Chinese market before the extra demand could have been so easily supplied," and that the quantity exported was very small in proportion to that consumed by the Chinese themselves (Fortune 1852: 28).

The Production and Distribution of Silk Textiles

The most common types of silk fabric were known by their generic names, such as *ch'ou* (silk cloth), *tuan* (satin), *chüan* (gauze), *sha* (thin gauze), *ling* (damask) and *chin* (brocade). The varieties under each category were literally innumerable, each locality boasting of its own specialties. The famous silk fabrics from Hu-chou, for example, included about a dozen varieties of different types and qualities. Who were the weavers of these fabrics, and how were the products marketed?

There were, no doubt, many village householders who wove small quantities of the silk produced by their own silkworms and who depended on the immediate sale of their cloth to make ends meet. However, the prevalence of the sale of raw silk by small producers indicates that a considerable portion of the textile manufacturing was done away from the premises of the household that had produced the silk; at least, it would be reasonable to suggest that the sericulturist and the weaver were quite often not the same person. The production of silk fabrics was, in fact, even more complex than the production of raw silk.

In general, silk weavers were classified into two groups, the "self-

---

* *Lu-an fu chih* (Gazetteer of Lu-an Prefecture), ch. 8; the importing of Szechwan silk for the looms of Shansi Province was an established practice by the late Ming (Li Chien-nung 1957: 48; *Ch'i-chiang hsien chih* [Gazetteer of Ch'i-chiang District, Szechwan], Tao-kuang edition, ch. 10: 22, in P'eng Tse-i 1957: 221.)

employed weavers" and the "putting-out weavers," the latter working with materials furnished by monied entrepreneurs who were often merchants dealing in silk textiles. The putting-out system flourished in the lower Yangtze–Lake T'ai region, where local histories have recorded the spread of silk-textile production along with the growth of sericulture from the last decades of the sixteenth century onward. The weaving of "silk cloth and figured gauzes," for example, gained impetus in the Wu-chiang district in late Ming times, so that wealthy investors hired workers to weave for them, and the poorer classes did the weaving themselves with the help of their children (P'eng Tse-i 1957: 221–22). By the eighteenth century, silk-weaving and trade in silk fabrics had transformed the villages of Chen-tse and Sheng-tse (both under the jurisdiction of Wu-chiang) into busy and prosperous towns, and some time during the Ch'ien-lung reign Chen-tse was separated administratively from the magistracy of Wu-chiang and granted the status of a district.

No one knows how many independent weavers (*chi hu*, literally "loom households") there were or what the ratio of these producers was to those who took put-out work to do in their own homes. Such accounts as that of P'u-yuan, a silk town in the Hu-chou area, telling us that "here lights of a myriad households shine at night, the people largely earning their living from weaving silk cloth and gauze" (*ibid.*: 216), give no indication of the actual structure of the industry.

The close and direct link between the cottage producer and the silk merchant, however, has been clearly depicted in a number of sources. An eighteenth-century work on P'u-yuan describes the large variety of silk fabrics that were traded at the local market, and explains that "ninety percent of the households in our town are weavers. . . . The silk cloths are bought from them by the very wealthy, and stored to await the buyers from the national and provincial capitals. . . ."[*] This passage might mean that the weavers were independent workers who were a class of highly skilled artisans in the countryside. However, it cannot be assumed that these individual artisans, even if they were self-employed weavers, were always economically self-sufficient. Many of these weavers were apparently indebted to silk brokers who lent them the necessary capital to buy the raw materials for manufacturing the fabrics (Shih 1968: 62).

Because the production of silk textiles in the Hu-chou and Soochow regions was so diffused, the rise of middlemen was a reasonable development. The "silk-cloth broker" (*ch'ou ling t'ou*) made his living from the fees he received for selling the cloth woven by the small producer to the commercial buyer. He was in all likelihood a local man with con-

---

[*] Hu Cho, *P'u-chen chi wen* (An account of the town of P'u-Yuan), Ch'ien-lung edition, "Introduction," in P'eng Tse-i 1957: 218.

nections among the producers as well as among the merchants. He would have to know the varieties and qualities of the many local fabrics in order to be able to fill satisfactorily the orders of the merchants who had come from some distances to buy silk.*

Aside from the weavers, whom we might call "cottagers," there was clearly a group of skilled artisans who were wage-earners. Although not the only locality where the practice was in use, Soochow provides us with the most extensive written records concerning this aspect of the industry. A well-known passage from the *Gazetteer of Soochow Prefecture* depicting the hiring procedures there during the K'ang-hsi and Ch'ien-lung periods (1662–1723 and 1736–96) reads as follows:

The inhabitants of the eastern section of the prefectural city [Soochow] are all textile workers. . . . Each weaver has a special skill, and each has a regular employer, who pays him a daily wage. If anything should happen [to the regular weaver, the employer] will get a worker who is without regular employment to take his place; this is known as "calling a substitute." The weavers without regular employers go to the bridges at dawn each day to await the calls. Satin weavers stand on Flower Bridge, damask weavers on Kuang-hua Temple Bridge, and spinners who make silk yarn at Lin-hsi Ward. They congregate by the score and by the hundred, scanning around expectantly with outstretched necks, resembling groups of famine refugees. They will stay until after the breakfast hour. If work should be curtailed at the silk textile establishments, these workers would be without a living.†

According to a document of late 1734, most of the weaving establishments of Soochow operated with hired craftsmen; the owner of an establishment furnished the funds and paid the weavers according to the type and amount of work put in.‡ A similar situation prevailed in Nanking, where satin was the principal fabric produced. The owner of the workshop was called a *chang-fang* or accounting house, with whom the weavers settled all accounts. The weavers were said to "put up the material," but more often they worked with silk provided by the *chang-fang*. The finished satin was received by the latter, and the weavers were paid according to the quality of workmanship. Small weavers without any

---

* Ho Ping, "Sheng-tse chih fang ch'ou yeh" (The silk weaving industry of Sheng-tse), Kuo chi mao i tao pao (International trade reports), 4 (1933), 5: 36, in P'eng Tse-i 1957: 220; see also Shih 1968: 62.

† KCTSCC, "K'ao kung tien" (Section on industries), ch. 10, "Textile production." The Ch'ien-lung edition of the *Gazetteer of Soochow Prefecture* contains a similar passage (see below); see Shih 1968: 77, on a similar situation in the Nanking silk industry.

‡ Text of an account recording the government order against work stoppages by weavers in the districts of Ch'ang-chou and Yuan-ho (both in Soochow Prefecture), in P'eng Tse-i 1957: 214; Fu I-ling 1956: 12.

capital to invest, therefore, were dependent on the accounting houses for their livelihood (Shih, 1968: 77–78). This method of organizing the textile industry was regarded as a way to fulfill mutual needs, with the quality of the product a major criterion in the determination of wages.

However, the workers who stood on the bridges at dawn may not have felt that their needs were being met. Even at the height of the silk-weaving industry there appears to have been an oversupply of labor, which undoubtedly goes far to explain the rise of artisans' organizations that instigated strikes in the early eighteenth century. The same document of 1734 explains the unstable labor situation in somewhat different terms (PKTL: 3):

> But there are some lawless fellows who, having been dismissed by their employers on account of their inferior workmanship, have nurtured a feeling of hatred and jealousy in their hearts, and begun to organize into gangs. They incite work stoppages and demand increases in wages, so that the establishments are compelled to close down their looms and the weavers lose their livelihood.

The silk weavers' strikes were successfully suppressed in 1734, but they broke out again later. Even the highly concentrated silk industry in Soochow Prefecture could not employ all the skilled weavers who lived there during the eighteenth and early nineteenth centuries. In 1822, nine decades after the document referred to above had been inscribed in stone, another one depicting the disputes between the silk establishments and the weavers was published. The authorities emphasized the need for weavers to live on their contracted wages only, forbidding them to organize strikes or sell the raw materials or the woven products for their own benefit (*ibid.*: 13–14). In Hangchow, any activity that might give workers a chance for collective action—such as organizing for the annual spring ritual of dramatic performances—was to be sponsored not by the workers, but by the owners of the silk workshops. Workers' organizations for the purpose of demanding higher wages or volunteering as arbitrator in labor disputes were prohibited. A weaver not in good standing with one employer was to be barred from employment by others.[*]

In spite of such internal frictions, however, the silk-textile industries at the producing centers continued to function as the main economic assets of these areas. Mid-nineteenth-century accounts by visitors em-

---

[*] In 1845 the prefectural government of Hangchow approved the document here summarized; see TPCIMY, Second collection: 359. Before the Taiping wars there were an estimated 10,000 looms in Hangchow (Shih 1968: 79); cf. du Halde's estimate of 60,000 employed in Hangchow in silk manufacturing (Fortune 1852: 37).

phasize the place of silk in the economy of Soochow and Hangchow (Hedde 1845: 584–87; Fortune 1852: 36–37).

Silk-textile manufacturing did not become important in the Canton area until the early part of the eighteenth century, but it soon developed into a major industry, and enough silk was produced in the Shun-te district so that several varieties, including pongee, were regularly sold to other provinces. The demands of foreign trade led directly to the growth of silk-weaving in the city of Canton itself, where a large number of textile-manufacturing establishments were dependent on the export trade for their existence. A strike called by some of the silk weavers in Canton in 1850 and 1851 immediately produced delays in the delivery of foreign export contracts.*

There is evidence that as the nineteenth century wore on and the general economy deteriorated, the fortunes of the silk-textile handicrafts-men progressively declined. In a situation of lessened opportunities, the competition for livelihood became acute among the artisans who plied trades connected with the silk industry, especially in localities where there had been a concentration of such work. A joint order issued by the magistrates' offices of the three districts of Ch'ang-chou, Yuan-ho, and Wu (all under the jurisdiction of Soochow Prefecture) in 1898 indicates that the economic decline manifested itself among the group of highly specialized artisans known as loom-makers and repairers in two ways. First, the traditional territories of specialization, based on the two distinct styles of loom—Soochow and Nanking—were more jealously guarded by their respective practitioners, and incidents of expansion into the other's territory thus became more serious. When Soochow-style satin-loom-makers and -repairmen saw that their territory was invaded by "unscrupulous men" of the Nanking-style looms, they lodged a complaint with the district government, and after due investigation the intruders were enjoined to respect the traditional limits of handicraft activity (PKTL: 18–19).

Second, there had been hereditary succession to the weavers' craft at the Imperial Silkworks in Soochow (PKTL: 7) for many years. The practice appears to have spread to other areas and to private factories. In a line of work that offered rather inelastic opportunities, in which particular skills were handed down from generation to generation, and in which it was considered necessary to enforce rigidly the observation of the work rules, such a development is not surprising. More important, each of these artisan families had its own hereditary patrons, thus achiev-

---

* CR 20, 7 (July 1851): 506–7. The strikes resulted largely from business rivalries among export merchants who were also the owner-operators of weaving establishments.

ing a certain degree of economic security even though opportunities had ceased altogether to expand. Thus, those who flouted the custom "of the past several decades" by trying to get work from other men's patrons were plainly regarded as a threat to the others' livelihood and were told by the authorities to desist from their unorthodox conduct or face punitive measures.

The Imperial Silkworks

The Imperial Silkworks (*Chih tsao chü*) were government textile manufactories inherited from the Ming period. There was a Court Weaving and Dyeing Office in Peking (abolished in 1843), and three Imperial Silkworks located in Soochow, Hangchow, and Nanking, respectively, supervised by the Office of the Imperial Household. Since the satin and silk cloths needed for various purposes by the Court—from Palace draperies and the silk cloths given to officials on numerous occasions each year, to silk fabrics used for border trade (in 1768, for instance, 12,050 bolts of silk stuffs were exchanged for horses and other livestock in Sinkiang)—were provided by the three Imperial Silkworks from early Ch'ing until they went largely out of function in 1894,* the organization of this particular aspect of the silk industry is well documented. Information on these government establishments has helped to throw light on the internal relationships of a considerable segment of the silk industry in the lower Yangtze–Lake T'ai region (P'eng Tse-i 1963: 91–116).

A basic policy for securing the materials for the looms of the Imperial Silkworks was decided upon in 1653, when it was ordered that raw silk was to be purchased from the producing districts with funds annually appropriated for this purpose, costs of transportation as well as the price of the silk being included in the allocations.† The artisans were hired for wages, paid either by the piece or on a daily or monthly rate and supplemented in most cases with food allotments paid in kind (Shih 1968: 16–18). The daily rate of wages for any individual worker was calculated according to the time and the number and types of artisans needed for the completion of a piece of work. The schedules of both

---

* Shih 1968: 25–26. In addition, Sung-chiang Prefecture, though without a regular government textile factory, was responsible for delivering 3,000 bolts of damask and gauze once every seven years. A like amount was required of Soochow and Hangchow in addition to their other quotas of silk fabric. All other varieties of silk cloths were to be sent to Peking as the need for replenishing the stores at the capital arose (KCTSCC, "Shih huo tien," ch. 310).

† Shih 1968: 21; KCTSCC, "K'ao kung tien," ch. 10, KCTSCC figures for 1677 show that the funds allotted to the Silkworks to cover raw materials, wages, and administrative costs came out of the income from miscellaneous taxes levied by the Board of Revenue and the Board of Works; each of the Silkworks had its individual and separate "budget," out of a total of 452,300 taels.

the cash wages and the food allotments were standardized for the three Silkworks with slight local variations (Shih 1968: 16; P'eng Tse-i 1963: 97–105). Through the height of the Ch'ing period, the three Imperial Silkworks maintained each year an average of approximately two thousand looms and seven thousand artisans and laborers of all types (Shih 1968: 14; KCTSCC, "K'ao kung-tien," ch. 10).

Looking at the official figures, one might conclude that the Silkworks were employers and the weavers and others their skilled employees. But the operations of the Imperial Silkworks were somewhat more complex than that. From the Shun-chih period (1644–62) on, an extremely close link was established between the government Silkworks and the private weaving workshops of various sizes. In brief, the responsibility for producing the required amounts of silk textiles was assigned by the Silkworks administrators to the private weavers, who fulfilled their contractual obligation in two different ways. They either contracted to have the stuff woven in their own places (by themselves or with additional hired workers) and delivered the finished product to the Silkworks, or they undertook to supply the Silkworks with skilled artisans to do the weaving on the government premises. In either case the wages were paid out of government appropriations.*

There are accounts from several periods of this contractual relationship between the government establishments and private handicraft. The three examples offered here are from Soochow. In *The History of the Imperial Silkworks at Soochow*, the author states that "According to tradition, special Court robes are woven and provided by selected well-to-do weavers; poor weavers are not assigned to this duty" (P'eng Tse-i 1957: 214).

The revised *Gazetteer of Yuan-ho District* (in Soochow Prefecture) of the early eighteenth century amends the passage on Soochow weavers (see above) at two places (*ibid.*: 214–15):

The inhabitants of the eastern section of the [district] city are all textile workers, and the weaving establishments [lit. "loom households"] are registered with the authorities, thus having an official status. The workers are hired for a daily wage, and each has a regular employer. . . . In former times [the workers] made a rather good living, but nowadays many are unemployed. Furthermore, the weaving establishments required to supply the government with their product are sometimes unable to meet the quota and thereby fall into arrears with the authorities; very frequently they are unable to make up for the amounts owed.

---

* P'eng Tse-i 1963: 92–93. Some modifications had been made in the early days of the Manchu rule, but the basic framework outlined above persisted throughout the Ch'ing period.

Here we are given two significant points regarding the Soochow textile world: (1) the loom households had to be registered with the government authorities as a part of their contract, thus placing themselves formally under official control, and (2) the obligations of the weaving establishments to supply the government with textiles were strictly defined and had a direct bearing on the life of the weavers themselves.

According to a nineteenth-century *Gazetteer of Soochow Prefecture*, the more elaborate and costly fabrics—including dragon robes, brocades, satins, and silk cloths and gauzes—were woven at the Imperial Silkworks. For more ordinary kinds of silk stuff, the raw silk was purchased by the Silkworks, turned over to "the people" (*min chien*) to be dyed and woven, then delivered to the Silkworks, which in turn sent it up to Peking. The finished product had to conform to the specifications laid down by the government; otherwise, the officials in charge were to be punished (*ibid.*: 81–82).

It would appear, therefore, that the "government-registered" textile producers were actually serving a dual function. They were responsible for maintaining their own establishments as a part of the private economy while at the same time serving as contractors for the Imperial Silkworks in order that this portion of government requirements might be fulfilled. In the latter capacity it was also their duty to hire the necessary artisans who were given government material and wages, and who produced the required textiles on government looms on the premises of the Silkworks (P'eng Tse-i 1963: 112–14). Thus, while the silk textile industry in Soochow, Hangchow, and Nanking was a flourishing private enterprise, it was also, through most of the Ch'ing dynasty, directly linked to the government procurement program. The skilled weavers crowding the bridges in Soochow city, awaiting calls for the day, for example, were wage-earners whose livelihood was very often directly derived from the operations of the Imperial Silkworks in that city. At Nanking, the "tribute satin" (*kung tuan*) destined for Peking was a noted local product, the government demand for which contributed to the flourishing textile industry there. At the height of prosperity in the eighteenth century the total number of looms in that city was about 30,000 (P'eng Tse-i 1957: 215).

Foreign Trade and Early Efforts at Modernization

Throughout the eighteenth century the exports of raw silk and silk piece-goods increased steadily, especially the exports of raw silk (see above, Table 3). In the first half of the century, the export of raw silk to Britain, the largest foreign customer, was no more than 300 to 400 piculs per year, but by the 1750's the increase in exports had made its effects felt in the Lake T'ai silk district. The prices of 1757 reached a new peak of between 225 and 250 taels per picul, and such prices meant an increase in the cost of raw materials for the domestic textile manufacturer. Interpreting the high prices as a result solely of enlarged foreign exports, the Ch'ing authorities extensively debated curtailing exports in 1759. One of the most ardent advocates of such a measure was An-ning, the Commissioner of Textiles of Soochow, whose main concern was to obtain raw silk at a reasonably low price for the local weaving establishments. Ultimately, in 1762, a stringent set of regulations went into force that limited silk exports to varying amounts at the different ports. These rules applied to Chinese coastal vessels and to ships from nearby tributary states, as well as to Western ships. The maximum amount permitted for each ship was 5,000 catties (50 piculs) of local (i.e. non-Chekiang) silk and 3,000 catties of late Hu-chou silk (the higher-quality early variety could no longer be exported). Silk fabrics might be substituted for raw silk, but with a 20 percent reduction in the weight allowed. However, since these restrictions failed to lower silk prices in the home market, whereas the export trade (which had been adding a million taels a year to the economy) was obviously being hurt, the government lifted the prohibition in 1764, and the export trade in silk was allowed to develop as it would.*

By the 1770's, the total amount of silk exported annually in British and European ships was about thirty-seven hundred piculs. The Chinese merchants from Canton who sold the silk to foreign buyers first contracted to furnish a stated amount of silk at a negotiated price, and then sent purchasing agents, usually provided with 50 to 80 percent of the purchase price, into the producing areas to secure the silk.† These agents were the "Canton and Fukien buyers" referred to in contemporary records. In addition, some of the merchants from other cities such as Soochow and Hangchow bought silk not merely to meet the needs of their local textile manufacturers, but also for "selling to Canton" (Shih 1968: 116, n. 3). Thus, the export portion of the silk from the lower Yantze–Lake T'ai region was actually channelled to the point of foreign purchase through a number of different routes.

The Treaty of Nanking (1842) ushered in an era of significant changes in the pattern of the silk export trade. One was the vast expansion of the volume exported, from a little over 12,000 bales (8,640 piculs) just before the First Anglo-Chinese War to 80,000 bales (57,600 piculs) in 1857

---

* Shih 1968: 102, 116–17 (notes 4 and 5).

† Morse 1925, 2: 11, 29. A report dated 1787 reads: "Raw silk, too, is always contracted for, bought and shipped by the unit of the bale . . . but the price is quoted and paid according to the actual net weight" (*ibid.*: 126).

(Shih 1968: 103). A second was the shift from Canton to Shanghai of the greatest volume of the export trade in silk.* Third, to satisfy the expanded demand of European and American silk-textile industries and the requirements of the highly mechanized modern power looms abroad, newer techniques of silk-reeling were adopted. It was perhaps natural that the first modern filatures were located in the two areas that led in silk exports—Shanghai and the environs of Canton—with most of the filatures eventually centered at Shanghai. The silk produced in the Shun-te area was exported through the nearby ports of Canton and Lappa.

The export business was usually handled by foreign merchants who bought from Chinese dealers at the ports; some Chinese owners of filatures in the late nineteenth century also had their own agents at the treaty ports to operate their own export trade (Allen and Donnithorne 1954: 61). Even after the modern reeling techniques had been adopted, the Chinese silk industry still suffered from the lack of many modern business techniques, a major one being standardization. For example, the technique of showing samples of silk piece-goods to prospective buyers and, upon receiving the order for specific items, having merchandise made that corresponded exactly to the samples was still not in use toward the end of the century, and "large orders" were lost because would-be purchasers could not see samples before buying (IMC: 209).

Standardization of the quality of raw silk proved to be of vital importance to the future of the trade, since throughout the nineteenth century European and American textile producers had steadily mechanized their plants, and now the production of textiles could be successful only if the silk was of a uniform quality suitable for the machines.† The first steam filature, with about a hundred reeling machines, was set up by Jardine, Matheson and Company, at Shanghai in 1862, but the venture was unsuccessful and the plant closed down in 1866 (Sun 1957: 67; Shih 1968: 83). The failure of this early filature has usually been attributed to the lack of sufficient technically trained labor, and to the obstructions raised by traditional "middlemen" who feared the competition of the new industry. The middlemen have been blamed especially for the

* Canton, however, remained one of the leading ports for silk export: in 1901 it exported 36,430 piculs of raw silk (as compared to 11,526 piculs in 1881–82), as well as a variety of silk piece-goods. See IMC: 176; Shih 1968: 42. A decade earlier the IMC recognized that the Western firms had been handling and controlling the great bulk of the import-export processes of the silk trade (Allen and Donnithorne 1954: 43).

† Allen and Donnithorne 1954, p. 62. The triumph of the power loom in the textile industries of the West was foreseeable by mid-century, as more and more firms converted to power and mechanization gained a kind of momentum (Charles Singer et al., *A History of Technology* [London and New York, 1958], 5: 580).

difficulties the filatures (the first as well as later ones) encountered in securing enough cocoons (Shih 1968: 85–88; Allen and Donnithorne 1954: 65; Sun 1957: 71). Although it is possible that old established interests could control the supply of a necessary raw material to a newcomer, one must also look to the larger scene, and seek to explain the halting beginnings of modern silk reeling at Shanghai by reference to contributing factors of a less personal nature. Two fundamental aspects of the circumstances surrounding these industrial ventures must be noted. One was the effect of the Taiping wars, which severely devastated and depopulated the prime silk districts of southern Kiangsu and northern Chekiang; the other was the new type of demand that a steam filature, capable of faster and year-round operation, imposed on the traditional pattern of the supply of cocoons, which in the lower Yangtze–Lake T'ai region were strictly a seasonal product. The year-round demand—or alternatively a very much enlarged demand during the silk season for stockpiling—would seem to have created a new situation for the rural silk producer, especially during the wars and their aftermath.

The adverse effect of the Taiping wars on the productivity of the countryside must not be minimized. Hu-chou, for example, lost so many people during the war years by death or by emigration that much of its land—including mulberry land—was untended until after 1865. Settlers from other regions were needed for the economic recovery of this area. Even after the war ended, not all of the skilled silk producers returned, and there was apparently a setback in the silk output for a number of years.* Baron von Richthofen's description of post-Taiping Chekiang and southern Anhwei specifically points out that in the desolate landscape "plantations of old mulberry trees, half of them decayed from want of care, tell of one of the chief industries of the former inhabitants. . . . " (Ho 1959: 243). There could have been, therefore, a genuine shortage of cocoons in the 1860's, perhaps even in the early 1870's, that proved to be a hindrance to the new filatures.

A further legacy of the wars was the government's striving for fiscal solvency. In time a heavy duty came to be levied on cocoons, a measure that raised the price of cocoons to the point where foreign silk interests thought it necessary to protest (Sun 1957: 72).

When silk production recovered from the immediate effects of war

---

* NYS 1: 392; Ping-ti Ho 1959: pp. 154–55; Ch'üan and Wang 1961: 156, Table 4, "Population changes in the provinces during the Ch'ing period." The population indexes for Chekiang in 1761, 1850, and 1898 are 100, 195, and 77 respectively. The last figure represents a population of 11.9 million for the entire province, as against more than thirty million in 1850.

and the dislocation of populations, it was distributed largely according to the old pattern of priorities, with a large portion going into foreign trade. Hand-reeled raw silk was exported to meet the steady demands of foreign buyers, the amount increasing even without benefit of modernized reeling. In 1876 the total amount of raw silk exported was reported to be 76,000 piculs, a record to date.* Ironically, the 1870's were a period in which the Chinese silk industry could have moved ahead and retained its leading position in the world market. The opportunity was there. The foreign demand overseas continued to increase, especially when silkworm disease struck the silk industries of France and Italy about 1850 and continued to plague them into the 1870's (NYS 1: 393). Furthermore, at that time the modernization of Japan's silk industry had barely begun, whereas China's silk industry within the next two decades had begun to move ahead. Steps were taken to eliminate silkworm disease, and the government started a program to propagate sericultural knowledge (Allen and Donnithorne 1954: 63). But the opportunity was missed. For the Chinese silk industry the lack of progress was part and parcel of a general lack in modernization and industrialization throughout the Chinese economy. The basis of the silk industry—the production of raw silk—remained diffuse and institutionally as well as technically antiquated. Neither the government nor private investors made more than sporadic attempts to change the situation, and the problem of insufficient capital investment was endemic.

In the Shanghai area, modern filatures began to be established on a more solid basis by 1880. Of the three such plants that existed in Shanghai in 1882, two had been founded by foreign interests—the American firm of Russell and Co. set one up in 1879, and the British firm of Jardine, Matheson and Company set one up called Ewo in 1881—and one by a Chinese investor named Huang Tso-ch'ing, a native of Hu-chou who had been in the silk-reeling business in Shanghai since sometime in the 1870's (Sun 1957: 69). The total number of machines was only 308, giving employment to approximately fifteen hundred workers, most of whom were women recruited from the surrounding countryside. Growth was rapid, and by 1908 there were between thirty and thirty-five filatures operating in Shanghai with a total of some eight thousand reeling machines and a working force of over twenty thousand laborers, including both women and children. In the same period a few filatures had

---

* NYS 1: 392. According to Allen and Donnithorne 1954: 42–43, by the 1880's much of the export trade was done by commission, silk now being sold on orders from Europe. This practice undoubtedly gave further incentive to the distributors who specialized in selling abroad.

also been set up in Soochow and Hu-chou, some by foreign companies. These modern plants supplied the bulk of the silk exported at Shanghai and contributed to a boom in silk production in the Lake T'ai region (NYS 1: 392; Shih 1968: 84, 90, 94, 100).

Simultaneously, silk reeling in the area around Shun-te was also undergoing changes. Ch'en Ch'i-yuan, a native of Nan-hai district, traveled in Europe and America and researched the markets for the sale of Kwangtung silk there. He had reportedly been to Annam on business and come to know French silk. In 1873 he established a modern steam filature in Macao and hired women workers to operate the machines, producing silk for export to Western countries. The productivity of these machines was triple that of hand-reeling, and the resulting uniform product fetched a price a third higher than that of the old-style raw silk. Ch'en then set up a plant in his native district "in order to lead the way." Resentment of the handicraftsmen against the new machines began to make itself felt. After a bad crop in 1881 further reduced the income of the traditional producers, they could no longer contain their resentment of the new filature. Blaming all their troubles on it, they attacked Ch'en's plant and damaged the machines. The riot was easily quelled by the local constabulary, and Ch'en's filature resumed operations, producing two types of silk that met international standards and secured a handsome profit. Ch'en's success eventually convinced others of the advisability of modernization. The improved silk-reeling establishments that were subsequently set up in the Shun-te silk region included plants of varying sizes and degrees of mechanization, from a modified pedal method of reeling the fibers off the cocoons to a mixture of mechanization and traditional techniques; many of the plants were small-scale filatures that did not require a large initial investment. Soon after the turn of the present century there were reportedly about 110 filatures in the entire silk-producing area of southern Kwangtung. The largest plants employed between 500 and 600 workers each, whereas the smallest ones had a work force of a hundred or fewer. The completely mechanized filatures were of the larger type, operating with an estimated average force of about five hundred women, whose annual wages totalled approximately $26,000 in local currency (Shih 1968: 35–36; *Shun-te hsien-chih*, ch. 1: 25–26; ch. 24: 28).

Summary and Conclusion

As the Ch'ing period came to a close, the silk industry in China was still by no means fully modernized. The main producing areas did not differ greatly from the way they were in early Ch'ing times, except that the Lake T'ai and the Shun-te regions had been stimulated to further expansion during the intervening centuries. Small producers of raw silk abounded in the rural areas in many provinces, but their fate was closely related to other factors in the economy. In pre-modern times one of the most influential of these factors was the wealthy silk merchant, who often both lent money to the peasant sericulturist and invested in the textile workshops, where a large portion of weavers found their livelihood. In the lower Yangtze–Lake T'ai region, government orders traditionally played a significant part in the silk-textile manufacturing industry.

During the nineteenth century the domestic market apparently failed to expand. This was fundamentally an outcome of an increasingly unfavorable man-land ratio, bringing with it the popular unrest and, eventually, the major military upheavals that created further problems in productivity and fiscal stability in the second half of the century. That the silk textile industry was in a stagnant state can be gauged from the loom-makers' dispute cited above: it was a clear indication of restricted opportunities in one of the leading centers of the silk industry. In the 1890's the Imperial Silkworks were phased out, and relatively dependable government orders became entirely a thing of the past. In addition, a general trend of rising prices in the economy as a whole toward the beginning of the twentieth century raised the price of raw silk, and this increase brought about a contraction in the manufacture of silk textiles. By 1911, for example, the number of silk workers in Hangchow had dwindled to some twenty thousand (Shih 1968: 107), about a third of the pre-Taiping estimate.

The decline in domestic consumption, however, was offset by increases in the export trade after 1842. Foreign markets became a dominant element in the scene, and the silk produced in the Hu-chou and Shun-te areas was channelled primarily toward export. At Hu-chou (renamed Wu-hsing after 1912) sericulture had recovered sufficiently by 1870 so that the area retained its important position in the silk industry, and from that date until after World War I, silk producers prospered mainly through exports. In 1921, for example, sericulture accounted for 70 percent of the total income of the rural families there, and rice only 30 percent. When there was a drop in silk exports in 1934, these proportions were reversed (Hou 1965: 193–94).

Although China's exports of raw silk had increased steadily in absolute quantity since 1842, Chinese silk began to lose ground relative to

Japanese silk in the world market after 1900.* This ineffective showing
of Chinese silk has been attributed to the lack of adequate modernization and of effective government leadership. Efforts to improve the reeling operation through the establishment of modern filatures, undertaken
first by foreign firms, then by private Chinese interests from the 1870's
onward, were rationally located in the traditional silk regions. The Chinese investors were usually natives of these areas with a long-standing
interest in silk—the lower Yangtze–Lake T'ai region, Shun-te, and such
provinces as Shantung, where tussore silk had grown into a major export
item. However, their efforts were uncoordinated and their financial resources not large enough to reverse an industry-wide trend.† Modernization of both reeling and weaving was taking place, but not on a sufficient scale to make an appreciable impact in international competition.
The government's attempts during the last quarter of the nineteenth
century to propagate sound sericultural knowledge and to encourage
mulberry cultivation were confined to age-old, well-used methods that
were appropriate to the traditional decentralized form of the industry.
They reflected no integrated plan and urged no uniform standards. Government policy-makers seemed not to realize that a modern silk industry
would require fundamental institutional changes. Even if they had seen
the need, they would probably have been unable to meet it because of
the political and financial state of China. That sericulture and the manufacture of silk textiles continued to function as well as they did under
those circumstances was perhaps indicative of their basic vitality; that
they had nevertheless not developed into a healthy modern industry
was, at the same time, symptomatic of China's difficulties in coping with
the challenges posed by economic modernization.

* Shih 1968: 104–5, and 111–15. Shih's tables show increases in the export of
raw silk from 13,220 piculs in 1845 to 107,584 piculs in 1917 and in silk piece-goods
from 4,008 piculs in 1867 to 28,539 piculs in 1912. Japanese products began to
overtake the Chinese during the decade of the 1900's, with an appreciable difference showing by 1913. Standardization, close government supervision, and mass-
production techniques were the factors favoring the Japanese producer as an international competitor, even though—as a Chinese Maritime Customs report pointed
out in 1901 (Allen and Donnithorne 1954: 66)—the Japanese product "has not
quite the strength of thread" that Chinese silk has.
† Shih 1968: 85–86, 98. The amount of capital needed to set up a filature with
300 workers was estimated to be about 70,000 taels. Many of the Chinese plants
were below this size, as the 1912 average of 236 workers per plant shows. Most
Chinese filatures were capitalized at under fifty thousand Mexican dollars, which
was less than 40,000 taels (see Allen and Donnithorne 1954: 66). The shortage of
liquid capital placed some of the Chinese-financed filatures in a precarious state
almost from the beginning.

Cotton Culture and Manufacture
in Early Ch'ing China

CRAIG DIETRICH

Just as two people can describe the same glass of beer as half full or half empty, scholars have variously characterized traditional economic organization in China. Taking a twentieth-century perspective, some scholars compare traditional China with modern societies and emphasize its shortcomings. Ch'ing China, as they never tire of pointing out, did not possess, nor was it rapidly developing, machine technology or natural science. But if focusing on the empty space in the glass is valid, so is examining its actual contents. The present paper deals with the interaction of traditional technology and other economic conditions that gave rise to the patterns we dimly see in the surviving records.

This study deals with the growing of cotton and the manufacture of cotton cloth in the Ch'ing period prior to about 1820, with some reference to earlier times. Of course cotton was only one aspect of traditional Chinese economic life, but in most places textile production probably overshadowed all other economic activities except for the production of food. Thus, information about cotton has some relevance to a general understanding of traditional economic organization. The main point this paper makes about the cotton industry is that although it was not modern, neither was it primitive. The history of the introduction of cotton into China suggests a capacity for change that is at odds with the stereotype of timeless China. By the time of the Ch'ing, change had slowed, and no revolutionary mechanical or organizational developments appeared during that period. Indeed part of the industry could be described as simple and changeless. But another part reveals itself to be differentiated and adaptive. The industry possessed, for example, a range of techniques and organizational forms that permitted cloth to be made both by self-sufficient families and by a system of market-oriented specialists.

Cotton Culture

Cotton was not native to China, nor was it a part of early Sinitic culture. However, in the two or three centuries of the late Sung, the Yuan, and the early Ming, it ceased being an exotic commodity in China and became the single most important source of fiber there. It did so because it combined durability, versatility, and other desirable characteristics with cheapness—a combination that makes it still the world's most important cloth fiber, natural or man-made (Cook 1964: 35). Cotton is easily washable and can withstand long wear and repeated washings. It is absorbent, and thus comfortable next to the skin. Loosely woven, it is a cool cloth for warm weather; tightly woven, a warm cloth for cold weather. It can be woven into many different kinds of fabrics. Cotton is pleasant to the touch and appealing to the eye. It takes dye well.

Silk is stronger, and wool is warmer, but none of cotton's competitors combines so many desirable qualities with cotton's additional advantage, cheapness. Cotton is cheap partly because the plant yields far more fiber per acre than other fiber plants (Yabuuchi 1959: 108–9). But this cheapness depends on efficient techniques for transforming the fiber into yarn. In the first millennium A.D. only tedious ways of ginning, fluffing, and spinning cotton were known. In this period, despite China's many contacts with South Asia, where cotton was used, the plant did not become important in East Asia (Yü Ching-jang 1954c: 17–18). But some time after A.D. 1000, improved methods of processing the fibers appeared in India and became known to the Chinese. After that, cotton began to displace other textiles in China.

A mid-fifteenth-century scholar sketched the spread of cotton in China in the following terms (Ch'u Hua 1937: 1):

> Although cotton entered China as tribute from the Han period through the T'ang, it was not yet cultivated, the people did not yet make clothes from it, and the government did not yet tax it. Its cultivation spread [to China] in the Sung and the Yuan. Kansu-Shensi and Fukien-Kwangtung were the first regions to profit from it. This was because Fukien and Kwangtung carried on trade with seagoing ships and Kansu and Shensi bordered on Central Asia. However, cotton was still not included in taxes. Thus the "Treatises on Fiscal Policy" in the Sung and Yuan [dynastic histories] do not mention it. In our [Ming] dynasty, however, it has spread throughout the Empire. It is used a hundred times more than silk or hemp.

Generally, modern scholars accept the pattern of transmission stated here, although there is disagreement over chronology and over the species of cotton plant involved (Shih Hung-ta 1957: 19; Ch'üan Han-sheng 1958: 25–26; Schafer 1963; 204–6, 326–27; Yü Ching-jang 1954c: 17–18). The Chinese knew about cotton cloth as early as the Western Han period. By that time the plant had spread from its original home in western India to Central Asia and, probably not much later, into Yunnan (Yü Ching-jang 1954c: 17–18), but these varieties of the plant did not move into the heart of China. Perhaps by the T'ang, certainly by the Northern Sung (*ibid.*), a perennial variety of the species *Gossypium arborium* was established in Kwangtung and Fukien, having come through Southeast Asia. One scholar believes that by the late T'ang, cotton cloth was being made by the Han peoples in Ling-nan Province around Canton (Schafer 1963: 205). Others are skeptical of such an early date (Yü Ching-jang 1954c: 17–18). In either case, these were remote southern provinces, far from the heartland of the Empire. Moreover, their variety of cotton was the perennial tree, whereas the developed Chinese cotton industry depended upon the annual shrub variety (*Gossypium arborium*, var. *neglectum*) (Yü Ching-jang 1954a: 4). The climate of southern China is too wet to be well suited to the cultivation of this shrub. It was the spread of the annual variety into the Yangtze region that signaled cotton's real rise in importance. Historians agree that this occurred in the late Sung or early Yuan. In the following two centuries, during the Yuan and the early Ming, the spread of this plant revolutionized Chinese textiles. By the eighteenth century, cotton had long been the foremost of Chinese fibers. As Li Pa, a prefect in Fukien Province, wrote in 1760 (Ho Ch'ang-ling 1963, ch. 37: 17):

If we search for [the fiber] that is most widely used, that is most reasonably priced and labor-saving, that is suited both to cheap and to expensive textiles, that benefits rich and poor alike, [we will find that] only cotton has all these exceptional qualities. . . . In all the places that my feet have left their traces there was no man who did not wear cotton and no soil that was not suited to its production.

Other evidence shows that Li Pa's claims were only slightly exaggerated. *Hsien* (county) and prefectural gazetteers, which began to proliferate in the sixteenth century, usually contain a section on "local products." By looking at a large number of such sections, it is possible to reach some conclusions about the dissemination of cotton. From an unpublished study (Dietrich 1970, chap. 3) of several hundred such sources, I concluded that between three-fifths and four-fifths of all *hsien*, both in the late Ming and in the early Ch'ing periods, manufactured some cotton cloth. When the *hsien* were grouped by provinces, the samples were too small to yield narrow confidence intervals, but it was clear that for most provinces at least half of the *hsien* produced cotton cloth. Similar but more impressionistic studies have been done by Japanese scholars, who also found that by the late Ming period cotton culture and manufacture were already widespread (Nishijima 1966: 765–70; Amano 1954a, *passim*; Amano 1954b, *passim*). Thus Li Pa's sweeping statement squares with other historical evidence.

Since the dissemination of cotton was not a particularly glorious enterprise, surviving documents tell us little about it. The first Ming emperor, T'ai-tsu, did issue an edict to the effect that, among other crops, cotton was to be widely cultivated (Amano 1954a: 20–21). But a more immediately influential figure was the Taoist nun, Huang. In the late thirteenth century, she is said to have brought efficient techniques for ginning and spinning cotton from Hainan Island into the lower Yangtze area. The people of Wu-ni Ching, the village near Shanghai where she settled, considered her contribution to their prosperity so great that they erected a shrine to her (*Hua-t'ing hsien chih* 1521, ch. 3: 15a).

Local officials may have played an important role in disseminating the fiber. Most references date from the Ming and Ch'ing periods, but there could well have been earlier instances. There is the case of Magistrate Li Chung-shun of Ju-kao Hsien in Kiangsu, who in 1621 discovered that the people in his *hsien* did not know how to spin or weave. Like most officials of his time, he felt that it was very bad for any region to depend on others for its food or textiles. He exhorted the people to plant cotton and to make spinning wheels and looms, and he brought experts in to teach them the necessary skills. Later, a gazetteer of the Ch'ing period singled out the manufacture of cotton cloth as the *hsien's* most profitable occupation (Amano 1954b: 76). Of course local magistrates could do nothing without favorable natural and economic conditions, as the case of Lu Jo will show. Fifty years before Li Chung-shun's successful campaign, Lu taught the villagers of Jui-chin Hsien in Kiangsi to plant cotton. But conditions were not favorable and cotton culture was soon abandoned (Amano 1954a: 31).

During the Ch'ing period, in contrast to the dynamic growth it experienced during the Yuan and Ming dynasties, the cotton industry seems to have settled down into a stable pattern. The general pattern of geographical distribution seems to have been established by the end of the Ming period and to have changed little during the Ch'ing (Dietrich 1970, chap. 3). The technology had also apparently reached a plateau. The hand-powered, individually operated equipment used to process the fiber had approached the limits of possible improvement by the end of the Ming period, although the Ch'ing may have witnessed minor refinements. Two innovations, theoretically compatible with traditional Chinese textile technology, did not appear: the "Saxony" type of spinning wheel with a flyer and the flying shuttle on the loom.

Cotton Technology

The technology of the manufacture of cotton textiles deserves to be considered in some detail. The following paragraphs describe the processes involved in cotton manufacture as it existed in Ch'ing China, detailing the implements used in each process and sketching the history of their development.

Ginning. The fibers make up only about a third of the weight of a cotton boll, the rest being made up of seeds attached to the fibers. The first step in the manufacturing process is to remove these seeds. The time-consuming procedure of picking them out by hand made cotton very expensive, and as early as the Sung the Chinese adopted a more efficient method. They used a small iron roller a few inches long and tapered toward the ends. Placing picked cotton on a board, they would roll this tool over it, forcing the seeds loose from the fiber (Ssu-ma Kuang 1927, ch. 159: 7a). Soon there appeared a still better method, probably originating in India (Needham 1965: 204; Dietrich 1970, chap. 2). Two rollers an inch or two in diameter were mounted close together in a frame to make a device that resembled a clothes wringer. When rotated, these rollers would pull the fibers through but not the seeds. On early-fourteenth-century models, two cranks, one on each side of the frame, powered the rollers. According to the Chinese sources this machine was commonly operated by three people, two to turn the cranks and a third to feed cotton into the rollers (Wang Chen 1956: 508), although two operators would seem to have been sufficient. Later a treadle was linked to one of the cranks, permitting a single person to operate the gin. While he turned one roller with his foot on the treadle, he could turn the second roller with one hand and feed cotton bolls in with the other (Sung Ying-hsing 1955: 96). Some time before the eighteenth century, a flywheel came to be attached to the treadle-powered roller to sustain its rotation (Needham 1965: 122–24). Figure 1* shows two eighteenth-century devices with four-spoked "flywheels," but apparently without treadles. Modified in these various ways, the gin remained an integral part of Chinese cotton technology until modern times.

* All illustrations are from eighteenth-century woodblocks published in rearranged form in the early nineteenth century (Fang Kuan-ch'eng 1809, chs. 1 and 2).

Bowing. After ginning, the fibers are still in bunches. If they have been transported any distance, they are matted together in bales or bags. Dust, bits of stem, and other debris mingle with the cotton. It was probably in India that a bow similar to the archer's bow was first adapted to loosen the fibers, tease them into a fluffy state, and at the same time shake out foreign matter (Needham 1965: 127). The operator brought the vibrating bowstring into contact with a pile of cotton. Repeated contact produced a mass of white fiber, fleecy and free of contaminants. The earliest bows were small and were probably vibrated by plucking (Ssu-ma Kuang 1927, ch. 159: 7). Later they became larger and were vibrated by rhythmic blows of a mallet. The heavier bows came to be suspended from flexible poles or short poles attached to the operators as in Figure 2.

Spinning. In preparation for spinning, cleaned cotton is formed into a "roving" perhaps an inch in diameter and a foot long. To turn this into yarn, the spinner must attenuate it, or draw it out, to a uniform thinness. At the same time he must impart twist, which provides strength and elasticity and enables the many short fibers to cling together in a continuous filament.

Several ways of spinning were used in Ch'ing China, differing in the tools and skills they required and in the quantity and quality of the output they yielded. The simplest spinning device in common use was the suspended spindle, essentially just a small weight, heavy enough to sustain the whirling motion imparted to it but light enough not to pull apart the forming thread on which it hung. The operator would draw out a bit of the roving and attach it to the spindle. He would then twirl the spindle and release it. It would hang, whirling, while he attenuated the roving with his hands. When that length of yarn was drawn out and twisted sufficiently, he would wind it onto the spindle itself and repeat the operation until the roving was used up. This method at its best is said to be unexcelled for producing fine and even yarns (Kissell 1918: 7; Cook 1964: 36), but it lacks the ease and speed of the spinning wheel.

The spinning wheel was probably developed in India around the thirteenth century (Needham 1965: 106; Kissell 1918: 11). As it existed in China, it was an exquisitely simple and effective combination of crude materials like twine, sticks, and bamboo leaves. Over the rim of a crank-turned wheel ran an endless cord that imparted the wheel's motion to a spindle mounted approximately parallel to the wheel's axle and to the ground. Being much smaller in diameter than the wheel, the spindle whirled rapidly. The spinner would draw out a bit of the roving and attach it to the spindle. Set in motion, the spindle would impart twist to

FIGURE 1. GINNING RAW COTTON

FIGURE 2. BOWING RAW COTTON TO LOOSEN THE FIBERS

FIGURE 3. TWO SPINNERS USING WHEELS

FIGURE 4. SIZING THE WARP IN PREPARATION FOR WEAVING

FIGURE 5. WARPING THE LOOM

FIGURE 6. WEAVING

FIGURE 7. DYEING, WASHING, AND CALENDERING CLOTH

FIGURE 8. GROWERS SELLING RAW COTTON TO A BROKER

the fibers at the same time that the operator attenuated the cotton by drawing the roving away from the device. The distance between his outstretched arm and the spindle was all the yarn that he could spin at one time. When that much was formed, he would raise his hand so that the yarn made a right angle with the spindle and wound onto it. He repeated this operation until the roving was used up (Kissell 1918: 11–13, 36ff; Hommel 1937: 169–73).

This was the major type of wheel used in Ch'ing China. Although it was considerably more efficient than the suspended spindle, yarn making was still a time-consuming job, accounting for more than half the labor in a piece of cloth. In the lower Yangtze area the strong demand for yarn stimulated the invention of the compound wheel. It used the same principle of transferring motion from wheel to spindle, but in this machine three spindles mounted directly above the wheel were driven by a belt that ran around the rim of the wheel and over the spindles themselves. Figure 3 gives a general impression of what spinning wheels looked like, but the details are obscure. To imagine how a wheel worked from this illustration truly requires us, as Confucius put it, to take "one corner of a subject and discern the other three." The "rim" of the wheel, for example, consists of a cord, attached to the ends of the spokes. The spokes are inserted into the axle alternately in two rows so that the "rim-cord" connecting the ends of the spokes zigzags from one spoke to the next. The other cord, the one that turns the spindle, rests on this "rim-cord." The illustration also fails to show the spindles clearly. The spindle of the wheel in the foreground would be below the spinner's left arm. Here is a modern description of its operation, which seems to have demanded considerable skill (Hommel 1937: 172):

The spinner holds three rovings with the left hand between thumb and forefinger, the yarns resulting from the rovings then pass between fore-finger and middle-finger, between middle-finger and ring-finger, between ring-finger and little finger respectively. They are next guided through the same fingers respectively of the right hand, whence they pass to the ends of the three spindles. The spinner holds in the right hand . . . a wooden stick. . . . This stick comes into play when the yarns have been spun as long as the left arm can conveniently be stretched out, away from the spindles. Then the spinner withdraws the fingers of her right hand from the yarns and pushes the yarns with the stick towards the right side of her body until the yarns form with the spindles approximately a right angle, when the yarns cease to twist (spin) and begin to wind around the spindles.

The spinner powered the wheel by working a treadle-board with the feet. A skillful operator could make twice as much yarn as a spinner on

an ordinary wheel, but lost some control over the evenness and fineness
of the product (Yen Chung-p'ing 1963: 10). Two-, four-, and even five-
spindle models were tried, but the three-spindle machine proved to be
the best compromise between quality and quantity of output (Hsu
Kuang-ch'i 1837, ch. 36: 14b; Ch'u Hua 1937: 9).

Weaving. Yarn straight from the spindle was not yet ready for weaving.
Depending on the scale of operation, different types of reels, spools,
frames, and cranking devices were used to combine several yarns into
long, multiple-ply thread suitable for warp. For example, there was a
single, hand-turned reel for taking yarn from the single-spindle wheel
(Hsu Kuang-ch'i 1837, ch. 35: 25ab). There was also a crank-operated
reeling frame that could draw yarn from eight spindles at once (*ibid.*:
26ab). Secondly, warp threads needed sizing—a coat of starch to stiffen
them and protect them against the friction of the weaving process. There
were various methods of sizing (Fang Kuan-ch'eng 1809, ch. 2: 10b),
one of which is illustrated in Figure 4, where the woman in the upper
left can be seen brushing starch on the cloth.

As early as the Han, the basic principles for plain and fancy looms
had appeared. By the Ch'ing these devices had evolved into three main
types: horizontal, "waist," and draw looms. The type of loom most often
used for ordinary cottons was the horizontal loom (Wang Chen 1956:
525; Hsu Kuang-ch'i 1837, ch. 36: 17ab; Hommel 1937: 180). As the
name suggests, it provided a horizontal warp that was wound around a
revolving "beam" at the rear of the loom. The completed cloth was
wound onto a revolving "cloth beam" just in front of the weaver. Both
beams are clearly discernible in Figure 5, which illustrates the process
of warping the loom. Alternate separation of the two groups of warp
threads was achieved by two heddles that were raised by pressing with
the feet on treadles. Figure 6 shows the heddles and the treadles, but
not their functioning or their relationship to one another. Figure 6 shows
in front of the weaver a batten, through the teeth of which the warp
threads passed, and which was used to tamp each weft thread into the
web. On many looms this batten was suspended from light bamboo
poles. Finally, the bobbin shuttle was used. One is visible in the hand
of the weaver in Figure 6.

A second type, the "waist" loom, was more closely related to the original Han models (Sung Po-yin 1962: 26–27). The warp was not mounted
horizontally, but slanted upward, away from the weaver, and there was
but one heddle to create the "shed" between the two groups of warp.
This heddle was raised and lowered by a rocker assembly attached to a
treadle. When the heddle was lowered, a second shed was automatically

formed by a permanent "shed bar." Like the horizontal loom, the waist loom had a revolving warp beam and a revolving cloth beam, but the latter was attached to the weaver himself by a wide girdle or strap around the lower back. Leaning back against this strap, he kept the warp taut. The waist loom was used mainly in Kiangsi Province and was probably less effective than the horizontal loom for making even, uniform cloth (Sung Ying-hsing 1955: 93, 643; E-tu Zen Sun 1966: 56, 71; Dietrich 1970, chap. 2).

The Chinese used the draw loom to weave cottons in elaborate patterns. Because of the many heddles needed on this kind of loom, it required two operators, one to pass the shuttles back and forth, one to operate the heddles. Since it was suited only for making luxury textiles, it probably accounted for only a small fraction of the cotton looms in use at a given time (Dietrich 1970, chap. 2).

Finishing. Some cloth was taken from the loom, washed, and fashioned into garments without any further processing, but much was turned over to dyers and other finishers who enhanced the beauty of the final product. Dyers could achieve a variety of solid hues. They used mainly vegetable materials: indigo for blue, safflower for red, sappanwood for red and purple, berberine wood for yellow, lotus-seed shells for brown, and *huai* flowers for green. Two important mineral dyes were ferrous sulfate for black and cinnabar for vermilion. Alum sometimes served as a mordant. For equipment, dyers and bleachers needed vats, stoves, sheds, and drying racks, some of which are visible in Figure 7. Their most valuable asset, however, was their knowledge of dyes and mordants, learned from their masters, guarded jealously, and passed down to sons and apprentices (E-tu Zen Sun 1966: 74; Hommel 1937: 90).

Even more specialized were the techniques of "resist-dyeing" and printing. For resist work, artisans brushed lime mortar onto cloth through a stencil, creating a pattern. When it dried, they dipped the cloth in blue dye, careful not to crack the mortar that "resisted" the pigment. It would later be scraped off. The resulting two-color patterns were widely known as a specialty of the lower Yangtze region (Ch'u Hua 1937: 10–11; Hommel 1937: 90). Printing cottons was of course related to the techniques of stone-rubbing and printing. The craftsman placed the cloth over carved wooden blocks, forced the textile into the depressions in the block, and passed over it with paints or dyes. Using several woodblocks, he could achieve multicolored patterns (Ch'u Hua 1937: 11).

Finally, fabrics were often calendered to give them a glossy surface. The principle was the same as that of modern calendering—applying pressure to cloth between smooth, hard surfaces. A man can be seen calendering in Figure 7. The tools used were "a stone base plate," "a roller of very hard wood," and a "peculiarly fashioned heavy stone which is placed upon the roller to move it back and forth upon the base plate." According to Hommel's modern description of the operation, cloth is laid (1937: 191)

under the roller on this curved base plate. . . . Then the heavy notched stone is tilted upon the roller so as to move the latter back and forth until the strip of cloth under pressure shows the desired gloss. The apparatus is operated by a barefoot worker who jumps on top of the stone and with one foot on each of its horns dexterously does the tilting. . . . Fold upon fold is thus fed under and over the roller until the whole bolt has been calendered.

Invented in the Ming, or possibly earlier, calendering became especially common in the Ch'ing period (Yokoyama 1960 and 1961, *passim*; Ch'u Hua 1937: 11).

Thus in two or three centuries the Chinese had adapted and improved the gin, the bow, and the spinning wheel, all imported from South Asia, and combined them with appropriate Chinese devices such as reels, looms, and calendering stones. The result was a technology suitable for a range of productive organizations, from the single family to highly differentiated, market-oriented entrepreneurs.

Social Organization of Production

No comprehensive study of the social organization of cotton production in Ch'ing China has been written, and perhaps none is possible. The data are scattered and of uneven quality, but enough information has been assembled so that some broad descriptive strokes can be drawn. It is possible to see, for example, that a complete picture would have to show wide variations in the forms and functions of productive units. No single "typical" pattern can be discerned in the organization of the cotton industry. There was a diversity of forms ranging from simple peasant self-sufficiency to operations specializing in one stage of production and integrated with other specialists through brokers and merchants. Perhaps what comes nearest to a common pattern is the location of cloth-making activities within the family. But there were important cases where this was not true. Moreover, family-bound units of production participated in the cotton industry in different ways.

Much of China's cotton cloth was manufactured in undifferentiated or only slightly differentiated peasant agricultural settings. This segment of the industry fits the anthropologist's general description of a peasant economy, "with a simple technology, productive units which are multipurposed and derived from other forms of social organization, and with a division of labor based chiefly on sex and age" (Nash 1964: 174). These were peasant families using their own labor, especially that of their women, to meet their own needs for textiles. Some Shantung and Hopei gazetteers illustrate the variations on this kind of organization. In Te-p'ing Hsien it was said that where the roads did not permit peddlers and merchants to pass, the men tilled the soil and the women wove cloth (*Te-p'ing hsien chih* 1796, ch. 1: 9b). A similar picture of self-sufficiency was presented in the gazetteer for Hopei's Hsing-t'ang Hsien where, it was said, raw cotton and cloth were produced in all villages. What these villages grew and wove was said to be of coarse quality and suited only for their own needs (*Hsing-t'ang hsien chih* 1763, ch. 3: 10a). The gazetteer was not specific, but cloth-making there was probably women's work. The phrase "men till, women weave" (*nan keng nü chih*), is common in the gazetteers, but there were variations. In Shantung's Ch'i-hsia Hsien, where the people were said to produce cotton only to clothe themselves, and where all members of both gentry and peasant families worked to make the cloth, there were no distinctions between men's and women's roles (*Ch'i-hsia hsien chih* 1754, ch. 1: 14b). Another Shantung gazetteer (*Teng-chou fu chih* 1674, ch. 8: 12b) mentioned this variation as well as another: when the family produced a small surplus beyond its own needs, it sold the excess cloth on the village market.

The sources rarely discuss the implements used by such producers. It can be tentatively assumed that they used the simpler equipment such as the hand roller to separate seeds, the suspended spindle (or perhaps the simple spinning wheel), and the less efficient looms. On the last point a Kiangsi source is suggestive. It notes a local distinction between "woman-loom" cloth, a coarse material for family use, and "waist-loom" cloth, a commercial textile (Amano 1954b: 78). No description is given of the "woman loom," but it was presumably something more primitive than any of the three types described above.

The wide dissemination of cotton culture and manufacture reflected in these sources suggests that family production for family needs was the dominant pattern in the Ch'ing cotton industry, since commercialization would have concentrated production in certain places. The sources are not conclusive on this point, because they present an overall view of a given *hsien* and may overlook specialization in towns and villages within it. But it can at least be said that, whatever degree of specialization may have characterized part of the traditional cotton industry, there was another important part that was undifferentiated and widely spread among peasant households.

One of the sources cited above mentions families selling small quantities of surplus cloth in the village market. This represents something of a halfway point between self-sufficiency and commercial production. It would not be easy to describe the degree of market-orientation that distinguishes one from the other. But the sources leave no doubt that an important part of the industry made goods primarily for sale. Such an orientation implies specialization, which could be carried to the point where a production unit performs all the steps of the process but concentrates on cotton to the exclusion of other fibers. Or it could be carried further, to concentration on one or two steps. In this part of the industry, the variation in organizational forms was greater than in the family or self-sufficient sector. Before describing this variation, however, I want to discuss the possible effect of the prevailing technology on specialization.

Figure 8, showing peasants selling their bags of cotton to a broker, illustrates differentiation at the first stage of production, or between growers and processors. This separation was not universal, even in communities that specialized in making cloth. But it did appear often, as in Wu-hsi Hsien, whose people spun and wove energetically but grew little of the fiber they used (Huang Ang 1896, ch. 1: 6b). This kind of differentiation was mandatory in regions poorly suited to growing cotton: such regions necessarily imported much of the raw material for their spindles and looms. Southern China, especially, depended for its supply on more northerly provinces, a dependence that paved the way for the introduction of foreign cotton. In the late eighteenth century the English found southern China a ready market for India's raw cotton. It quickly became a major item of trade, at first more important than opium for balancing imports of Chinese goods (Ubukata 1939: 262).

Ginning was often done by the cotton brokers. This made good sense if the fiber was to be shipped, because extracting the seeds, as already noted, greatly reduces the weight of the cotton. Figure 1 has an accompanying plate, not reproduced here, that shows two other workers, both men, ginning. The presence of male workers suggests that the artist was depicting a specialized enterprise, perhaps connected with a broker. Professor Nishijima found evidence of a connection between brokers and ginning (Nishijima 1966: 827–33; see also Gamble 1954: 294–98). Ginning was also sometimes linked with the next step, bowing. For example, in Chekiang's Jui-an Hsien the same people ginned and bowed cotton and then formed it into rovings for sale to spinners (*Jui-an hsien chih* 1809, ch. 1: 39a). However, bowing could be done separately. For instance, a seventeenth-century Kiangsu man got his start toward wealth by bowing cotton (Fu I-ling 1963: 47). The fact that the two bowers in Figure 2 are men points toward specialization, but whether they belong to the same unit of production as the ginners in Figure 1 is not clear.

There are many references to specialized spinning. One such source, a late Ming gazetteer, suggests an economic reason for this particular specialization. It says that "the poor people lack funds and cannot weave cloth. Daily they sell several ounces of yarn to make a living" (Fu I-ling 1963: 83). That is, people without enough money for a loom, or for the relatively large amounts of cotton needed for making cloth, bought small amounts of fiber to be spun into yarn and sold immediately. Some spinners produced only warp, which they did by reeling and twisting together several strands of good-quality yarn (*ibid.*). The eighteenth-century *Mu mien p'u* says of the Shanghai area (Ch'u Hua 1937: 9): "There are those who only sell yarn. If they work night and day and produce about one *chin* of yarn, they are able to support themselves. Good spinners normally use three- or four-spindle [wheels]. They at least use two-spindle [wheels]."

Specialization in weaving presupposes a certain degree of specialization in spinning. A late-nineteenth-century source for a *hsien* in Kiangsu notes that the northern and eastern villages had established themselves as producers of high-quality yarn. They sold it to the southern villages where it was woven into a good-quality cloth (*Chia-ting hsien chih* 1882, ch. 8: 8b). An eighteenth-century Chekiang gazetteer says that women who lived close to the towns all made weaving their occupation (Terada 1958: 56). Such a woman is the subject of a poem called "Complaint of the Weaving Wife," a translation of which appears in the next paper in this volume (see p. 160).

Finishing operations were specialized as a matter of course. This was because dyeing and other finishing processes required special, sophisticated skills and equipment and because they were commercially oriented. Figure 7 shows dyeing, washing, and calendering being carried on in connection with a retail establishment, but merchandising was often organized separately. The finishing operations themselves might be broken down into specialties, as the following passage shows (Ch'u Hua 1937: 10):

Among dyers there are blue shops (*fang*), which dye sky blue, deep blue, and moonlight blue; there are red shops, which dye deep red and pink; there are bleaching shops, which turn coarse yellow into white; there are miscellaneous color shops, which produce yellow, green, black, purple, old copper, gray, scarlet, camel, toad green, and Buddha-face [gold?].

Finally, in the lower Yangtze area the single process of calendering was an important industry. In the Soochow area alone, it employed many thousands of workers, who processed cottons in very large quantities (Yokoyama 1960; 1961: *passim*).

Except in the finishing trades, the specialized units of production in the manufacture of cotton textiles were variations on the family enterprise. There is little evidence of operations on a larger scale. The lower Yangtze was the most important cotton-producing region, and there, if anywhere, more differentiated organizational forms should appear. But in Kiangsu agricultural settings, where spinning and weaving were by-occupations to tilling the soil, these activities were organized around the peasant household, as is reflected in an eighteenth-century gazetteer for the *hsien* of Wu-hsi and Chin-kuei. There, cotton manufacture was a very important part of the village economy. The villagers "in the spring, closed [themselves into] their homes to spin and weave" (Huang Ang 1896, ch. 1: 6b). Nor was it different in towns and cities, except that households may sometimes have owned more than one loom and used hired weavers (Nishijima 1966: 856–80; Terada 1958: 68). The sexual division of labor often broke down within the specialized household. Again in Wu-hsi and Chin-kuei Hsien in certain villages that were agriculturally poor and depended on selling the textiles they made, the peasants "did not make a distinction between male and female [work] and in their households wove cloth and spun raw cotton to the exclusion of other pursuits" (Huang Ang 1896, ch. 1: 7b). This was all the more likely to be the case in urban households (Nishijima 1966: 860). An interesting variation on the family enterprise occurred in Nan-kung Hsien, Hopei, where families on the same lane would construct a communal cellar in which to spin. In this way they counteracted the bad effects of the region's low humidity. But this was nothing more complex than a group of independent family operations working under one roof (Amano, 1954a: 38; Ch'üan Han-sheng 1958: 29–30).

In the finishing trades, organization of production assumed more complex forms. In eighteenth-century Soochow, there was a kind of finishing enterprise called *tzu-hao* (Fu I-ling 1963: 129): "A *tzu-hao* includes washers, dyers, inspectors (*k'an-pu*), and traders. One *tzu-hao* commonly numbers ten specialists (*chia*). They rely on this for their livelihood." But the calendering operations gave rise to the most interesting organizational forms. In Soochow Prefecture, ten or twenty thousand workers, perhaps even more, worked at calendering under the supervision of a group of bosses called *pao-t'ou*. The bosses received the cloth and the calendering contracts from merchants. The relationships among these three groups do not precisely fit such common categories as employee, artisan, contractor, capitalist. But the roles had clearly become differentiated from other social institutions such as the family, and the relationships among the parties remained largely impersonal and monetary.

The workers were not employees. They rented their equipment and lodging from the bosses. But neither could they be considered independent artisans, since they owned no tools or equipment and since the skill of calendering was easily acquired. They were always required to work under supervision of the bosses. They resemble a proletariat in some ways. Without family or property, they had very little economic or social leverage with which to promote their interests. They sometimes agitated and even rioted for better piece rates, but they were rarely successful. The rich and powerful viewed them uneasily as bothersome sources of unrest and criminality.

The bosses were not exactly employers. The money they gave the calenderers came from the merchants. Moreover the equipment was probably owned by a fourth group, not the bosses. On the other hand, they carried a burden beyond that of foremen or straw-bosses. They were responsible for the cloth entrusted to them by the merchants and for the completion of the calendering process. Moreover, since the merchants cleared their accounts with the bosses only three times a year, the bosses had to have the working capital to pay the workers and rent the equipment.

The merchants exercised considerable control over the calendering industry without assuming any direct managerial responsibility. They got the government to establish rates of pay for calendering and to enforce rules for the organization of the trade. To the bosses they left the task of parceling out the work and managing the workers. The whole organization resembled a modified putting-out system, wherein merchants entrusted raw material (cloth) to laborers through the intermediary of bosses. After processing, the laborers returned it, through the same intermediary, to the merchants (Yokoyama 1960; 1961, *passim*).

The importance of merchants was not confined to the calendering industry. Since the activities of the innumerable spinners and weavers were not integrated with one another in any organizational structure, it was the merchants, both local and regional, who held the industry together and allowed it to function as a system. The merchants' operations followed no uniform pattern: the sources refer to a variety of merchant types. There were great interregional merchants who dealt only in bulk quantities of cloth and who bought it from networks of smaller buyers and brokers. The following late-Ming passage describes such a network that dealt in cottons from Sung-chiang Prefecture (Terada 1958: 59):

Those who come from several thousand *li* away bringing great capital to exchange for cloth are called *piao* merchants. Those who take this capital and buy up cloth are called "shop households" (*chuang hu*). The villagers sell to the shop households, who in turn sell to the *piao* merchants.

An eighteenth-century Shanghai treatise on cotton portrays a similar system and suggests that there could be a permanent patron-client relationship between the merchant princes and their suppliers (Ch'u Hua 1937: 10).

Locally, merchants integrated the different parts of the cloth-making process that were scattered among many households. Some sources suggest a kind of putting-out system. The epitaph of an early Ch'ing native of Soochow Prefecture, Tu Ch'i-t'u, says that he supplied the women of Tung-t'ing with raw materials and equipment (Terada 1958: 63). The producers of summer stockings in Sung-chiang Prefecture doled out piece work to women who could not weave (Fu I-ling 1963: 38, 102). However, Tu Ch'i-t'u's epitaph may actually refer to an act of charity, and the making of summer stockings did not involve weaving the cloth itself.* Something like putting-out is also suggested by an eighteenth-century writer, whose Uncle Hun set up a shop in Wu-hsi Hsien where he traded raw cotton (or perhaps yarn) for cloth. Uncle Hun for some reason was partial to a certain young girl who "always brought in her cloth to exchange for raw cotton." He habitually and willingly made the exchange greatly in her favor (Terada 1958: 62; Ch'üan Han-sheng 1958: 32). This may have been a putting-out relationship where the worker rather than the merchant did the travelling.

There is also evidence of impersonal market relationships. An example is the following late-Ming passage reproduced in an eighteenth-century gazetteer for Chekiang Province (Fu I-ling 1963: 42):

Merchants from nearby prefectures gather in our area to deal in raw cotton. At dawn the local people take their output of cloth or yarn into the market to exchange for raw cotton. This they in turn prepare, spin, and weave, and then return the following morning bringing [the cloth and yarn] to trade.

The Chinese character here translated by "exchange" is *i* ("trade") rather than some character meaning "sell," but there is no suggestion of a fixed relationship between the merchants and the spinners and weavers. The

* I am indebted for these observations to Professor Mark Elvin of the University of Glasgow.

passage (earlier) refers to many shops (*lieh-ssu*), suggesting that there was competition among buyers. In Chia-ting Hsien in the Ming and early Ch'ing, there were complaints that merchants, including cloth brokers (*pu-chuang*), were giving out bad coin (Nishijima 1966: 884). This also suggests fluid, impersonal market relationships.

Geographical Specialization

Whereas cotton production by individual families was widely disseminated, as noted above, the specialized sector of the industry became concentrated in certain areas. Even the growing of cotton came to be the specialty of certain small areas and a few large regions such as southern Kiangsu and northern Chekiang, eastern Shangtung and southern Hopei, Hupeh, and Honan. These regions exported fiber to other areas, especially Fukien, Kwangtung, Kiangsi, and possibly Hunan Provinces in the south, and Shensi, Shansi, and Szechwan Provinces in the north and west (Dietrich 1970, chap. 4). Growers in the exporting regions probably knew more efficient and productive techniques than did those who cultivated the fiber for local consumption. The chapter on cotton in the seventeenth-century agricultural treatise, *Nung cheng ch'üan shu*, describes seed selection, soil preparation, the spacing, fertilizing, and pruning of plants, and pest control as very highly developed in the important growing regions of Shantung and northern Chekiang (Hsu Kuang-ch'i 1837, ch. 35: 2b–10b; Amano 1954a: 34–45).

There were also areas that specialized in the making of cloth and exported textiles, usually high-quality goods, to other regions. By all odds the most important was the lower Yangtze area around Sung-chiang Prefecture. This center was served by no fewer than three important water routes. Cloth went up the Grand Canal to northern Kiangsu, to the Shantung entrepôt at Lin-ch'ing, and to the capital and the regions beyond. Cottons travelled up the Yangtze to be sold in Kiangsi, Anhwei, Hupeh, and Shensi. Thirdly, goods moved down the coastal route to Fukien and Kwangtung (Dietrich 1970, chap. 3). Some of the lower Yangtze products achieved wide fame and were used as standards of excellence in other regions (Hsu Kuang-ch'i 1837, ch. 35: 12b–13a). In the Ming, the "shuttle cloth" (*so-pu*) of Sung-chiang Prefecture won the ultimate distinction—it was used for the emperor's underwear (Lu Jung 1936: 1).

The area including western Shantung and south-central Hopei also qualified as an interregional exporter of cotton cloth. Lin-ch'ing was not only a distribution center for cloth from other provinces, but was itself the center for several nearby cotton-making communities that sold their products to the capital and the northern border. The region also shipped cloth to Liaotung. Towns in Hopei's Cheng-ting Prefecture exported it into Shensi. And two other Hopei *hsien*, Nan-kung and Su-ning, produced large amounts of cloth, possibly for export, although the sources are not explicit on this point (Dietrich 1970, chap. 3).

A third important region may have flourished in Hupeh Province near the confluence of the Han and the Yangtze Rivers. Serving the western provinces, this region was probably much less productive than the two just mentioned. Cotton goods from Hupeh were sold in Shensi, Honan, Szechwan, and Kwangtung (*ibid.*). Besides the large exporting areas, there were smaller centers that seem to occupy lesser niches in a hierarchy of specialized cotton-making areas. A source for Cheng-yang Hsien in southern Honan indicates that it sold its wares as far away as northern Anhwei and Shensi, thus sharing some of the markets of Hupeh and perhaps of the lower Yangtze as well. Shansi had a cloth center in Yü-tz'u Hsien that sent its cloth as far away as Peking. Other secondary centers included Wei-yuan Hsien in Szechwan, Sian (the capital of Shensi), and Fan-ch'ang Prefecture in Anhwei. All probably served limited markets in nearby prefectures or occasionally in neighboring provinces. If surviving records were more numerous, the list could no doubt be expanded. Other *hsien* are known to have produced specialty textiles that were probably sold outside the immediate locality (*ibid.*).

Some sources also give information on the cotton industry within a given *hsien*. They reveal a consistent tendency for the makers of cloth to congregate in one or two places in the *hsien*. A few villages, suburbs, or parts of a city are commonly found to produce a major portion of the *hsien's* cloth output. Of the various regions, the lower Yangtze is mentioned by the largest number of such sources. The seventeenth-century gazetteer for Sung-chiang Prefecture states that all the higher (i.e., poorly watered) villages and those along the sea planted cotton, and the women wove it. The best cloth came from East Gate (*Sung-chiang fu chih* 1663, ch. 4: 9b, 13b). Chu-ching Town became a center for the making and trading of cloth in the late Ming. An early-nineteenth-century gazetteer of the town states that those who spun or wove cotton were numerous as scales on a fish (*Chu-ching chih* 1802, ch. 1: 12a). Nan-hui Hsien contained several places where cotton cloth was a specialty, such as Chou Landing and New Market (Amano 1954b: 75). The famous summer stockings of *yu-tun* cloth were made in Sung-chiang Prefecture out of material woven in a place just to the west of the prefectural city (Fu I-ling 1963: 75 [n. 13], 85). Similar specialization occurred in Soochow Prefecture, northern Chekiang, the Shantung-Hopei region, and Hupeh. A few scattered references from Honan and Shensi suggest similar local concentrations of cotton manufacture (Dietrich 1970, chap. 3).

The forces that produced this kind of localization persisted in modern China. A study done in the 1930's in Hopei's Ting Hsien revealed a pattern similar to that of Ch'ing communities. In Ting Hsien, cotton was the most important local manufacturing industry. All but 16 of the 453 villages engaged in at least some spinning, and all but 75 had at least some weaving, but there was a heavy concentration of growing, spinning, and weaving in the third and sixth districts of the *hsien*. They grew 83 percent of the cotton, ginned 77 percent of it, and spun and wove about 65 percent of the yarn and cloth produced in the *hsien* (Gamble 1954: 294).

Conclusion

This article has tried to show that, although the technology of Ch'ing cotton culture and manufacture was pre-modern, the structure of the industry was neither simple nor inherently inflexible. Across the Empire a variety of patterns can be discerned in the kind of equipment used, the way growers and processors interrelated, the way cotton fit into other economic and social pursuits, and the way the industry was organized geographically.

The High-Level Equilibrium Trap: The Causes of the Decline of Invention in the Traditional Chinese Textile Industries

MARK ELVIN

In his famous *Treatise on Agriculture*, first printed in 1313, Wang Chen described a machine for spinning hemp thread, the motive power for which could be provided by a man, an animal, or a water wheel (ch. 22: 4a, ch. 19: 13a). Its thirty-two spindles, he said, could spin a hundred catties (or approximately 130 pounds) of thread in twenty-four hours. This machine effected a saving in labor costs, for it was "several times cheaper than the women workers it replaces." Moreover, the kind driven by water power was "far more convenient than the land-based machine." As he wrote in a poem, "It takes a spinner many days to spin a hundred catties, but with water power it may be done with supernatural speed."

These spinning machines were widespread, unlike some famous early inventions such as Polzunov's steam engine of 1766 or Papin's steamboat of 1707, which failed to find acceptance because of an underdeveloped economic environment. "This device," said Wang of the ordinary variety, "is used in all those parts of North China where hemp is manufactured." Of the water-driven version he added: "Many of these machines have been installed in those places in the North China plain which are near to running water."

Anyone reading Wang's description of this machine and looking at those pictures of it which have survived* is irresistibly reminded of Hargreaves' spinning jenny and Arkwright's spinning frame; and it is natural to wonder why it was eighteenth-century England that was the scene of an industrial revolution in textile manufacture and not fourteenth-century China. The sense of mystery deepens when one discov-

---

* Wang Chen 1313, ch. 22: 4a, ch. 19: 13a; Wang Ch'i 1609, *ch'i yung* section, ch. 9: 3a; Hsu Kuang-ch'i 1843, ch. 36: 14ab, ch. 18: 16ab; Amano Motonosuke 1967: 366, 453.

ers that by the beginning of the seventeenth century the machine had disappeared (Li Ch'ung-chou 1959: 29) and that, so far as is known, the accounts given of it in Wang's and other books inspired no one in the centuries after its invention to attempt an imitation or improvement. Why should this have been so?

It appears justified to assume that the appearance of an invention depends mainly upon two preconditions. These are that the inventor should have the prospect of making a profit by satisfying some particular economic need, and that a suitable stock of scientific knowledge should be available for him to draw on (Schmookler 1966: 206–9). An invention will be brought into use if there is a greater profit to be had by so doing than by adopting or retaining any other known technique of production. Given these assumptions, it seems reasonable to look for the explanation of the *abandonment* of a successful invention such as the hemp-spinning machine in some change in the balance of economic forces. Similarly, it seems possible to hypothesize that if the flow of new inventions as a whole comes to an end in a society, this is the consequence of (1) a change in the balance of economic forces such that possible inventions are now unprofitable, or (2) an inadequacy in the stock of scientific knowledge such that profitable inventions are for the moment impossible, or else (3) a combination of (1) and (2).*

It may be noted in passing that what has already been said will serve as the outline of a proof that in certain structural respects—possibly even the most important structural respects, since technological advance is the key to sustained economic progress—the traditional Chinese economy *must* have altered in some fashion between the early fourteenth century and the early nineteenth century.

At all events, if we accept the presuppositions made above, the following tasks then remain to be accomplished: to determine the pattern of economic forces that initially induced Wang Chen's hemp-spinning machine, and the stock of scientific knowledge that made it possible; to discern how in subsequent centuries this pattern of economic forces changed; and to decide whether or not the limitations of the stock of scientific knowledge available to the Chinese constituted a serious obstacle to the next few steps of technological advance.

On the answer given to the last of these questions depends whether or not the problem of technological stagnation can be treated within the relatively closed causal system of economics. If it can be shown that the limitations of Chinese scientific knowledge were not a serious obstacle

---

* A strong enough economic incentive may lead to a successful search for the knowledge required.

to immediate technological progress, then there is no need to venture into the history of science. If, on the other hand, it can be shown that these limitations were an obstacle, then economics does not offer a wide enough conceptual framework. The view taken here, for which the arguments will be presented in due course, is that an approach simply in terms of economic theory can go a long way toward explaining the waning of Chinese technological creativity after about 1350; but that this is not, by itself, quite adequate. Science declined in China at the same time as practical invention, and there was clearly some subtle intellectual transformation taking place in the fourteenth century. A few remarks on this are a necessary background to the main subject.

From the beginning of the Han dynasty until the last years of the Yuan dynasty China produced an astonishing series of discoveries in mathematics and natural science. By the latter period, thanks in part to the invention of printing and the publication of popular works on elementary arithmetic, she was the most literate and the most numerate nation in the world (Yabuuchi 1967a: 81–86). It is one of the great puzzles of history why the spirit of inquiry should thereafter have begun to fail.

The successive invasions by the Chin Tartars and by the Mongols in the twelfth and thirteenth centuries are no explanation. Much interesting work was done under these foreign dynasties, especially in theoretical medicine and in algebra. Perhaps the possibility should not be ruled out that military disorders did fatally disrupt the continuity of the scholarly communities in the northern part of the Empire, where most of the creative effort was concentrated; and that the last brilliant achievements were either the work of northerners who had fled south, like the algebraist Chu Shih-chieh, or of southerners inspired by northern emigrés, like the physician Chu Chen-heng, both alike unable to find colleagues or successors. Yet the change of spirit in the fourteenth century is striking, and not confined to science. The tradition of Sung painting, which Max Loehr has aptly described as "the last word in objective and highly differentiated images of the visible world," and sometimes possessed of "an almost scientific character" (1964: 191–93), gave way to a more introspective, calligraphic art much less concerned with representing the appearance of nature. Confucian philosophy developed in a direction that was both practical and intuitionist, perhaps because of the difficulties involved in the logical derivation of ethical principles from purely naturalistic and immanentist assumptions (Iwama 1968). Secular concerns triumphed, and the decline of the reformed Taoism which had inspired much work on algebraic theory epitomizes the passing of a nature mysticism which had found in scientific pursuits the promise of unravelling the secrets of the universe.

The effect of the new *Zeitgeist* can be demonstrated from the case of mathematics. In Ming China, through two and a half centuries, no advances were made on the work of the great algebraists of the Chin and Yuan dynasties; but when Chin and Yuan books on mathematics were imported into Japan around the end of the sixteenth century, they gave rise at once to vigorous new explorations. It was on borrowed Chinese foundations that the Japanese mathematicians of the seventeenth and eighteenth centuries, above all Seki Kowa and Ajima Chokuyen, developed the theory of determinants and a form of the calculus (Smith and Mikami 1914). Chinese mathematics had not reached an intellectual impasse inherent in its own nature, as Needham and Cajori have suggested (Needham 1959: 151–52). Rather, the Chinese after the Yuan dynasty were insufficiently interested, for reasons that are still to be determined, in exploiting its potentialities.

It is hard to believe that this changing *Zeitgeist* did not have some connection with the story of economics and technology which follows.

The Medieval Chinese Economic Revolution

Between the tenth and the fourteenth centuries the Chinese economy was transformed.

There was a rapid increase in agricultural productivity. Rice cultivation, with its high yields per acre, benefitted from improved techniques of irrigation and a greater use of treadle pumps and norias (peripheral pot wheels). Much more fertilizer was used. A wider range of seeds was developed, permitting a variety of multiple cropping patterns. Iron farm tools became almost universal and several new tools were invented. Advanced practices, most of which originated in the province of Liang-che (modern Chekiang and southern Kiangsu), were disseminated through printed books, official proclamations, and the circulation of a concerned and informed bureaucratic elite (Sudō 1962).

Water transport witnessed a number of small but cumulatively critical technical improvements. Safe ways were found of passing through or circumventing the dangerous places in major rivers that had hitherto made through transport, and hence a continuous network of routes, difficult or impossible. The construction of canals and lockgates became more skillful, culminating in the early fifteenth century with the successful rebuilding of the section of the Grand Canal that runs over the western spurs of the Shantung hills. Better ships were built, fastened with iron nails, waterproofed with t'ung oil, safeguarded with watertight bulkheads, and steered by axial rudders. Ocean navigation was made more reliable by the use of the mariner's compass and the navigator's manual. In consequence, the volume of traffic grew dramatically (Shiba 1968, chap. 2; Li Chien-nung 1957: 110 ff).

The amount of money in circulation rose at least ten times in these three or four centuries. Paper money was invented, and so were many types of credit instrument for official and private use. Merchants regularly employed credit in their dealings with each other, and the use of money penetrated into many, probably most, of the back-country villages.*

A national market was established not only in the specialty products of certain localities but also in a number of basic commodities, although some areas with poor communications were not as yet fully integrated into it. There appeared a measure of regular regional interdependence in food-grains, and a much higher degree of intermittent interdependence in years of localized poor harvests. The number of periodic rural markets grew rapidly, and many peasants took up commercially oriented handicrafts, forestry, pisciculture, and mining on a full- or a part-time basis. Mercantile organization became more complex. There were specialists in collection, transportation, warehousing, brokerage, wholesaling, retailing, and various combinations of these functions. The swelling volume of trade made it for the first time worth while for the government to set up a regular network of internal customs offices (Shiba 1968, chap. 3; Katō 1953, 2: 193).

The greater productivity of agriculture, the reduced costs of transport, and the enhanced importance of commerce combined to create a higher level of urbanization and many more large cities than ever previously. The Chinese city was no longer simply and invariably a center of administration and consumption financed primarily through taxes. It might now sometimes have a predominantly commercial or even, as in the case of Soochow, a predominantly industrial character (Shiba 1968, chap. 3, part 1).

Ferrous metallurgy took great strides forward with the general use of coal and (possibly) coke in North China for smelting, and per-capita production rose rapidly. Large-scale government and private enterprises which, with their hundreds of furnace-workers and thousands of ancillary workers, were not to be surpassed in size anywhere in the world until the creation of the Urals iron industry in the eighteenth century,

---

* Twitchett 1963: 78; Miyazaki 1943: 145; Shen Kua 1086–91, ch. 12; L.S. Yang 1952: 51–61; Katō 1953, 2: 1–164, and 222–34; Franke 1949, chap. 3; Shiba 1968: 369–70.

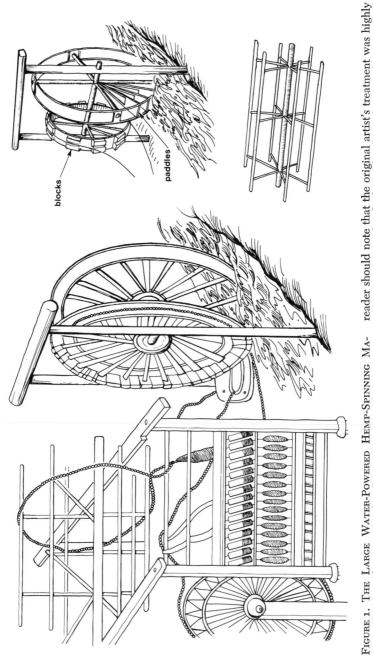

labels: blocks, paddles

FIGURE 1. THE LARGE WATER-POWERED HEMP-SPINNING MA-CHINE (Wang Chen 1313). This illustration is based on a micro-film of the Ssu k'u ch'üan shu manuscript edition, redrawn in order to make the main features more readily apparent. The reader should note that the original artist's treatment was highly impressionistic. The flanking sketches, showing the presumed alignment of the wheels and the possible structure of the reeling frame, are based on other illustrations in Wang Chen's book.

were complemented by an army of petty smiths working in the country-side at the manufacture of farm tools and sometimes weapons.*

To these should be added the communications revolution brought about by woodblock printing. This technique had been invented in the ninth century but did not become important, or remunerative as a business, until toward the middle of the eleventh century (Carter 1925; Yoshida 1967: 267–76).

The spinning machine described by Wang Chen thus appeared in the latter part of a period when per-capita income was rising and the demand for hemp cloth, the material used for ordinary clothing, presumably was also rising. Given the relatively high level of commercialization, there would obviously have been attractive profits for anyone who could produce this cloth more cheaply and in larger quantities. It may be hypothesized for the moment that the immediate cause of the invention lay simply in this. It was a response to a challenge, just as, in a different way, the use of coal in iron-smelting was a response to the fuel crisis caused by the deforestation of North China.

What of the stock of practical scientific knowledge required?

The basic document here, and probably the only independent source, is Wang Chen's description of the mechanism. Wang tells us that the water-powered machine, shown in Figure 1 here, was similar in every respect insofar as the spinning mechanism was concerned (Wang Chen 1313, ch. 22: 4a):

The Large Spinning Machine. It is so constructed as to be more than 20 feet long and about 5 feet wide. A wooden framework is first built as a base, and uprights about 5 feet in height are erected at each of the four corners. Through the center runs a horizontal cylinder. Light struts complete the structure at the top. The iron axle of the long reeling-frame onto which the hemp thread is wound rests in two ridged grooves in these struts. Next, a long wooden baseboard is fixed to the main frame. Sockets set into it receive the iron bearings at the bottom of the bobbin-rollers. (These are tubes made on a lathe and 1 [Chinese] foot 2 inches long and 1 foot 2 inches around. There are 32 of them, and the thread is wound [or "twisted"] inside them. Iron rings at the ends of rods are used to hold the tops of the bobbin-rollers steady. Furthermore, on the front of the top strut is set a line of small iron forks which separately seize the rovings and transmit them upwards onto the long reeling-frame. What is more, to the left and the right [of the framework] are two wheels set on separate strands. They are joined by a leather driving-belt. On its lower traverse it passes along the line of bobbin-rollers, and on its upper traverse shuttles past the revolving drum of the reeling-frame. Motion is im-

---

* Hartwell 1962, 1966, 1967; Miyazaki 1957; Yoshida 1966; Sudō 1962: 207–24. There is disagreement over the size of the increase in iron production.

parted to the large wheel on the left-hand side either by a man or by an animal. The driving-belt is moved by the rotation of the wheel, and every part of the mechanism is set in motion. The upper and lower portions respond to each other at the appropriate relative speeds. In consequence they cause the rovings to be stretched and wound upon the reeling-frame.

Wang's keen delight in the automatic nature of the process is evident from the poem which he appended to the foregoing description:

> There is one driving-belt for wheels both great and small.
> When one wheel turns, the others all turn with it.
> The rovings are transmitted evenly from the bobbin-rollers.
> The threads wind by themselves onto the reeling-frame.

The literary evidence thus does not permit us to establish directly the precise details of the mechanism. Certain inferences are, however, possible. Firstly, it seems certain that *hollow* spindles (the "bobbin-rollers") were used. Otherwise the arms carrying the iron rings to steady the tops of the rollers would have interfered with the free upward passage of the thread. Secondly, the transfer of power merely by a tangential contact between the belt and the rollers, as seems implied by the text, would have been grossly inefficient, even with a heavy belt. Some method of increasing the angle of lap must have been used, although no hint of this is given. Thirdly, the reeling-frame must have been turned by a secondary belt twisted through a right angle and passed around a smaller drum turned by the main belt. This secondary belt can be clearly seen at the right-hand end of the reeling-frame in Figure 1. The relative sizes of the frame and the drum would have been such that the speed of the reeling-frame was reduced to the requisite extent.

The iconographic evidence is too corrupt to be of much help, and in some respects it is contradictory. In particular, one of the two main traditions shows the rovings on separate spindles below the bobbin-rollers whereas the other shows them wound on the lower part of the bobbin-rollers.* Figure 1 belongs to the first tradition, which seems to me on grounds of feasibility to be the more plausible, and a reconstruction of the mechanism appears in Figure 2.† The hollow bobbin-

---

* These two traditions are exemplified by the pictures in Amano 1967: 366 and 453 respectively. They appear to reflect a difference between the water-powered machine and the land-based machine. Why this should be so is not at all clear. Cf. Hsu Kuang-ch'i 1843, ch. 36: 14ab and ch. 18, 16ab.

† Douglas Steen, Esq., of Douglas Steen and Associates (Dundee), John Grant, Esq., of Simon-Litwin, Ltd. (London), and David Holm, Esq., of the University of Glasgow, provided valuable technical insights.

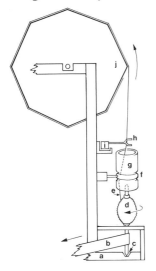

FIGURE 2. POSSIBLE RECONSTRUCTION OF THE HEMP-SPINNING MACHINE DESCRIBED BY WANG CHEN (1313). A spindle-shaft (*c*) rests on a baseboard (*a*), and is rapidly rotated by a driving-belt (*b*). A bobbin (*d*) carrying the roving is set loosely on the spindle-shaft, and a bobbin-roller (*g*) is firmly attached to the top of the spindle-shaft and rotates with it, held steady by an iron ring (*f*). The roving (*e*) is drawn off the bobbin into a duct in the bobbin-roller, from which it passes through a small iron fork (*h*) to the reeling-frame (*j*). The horizontal beam (*i*) on which the fork is set moves slowly back and forth so that the yarn is laid down in broad bands on the reeling-frame.

roller would thus have functioned much like the flier on a modern silk-spinning machine, in which the thread is also drawn upwards off a spindle onto a horizontal reel. The only difference, but an important one, is that on the Chinese machine the bobbin-roller was probably attached firmly to the rotating shaft, with the sleeve carrying the roving left loose to turn freely, whereas in modern silk spinning it is the flier which revolves independently, and the bobbin below it bearing the thread which imparts the twist.

The hemp-spinning machine was clearly derived from the Sung silk-reeling machine. This device consisted essentially of a large open-work reeling-frame worked by a treadle. A number of filaments were drawn simultaneously from cocoons immersed in a tub of boiling water, passed through eyelets and then through hooks on a ramping arm that derived its oscillating motion from an eccentrically placed lug on a pulley driven by a belt linking it with the rotating axle of the reeling-frame, and then laid down in broad bands on the frame.* For hemp spinning, a spindle carrying the roving was substituted for the cocoon wound with silk fiber. The novel elements were of course the hollow bobbin-rollers and the belt which made them spin round. In terms of the analogy with the silk machine, the former may be considered as eyelets set off-center in rotating disks. The morphological evolution is neat and impressive.

The silk-reeling machine was itself the product of the Chinese medie-

---

* Illustrations may be found in Needham and Wang 1965, IV. 2, Plate CLIV facing p. 107, and in Sung Ying-hsing 1637 (1966): 46.

val economic revolution, and probably dates from the tenth or eleventh century. Thus the technique which provided the unknown inventor of the hemp-spinning mechanism with his basic conception was absent until two or three hundred years before his time. Furthermore, the production of a variety of motions at differing speeds from a single power source, either by means of gearing or by means of belt drives linking wheels of different sizes, did not begin to be widely understood and exploited until Sung times. The most spectacular·example of this new skill was the well-known hydraulic clockwork of Su Sung and his successors, but there were plenty of humbler instances, notably the ordinary spinning wheel, which was in widespread use in China by the thirteenth century.

We may conclude that the pattern of economic forces and the state of scientific knowledge in the latter part of this century were such as to make the invention of the hemp-spinning machine both immediately intelligible and no more fortuitous than any invention must, in the nature of things, always be.

The technological level of this machine was about that of those used for the respinning of flax and the spinning of silk in Europe about 1700. The device described in Diderot's *Encyclopédie* for retwisting flax thread, shown here in Figure 3, may be instanced in support of this assertion. Its resemblance to Wang Chen's machine is instantly apparent. A continuous belt turns a line of bobbins, surmounted by freely turning fliers, from which the spun thread rises through guides to be wound on an open-work reeling-frame. The suspicion of a Chinese origin, either directly or perhaps through the comparable machinery used for silk thread, is hard to resist although not easy to reconcile with the apparent disappearance of such machines in China by the seventeenth century.

However this may have been, the burgeoning mechanical genius of modern Europe had already laid its hand on the machine shown in Figure 3. The transfer of power from the belt had been improved by the use of counterset rollers (5 in *fig.* 4); a screw device had been inserted to allow the operator to tighten or slacken the belt as he desired (left-hand end of *fig.* 5); the relative speeds of bobbins and reeling-frame had been regulated by gearing rather than by a second belt; little lead weights had been fixed under the bobbins to ensure the regularity of their rotation; sockets of glass had been sunk into the pieces of wood marked *i* in *fig.* 4. Earlier versions probably resembled the Chinese model more closely, whether or not they were actually derived from it.

Further improvements were to come. Irregularities in the speeds at

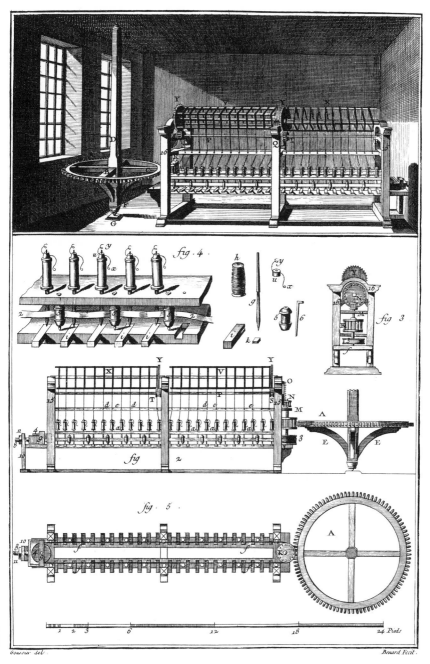

Goussier del. Benard Fecit.

FIGURE 3. EUROPEAN MACHINERY OF THE EARLY EIGHTEENTH CENTURY
FOR RETWISTING FLAX THREAD

SOURCE: *Encyclopédie*, Planches, t. iii, Fil

which the bobbins rotated, resulting from irregularities in the transfer of power from the belt, led to the invention of a machine with the bobbins in a circular array, so as to increase the angle of lap. Later still, when difficulties arose from the varying distances of the bobbins from the reeling-frame on account of the circular layout, the bobbins were arranged in an oval (Diderot 1765: 787–78). None of these simple and useful advances, including the use of gearing, was out of the reach of Chinese skill in the fourteenth century; but there is no evidence that efforts were ever made in these directions. It is thus possible to concede the obvious—namely that in Europe by the first half of the eighteenth century mechanical skills had developed well beyond those of China in the fourteenth century, and that this higher level of skill was without doubt of great importance for the advance of industry at this time—and yet to maintain the crucial analytical point that the Chinese failed to make anything like the fullest use of their fourteenth-century skills. Why?

Changing Patterns in the Supply of Raw Materials and
Labor, 1300–1800

At this point our analysis becomes more complicated, essentially because we are shifting from explaining what did happen to trying to explain what did not.

The first problem that confronts us in this connection is why the technique of mechanized hemp spinning was not rapidly transferred to the cotton industry. Cotton was of negligible economic importance in China before the thirteenth century, but made great advances after about 1200. It was preferred to hemp and ramie because of its greater warmth, lightness, and capacity to absorb moisture. About ten times as much cotton fiber can be grown on a given acreage as hemp, and so where the cultivation of hemp gave way to that of cotton there was for a time a glut of raw material. This prompted the introduction of several new machines. Of outstanding importance were the treadle-driven multi-spindle spinning wheel and the cotton gin, both of which appear to have originated outside China, perhaps in Indochina or India. The way in which a suddenly increased supply of raw materials could foster mechanization emerges clearly from Wang Chen's account of the latter machine. "In times past," he says, "rollers were employed [to strip the seeds from the fibers]. Nowadays, the gin is used. . . . It is several times more advantageous than the rollers. . . . Even if there is a large quantity of cotton, the use of this method permits one to get rid of the seeds immediately and to keep a backlog from piling up" (Wang Chen

1313, ch. 21: 16b). Without substantial modification the hemp-spinning machine was not suitable for spinning the much shorter cotton fibers but it is surprising that, once the feasibility of machine spinning had been established, there was not a determined and ultimately successful search for a way to do the same thing with cotton.

Three observations are pertinent at this point. Firstly, the medieval economic revolution mentioned above failed to achieve a compound-interest kind of growth; and, as it lost momentum, the early gains in per-capita income were largely obliterated by continuing population growth. In some sectors of the economy, such as iron, there was even a fall in total output. In others, such as agriculture, the best practices may have continued to spread over a wider geographical area. But after about 1350, with a handful of minor exceptions, there were no new inventions in any field. Moreover, as we have already noted, Chinese science after this time was almost wholly drained of its creative power. Finally, the relative glut of raw cotton did not last for long. By the sixteenth century there was already an acute shortage in the lower Yangtze Valley, then the main center of the industry, and the shortage intensified with the passing of time. It would therefore appear that there was only a short period after the spread of cotton cultivation in China, perhaps no more than fifty years in all, during which the conjuncture of intellectual and economic forces was still highly favorable to invention in the cotton industry. Conceivably, this was simply not long enough.

Did the limited supply of raw material place a barrier in the way of labor-saving invention?

By the early seventeenth century a gazetteer for Sung-chiang Prefecture could observe that "Sung-chiang cotton cloth clothes the Empire . . . , but most of the raw cotton used in it is grown in the North" (Nishijima 1947: 125). A contemporary gazetteer for Chia-ting, a Kiangsu *hsien* almost wholly given over to the cultivation of cotton, also noted, "Every part of Honan and Hukwang [Hupeh and Hunan] knows how to grow it. They load their bales of it into an unending line of boats and come down to Kiangnan to sell it" (*ibid*.: 126). According to a late Ming gazetteer for Yen-chou in Shantung, "The land here is suited to cotton. Merchants sell it in Kiangnan, where they have set up shops. It is more than twice as profitable as growing grain" (*ibid*.: 126). In 1594 an official called Chung Hua-min wrote that he had "seen half of the rich lands of Honan planted with cotton, all of which is sold to merchants for them to sell. In consequence, all the inhabitants have to buy their clothing" (*ibid*.: 127). Thus, by an irony of fate, the areas that had once produced the most advanced spinning technology in the world were now reduced to supplying raw materials for the Kiangnan textile industry. There was, presumably, no longer enough demand for hemp cloth to make mechanized spinning worth while. The botanical revolution represented by the cotton plant had triumphed over the mechanical revolution represented by the hemp-spinning machine.

The southeastern coast and Kiangsi were even more dependent upon interregional imports of raw cotton. Thus a Ch'ing dynasty work on Kwangtung observed that cotton fabrics from Sung-chiang and Hsien-ning in Hupeh were "the chief articles of trade, together with raw cotton," for "Kwangtung does not produce enough raw cotton to meet the requirements of its ten prefectures" (*ibid.*: 128). Chu Hua, the famous Shanghai cotton expert, wrote that Fukienese merchants did not buy cotton cloth, "but only our ginned cotton, with which they return home, their thousands of multi-decked boats laden to capacity with sacks." "The people of their province," he added in explanation, "are capable of spinning and weaving for themselves" (Chu Hua: 11b). According to an early Ch'ing gazetteer for Hsin-ch'eng Hsien in Kiangsi, "Our raw cotton is provided by Honan and Kwangtung. The local people grow a certain amount but not much" (Nishijima 1948, part 2: 28). A gazetteer for Jui-chin Hsien also tells a story that suggests a perpetual quest for raw materials: "No cotton was formerly grown in Jui-chin, all of it being purchased from merchants. In 1569 the magistrate of the *hsien*, Lu Jo-yü, recruited people to buy cotton seeds in the neighboring prefectures and teach others how to grow the plant. The ground was unsuitable and it did not thrive. Now it no longer exists" (*ibid.*: 28). Shensi's dependence on imports is mentioned in Ch'en Hung-mou's notes on Ku Yen-wu's *Records of Knowledge Day by Day*: "Raw cotton and cotton cloth come from Hukwang. The poor people do not have enough to eat, but even so they sell their grain so as to be able to make clothing" (*ibid.*, part 1: 14).

In the seventeenth and eighteenth centuries Shantung and Chihli (Hopei), which had in former times specialized in exporting raw cotton, began to weave their own cloth, taking advantage of local supplies unburdened by transport costs. Hsu Kuang-ch'i noted that the cheapness of raw cotton in Su-ning in Hopei made it possible to weave there a cloth as good as the medium quality from Sung-chiang, and at sixty to seventy percent of the price.* This expansion of the North China tex-

---

* Hsu Kuang-ch'i 1639, reprint, 2: 708. An important reason for the development of cotton-spinning in the dry northern climate was the discovery that subterranean workshops would provide the necessary humidity.

tile industry put pressure on the Yangtze Valley industry to find new sources from which to import raw cotton and to increase its own output of the fiber.

Manchuria became a major supplier. In 1746 the Ministry of Works reported that bannermen (Manchu military men) and commoners were "selling their entire crop to merchants, losing the use of the cotton they have grown, and having besides to meet the expense of buying cloth every year" (Katō 1953, 2: 608). Slightly later, China began to import large amounts of raw cotton from India. The annual import averaged 27.4 million pounds between 1785 and 1833 (Ch'üan 1958: 31), and reached a maximum of 45.6 million pounds in the latter year. This was more than ten times the total yearly consumption of Britain at the time of the invention of the spinning frame (Hatano 1961: 521; Baines 1835: 346).

In the lower Yangtze region, the pressing need for more cotton led to an increased use of fertilizers. Even by the seventeenth century, this technique was being pushed close to the limits of its effectiveness, as may be seen from the remarks of Hsu Kuang-ch'i on the subject (Hsu, 2: 704; cf. 709–10):

Manure, ashes, bean cake, or fresh mud should be put onto cotton fields before the seed is planted. How much depends on the relative fertility of the land. On no account *throw* chopped-up bean-cake onto the soil. Spread it equally plot by plot. In our region, when planting seeds closely, on no account use more than ten bean cakes [per *mou*], or more than ten piculs of manure. Otherwise it is to be feared that the land will be too rich and the cotton will grow without bearing bolls or, even if it does have them, will be infested with pests.

In his *Cotton Manual*, written a century later, Chu Hua stressed that "the fecundity or barrenness of the land depends on the quantity of fertilizer and labor expended" (Chu Hua: 4b). The bean-cake trade from Honan and Shantung to Kiangnan was already significant in the sixteenth century, and imports of the fertilizer grew greatly with the opening up of the Manchurian trade in the late seventeenth century and the early eighteenth century. A fleet of about thirty-five hundred ships, each carrying between 65,000 and 400,000 pounds of cargo, made several trips a year between Shanghai and Manchuria exchanging southern cotton cloth and tea for northern beans, bean cake, and wheat (Fujii 1953: 20; Nakahara 1959: 76; Yamaguchi 1958: 57).

Interesting light is shed on the possible shortage of cotton by the manner in which, after China had been opened to more extensive foreign trade in the nineteenth century, imports of Indian yarn created new textile industries in several parts of the country. In 1898 the Japanese consul at Amoy reported (Hatano 1961: 526):

No cotton is grown in the environs of Foochow. The inhabitants were formerly ignorant of the art of weaving cotton cloth, and so depended for clothing materials entirely on Kiangsu and Chekiang. Cotton yarn has recently begun to be imported from India, and many more women have mastered the art of weaving. There are said to be more than ten thousand looms at present in the various parts of Foochow Prefecture. . . . In the Chiang-wei area [in Hai-ch'eng], which was previously without any sort of industry, the people have gradually become acquainted with the weaving of cloth. Their share of the cotton yarn imported into Amoy is an important one. This is enough to enable one to see how much the import trade in foreign yarn has helped the development of industry among the Chinese people. . . . There was formerly a surprising absence of cotton cloth manufacture in the eastern part of Kwangtung, but imported yarn has recently been in great demand.

The consul's report seems to contradict Chu Hua's remarks quoted above on eighteenth-century imports of cotton into Fukien. Is it perhaps possible that part of the Fukienese cotton industry temporarily disappeared because of the lack of raw materials?

Land that was used to grow cotton was also land that could be used to grow food-grains. By the eighteenth century most of the land in China that was cultivable with the technology of the day was already being cultivated, and the pressure of population meant that no more than an essential minimum of the new land being opened up could be spared for growing a clothing fiber. Any expansion in the per-capita supply of raw cotton, and possibly even maintaining existing levels, with this rising population and a relatively limited resource base, would have meant increasing a per-acre agricultural productivity that was probably already the highest in the world, or increasing imports of food or of cotton. The Chinese had no such vast new sources of cotton as the British found in the West Indies and South America, which, added to imports from older sources in the Levant, made possible a *tripling* of British consumption between 1741 and 1771–75.

We can now return to the question asked above, "Did the limited supply of raw material place a barrier in the way of labor-saving invention?" The conclusion that it did would seem to impose itself, if two assumptions be granted. The first of these is that situations in which invention is profitable are usually the result of sizeable changes in the balance of economic forces such as supply and demand. The question whether or not the Chinese per-capita cotton supply was minimally sufficient is therefore of little importance compared to the question whether or not it could have been rapidly expanded, as the British supply was. At the national level, the answer is obviously "No." For one thing, the Chinese economy was too big even relative to *world* cotton supplies in the eighteenth century. In order to maintain that there could have been no rapid expansion at the local level, either, we must further be granted the second assumption referred to above: that by this time the commercial development of China was sufficiently advanced for local effects to be largely evened out by interregional trade. What China thus needed was something not within the bounds of technological possibility—namely, a machine that would produce cotton cloth with half the previous input of raw cotton rather than half the previous input of human labor.

This in turn raises the question of labor costs. Did their relative share in the cost of textiles perhaps fall with time? The balance of probabilities would seem to be that they did.

As cotton replaced hemp as the main fiber used for everyday clothing, the center of the Chinese textile industry shifted from the North to the Yangtze delta. This was a shift away from a region of relatively sparse settlement based mostly on dry farming to a relatively densely populated region based on irrigated rice cultivation. A long-term decline in the northern population, which continued until the end of the thirteenth century, may also have made human labor increasingly expensive in the north. The main demographic trends are shown in the accompanying table, which gives the official figures for the numbers of households in the north and in the south. Even by Mongol times there was an abundance of cheap labor in Kiangnan. Here, the poet Yuan Chüeh remarked, "men did the work of animals" (Shiba 1968: 67). With the passing of the centuries the southeast grew still more overcrowded. A flow of outmigrants began to leave the area, and the lands of the Yangtze delta, once

CHANGES IN THE REGIONAL DISTRIBUTION OF THE CHINESE POPULATION

	Millions of households	
Date	North China	South China
A.D. 742	4.9	4.1
A.D. 1080	3.0	10.6
A.D. 1223	n.a.	12.7
A.D. 1290	1.4	11.8
A.D. 1393	2.3	8.4

SOURCES: Katō 1953, 2: 330–31, 332–33; Franke 1949: 128; and P. T. Ho 1959: 10. Compare the population graph in Miyashita Saburō, "Sō-Gen no iryō" (Medical care in Sung and Yuan times) in Yabuuchi 1967b: 127.

NOTE: The areas designated "North China" and "South China" are only approximately identical for the different periods.

the granary of the Empire, became dependent upon regular imports of food-grains from Hunan, Hupeh and Szechwan (Fujii 1953, part 1: 21, 31). The population density in Kiangsu by the eighteenth century was over eight hundred persons to the square mile. By the middle of the nineteenth century it was over a thousand, there being less than a third of an acre of arable land per inhabitant (Ch'üan 1958: 28). It is therefore reasonable to assume that to the degree that farming provided a less and less adequate living for the peasants, their labor and that of their womenfolk could be had for a lower and lower wage. This applies to subsidiary or seasonal labor combined with farming, and as we shall see this sort of labor was the mainstay of the cotton industry; but the absence of attractive alternative employment on the land, and the competition of the peasant part-timers, would also have tended to force down the wages of full-time textile workers.

The low level of wages in the cotton industry was notorious. Hsu Hsien-chung, a scholar and official who flourished in the sixteenth century, made the following observations (Li Wen-yao 1750, ch. 5: 696):

The people of this *hsien* [Shang-hai] manufacture cotton cloth and thread. When peasants are in difficult straits, they are able by these means to obtain a measure of relief. Yet their lives are extremely wearisome. [The spinning or weaving of] cotton is not to be compared with the rearing of silkworms, the reeling of silk, and the working of hemp and ramie undertaken in the nearby *hsien* and prefectures, in which a lesser expenditure of effort brings double the returns.

In the Yangtze Valley industry after the sixteenth century, the costs of imported raw cotton and imported bean-cake fertilizer must have driven up the percentage of the price of the final product represented by the cost of materials. The comments made in 1898 by Japanese investigators of the rural cotton industry around Shanghai are also suggestive: "They do not in the least welcome orders on special occasions which need imported machine yarn for warp and weft. We have heard that the reason is that they dislike having to buy all the raw materials and not using their home-grown cotton" (Hatano 1961: 531). According to Chu Hua, the most skillful spinners in the Yangtze delta used wheels with four spindles, while the ordinary run of spinners used three (Chu Hua: 9ab; Chang Ch'un-hua 1839: 15a). They were therefore several times more productive than their English counterparts prior to 1769. Multi-spindle wheels were found in a few other places, such as Lo-an in Kiangsi, but they were not generally used across the nation although they had been known for four or five hundred years. That this should have been so indicates that no one can have been particularly preoccupied with reducing labor costs in the manufacture of cotton textiles.

To sum up, between Yuan and Ch'ing times the underlying pattern of resource-availability in the textile industry changed in such a fashion as to make the induction of invention less rather than more likely. In the cotton industry there was a shift from a moderate surplus to a relative scarcity of materials. As southern cotton ousted northern hemp, the key area for the manufacture of cloth for mass consumption moved from one with a relative shortage to one with a relative abundance of labor. The later revival of the northern industry in the seventeenth century came at a time when the north was much more populous than it had been in Yuan times. It is curious, though, that the great epidemics of 1586–89 and 1639–42, which so drastically reduced the populations of the North China plain and of Kiangnan (Imura 1936, part 3: 14–24), seem not to have led to any search for labor-saving machines. Bearing in mind, then, that the picture is complicated by such considerations as the foregoing, we may cautiously conclude that labor's share in the cost of finished cloth fell after late medieval times.

Two further issues now arise. The total Chinese output of cotton cloth was so big that, even without any increase, it would have lent itself well to mechanized production. The use of machinery would have conferred a competitive advantage on those who used it, especially in the spinning sector where the productivity of an operative can be quite easily multiplied from ten to forty times. Why, then, was machinery not introduced? And why was there not at some time a rapid growth in the total demand for cotton cloth, straining existing productive capacity and making the invention of better techniques attractive, even imperative? To answer the first question we need to take a closer look at the organization of the cotton industry; and to answer the second we need to survey the dynamics of the late pre-modern Chinese economy as a whole. The next two sections will therefore be devoted to these two topics respectively.

Commerce as a Substitute for Management: The Divorce of Market and Technique

It is far from clear how the hemp industry was organized in Sung and Yuan times, but it seems likely that at least three systems were used. Where the peasants were serfs or tenants tied to the soil and obliged to perform various services for their landlord, their womenfolk probably sometimes produced cloth for the market under the discipline of a manorial regime. Manors produced much of the grain sold through commercial channels, and also marketed fruits such as lychees (Sudō 1954: 340; Shiba 1968: 205). I have as yet found no text from before Ming times referring to the sale of manorial hemp or cotton, but Mao K'un's description of his parents, who lived in the late fifteenth century, probably affords us some idea of the kind of organization involved: "When I was a boy, . . . I was also accustomed to seeing my mother personally direct the women serfs at weaving in their own houses, starting by lamplight and finishing by lamplight. . . . Purchasers offered high prices in competition with each other to buy what they had woven" (Fu 1963: 65). It would be a plausible supposition that the majority of hemp-spinning machines, capable of producing up to 40,000 pounds of yarn a year, were owned by manor lords or other well-to-do persons who made them available to the peasantry for a cash fee or a percentage of the yarn. Serfs would no doubt spin their master's hemp from time to time. Wang Chen's remarks strongly suggest that the machine was not treated as industrial equipment, to be kept steadily at work so as to maximize the return on the capital invested in it: "When it so happens that many families have much spinning to do, they gather by the machine, weigh the material to be spun, and share out [*pro rata*] the thread produced. The work is finished without hard toil" (Wang Chen 1313, ch. 22: 4a).

Rather better documented is a system by which merchants coordinated the work of scattered rural producers, probably mostly in regions (such as the Chekiang mountains) where the manorial system was weak or nonexistent. The earliest reference seems to be a decree of 1168 concerning silk (Shiba 1968: 283):

In I-wu Hsien in Wu-chou [Chin-hua] there are scattered storehouse proprietors and brokers who undertake the buying and selling of silk. . . . Previously, the people in the hilly valleys of I-wu made their living by weaving thin silk. The magistrate of this *hsien* detained all the storehouse proprietors of eight communities, made a note of their names, and confiscated the silks which they had woven. As a result the people suffered greatly.

In the latter part of the twelfth century Hung Mai described what was probably a comparable system in the hemp industry:

Ch'ien T'ai was a commoner from Fu-chou [in Kiangsi] who made his fortune by selling hemp cloth. Every year he advanced capital as a loan to spinners in the *hsien* of Ch'ung-jen, Lo-an and Chin-chi. In the *hsien* of Chi-chou Prefecture he had brokers to take charge of his affairs. In the sixth month he would go in person to collect the cloth from them, only returning late in the autumn. This went on for a long time.

He also advanced money to his brokers so that they could build store-houses that would hold several thousand lengths of cloth (Sudō 1962: 355).

I have no evidence at present on the organization of production in the northern hemp industry, but commercial transactions seem often to have been on a large scale. Hung Mai recounts the story of a Mr. Chang of Hsing-chou in present-day Hopei who bought 5,000 lengths of hemp cloth on credit from a man whose life he had formerly saved, and rose to fortune when his grateful creditor refused to accept payment (Katō 1953, 2: 223–24).

The third system was that of individual peasant production for sale at the local market. The eleventh-century poet-monk Tao-ch'ien mentions a market in Kiangsi where "They bring hemp cloth and paper made from wood-pulp, / Or drive before them chickens and sucking pigs" (Shiba 1968: 371). And a gazetteer of the early thirteenth century observes: "Ch'iang-k'ou cloth is made of hemp [or ramie], being produced in Yen [Sheng Hsien in Shao-hsing]. It is very roughly woven, but merchants and peddler-women constantly compete to get it so that they can sell it to the men of Wu [Soochow]" (Sudō 1962: 339).

After cotton had replaced hemp as China's basic textile, the first two of these three systems seem gradually to have disappeared. The demise of the manorial organization was presumably connected with the final extinction of serfdom and serf-like tenancy in the course of the seventeenth century (Elvin 1970: 104–8), and is thus not particularly surprising. The decline of what amounted to a sort of putting-out system (not a true putting-out system since the advances were of money, not materials) is more surprising. The explanation seems to be that the market network in the areas where cotton cloth was manufactured had reached such a density, surpassing in this respect even eighteenth-century England,* that putting-out as a means of coordinating producers simply became unnecessary. Advances to producers, and some degree of direct merchant involvement in production, seem to have existed in eighteenth-century China only under special circumstances such as those of the tea industry, which was in the back-country with poor communications and few local markets. They also existed after the eighteenth century in the silk industry, when a growing foreign demand had so far inflated the price of raw materials that a substantial working capital was required to buy them (Hatano 1961: 37–38, 80, 112–12, 120–21; Fu 1956: 12).

---

* This is a general impression based on reading Defoe and Richardson 1753.

I have described elsewhere the development of water transport and market towns in Sung-chiang (Elvin, in press). Here it remains to try to substantiate the assertion just made concerning the almost total absence of putting-out in this later period.

By the seventeenth and eighteenth centuries it was normal for spinners or weavers in the countryside to make *daily* trips to market to buy their raw materials, a practice that would not have been possible had markets still been merely periodic here. According to a late Ming gazetteer for Hu-chou (Fu 1963: 42):

Merchants from other prefectures buy raw cotton and set up shops on our land. The poor people take what they have spun or woven, namely thread or cotton cloth, and go to the market early in the morning. They exchange it there for raw cotton [or yarn] with which they return to spin or weave as before. On the morrow they again take it to be exchanged.

The Ch'ien-lung gazetteer for Shang-hai Hsien says much the same in the eighteenth century (Li Wen-yao 1750, ch. 1: 21a):

It is not only in the country villages that spinning is to be found, but also in the capital of the *hsien* and in the market towns. In the morning the village women take the thread which they have spun and go to the market, where they exchange it for raw cotton, with which they return. The following morning they again leave home with their thread, never pausing for an instant.

The literary evidence shows a world of peasants who either grew their own cotton or relied on the markets for it. No mention is made of putting-out. Here is Hsiung Chien-ku's *Cotton Song*, written some time in the Ming dynasty (*ibid.*: 22a):

In the fall sun, when twigs are bare and harvest in,
The drab, patched sacks spill over with white bolls
Which peasant women bear off home in baskets,
And set their families' fingers to the looms.
The older boys want jackets, the young ones trousers;
But debts take half and taxes take the rest.
Cotton in panniers hangs in the smoking fire,
The weevils and their broods come scurrying forth.
Like pearly snow it comes from the iron rollers,
Softer than autumn river-mist at one snap of the bow.
Hollow within and light without, it's twisted into rovings.
Then, day and night, the treadle wheel sings its disjointed song.
The wheel once still, the thread's rushed to the loom;
And they wonder who will wear what they have woven.

Tung Hsien-liang's *Weaving Song*, also written in the Ming dynasty, tells of the purchase of supplementary raw material (Nishijima 1966: 846):

> He tends his cotton in the garden in the morning,
> In the evening makes his cloth upon the loom.
> His wife weaves with ever-moving fingers;
> His girls spin with never-ceasing wheels.
> It is the humid and unhealthy season
> When they finish the last of the cotton from their garden.
> Prices go up and up, if outside merchants come to buy;
> So if warp's plentiful a lack of weft brings grief.
> They therefore buy raw cotton and spin it night after night.

Finally, Hsu Hsien-chung's *Prose-poem on Cotton Cloth*, written in the middle of the sixteenth century, gives a vivid picture of peasant dependence on the market (Li Wen-yao 1750, ch. 5: 69b–70b):

> Why do you ignore their toil? Why are you touched
> Only by the loveliness that is born from toil?
> . . . .
> Shall I tell you how their work exhausts them?
> By hand and treadle they turn the rollers of wood and iron,
> Feeding the fiber in between their fingers;
> The cotton comes out fluffy and the seeds fall away.
> The string of the cotton bow is stretched so taut
> It twangs with a sob from its pillar.
> . . . .
> They draw out slivers, spin them on their wheels
> To the accompaniment of a medley of creakings,
> Working through darkness by candlelight,
> Forgetful of bed. When energy ebbs, they sing.
> The quilts are cold. Unheard, the waterclock flows over.
> . . . .
> Then in the freezing cold they send the shuttle flying.
> One up, one down, the warp-threads through the heddles run,
> And as the footbar moves they rise and fall in turn.
> A thread snaps; and is painfully joined again.
> . . . .
> The chill night stretches out
> As one foot, then another foot, is done.
> The hens are cackling in the morning cold
> When the piece is wound off the roller
> And they hurry to market.
> . . . .

When a woman leaves for market
She does not look at her hungry husband.
Afraid her cloth's not good enough,
She adorns her face with cream and powder,
Touches men's shoulders to arouse their lust,
And sells herself with pleasant words.
Money she thinks of as a beast its prey;
Merchants she coaxes as she would her father.
Nor is her burden lifted till one buys.

I have not yet found a poem from the Ch'ing dynasty explicitly describing this sort of market-dependency in the Sung-chiang rural cotton industry. The nearest to it is Tung Hung-tu's moving *Complaint of the Weaving Wife*. It speaks of the pressure exerted on the peasants by the landlord and the tax-collector but, perhaps significantly, makes no mention of a putter-out coming to collect his goods (*ibid.*, ch. 1: 22b–23a):

Hungry, she still weaves.
Numbed with cold, she still weaves.
Shuttle after shuttle after shuttle.
The days are short,
The weather chill,
Each length hard to finish.
The rich take their rent,
The clerk the land tax,
Knocking repeatedly with urgent insistence.
Her husband wants to urge her on,
But has no heart to do so.
He says nothing,
But stands beside the loom.
. . . .
The more she tries to get it done,
The more her strength fails her.
She turns away, choking down tears,
And consoles herself they are still better off than their neighbors,
Wretched and destitute,
Who having sold their loom
Next had to sell their son.

There is, however, a little evidence suggesting that a putting-out system existed. The most important is a tombstone inscription written by Wang Yuan late in the seventeenth century for Hsi She-jen, a member of a family of cotton merchants (Hatano 1961: 42, 80):

I made several trips to Tung-t'ing Tung-shan. . . . At that time the women in the hills had no subsidiary occupation and ate in empty-handed idleness. Much later, weaving became known and was to be met in every highway and byway. When I asked who had brought this about, they told me, "She-jen taught it to girls whom he recruited in the neighboring prefectures." I asked them where they got raw cotton, and also their spinning wheels and looms. They answered, "She-jen gave them."

There is also an account of the Sung-chiang sock industry by Fan Lien, though this seemingly refers to sewing rather than to spinning or weaving (Fu 1956: 11):

Formerly there were no shops for summer socks in Sung-chiang. Most people wore felt socks in the hot months. After the Wan-li reign-period [1573–1619] *yu-t'un* cotton cloth was used to make thin summer socks which were extremely light and attractive. People from distant places competed to purchase them. As a result, more than a hundred shops for summer socks were opened in the hinterland to the west of the prefectural capital; and men and women throughout the prefecture made their living from the manufacture of these socks, the supplies for which they obtained from the shops. It was a new occupation of benefit to the people.

Unfortunately, neither of these passages gives an altogether clear picture of the kind of organization involved. Until official documents and belles lettres of the seventeenth and eighteenth centuries have been systematically combed for materials referring to the cotton industry, further progress on this point is impossible. For the present, the evidence, such as it is, unambiguously favors the view that a market-oriented structure predominated.

Genuine putting-out did develop around Foochow by the end of the nineteenth century, as is indicated by the remark in a Japanese report on the cotton industry there that "the weavers may be regarded as being under the yarn merchants" (Hatano 1961: 534–35). It was also, of course, commonplace in the Kao-yang cotton industry in the Republican period (*ibid.*: 538–39, 544–46). The first of these instances is of some significance, relating as it does to a traditional context, although the industry itself was largely new (see page 152 above), but the second is probably too late for any useful conclusions to be drawn from it about traditional times.

If, then, the rural cotton industry was based mainly on subsidiary labor, often with a marked seasonal aspect, and if it was coordinated on a large scale through a market mechanism, several deductions about the lack of stimuli for invention follow immediately. Firstly, if income from spinning and weaving constituted only a portion of the total income of a peasant household, and if their simple equipment lay unused for substantial parts of the year, it is evident that both rising and falling demand for cotton textiles would exert a much weaker pressure on the technology of the industry than in the case where workers were mostly full-time and coordinated through a putter-out. For consider—when demand was rising there would be an enormous reserve productive capacity in hundreds of thousands of peasant households that could be brought into play as needed by diverting labor from agriculture as price levels determined its marginal return. And, when demand was falling, only a portion, perhaps quite a modest portion, of the total composite income of each peasant household would be adversely affected, and the damage could be further reduced by directing labor to some extent back into farming. Thus there would be no great prospective rewards for inventors in times of boom, and few penalties in times of slump would be severe enough to drive the inefficient permanently out of business.

Secondly, the very excellence of the market mechanism made it unnecessary for cotton cloth merchants to become directly involved in production. They could keep almost all their capital in relatively liquid form as working capital and avoid tying it up in the form of fixed capital. This gave them much greater potential freedom of action, and spared them the problem of the embezzlement of materials by spinners and weavers. In the absence of any marked benefits to be had from acting otherwise, this arrangement must have been congenial to the merchant temperament.

Thus those with the keenest awareness of market forces, and possessing the capital and skills to foster new initiatives, were so situated that they were very unlikely to have any deep personal appreciation of how their product was manufactured and any ideas as to how it might be improved. Insofar as the rural cotton industry had a structure of the sort outlined above, it is possible to argue the paradoxical proposition that the countryside was both overindustrialized and overcommercialized.

Was the organization of the urban cotton industry significantly different?

There is reason to suspect that it may have been. At least in the hemp and silk industries there were weaving shops with hired labor. Consider, for example, the following remarks of Chang Han, who came from Hangchow (Fu 1963: 46–47):

My ancestor I-an was of modest social status, being a dealer in wines. In 1471 there were floods . . . and he abandoned this business and bought a loom. He wove all kinds of hemp [or ramie] cloth, exceedingly finely worked. Whenever he had finished a piece, people would compete to buy it, and he made a profit of twenty percent. After twenty years he bought a second loom; and finally he had more than twenty of them. Outside his doors there was a constant crowd of merchants, and he still could not supply them with all they needed. As a result the family became extremely rich. Four of my forebears later continued in this business and each amassed several tens of thousands of ounces of silver.

It is of course only likely, not certain, that this passage refers to urban production. There was a somewhat comparable situation in the silk industry, if the report made by Ts'ao Shih-p'in on the disturbances among the silk-weavers of Soochow in 1601 may be taken as a guide (*ibid.*: 89–90):

Very few [of the Soochow people] have a regular [agricultural] livelihood, but in every family one will find looms and woven silk. The "loom households" provide the capital, and the weavers provide the labor, each relying upon the other to prolong their days. . . . [Besides setting up customs stations which interfered with trade, the followers of Sun Lung, the eunuch director of taxes] also recklessly proposed taxing every loom 0.3 of an ounce of silver. All the loom households closed their doors, and the weaving workers, who were faced with the prospect of death by starvation, responded at once (with a riot). . . . The people without families who wander around in search of a living cannot make plans in the morning for the evening of the same day. If they find employment, they live. If they lose employment, they die. When the dyeing shops closed, I saw several thousand dyers scattered. When the loom houses closed I saw a further several thousand weavers scattered. These were all worthy people who supported themselves by their own efforts.

The daily labor-markets in Soochow and Hangchow at this time, described elsewhere in this volume (see pp. 96–97), are also evidence of the extensive use of hired workers in the silk industry (Hatano 1961: 74: Fujii 1953, part 1: 18).

Incontrovertible proof of a comparable system in the Kiangnan urban cotton industry is lacking, at least for the moment. The most suggestive text is the following passage from a writer of the early nineteenth century (Terada 1958: 66–67; Fu 1963: 130):

Mr. Wang from Hsin-an set up the Beneficial and Beautiful wholesaling firm by the Ch'ang Gate of Soochow city. He was a cunning business man. He gave secret orders that tailors who used his firm's cloth should be rewarded with 0.02 of an ounce of silver. The tailors, greedy for this small profit, all extolled the beauties of Wang's cloth, and users competed to buy it. He calculated that [normally] he sold about a million full lengths each year, making a profit of a hundred cash per length [i.e. a total profit of 100,000 strings of cash], and that if he laid out 20,000 ounces of silver [in rebates to tailors] in addition to the cloth, he increased his [gross] profits to 200,000 strings of cash [or, in other words, he doubled them]. For ten years he was the richest of all merchants, and his cotton cloth was sold ever more widely throughout the Empire. He subsequently went on a tour of duty as an official, and, having to relinquish the business, consigned it to a relative called Ch'eng. Ch'eng later returned it to Wang, and for some two hundred years now there has been no place, either north or south, that has failed to consider Beneficial and Beautiful [cloth] to be lovely.

The figures in this passage are almost certainly notional rather than realistic. In the first half of the seventeenth century, when Mr. Wang flourished, the price of a full length of good-quality Kiangnan cotton cloth was between 0.15 and 0.18 of an ounce of silver (Yeh, ch. 7: 5a–6b). Because of the rapid rise in the exchange ratio of copper to silver during the last years of the Ming dynasty, it is possible to determine the percentage profit represented by a hundred cash only for specific years. As of about 1628 the ratio used in the provinces would have made a hundred cash equal to 0.09 of an ounce of silver (*ibid.*, ch. 7: 16a). At 0.18 of an ounce per length this means a profit of 100 percent over cost, which is surprising though not necessarily completely unbelievable.

What is clear is that something like four thousand weavers, and several times that number of spinners, would have been needed to produce the million lengths of cloth which Mr. Wang sold in a normal year, for it took a weaver between one and two days to weave a standard forty-foot length (Li Wen-yao 1750, ch. 1: 21a). Unless the reputation of Beneficial and Beautiful rested solely on Wang's skill in public relations, he must have exercised some control over its production. Did this control extend to weaving? Or did he simply rely on the superior talents of his purchasing agents, and his own care in arranging for the dyeing and finishing of the cloth? It is almost certain that the latter was the case. Wang was one of a number of cotton wholesalers outside the Ch'ang Gate of Soochow, and organizing dyeing and finishing seems to have been their principal concern (Yokoyama 1961).

What is more, the structure of this dyeing and finishing industry seems to have been deliberately designed to prevent merchants from participating directly in production. Its essentials were described by Li Wei, Governor-general of Chekiang, in a memorial of 1730 (*ibid.*, part 1: 337–38):

In the prefectural capital of Soochow . . . the green and blue cotton cloth from the various provinces is bought and sold. After it has been dyed it has to be given luster by being calendered with large stone foot-rollers. There is a class of persons called "contractors" who make ready large stones shaped like water chestnuts, wooden rollers, tools, and rooms. They gather together calenderers to live there, and advance them firewood, rice, silver, and copper cash. They receive cloth from the merchant houses to be calendered. The charge per length is 0.0113 of an ounce of silver, all of which goes to the aforesaid workers. Each of them, however, gives to the contractor each month 0.36 of an ounce of silver as representing the rent for the workspace and the tools. . . . Formerly, there were only seven or eight thousand men in the various workshops. . . . Now a careful investigation of the area outside the Ch'ang Gate of Soochow has shown that there are all together over three hundred and forty contractors, and that they have set up more than four hundred and fifty calendering establishments, in each of which several tens of men are employed. There are over ten thousand nine hundred calendering stones, and the number of workers must equal this.

There were therefore three main groups involved in the process of production, namely the cloth merchants, the contractors, and the artisans. There may also have been a fourth, peripheral, group consisting of landlords who owned and leased the premises on which the work was done. The relationships between these three (or four) groups presented an odd combination of organizational fragmentation and structural rigidity.

At the head of the pyramid stood the Soochow cotton cloth wholesalers (like Mr. Wang), of whom there were about seventy at the beginning of the eighteenth century. They drew their supplies either from their own branch shops or from cotton dealers in major towns such as Wei-t'ing. According to a gazetteer of the early nineteenth century, "The cotton cloth shops are in the eastern market of Wei-t'ing. Outside merchants from various areas and the wholesalers from the Ch'ang Gate of Soochow all have shops here for buying" (*ibid.*, part 2: 460). These latter, in their turn, were supplied by merchants operating in the smaller market towns. Thus an early-nineteenth-century inscription observes (*ibid.*):

Sung-chiang Prefecture is an area which produces cotton cloth. The people of the towns and villages of Shang-hai depend upon the weaving and sale of cloth for their living. It is therefore decreed that the cotton cloth shops, and those who buy and sell cotton cloth in the villages and in the market towns, shall not henceforth prettify their cotton cloth with flour, and that the cotton cloth brokers and the cotton cloth wholesalers shall not purchase cloth so powdered.

Two levels in the market structure thus normally intervened between the Soochow wholesaler and the weavers of his cloth.

The wholesaler was also separated from those who performed the finishing work by the contractors. These intermediaries had a legal monopoly of the right to allocate work to the artisans. No one might enter the business unless he had been guaranteed by those already engaged in it. In return for this privilege the contractors had to assume full liability for cloth entrusted to their care. According to an inscription of 1644, "If any of the calenderers steals or absconds with stolen materials, or acts in an evil manner, then the responsibility shall fall upon the contractor. It shall be no concern of the wholesalers or of the proprietors of the dye-shops" (*ibid.*, part 1: 339). An inscription about fifty years later stressed that "when the contractor receives the cloth and passes it on, the personal record of the calenderers, and any loss or damage to the goods, shall be the concern not of the cloth merchant but of the contractor" (*ibid.*: 342).

These arrangements seem to have been devised by the wholesalers themselves, wealthy businessmen with considerable influence over the local officials. Rates of pay, both to the contractors and to the artisans, were fixed at a level favorable to the merchants until some time in the 1860's. The latter obviously counted on playing one contractor off against another in order to obtain the best service. Early in the nineteenth century the wholesalers strenuously resisted the efforts of the contractors to ensure a higher degree of predictability in their operations by having the wholesalers advance them money for work to be done later (their pretext being the difficulties created by rising rice prices). In 1834 the wholesalers had a decree issued (*ibid.*, part 2: 463):

The workshop proprietors [contractors] undertake to calender cloth for the wholesale firms. This resembles the way in which a tenant undertakes to cultivate a field for its owner. If the tenant is in arrears with his rent, the owner may dismiss him and engage someone else in his place. If the artisans in some workshop do not give a high enough luster to the cloth, how can it be that the merchants should not be able to go elsewhere?

This is a striking example of the substitution of commerce for management.

The immediate reason for the creation of the contractor system seems to have been labor discipline. The calenderers were an unruly lot, and after they had struck in 1670 for higher wages it was laid down by the local authorities that "henceforth all the calenderers must submit to the supervision of the workshop heads [contractors], and the workshop heads must submit to the control of the merchants" (*ibid.*, part 1: 339).

During the early eighteenth century further restrictive measures were imposed on the artisans. These included the compulsory formation of groups whose members were mutually responsible for each others' behavior, and the imposition of severe restrictions on the hours during which calenderers might go out and about.

The exact status of the artisans is hard to define. In one sense they were independent craftsmen employed not by a contractor but through him. In another sense of course they were highly dependent on the contractor, not only for the provision of work, tools, and a workplace, but also for money to buy food and other necessities until they were paid. The actual payments were also channelled through the hands of the contractor, which made it possible for him to retain more than the amount to which he was legally entitled.

Further research is needed to find out whether this strange Soochow system was unique or had counterparts elsewhere. In either event it epitomizes the divorce, so characteristic of the cotton industry in late traditional China, between the merchant's concern with the market and the artisan's concern with production.

Chang Han's prosperous ancestor I-an, with his twenty looms for hemp cloth, must have had some counterparts among the urban cotton weavers; but on the whole it seems reasonable to conclude that an industry enormous in the aggregate was created not by expanding the size of the units of production but by coordinating a growing multitude of small producers through a market mechanism.

Toward a High-Level Equilibrium Trap

After the later sixteenth century the structure of the Chinese cotton industry clearly made invention less likely than before. Organization through the market instead of a putting-out system, the tendency to separate selling from producing, and, it should be added, the disappearance of a class of manor-lords whose supervision of their serfs and tenants had given them a personal interest in technology, all combined to reduce the numbers of those equipped by experience, resources, and education to become inventors or sponsors of invention. But such people can hardly have disappeared altogether. An invention like the spinning jenny was certainly not beyond the capacity even of those peasants and ordinary city-dwellers whose wives engaged in part-time spinning and weaving, and who indeed sometimes engaged in it themselves (Nishijima 1947: 131). Why, then, did no spinning jenny appear? We can only assume that at this later date economic forces in general no longer combined in such a way as to reward inventive success with fortune.

In particular, why at some point did the economy not generate a demand for cloth that was rising fast enough to smash through the institutional and structural barriers to invention? The answer to this cannot be the usual one, namely the lack of a large enough market. The market for the cloth produced in the Yangtze delta was demonstrably enormous. The geographic range of the trade was about eight hundred miles from north to south, and on a Western European scale the south Kiangsu cotton manufacture would have been a flourishing international export industry. Here, by way of illustration, is a part of Yeh Meng-chu's account of Shang-hai Hsien in the later seventeenth century (Yeh, ch. 7: 5a–6a):

Cotton Cloth. Our *hsien* used to produce three grades. . . . The broadest and finest of them was called Standard Cloth. The best was made in the town of San-lin-t'ang, the next best in the town of Chou-p'u, and that made in the capital of the *hsien* was the poorest. All three qualities went to Shensi, Shansi, and the border areas. . . . Rather narrower and longer than Standard Cloth was the kind called Midloom. It went to Hupeh, Hunan, Kiangsi, Kwangtung, and Kwangsi. The price was the same as that of Standard Cloth.

Under the preceding dynasty [the Ming] a thriving business was carried on in Standard Cloth. The wealthy merchants who came to purchase it each possessed a capital of many tens of thousands of ounces of silver. The richest may have had several hundreds of thousands, the poorest perhaps ten thousand. For this reason the brokers treated the cotton cloth merchants as if they were princes or marquises, but at the same time struggled against them as if they had been a hostile army. No broker who did not enjoy the backing of a powerful family could stand up to them. Few merchants bought Midloom, and those that did had a limited supply of capital. Thus not much of this cloth was produced. Under the present [Ch'ing] dynasty few of the great merchants who dealt in Standard Cloth have continued to come. Recently none of them has brought more than ten thousand ounces, and some have brought as little as two or three thousand. Their profits have also been limited. The trade in Midloom has, on the contrary, prospered. Those who used to deal in Standard Cloth have now turned to Midloom. . . . There also used to be a very narrow and short variety called Smallcloth. It was little more than a foot wide and did not exceed sixteen feet in length. It was only sold to places like Jao-chou in Kiangsi. . . . After 1669 the Jao-chou merchants stopped coming, and Smallcloth consequently disappeared.

The responsiveness of the traditional industry to the ebb and flow of market forces is clearly apparent.

Also apparent from Yeh Meng-chu's observations is the degree to which the welfare of the delta region was linked with long-distance commerce. He wrote of the troubles in North China in 1641 (*ibid.*, ch. 1: 10b):

Half of the profits of Sung-chiang Prefecture depend upon spinning and weaving. After Shantung had been afflicted with famine and rebellion, and Honan had been even worse disrupted, the people of our region exchanged their children to eat or broke up corpses to steam them. The cotton cloth merchants failed to come, and the inhabitants of Sung-chiang could only stand and wait to die.

Likewise in 1644, "The merchants did not come and the prices of goods rose like boiling water" (*ibid.*: 12a). Except, of course, for the price of raw cotton, which temporarily plummeted to about a third of its former level (*ibid.*, ch. 7: 4b–5b).

The inhibition of mechanical invention in the Chinese cotton industry cannot therefore be attributed to the smallness of markets or the weakness of commercial influences. Nor can it have been due to primarily technical difficulties. Except for the concept, embodied in Arkwright's spinning frame, of rollers turning at different speeds to attenuate a roving, the Chinese in the fourteenth century already had all the mechanical knowledge needed to turn their primitive spinning machines into quite efficient means of mass production. The real key to the problem almost certainly lies elsewhere. The Chinese economy as a whole was caught in what may be called a high-level equilibrium trap:* a situation to which most of the usual criteria of "backwardness" do not apply, yet characterized by a technological immobility that makes any sustained qualitative economic progress impossible. A full analysis of this trap is given in my forthcoming book *The Pattern of the Chinese Past*. Here, for reasons of space, it is possible to offer only a summary of that analysis.

The basic idea is that stimulus to invention in the economic field usually takes the form of a change in the pattern of supply and demand. This change creates both new difficulties and new opportunities. The response to these challenges does not necessarily have to be technological; it may be organizational, political, or even military. Sometimes a response of the latter kind will simply re-establish equilibrium. In most cases, however, the effect of the response will be to alter yet again the pattern of supply and demand, and so set fresh challenges to individual and collective ingenuity. But if, for whatever reason, the flow of such causally interlocking changes comes to an end, there will also be an end to economically significant invention. It will not reappear until some extraneous event (such as the impact of the West on China in the nineteenth century) disrupts the equilibrium.

* The concept of the high-level equilibrium trap first arose in the course of conversations with Dr. Radha Sinha of Glasgow University in 1968.

There were several reasons why such an equilibrium became established in China between the fourteenth and the eighteenth centuries. The most important of these was the growing pressure of population on arable land. This meant that the surplus product available for generating demand above the level of subsistence was progressively reduced. It is important to distinguish here between three phases. During the first of these, from about 600 to 1300, the expansion of the Han Chinese into the new lands of central and southern China, and the development of wet-field rice cultivation there, had made agriculture into a leading sector, transmitting the effects of its increased productivity throughout the economy. After about 1300 this was no longer so. The recovery of the north after the period of Chin Tartar and Mongol domination needs further study, but in general it is true to say that agriculture now only expanded more or less in step with population growth. Improved techniques were no longer invented, but what may be termed "the level of practice" improved. The best techniques were more widely diffused; productivity was raised by increased inputs of labor per acre, by more capital formation (particularly in the form of irrigation projects), and by better organization (notably a denser market network and freer forms of land tenure). During this second phase, however, agriculture had lost its former capacity to act as a leading sector. The third phase set in gradually between 1600 and 1800, spreading from region to region, and not becoming firmly established on a national scale until the latter date. In this phase the pressure of population on land led to a serious problem of mere subsistence. New land brought under the plow was of a sharply declining quality, and the potentialities of better practice for increasing output per acre were virtually exhausted. Further increases in productivity could be accomplished only by a radically new technology based on inputs created by an industrial revolution that as yet did not exist: chemical fertilizers, scientifically bred seeds, motorized farm machinery, concrete, and electricity.

In the accompanying diagram (Figure 4) Dr. Radha Sinha of Glasgow University has symbolized in simplified form the progress of the pre-modern agricultural sector to the high-level equilibrium point at the end of the second phase. The function of the diagram is to distinguish between intermediate equilibria (here symbolized by the points E_1, E_2, etc.) and the high-level equilibrium trap (E_T). For the sake of convenience the total area of arable land is taken as constant. The potential output of the best pre-modern agricultural technology for a given input of labor under the best practice is represented by the curve $OAFE_TT$. The series of short curves P_1, P_2, etc., shows potential output for the best technology with less than the best, but improving, practice. By "practice" at any point must be understood a given *mix* of inputs per acre (labor, fixed capital, fertilizer, and so forth), and a given level of organizational efficiency. The quality of the inputs, as between one mix and another, does not vary. No attempt is made to represent actual output, which may be thought of as a composite formed of the curves P_1, P_2, etc., the exact shape being determined by historical accident. The straight line OS shows the amount of farm output needed for the subsistence of a given population. There is an oversimplification here in that "Labor" is being made to mean both "hours of work" and "mouths to feed," which are not at all the same. The excuse for this sleight-of-hand is that it allows the potential surplus with best, and with less than best, practice to be conveniently represented by the distance beween OS and the curve $OAFE_TT$, and between OS and the appropriate curve P, respectively. The lines AC and BC are an example.

So long as output remains above OS, there is a surplus and hence an element of dynamism in the economy. At the intermediate equilibrium points E_1, E_2, etc., however, the surplus disappears, and the level of practice must be improved if the population is to be maintained above subsistence level. Only when the point E_T is reached is this escape route barred: increased inputs of labor, capital, and organization yield no returns. Pre-modern technology and practice are both at a maximum. The Chinese farm economy had not actually reached E_T in 1800, but

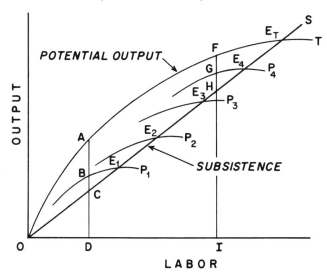

FIGURE 4. THE HIGH-LEVEL EQUILIBRIUM TRAP

it had approached it so closely that the surpluses created by improved practice had become much smaller relative to total output than in earlier times (contrast BC/CD with GH/HI), and their influence in creating new demand had been much diminished.

Pre-modern water transport in China went through the same kind of evolution as agriculture. By the early twentieth century it could carry most goods more cheaply than railroads over comparable routes (Koizumi 1943: 70–72). When the modern transport revolution came to China, its full effects were reserved for the peripheral inland areas not served by good water transport.

Another aspect of the trap was the huge size of the Chinese economy. By itself, bigness has no great significance. The crucial additional factor in China's case was that the country was not just a loosely-knit collection of local economies, but an economic unit effectively integrated by trade. (This integration, too, was the outcome of a high level of pre-modern development.) The consequence of great size combined with economic unity was that, in absolute terms, a much larger stimulus was needed to provoke a response than in, let us say, the eighteenth-century British economy. Presumably, therefore, it was less likely to occur.

China's foreign trade in cotton textiles may serve as an example. Exports out of Canton rose from 0.37 million lengths a year in 1786 to almost 3.4 million lengths in 1819 (Ch'üan 1958: 40). But this was a negligible percentage of total Chinese output. Mr. Wang, one of about seventy Soochow wholesalers, handled 40 percent of this amount at his peak. Neither the growth of the export trade, nor its demise in the 1830's as a result of British competition, can have affected the Chinese cotton industry very much.

The great size of the economy (given its commercial integration) also worked against the creation of atypical local effects. In the absence of overall rapid change, pressures building up in a single locality can easily be relieved by merely marginal adjustments made through the rest of a large economy. Overall growth was held back primarily by a long-established combination of low farm productivity per capita and very high productivity per acre. This was not the case in the small, and recently backward, economy of eighteenth-century Britain.

The Commercialization of Agriculture in Modern China

RAMON H. MYERS

Since the 1890's the peasant economies of mainland China and Taiwan have become increasingly dependent on the market. The marketed surplus, or the amount of its crop that each farm family chose to place on the market for sale to obtain cash, rose over time and became a higher proportion of total agricultural production. The process by which the marketed surplus increased, defined below as the commercialization of agriculture, was associated with unimproved, and sometimes deteriorating, living standards and overcrowding of villages for the mainland Chinese peasantry, but with rising real income and greater welfare for the Taiwanese peasantry. In mainland China the marketed surplus was gradually increased by improvements in transport and expanding trade that enabled farms to adopt new cropping systems, engage in crop specialization, and apply more labor to the production of certain cash crops. Very little change in farming technology occurred, however. In Taiwan the marketed surplus increased in the same way, but substantial technological change occurred as well: farmers began to use new seeds, inorganic fertilizers, and irrigation; in essence, a fertilizer-seed revolution had begun.

This essay* examines the economic behavior of family farms as they began to produce an expanding marketed surplus in pre-war China and Taiwan after the 1890's. The first section shows that Taiwan gradually surpassed the Mainland in its agricultural growth rate for both food and industrial crops. Section two demonstrates that in spite of diverging farm production and trade performances between the two systems and different geographical conditions and cropping practices, the char-

* I want to thank the East Asian Research Center, Harvard University, for its support of the research on which this study is based, and the Ford Foundation for enabling me to finish writing this essay in 1970–71.

acteristics and the economic behavior of their family farms remained quite similar. Section three shows that the dependency of the family farm on the market increased during the period discussed until peasants in both systems marketed roughly half of what they produced. This section also shows that small farms specialized in one or two crops and purchased much of their food, including food-grains, from the market. Large farms, by contrast, did not carry specialization so far and produced more of their own food-grains and other food. Thus, although large farms produced a larger absolute surplus for the market, small farms marketed relatively more of what they produced and were more dependent on the market than large farms. The final section argues that commercialization affected family farms differently in the two systems because technological change accompanied the process of commercialization in Taiwan but not in mainland China. Mainland farms increased their production and their marketed surplus, but within the limits prescribed by traditional farming technology. Commercialization of agriculture permitted this agrarian system to support a larger rural population and an expanded urban economy without any noticeable changes in rural living standards and welfare. The mainland peasant economy clearly possessed responsive elements capable of supporting the same rural transformation that occurred in Taiwan; but without peace, stability, and a sustained government program to promote technological change in agriculture, these elements could not operate as they did in Taiwan. In Taiwan, the Japanese colonial government promoted organizational changes that led to a new farming technology for the peasantry and produced a real agricultural revolution.

Agricultural Production and Trade, 1890–1937

Between 1890 and 1937, the rural population of China grew 1 or 2 percent a year,* whereas the largest cities grew between 3 and 5 percent a year (K'ung 1965: 209–29). Exports, of which raw and processed agricultural products made up about two-thirds, increased about 2.1 percent a year (Cheng 1956: 258–59). Chinese agriculture managed to keep pace with all this growth without becoming excessively dependent on imported food (Myers, 1970, part 4). Food imports rose immediately after the first world war, but increased greatly thereafter only during periods of civil war or natural calamity, as in 1922–23, 1926–27, and 1931–32 (Ou 1934, Appendix). After 1933 they declined, only to rise again after the outbreak of war (Inspector General of Customs,

---

* These estimates of rural population growth were derived from C. M. Chiao and J. L. Buck (Chiao and Buck, 1928, 219–35). They conclude that China's rural population was increasing 1.43 percent a year or doubling every 70 years.

1934–40). This is a remarkable performance for a farming system that received virtually no government assistance and relied exclusively upon traditional farming technology.

Since 1900 Taiwan's population has risen fourfold, yet farm production has more than kept pace with demand, and surpluses have accumulated to permit an expansion of farm exports. The total value of exports grew tenfold between 1910 and 1940 (Myers 1969a: 27). During this period the six leading agricultural exports made up approximately four-fifths of this total, with rice and sugar the major contributors. In 1910 rice exports to Japan were 104,000 metric tons, or 17 percent of the island's total rice production. Twenty years later rice exports had trebled, and comprised 30 percent of the island's total production, whereas by 1937 the export volume had reached 692,000 metric tons a year, or half of all the rice grown in that year (*ibid*.: 27). This large increase was achieved without any reduction in the level of domestic consumption, although the population nearly doubled during the same period. In the case of sugarcane, production trebled between 1910 and 1937 and exports of sugar increased in the same proportion, while per-capita sugar consumption rose slowly. Between 1910 and 1944 the total value of imports trebled, but imports of food and fibers averaged somewhat less than half the total before 1930, and even less by 1940 (*ibid*.: 28). While imports of fibers represented a fairly constant proportion of the total over most of the period, a trend toward self-sufficiency in food emerged between 1910 and 1940. Between 1905 and 1943 the total population of Taiwan increased 1.84 percent a year whereas agricultural production increased an average of about 3.45 percent a year (Hsieh and Lee 1958: 4), or nearly twice as fast as population.

Characteristics of the Family Farm and Economic Behavior of Farmers

Although the Chinese and Taiwanese patterns of farm production and levels of farm income steadily diverged after 1900, basic rural institutions and the economic behavior of family farmers were similar in the two areas, and remained so. Land and other property continued to be divided equally between the male heirs in each farm family (Myers 1969b: 349–70). Land continued to be pledged to obtain short- and long-term credit. Finally, land continued to be leased and rented for short terms, mainly by oral contract. Tenants paid their rent in cash or in kind, according to local custom.

The characteristics of farm households and economic behavior as related to creating a marketable surplus were also similar in the two farming systems. First, farm size and wealth (value of property and

TABLE 1. FARM DEFICIT OR SURPLUS IN 1951 AND 1961

Land ownership (*chia, ca.* 2.5 A.)	Agricultural earnings N.T.$	Total farm expenditures N.T.$	Farm surplus or deficit N.T.$
1951 (391 farms):			
.99 or less	$8,048	$9,012	−$964
1.0–1.99	11,320	12,112	−792
2.0–2.99	16,629	16,633	−4
3.0–5.99	19,883	18,892	+991
6.0–13.00	23,852	23,704	+148
1961 (223 farms):			
.49 or less	24,631	28,437	−3,806
.5–.99	38,105	38,703	−598
1.0–1.99	54,855	53,320	+1,535
2.0–2.99	78,161	74,280	+3,881
3.0–5.99	115,792	92,116	+23,676

SOURCE: Calculated from data in Department of Agriculture and Forestry 1952, 1962.

farm assets) correlated positively with household size and number of man-equivalents available for farm labor (Buck 1937b: 297, 300). Since farmers derived income from activities on and off the farm, a large, healthy household labor force was indispensable for maintaining and increasing such income. As more income was earned, a household could acquire more land and augment the farm's wealth.

Second, non-farm cash income was very important for enabling farmers to cover their expenditures. Large farms typically covered costs and even produced a modest surplus. Small and medium farms could cover costs only when farm income was supplemented by non-farm income. Only after 1950 in Taiwan does a trend emerge for small farmers to cover costs and even obtain a small surplus from farm income alone. When survey data for 1951 and 1961 are compared, we observe that by the end of that decade farms of 1–2.99 hectares finally began to cover their costs and obtain a surplus from the year's farming operation (see Table 1).

Third, peasants borrowed money according to their capabilities to repay debt and their credit rating with moneylenders. When debt is considered by farm size, the large farmers appear to be more heavily in debt, often two and three times as heavily as the owners of the smaller, poorer farms. In a sample of 184 farms surveyed in two villages of Hopei in 1931, wealthy farms of 60 *mou* and above constituted only ten percent of all households but accounted for a third of the total debt. The poorest farms, under 20 *mou* and making up half the total sample, accounted for only a fourth of total indebtedness (Feng 1936, 2: 650). This pattern prevailed in Taiwan as well (Taiwan sōtokufu shokusankyoku 1924: 156–204).

Fourth, consumption and investment patterns of family farms in the two systems were remarkably similar. When the demand for certain food and industrial crops increased because of improved transport, expansion of trade, and urban growth, peasants responded by specializing in these products and marketing their surplus, as they obviously expected this increased demand to continue for some time.

As peasants increase their marketed surplus, their money income increases. If total household earnings (farm plus non-farm income) rise, do peasants then consume more or save more to invest in land and other forms of capital?

Several consumption patterns should first be mentioned before answering this question. First, per-capita expenditures for food, clothing, furniture, luxury items, education, and transport were higher for upper-income than for lower-income farms. Table 2 illustrates this pattern with data showing expenditures by farm size from a 1935–36 study of a village in Shansi Province. Second, high-income farmers not only consumed more food, but consumed higher-quality food than low-income farmers. In Table 3 I have shown this pattern in data from a sample of 36 Taiwanese farms surveyed to determine the quantity of food consumed per person per day by farm size.

TABLE 2. FOOD EXPENDITURES AND HOUSEHOLD EARNINGS IN NINETY-NINE
HOUSEHOLDS OF PAI CHIA WU VILLAGE, SHANSI (1935)

Category	Farm-size category (mou)				
	5–30	31–50	51–130	131–300	Average
Number of households	44	36	10	9	
Average farm size (mou)	14.5	33.8	106.0	192.0	35.7
Average number of persons per farm	3.8	5.6	7.2	9.2	6.3
Farm income (yüan)	93.70	131.07	446.57	834.96	376.57
Non-farm income (yüan)	32.05	21.11	28.00	44.00	31.29
Total household earnings (yüan)	125.75	152.18	474.57	878.96	407.86
Household consumption outlays (yüan)	91.45	148.48	321.10	627.12	297.04
Average food expenditures per farm (yüan)	57.63	93.10	214.07	395.00	189.95
Food outlays as a percent of outlays	63.0%	61.1%	45.1%	44.9%	53.3%
Average consumption expenditure per person (yüan)	24.19	26.50	44.60	68.16	47.15
Average earnings per person (yüan)	24.79	27.37	66.37	95.54	53.51
Food outlays per person (yüan)	15.24	16.74	29.94	42.93	26.21

SOURCE: Calculated from data in Tōa keizai chōsakyoku 1936.

TABLE 3. DAILY PER-CAPITA FOOD CONSUMPTION BY FARM SIZE IN TAIWAN, 1920

Farm size (chia)	No. of farms	Av. farm size	Rice (liters)	Sweet potatoes (grams)	Daily per-capita consumption					
					Veg. (grams)	Meat and fish (grams)	Veg, oil, etc. (grams)	Flour, bean curd (grams)	Salt and sugar[a] (grams)	Tea (liters)
3.60–11.85	12	5.65	.93078	485.93	395.85	72.39	9.26	48.12	16.42	2.58
1.96–3.59	12	2.57	.75762	907.76	495.11	108.87	13.78	56.33	24.58	0.29
1.95 or less	12	1.50	.79830	1,335.38	367.61	74.50	14.19	40.93	15.47	0.25
Average		2.91	.82890	910.88	419.51	85.13	12.41	48.45	18.82	1.04

SOURCE: Taiwan sōtokufu shokusankyoku 1921: 4–5.
[a] Miso is included in the figures for salt and sugar.

In Table 2 farm size correlates positively with persons per household; farm income and total earnings rise with farm size. Food expenditures per farm and per capita also rise as farm size and earnings increase. However, wealthy farms spend a larger share of their outlays for non-food items than do small farms. In Table 3 the larger and wealthier farms have a higher per-capita rice consumption than do small farms. Poorer families consume more sweet potato than rice, consuming a food they consider inferior food in order to market their rice. In North China after World War I poor peasants began switching to potato to free more land to grow cotton and wheat, which could be sold to buy more food than they could produce on their few small plots (Chūgoku 1957: 514). Family farms in both systems cultivated food crops that had high yields per acre and high caloric value in order to free land for high-value cash crops. Wealthy farms in both systems ate better and maintained higher living standards than did poorer farms. The fact that wealthy farms spent a smaller fraction of total expenditures upon food than did poorer farms suggests that as incomes and expenditures rise, a smaller fraction goes for food. Such a pattern does not necessarily mean that a higher fraction of additional income is saved. However, the following analysis shows this to be the case.

I have selected cash-income and expenditure data from mainland and Taiwan farm surveys conducted between 1920 and 1940 to show how expenditure patterns changed as income increased.* I present the statistical findings in Table 4 for seven samples of farms in northern and central China, where data were expressed in Chinese currency and for ten samples in northern China, Manchuria, and Taiwan, where data were expressed in Japanese currency, a total of 652 farms. The results are divided into geographical and currency groupings and arranged according to increasing village income within each grouping. About half of the samples yielded coefficients of determination (r^2) higher than 0.5,

---

* The association of income and expenditure was determined by solving the following linear relationship (Blyth 1969: 357):

$$E_{ij} = a_{ij} + b_j Y_i$$

where E_{ij} is the expenditure of the ith family for the jth commodity, Y_i is the cash income of the ith family, and a_{ij} and b_j are the constant parameters for the cash expenditures. The constant a_{ij} can have a zero, positive, or negative value; it may represent subsistence consumption, or it may serve to fix the level of income at which cash outlays for a commodity begin. The variable b_j represents the typical marginal propensity to consume and denotes the fraction of additional income spent on consumption; $1–b_j$ represents the marginal propensity to save. When data are fitted to this equation and the parameters obtained, we can observe whether peasants spend or save the larger share of the increase as their income rises by noting whether the marginal propensity to consume has a high or low value.

TABLE 4. AGGREGATE MARGINAL PROPENSITY TO CONSUME AND SAVE
(CASH INCOME)

Village sample	Marginal propensity to consume	Coefficient of determination (r^2)	Cash income per household	Marginal propensity to save
Mainland farms (value unit: *yüan*)				
Yen chia shang, Ch'ang-shu Hsien, Kiangsu (1939)	.25	.240	100.8	.75
Ta pei kuan, P'ing-ku Hsien, Hopei (1936)	.10	.319	120.0	.90
7 villages, Wu-hsi Hsien, Kiangsu (1940)	.72	.680	167.3	.28
Liang k'o chuang, Ch'ang-li Hsien, Hopei (1936)	.37	.614	169.5	.53
Mi-ch'ang, Feng-jun Hsien, Hopei (1936)	.23	.676	259.1	.77
T'ou tsung miao, Nan-t'ung Hsien, Kiangsu (1940)	.29	.715	378.6	.71
4 villages, Sung-kiang Hsien, Kiangsu (1939)	.29	.441	550.5	.71
Mainland farms (value unit: *yen*)				
Ma, Honan (1939)	.32	.575	589	.68
Mi-ch'ang, Hopei (1938)	.30	.647	666	.70
Wu-kuan, Hopei (1940)	.26	.448	885	.74
Mi-ch'ang, Hopei (1939)	.30	.409	1,172	.70
17 Russian farms, North Manchuria (1938)	.35	.649	2,517	.65
Taiwanese farms (value unit: *yen*)				
50 rice farms (1931)	.50	.431	960	.50
22 rice farms (1937)	.25	.230	1,333	.75
25 sugar farms (1921)	.26	.154	1,339	.74
68 sugar farms (1921)	.44	.887	1,676	.56
28 sugar farms (1931)	.22	.261	3,146	.78

NOTE: In each case the t-test was performed, and the results show each to be significantly different from zero at the .05 level.

a result that suggests a fairly close association between cash expenditures and income. In most of the mainland and Taiwanese samples, the propensity to save is high. These results indicate that even where cash income is high, the propensity to save remains high.* The fact that the saving pattern of farms in the two systems is similar is all the more striking since Taiwanese farms were experiencing a gradual rise in real income per capita during this period.

* Plotting the coefficients for marginal propensity against cash income by village sample yields a curve (Myers n.d., chap. 6).

Dependence on Markets

It remains now to show the dependence of family farms on the market and the consequences of that dependence for farm production and income over a period of time. Market-dependency can be measured in two ways. The usual procedure is to calculate the percentage of farm earnings formed by farm receipts, where farm receipts is the income earned in cash from exchanging output on the market, and farm earnings are farm receipts plus the value of products and services produced and consumed on the farm valued at market prices (farm privileges). As farm earnings rise, this percentage usually rises and can be referred to as the commercial index. A rising index attests that peasants are marketing a larger share of their output, receiving more cash income, and becoming more dependent upon the market. A high commercial index is interpreted to mean that peasants have become highly responsive to market change, innovative, and quick to adopt new ideas and techniques. A low index is supposed to reflect the opposite situation or pattern of behavior. It is never clear at what point on the index farms are supposed to begin to exhibit commercial as opposed to subsistence farming behavior (Miracle 1968: 292–310), partly because the index figure is nearly useless unless related to the cropping patterns, the farm prices, and the level of farm technology in the area being studied.

Market-dependency can also be measured by noting how much farmers purchase for their personal use and for use in operating their farms. This amount is determined by the availability of goods the farmers desire and by the terms of exchange between these goods and those they sell. If farmers see over the period of a year or more that goods are becoming scarce and will thus cost a larger part of their marketable surplus, they may simply consume more of what they produce and market less. If they perceive that goods are plentiful, and of a quality superior to that of the usual assortment, they may be encouraged to sell and buy more, thus pushing the commercial index upward. However, this can occur only if output can be increased to enlarge the marketed surplus.

Did the commercial index for farms throughout China and Taiwan rise after the 1890's, and if so, how high had it risen by the 1920's and 1930's? Unfortunately we do not have the comparative data for single villages or rural communities that would allow us to determine precisely how much the commercial index rose over this period. However, enough evidence exists to allow us to infer that the commercial index did indeed rise after the late nineteenth century.

Let us assume a largely rural economy without foreign trade, an urban

population growing at the same rate as the rural, and a certain combination of food and industrial products exported to the urban sector.
These conditions resemble those of China before 1890. Let us assume
now that transportation improves and foreign trade begins because of
commercial contact with the West. New market demands are suddenly
imposed upon the village economy, and prices of certain crops begin
to rise. Let us assume further that villages cannot increase their cultivated acreage because all the good land is already being farmed, and
they have no means to reclaim poor land. Farmers are encouraged to
specialize in certain crops because they will bring more income than
others, and because improved transport and marketing have made certain goods—including those they still need but no longer produce—
available at prices they can afford. Some areas produce mainly food,
while others produce mainly industrial crops. The economy begins to
export more industrial crops (raw or processed); urban population increases faster than that of the villages because new employment opportunities attract peasants to the cities. Urban demand for food rises but
is satisfied by drawing more food from the countryside and by importing
food from abroad when the harvest has been poor. These conditions
approximate the China of 1890–1937.

As China's growth rate in food production matched that of population while the growth rate in industrial-crop production also rose,
family farms must have increased both their total production and the
proportion of their marketed surplus. For example, farms in Region A
began to reallocate some of their land and labor so as to produce less
grain but more industrial crops, while farms in Region B did exactly
the opposite. Let us assume that farmers in Region A obtained increasing returns for their labor but farmers in Region B received the same
constant return for their labor; greater specialization would result in
larger output of industrial crops and greater exchange (see next section). If per-capita grain consumption remained constant in the two
regions over this period, and if no grain was brought in from the outside, then the marketed surplus of individual farms for both grain and
industrial crops had to rise.

According to a study by Dr. Friedrich Otte, coastal urban centers
became dependent on imports of cereals from abroad only when the
grain supply from the countryside was interrupted by poor harvests or
by civil war. Otte also pointed out that the Chinese farmer had responded quickly to market demand to cultivate crops he could sell at
more advantageous terms of exchange (Otte 1928: 369):

The Chinese farmer is fairly quick to notice his own advantage provided he is left alone and is sure that the fruits of his labor become his. One need only point to the tremendous increase in the cultivation of groundnuts in the neighborhood of the Tsinan-Tsingtao railway, or of soya bean and wheat along all the Manchurian railway, or to the transformation of agriculture around Shanghai: wheat and cotton instead of rice, in order to realize that the passiveness even of the northern Chinese farmer is by no means due to dullness of perception.

The cultivated area devoted to barley, indigo, kaoliang, millet, rice, and sugarcane gradually declined after 1900, whereas that devoted to sweet potato, soy beans, sesame, peanut, rapeseed, cotton, and corn increased (Buck 1937a: 217). Sweet potato and corn yield more calories per unit of land, so that growing them releases land for industrial crops like cotton, rape, peanut, sesame, and soybeans. The legume soybean not only provided the peasant with cash but restored nutrients to the soil because of its nitrogen-fixing properties. In North China the cultivation of cotton and sweet potato steadily increased, and in central China peasants used more land for oil-seed-bearing crops (Murakami 1941: 1–44). For Shantung and Hopei I have measured the change in land use and found that in 40 out of 108 *hsien* in Shantung, the four crops with the largest cultivated area in 1910—none of which would be considered a cash crop—were replaced by one or more cash crops by 1930. In 50 out of 129 *hsien* of Hopei the same change occurred (Myers 1970: 190–93).

By the 1920's and 1930's, family farms were heavily dependent upon markets. A Russian survey of Chinese family farms in northern Manchuria (1922–24) found that 48 percent of their farm output was marketed (Mantetsu Taiheiyō 1931: 60). Between 1921 and 1925 John L. Buck collected similar data for family farms in northern and east-central China, and found that average farm receipts exceeded 50 percent of total farm earnings whether the family rented, owned part and rented part, or owned all of the land it cultivated (Buck 1930: 65–80). For east-central China, farm receipts amounted to about two-thirds of farm earnings (*ibid.*: 65–80). The percentage of total inputs purchased from the market by farms exceeded 40 percent for owner-cultivator and owner-cultivator-tenant. When farms in Manchuria, North China, and Taiwan are compared for their market-dependency, the average percentage of total farm earnings that is gained from the farm itself ranged from a low of 40 to a high of 70 percent (Myers n.d., chap. 3, table 2). If these sample data were drawn only from villages located near county-seat markets or large towns, the high rural market-dependency claimed so far might be considered exaggerated. The data are drawn from all sorts of villages, however. It should be pointed out, moreover, that considerable variation in market-dependency existed even in districts located along major railway lines, where high, perhaps uniform, market-dependency would be expected. A survey of *hsien* along the Hankow–Peking railway line revealed that for prime crops such as wheat, the marketed surplus ranged from 19.7 to 90.7 percent of farm production (Ch'en Pai-chuang 1936, statistical appendix). The same wide range characterized the marketed surplus for fibers and oil seed, although the average commercial index of all districts for all crops was uniformly high. Simply being close to a railroad did not mean that the peasant always marketed a high percentage of all crops. The degree of crop specialization varied from area to area and even from farm to farm with varying soil conditions, market demand, and labor supplies. In many of these districts off-farm employment gave peasants high wages, so that many farms could not get enough workers to cultivate the cash crops requiring more intensive labor than conventional food crops. Finally, a farmer planted many kinds of crops, of which one or two might be marketed in their entirety but the remainder would be consumed on the farm. The commercial index for a given crop might be very high, but when all crops are taken together the index would be lower. Sidney D. Gamble surveyed four hundred farms in Ting Hsien of central Hopei in 1927 and found that only 25 percent of total farm production was marketed. But when wheat, peanut, cotton, and sesame were considered separately, the marketed proportions ran 42, 93, 86, and 92 percent respectively (1945: 356).

As for the economic behavior of different-sized farms and their market dependency, survey data strongly indicate that as farm size increased, farm receipts rose and large farms earned between two and five times as much as small farms (Myers n.d., chap. 3). Small farms tended to market a higher percentage of what they produced than did large farms. This assertion seems valid on the basis of scattered data showing small farms allocating a higher percentage of their land and labor to industrial crops than did large farms. Table 5 presents data from village surveys to show how the percentage of land farmers allocated to different crops varies according to farm size. The trend is for small farms to use a higher percentage of their land for cash crops than do large farms.

This does not mean that small farms provided the largest share of the total marketed surplus from villages. Village farm survey data indi-

TABLE 5. LAND ALLOCATION BY FARM SIZE FOR VARIOUS VILLAGES IN NORTH
AND EAST-CENTRAL CHINA (1930's)

Area and village	Size of farm (*mou*)	Average size of farm (*mou*)	Allocation of land (*percent*)		
			Cotton	Grain	Vegetables
Mi-ch'ang Village, Feng-jen	41–100	72.7	52%	34%	14%
Hsien, Hopei (1937)	21–40	26.7	56	36	8
	less than 20	13.2	70	28	2
Ma-ts'un Village, Huo-Lu	46–60	51.3	25	49	26
Hsien, Hopei (1939)	31–45	42.1	20	51	29
	0–30	15.4	25	35	40
			Cotton and peanuts	Grain and vege- tables	
Ta wei chia t'un Village,	180–above		32%	68%	
Kwantung (1936)	61–179		29	71	
	31–60		38	62	
	less than 30		38	62	
			Cotton	Grain and vege- tables	
T'ou tsung miao Village,	6.0–8.0	6.3	43%	56%	
Nan-t'ung Hsien,	3.0–5.9	4.2	40	60	
Kiangsu (1939)	1.0–2.9	2.3	58	42	
	less than 1.9	0.9	48	52	
			Cotton	Rice	Other foods
Yao-ching Village, Tai-	15.0–25.0	20.1	25%	67%	8%
ts'ang Hsien, Kiangsu	10.0–14.9	11.9	36	58	6
(1939)	3.0– 9.9	6.1	32	66	2
	0.0– 2.9	1.7	10	85	5
			Cotton	Wheat	Rice
Village near Shanghai	16–25	18.5	36.7%	20.5%	21.6%
(1932)	9–15	12.4	38.1	18.4	20.8
	0–8	6.1	33.5	24.8	12.2
			Cotton	Peanuts	Millet
Village near Tsingtai	21–30	24.8	8.0%	5.0%	11.5%
(1938)	16–20	17.8	30.9	12.9	29.7
	11–15	12.5	28.9	11.1	24.6
	6–10	6.5	37.8	12.5	23.5
	0–5	2.3	25.0	62.7	11.1

SOURCE: Data for the villages are drawn from the following sources, respectively: Hoku-Shi jimmukyoku chōsabu 1939: 7; Hoku-Shi jimmukyoku chōsabu 1941: 6; Suzuki Kohei 1936: 183; Mantetsu Shanhai chōsabu 1941, Tables 1 and 4.1; Mantetsu Shanhai jimmusho chōsashitsu 1940, Tables 8.1 and 9.1 in Statistical Appendix; Feng Ho-fa 1936, I: 241–301; Mantetsu Hoku-Shi jimmukyoku chōsabu 1939: 40–45.

cate that large farms, households owning more than 15 and 20 *mou* and usually comprising less than a quarter of village households, supplied between two-fifths and three-quarters of the share of crop output placed on the market. In Liang k'o chuang Village of Ch'ang-li Hsien in Hopei (1936) 28 percent of the households—and these farms exceeded 20 *mou* in size—marketed 71 percent of the peanuts they grew (Minami Man-shū 1938, tables 4, 12, 13). Peanut was the primary cash crop in this village. In nineteen villages surveyed in northern Manchuria in 1934, soy bean, wheat, and oil-seed-bearing crops were found to be the primary cash crops marketed throughout this region. Again a disproportionately small share of farms, usually less than one-third of the village, marketed nearly the entire amount placed on the market (Kokumuin jitsugyōbu, 1936). In an island-wide survey of 68 rice farms conducted in 1921–22, approximately one-third of the sample, consisting of large farms (four *chia* and above) marketed 43 percent of all rice sold by these sample farms (Taiwan sōtokufu shokusankyoku, 1923: 26–29). This same share of farms marketed 72 percent of all vegetables sold.

From these scattered survey findings the statistical evidence strongly suggests that farms on both the Mainland and Taiwan depended greatly upon the market and can be classified as "semi-commercial and commercial" farms, highly integrated into a market economy (Wharton 1969: 13). In both farming systems, large units supplied a disproportionate share of the marketed surplus. Small farms also contributed to the marketed surplus because these peasants could survive only by specializing in cash crops in order to buy the extra food their small holdings could not provide. The large proportion of village farms working less than 10 or 20 *mou* simply had to purchase additional food from the market with cash earnings from sales of fiber or oil seed, wages, or remittances. The smaller the farm, the more specialized its use of resources and production. This development made more and more farms increasingly dependent on the market. The larger the farm, the more diverse its output, and the longer it could hold a large portion of its crops, waiting long after the harvest until crop prices reached their annual high before selling.

The Effects of Commercialization on Family Farms

Prior to the 1890's, market towns and cities on the Mainland demanded less food and fewer industrial crops; aside from cotton yarn and cloth, a mass market for consumer goods supplied by raw materials from agriculture still did not exist (Nishijima 1966: 729–903). After the 1890's, foreign trade and the development of treaty ports increased the demand for agricultural products, and their prices began to rise more rapidly. Family farms responded by specializing in certain crops, the choice of crop depending upon regional climatic, soil, and commercial circumstances. Initially, these farms obtained more income from the market than they had before. Consider, for example, the hypothetical case of two family farms that have traditionally devoted two-thirds of their labor to producing food-grains and one-third to producing an industrial crop. If returns for labor expended now increase for the industrial crop, one of the two farmers may decide to specialize in it, devoting all his land and labor to producing it. If other farmers in the area make the same decision, food-grains may become relatively scarce, and the second farmer may decide to specialize exclusively in them. Complete specialization of this kind was rare, but where it did occur, the absolute marketed surplus of the industrial crop, the relative surplus marketed by the industrial-cropping farmer, and the market-dependency of both farmers would all increase, even if specialization did not increase total output. And since specialization usually does increase total output, the marketed surplus of the food-growing farmer would also increase, and both farmers would obviously receive more for their marketed surplus each year than before (cf. Shand 1965: 199).

Meanwhile, as the best practices of traditional farming technology became diffused throughout the countryside, output was also increased. Selecting better native seed, using soybean curd and ashes with traditional fertilizers, and employing better methods of pest-control are a few such examples of these practices (Amano 1962: 632–39). Finally, farmers began to grow food crops requiring less land than their old crops to fill the family's food needs. Land was thus freed for cash crops, and a new crop-rotation pattern and form of specialization was created. Peasants throughout China increased their marketed surplus in one or more of these three ways. The food-grains and industrial crops flowing through rural and urban markets were purchased either by farmers and urban consumers or by entrepreneurs in the export trade, by food-processing businesses, or by industries that used them as raw materials. The agrarian system supported an increase in population, a gradual transfer of labor to urban employments, and an expanding foreign trade. Several examples show how these developments came about.

In 1900 peasants began migrating in great numbers to I-t'ung Hsien of Kirin Province. The population grew from somewhere around 100,000 (my estimate) to 350,000 by 1930, so that although land was reclaimed to accommodate new families, nearly 60 percent of village households were still without land in 1935 (Sarai 1937: 61–152). Farmers marketed about 60 percent of their soybeans, about half of their kaoliang, 80 percent of their rice, and often some millet. Some large landowners had mortgaged and eventually sold their land, so that there remained a smaller number of such landlords than a half-century before, and their holdings were smaller. The migrants who settled in I-t'ung before 1910 had acquired farm land by specializing in soybean production on rented land. They in turn employed immigrant workers, of whom many obtained enough cash to rent land to secure a small toehold in farming. Because soybean exports continued to increase, the agriculture of the area successfully absorbed wave after wave of immigrants.[*]

Wu-tien Village of Liang-hsiang Hsien in Hopei was located only a kilometer from the *hsien* seat (Chūgoku 1957, 5: 407–651). Between 1910 and 1942 the number of households in the village had risen from 40 to 70, and only 20 of these 70 households could depend entirely on farming. These 20 households owned an average of 40 *mou*, whereas the remainder owned an average of 10 *mou*. The smaller family farms sent their young men to work outside the village to supplement their income from the farm. In Wu-tien the peasants specialized in wheat as their prime cash crop and grew maize, millet, sweet potato, and vegetables on their remaining land. They marketed their wheat to buy millet and kaoliang. About a half-century before, most farms were said to have been self-sufficient. But the population increase, the consequent decline in farm size, and occasional poor harvests forced more households to specialize in food-grains as cash crops, to work outside the village and to adopt crops like the potato—which they considered inferior to millet and corn—as a food supplement.

The village of T'ou tsung miao, located in Nan-t'ung Hsien of Kiangsu, produced cotton, assorted food-grains, and vegetables (Nantsūken 1941). T'ou tsung miao contained 94 households of nearly 400 people. The village specialized in cotton, which comprised about 40 percent of the first crop each year. Farmers planted yellow beans between their wheat, cotton, and other crops in both cropping periods. Family farms smaller than 3 *mou* depended heavily upon handicraft weaving and off-farm earnings to support themselves, but larger holdings retained their labor for farming and weaving. Only a few households supplied all their food needs from their own land; most specialized in some industrial crop and bought food from the market. The typical farm bought nearly one-fifth of its wheat and four-fifths of its rice.

In Taiwan, expanding foreign trade, improved transport, and urban

---

[*] It should be noted that the rate of tenancy was extremely high in southern Manchuria around the year 1900, because new arrivals had not yet been able to buy their own farms. An expanding market for agricultural products, however, soon

growth encouraged peasants to cultivate more land and become more specialized producers (Myers and Ching 1964: 555–70). The same process of commercialization was at work on Taiwan as on the Mainland, with one major exception: new farming information, techniques, and supplies were made available by the Japanese colonial administration, and the Taiwanese peasants gradually learned a new farming technology.

The colonial government deserves credit for leading and financing agricultural development in general and for making improved rice and sugarcane seeds and inorganic fertilizers available to the majority of peasants in particular. The fertilizer-seed revolution launched by the colonial administration rested upon a system of research stations and farmers' associations established throughout the island as early as 1908 (Taiwan shokusankyoku 1933, chap. 1). Local government took the initiative in financing and developing irrigation projects, and by the late 1920's several large projects were being completed in the south. Peace and social stability reigned throughout this period, so that commercialization and rapid technological change mutually reinforced each other and enabled peasants to increase yields dramatically.

On the Mainland the absence of any sharp break with traditional farming practices and technology must be attributed mainly to political instability and war. For a brief period between 1928 and 1937, the KMT enjoyed some control over the countryside and launched an agrarian program quite similar to that of the Japanese in Taiwan (Ka-Hoku sangyō kagaku kenkyūjo 1937, chaps. 1–4). But a decade was too short to produce a sustained technological revolution in Chinese farming. The peasants continued to rely upon age-old farming practices, and specialization and exchange continued to take place. The commercialization of agriculture, initiated by new market-demand forces after the 1890's, clearly played a positive role in increasing output. The increase was a modest one, nothing like that occurring in Taiwan during the same period.

It is a moot question whether the peasantry responded to new mar-

---

enabled many of them to move upward to owner-cultivator status. As newer immigrants arrived to settle the central and northern areas of the province, the rate of tenancy rose higher in these areas than it was in the south. The following figures for the 1930's reflect this pattern. In southern Manchuria where commercialization was classified as high (on an arbitrary index based on development of transport, banking, and trade), a survey of ten villages indicated that 71.3 percent of the households were owner-cultivators, whereas only 28.7 percent were tenants. The comparable figures for central (ten villages, commercialization moderate) and northern (seventeen villages, commercialization low) Manchuria were 31.1 *vs.* 68.9 percent, and 50.7 *vs.* 49.3 percent, respectively (Nichi-Man nōsei kenkyūkai 1940: 307).

ket demand because they saw the chance of monetary gains or because population pressure and rural misery compelled them to increase their marketed surplus to stay alive. Throughout Chinese agricultural history peasants gradually changed their systems of land use and cropping as new crops appeared on the scene, as irrigation developed, and as traditional farming technology improved. The adoption of wheat in North China in the late T'ang period, the cultivation of cotton in both the north and south after the thirteenth century, and the adoption of new food crops obtained from the Philippines during the Ming and Ching periods brought about changes in systems of cropping and land use. What cannot be ascertained with any certainty is whether population pressure on the land compelled the peasantry to shift from short-fallow cultivation to annual cropping, and finally, in many areas, to multicropping.* In each system of land use, idle labor certainly existed at one period or another of the farming cycle. Depending upon the farmer's skill, health, and diet, increasing returns to labor quite likely existed as well. If this was the case, the impetus to adopt a new cropping system requiring more labor need not have been population pressure on the land, as an ample labor supply would already have existed. An increased demand for crops in the market would appear more important initially, and this would have manifested itself in rising farm prices, in the availability of new seeds, fertilizers, and techniques, and in the appearance of new consumer goods that farmers could afford to buy.

If a system of land use changes in response to new demands and to improvements in transport and marketing, then family farms have apparently adopted new crops or are specializing their land and labor in the production of certain traditional crops. As the marketed surplus rises, so too does population. What now becomes critical is the relationship between output, marketed surplus, and population as commercialization continues. If, as in the case of mainland China, yields increase modestly while population continues to grow at a relentless rate of, say, 1.5 percent per annum, population pressure on the land becomes intense and must be considered an important factor in explaining why the peasant continues to try to increase his marketed surplus. Such conditions were definitely present in North China after World War I, as indicated by the decline in average farm size, the adoption of sweet potato as a supple-

---

* Boserup has argued eloquently that the shift toward annual and multi-cropping systems in peasant economies throughout the world was caused in the main by population increase, and quite likely by population pressure on the land (1965, chap. 8). Although her taxonomy of agricultural development is both useful and interesting, she has ignored factors of demand that have influenced the sequence of land-use systems.

mentary food crop, and the gradual decline of animal husbandry (Murakami 1941: 40–44). The farms of many peasants had become too small to support both animals and human beings unless most of the land was used to grow an industrial crop to exchange for food.

In Taiwan, technological change occurring simultaneously with commercialization enabled farmers to increase their yield per acre and thus their total production significantly, so that although the population was increasing even more rapidly than China's, the long-run trends observable in North China were not evident there. After 1950 average farm size did decline, but economic conditions continued to improve in both rural and urban sectors of the economy. An agricultural revolution followed by rapid industrialization greatly improved peasant living standards despite the rapid population growth that was taking place.

The process of commercialization in mainland China between 1890 and 1937 was interrupted severely only once—during the commercial and monetary deflation of 1930–33. The peasantry suffered greatly and there is every indication that for a time increased numbers of peasants lost their land and became tenant farmers in a given year. The catastrophic decline in farm prices hurt especially those already in debt and others who suffered poor harvests and had to borrow to buy grain. Taiwan was relatively insulated from world depression because of her trade and monetary relationship with the Japanese Empire. Aside from this brief period, mainland agriculture enjoyed a mild secular inflation in which farm prices, in the main, rose a little more rapidly than the prices of goods peasants habitually purchased from the market. Without this commercialization process, peasants could not have increased their production sufficiently to support the population growth and urban expansion that was going on at the same time.

The Sociology of Irrigation: Two Taiwanese Villages

BURTON PASTERNAK

Our approach to the study of Chinese culture and society, long marked by an over-reliance on casual observation and easy generalization, is at last becoming more systematic and more specific. Chinese cultural phenomena are being observed in particular times and places as Sinologists try to learn how sociocultural variants arise and how they are integrated into the larger culture.

This paper considers only one very limited aspect of Chinese society: the management of a single natural resource, water, in two Chinese villages of southwestern Taiwan. The general question involved is how a community's handling of its essential resources affects its sociocultural adaptation. The specific question—and the subject of this paper—is how a community's irrigation system influences such cultural patterns as conflict and cooperation, labor supply and demand, and even family size and structure. Data from a Chinese village on the Chia-nan Plain will be presented in some detail and compared briefly with data from a village on the Ping-tung Plain.*

* The village of Chung-she on the Chia-nan Plain is inhabited by 1,115 Hokkien-speaking people in 194 households. Twenty surnames are represented, but three of them account for half of the village households. The village is compact and nucleated, with each surname group tending to concentrate in a particular portion of the village. The village of Ta-tieh on the Ping-tung Plain is a nucleated, multi-surname, Hakka-speaking community with a resident population of about 1,600 people in 265 households. There is no marked tendency for people with a single surname to concentrate in one part of the village. Neither the ethnic difference (discussed later) nor the difference in physical grouping of the population between the two villages is highly significant for the comparison to be presented here, and the villages are otherwise quite similar. The Chung-she data were collected in the course of a community study undertaken in 1968–69 with the support of the National Science Foundation. The Ping-tung data, collected between 1963 and 1965 with the aid of a Foreign Area Fellowship, have appeared elsewhere (Pasternak 1968), and are presented here only for purposes of comparison.

Considerable attention has already been given to the social correlates of irrigation, particularly at the level of the State (Eisenstadt 1958; Geertz 1970; Leach 1959; Orenstein 1956 and 1965; Pan-American Union 1955; Pasternak 1968; Steward 1955; and Wittfogel 1957). Most familiar, perhaps, is the work of Karl Wittfogel who, in his monumental work *Oriental Despotism*, investigates the sociopolitical concomitants of particular technological environments. Wittfogel believes that dependence on integrated irrigation systems tends to generate despotic states and elaborate bureaucracies. These bureaucracies develop, he argues, because so much labor is required first to construct and then to maintain irrigation facilities—labor that must be recruited and coordinated—and because considerable planning, supervision, and authority are required to keep such a complex system running. I do not intend to discuss the first part of this argument except to note that integrated irrigation systems may be constructed piecemeal and without benefit of the elaborate bureaucratic forms Wittfogel describes (see Leach 1959: 2–25) and that even if a complicated bureaucracy evolves while a system is being built, it may be abandoned once construction is complete. I will be concerned from time to time, however, with the second part of Wittfogel's argument—that the distribution of water and the adjudication of conflicts over water require a managerial presence, specifically of a bureaucratic sort.

There is a threshold of complexity in irrigation systems at which cooperation* must give way to coordination; at which those served by the systems relinquish their decision-making power and their direct role in settling disputes. Authority and responsibility for these vital functions are then transferred to managerial structures of one sort or another. This is not to say that cooperation is then absent, but rather that it is no longer the dominant pattern of operation. The transfer to managerial coordination is not simply dependent on the size of the irrigated area. It is also—and more directly—dependent on the number of farmers drawing water *from a single source*. Where so many farmers are involved that face-to-face relations break down, management of some kind becomes necessary. Otherwise, the system may be disrupted by constant conflict, and much of the community may be deprived of water.

Conflict and Cooperation

In any densely populated rice-growing community, frequent conflicts over water would certainly not be surprising, if indeed they were not

---

* This word as used here and elsewhere in this paper denotes joint activity jointly decided upon.

taken for granted. What might be surprising on first thought, however, is the precise and almost paradoxical relationship between such conflict and the means developed to manage it. For the very existence of feuding seems to stimulate the emergence of both cooperative networks and managerial structures to preclude or at least restrain overt expressions of hostility. And the greater the danger of such hostile outbreaks, the more extensive and powerful the networks and structures seem to be.* Exactly what they will be like in a particular case will be influenced by the character of the factors that generate them—that is, by the nature of the specific irrigation system involved.† Changes in the system will, of course, cause changes in the kind and intensity of conflict prevalent in the community and, consequently, in the means of dealing with it.

With this in mind, let us consider a specific irrigation system and a specific community, the Chia-nan Irrigation System and the village of Chung-she on the Chia-nan Plain of southwestern Taiwan. The plain, which includes the *hsien* of Tainan, Chiayi, and Yunlin and the city of Tainan, has a total area of approximately 4,884 sq km, or virtually one-seventh that of the island. Rainfall on the plain is unevenly distributed throughout the year (roughly 80 percent of the mean annual precipitation of 3,000 mm falls between May and September), and underground water is not abundant, but the region is otherwise well suited to agriculture. About two-thirds of it is flat and fertile, and the temperature does not normally fall below 17° C. except in January. The area is often referred to as "the granary of Taiwan."

Chung-she Village lies in the southeastern portion of the plain. According to my census in 1968, 174 of its 194 households cultivated land, 104 of them as full owners (161 households owned at least part of the land they farmed). Its total cultivated area was 249 hectares in 1968. The principal crop has always been rice.

Before the Chia-nan Irrigation System was built, a small part of Chung-she's farmland drew water from public or private ponds scattered about the landscape. The farmers dependent on each pond functioned as a group to obtain "common water," and to manage disputes arising over it. The larger ponds had radiating canals. When the water in such a pond was sufficient, the canals drew water in a scheduled sequence, with farmers at the shallow end operating foot-treadles or

---

* Arend Lijphart (1968) has made a similar point with respect to the accommodation of pluralism at the national level.

† For a discussion of the various irrigation systems on Taiwan, see Chen 1963: 140–71.

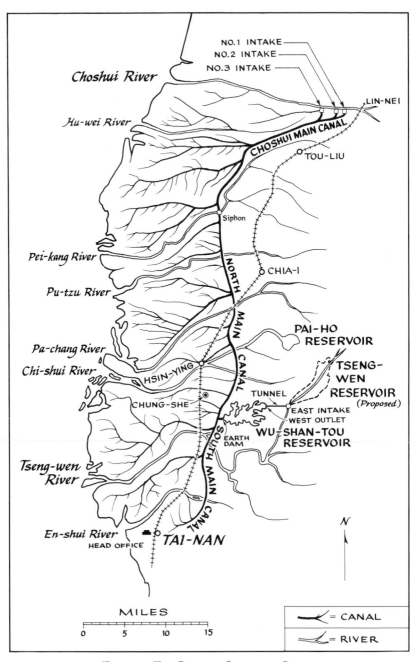

NO.1 INTAKE
NO.2 INTAKE
NO.3 INTAKE

Choshui River

LIN-NEI

Hu-wei River

CHOSHUI MAIN CANAL

TOU-LIU

Siphon

Pei-kang River

NORTH MAIN CANAL

CHIA-I

Pu-tzu River

PAI-HO
RESERVOIR

Pa-chang River

Chi-shui River

HSIN-YING

TSENG-
WEN
RESERVOIR
(Proposed.)

TUNNEL

CHUNG-SHE

EAST INTAKE
WEST OUTLET

WU-SHAN-TOU
RESERVOIR

SOUTH MAIN CANAL

EARTH
DAM

Tseng-wen
River

En-shui River
HEAD OFFICE

TAI-NAN

N

MILES

0   5   10   15

= CANAL

= RIVER

FIGURE 1. THE CHIA-NAN IRRIGATION SYSTEM

opening gates before those at the deep end. The drawing period for each farmer was determined by the area of his fields, and measured by burning incense sticks. When water in the pond was low, however, each canal might draw water without regard to schedule. The only rule was that water would be taken only by foot-treadle. Farmers located at the deep end of a pond sometimes broke this rule. While pretending to pedal, they would covertly open a gate, forcing farmers at the shallow end to pedal furiously, and causing conflict. Farmers who were caught at this trick were denied access to the water in the canal. The smaller ponds were usually capable of supplying water only to the fields immediately surrounding them. So few farmers were involved that there was no need for schedules; each field-owner and his family simply treadled at will. Cooperation was not necessary.

Most of the fields cultivated by Chung-she villagers during this period depended exclusively on rainfall, and were referred to as *k'an-t'ien t'ien*, or "fields that depend on the heavens." Generally speaking, then, either all farmers had water, or no farmers had water. Before 1920, cooperation and conflict in irrigation were minimal and involved only individuals. Households needed to cooperate for only a few purposes, such as providing drainage for each other's fields, or equalizing the supply of water by passing it from one field to another. Theft of water was rare, and usually involved farmers cultivating fields irrigated by ponds. There was a saying that "a good field is made by a good field-neighbor; a good house is made by a good house-neighbor."

Some canals were built on the Chia-nan Plain early in the Ch'ing period.* These were mostly small, private canals that drew water from nearby rivers to irrigate the owners' lands. The total irrigated area at that time has been estimated at only 5,000 hectares. The great change came when Japanese authorities bent on extending the cultivation of sugarcane devised a plan to irrigate and provide drainage for 150,000 hectares of farmland on the plain (expanded by the Nationalists to over 160,000 hectares). The canals constructed under this plan between 1920 and 1930 constitute the largest integrated irrigation system on the island, the Chia-nan Irrigation System (see Figure 1). It has over 10,000 km of irrigation canals, nearly 7,000 km of drainage canals, and over 300 km of sea and river dikes.

* The following general introduction to the Chia-nan System is based on numerous documents, the most important of which are: Chen 1963: 160–66; Hsieh 1964: 168–71; *Brief Introduction of Chia-nan Irrigation Association*, 1967; *Report on the 1964 Irrigated Land Survey of Irrigation Associations in Taiwan, The Republic of China* 1965: 325–50; *Tai-wan Sheng t'ung chih Kao* 1955: 200–211; *Tai-nan Hsien-chih kao* 1960; and *Chia-nan ta-chün hsin-she shih-yeh kai-yao* 1921.

Most of its water is drawn from two sources, the Tseng-wen and Cho-shui rivers. Water from the Tseng-wen is led into the Wu-shan-tou Reservoir, which covers some 6,000 hectares. From there, water is conducted into the south and north sections of the main canal. At the northern end of the system, water is drawn from the Choshui River at three intakes, combined, and then conducted into the Choshui section of the main canal. A large diesel facility called a siphon connects the Choshui and north sections of the canal so that a deficiency in one can be remedied by drawing water from the other. The main canal feeds lateral canals that in turn provide water to lesser canals and to farm ditches throughout the plain.

The water supplied by the Chia-nan System is not sufficient to allow the cultivation of rice every year throughout the entire region. For this reason, a three-year rotation schedule has been established for about 75 percent of the system (122,167 hectares), including the area cultivated by Chung-she Village.* The rotation area is divided into *hsiao-ch'ü,* or "small areas," of about 150 hectares each, which are in turn divided into three roughly equal sections. In any one year only one section is to be planted to rice, while the second is to be planted to sugarcane, and the third to a crop that requires even less water, perhaps none at all from the system. The intent of this plan is to give every farmer equal access to the available water.

Putting the plan into effect is a complex matter, as the operation of the Wu-shan-tou portion of the system (serving Chung-she) may illustrate. Water is furnished to the main canal every day from June 1 to October 10.† All the water in the canals during this period is intended for the rice-growing areas. During December, all gates are opened for a period of approximately twelve days. Water supplied during this period is intended for the irrigation of dry crops. For fifteen days in February or March, the canals are again filled to supply water for the cultivation of sugarcane. When newly released irrigation water has reached the terminal points of the main canal, and when water levels have been determined to be correct, all gates exiting from them are simultaneously opened. Two or three times a day while these gates are open, the water level is checked at various points along the canal and adjustments are made to keep it constant. As water is led into each

---

* *Report on the 1964 Irrigated Land Survey,* pp. 328–29. There are two other basic irrigation patterns on the plain. A so-called combined irrigation pattern, using additional sources of water such as pumps and ponds, allows one or even two crops of rice each year on 12,246 hectares. And 26,371 hectares of farmland are independently irrigated by small streams, ponds, and lakes.

† All agricultural dates used here and elsewhere in this paper are solar dates.

lateral canal, gates exiting from it are partially opened, starting from the top gate and working down to the last one, as water passes each gate. When the water has reached the end of the line, the level of water at various points along the lateral canal is checked and adjusted accordingly. Thus, all gates in the system are actually kept open at the same time, and their apertures are adjusted as necessary.

The preceding description illustrates the integrated nature of the irrigation operation and the high degree of coordination that is required. The coordinating body is the Chia-nan Irrigation Association.* Below the system level, however, cooperation prevails. The local irrigation station hires one or two villagers each year and assigns them to manage water distribution in a "small area." In fact, however, these men do little more than make ritualistic patrols. The actual channelling and distribution of water is handled by the farmers themselves.

In fact, it would probably be fair to say that cooperation in the handling of water resources is more prevalent in Chung-she today than it was before the irrigation system was built. Most village households own from two to four fields located in different places. When fields were watered by rainfall, as already noted, households needed to cooperate in only a few ways, such as providing drainage or equalizing the supply of water by passing it from one field to another. Theft of water was rare, and usually involved farmers cultivating fields irrigated by ponds. For the most part, either all farmers had water or no farmers had water. Since completion of the Chia-nan System, water is supplied to fields on a schedule and from a localizable source. Since each field has to be filled and drained several times during the growing season, and since not all fields border on canals, it is clear that a farmer must articulate his activities with those of other farmers. Not only must he cooperate with the owners of adjacent fields, but he must also arrive at understandings with farmers farther up the line on the canal, who receive water first.

In addition to cooperating in the day-to-day operation of the irriga-

---

* The twenty-six irrigation associations of Taiwan are approved and supported by the government, but self-administered. Empowered to levy workers, to acquire land, and to collect fees from farmers within their jurisdictions, they are administratively responsible for maintaining local irrigation systems and for arbitrating irrigation disputes. The irrigation association of a district lying entirely within the jurisdiction of one *hsien* or city is supervised primarily by the government of that *hsien* or city and only secondarily by the Water Conservancy Bureau of the Provincial Department of Reconstruction. Just the reverse is true where a district involves more than one local jurisdiction. The members of each association elect representatives to a representatives' congress. The congress in turn elects a supervisory committee and a president, who appoints a general manager and who serves as the association's *de facto* representative to the Joint Council of Irrigation Associations.

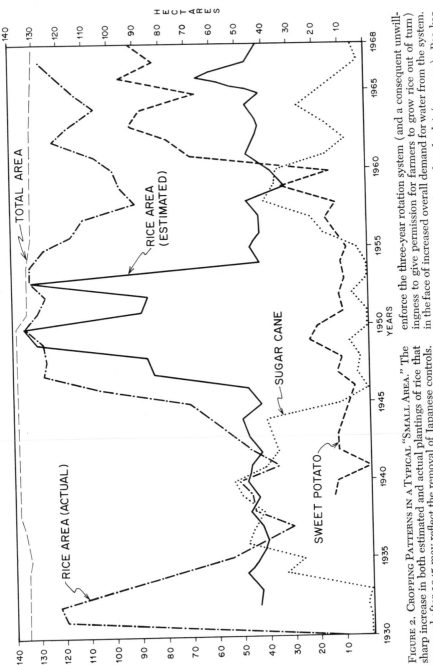

FIGURE 2. CROPPING PATTERNS IN A TYPICAL "SMALL AREA." The sharp increase in both estimated and actual plantings of rice that occurred after 1945 may reflect the removal of Japanese controls. The sharp drop in estimated plantings that occurred about 1954 may reflect a renewed attempt by the irrigation association to enforce the three-year rotation system (and a consequent unwillingness to give permission for farmers to grow rice out of turn) in the face of increased overall demand for water from the system. SOURCES: Shui-tao tso-fu kwan-hsi shu-lei (1930–37); Pao-kao shu-chui (1937–47); Chung-yao shu-lei (1948–68).

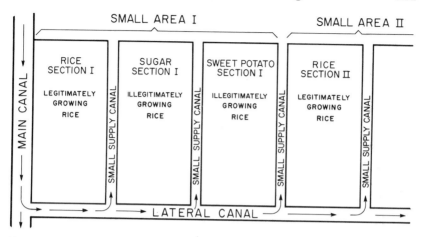

FIGURE 3. AN IRRIGATION MODEL FOR A "SMALL AREA." Arrows indicate direction of water flow.

tion system, many farmers cooperate to steal water (see below). They even establish complicated rotation schedules among themselves. Figure 2 suggests the extent of water-theft in one typical "small area" in Chung-she. Actual plantings of rice during much of the period since 1930 have far exceeded official estimates (the forty-five hectares scheduled to grow rice plus those areas given special permission to grow rice out of turn). This excess area could have been watered only with water illegally diverted from the irrigation system. It should be noted that the mean hectarage cultivated by individual households in this area has steadily decreased since 1935, and that the smaller a farmer's holding, the more likely he is to feel compelled to plant rice every year rather than sugarcane, in order to be sure of feeding his family.*

The potential for conflict in Chung-she has obviously increased greatly since the Chia-nan System was built. Yet conflict over water in the village has not increased in the proportions that might have been expected —except possibly for disputes arising from thefts of water. And means have evolved for managing even these, as the following actual cases will illustrate.

Case 1. As noted above, "small areas" like the one schematically represented in Figure 3 are subdivided into three sections of about 50 hectares each. According to the rotation plan, each of the three sections

* There are other reasons for the persistent preference for rice that can be seen in Figure 2: sugar prices have not always been stable; rice produces a crop in four months, whereas sugarcane takes eighteen; and the cultivation of rice allows more effective use of family labor during the year.

should be cultivating a different crop as the diagram shows, but all three are in fact growing rice. When a farmer in the section scheduled to grow sugarcane needs water, he will watch the fields. Each farmer in the legitimate rice-growing section will come to his field shortly before his turn to draw water, so there will usually be at least one farmer there at any given time. The would-be thief will ask him whether he needs all the water he is entitled to, or whether he needs the entire period of his turn. If he does not, a small part of his share can be diverted through small ditches and drainages. When water is plentiful, the legitimate rice-growers may not even bother to come to their fields early. In this case, the thief will simply divert water to meet his needs. Relations between farmers within the "small area" are face to face.

Case 2. Problems sometimes arise between "small areas." Suppose, for example, that many farmers scheduled to grow sugarcane in "Small Area" I draw water out of turn. This will cause shortages farther down the line in "Small Area" II as the level of water in the lateral canal falls below that of the exit gates. Such a situation brings large blocs of farmers into opposition and might lead to violence. But the customary way of handling the situation avoids violence by avoiding the direct expression of hostility. One or more of the legitimate rice-growers being deprived of water will complain to the irrigation station. The clerk at the station will then telephone the clerk at the nearest canal-management station, who will consult his counterparts at higher-level canal management stations. Water levels at each station—closely watched in any case to guard against theft—will be checked until the diversion is located and corrected. The relations between "small areas" are therefore indirect. Face-to-face encounters occur between agents of the irrigation association rather than between the two groups of farmers themselves. A potentially hostile situation is managed by taking it out of the hands of those directly involved in it.

Case 3. One night a certain Mr. Huang diverted water from an adjacent section of his "small area" into the supply canal leading to his field. Before it reached his field, however, this stolen water was diverted again, by a canal block placed by one Mr. Ts'ai. When Mr. Huang discovered the block, he went to work at once to remove it. Mr. Ts'ai saw him and came over to stop him. Mr. Huang complained that this was *his* stolen water. After some pushing and shoving, they finally agreed to take turns using the water. Mr. Huang was allowed to draw first.

Case 4. In one case there was a potential for conflict between larger areas, i.e. between areas dependent on separate laterals. One year, about eighteen farmers owning seven or eight hectares of land in a single section of the East Chung-she "Small Area" met informally in the fields and in front of village shops. These farmers were all growing rice out of turn and needed water. Not enough water was available in their immediate vicinity, so they agreed to cooperate in drawing water illegally from a lateral canal to the north. At the specified time, designated farmers brought a gas pump, a siphon, and hoses. The owner of the pump received a fee from all other members of the group.

The diversion was accomplished as follows. A siphon was set up at Point A on the Lin-feng-ying Lateral Canal (see Figure 4). Water was lifted from the canal and led through a small drainage canal to the medium drainage canal indicated on the map. The medium canal was blocked at Point B so that water south of the block would rise and flow southward (the reverse of normal flow in this canal). All who were to benefit from the diversion helped build the canal block. The gas pump was installed at Point C to lift water from the medium drainage canal into a small drainage canal that ran along the edge of the area to be watered. At Point D the water was diverted by another cooperatively constructed block into the first field to be watered. From there it was led to the other thieves' fields in a sequence previously agreed upon

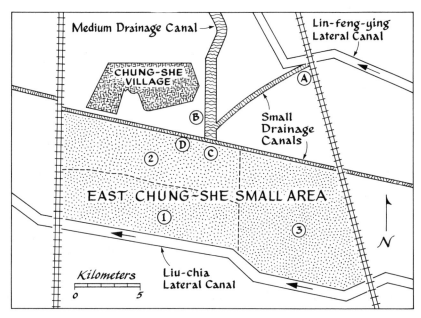

FIGURE 4. A CASE OF WATER THEFT IN THE EAST CHUNG-SHE "SMALL AREA." Arrows in lateral canals show direction of water flow.

by all. The pump used in this operation was left in place and watched by one of the group members day and night. Only the siphon was removed after each night's use.

Farmers dependent on the medium drainage for irrigation noticed that water had suddenly vanished from it. They immediately reported the fact to clerks of the irrigation association, who eventually located the block and had it removed. Thus was averted a conflict that might eventually have involved farmers in several villages and might even have disrupted a large portion of the system.

The Chia-nan Irrigation Association has taken several steps specifically designed to reduce conflict over water. The various farm ditches served by a single small-supply canal initially drew water simultaneously. But the water flowed so slowly that much of it seeped away, and it took a long time to irrigate the area supplied by each ditch. Farmers with fields located at terminal points had to wait a particularly long time. Besides, farmers whose ditches were higher on small-supply canals were in a position to draw water faster at all times and to draw more water in times of shortage. Water passed their ditch entries first, and the openings could be widened to let in a greater quantity of water. Conflicts therefore arose between the owners of ditches fed by a single small-supply canal.

A year or two after the Chia-nan project was completed, however, a plan was devised whereby each ditch received water by rotation. The time allotted for each ditch depended on the type of soil and the total area to be watered, and was measured by burning incense sticks. All the water in the small-supply canal could now legally pass into the entitled ditch. The water flowed faster, and less of it seeped away.

When conflicts arose because certain farmers sheltered their incense sticks to make them burn more slowly, alarm clocks were introduced to standardize timing. The first farmer on a ditch would open it and draw water. Because conflicts over timing arose between farmers along a single ditch, the irrigation station devised rotation schedules for each ditch. When the last farmer on the schedule had drawn his share, he passed the clock to the first farmer on the next lower ditch, who opened its entry and closed that of the upper ditch. If anyone claimed that the clock was running slow, it would be checked against the one in the local train station.

In a further attempt to reduce conflict over water, the irrigation station created the water patrol a few years after the Chia-nan System was completed. Steam-powered tillers used in the planting of sugarcane worked very deep, causing the soil to absorb great quantities of water during a short period. Simultaneous drawing of water from a small-supply canal, such as was still being practiced in rice areas, was no longer possible. Rotation among ditches in the sugarcane areas was therefore established early, and the patrol was set up to supervise it and to watch for flooding in the canals. It was later extended in modified form to rice areas as well.

In summary, then, the extension and integration of irrigation that occurred when the Chia-nan Irrigation System was built required a parallel expansion of the cooperative and managerial networks previously developed by the farmers of the Plain. Bernard Gallin has described the same sort of expansion in Hsin-hsing, another Taiwanese village. In that village, as in Chung-she, the extension of canal irrigation during the Japanese period made water available to a greater number of farmers, extended the area of interdependence, and broadened cooperative networks (Gallin, 1966).

The experience of Chung-she and Hsin-hsing contrasts sharply with that of Ta-tieh Village on the Ping-tung Plain farther to the south (Pasternak 1968). Before 1956, the 220 hectares of farmland cultivated by Ta-tieh farmers were tied into an integrated irrigation system. Conflict over water in this area, already sharp because of population pressures and ethnic rivalry, was intensified early in the twentieth century when subsurface dams and new canals built upstream for the benefit of a new sugar factory deprived the system of much of its water.

Beginning in 1956, pumps designed to tap underground water were installed at various points along the canals in Ta-tieh and the rest of the Ping-tung system. These pumps were intended to counterbalance the drying up of older sources and to ensure more equitable and timely distribution of water for irrigation. An unintentional effect of introducing the pumps has been to split the system into more or less independent units, each drawing most of its irrigation water from a single pump, and there have been noticeable sociocultural adaptations to this change. Conflict over water has significantly diminished, and cooperative networks have contracted. The irrigation association still functions, and a small-group chief is still elected every three years to collect irrigation fees, to disseminate information passed down from the irrigation association, and, theoretically, to help arbitrate water disputes arising within each large-canal system. But the real authority lies in the hands of natural groups consisting of the twenty to twenty-five farmers who draw water from a single pump. It is within and between these groups that rotation and other forms of cooperation mainly occur.

Each pumping station is assigned a watchman by the irrigation association, but the selection usually follows the recommendation of pump-group members. The watchman is responsible to the members of the group he serves for the day-and-night security of his pumping station. During the dry season, especially during periods of severe drought, a pump group may also employ one or two field watchmen to ensure an equitable distribution of water day and night. Such watchmen are paid directly by the owners of the fields they guard. Once a rotation schedule has been agreed upon, usually by drawing lots at a group meeting, these watchmen must see that it is followed. They cannot change it without unanimous prior authorization from the group. During periods of really severe drought, farmers stay in their fields all night to double-check the watchmen.

Where local groups of farmers request it, the irrigation association may investigate the feasibility of and arrange loans for the construction of special pumping devices. The association then assumes responsibility for the maintenance of these facilities, passing both construction and maintenance costs on to the farmers. The irrigation association also assumes responsibility for major water projects such as dikes along the river, but its presence is rarely felt in the areas of water distribution and conflict resolution at the local level. These activities are normally regulated and managed on a face-to-face basis within and between pump groups. Major decisions are enforced by public opinion.

Labor Supply and Demand

Before the Chia-nan Irrigation System was built, the labor supply in Chung-she consisted of the farmers and their grown sons.* Only a few wealthy families had permanent laborers attached to their households or living elsewhere in the village. The demand for labor was characterized by brief but intense peaks followed by relative lulls. Rainfall, unevenly distributed throughout the year and lasting only barely long enough at certain critical points in the rice cycle, had to be taken advantage of when it came. Every farmer was reportedly ready to begin preparing his rice fields (about 2.5 hectares in the second cropping season) as soon as the rains began. During the few days when the fields were actually wet enough to allow proper preparation, he and his sons and their buffalo would work as hard and fast as they could. But work as they might, they would sometimes not finish in time and would have to plant a faster-growing but lower-yielding strain of the native *tsai-lai* rice.

---

* Before the second World War, Hokkien women did not work in the fields.

When rice seedlings reach the proper stage of development, they must be transplanted within a certain period of time (see below), or they will be lost. Even if rainfall was adequate, the farmer and his sons had to work steadily to finish the job in time. Obviously under these circumstances there was no labor available for exchange or for hire within the village. Nor was there labor that could be brought in at these crucial times from villages just to the north, south, or west. As in Chung-she, farmers in these areas were under pressure to prepare their fields and plant their crops with the rains. Labor could not even be imported from areas farther away where the planting and harvesting times were different, because transportation was so expensive. In 1920 a round-trip train ticket from the city of Tainan to Chung-she, for instance, cost the equivalent of 50 catties of rice. The average yield per hectare at that time was only 1,000 catties. The only hired labor in the village of Chung-she consisted of a few work teams from the western coastal areas brought in to help with the second-season harvest of rice.

The Chia-nan Irrigation System has changed all this. More land is irrigated and can therefore be more intensively cultivated. Yields per hectare are higher. Fields are no longer perpetually flooded, and each rice crop must be weeded at least three times, instead of once as before. The total demand for labor has accordingly increased. However, the prolonged availability of water has spread this demand over a longer period of time. Farmers do not all have to carry out the same operation at the same time, and the peaks in demand are considerably less sharp.

Exactly the opposite happened in Ta-tieh (Pasternak 1968). In a system where farmers once received water in sequence, water was suddenly available to most villagers at about the same time of year, so that households were in a position to prepare, transplant, and harvest their fields almost simultaneously with everyone else. Peak periods of demand for labor (when rice is transplanted or harvested and when beans are planted) were therefore contracted.

Interestingly enough, these opposite patterns of demand for labor have not produced opposite patterns of labor supply: both villages began to hire far more labor than before. An increase in the hiring of labor would be predictable in Ta-tieh, where peak periods of demand were suddenly created. In Chung-she, however, where these peak periods were considerably eased, it might be thought that the villagers would begin to exchange labor. On the contrary, they began to hire workers for transplanting, for routine care of plants, and for harvesting. Brokers even appeared in some villages in the area to accommodate the new demand for hired labor. Perhaps the best explanation for this similarity is that in both villages the irrigational changes I have been describing brought substantial increases in annual income for most residents.

Family Form

By blunting and extending peak periods of demand for labor, the Chia-nan Irrigation System may have removed an important impediment to family division in Chung-she. Let us consider this possibility more closely.

Rice nurseries are seeded from mid-May to mid-June (solar). The seedlings are ready for transplanting thirty days later, by mid-June to mid-July. It is important to remember that once the seedlings are ready, they must be transplanted within twenty days. It should also be remembered that before the Second World War, field labor in this Hokkien area consisted exclusively of males. This custom placed an important limitation on available labor, one not present in Ta-tieh, for the Hakka traditionally have had no such restriction. With these facts in mind, and considering only the amount of labor needed to plant rice on each holding, let us now look at a model joint family and weigh the advantages and disadvantages of dividing it.*

The family contains three males capable of field labor: two married brothers, A and B, and A's son. Like other such families in the village, it owns two buffalo and cultivates about two hectares of land. If the water supply is adequate, two of its three workers using its two buffalo can prepare the two hectares for transplanting in twelve to fifteen days. Three workers can transplant the entire holding in seven days. At worst, if they wait until their entire holding has been prepared before beginning to transplant, the family can prepare the land and transplant the seedlings in nineteen to twenty-two days.

If the brothers set up separate households, Brother A would now have one buffalo, two workers, and one hectare of land. One man and one buffalo could prepare the land in twelve to fifteen days, and two men could complete the transplanting in five days. Brother A and his son could therefore get their crop planted. Brother B, however, could not quite make it alone. He would need twelve to fifteen days to prepare the soil plus an additional ten and a half days to transplant. He would actually have to wait until his entire holding had been prepared before

* A joint family is one in which there are two or more married siblings. A nuclear family consists of one married couple and their children. Where a family contains members not normally associated with a nuclear family, but does not meet the criterion for a joint family, it is referred to in this paper as an enlarged family. For purposes of this discussion it will be assumed that neither hired nor exchanged labor is available.

transplanting, and the total period required could by no means be less than twenty-three to twenty-six days.

Obviously it would be easy to lose a rice crop at this stage. If during the allowable twenty days for transplanting there are fewer than fifteen days with sufficient water for preparing fields, all farmers will lose their crops. If there are between sixteen and twenty days of rain, the amount of labor available will determine the outcome. According to my informants in Chung-she, rice crops were often lost at transplanting time before the Chia-nan System was built. Even more risky is the period just before and just after the rice forms heads. If there is not a single substantial rain for ten days before or twenty days after heading, the crop will be ruined. Lack of rain at this time, according to my informants, was an even more frequent cause of crop failure before the Chia-nan System was built.

A farmer who lost his crop of rice would have to plant a crop of sweet potatoes immediately to tide him over until the next year's rice harvest. Since clay soils, particularly under drought conditions, are far from ideally suited to the cultivation of sweet potato, most village families kept about 0.3 hectare of sandy soil within their holding as insurance against just such drought conditions. Upland rice could be planted on this area in March and harvested in August (i.e. in time to plant a crop of sweet potatoes).

It is when a farmer loses his rice crop because of prolonged drought that the disadvantages of family division become most apparent. Let us assume that the model joint family just discussed has lost its crop of rice because of insufficient rainfall. Since 0.3 hectare of sweet potatoes would be barely enough to sustain the family until the next harvest, it is imperative that the entire area be planted. Two men using two buffalo can prepare 0.3 hectare for ridge construction, manuring, and planting in four and a half days.* Three workers can build ridges in the field and spread the manure in one day, and can then do the planting in two afternoons. The soil will therefore have to be moist enough for this work for at least seven days.

Should the brothers divide their family and their holding, each would now have one buffalo and 0.15 hectare of land suitable for such an emergency planting. Brother A could use his animal to prepare the land in four and a half days. He and his son would need an additional day for

* Labor requirements were determined by interviewing villagers. If these requirements appear higher for the same task in one instance than in another, this is because the number of laborers available determines whether everything must be done in sequence (one laborer) or whether parts of certain tasks can be done simultaneously (two or more laborers), and therefore determines the amount of time needed for any step in cultivation.

ridging and manuring and three afternoons for planting, a total of at least eight moist days. In what informants called a dry year, a farmer dependent on rainfall could rarely hope for more than seven sufficiently moist days between mid-August and the end of September. There might even be fewer than seven. Brother A would thus be hard pressed to plant his entire holding within the allotted period, and Brother B would find it impossible (he would need at least eleven moist days). If they remained members of a joint family, on the other hand, their chances would be considerably improved.

If Brother B's wife whispered her displeasure at having to feed and support the sons of her husband's brother, therefore, her husband might well reply, "And who then would work in our fields when the year is dry?" Whereas in good years a younger brother might have more to gain from an early division of the family, in dry years he would have more to lose.

A more reliable water supply, the introduction of the power tiller, and the increased availability of wage labor (and of the means for hiring such labor) have all served to remove these obstacles to family division. Rice has become a reliable crop, and the sweet potato is no longer a crisis crop. Before the Chia-nan Irrigation System was built, the noon-time earth was so hot and dry that sweet potato stems had to be planted in the afternoon to survive; today, the continuously moist earth allows planting in the morning as well. Also, the soil can be prepared much more rapidly now. One man with buffalo and plow needed thirty days just to get one hectare ready for ridging and manuring. With a power tiller he can do it in twenty-four hours. There are, essentially, no more dry years. Thus it is not surprising that in Chung-she today the younger brother usually initiates the division of a joint family.

We have been dealing with a model family, but one of a type that was fairly well represented in the village before 1930. To be sure, there were families with more or fewer working males; but there were also families with more or less land (and a proportionately greater or lesser demand for labor)—and years with more or less rain. The illustration suggests the adaptive advantage of joint families prior to the completion of the irrigation system.

Another of the system's consequences has been a dramatic decline in the number of *ju-chui*, men who marry matrilocally and allow one or more of their sons to adopt the surname of their wives. Though now uncommon in Chung-she, such marriages were formerly even more common than male adoptions. Since *ju-chui*, unlike adopted sons, enter their new families as adults capable of field labor, and since many are known to have entered families that already had a male heir, it seems clear that the main motive of families taking a *ju-chui* was to obtain labor—not only or even primarily for day-to-day needs, but for the sort of need that might arise in a crisis. Indeed, in virtually all cases known to me, *ju-chui* entered families deficient in adult male labor; and in some cases *ju-chui* marriages resulted in joint families. *

Although I cannot demonstrate beyond any doubt that families in Chung-she Village deliberately put off dividing in order to have enough labor for times of crisis, the evidence points that way. A preliminary examination of Japanese household registers dating from 1905 indicates that before the Chia-nan project was completed in 1930, most village families, tenants as well as landlords, with two or more adult sons achieved the joint form before dividing.† Although the data await finer quantitative analysis, it appears that families divided at a much slower rate between 1905 and 1930 than they did after 1930.

This suggestion is supported by Japanese census figures. As Table 1 indicates, the number of resident households in Chung-she rose much more gradually between 1920 and 1935 than between 1935 and 1968. The table indicates no comparable disparity between the two periods for Ta-tieh Village. Households in Chung-she thus apparently proliferated more slowly than in Ta-tieh during the first period, but considerably faster than in Ta-tieh during the second. Note also the dramatic drop in the percentage of joint families in Chung-she for a comparable period, shown in Table 2.‡

---

* Such marriages have always been rare in Ta-tieh, and contracted strictly for the purpose of acquiring a male heir to carry on the family line.

† Great care must be exercised in using household registers as a source of information on family form in Taiwanese villages. One difficulty is that their recording of migration is incomplete. This deficiency is greater today than it was during the Japanese occupation, when people usually moved only from one village to another and registers were maintained by local police officers who knew everyone in the villages under their charge. In recent years people have tended to move to large cities, and the registers are now maintained by the township office, which is ill equipped to keep up-to-date records. Another difficulty in using the registers is that false reporting of family division—both registering divisions that have not taken place and failing to register divisions that have taken place—has been common from the beginning of the Japanese period to the present. My own censuses in Ta-tieh and Chung-she have indicated considerable error in the data on family form in contemporary household registers of both villages.

‡ My copies of the household registers for Ta-tieh prior to 1946 are incomplete. Thus I am unable to compare the two villages before that year. A simple arithmetic mean obtained by dividing total resident population by number of households would not be satisfactory, since the actual distribution curves would probably be skewed differently in the two villages by the presence of unknown numbers of very large or very small households.

TABLE 1. CHANGES IN POPULATION AND NUMBER OF HOUSEHOLDS IN
CHUNG-SHE (1920–68) AND TA-TIEH (1920–64)

Village and category	1920	1935	Percent change since 1920	1964	1968	Percent change since 1935
Chung-she						
Households	78	87	11.5%	—	194	122.9%
Population	364	565	55.2	—	1,115	97.3
Ta-tieh						
Households	148	189	27.7	265	—	40.2
Population	809	1,051	29.9	1,602	—	52.4

SOURCE: Figures for 1920 and 1935 are based on the Japanese censuses for those years. Figures for 1964 and 1968 are based on my own censuses and apply to units comparable to those of 1920 and 1935.

That Ta-tieh is a Hakka village and Chung-she a Hokkien village is seemingly no help in explaining their differences in family form. There is no reason to suspect, for example, that the Taiwanese Hakka as an ethnic group are any more or less prone than the Hokkien to live in joint families. Whereas in Ta-tieh joint families have constituted about 5 percent of all households for at least a generation, Cohen finds that in Yen-liao (another Hakka village on Taiwan) they constitute about 32 percent of all households (Cohen 1967: 638); and Gallin's figure for Hsin-hsing, a Hokkien village, is 5 percent, the same as Ta-tieh (Gallin 1966: 138).

Some years ago, Karl Wittfogel noted a propensity for nuclear as opposed to joint families in societies with large-scale irrigation (1935: 42f, 48f, and 1938: 7–8). More recently, using data on fifty-nine Indian villages, Henry Orenstein found a significant negative correlation between availability of large-scale irrigation and percentage of joint families (1956: 317). He was not entirely successful in explaining this correlation, but he attributed it primarily to the "immediate economic consequences" of irrigation (Orenstein 1956: 318–19).

Irrigation often accentuates the importance of cash crops and a money economy. Where income is primarily for direct consumption, the joint family stores its produce in one unit and uses it when needed. But when a large part of income is in cash, its joint use becomes complicated, and it is a fact that a number of joint families are divided because of quarrels over the disposition of money income.

For Taiwan, a comparable focus on cash income would probably be too narrow. Cohen, for example, found the joint family thriving in Yen-liao, where tobacco is an important cash crop. He ascribes the persis-

TABLE 2. FAMILY FORM IN CHUNG-SHE AND TA-TIEH

Family form	Chung-she				Ta-tieh			
	1946		1968		1946		1964	
	Number	Percent	Number	Percent	Number	Percent	Number	Percent
Joint	10	9.2%	3	1.6%	10	4.8%	13	4.9%
Enlarged	43	39.4	51	26.4	80	38.5	94	35.6
Nuclear	53	48.6	135	69.9	110	52.9	147	55.7
Other	3	2.8	4	2.1	8	3.8	10	3.8
Total	109	100.0%	193	100.0%	208	100.0%	264[a]	100.0%

SOURCE: Household registers and my censuses.
[a] The household made up of residents of the village temple has been excluded from these calculations, since the members are in no sense related.

tence of joint families in Yen-liao to "the interdependent nature of the various economic activities undertaken by different family members." Specifically, a joint family is less likely to be divided where "the limited possibilities remaining to each unit would not bring total returns as great as those derived from the total investments of the family as now constituted," or where "division would also mean a reduction in total income from present enterprises" (Cohen 1967: 642–43). The persistence of joint families in Chung-she before 1930 would appear to be explainable in exactly these terms.

If this explanation has merit, it may help resolve long-standing disagreements over the conditions under which "Chinese families" achieve joint form during their developmental cycle. If, for example, we could compare the dynamics of family development in areas dependent on rainfall and areas dependent on irrigation, we might find that, other conditions being equal, families in rainfall areas are more likely to achieve and retain joint form than those in irrigated areas. At a minimum, I have shown that changes in local irrigation patterns can lead to significant sociocultural adaptations. A proper understanding of this relationship in its many forms and aspects should throw light on sociocultural differences not only in Chinese society, but in all societies that practice irrigation.

Marketing on the Changhua Plain, Taiwan

LAWRENCE W. CRISSMAN

The material to be presented here was gathered in the course of fifteen months' field research in southwestern Changhua Hsien, Taiwan, in 1967–68.* The principal aims of my fieldwork were to define the central-place hierarchy† in that region of the island, to establish the marketing habits of the rural population, and to discover the extent to which marketing behavior influences other aspects of local social organization. The impetus for the project was G. W. Skinner's monumental series of articles entitled "Marketing and Social Structure in Rural China" (Skinner 1964, 1965), which presents models for the distribution and organization of traditional and modern rural markets in China and offers important hypotheses concerning various social concomitants of Chinese marketing systems. In the process of investigating the situation on the Changhua Plain, I became aware that it differs significantly from Skinner's published descriptions of traditional and modern China. The situation I found is interesting in its own right, and consequently the bulk of this article presents a descriptive analysis of the present central-place hierarchy and associated marketing behavior in southwestern Changhua Hsien. The discussion at the end of the paper provides a brief history of the development of the system found in Changhua Hsien, and offers some possible explanations for the most striking differences between it and Skinner's models for mainland China.

Changhua Hsien lies on the west coast of Taiwan roughly halfway

* My fieldwork was sponsored by the Cornell Committee of the London-Cornell Project for East and Southeast Asian Studies, to whom I am very grateful. I am also indebted to the Center for Advanced Study, University of Illinois, Urbana-Champaign, for a fellowship that enabled me to bring this article to its present form.
† See Berry 1967 and Marshall 1969 for overviews of central-place theory.

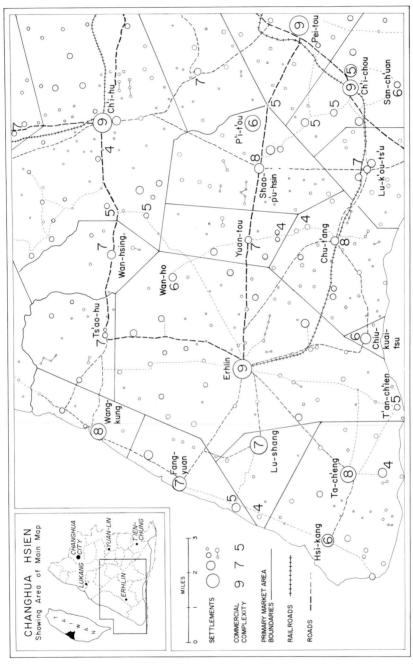

CENTRAL PLACES AND PRIMARY MARKETING AREAS IN SOUTH-WESTERN CHANGHUA HSIEN, TAIWAN. Within the lines indicating the area of the main map on the inset, the *hsiang* surrounding Erhlin Chen are, reading counterclockwise from the upper left, Fang-yuan, Ta-ch'eng, Chu-t'ang, and P'i-t'ou; part of Ch'i-chou Hsiang occupies the lower lefthand corner.

between the northern and southern extremes of the island. Except for a single township lying to the east of the northern promontory of the well-defined range of low hills that marks its eastern boundary, Changhua consists of a very low and level alluvial plain shaped approximately like an isosceles triangle with its apex to the north, measuring 40 km east to west along its base and 45 km north to south on each side. The principal channel of the Choshui, Taiwan's largest river, forms the *hsien's* southern boundary. Since the Choshui has only two crossings, in one place by road traffic and in another by rail, both bridges being near the eastern edge of the plain where the river flows through the hills, it effectively seals off the southwestern portion of the plain to traffic from the south. Except in a narrow band along the coast of the Taiwan Straits where little rain falls, much dust blows, and peanuts and sweet potatoes are grown, the crop land of the plain is principally given over to paddy fields producing two crops of rice and one of vegetables, rapeseed, or wheat annually. The *hsien's* population of just over one million lives far above mere subsistence levels despite an average population density of over 1,000 persons per square kilometer.

My study was based in the town of Erhlin, the largest center in the southwestern corner of the plain. In addition to Erhlin Chen (township), the primary field area included Fang-yuan Hsiang, Ta-ch'eng Hsiang, Chu-t'ang Hsiang, and P'i-t'ou Hsiang (townships). Together these five townships comprise another triangular area stretching 25 km east to west along the Choshui River and 25 km to the north along the coast. This region has relatively poorer soil and less readily available water than the remainder of the *hsien*, and consequently a fair amount of sugarcane is grown. The smaller triangle, my field area, occupies about a third of the plain, but contains fewer than 200,000 people at an average density of only 600 persons per square kilometer.

The five townships making up the field area many be identified on the inset map in the upper lefthand corner of the large map. The inset also identifies several large towns outside the field area that are mentioned in the text. The main map contains all of the field area but the northern tip of Fang-yuan Hsiang. The upper and lower right-hand corners display regions outside the field area. The circles that represent settlements have been drawn approximately to scale, so that their size is proportional to the population of the places they represent. Small circles joined by solid lines indicate long, narrow villages. All roads shown on the map are suitable for automobile traffic, but they vary in width, state of repair, and traffic load, as indicated by the length and strength of the dashes in the broken lines that mark them. An extensive network of trails and paths suitable only for motorcycles, bicycles, or oxcarts was omitted from the map for the sake of clarity. The heavy solid lines shown on the main map represent the boundaries between primary marketing areas. Except where such boundaries follow significant water courses, they have been abstracted into straight lines, and as many as possible were made to meet at common points. A number within or beside a circle indicates that settlement's position in the central-place hierarchy as defined in Table 1, p. 222 below.

The Problem

The most striking feature of the economy of rural Taiwan is its extreme commercialization.* Increasingly since the Second World War, even villages have acquired permanent stores, and at present they are found in a full three-quarters of all settlements, including some quite small hamlets. There are, in fact, so many such stores that turnover and profits are low, and it is difficult to support a family solely by operating one. Larger villages have them in a rough ratio of one per twenty-five to fifty households. These "village stores" are usually operated by natives of the place, either prosperous farm families or, occasionally, land poor who have amassed the necessary liquid capital. They are sometimes housed in unused rooms in a family courtyard but more commonly occupy ramshackle structures of wattle-and-daub and bamboo. A few are found in permanent brick shop buildings of modest dimensions.

Village stores sell daily necessities and luxuries such as cooking oil, noodles, cake and candy, soap, matches, cigarettes, wine, soda pop, betel nut, canned goods, children's toys, spirit money, incense, and fresh fruit and sugarcane in season. Occasionally they carry fresh vegetables, small household goods, and a few farm supplies. Most of these items cost about 20 percent more than in the nearby towns where village stores obtain them, but people buy in village stores anyway, especially for small purchases, because they are nearby and, most important, because credit is easily obtained.

The social functions of village stores are at least as important as their economic roles. Idlers are usually to be found sitting around in front of them chewing betel nut and gossiping, and at night they often provide an arena for gamblers. In a moderate-sized village with several stores, some are social centers for women as opposed to men, or for one

* It can, in fact, be argued that because of their dependence on purchased foodstuffs, manufactured articles, and world markets, the Taiwanese are no longer peasants in the strict sense of the term. They are not farmers in the modern Western sense, either, but probably belong somewhere in between in a category that Barbara E. Ward has called "post-peasants" (Ward 1967).

political faction as opposed to another. More than one village store in a very small place is usually an indication of divisive political factionalism.

Some villages contain other businesses in addition to village stores. Over a third have mills where rice is husked and polished. These mills contract with farmers for their surplus, and then resell it to rice merchants in the towns and cities. One village in four has people who sell insecticide, often on consignment, and one in five has a barber or barbers serving school children and thrifty farmers. Approximately 10 percent of the villages in the field area contain small collections of shops and stalls that may include grocery stores,* beauty parlors, fresh vegetable stands, hot-snack and meal stalls, and occasionally pork sellers, modern Western-type drugstores, and even pool halls. These businesses are sometimes spread throughout a village but are more often found clustered together, forming an embryonic central place.

Four places in the field area have approximately twenty-five businesses each, and one of these even has a small covered market place for fresh fish and vegetables. At least three or four places that must be considered to be market towns because they have a large number of diverse shops (50 to 150) and because people from nearby villages obviously go there regularly to shop, may also be thought of as villages because the vast majority of their population is no more involved with business activity than other farmers living down the road in places that are not developed commercially. The Ta-ch'eng township seat has well over two hundred businesses, two large retail markets, some light industry using power machinery, and numerous government offices, yet the bulk of its population of approximately 5,000 are farmers indistinguishable from those who do not happen to live in a town. Even Erhlin Town, indisputably a high-level central place with over eight hundred businesses, has ordinary farmers living on its streets and alleys, as do other similar places.

How, then, can towns be distinguished from villages? For the purposes of this paper, at least, they need not be. The two categories are not mutually exclusive. This is not simply because there is a continuum embracing villages and towns, but, more importantly and more analytically, because two different aspects of a settlement are involved in the two terms. "Village" denotes a compact rural settlement of peasant farmers or perhaps fishermen, while "town" denotes diverse economic

---

* Distinguished from village stores by more elaborate premises and a concentration on foodstuffs alone, including dried fish, pickles, powdered milk, and a large amount of canned fish, meat, and fruit.

functions and centrality. Whether a given place with both attributes should be referred to as a village or a town depends on which aspect of the settlement enters discussion. In the ensuing analysis of the central-place hierarchy in Changhua Hsien, the relevant aspect is commercial complexity, and settlements will be classified on the basis of the range of goods and services available in them.

A shop census was taken in order to make sense out of the bewildering variety of businesses found in various settlements. The location, size, and condition of every shop in all the towns and commercially important villages in the field area were recorded, along with a list of the principal items sold in each. Permanent peddlers' stalls and various small stands were included, as were small handicraft factories and all other businesses. In addition, frequency counts of items sold or produced and separate counts of the number of businesses were made in the towns of Lukang, Ch'i-hu, Pei-tou, and T'ien-chung, places of the same general size and complexity as Erhlin, but located outside the field area. The same was done in the town of Ch'i-chou and, in order to increase the number of places with 15–35 businesses in the sample, in the three developed villages in Ch'i-chou township, which lies just outside the field area to the southeast. A questionnaire designed primarily to elicit marketing behavior was administered in every village with more than ten households in Erhlin Chen and Fang-yuan, Ta-ch'eng, Chu-t'ang, and P'i-t'ou Hsiang. The replies to this questionnaire yielded information on business establishments present in ordinary villages in the field area. Altogether the sample contains 207 places.

The Hierarchy of Commercial Complexity

Analysis of the 156 items that were recorded as occurring in three or more of the places in the sample readily yielded a Guttman Scalogram* of gigantic proportions, which is summarized in tabular form in Table 1. The scale ranks the settlements in the sample along the single dimension

---

* A technique whereby individual cases and their attributes are simultaneously ranked on the basis of the number of occurrences each produces in the other. The assumptions inherent in the device are the existence of a continuum uniting the cases, and the representativeness of the items measured. The result is a unidimensional scale that orders the cases in terms of the quality inherent in the attributes. In a perfect scale, all the cases in a given scale step exhibit the item defining the step and all other items similarly associated with lower steps, but do not manifest items found in higher steps. The legitimacy of a Guttman scale is measured by the (non-statistical) Coefficient of Reproducibility, a measure of gross error that should be above .9 for an adequate scale, and by the (also nonstatistical) Coefficient of Scalability, a more sophisticated measure of relative error that should be .6 or more for a good scale (Guttman 1950; Menzel 1953).

of commercial complexity. It was constructed by scrupulously minimizing inclusive errors at the expense of exclusive errors so long as total errors were not thereby increased. No items were discarded for causing a disproportionate number of errors, although eleven could have been dropped for that reason according to normal scaling procedures. All eleven occur at the most complex end of the scale and can be explained by the lack of higher-level centers in the sample. In my estimation, only three additional steps would be required to encompass places like Changhua, Taichung, and Taipei, which are representative of all other Taiwanese cities.

Except for the most complex towns in the sample, which account for the aberrant items just discussed, only seven of the 207 places exhibit a disproportionate number of errors. These seven occur in the middle range of the scale (steps 2–6), and all but two lie directly on principal roads whose constant streams of potential customers have apparently induced merchants to offer goods normally associated with higher-level centers. The complete scale has a Coefficient of Reproducibility of .991 and a Coefficient of Scalability of .776. If aberrant items were discarded, the latter figure would be .787.

The significance of the scale is its ability to rank all the various settlements in the sample along the single, definable dimension of commercial complexity. Hamlets without a single shop, villages of all sizes with a wide range in the number of businesses they contain, places that have only recently begun to function as central places, and small, medium, and large towns, some with over a thousand businesses, are all included and together constitute a single, demonstrable hierarchy.

As a result of the distribution of items in places, the scalogram is not symmetrical. At the lower end each item discriminates a large number of places, whereas at the upper end numerous items define each place. Altogether the scalogram has thirty-three steps—too large a number to be useful. Consequently, only ten major steps are recognized in Table 1. The others are indicated by specific items and number of cases in steps 0 through 5 and by names of towns in steps 6 through 9.

The ten major steps, which define the central-place hierarchy in the southwestern corner of the Changhua Plain, were not chosen arbitrarily. The principal criterion used to determine their demarcation is the occurrence of items with few or no errors. This alone is sufficient to establish steps 1–6. Step 7 was put where it is rather than one case higher, where it would also be defined by four items with relatively low error, on the basis of the pattern exhibited by exclusive errors, a criterion that is also useful in corroborating the demarcation of steps 5, 6, 8, and 9. The last

TABLE 1. GUTTMAN SCALE OF COMMERCIAL COMPLEXITY RANKING 207 SAMPLE SETTLEMENTS IN 10 MAJOR STEPS AND 33 SUB-STEPS

Major step	Percent of sample discriminated	Number of cases in the step	Items	Number or names of cases in sub-steps	Errors in lower steps	Exclusive errors in same step	Inclusive errors in same step	Errors in higher steps
0	100%	48	Ten or more households	1	0	0	0	0
1	76.8	82	Village store	1	0	0	0	0
2	37.2	32	Rice mill	24	1	0	0	3
			Insecticide	8	13	0	0	2
3	21.7	10	Barber	1	7	0	0	3
4	16.9	5	Grocery store	2	0	0	0	2
			Fresh vegetables	1	1	0	0	3
			Animal feed	2	3	0	0	7
5	14.5	8	Hot snacks	2	1	0	0	0
			Western drugs	3	1	0	0	2
			Bicycle repair	2	5	0	0	2
			Chinese drugs	1	2	1	0	1
6	10.6	6	Fresh pork	Hsi-kang	2	0	1	0
			Beauty parlor	Wan-ho, P'i-t'ou	5	0	0	0
			Western doctor	San-ch'uan	0	0	0	3
			Sandals	Chiu-kuai-ts'u	1	1	0	2
			Bicycle sales		5	1	0	0
			Dressmaker	Ch'eng-kung	5	2	0	0
			Fruit parlor		0	0	0	2

222

Business type				
Yuan-tou				
Household goods	0	0	0	0
Stationery	0	0	0	0
Cloth	0	1	0	0
Gas and oil	0	1	0	4
Lu-shang				
Bamboo yard	0	1	0	2
Fresh fish	0	0	0	3
Clothes	0	0	0	1
Electric appliances	0	0	0	0
Ts'ao-hu				
Bakery	0	1	1	0
Watches and clocks	0	0	1	0
Wan-hsing				
Concrete casting	0	0	1	3
Sewing school	1	0	0	1
Laundry	0	1	0	0
Cosmetics	0	1	0	0
Lu-k'ou-ts'u				
Restaurant	0	0	0	0
Photographer	1	0	0	0
Blacksmith	1	0	0	0
Fang-yuan				
Peanut oil mill	0	0	2	2
Rice and grain	0	0	1	1
Tailor	0	0	2	0
Ice maker	1	0	2	0
Hardware	0	0	2	0
Ice-cream maker	1	0	0	1
Lending library	1	0	1	0
Carpenter	1	0	1	0
Concrete tiles	0	0	0	0
Hotel	0	0	0	0
Religious articles	2	0	0	0

7   7.7   6

TABLE 1.—*Continued*

Major step	Percent of sample discriminated	Number of cases in the step	Items	Number or names of cases in sub-steps	Errors in lower steps	Exclusive errors in same step	Inclusive errors in same step	Errors in higher steps
8	4.8	4	Movie theater	Wang-kung	0	0	0	0
			Tea house		0	0	0	0
			Metal & plastic		4	0	0	0
			Pool hall		3	0	0	0
			Bamboo furniture		2	0	0	0
			Farm implements		2	0	0	0
			Sheet metal		3	0	0	0
			Farm supplies		1	0	1	0
			Furniture maker		1	0	1	0
			Hospital		1	0	1	0
			Sewing supplies		1	0	1	0
			Knitting		1	0	1	0
			Diesel motors		0	0	0	0
			Electric motors		0	0	0	1
			Motorcycle repair	Shao-p'u-hsin	5	0	0	0
			Dentist		4	0	0	0
			Fertilizer sales		4	0	0	0
			Welding		3	0	0	0
			Notary public		2	0	0	0
			Spirit-money maker		2	0	0	0
			Seal carver		1	0	0	0
			Taxicab company		0	0	0	0
			Water pumps		0	0	0	0
			Machine shop		0	0	1	0
			Yarn		0	0	1	0

Establishment				
Ta-ch'eng				9
Cotton bedding	0	0	1	6
Shoes	0	0	1	2
Pneumatic tires	0	0	1	1
Spectacles	0	0	1	0
Mosquito nets	0	0	1	0
Sewing machines	0	0	0	0
Fortune-teller	0	0	0	0
Seeds	1	0	0	0
Chu-t'ang				2.9
Paint	0	0	0	0
Electric contractor	0	0	0	0
Motorcycle sales	0	0	0	0
Sawmill	0	0	0	0
Luggage	0	0	0	0
Ch'i-chou				6
Fancy gift food	—	0	0	1
Sign painter	—	0	0	0
Goldsmith	—	0	0	0
Coal yard	—	0	0	0
Charcoal	—	0	0	0
Automobile repair	—	0	0	0
Television sets	—	0	0	0
Books and magazines	—	0	0	0
Records	—	0	0	0
Table and chair rental	—	0	0	0
Chinese doctor	—	0	0	0
Savings association	—	0	0	0
Pawn shop	—	0	0	0
Wedding gown rental	—	0	0	0
Wholesale betel nut	—	0	0	0
Rickshaws	—	0	0	0
Three-wheeled carriers	—	0	0	0
Cooper	—	0	0	4
Midwife	—	0	0	4

TABLE 1.—Continued

Major step	Percent of sample discriminated	Number of cases in the step	Items	Number or names of cases in sub-steps	Errors in lower steps	Exclusive errors in same step	Inclusive errors in same step	Errors in higher steps
9 (Continued)			Wine house		1	0	0	—
			Truck company		1	0	0	—
			Tools		2	0	1	—
			Plumbing contractor		1	0	0	—
			Jewelry		1	0	0	—
			News dealer		1	0	1	—
			Knitting school		1	0	1	—
			Chicken hatchery		0	0	1	—
			Large toys		0	0	1	—
			Electric fans (only)		0	0	2	—
			Electric parts		0	0	0	—
			Building contractor		1	0	0	—
			Tatami	T'ien-chung	3	0	0	—
			Metal working		1	0	0	—
			Coffin maker		1	0	0	—
			Diesel cultivators		1	0	0	—
			Bamboo basket maker		4	0	0	—
			Pictures and mirrors		1	0	0	—
			Window maker		1	0	0	—
			Medical laboratory		0	0	0	—
			Ice boxes		0	0	0	—
			Printer		0	0	0	—
			Insurance agent		0	0	0	—
			Tombstone carver		0	0	1	—
			Fodder chopping		0	0	1	—
			Tea store		0	0	1	—
			Scales		0	0	1	—
			Embroidery		0	0	1	—

Specialty	Town				
Noodle maker	Pei-tou	3	1	0	—
Concrete stoves		2	0	0	—
Auto batteries		2	1	0	—
Insecticide sprayers		1	0	0	—
Border sewing		0	0	0	—
Sandal maker		0	0	0	—
Pickling urns		0	0	1	—
Furniture factory		0	0	1	—
Cement	Lukang	1	1	0	—
Electric motor repair		0	1	0	—
Sausage maker		0	0	0	—
Coal ball maker		0	0	0	—
Chinese boxing	Erhlin, Ch'i-hu	0	1	0	—
Veterinarian		0	1	0	—
Cobbler		1	1	0	—
Large hotel		0	2	0	—
Fur coats		2	2	0	—
Women's underwear maker		2	1	0	—
Fodder-chopping machines		1	1	0	—
Commercial bank	0	0	3	0	—
Mattresses		0	3	0	—
Drug manufacturer		1	3	0	—
Bathhouse		1	2	0	—
Mushroom spores		2	2	0	—

NOTE: Ch'eng-kung (in step 6) does not appear on the map. It is located in eastern Ch'i-chou Hsiang southwest of T'ien-chung Town. The sub-step containing no towns and following the one containing Erhlin and Ch'i-hu includes items that occurred in three or more of the towns in the sample, but occurred irregularly. They either belong to the next higher step, or are wholly aberrant.

227

place in step 6 has only four exclusive errors, whereas the first place in step 7 has ten, about the same number as the next higher place. This pattern reflects the fact that most items in the scale are found in all the places in a given step and those higher, randomly in the next step down, and infrequently or not at all in still lower steps.

This phenomenon, which makes it possible to construct a Guttman scale at all, is readily explicable. In Taiwan's rapidly expanding economy, commercialization and personal incomes are both increasing. As a result, more and more goods and services are being offered at more and more places. Newly available goods and services, such as television sets, electric motor repair, bakeries, shoes, and taxi service, are always introduced first in high-level central places, and only eventually become available in lower-level centers, depending on demand and entrepreneurial optimism. A given item or service may have sufficient demand to become a consistent and permanent offering in towns at a certain level and above, but will appear sporadically at lower levels for an extended period until increased overall demand allows it to become firmly established at the lower level. Alternatively, demand for an item or service may stabilize at a level such that businesses offering it are not viable in places below a given rank in the hierarchy. In such cases it may disappear entirely from lower levels as merchants go out of business or change their lines, or it may linger on as a marginal item supported by profits from other items in those places where it has been tried, but it will not be introduced at other places in that same level because no one is willing to risk the necessary capital. The same alternatives apply to traditional occupations such as those of bamboo furniture makers, tea merchants, and coopers, as craftsmen respond to the growing economy by attempting to establish themselves in growing low-level centers. The random occurrence of most items in steps immediately below the ones to which they are specific demonstrates that the major steps indicated on Table 1 represent coherent levels of commercial complexity, and corroborates the other evidence used to establish them.

The clumping of low-error items and the pattern of exclusive errors exhibited by cases is sufficient to establish steps 8 and 9. However, these two steps are less distinct than they might be, for reasons that lie in the history and situation of the particular towns that appear on either side of the two breaks.

Fang-yuan, the most complex town in step 7, is in many ways a unique place. It was one of the first places in the field area to be settled by Chinese immigrants in the early seventeenth century and enjoyed some activity as a port in the eighteenth. When the Japanese came to the island its population was far larger than Erhlin's, and it continued to have a customs house for a brief period. In the early years of the Japanese occupation it was given a variety of administrative functions, and since 1910 it has been a township seat. It is now the administrative center for a township with a population of nearly 50,000. Nevertheless, it has failed to develop commensurately with similar places elsewhere, probably because it is not centrally located, it is too close to Erhlin, and its environment is dry and inhospitable. About half of the eleven items found in Fang-yuan but absent in other towns in step 7 are related to its administrative status, a factor shared by all but one of the towns in steps 8 and 9.

Wang-kung, the least complex town in step 8, is located four and a half kilometers north of Fang-yuan along the coast in the same township. It lacks two of the items found in Fang-yuan and other places in step 8, but contains fourteen items that are absent in Fang-yuan and present in almost all of the other places in steps 8 and 9. It has developed from practically nothing since the Second World War, and has a certain momentum of growth that is completely absent in Fang-yuan, where no new building has been put up for years.

The extensive commercial development of Wang-kung may be explained in part by heavy immigration into the surrounding area since the Second World War. The poor and sandy soil of the region, deposited by the Choshui River in one of its peregrinations in the early years of this century, discouraged all but a few Taiwanese from living there. During the late thirties and early forties, however, Japanese colonists came and established farms. When the colonists were repatriated after the war, many landless Taiwanese moved in to take their place. The population of the area is now several times what it was at the end of the war, principally because of the use of electric or diesel pumps on irrigation wells. Most of the newcomers to the area report doing most of their marketing at either Lukang, a step-9 town far to the north, or Ts'ao-hu, a step-7 town five kilometers from the coast, but I consider them nonetheless to be important in Wang-kung's development. Also, the population of the town alone is nearly 9,000, enough in itself to support all the businesses in a small town. These conditions, plus its location approximately equidistant from three large towns in an area where there is only one other settlement in steps 4 through 9 (Ts'ao-hu), no doubt account for its commercial development.

Ch'i-chou, the smallest and least complex town in step 9, is also peculiar. It owes its development primarily to being the island headquarters for the Taiwan Sugar Corporation. The company maintains an extensive residential enclave for its executives that resembles American military housing projects. Until very recently there was a large sugar mill, but it was sold to South Vietnam. Ch'i-chou still has a large flax-processing plant and is located on the main north-south highway only a few miles from the only road bridge across the Choshui River.

The functional complexity exhibited by Ch'i-chou is clearly closer to that of other places in step 9 than of places in step 8. It is marked by thirty-one items found in the rest of the large towns, in contrast to five items that isolate the most complex place in step 8, and sixteen items that mark the next higher place in step 9. Ch'i-chou also has wholesale functions equivalent to those of other places in step 9, although it does not have a central role in transportation. That is held by Pei-tou, a very old town located only two and a half kilometers to the northeast just off the main highway.

Pei-tou has been a market center for 250 years, and until well into this century was the largest and most important place in Changhua Hsien after the capital and the port of Lukang. Under the Japanese administration it had a position intermediate between the provincial government in Taichung City and all the townships in the field area. Until just before the war it was also the only large town in southern Changhua Hsien, and people from Erhlin report having gone there to buy things they could not get locally. Since the Second World War, however, it has not kept pace with the newer towns in step 9 and now has fewer shops than any in the *hsien* except Ch'i-chou and Ho-mei, a textile center in the north. Ch'i-chou appears to be usurping many of Pei-tou's central-place functions. It is much newer and has only half as many businesses, but it is growing rapidly, whereas Pei-tou is stagnating.

I cannot fully explain Pei-tou's relative decline on the basis of the data I have, but certainly the conditions that have promoted Ch'i-chou have worked against Pei-tou. There is room in the central-place hierarchy for only one step-9 town in that neighborhood, but it is unlikely that Pei-tou will ever lose its status completely. There is, however, no inherent reason why central-town functions cannot remain divided between the two narrowly separated centers for the foreseeable future. As a matter of fact the businesses growing up along the two and a half kilometers of heavily traveled national highway between the two towns may soon join them. In the discussion that follows, Pei-tou and Ch'i-chou will usually be treated separately, but it should be borne in mind that they divide the market for high-level goods in the surrounding area.

Given the wide range of goods and services used to rank the sample settlements along the dimension of commercial complexity, it would be possible to select items that relate to specific aspects of the economy, such as transport, agriculture, entertainment, or medicine, or that represent modern as opposed to traditional activities or techniques, and use them to construct scales that would rank the places along a variety of more specific dimensions. Although such limited scales would place some settlements in relative positions slightly different from those they occupy on Table 1, the same major steps result, indicating that economic development in this part of Taiwan has been uniform and that there are no significant distinctions within the single dimension of commercial complexity.

When the frequencies with which particular items are found in individual places are considered—data that scalogram analysis ignores—differential emphases become apparent, but they do not affect ranking. For instance, Erhlin has an inordinate number of so-called tea and wine houses that are actually houses of assignation. Although there are more such houses in Erhlin than in any other place in the *hsien*, including Changhua City, Erhlin is not therefore considered more complex.

Correlations

The integrity of a Guttman scale can be demonstrated by internal evidence such as that discussed above, but its validity, that is, its relation to the real world (in this instance the central-place hierarchy on the Changhua Plain), must be shown empirically by reference to attributes that are not contained in the scale itself. This is done in Table 2, which presents correlations between the ten major scale steps and other measures, all of which were divided into the same number of categories as the steps to which they were compared. The categories were delimited so that they had as nearly equal numbers of cases as the data allowed.

The way in which the Guttman Scale of Commercial Complexity was

TABLE 2. CORRELATIONS (KENDAL'S TAU BETA) BETWEEN COMMERCIAL COMPLEXITY AND OTHER ATTRIBUTES

Commercial complexity	Number of commercial functions	Number of businesses	Number of households
Steps 0–3	.900	.797	.498
Steps 4–6	.706	.731	.574
Steps 7–9	1.000	1.000	.615
Steps 0–9	.934	.871	.626

NOTE: All of the measures are significant at the .0005 level or higher. Kendal's Tau beta is a rank-order correlation coefficient that ranges between −1 and +1; 0 indicates complete lack of association, and ±.5 and above represents a strong relationship. Significance levels are determined by reference to normal distributions, not Chi-square (Siegel 1956: 213–23).

constructed automatically creates a very close (nearly tautological) relationship between number of commercial functions (goods and services) and scale rank (Tau beta = .934). The correlation is not quite perfect because the ranges of numbers of functions exhibited by places in the lower scale steps overlap to a limited extent, primarily due to cases with a high proportion of exclusive errors. These are concentrated in steps 4–6, and as a result the correlation between scale rank and number of functions is relatively low (Tau beta = .706) for the nineteen cases in those steps.

The principal advantage of a scale of commercial complexity over a count of commercial functions is that the added information it contains allows a continuous variable to be broken down into a manageable number of discrete categories. In addition, the ordering of cases in the scale is more rigorous than simple rank order by number of functions, because it discriminates against the random introduction of goods at inappropriate levels of the hierarchy that can unduly inflate the number of functions found in particular places.

The correlation between commercial complexity and number of business establishments is nearly as good as the one with number of goods and services (Tau beta = .871), but is not at all tautological. The replication of equivalent small units is fundamental to Chinese business practices (DeGlopper's paper in this volume) and numerous businesses offering identical goods are found in the same places at all levels of complexity. Also, a single business establishment commonly offers several distinct lines of goods or services. For example, insecticide, fertilizer, and animal feed are frequently sold in rice mills.

At the lower end of the scale the relationship between commercial complexity and number of businesses suffers somewhat (Tau beta =.797) because village stores and rice mills tend to replicate in settlements with large populations. In the middle of the scale the association suffers slightly more (Tau beta = .731) because of a similar replication of like units and, in addition, the existence of some higher-level functions. At the upper end of the scale, the relationship is perfect despite both of these tendencies toward error, because the absolute numbers of businesses are so much larger.

As is evident from Table 3, which lists the attributes of towns in steps 6–9, not only do the numbers of businesses associated with places in the three highest steps fall into discrete ranges (as do numbers of commercial functions), but the intervals separating adjacent steps are nearly as large as or even larger than the range exhibited by the lower of the two. This finding establishes a definite size hierarchy, as opposed to a

TABLE 3. ATTRIBUTES OF TOWNS IN STEPS SIX THROUGH NINE,
LISTED IN ABSOLUTE RANK ORDER

Scale step	Town	Number of commercial functions	Number of businesses	Population	Ratio of businesses to population
9	Ch'i-hu	150	1000	12,000	1:12
9	Erhlin	147	850	10,000	1:12
9	Lukang	144	1075	28,000	1:26
9	Pei-tou	138	725	12,000	1:17
9	T'ien-chung	141	725	9,300	1:13
9	Ch'i-chou	119	400	7,000	1:18
8	Chu-t'ang	87	230	1,700	1:7
8	Ta-ch'eng	82	240	5,000	1:21
8	Shao-p'u-hsin	74	165	2,100	1:13
8	Wang-kung	66	165	8,800	1:53
7	Fang-yuan	56	110	6,500	1:59
7	Lu-k'ou-ts'u	43	90	4,500	1:50
7	Wan-hsing	38	70	5,000	1:72
7	Ts'ao-hu	37	60	2,000	1:32
7	Lu-shang	36	80	6,000	1:75
7	Yuan-tou	30	60	2,000	1:32
6	Ch'eng-kung	21	33	2,800	1:100
6	Chiu-kuai-ts'u	17	26	2,800	1:112
6	San-ch'uan	11	17	2,000	1:125
6	P'i-t'ou	17	37	6,300	1:180
6	Wan-ho	15	12	2,300	1:190
6	Hsi-kang	17	28	4,000	1:133

NOTE: Of the six places in step 9, only Erhlin is in the field area. The others lie just outside the field area to the north and east, and were included for comparative purposes, as were Ch'eng-kung (not shown on the map) and San-ch'uan in step 6, both of which are in Ch'i-chou Hsiang to the southeast of the field area. Altogether, 155 possible items were found in three or more places in the sample. Lukang and Pei-tou in particular had numerous items that were not scaled.

continuum of sizes, for towns in scale steps 7, 8, and 9. The demonstration of a size hierarchy absolutely aligned with the scale of commercial complexity allowed towns on the Changhua Plain that were not included in the census or in the sample to be assigned to a place in the central-place hierarchy purely on the basis of the number of business establishments they contain. These numbers were ascertained quite quickly and fairly accurately by riding a motorcycle up and down every street and alley of each town, counting shops and stands.

The relationship between commercial complexity and population size is highly complex and statistically rather poor (Tau beta = .626), even at the most complex end of the scale (Tau beta = .615). Some partial explanations for this situation can be offered. In the first place, not every one who lives in a town is engaged in business. There are also farmers, fishermen, and day laborers. The ratio of businesses to population, shown for steps 6–9 in Table 3, can be used as a rough measure of the proportions. As is apparent from the table, there is wide variation in the ratios exhibited by places in the same scale step. Averages for the various steps do, however, demonstrate a definite negative relationship with commercial complexity. Places in step 9 have roughly one business per 15 people; towns in steps 8 and 7, one per 25 and 50 people respectively; and places in step 6, one per 140 people. The relatively high ratios in step 9 belong to old towns (Lukang and Pei-tou) with many farmers or fishermen and the rudiments of an urban próletariat, or result from unique factors such as the white-collar staff of the sugar company head-quarters in Ch'i-chou. High ratios in steps 7 and 8 indicate relatively recent commercial development of places that were large agricultural villages before the war. Low ratios in the same steps reflect commercial development in relatively small places located at strategic transportation nodes.

Another, perhaps more fundamental, explanation for the disparity between population size and commercial complexity in steps 7–9 is the fact that businesses associated with high-level central places are primarily dependent upon surrounding rural populations rather than on their own residents. Table 4 below, which lists attributes of marketing areas, shows that there is a fairly clear relationship between a town's commercial complexity and the number of people who live in its primary marketing area. The same is true to a very limited extent in regard to the rudimentary central places in steps 4–6.

Certain positive statements can be made about the relationship between a settlement's population and its commercial complexity. For instance, all places in step 9 have over 7,000 people, all but one place in steps 6–8 (Chu-t'ang in step 8 with 1,700) have more than 2,000, and only three out of thirteen places in steps 4–5 have fewer than 1,000 (two of the three have fewer than 200). However, such statements need to be balanced by calling attention to two places in step 2 with more than 2,000 people and seventeen places in steps 1–3 with between 1,000 and 2,000. Of the 197 places in the field-area sample (which does not include hamlets with fewer than ten households or the ten places in steps 4–9 brought into the total sample to provide comparative data for the middle and high end of the scale), there are forty-two with populations in excess of 1,000. Nineteen, or 45 percent, of these have no appreciable commercial development (steps 0–3).

Some characteristics shared at least partially by places in steps 4–6 are relatively large population, distance from higher-level towns, and location on heavily traveled roads (which largely account for the three minor centers with very small populations). Places in step 6 have at least two, and commonly all three, of these characteristics, whereas those in steps 5 and 4 have one or two of them in weaker combinations. It is also true that villages in steps 0–3 are small on the average (mean size is from 55 to 59 households, with a principal mode at 30–34 and minor modes at 15–24, 50–64, and around 150 and 200 households), that some are quite close to high-level towns, and that some can be reached only by oxcart trails and footpaths. Nevertheless, some places in steps 0–3 have characteristics in common with the majority of those in steps 4–6.

Several hypotheses that might have accounted for differential commercial development in villages and rudimentary central places proved under statistical analysis to be untenable. Neither distance from a settlement to the closest town in step 9 nor distance from a settlement to towns in steps 7–9 had any bearing on the scale rank of places in steps 0–6 (respectively, Tau beta $= -.074$ and $.006$ at significance levels of $.06$ and $.4$). Correlations between commercial complexity and location on a main road (Tau beta $= .181$ at the $.0001$ level) and location on either a secondary or a main road (Tau beta $= .299$ at the $.00004$ level) were also too poor to be meaningful explanatory factors, although the second measure approaches importance. Most places in steps 4–6 developed on fair roads or have had roads to them improved, but the same is also true for many places in steps 0–3. Distance from the coast, which influences the proportion of dry to wet fields, proved to be irrelevant as well.

I could find no specific reasons why some places begin to develop and others in similar circumstances do not—why people will risk their capital in one village and not in another much like it. Given a certain number of potential customers, due to a strategic location or a large local population, a village will begin to develop central-place functions only to the extent that individuals are willing to invest their capital in businesses located there. It may require more capital and be more difficult, in terms of finding a location and competing with established firms, to open shop in a town rather than in a village, but these factors are outweighed by the greater probability of commercial success for new businesses in well-established centers. In general, shops located in villages are operated by locals who see a chance to obtain their friends' and relatives' custom and who are prepared to put up with marginal or no profits for years while it develops, if it ever does. Outsiders who move into a village and initially have a hard time getting customers soon move on.

Whether or not anyone is willing to risk money by establishing a rice mill, grocery store, or bicycle repair shop in any particular village is to a large degree fortuitous, although there is a snowball effect such that, for instance, a beauty shop is far more likely to be started in a place that already has a drugstore, a snack seller, and a vegetable peddler than in a neighboring village that has only village stores and perhaps a mangy barber. Local political machinations also seem to influence commercial development, leading more often to the replication of existing businesses than to the introduction of completely new ones, however.

The finding that there is only a relatively weak relationship between the size of a settlement's population and its central-place functions points to the inadvisability of categorizing places as towns simply on the basis of the number of people they contain. It is especially dangerous to use published census figures in any such classification because the administrative districts used for census purposes do not often coincide with the social or even the geographical boundaries of settlements. As has been demonstrated, the number of businesses found in a place is a far better indicator of commercial complexity than is population, especially at higher levels of the central-place hierarchy where measures of centrality have greater social significance. Numbers of businesses are also relatively easy to ascertain in the field, although it must be cautioned that informants are very unreliable in this regard.

Correspondences with Traditional China

In the preceding pages I have defined the central-place hierarchy found in southwestern Changhua Hsien, I have examined a number of correlations with other features of the settlements in my sample, and I have provided some discussion of several factors related to differential commercial development. On the basis of familiarity with other regions of Taiwan, I am convinced that the same levels of commercial complexity are found throughout the island, although the details of the Guttman scale presented in Table 1 may not be representative of any other specific area.

As a prelude to the ensuing description of marketing behavior in southwestern Changhua, it will be convenient to align the Taiwanese central-place hierarchy described in Table 1 with the hierarchy of markets Skinner has defined for mainland China. This will allow the use of similar terminology and will provide a guide to corresponding orders of magnitude. Given the differences in time, space, and conditions between Taiwan and the systems Skinner describes, functional criteria must be used to identify the Taiwanese counterparts of traditional Chinese markets. Retail marketing patterns are the most obvious and relevant.

A survey was undertaken to determine where people in the field area do their marketing.* The places reported for the 185 villages in the sample are contained in scale steps 7, 8, and 9 with only two or three very minor exceptions. It is therefore reasonable to equate these steps with Skinner's hierarchy of market towns and, specifically, the lowest of the three, step 7, with his standard market towns. The towns in step 9 are much older and larger than the others, are the main sources of wholesale supply for village stores in their hinterlands, and are all at the centers of radiating networks of roads served by bus routes originating in them. They therefore meet all the conditions for Skinner's central market towns. If these two identifications are correct, then the towns in scale step 8, which are in the middle range both in size and in function, can logically be classed with Skinner's intermediate market towns.

Places in scale steps 4, 5, and 6 are either collections of shops located on main roads or large villages that have only recently begun to acquire a fair variety of businesses. Most are clearly incipient small market towns, corresponding perfectly to what Skinner calls minor markets. Steps 0 through 3 contain villages of various sizes that cannot be considered even rudimentary central places. Places such as Changhua City and Taichung City (which were not included in the sample) are clearly in separate classes above the towns contained in the sample, and can be identified as local and regional cities, respectively.

Because of the basically different circumstances found in Changhua, notably in this instance a commercialized, modern economy and the lack of true *markets* consisting of large periodic congregations of peasants and peddlers, it is perhaps best to employ a terminology slightly different from the one Skinner applied to the Mainland. In order to distinguish the Taiwanese marketing system, towns in scale step 9 will be called "central towns," those in step 8 will be called "intermediate towns," and those in step 7 will be called "standard towns." "Minor towns" will be those in steps 4 to 6.

Taiwanese Retail Marketing Patterns

The interview schedule mentioned above asked where people in each village shop most frequently, what percentage (in increments of 10 percent) of marketing they do there, and how often a member of each household goes, on the average. Similar questions regarding the second

---

* Interviewers, all of whom were local people having contacts throughout the areas assigned to them, sought out someone in every village with more than ten households (only about a dozen have fewer), and asked him where fellow villagers did their buying and selling. There were usually several people present when the questions were asked, and the answers typically represent a consensus of many responses.

and third most frequent places were asked in order.* Respondents were also asked where they bought twelve items known to be associated with different levels of towns. Their replies were used as a check on the preceding general responses. Correspondence between answers to the two sets of questions was quite good.

Only a third of the respondents reported that their fellow villagers do all of their marketing at a single place. The remainder specified two or three towns, but almost invariably indicated that their custom is not divided equally between them. With only two exceptions out of 185 villages, at least 50 percent of all marketing is done at a single town, although by no means the closest one. Of those respondents who indicated two or three towns, about half reported that 70 percent of all marketing is done at one place, somewhat fewer than a quarter reported 60 percent, and a like number reported 80 percent. Only a handful reported 90 percent.

Since half of all responses indicate that 70 percent or less of marketing is done at one place, it is clear that there is no counterpart in Changhua for the clearly demarcated, discrete standard marketing areas described for traditional China. It will therefore be convenient to use the term "primary marketing area" to refer to the region around any town that contains villages that do more than 50 percent of their retail marketing in that town. Primary marketing areas are shown on the main map on page 216. As noted above, the boundaries shown have been straightened and regularized except where they follow significant watercourses. The place where a village does 50 percent or more of its marketing will be referred to as its "primary town," no matter whether the town is classified as standard, intermediate, or central on the basis of commercial complexity. Definitions of "secondary areas" and "secondary towns" follow logically, involving reports of 40 percent or less.

The nature of primary marketing areas and the ways in which secondary marketing areas overlap with them can be illuminated by a description of the spatial distribution of percentages of marketing reported done at various places. All villages that were reported to do 90 or 100 percent of their retail buying at a single place are clustered around Erhlin, the only central town in the field area, or around the two largest intermediate towns, Ta-ch'eng and Chu-t'ang. Erhlin accounts for a majority of them. Well over half of the reports of 80 percent come from villages that are located in loose rings on the margins

---

* Only one or two out of the nearly two hundred responses (more than one response was obtained from some villages) reported that their fellow villagers regularly shopped in more than three towns.

of the core clusters of 90 and 100 percent. Otherwise, no patterns can be discerned: reports of 50, 60, and 70 percent and the remainder of the 80 percents are distributed at random outside the core clusters of 90 and 100 percent except in trivial and readily explicable pockets. There are, for instance, no clusters of 80 or 70 percent surrounding standard towns.

The only minor town in the field area that was reported to have a primary marketing area is Chiu-kuai-ts'u. Its area includes only itself and one hamlet, and inhabitants of both reportedly do 60 percent of their business in its twenty-six shops. Two other minor towns account for only a small percentage of the custom of their own large populations. The remaining minor town for which marketing information is available is one that has recently emerged near a new wholesale vegetable market. There were no reports that any village patronizes this town, most likely because the only people who shop there are the growers of the specific vegetable sold in the market, and they live scattered around in many villages in the region.

Percentages of marketing done in secondary towns do show regular patterns in their distributions. People who live in villages outside the 90- and 100-percent cores surrounding central and some intermediate towns but still within their primary areas go to smaller places, which are appreciably closer to them, for about 20 percent of their retail needs. This behavior accounts for approximately one quarter of responses from 10 to 40 percent. The remainder of such responses represent villagers in the primary areas of standard and intermediate towns who find it necessary to visit higher-level centers for around a third of their purchases. This average figure masks the seeming ability of towns such as Ta-ch'eng and Chu-t'ang to supply everything needed often enough to be remembered offhand in response to the questionnaire. Higher-level marketing done by people living in the primary areas of standard towns is usually divided between the closest intermediate town (15 to 25 percent) and the closest central town (10 to 20 percent) unless a central town is closer than any intermediate town, in which case all higher-level marketing is done at the central town. There is also a definite tendency for people to do up to 10 percent of their marketing at their township seat even if they live rather far away from it and there are closer towns at the same level of complexity. This tendency is explained by their need to go there anyway from time to time for a variety of official or political purposes.

If the marketing percentages discussed above are looked at in terms of the secondary areas they define, the patterns they manifest can perhaps be visualized more clearly. The secondary areas of central towns extend almost precisely halfway toward other central towns, overlapping the primary areas of intervening intermediate and standard towns. With the possible exception of the villages that were reported to do all marketing at one of the two largest intermediate towns, every village and town is contained in the secondary area of a central town. A few villages reported shopping in more than one central town, but the zones of overlap between central-town secondary areas are very narrow, and as a general rule villages belong to the secondary area of their closest central town.

The secondary areas of intermediate towns permeate the primary areas of adjoining standard towns, extending roughly halfway toward other intermediate towns and somewhat less than halfway toward adjacent central towns. The secondary areas of intermediate towns do not overlap with each other, but do overlap with central-town secondary areas within the primary areas of standard towns. Villages located near the center of primary marketing areas of central (and some intermediate) towns do not belong to the secondary area of any intermediate or standard town. The secondary marketing areas of standard towns extend, with rapidly diminishing strength, rather less than halfway toward neighboring higher-level towns, and can be viewed as infringements that take a small amount of patronage away from more distant, larger places. The same is true of the overlap of intermediate-town secondary areas with the primary areas of central towns.

The last column of Table 4, p. 244, lists the average percentage of marketing done by inhabitants of primary marketing areas belonging to towns in the field area. It shows that standard towns receive an average of less than 70 percent of the patronage of people living in their primary areas, whereas intermediate and central towns provide for an average of 80 percent (as much as 90 percent in some cases) of the marketing needs of people living in their primary areas. One reason for this is that standard towns on the Changhua Plain cannot provide everything that the rural population needs or wants. In this regard, they are not equivalent to standard markets in traditional China, which were capable of supplying all peasant needs. In traditional China intermediate markets supplied elitist and luxury goods to the local gentry—the educated, wealthy, and leisured class. The 30 to 40 percent of patronage taken from standard towns by higher-level centers comes from literate, prosperous "post-peasants" with plenty of spare time. What with transistor radios, record players, motorcycles, white buck shoes, pastries, canned goods, small diesel-powered two-wheeled tractors, electric pumps for irrigation and running water, sewing machines, and all the other material paraphernalia of world culture, the life-style of today's affluent Taiwanese farmer is as far removed from that of a Ch'ing dynasty scholar-official as is a modern Frenchman's from that of Louis XVI. Yet in terms of marketing behavior he is far more akin to the Ch'ing gentry than to the traditional Chinese peasant in that standard towns cannot supply the myriad goods he occasionally purchases.

There are other reasons as well why the Taiwanese are prone to frequent higher-level towns rather than their closest standard town. The last column of Table 4 displays an interesting peculiarity: villagers in Shao-p'u-hsin's primary area do markedly less shopping there than do people living in the primary areas of the two largest intermediate towns, Chu-t'ang and Ta-ch'eng (66.5 percent as compared to 85 and 90 percent, respectively). An analysis of this anomaly provides another insight into the nature of retail marketing habits in modern Taiwan.

The number of goods and services available in these three intermediate towns may have an effect on the frequency with which they are patronized. Although difficult to evaluate conclusively, this factor does not seem to be of any great significance. Only eight items absent in Shao-p'u-hsin can be found in both of the other two. On the other hand, each town offers four or five items that cannot be purchased in either of the others. In addition, Ta-ch'eng lacks five items found in Chu-t'ang, yet it is patronized more frequently by villagers in its primary area than is Chu-t'ang.

Part of the answer to the problem posed by Shao-p'u-hsin's lower average certainly lies in the amount of patronage drained off by adjacent towns at different levels. Shao-p'u-hsin is located within eight kilometers of four central towns (counting Pei-tou and Ch'i-chou separately), whereas Chu-t'ang is close to only two central towns (unless Hsi-lo at the southern end of the only road bridge across the Choshui River is considered), and Ta-ch'eng is isolated in a corner formed by the river and the sea with only Erhlin nearby. Erhlin is the only central town reportedly patronized to any appreciable extent by villagers in the primary areas of Ta-ch'eng and Chu-t'ang. An appreciable number of people who live in Shao-p'u-hsin's primary area, however, are reportedly drawn away from it toward central towns in three directions: west to Erhlin, north to Ch'i-hu, and east to Ch'i-chou and Pei-tou. Many of the people living around Chu-t'ang and (particularly) Ta-ch'eng must pass through these places on their way to Erhlin, and if what they need is available at the first stage in their journey they are unlikely to continue. By contrast, the people living in Shao-p'u-hsin's primary area do not need to pass through it on their way to any central town.

The percentage of marketing drawn off by neighboring lower-level towns is also significant. The two standard towns adjacent to Shao-p'u-hsin attract business from seven villages in its primary area. They represent 35 percent of the villages reporting, enough to bring Shao-p'u-hsin's average down considerably. Chu-t'ang is also adjacent to two standard towns, but only one attracts business from one of its villages. No standard town takes business away from Ta-ch'eng. Chu-t'ang has an average 5 percent below Ta-ch'eng's because people living in villages near the minor town of Chiu-kuai-ts'u go to Erhlin for about 40 percent of the things they buy. The analogous area in Ta-ch'eng Hsiang, around the minor town of T'an-ch'ien, is a part of Erhlin's primary area, not Ta-ch'eng's. Seven out of ten neighboring towns at various levels draw patronage from twenty-two villages (about one-third of the total) on the periphery of Erhlin's giant primary area, but they barely succeed in reducing its average marketing percentage below 90 percent, a testament to the attraction that central towns have for Taiwanese peasants.

The consideration of surrounding towns at various levels is enough to account for the differences in percentage of marketing done at towns in the field area, but does not go to the heart of the problem that Shao-p'u-hsin presents. The question remains: what is wrong with Shao-p'u-hsin? Why does no village in its primary area report marketing there exclusively, as a fair number of villages do for Ta-ch'eng and Chu-t'ang? People living right around Ta-ch'eng and Chu-t'ang must occasionally go elsewhere to buy a television set, order a tombstone, pawn a ring, get their urine analyzed, or do other things that cannot be done in an intermediate town, and one must suppose that such concerns arise no less often for these people than for the people living near Shao-p'u-hsin. Yet they are significantly more inclined to patronize their primary town than are the villages in Shao-p'u-hsin's area.

The necessary and sufficient reason for the difference is the Taiwanese penchant for passive entertainment by crowds and noisy activity of any kind. Shao-p'u-hsin is simply not a very satisfying town. It has fewer shops than either Chu-t'ang or Ta-ch'eng, it has only two intersecting streets with generally poor-looking shops strung out along them for a considerable distance, and it is one of the dullest places around. No crowds, no activity, no life! And something more stimulating than the "monotony and vacuity of village life" (Smith 1900) is one of the main reasons why the Taiwanese go to town as often as they do.

They go all the time. The roads are filled with constant streams of bicycles, motorcycles, oxcarts, buses, and even pedestrians. However, it is not possible to assess marketing behavior by counting the number of people loaded on each bicycle or the number of straw hats wandering around in the streets. According to the information obtained in the survey, adults go to their primary town about every second day on the average, and in many households one member goes every day. In addition, people living in the primary areas of standard towns go to their intermediate town about once every four or five days, and to a central town once a week or so. People living in the primary areas of intermediate towns go to their central town just as often.

Except for daily inspections of growing rice, field work between transplanting and harvest is done by women who can be hired for less than half an American dollar for a back-breaking day of crawling around on all fours in the mud, pulling weeds. Thus farmers, and rural housewives who need not stoop for their daily rice, have plenty of time to go shopping. They are not limited to brief periodic bursts of marketing activity but can find businesses open every day of the year, including the New Year, and from dawn until well into the night. Shopping expeditions usually involve visits to favorite gathering places, a squat for a chew of betel nut during which the latest juicy story is passed along, and perhaps a movie or a glass of tea to round out the day.

When Taiwanese peasants decide where to go to do their shopping they are not necessarily guided by the factors that go into making up the "rational economic man" so beloved of economists and classical central-place theorists. With time on their hands, money in their pockets, and buses, motorcycles, and bicycles readily available, they are apt to ignore time and distance factors and pay attention to entertainment value. There is no question about the fact that central towns with their gaudy streets, bustling crowds, blaring moviehouse sound tracks, and the even chance they afford to witness a funeral, a fight, or the girls in a teahouse, are eminently more appealing to the Taiwanese than the dusty streets, tawdry shops, and sleeping dogs that typify standard towns. Such "non-rational" factors go a long way toward explaining why customers are not drawn to Shao-p'u-hsin, which except for its size and complexity in many ways resembles a standard town. They also have a profound effect on the size and shape of all primary marketing areas.

Size and Shape of Primary Marketing Areas

Certain facts pertaining to the primary marketing areas of towns in the field area are presented in Table 4. The number of villages recorded

TABLE 4. CHARACTERISTICS OF PRIMARY MARKETING AREAS IN THE FIELD AREA

Scale step	Towns	Number of villages	Area population	Area in sq km	Average percentage of marketing
9	Erhlin	60	45,000	89	89%
8	Chu-t'ang	28	18,000	23.8	85
8	Ta-ch'eng	27	24,000	34.2	90
8	Shao-p'u-hsin	22	22,500	25.5	66.5
8	Wang-kung	6	10,500	9.25	72
7	Fang-wang	5	13,350	13.0	70
7	Lu-k'ou-ts'u	12	9,700	18.4	65
7	Wan-hsing	6	5,700	19.0	72.5
7	Ts'ao-hu	11	7,000	17.5	67
7	Lu-shang	5	6,250	11.3	70
7	Yuan-tou	8	7,200	13.7	63
6	Chiu-kuai-ts'u	1	2,900	1.75	60

for each town includes small hamlets, but not the towns themselves. The figures representing populations are very close estimates based on household registration records, and include the inhabitants of the towns as well as those of the villages. In those instances in which the number of villages is small but the population is considerable, the towns themselves have exceptionally large numbers of people. The sizes of the areas were computed with the aid of the straight lines drawn on the main map on page 216. Average percentages of marketing come from the responses to the questionnaire.

In general, Table 4 shows that the population and size of primary marketing areas fall into definite ranges that are clearly associated with position in the central-place hierarchy. There is only one truly anomalous case, and that is Wang-kung. This place, whose rapid growth since 1950 was discussed earlier, has only recently become an intermediate town. In each of the columns its figures are well within the range for standard towns, and if these were the only criteria used, it would have to be so classified. Table 1, however, clearly demonstrates the validity of considering it to be an intermediate town.

The large variation in the size of primary marketing areas is of great significance, and presents a marked contrast with Skinner's models for the traditional Mainland. The average size of the primary areas centered on the seven standard towns in the field area is 13.5 sq km, just half that of the primary areas centered on the three normal intermediate towns, and 60 percent of the average of 22.2 sq km that results when Wang-kung is included. Erhlin's primary area, 89 sq km, is nearly five times as large as the average for all the other eleven towns in the sample, and it is not unique among central towns on the Changhua Plain in having a very large area.* The population of primary areas follows precisely the same pattern as size at all three levels of complexity.

The primary areas of high-level towns are so much larger than the primary areas of low-level towns simply because people prefer to go to larger places. The reasons I have given for this preference—availability of more goods and services, and entertainment value—need to be put into spatial and practical perspective in order to make their effect on the size and shape of primary areas manifest.

When villagers living close to a standard town but roughly between it and a more distant central or intermediate town are asked why they shop in the larger place most frequently, their reply is that they do occasionally go to the nearby place if they need to get their bicycle or oxcart fixed, or if they know exactly what they want and are sure that it will be available. Otherwise, they would rather go the greater distance and be sure of getting what they want than go to the little place first and then have to backtrack to reach the larger one. They often do not mention explicitly that they find standard towns a dull lot whereas they are certain to be entertained in some way or other if they venture to a larger town, but this is evident from other contexts.

These considerations do not apply to people who must travel through a standard or intermediate town to get to a larger place. They may find what they are after, meet a friend with some new gossip, witness a scene, or satisfy their needs in some other way in the small place without having to go all the way to a big town. Also, the round trip to a higher-level town is much longer for such people; they have to make what is in effect two trips to get there.

The choice of which town to visit depends not only on relative distances and attractions, but also on the ease with which the towns in question can be reached. This involves practical considerations of roads and trails and available means of transportation. Some people walk to town, especially if the journey is a short one and they can take a relatively direct route along paths and paddy bunds (dikes), which usually connect any village with the closest town. Most people, however, have some form of mechanical transportation at their command. Bicycles and

---

* My estimates for the primary marketing areas of other central towns on the plain are: Lukang, 86 sq km; Ch'i-hu, 67 sq km; T'ien-chung, 36 sq km; Pei-tou, 27 sq km; and Ch'i-chou, 36 sq km. The average (including Erhlin) is 57 sq km if Pei-tou and Ch'i-chou are counted separately and 68 sq km if their areas are combined. Changhua City and the other two central towns in the *hsien* have primary areas that are well within the same size range.

motorcycles can be taken almost anywhere that people can walk, but of course they provide a much greater advantage when used on major trails and roads. Oxcarts and trailers pulled by two-wheeled tractors are limited to trails and roads, and the buses that run frequently between all towns are limited to the roads. It is not possible to go directly from all villages to the surrounding towns by roads and trails. Detours, sometimes of considerable length, are often involved in getting from one place to another except by foot or perhaps by bicycle. The main map at the beginning of this paper displays roads suitable (sometimes marginally) for four-wheeled vehicles. It can be seen that there is a complex pattern of roads radiating out of Erhlin, which is typical of central towns in this regard. Most intermediate towns (Chu-t'ang, for instance) have similar, if more rudimentary networks. Standard towns, on the other hand, are typically located on single roads between higher-level towns, or at the intersection of two such roads.

The effect of roads and available mechanical transport is that in many cases it is easier and more convenient for villagers to shop in more distant higher-level towns than in closer lower-level towns. This factor, coupled with the far greater attraction that high-level towns hold for the Taiwanese, has led me to formulate a "gravitational" model for the location of central places and the size and shape of their marketing areas.*

Lines of attraction, partially composed of "non-economic" factors, follow the roads (strongly) and paths (weakly, and with rapidly diminishing strength) that radiate out of central places. The effect of this attraction on the marketing areas of satellite lower-level central places is to cause them to sweep away from higher-level central places like comet tails, or to be squeezed into long and narrow fields perpendicular to the roads between two higher-level towns. These effects can be discerned on the map in the cases of Lu-shang and Ts'ao-hu, and Yuan-tou and Wan-hsing, respectively.

Under the influence of the forces involved in this gravitational or "attraction" model, the boundaries between primary marketing areas of towns at different levels in the central-place hierarchy are not anywhere near halfway between the two places. Boundaries between the primary areas of central and standard towns, for instance those between Erhlin and Ts'ao-hu or Yuan-tou, are *very* close to standard towns, even approaching the limits of the settlement itself in some instances. Boundaries between central and intermediate towns and those between inter-

---

* As contrasted with the marketing, transport, and administrative models introduced into central-place theory by Christaller (1966).

mediate and standard towns are not affected to the same extent because of lesser relative differences in attractions and convenience. This can be seen in the boundary between Erhlin and Chu-t'ang and the ones between Chu-t'ang and Yuan-tou or Lu-k'ou-ts'u, which are more nearly, but still not exactly, midway between the respective towns.

The relationship between primary retail marketing areas and administrative districts deserves brief mention here. The two are in some cases nearly congruent, but for etymological (and ideological) reasons, educated Chinese as well as peasants often assert that they are invariably identical. They obviously cannot be the same in all or even in most cases, however, because there are far more towns than administrative areas (*hsiang* and *chen*, or "townships," in this instance). In addition, *chen* administrative seats (which are almost invariably central towns) are often located at the very edge of their districts, and the people living in the adjoining areas of neighboring *hsiang* naturally do their marketing there. *Hsiang*, which often (but by no means always) have intermediate towns as their centers of government, sometimes correspond fairly closely with the primary marketing areas of the principal towns they contain. The reason for this is a simple historical one: the Japanese set them up that way when they determined the final form of the units of local government in 1920, having experimented with the idea during the preceding ten or fifteen years, and township boundaries have not changed since.

Wholesale Marketing Areas

The only important wholesale function performed by market towns in Changhua Hsien is supplying village stores with their small stocks. Government monopolies (salt, tobacco, and alcohol) are located in *chen* administrative centers, and all retailers of these items must fetch what they need. Otherwise, merchants in standard towns order their stock through traveling salesmen or directly from wholesalers or producers in local and regional cities just as merchants in intermediate and central towns do. Merchandise is delivered to shops by mail, by rail, or by the fleets of trucks and three-wheeled carriers that ply the highways and back roads.

At the same time that interviews were conducted in villages to discover the details of retail marketing, the operators of village stores were asked where they obtained their merchandise. The responses show a bewildering variety of sources. A typical village store obtains its soda pop from Yuan-lin (a large central town south of Changhua City) or Pei-kang (fifty miles to the south), its sugarcane from a neighboring village, its spirit money from the closest intermediate town, its cookies from a nearby standard town, and its cigarettes and wine from the closest central town. Villages along the coast get their supplies from far fewer places, but that is because there are fewer suitable sources nearby. Stores located in the eastern part of the field area are served by five or six towns as a matter of course.

It is difficult to generalize about such diverse phenomena, but the patterns occurring in the field area are roughly as follows. Erhlin provides 75 to 80 percent of the goods sold in village stores in its primary retail marketing area, and throughout southern Fang-yuan and Ta-ch'eng Hsiang as well, because of the lack of competition from other central towns. Where it has competition, in other parts of its secondary retail area, it supplies only about 25 percent of such goods. The same appears to be generally true of other central towns in both their primary and their secondary retail areas. If a town specializes in certain products, as Yuan-lin does in fruit, its wholesale area will extend far beyond its retail areas, but the percentage of goods it supplies in those fringe areas will be far lower than within its secondary area. Intermediate towns provide 25 percent of the goods to stores in their primary retail marketing areas, but very little beyond. The remainder comes from all over, occasionally from standard towns but usually from central towns and local cities, some of them quite far away. Some items, such as cake and cookies or soda pop, are usually delivered on a regular schedule, but most are fetched by the proprietors themselves as they need them.

Produce Marketing Areas

The same people who were asked to describe the shopping habits of their fellow villagers were also questioned about the marketing of produce. They were asked where and in what amounts the three major crops—rice, peanuts, and sweet potatoes—were sold or, if they were sold in the village, where the people who bought them came from. They were asked what percentage of the rice crop was disposed of through the farmers' association, as well as what subsidiary crops people in the village might raise, and how they were sold.

Rice is by far the largest crop in the region, except near the coast where the land is too dry. The bulk of the harvest is turned over to the government-controlled farmers' association in payment of land tax, as installments on fields purchased under the land reform, or in exchange for fertilizer. There is a farmers' association warehouse in every township seat, and branch offices are maintained in many of the smaller towns, which thereby gain a role in produce marketing that would not otherwise be theirs. Rice that is not given over to the government or required for home consumption is sold to rice mills. Those located in villages do not buy as much in proportion to their numbers as do those in towns. Rice mills and grain dealers in intermediate and central towns get most of the excess produced in their primary areas, usually picking it up by truck from the farmers. Rice mills often lend money against unharvested rice as a means of ensuring that they will eventually get their hands on some of it.

Peanuts, which are grown throughout a coastal belt five to ten kilometers wide, are commonly sold to the numerous peanut-oil mills in Fang-yuan. It therefore has a produce-marketing area out of all proportion to its primary retail area. Oil mills are found in all central and intermediate towns and in a few standard towns, and they take some of the peanut crop from surrounding areas. Flax, grown for fiber or for linseed oil, is invariably sent to the factory in Ch'i-chou, which as a result performs produce-marketing functions for places well within Erhlin's primary retail area. Other special winter crops, such as garlic, rapeseed, wheat, and a wide variety of green vegetables, are sold on contract, often to buyers from large cities who load them onto trucks at the edge of the fields. The American government buys green tomatoes in this manner and ships them to Vietnam.

Watermelons are the only fruit extensively cultivated in the field area. Some melons are hawked on the streets of local towns, but most are either sold on contract or taken to the wholesale fruit markets in Ch'i-hu or, especially, Yuan-lin. The wholesale produce markets in these two places also collect a variety of vegetables for shipment to the cities. In addition, they sell vegetables from other parts of the island, and much of the produce sold in local markets comes from these towns, the remainder being grown by the permanent market sellers themselves.

Mushrooms and asparagus, which are canned for export, have been introduced into the region within the last five years and have added greatly to the prosperity of Erhlin in particular. They are disposed of by contract to the farmers' association or to private brokers who work for canning plants in the region. Large baskets filled with either vegetable can be seen soaking in foul water-buffalo wallows while waiting to start their long journey to the shelves of foreign supermarkets.

About the only things that people bring to town and sell to whoever will buy are excess sweet potatoes, peanut and sweet-potato vines to be used as pig fodder, and a spinach-like green that is brought to town at dawn by women eager for the few cents it will bring.

Produce-marketing areas are basically similar to primary retail marketing areas, but the pattern is blurred by the factors discussed above. Given the existence of farmers' associations, contract sales, and, one suspects, speculators in commodity futures, market towns on Taiwan are far from the sort of place that "functions in the first instance to exchange what the peasant produces for what he needs" (Skinner 1964). The Taiwanese exchange what they produce wherever they can for as much money as they can get, and then buy what they want wherever it it is conveniently available.

Mainland Marketing Systems

The preceding pages describe the hierarchy of central places in southwestern Changhua Hsien and the marketing areas served. As a description the study can stand alone, but it becomes meaningful only when placed in comparative and historical perspective. Since Taiwan is still culturally Chinese despite fifty years of Japanese colonial occupation and twenty-five years of influence by American aid and involvement with the world economy, mainland China is the obvious place with which to begin making comparisons. At this point it is therefore necessary to introduce G. W. Skinner's models (Skinner 1964 and 1965) for traditional and modern marketing systems in rural China. They greatly aid the following discussion of historical developments in the marketing system on the Changhua Plain.

The basic units in the model that Skinner has provided for traditional Chinese marketing are *standard markets*, where peasants sell their produce and buy necessities on set market days that follow periodic schedules. Typically, each peasant household sends at least one of its members to the nearest standard market each day that the market convenes. There they do business with peddlers who move on a circuit between neighboring markets collecting produce and dispensing essential wares. Peasant participation in the marketing system is in general limited to the single closest standard market, and their social horizons are limited to the standard marketing community centered on their standard market. Standard marketing areas, the spatial expression of standard marketing communities, are discrete. That is, they are clearly bounded and do not overlap. In addition, as a corollary of the proposition that all peasants patronize their closest standard market (a basic assumption in classical central-place theory), standard marketing areas completely fill the landscape and are equivalent in size in any locality. They must therefore be hexagonal, at least in principle. Large areas of China were found, empirically, to have an average of around eighteen villages in each one, which is in accord with the geometry of the models.

The next level in Skinner's hierarchy of traditional Chinese central places consists of *intermediate markets*, where the peddlers who move between standard markets sell the produce they have collected to permanent dealers and purchase new wares from wholesale merchants. Intermediate markets also provide elitist goods and services for the local gentry, and they, along with the peddlers, integrate standard marketing communities into intermediate marketing communities with associated intermediate marketing areas. Intermediate market towns not only provide the setting for intermediate markets but also host standard markets, in every way equivalent to those held in standard market towns, for the peasants who live nearby. The two levels of markets are held on different, although interrelated, periodic schedules.

At the next level in the hierarchy, *central market towns* host central markets in addition to intermediate and standard markets. Central market towns have important wholesale functions for their dependent intermediate markets, occupy strategic sites in communication and transportation networks, and provide a wider array of goods and services than lower-level centers. *Local* and *regional cities* come above central market towns, and similarly provide all the functions of lower central places. There are *minor markets*, best defined as incipient standard markets, at the very bottom of the system of central places.

When the vagaries of local geography are reduced by abstraction, market towns can be seen to be located at the apexes of congruent equilateral triangles, and market areas at all levels can be conceived of as regular hexagons. Higher-level marketing areas overlap lower-level areas, but have different functions. There is no overlap between the areas of two towns at the same level, although some lower-level centers are located on the boundaries of higher-level areas and are therefore served by more than one higher-level central place. Two geometric arrangements satisfy all these conditions, and both have been found to exist empirically, one being associated with rough topography where road-building is difficult and the other with densely settled plains. In all these regards, Skinner's models follow classical place theory as formulated by Christaller (1966).

Under normal circumstances, the only change that occurred in traditional Chinese marketing systems was intensification due to increased population densities. Minor markets became standard markets, standard markets became intermediate markets, and so on. Whole systems were simply replicated on a smaller scale. The advent of railroads and, later, of motor vehicles gave rise to developments of a different nature, which Skinner calls modern change. As he describes it, when transportation becomes radically more efficient, standard markets decline and die out. Their economic (although not their social) functions are taken over by higher-level towns, the beneficiaries of the new technology. Standard marketing areas disappear, and are replaced by trading areas centered on intermediate and higher-level towns, where permanent shops, open daily, replace periodic markets (Skinner 1965).

Historical Development in Changhua Hsien

The field area encompasses only a third of the Changhua Plain. At the turn of the century it contained only four central places, too few to serve as the basis for confident statements about historical changes in the marketing system. For the purpose of historical reconstruction it was necessary to expand the area of inquiry to the whole plain. All central places with more than twenty shops on the entire plain were surveyed to discover how many shops they contained, and on the basis of the known relationship between number of shops and scale steps 7 through 9, towns outside the field area were assigned to levels in the hierarchy of commercial complexity.

A reasonably accurate reconstruction of the time ranges in which the towns first developed and in which they attained various levels of complexity was arrived at on the basis of the numbers of shop buildings built in the architectural style of particular time periods. Reports of informants, local histories, old maps, inconclusive statistical compilations for various dates during the Japanese Period, and a scale of commercial complexity for the field area for 1950 were also taken into account. Although some information is available beginning in 1830, the first decade of the twentieth century is the earliest period for which a clear picture can be obtained. This is close enough to the time when Taiwan was a part of traditional China to allow the assumption that the situation as it was then represents the period before exogenous influences were manifest to any significant degree.

Around 1900 there were fourteen central places on the Changhua Plain: one local city, Changhua; two central towns, Lukang and Peitou; two intermediate towns, Yuan-lin and Erhlin; and nine standard towns including Fang-yuan and Shao-p'u-hsin. Their locations were roughly in accord with one of Skinner's geometric models, there being one standard town on each of the trails between higher-level centers. This arrangement is supposed to occur where topography is rough and transportation costs are high, not in flat areas like the Changhua Plain, which is remarkably level. However, the Changhua Plain was not easy to move around on. There were no roads, only miserably muddy or dusty paths. In addition, travelers were threatened by highwaymen and by endemic feuding between surname groups. In regard to ease of transport, then, the plain was similar to hilly regions of traditional China, and this may explain why central places were distributed as they were.

The location of towns is only one way in which the situation in Changhua departs from Skinner's models for the traditional Mainland in the period under discussion. Although it is impossible to determine the boundaries between marketing areas at that time, there is evidence that areas were far larger than Skinner's models allow for. The field area contained well over a hundred, and most probably over 150, settlements, which were served by only four central places. The ratio between density of settlements and density of central places was similar throughout the plain. Density of population, however, was not nearly so great as in a comparable area of the Mainland. This was perhaps partially due to the fact that Changhua was still in some respects a frontier region for Chinese settlers, even though some Chinese had been there for over two hundred years. A more important reason, certainly, is that before the Japanese instituted public health programs Taiwan was by all accounts a very unhealthy place to live because of malaria and other endemic diseases. The number of settlements per marketing area may not be so significant as numbers of people, but in any event marketing areas in Changhua were very large in terms of area and numbers of villages in the early 1900's.

The most crucial way in which traditional marketing in Changhua differed from marketing in traditional China was that Changhua apparently had no periodic markets. Periodic markets were an essential feature of traditional mainland marketing systems, yet I could discover no evidence for periodic marketing in the field area or surrounding parts of the island. There were periodic cattle markets in what are now central towns, which were continued under the Japanese for the convenience of tax collectors and which in fact still operate under the old schedules. They are limited to the sale of cattle at present and, according to informants, always were. No periodic marketing schedules are mentioned in local gazetteers and informants do not remember any periodic markets. This of course is negative evidence only and does not prove in any strict sense that periodic markets did not exist, but I am convinced that they did not.

The absence of periodic markets in Changhua demands some sort of explanation. Periodic markets were ubiquitous in mainland China, and are found widely throughout the world in peasant societies because of their functional advantages: customers do not have to go so far to market and sellers have more potential customers. A clue as to the reason why these advantages could not be realized in Changhua is provided by reports from all over the world of periodic marketing being disrupted in times of civil disturbance. Central Taiwan was more or less permanently unsettled from the time Chinese immigrants first arrived until the Japanese occupation was well established. In the beginning there was fighting with the aborigines, followed by fighting between Hokkien and Hakka Chinese, fighting between Hokkiens from different parts of Fukien Province, and fighting between different surname communities. Pirates (who were otherwise local fishermen) infested the coast, and robbers and bandits (who were otherwise local peasants) roamed inland. Informants in the field area still recall that people named Chen living around Wang-kung used to make it very difficult for people named Hung living around Fang-yuan to trade in Lukang, the major local port to the north. Armed expeditions of Hungs would attempt to break through the blockading Chens. Sometimes they were let through in order that they could be robbed of their purchases on their return. Under such conditions periodic marketing was just not possible.

Even without a settled system of marketing, peasants need to sell a certain amount of produce and purchase certain essential goods and services they cannot themselves supply. Peddlers appear to have provided for this need. There was a tradition on Taiwan, which still exists to a certain extent, of itinerants who went out from towns to villages. These people were mainly natives of rural areas who, in agricultural slack periods (or if not farmers, year-round), went from village to village giving haircuts, sharpening plows, selling cloth, medicine, vegetables, and fish, and providing other necessities for their neighbors. It would have been easier for such individuals than for entire local populations to buy safe passage through hostile territory or otherwise protect themselves on the way to and from market towns. If villagers could not go to market perodically, the market could come to them intermittently on the backs of peddlers. When large amounts of produce needed to be sold or large purchases made, armed expeditions could be sent to town. Towns at all levels would need to contain permanent businesses to serve the itinerant peddlers and shopping expeditions, and that in fact appears to have been the case in Lukang, Pei-tou, and even Erhlin. The total amount of marketing that could be done under such conditions was of course limited, and this perhaps explains why there were so few central places and why their marketing areas were so large. Such conditions would also preclude the existence of marketing *communities* in any significant social sense.

Just as the marketing system in traditional Changhua differed from marketing in traditional China, so the change it underwent under the Japanese (and subsequently) differed somewhat from that which occurred in twentieth-century China. In regard to the rural marketing system there were four relevant aspects to the Japanese occupation of Taiwan. First, civil order was guaranteed by an efficient, if somewhat ruthless, police force, with the result that feuding was stopped and travel became safe. Second, public health measures reduced the death rate, and the population grew tremendously. Third, large commercial sugar farms and some local industry were established and the economy became increasingly commercialized. Fourth, transportation was radically improved. In the first decade of the twentieth century, the first real roads in Changhua Hsien were built between existing towns, and a railroad linking Taipei and Tainan was run along the eastern edge of the plain. Between 1920 and 1940 major roads were improved to all-weather condition, additional minor roads were built, bus service was begun, and narrow-gauge spur lines were run from the main railroad to Lukang, Ch'i-hu, and Erhlin. The effect of all these factors on the marketing system was to preclude the intensification of central places in a traditional mode and to initiate modern change.

There is one crucial difference between the process of modernization described by Skinner for the Mainland and that which occurred on the Changhua Plain. No standard towns declined or died off. On the contrary, six completely new towns were established between 1910 and 1940, and all but two of the standard towns that existed in 1910, as well as three that developed from practically nothing along the railroads, had achieved intermediate- or central-town status. The ratio between standard and higher-level towns, which was 9:5 in 1910, changed to 9:8 by 1930 and had become 5:15 by the end of the Second World War. By 1967–68, when my study was made, Ch'i-chou had become a twin central town with Pei-tou, three existing standard towns had become intermediate towns, and twelve completely new standard towns and one new intermediate town (Wang-kung) had appeared, yielding a ratio of 14:19 between standard and higher-level centers.

Except for the failure of standard towns to die out (and indeed the appearance of six new ones), the situation in Changhua before the Second World War was approximately similar to Skinner's model for modern change on the Mainland, in that intermediate- and higher-level trading areas predominated. However, the appearance of so many new standard towns since the war represents a departure from Skinner's model that makes it necessary to speak of standard trading areas—the primary retail marketing areas discussed at length above. Between 1950 and 1967 lower-level towns grew faster than higher-level towns, although even central towns approximately tripled in size. Whether most of the existing standard towns will eventually attain intermediate status is problematical, and it is possible that intermediate trading areas will at some point in the future again be the norm, although the number of new minor towns that are appearing make that unlikely, and I am reasonably confident that the present rough parity between standard and higher-level towns will continue.

The reason why, on Taiwan, new standard towns have continually appeared and low-level towns have gradually achieved higher levels of complexity is that tremendous increases of population have occurred simultaneously with the modernization of transport and the commercialization of the economy. In seventy years Changhua has become as densely populated as comparable areas of the Mainland. The marketing system has not only become modernized, which led to the development of intermediate trading areas on the Mainland, but also intensified at the same time in response to multiplying population and rising personal incomes. The result is that standard trading areas have emerged along with intermediate and central trading areas.

Standard towns can compete (however disadvantageously) with higher-level centers because the wholesale and transport systems allow merchants located in them to acquire merchandise as easily and at the same prices as merchants in higher-level towns. Modernization of transportation has in fact gone much further on Taiwan than it did on the Mainland, where railroads and steamboats were the major innovations. Taiwan has experienced an enormous post-war increase in kinds and numbers of motorized vehicles—motorcycles, diesel-powered cultivators used for pulling wagons, three-wheeled gasoline-powered carts, trucks of all sizes, buses, and taxicabs. These all provide cheap and very efficient transport of people and goods, but unlike trains and boats they can go anywhere there are decent roads, and not just to stops along a rail line or a river. In addition, ubiquitous bicycles provide at least a three-to-one advantage in time and effort over foot travel, especially with heavy loads, and they can be taken practically anywhere. In conjunction with rapid increases in population and purchasing power, truly modern transport has allowed modern change in the marketing system on Taiwan to progress a step further than it did on the Mainland before the war, and new standard trading areas are the result.

Modern change has not, however, progressed to the point predicted by classical central-place theory. According to Christaller's models, low-level central places should appear at points equidistant from centers at the next higher level in the hierarchy: either equidistant from three such centers if the market principle applies and travel is assumed to be equally easy in all directions, or equidistant from two higher-level centers at the midpoints of transportation routes if the traffic principle applies. Lower-level centers should therefore outnumber higher-level centers in a ratio of 2:1 or 3:1, respectively. The new towns that have appeared on the Changhua Plain in this century have clearly been influenced by the traffic principle. Those that emerged before the war are on railroads or were chosen as sites for large sugar mills or textile industry, necessitating good roads. Those that have appeared since the war are without exception located on good, heavily traveled, all-weather roads between higher-level centers.

There are far fewer new low-level centers than are required by the traffic model, however. There are three reasons for this. First, the road network is not nearly so complete as the model assumes it will be. For instance, there are no roads between Ta-ch'eng and Chu-t'ang or Chu-t'ang and Shao-p'u-hsin. Second, density of traffic along roads is not constant—the most direct route between Erhlin and Ch'i-hu is in very poor condition, whereas the route that detours through Ts'ao-hu and Wan-hsing has been steadily improved until it is now surfaced in asphalt and carries a heavy traffic load. New central places do not emerge where there are no roads or where traffic is light. In addition, roads on Taiwan are not built or improved in response to local economic factors alone, but as a result of pork-barrel politics or bureaucratic decisions concerning plans for national development or defense. Traffic along alternate roads depends on ease of travel and on bus and taxi routes. Finally, marketing behavior that fits the gravitational model disadvantages lower-level centers and discourages their emergence and growth. In my opinion the great attraction of central towns explains why there is no intermediate town between Erhlin and Ch'i-hu and why there is only one standard town on the road between Erhlin and Pei-tou and only one on the road between Erhlin and Ch'i-chou.

Marketing areas shaped like space-filling, congruent, regular hexagons, demanded by both Christaller's and Skinner's models, are not possible even in the abstract unless the ratio between the number of towns in a given level of the central-place hierarchy and the number of higher-level centers is either 2:1 or 3:1, *and* unless the centers are located according to the associated regular geometrical pattern. Neither condition has ever existed on the Changhua Plain, with the result that marketing areas, even when abstracted as has been done to a certain extent in the main map on page 216, are irregular polygons of diverse order. In addition, because of the effect of differential attraction of towns at different levels, marketing areas are of radically different size, and appear always to have been so although actual differences in size cannot be demonstrated until the immediate pre-war period. Information pertaining to marketing habits during the Japanese occupation was collected by the same interview schedule discussed earlier. It shows that before such new standard towns as Lu-shang, Yuan-tou, and Ts'ao-hu began to divert patronage from Erhlin, the difference in size between Erhlin's primary area and the areas of intermediate towns such as Ta-ch'eng and Chu-t'ang and standard towns such as Fang-yuan was far greater than it is today. The gravitational model of marketing behavior is necessary to account for the size and (abstract) shape of marketing areas in southwestern Changhua.

Discussion

The marketing system in the field area can be adequately described in terms of the hierarchy of commercial complexity and associated marketing behavior. The historical development of the system can be explained in terms of modernized transport, commercialization of the economy, and population growth. The nature of its differences from Skinner's models for mainland China and from Christaller's central-place theories can be understood in light of Taiwan's separate history, local realities, and the gravitational theory of marketing behavior. The point I wish to make in conclusion is that the people of southwestern Changhua Hsien may not be unique in finding higher-level central places more attractive than lower-level ones, and that central-place theory needs to be re-examined in terms of customer preference for high-level central places.

Both central-place theory and Skinner's derivative models are predicated upon assumptions of economic rationality that preclude excess profits, marginal businesses, and competing firms in the same center. They also assume, prices being equal, that people will shop in the closest center that provides a given item. In my opinion, none of these assumptions is ever empirically valid. In addition, non-economic (often culturally specific) motivations strongly affect marketing behavior, particularly in regard to the size and shape of marketing areas, which in turn influence the locations, numbers, and development of various levels of marketing centers.

There is evidence for these contentions from at least certain parts of the traditional Chinese Mainland. Unfortunately, nothing definite can be said concerning possible overlap of standard marketing areas in China, but significant differences in the size of standard marketing areas associated with different levels of the central-place hierarchy can be demonstrated (Amano 1953: Katō 1936; and Yang 1944). Skinner mentions at one point that higher-level centers may have served slightly larger standard marketing areas than did standard marketing towns, partially because of advantageous prices, but he clearly did not envision such great differences as Amano reports for Kwangtung or as I found on Taiwan. In the field area, primary areas of standard towns contain an average of eight villages, primary areas of intermediate towns average twenty-one villages if Wang-kung is included and twenty-six if it is excluded, and Erhlin's primary area contains sixty villages. Average numbers of villages per marketing area over large regions, which is the only information normally available and therefore the information Skinner uses to support the fit of his models to actual cases, proves nothing about the relative size of marketing areas associated with towns at various levels. For instance, the average number of villages per primary area in the field area is just seventeen, close indeed to the eighteen villages per standard marketing area demanded by Skinner's models. The actual range, however, is from five to sixty villages. Amano reports a range of like magnitude.

Such great differences in the size of marketing areas invalidate the assumptions on which existing central-place theories are predicated. They also call for some sort of explanation. The gravitational or attraction model I have suggested for Changhua can be applied, with suitable modifications demanded by place, time, and culture, to the traditional Mainland of China and to any other area of the world where marketing behavior does not accord with existing models.

The Inculcation of Economic Values
in Taipei Business Families

STEPHEN M. OLSEN

This paper examines two major concepts—economic values and economic socialization—on the basis of questionnaire responses from a
study conducted in Taiwan during 1967–68.[*] Since both of these concepts are liable to confusion with economic concepts, it might be well
to consider at the outset how a sociologist would use them and how he
would understand the title of this paper.

In the concept of values we find the closest link between economics
and sociology. The development of sociology can, in fact, probably best
be understood as an attempt by nineteenth-century economic theorists
and economic historians to resolve their dilemmas, and social values as
the key they used. Values, as the term is used today, refers to the conceptions people have of what is or is not desirable, the bases on which
they choose among alternative courses of action (Kluckhohn 1951; Williams 1951: 374–82). Values may operate on a very generalized and abstract level, or at a more specific level, as when they specify the qualities considered desirable in people. The sociologist is interested in val-

[*] The study was supported by a fellowship from the Foreign Area Fellowship
Program of the ACLS and the SSRC, and by Dissertation Research Grant GS-1304
from the National Science Foundation. The Cornell University China Program
financed my analysis of the material gathered under a grant from the Ford Foundation. Extensive help was given me by the Taipei Municipal Bureau of Education and
its officials (especially Mr. J. P. Ch'iu, Deputy Director) and by the principals,
staff, and teachers of many Taipei primary and secondary schools. I would like to
express my thanks to Professor Murray Straus for his permission to use several measurement instruments from his study, only one of which is mentioned in this paper,
and also for his cooperation in supplying supplementary information and materials.
Professor Straus's approach to the theory of socialization, as developed in the cited
paper and elsewhere, has been important in shaping my own approach. The preparation of this paper benefitted from the editorial assistance of Nancy Olsen.

ues because they are shared and transmitted among people. Some values are significant because they are shared by nearly all members of a society; others, precisely because they are not so widely shared, because they differentiate groups in a society and serve to distinguish these groups from the rest of society. It is this latter type of value and this concept of the differentiating role of values in society that I will be talking about here.

I will argue that different occupational groups in the Chinese society of modern Taipei hold and transmit substantially different sets of economic values. To avoid confusion with economic concepts, I should point out that by economic values I mean those social values that pertain primarily to occupational roles.

Ryan (1961) has done an excellent descriptive and analytical study of the value system of a group of Chinese businessmen in a Javanese town, a study that is a model of sociological analysis as well as a source-book for students of specifically Chinese economic behavior. Using an essentially ethnographic approach, Ryan was able to delineate and categorize an integrated set of values for these businessmen: (a) values that governed behavior in social groupings, (b) values that governed behavior in occupational roles, and (c) more general values that stood in contrapuntal or corrective relationships to (a) and (b). Focal values (those that tie together a number of less general values) in the social sphere were found to be associated with kin-group membership and with being distinctly Chinese in an alien environment. In the economic or occupational sphere, a focal value of wealth ties together a complex of values—work, self-reliance, interdependence, trust, and frugality. A particularly valued type of personality is one that combines integrity with cleverness, nerve, and skill. Although this brief summary of Ryan's findings cannot do justice to the sensitivity of his analysis, it should nevertheless reveal that Ryan has made a real attempt to study a Chinese value system in an orderly manner.

It is difficult to know to what extent Ryan's findings may be taken as generally descriptive of Chinese economic values. The town he studied had a population of only 20,000, less than 10 percent of whom were Chinese. Had he studied a large, heterogeneous city, he might not have been able to discern a single discrete set of occupational values.[*] Moreover, the significance of living and working in a non-Chinese environment

---

[*] Prior to the study reported in this paper, I studied a very limited set of economic values and choices among an elite group of Chinese and Indonesian students in Djakarta, the capital city of Indonesia, and found that students who planned to enter different occupations expressed very different values (Olsen 1965).

cannot be ignored when considering the generality of Ryan's findings. The survey method, which was used to collect the data I will be presenting in this paper, is required when studying large, diverse populations. Taken together with intensive studies of smaller groups, such as Ryan's, and DeGlopper's in this volume, survey research can help form a comprehensive picture of Chinese values, particularly since this method allows one to discover the values that differentiate groups within Chinese society, as well as those values that are held in common.

Like the word *value*, the word *socialization* has very different meanings in sociology and in economics. The Social Science Research Council Committee on Socialization has recently provided a comprehensive survey of sociological research and theory on the subject (Clausen 1968), revealing that even among sociologists, the word can be variously defined, according to the emphasis of the researcher. To present the sociological definition and to reveal my own emphasis, I can do no better than to quote David Aberle (1961: 387): "Socialization consists of those patterns of action or aspects of action which inculcate in individuals the skills (including knowledge), motives and attitudes necessary for the performance of present or anticipated roles." As Clausen points out, such a definition emphasizes the social apparatus that inculcates ability and motivation to perform roles in a given social structure (1968: 4). It is the direct opposite in point of view from the kind of definition that focuses on the learning individual and sees social structure as emergent from individual behavior. Whichever kind of definition is used, however, if we limit our view to inter-generational socialization, we must agree with Clausen that, "In the last analysis, adult performance is the criterion by which the adequacy of the socialization apparatus is to be assessed" (1968: 5).

Since adults assume not just one but many roles in society, it is not surprising that research on socialization has been divided into several categories and that it has been pursued by workers in several disciplines outside sociology proper. Political socialization has been rather thoroughly explored by political scientists who are interested in adult political behavior (e.g. Sigal 1965; Wilson 1967). Socialization for sex roles has been studied by psychologists who are trying to understand adult sexual behavior, and socialization for kinship roles has been studied by some researchers on the family (Brim 1959) and on the influence of sibling position on child development (Sutton-Smith *et al.* 1964; Skinner 1966). Religious socialization has been described among groups that feel their children pulling away from their traditional religion (Thomas 1952).

Within sociology itself, the major interest has been in socialization linked to social class. Such an emphasis is understandable, since it is here that the strongest and most consistent differences in socialization can be empirically demonstrated, especially in the United States (Bronfenbrenner 1958) but also around the world (e.g., Danziger 1960a, 1960b; Prothro 1966; Pearlin and Kohn 1966). Until very recently, however, theoretical interpretation of the undisputed empirical facts was either unsatisfactory or lacking altogether. To the extent that there was interpretation, it relied largely on a conception of "status socialization" (Hodges 1964, chap. 9; Barber 1957, chap. 11). The logic of this approach is that there are clearly ranked, reasonably well-defined status groups in any complex society, each interested in maintaining or improving its relative positon. Especially for the higher status groups, this imposes an imperative on the socialization process, namely, training that will ensure "status maintenance" (Goode 1959).

More recently, a new interpretation of class differences in socialization has been put forward, along with some evidence that is at variance with the "status socialization" theory (Kohn 1969). According to the newer interpretation, differences in socialization are largely a function of the day-to-day occupational experiences of the head of the family, experiences that typically are different in different social classes. These occupational experiences affect a man's view of the world, which he ultimately transmits to his children. The factory worker, for example, whose work consists of doing precisely what he is told and permits of no individual decision-making, is much more likely to value obedience to authority than is the factory manager, who must take individual responsibility for his own decisions and who may value self-reliance in his children. The test cases for determining the relative explanatory power of the work-experience hypothesis and the status-socialization hypothesis appear when actual work experience and subjective class identification, respectively, are different from what is typical of people in a given "objective" class position. The evidence from such cases suggests that subjective identification, admittedly a difficult thing to measure, does not influence socialization values under these circumstances, but that the actual work experience does (Pearlin and Kohn 1966; Kohn 1969).

One advantage of the work-experience approach to class differences in socialization is that it can be used with occupational groups defined in ways other than those resulting from a division into hierarchically ranked social classes. In the United States, a number of studies (Miller and Swanson 1958; Johnson et al. 1961) have attempted to discover whether the socialization values and techniques of people in entrepreneurial occupations differ from those of people in bureaucratic positions, when social class position is the same. Methodological shortcomings preclude drawing any very definite conclusions from these studies, but they suggest, at the very least, that the work-experience approach is a meaningful one.

As the reader might expect from the preceding introduction, my primary interest in this paper is to try to determine which of the things that help prepare an individual to perform adult occupational roles are the result of the intended or unintended influence of the behavior of others toward him. Those things will constitute economic socialization as I define the term. Economic socialization can and should be seen as one of a set of socialization processes—sexual, political, kinship, religious, etc.—corresponding to the typical set of adult roles. Its primary reference here is to inter-generational socialization, and more specifically, to that taking place in the context of the nuclear family. Values are a very important part of economic socialization, but they by no means exhaust it. Conceptions of the world, objective knowledge, limitations on the range of acceptable choices—all may be very relevant to entrance into and effective performance of a particular occupational role. Because of their predominance in urban Chinese society and their pivotal significance in the social structure of that society, I am particularly concerned with the kind of economic socialization and the economic values characteristic of entrepreneurs.*

Although the sociological approach to socialization embraced in this paper emphasizes the means of socialization, and especially the patterning of experience in the nuclear family, I do not intend to assign a passive position to the socialized individual. I believe that a complementary and cumulative process is involved, one in which both society and the individual participate and one that is essentially probabilistic rather than deterministic. For example, the values expressed by a Taipei middle-school boy are often more closely related to the occupation he intends to enter than to his father's occupation, if the two are different. But this finding, which anticipates data to be described below, need

---

* In the study of traditional Chinese society, the nature of the entrepreneurial and bureaucratic elites and of their relationships to one another has always been of great interest (Eberhard 1962; Wittfogel 1957). In fact, it may be argued that the process of competition and accommodation between these two groups is one of the key features of the traditional social structure. This study, insofar as it succeeds in delineating a specifically entrepreneurial system of values for modern urban Taipei, may be regarded as a preliminary to an understanding of the modern relationship between these two groups.

not conflict with the conception of economic socialization as primarily the product of influences received in the nuclear family. First of all, the boy's values almost certainly reflect a long-standing pattern of inter-generational social mobility, perhaps modified by modernization. More important, however, is that in many cases an additive relation exists between simple value inculcation and the choices of the individual being socialized. Merton and his associates have coined the term "anticipatory socialization" (1957: 265–68) to describe the phenomenon whereby once an individual has identified himself with some future role, he tends to socialize himself, taking on the attitudes, values, and other characteristics he perceives to be appropriate to that role. Of course, this process operates within a context of earlier socialization and tends to be complementary to it.

Again anticipating results to be presented below, we may note a further complication in the process of value-transmission. As we shall see, there are many sons of Taipei businessmen who could inherit a respectable business but have no desire to do so. Although not analyzed in this paper, these "rejections," which may be seen as a function of the affective relationship between father and son, are assessable from the available material. Such an assessment would begin by recognizing that the socialization process is not uniformly effective and might call upon the psychodynamic theory of identification to help explain why. In this manner, a more complex model of economic socialization might be developed. Regrettably, such an analysis is beyond the scope of this paper.

Methodology and Sampling

As part of a larger study of socialization in Taipei City,* I wanted to get an idea what the "product" of socialization was like at a point fairly close to actual entry into an adult role. Therefore, I decided to study groups of adolescent boys;† specifically, students in the first and second years of senior middle school, 90 percent of them between sixteen and nineteen years of age. Such boys could be sorted into different educational streams and associated career and mobility paths. Moreover, much more complicated information could be gathered from the recipients of the socialization themselves, including their reports on the process, their expression of values and beliefs, and so forth.

---

* Results of the major part of the study, based on interviews with parents of sixth-grade primary-school boys, are reported in Stephen M. Olsen (1971). Results of a parallel study of socialization, also partly based on data collected in Taipei, are reported in Nancy J. Olsen (1971).

† Girls were excluded from consideration because of the complications introduced by sex role into the occupational choices, aspirations, and values of girls, when the subject is already complex enough for boys.

The major desideratum for this part of the study was that all major types of secondary education be represented. To this end, three senior middle schools were selected. Of the thirty-six senior middle schools in Taipei, twenty-four or two-thirds are considered "ordinary" or academic middle schools, though they may teach some vocational courses or have vocational sections, and twelve (including one normal school) are vocational schools. Of the vocational schools attended by boys, the majority (55.5 percent) are commercial or business schools. Thus, the three sample schools include two academic middle schools (one public and one private) and one vocational middle school (private). These schools are, respectively, Taipei Municipal (formerly Provincial) Chien-kuo Middle School, Yen-p'ing Middle School, and Yu-ta Commercial Vocational Middle School.

There is no question that, even within their respective categories, these particular three schools may have their peculiarities. For example, Chien-kuo is always mentioned as one of the two or three most prestigious high schools for boys in Taipei. Thus its students would be expected to come from a somewhat more elite group than do those in some other public middle schools. That it is indeed an elite school can be seen from Tables 1, 2, and 3. The families of Chien-kuo boys are predominantly non-Taiwanese, highly educated civil servants. On the other hand, even this predominance may not be so great as it would be in some of the high-prestige academic middle schools in Taipei, for Chien-kuo has a particular attraction for Taiwanese business and professional families that dates back to the Japanese Period.

TABLE 1. CHARACTERISTICS OF MIDDLE-SCHOOL SAMPLE, TAIPEI, APRIL 1968

Native place and educational background	Name and type of school			
	Yen-p'ing, private academic	Chien-kuo, municipal academic	Yu-ta, private commercial-vocational	Total or average
Total number in sample (grades 10 and 11 only)	(192)	(227)	(224)	(643)
Native place				
Taiwan	77.1%	39.2%	86.2%	66.9%
S. China	16.7	47.6	9.8	25.2
N. China	5.2	13.2	3.6	7.5
No information	1.0	—	0.4	0.4
Father's education				
College or above	21.9%	49.3%	5.4%	25.8%
Higher secondary	33.9	27.8	17.0	25.8
Lower secondary	13.5	7.5	23.2	14.8
Primary or less	23.2	11.5	46.4	27.2
No information	7.3	3.9	8.0	6.4

TABLE 2. DISTRIBUTION OF FATHERS' OCCUPATIONS IN THREE MIDDLE
SCHOOLS OF TAIPEI, BY SCHOOL, APRIL 1968

Father's occupation	Name and type of school			
	Yen-p'ing, private academic	Chien-kuo, municipal academic	Yu-ta, private commercial-vocational	Total or average
N	(192)	(227)	(224)	(643)
Public employees	34.4%	48.0%	18.8%	33.8%
Private white-collar employees	5.7	10.6	5.4	7.3
Other employees	12.0	11.9	17.0	13.7
Professionals	4.7	4.4	1.8	3.6
Shopkeepers	12.5	7.5	15.2	11.7
Owners and partners (factories and companies)	17.7	10.1	9.4	12.1
Other proprietors	7.8	2.2	16.5	8.9
Farm-owners and farm laborers	—	1.8	6.7	3.0
Father not present or no information	5.2	3.5	9.4	6.1
Total	100.0%	100.0%	100.2%	100.2%

NOTE: Totals greater than 100.0% due to rounding.

In any case, the predominance of mainland students in Chien-kuo is balanced by an even greater predominance of Taiwanese students in Yu-ta Commercial School, making the sample as a whole conform quite closely to the 63:37 ratio of Taiwanese and Mainlanders in Taipei as a whole (*Statistical Abstract of Taipei Municipality* 1965: 41–42, Table 14).

The educational distribution of fathers in the sample, however, probably does not correspond very well with that of all Taipei residents. Over half of the sample fathers are reported to have attended senior middle school or college. Although not directly comparable because of the wide range of ages included, official statistics for Taipei men twelve years old and over who are not in school show only 28.2 percent with a senior-middle-school or college education (*Taiwan Demographic Factbook* 1966: 98–99, Table 5).

There is no way of comparing the occupational distribution of the middle-school fathers (Table 2) with any official statistics.* From Table 3, however, a rough comparison can be made. The statistics for recent

* Most official statistics give breakdowns only by industry. At the time of this writing, the results of the 1966 decennial census had not yet been published, and the previous census report would have been of little use because of the massive changes that have occurred in the interim.

TABLE 3. OCCUPATIONS OF ALL EMPLOYED TAIPEI MALES AND OF THE
FATHERS OF THE MIDDLE-SCHOOL SAMPLE, APRIL 1968

Occupation	All Taipei, 1966[a] (268,948)	1965 fathers[b] (10,773)	Fathers of middle-school sample (535)
Agriculture, fishing, mining, salt production	6.5%	6.5%	5.8%
Manufacturing (including construction)	26.4	27.4	32.3
Commerce (including banking)	26.0	24.6	24.6
Public service (including education)	10.8 ⎫	11.3	⎰ 17.6
National defense	8.3 ⎭		⎱ 5.8
Professions	6.5	4.8	4.3
Transportation	8.2	9.6	6.0
Personal service	6.0	6.0	1.7
Other	1.3	9.8	1.9
Total	100.0%	100.0%	100.0%

SOURCES: *Taiwan Demographic Factbook* 1966: 72–73, Table 4; *Statistical Abstract of Taipei Municipality* 1965, No. 19: 75–78, Table 19.
[a] Twelve years old or over.
[b] Those having a child born in 1965.

fathers contained no separate category for national defense (the military). Leaving aside that difference, we find that the occupations of recent fathers are quite similar to those of all men in Taipei, suggesting that the widespread use of young unmarried labor is not sufficient to produce a distribution markedly different from that of a sample of fathers. Therefore, the differences between the middle-school fathers and the general population must be the results of selection. Workers in transportation and personal-service industries are noticeably few among middle-school fathers, although some are doubtless hidden in the "other employee" category. Public-service workers, by contrast, are obviously over-represented.* There is little doubt, then, that this sample of boys from the three Taipei middle schools is imperfectly representative of the population of the city as a whole. The question is whether the bias is in the selection of the sample, or in the class-selectivity that is characteristic of Taipei's educational system.

It is my belief that the unrepresentativeness of the middle-school sample reflects selection in the educational system, and not bias in the drawing of my sample. Between the universal and ostensibly free primary education and a senior middle-school education lie two very selec-

---

* The division into occupational categories appearing in Table 3, of course, does not give a full picture of the scope of government activities in Taiwan or in the sample, since large numbers of men listed as working in manufacturing, banking, and transportation are in fact public employees.

tive examinations and considerable monthly expense. Once the student passes the junior-middle-school entrance exam, he is past the major hurdle, but there is also an entrance exam for senior middle school. In this very competitive process, where extensive use of costly "supplementary study" or cram classes is the norm, one can well imagine that students from higher-status backgrounds would have an advantage. Although civil servants' salaries are low, often they are supplemented for children's educational expenses, and big private companies sometimes have similar arrangements for their employees. Clearly, a senior-middle-school education is reserved for a selected portion of the population of Taipei, though by no means solely for an upper-class elite.* It seems unlikely that the most carefully drawn sample of middle-school boys in Taipei would produce a background distribution more than marginally different from that shown in Tables 1–3. Therefore, I think we can accept the sample as reasonably representative of the population that sends sons to middle school, and consequently we can hope that conclusions based on data from the sample will not be far wrong.

We are on much less solid ground in talking about students from one kind of school as opposed to another. For example, of the five commercial schools in Taipei that have male students, three are public institutions. As such, they have more prestige than private schools. Thus, Yu-ta, being a private school, may not provide a fair sample of commercial-school students. Nevertheless, it may be worthwhile to look at the general pattern of differences between Yu-ta as a commercial vocational school, and the academic schools, particularly Yen-p'ing, which is also private and also heavily Taiwanese.

My study reveals a clear difference between the backgrounds of boys in the academic schools and those of boys in the commercial school. As we have already seen, very few Mainlanders go to Yu-ta, so government jobs are relatively rare among the students' fathers. However, another tendency within the Taiwanese group is superimposed on this basic difference. The commercial school recruits its students very largely from the lower levels of the Taiwanese community, particularly the small and very small entrepreneurs. Two elite groups, almost completely Taiwanese in origin, are either missing or markedly underrepresented—profes-

---

* This was the situation at the time of my study. However, President Chiang has subsequently decided to extend free education through the junior-middle-school level, in a program starting in September 1968 and scheduled for completion in 1971. By removing the major part of the expenses associated with a middle-school education, this decision should reduce the advantage now enjoyed by boys from higher-status homes, although some of the same competitive pressures will merely be shifted to the senior-middle-school entrance exam three years later.

sionals (mainly doctors) and medium- to large-scale businessmen. These groups are concentrated in the academic schools, somewhat more in Yen-p'ing than in Chien-kuo.

Some idea of the nature of the competition for places in middle school is important for understanding the different backgrounds and characteristics of students at particular schools. A single examination determines whether a student may attend middle school and, if so, which schools he will be eligible for. Since qualifications for private schools, and especially for private vocational schools, are lower than for public and academic schools, their students are, on the one hand, more likely to come from families whose incomes are somewhat lower or whose pressures for academic success have been less intense or less effective, or both. On the other hand, it should not be forgotten that the cost, including income forgone, of attending any middle school is considerable, so that students in private commercial schools are likely to be better off than the run of their age-mates.

Occupational Inheritance

Before turning to the major concern of this paper, the transmission of specific economic values, I want to discuss briefly another aspect of economic socialization: the extent to which the sons of entrepreneurs choose to continue the family business. Students at the commercial schools may be there as much because they have done poorly on the middle-school entrance exam as because they wish to prepare for a business career. In fact, only slightly more than half of the boys at Yu-ta (53.6 percent) intend entering any kind of business occupation.

Family background, however, has a very definite relationship to occupational choice, as shown in Table 4. Sons of businessmen, and particularly the sons of small shopkeepers, are more likely than boys of non-business backgrounds to indicate that they intend a business career. This finding contrasts strikingly with the fairly general rejection of entrepreneurial careers among boys in the academic schools.

The interesting tendency for sons of very successful businessmen to reject business careers suggests the possibility that a traditional Chinese pattern of social mobility survives in present-day Taiwan. For centuries in China, merchants who became wealthy enough to give one or more sons the necessary education encouraged them to enter the Imperial bureaucracy. Indeed, the practice of selling degrees (sometimes with the possibility of official appointments) that flourished at various times in Chinese history may have provided the opportunity for the merchant himself to move in that direction (Marsh 1962). The long-run signifi-

TABLE 4. OCCUPATIONAL CHOICE AND BUSINESS BACKGROUND IN THREE
MIDDLE SCHOOLS OF TAIPEI, APRIL 1968

		Business background			
Occupational choice	Total	Non-business background	All business-men	Owners/partners in factories, companies	Shop-keepers
Total sample (N)	(643)	(433)	(210)	(78)	(75)
Non-business	77.3%	82.0%	67.6%	76.9%	61.3%
Business	22.7	18.0	32.4	23.1	38.7
Academic schools (N)	(419)	(301)	(118)	(57)	(41)
Non-business	93.8%	96.7%	86.4%	86.0%	87.8%
Business	6.2	3.3	13.6	14.0	12.2
Commercial school (N)	(224)	(132)	(92)	(21)	(34)
Non-business	46.4%	48.6%	43.5%	52.4%	29.4%
Business	53.6	51.4	56.5	47.6	70.6

cance of the type of school attended and the expressed occupational
choice of contemporary Taiwanese students is a matter for separate
consideration; nevertheless there is an indication that very successful
entrepreneurs still encourage their sons to choose non-entrepreneurial
careers. However, they no longer direct them exclusively into bureaucratic careers, at least of the traditional governmental sort, but into the
increasingly prestigious and better-paid professions as well.

The economic values of the middle-school boys in these three schools
were assessed by means of a questionnaire. Because, so far as I could
determine, there was no previous scholarship indicating which values
might be held more strongly by one or another occupational group in
Chinese society, an instrument developed for use in the United States
formed the basis of my questionnaire. The "American Business Creed"
has received quite a lot of scholarly attention (see, for example, Sutton
et al. 1956), and from such sources Straus developed a quantitative
measure that could be used to assess the effectiveness of one kind of
economic socialization in different kinds of families (Straus and Sudia
1965). In the absence of an equally comprehensive and detailed description of the "Chinese Business Creed," I thought it worthwhile to apply
these measures of American business values to Chinese respondents.

The nature of the measures and their limitations in the Chinese context should be understood from the outset. Of a somewhat larger number used by Straus, seventy-four items were selected that could reasonably be translated and used in the Taiwanese context. These are simple
statements in reply to which the respondent is asked to agree, disagree,

or indicate uncertainty. Some of the statements are formulated as cognitive, in that they refer to perception of a state of affairs, such as "Most businessmen are honest," or "The only way to get ahead in the business world is to have 'connections.' " Such statements are not purely cognitive, of course, in that an evaluative context is implied for the statement of fact. Most of the items, however, are clearly evaluative in nature. They concern themselves with the relative desirability of two states of affairs, both usually more or less positive.* Examples of evaluative statements are, "People should be encouraged to invest their money in business rather than just saving it," and, "The best government engages in the fewest activities."

In constructing his measures, Straus was trying to elicit sixteen separate elements or value areas in the American Business Creed, ranging from a positive valuing of competition to a negative valuing of government regulation of business. Five or six items were included for each. In this study, a sufficient number of statements survived translation to allow me to talk about fifteen separate value groupings (see Tables 5–10). Most of the items relating to Straus's sixteenth area, welfare activities of the state, however, seemed irrelevant to the Chinese scene. In addition, very few of the items Straus designed to measure labor orientation or seeing things from the workers' point of view were appropriate to Taiwan, but this value can still be examined by looking at the responses to items originally designed to measure some of the other value areas.

The instrument was administered as part of a larger questionnaire in regular school classes. The students were told that their responses would be anonymous, that their names were not required, and that they should therefore feel free to express their personal opinions. If despite these assurances many students viewed the questionnaire as they would an examination, attempting to give "correct" answers, the appearance of significant differences among the groups may be regarded as all the more remarkable.

Summary scores for each value area are simple, unweighted averages of actual responses to the various items dealing with that value, where disagreement receives a score of 1, uncertainty a score of 2, and agree-

---

* This technique, known as "forced choice," is among the most favored in the sociologist's bag of tricks. One characteristic of a forced-choice question, that it shows relative preference among several generally positive alternative values, should be borne in mind in judging the significance of this study and of others using the same method. In using the method, relatively small differences between groups are to be expected.

ment a score of 3.* The scales are constructed in such a way that, according to the American Business Creed, businessmen would be expected to score higher than non-businessmen.

Antecedents of Economic Values

The procedure for analyzing each of the fifteen value areas will be to divide the sample into those whose fathers are proprietors of some kind of business (business background) and all others (non-business background), and to divide each of these groups further according to whether they are studying in a commercial or an academic middle school, according to whether or not the students themselves have chosen to become businessmen, and according to whether they are the sons of native Taiwanese or of refugees from the Mainland. Because these four variables (father's occupation, son's occupational choice, type of school attended, and native place) are not completely independent of one another, determining the precise effect of any one of them on economic values requires controlling the influence of the other three.

Columns 1 and 2 of Table 5 contain the simplest breakdown of the data. Average scores for the fifteen economic values are presented separately for boys from business (proprietorial) and non-business families as defined above. Assuming that American business values have analogs in the Chinese business subculture—admittedly an inferential leap—

---

* The Chinese term used for uncertainty (*pu i ting*) is unfortunately not so unambiguous as the English term. *Pu i ting* often implies as much about the nature of external reality as about the speaker's state of mind concerning it. This semantic factor resulted in an uncomfortably high proportion of "uncertain" responses, over 50 percent on some questions. However, when the various tables were computed again, including only students who indicated agreement or disagreement, the results remained the same in all essential respects.

Although a preliminary analysis showed that I could have used Guttman scales for most of the values discussed, as Straus did, I used simple averages for two reasons. First, I disagree with the basic assumption of cumulative scale analysis as it applies to attitude measurement, i.e., that responses not conforming to the cumulative pattern should be considered errors of measurement if they are not too common, and should be ignored in the summary measure. I believe, on the contrary, that an average of indicators of an attitude is a better predictor of who actually holds that attitude than one that takes into account the particular statements they endorse or do not endorse. This logic is also embodied in scores constructed from factor loadings in factor analysis, albeit weighted by relative contribution to the underlying factor. (The results of a factor analysis of these data are not included in this paper, but are available.) The second reason simple additive scores are used in this study is to avoid giving the impression that the measures used here are more elegant than in fact they are. In looking at the summary measures, if the reader remembers that they represent an average of the number of respondents saying "disagree" (extreme negative = 1), "uncertain" (precise neutrality = 2), and "agree" (extreme positive = 3), he is unlikely to be misled.

TABLE 5. SUMMARY VALUE MEASURES, BACKGROUND, AND KIND
OF SCHOOL ATTENDED

Value area and expected orientation	Background		Kind of school	
	Non-business	Business	Academic	Commercial
N	(433)	(210)	(419)	(224)
Positively valued				
Competition	1.89	1.86	1.91	1.82 ---
Work	2.45	2.52 +++	2.42	2.56 +++
Business, businessmen	1.90	1.96 ++	1.83	2.09 +++
Individualism	2.05	2.13 +++	2.00	2.22 +++
Investment	2.02	2.06	1.98	2.14 +++
Profit	2.06	2.06	2.06	2.06
Progress	2.39	2.40	2.35	2.47 +++
Risk-taking	1.79	1.82	1.76	1.86 +++
Small enterprise	2.15	2.15	2.16	2.13
Social utility of business	2.34	2.42 +++	2.33	2.43 +++
Universalism (impersonal business code)	2.18	2.14	2.19	2.13 −
Practicality	2.39	2.46 ++	2.35	2.53 +++
Negatively valued				
Government regulation	1.46	1.51 +	2.52	2.54
Labor	1.72	1.76	1.69	1.82 +++
Profit-sharing	1.56	1.73 +++	1.58	1.69 +++

NOTE: Averages based on possible scores of 1 (disagree), 2 (uncertain), or 3 (agree). Differences significant by t-test: +++(−−−) $p < .01$; ++(−−) $p < .05$; +(−) $p < .10$.

and that substantial inculcation of such values occurs in Chinese families, we would expect to be able to distinguish boys with business backgrounds from the other boys in the sample on the basis of their scores on these value measures.

In fact, on seven of the fifteen value measures, boys from business backgrounds do register reliably distinctive scores.* The seven include attitudes toward work *per se*; toward business and businessmen; toward government regulation or control, especially of business; toward individualism; toward profit; toward the proposition that business activities are

* The Chi-square and t-tests used to evaluate the statistical significance of the differences observed between groups in this study are part of the sociological ritual; but they are something more than ritual, even in this kind of exploratory research. They give us a kind of yardstick for judging which of the many such differences that any cross tabulation will generate are worth attention. From the number of cases studied and the overall variability observed in the responses, a standard is established below which differences between groups are considered unreliable. Differences that are statistically reliable may or may not be of substantive importance. That judgment must rest on other grounds.

socially as well as individually beneficial; and toward practicality. For six of the remaining eight values, there is either no difference or only an unreliable difference in the expected direction. However, for two values—competition and universalism, or an impersonal business code— the trend is opposite to what we would expect: there is a small and statistically unreliable tendency for sons of businessmen to see competition in negative terms and to profess particularistic rather than universalistic values more often than other boys.

Thus the evidence of Columns 1 and 2 may be said to support, albeit somewhat weakly, a simple relationship between a boy's family background and his economic values. The evidence of Columns 3 and 4 far more conclusively supports an equally uncomplicated but more interesting relationship between the type of school a boy attends and his economic values. (Here it should be recalled that boys are as likely to enter commercial school because their scores on the middle-school examination disqualified them for the academic schools as because they intend a business career. Moreover, as the table shows, fewer than half the commercial students in the sample come from business backgrounds.) When the kind of school attended is considered, the scores of those students attending the commercial school, regardless of family background, differ substantially from those of the other students on all but three of the fifteen values under consideration. The same differences noted between sons of business families and other backgrounds appear in the comparison of commercial and academic students, but in addition unreliable trends on six values seen when comparing sons of businessmen with sons of others become quite substantial when looking at students in the commercial school as compared with students in the academic schools. Investment as a value, an anti-labor orientation, progress as a reality and as a good, and risk-taking as a value are all unmistakably more common among the commercial-school students than among the students of the academic schools. The rejection of competition and the relative emphasis on particularism as opposed to universalism in a business code, seemingly somewhat stronger in boys from business backgrounds than in other boys, are significantly stronger in boys from the commercial school than in those from the academic schools. Thus, these values are probably an integral part of the pattern of business values found in urban Taiwan.

Three values do not show up as reliable differences in Columns 3 and 4 of Table 5—small enterprise as an intrinsic value, a positive attitude toward profit, and opposition to government regulation. As will be shown below, the first two of these do not appear to form part of a differentiated system of business values. As for the third, boys from business families show a significantly stronger tendency to oppose government activities of various kinds than do boys from non-business families, but no such difference shows up in the breakdown by kind of school attended. This finding suggests that the interaction between the influences of family and school should be examined. Columns 1–4 of Table 6 present the various combinations of family background and type of school attended, and Columns 5–8 abstract from them the reliable patterns.

As we would expect from the data just described, the more striking differences appear when the responses are grouped according to the kind of school attended. These differences can be seen most clearly when the responses of boys from non-business families in the two types of schools are compared (Table 6, Column 7), but boys from business families show them also in a less dramatic way. With the exception of a few values, boys in the commercial school do seem to exhibit a distinctive "business ideology," regardless of their family background.

A family business tradition, however, continues to exert a direct influence on the values held by the schoolboys of my sample. Columns 1 and 2 of Table 6 show that for at least six values, business background is important when the two types of schools are considered separately. Even in the academic middle schools, there is a distinctive value-emphasis characteristic of the sons of businessmen. It is, above all, individualistic and opposed to profit-sharing; it presupposes the social utility of business, opposes government regulation, and values risk-taking and work as ends in themselves.

Economic values in general have been shown to be closely related to individual occupational choice (Rosenberg 1957; S. Olsen 1965). This is also the case for the values and groups under consideration here, as shown in Table 7. The comparisons drawn in this table reinforce what has been learned from the breakdowns by family background and type of school attended, but this is largely because occupational choice is related to both of these variables. Although there is no reason to think that individual choice and family influence work in opposition to one another rather than in a cumulative way, it would be desirable to be able to sort out the influences of each of the three business contact variables and to see their independent influence on the economic values held by the respondents in this study. It would be particularly desirable to be able to hold type of school attended and occupational choice constant while looking at the direct effects of a business background on economic values. Although the sample is really too small to do so ade-

TABLE 6. SUMMARY VALUE MEASURES BY BACKGROUND AND KIND OF SCHOOL ATTENDED: COMBINED DATA AND RELIABLE DIFFERENCES

Value area and expected orientation	Combined data				Strength and direction of differences			
	Non-business background		Business background		Business vs. non-business background		Commercial vs. academic school	
	Academic schools	Commercial school	Academic schools	Commercial school	Academic schools	Commercial school	Non-business background	Business background
N	(301)	(132)	(118)	(92)				
Positively valued								
Competition	1.92	1.83	1.88	1.82			---	+++
Work	2.42	2.52	2.44	2.61		++	+++	+++
Business, businessmen	1.81	2.10	1.86	2.09			+++	+++
Individualism	1.98	2.23	2.07	2.21	+++		+++	+++
Investment	1.97	2.13	1.99	2.14			+	+++
Profit	2.04	2.11	2.11	2.00	+	--	+++	--
Progress	2.36	2.48	2.35	2.45	++		+++	++
Risk-taking	1.74	1.89	1.82	1.82	++		+++	
Small enterprise	2.17	2.11	2.15	2.15				
Social utility of business	2.31	2.41	2.40	2.45	++		+++	
Universalism (impersonal business code)	2.20	2.15	2.16	2.11				
Practicality	2.34	2.51	2.38	2.56			+++	+++
Negatively valued								
Government regulation	1.46	1.45	1.53	1.48	++		+++	
Labor	1.68	1.82	1.71	1.82			+++	
Profit-sharing	1.52	1.65	1.71	1.75	+++	++	+++	++

NOTE: Averages based on possible scores of 1 (disagree), 2 (uncertain), or 3 (agree). Differences significant by t-test: +++ (---) p < .01; ++ (--) p < .05; + (-) p < .10. The first column showing strength and direction of differences compares Columns 1 and 3; the second, Columns 2 and 4; the third, Columns 1 and 2; and the fourth, Columns 3 and 4.

The Inculcation of Economic Values in Taipei 279

TABLE 7. SUMMARY VALUE MEASURES AND STUDENTS' OCCUPATIONAL CHOICE

Value area and expected orientation	Non-business choice	Business choice
N	(497)	(146)
Positively valued		
Competition	1.88	1.88
Work	2.45	2.53 +++
Business, businessmen	1.88	2.07 +++
Individualism	2.05	2.19 +++
Investment	2.00	2.13 +++
Profit	2.05	2.09
Progress	2.39	2.41
Risk-taking	1.79	1.83
Small enterprise	2.16	2.12
Social utility of business	2.34	2.45 +++
Universalism (impersonal business code)	2.18	2.13
Practicality	2.38	2.53 +++
Negatively valued		
Government regulation	1.52	1.54
Labor	1.71	1.81 +++
Profit-sharing	1.59	1.71 +++

NOTE: Differences significant by t-test: +++ $p < .01$.

quately, Table 8 brings out quite clearly the patterns earlier tables would lead us to expect. In the academic schools, both for boys who have said they want a business career and for those who have not, sons from business (proprietor-father) families have a distinctive value pattern. They are opposed to any kind of profit-sharing and to government regulation; they are individualistic and particularistic; they value risk-taking, and they believe that business is socially beneficial. This evidence clearly supports the argument that differences in economic values originating in some aspect of the father's occupational experience are transmitted through socialization to the younger generation.

Table 8 has more to say than I can comment on at this time. However, we can note in passing that there seem to be significant "interactions" in the statistical sense. For example, the first four columns of Table 8 show that the emphasis on practicality and the anti-labor orientation, associated with the choice of a business career in Table 7, appear only among those students who also come from a business background. This kind of relationship supports a view of socialization as the combined influence of background and individual choice.

The commercial-school students (last four columns of Table 8) do not show the same consistency or magnitude of differences in their val-

TABLE 8. SUMMARY VALUE MEASURES AND FAMILY BACKGROUND FOR STUDENTS IN SAMPLE, BY KIND OF SCHOOL AND BY OCCUPATIONAL CHOICE

Value area and expected orientation	Academic schools				Commercial school			
	Non-business choice		Business choice		Non-business choice		Business choice	
	Non-business background	Business background	Non-business background	Business background	Non-business background	Business background	Non-business background	Business background
N	(291)	(102)	(10)	(16)	(64)	(40)	(68)	(52)
Positively valued								
Competition	1.91	1.88	2.10	1.90	1.80	1.75	1.85	1.88
Work	2.41	2.46	2.46	2.34	2.49	2.65 +++	2.54	2.58
Business, businessmen	1.81	1.87	1.93	1.80	2.08	2.05	2.12	2.12
Individualism	1.98	2.06 ++	1.86	2.15	2.22	2.20	2.24	2.22
Investment	1.97	1.97	2.08	2.09	2.13	2.13	2.14	2.15
Profit	2.04	2.10	2.12	2.16	2.07	1.99	2.14	2.00
Progress	2.36	2.34	2.13	2.42 ++	2.50	2.49	2.45	2.42
Risk-taking	1.74	1.82 ++	1.73	1.80	1.92	1.80 —	1.86	1.83
Small enterprise	2.17	2.16	2.04	2.14	2.12	2.14	2.11	2.15
Social utility of business	2.31	2.38	2.28	2.53 ++	2.39	2.41	2.43	2.48
Universalism (impersonal business code)	2.21	2.13 — —	2.03	1.67 — —	2.14	2.15	2.15	2.09
Practicality	2.34	2.35	2.34	2.56 +	2.51	2.52	2.51	2.59
Negatively valued								
Government regulation	1.46	1.52 +	1.56	1.61	1.46	1.54	1.44	1.43
Labor	1.68	1.69	1.65	1.84 ++	1.79	1.86	1.84	1.79
Profit-sharing	1.52	1.68 +++	1.56	1.91 ++	1.66	1.65	1.77	1.75

NOTE: Differences significant by t-test.

ues when we look at family background and occupational choice. There is one obvious reason for this. As we saw in Table 5, commercial-school students are already near the extreme on almost all of the values associated with what we may now call the Taiwan Business Ethic. Although some of the expected family-background relationships still obtain in an unreliable way, there are also some reversals. For example, whereas sons of business families are the group in the academic schools who are most committed to risk-taking as a means of attaining success, the group most committed to risk-taking in the commercial school are apparently the sons of non-business families. I will take up this kind of relationship in the discussion of the separate values. Thus, there may be interesting patterns of "interaction" in both parts of Table 8. However, the major conclusion must be that the economic values of the commercial-school boys of the sample are (1) closer to the Taiwan Business Ethic than those of the academic-school boys, and (2) more closely related to the kind of school attended than to the business or non-business nature of family background. It seems very likely that this is the result of implicit and explicit socialization in both kinds of school, a pro-business ideology in the commercial school meshing with and modifying the pro-government ideology presented in all the schools. However, no first-hand evidence is available concerning the ideological content of the middle-school textbooks or curricula, or the nature and extent of socialization occurring in the classrooms.

The results presented so far demonstrate that a business background in the family, attendance at a commercial school, and choice of business as a career are all related to a pro-business pattern of values in adolescent boys. Although kind of school attended is the variable most closely related to such a system of values, controlling for this, and for occupational choice, does not eliminate the effect of a business background on economic values. There remains, however, one possible complicating factor. In Taiwan, a businessman is much more likely to be a native Taiwanese than a Mainlander, a fact that is reflected in the present sample. Of the 210 sons of business proprietors, only 32 are Mainlanders. We will see below that among the values differentiating boys from business and non-business backgrounds are several with anti-government connotations. Such values might reasonably be expected to be held more often by Taiwanese than by Mainlanders, regardless of occupation. In order to determine the precise influence of a business background on economic values, it is necessary to control for native place. Although the small number of boys from mainland business families makes this

TABLE 9. SUMMARY VALUE MEASURES, GEOGRAPHICAL BACKGROUND, AND FAMILY BACKGROUND BY TYPE OF SCHOOL ATTENDED

Value area and expected orientation	Academic schools				Commercial school			
	Non-business background		Business background		Non-business background		Business background	
	Taiwanese	Mainlander	Taiwanese	Mainlander	Taiwanese	Mainlander	Taiwanese	Mainlander
N	(141)	(158)	(96)	(22)	(111)	(20)	(82)	(10)
Positively valued								
Competition	1.87	1.95	1.89	1.84	1.83	1.80	1.84	1.70
Work	2.44	2.40	2.43	2.48	2.52	2.49	2.61	2.62
Business, businessmen	1.82	1.81	1.84	1.94	2.11	2.02	2.10	2.07
Individualism	2.00	1.96	2.07	2.06	2.25	2.13	2.20	2.30
Investment	1.97	1.98	1.99	1.97	2.17	1.92	2.12	2.30
Profit	2.02	2.06	2.10	2.15	2.10	2.15	1.99	2.08
Progress	2.35	2.36	2.35	2.36	2.45	2.59	2.46	2.40
Risk-taking	1.72	1.76	1.82	1.83	1.88	1.89	1.83	1.72
Small enterprise	2.14	2.18	2.14	2.22	2.13	2.04	2.14	2.18
Social utility of business	2.28	2.33	2.38	2.50	2.41	2.38	2.45	2.43
Universalism (impersonal business code)	2.19	2.22	2.16	2.16	2.13	2.28	2.09	2.27
Practicality	2.33	2.35	2.38	2.40	2.53	2.38	2.55	2.62
Negatively valued								
Government regulation	1.49	1.43	1.53	1.53	1.46	1.40	1.50	1.31
Labor	1.68	1.68	1.70	1.79	1.82	1.80	1.81	1.90
Profit-sharing	1.59	1.47	1.73	1.65	1.65	1.69	1.75	1.82

The Inculcation of Economic Values in Taipei 283

kind of analysis difficult, it will still be possible to get some idea of the relative importance of occupational and geographical factors.

Table 9 compares the effects of these two variables separately for students in academic and in commercial schools. For boys in the academic schools, the pattern of results revealed in Columns 1–4 of Table 10 indicates very clearly that it is business or non-business background, rather than native place, that is the stronger source of values. Only in feelings of opposition to government regulation of business does being Taiwanese seem to weigh more heavily than being the son of a business proprietor. The associated value of opposition to profit-sharing is not unrelated to geographical background, but business or non-business background is the more important influence here.

Being opposed to government regulation is also more characteristic of the Taiwanese than of the Mainlanders in the commercial school. May we conclude, then, that a family business background plays no part in forming a student's attitudes toward government control of business? Inspection of the actual scores given in Table 9 shows that this is not the case, and that both occupational and geographical backgrounds have an effect on anti-government feelings. In the academic schools, it is the small number of sons of mainland business proprietors that prevents the difference between business and non-business backgrounds from reaching a level of statistical significance. Another factor is at work in the commercial school. Here the ten Mainlanders with business backgrounds show a uniform approval of government regulation. This anomalous attitude may indicate that the mainland businessmen who are their fathers resent the relatively more powerful Taiwanese businessmen, and feel that they need help from the Mainlander-controlled government. In any case, the other three groups of boys with business backgrounds (Taiwanese and Mainlander in the academic schools, and Taiwanese in the commercial school) all show stronger anti-government feelings than do boys with non-business backgrounds.

Whereas the results for students in the academic school were quite clear-cut, those for boys in the commercial school were contradictory and inconclusive. Geographical background seems more important for some values, business background for others; there are some reversals and a number of nonsignificant interactions. Such indeterminate results defy any easy interpretation. Perhaps it should be argued that the very scarcity of Mainlanders in the commercial school (twenty from non-business and ten from business backgrounds) explains their deviant scores and the "significant" findings. The most that can be said of the

TABLE 10. STRENGTH AND DIRECTION OF RELIABLE DIFFERENCES IN SUMMARY VALUE MEASURES: COMPARISON OF GEOGRAPHICAL AND BUSINESS BACKGROUNDS BY TYPE OF SCHOOL ATTENDED

	Academic schools				Commercial school			
	Taiwanese students		Business background		Taiwanese students		Business background	
Value area and expected orientation	Non-business background	Business background	Taiwanese	Mainlander	Non-business background	Business background	Taiwanese	Mainlander
Positively valued								
Competition							++	
Work				+				
Business, businessmen								
Individualism			+	+				++
Investment					+++			
Profit					−−		−−	
Progress								
Risk-taking			++					
Small enterprise			++					
Social utility of business		−		++		−		
Universalism (impersonal business code)								
Practicality					++			+
Negatively valued								
Government regulation	++			++		++		
Labor			+++				+	
Profit-sharing	+++							

NOTE: Differences significant by t-test; values as in tables above. The relationships between the columns of Tables 9 and 10 are as follows: the first column here compares Columns 1 and 2 of Table 9; the second, Columns 3 and 4; the third, Columns 1 and 3; the fourth, Columns 2 and 4. The pattern is repeated exactly for Columns 5–8 of the two tables.

responses in this particular breakdown is that if business background is not very consistently related to values, neither is native place.

Economic Values Considered Separately

The results presented so far show that much of the pattern of values characteristic of American businessmen is also associated in various ways with business culture as it exists in Taipei and that these economic values may be transmitted from one generation to the next. However, some exceptions and reversals appeared in the data, and these deserve discussion, along with those findings that follow the expected patterns.

The value of small enterprise. A positive valuing of small business enterprise, as the reader may have noted, showed no consistent relationship to any of the antecedent variables. When dealing with previously untested measures in a new setting, the researcher may interpret this sort of finding in at best two ways. The first would be to conclude that the concept being measured is irrelevant in the new context, so that respondents do not perceive the statements as being related in a cognitive sense or as being different in an evaluative sense. Such a conclusion might be of considerable substantive importance. The second would be to decide that the concept exists in the culture, but the measures or methods of analysis used are insensitive to it. This second interpretation would have only methodological significance.

Small business as the keystone of the free-enterprise system is a cliché to which businessmen in the United States all seem to subscribe, despite its daily increasing irrelevance. In Taiwan, as in other less developed societies, the cliché would seem to be far more vital: the dominance of small and very small commercial and industrial enterprises is one of the most obvious facts of economic life there. Yet we have seen that there is little evidence for the existence of a generalized evaluative concept relating to size of business among the sons of Taipei businessmen, nor do those who themselves have chosen business as a career, or who are studying in a commercial school, seem to have such a concept.

Of the six questionnaire items intended to measure the relative desirability of largeness and smallness in a business enterprise, only one reveals any reliable difference between groups with various kinds of business contact.* However, the summary measure does show one indication that the dimension of business size exists as a generally evaluated

---

* Those who planned to enter a business career were more likely than those who did not to agree that "Small business should be protected from the competition of large corporations" (79.5 percent *vs.* 64.2 percent; $p < .01$). The other five items pertaining to small enterprise as a value in itself were (1) Large corporations tend

concept in Chinese business culture. The sons of small businessmen, including shopkeepers and craftsmen, when compared with the sons of medium- and large-scale businessmen, show a statistically unreliable preference for small business (2.20 vs. 2.12, $p = .10$). These few differences, plus the internal consistency of the measure,* lead me to believe that a clearly defined cognitive concept with regard to size of business organization does exist in Taiwan, but either it is one on which the business community is internally differentiated, or it is largely irrelevant in the context of Chinese business life.

It could be argued that small business comes to be more highly valued when large-scale business threatens to overwhelm it—and even after it is overwhelmed—than in the early stages of industrialization and commercial expansion when its dominance is simply assumed, and when the chief reaction to the image of big business is probably admiration for its success. However, when the big business involved is state-controlled, as are most of the largest in Taiwan, a different evaluative concept is evoked. This concept will be taken up below in connection with the negative value placed on government regulation of business activities. Finally, the lack of a differentiated value on small business enterprise does not imply lack of concern for apparently related values such as competition, which will also be discussed below. It merely means that the value system has not been differentiated to the fullest extent possible. It also means that the Chinese avoid the strain that the value on small enterprise sets up within the American business value system, where it tends to contradict other major tenets of the system.

Profit. The value measure whose results appear in the row labeled Profit in the tables is composed of five individual items in which the respondent is given an opportunity to show a positive orientation toward profit-making.† No such orientation emerged as part of a differentiated business value-system in any of the simple breakdowns I examined, be-

---

to form monopolies and keep prices high; (3) It is dangerous for large corporations to buy out small business; (4) The small businessman is the cornerstone of the free-enterprise system; (5) Big business is almost always more efficient than small business; (6) Big business permits the development of better products at lower prices.

* Size was one of the dimensions that emerged in a factor analysis of the individual questions. This means that items concerning size are inter-correlated and at the same time not highly related to the other questions asked.

† (1) Businessmen get a higher income than they deserve; (2) Personal satisfaction is more important than material gain in operating a business; (3) There is no reason why businesses should be allowed to make profits on essential public services such as electricity and telephones; (4) Collecting interest on money is somewhat immoral, even though perfectly legal; (5) The desire to make a profit is a basic motivation on which the welfare of society depends.

cause of an interesting contradiction that is visible in Table 6 but more striking in the responses to certain of the individual items. For instance, respondents were asked to agree with, disagree with, or declare themselves uncertain about the proposition, "Businessmen get a higher income than they deserve." Among the 497 students who have chosen a non-business career, only 19.7 percent of those from business backgrounds (as opposed to 33.8 percent of the other boys) agreed with the proposition, whereas 25.4 percent of them disagreed, and 54.9 percent were uncertain (as opposed to 20 percent and 46.2 percent, respectively; Chi-square = 9.69; $p < .01$). Among the 146 students who intend to go into business, 26.5 percent of those from business backgrounds agree with the proposition and only 19.7 percent disagree with it, while 58.8 percent are uncertain. The comparable figures for boys from non-business backgrounds are 11.5 percent, 33.3 percent, and 55.1 percent, respectively (Chi-square = 9.58; $p < .01$).

On this particular item, then, it would seem that among boys who have chosen not to become businessmen, the sons of businessmen view profit more favorably than do the other boys. But among those who plan to become businessmen, it is the sons of non-businessmen who have the more positive view of profit. A similar finding obtains when comparing the responses of boys who attend the two kinds of school, sons of business families in the commercial school being less favorable to profit-making than boys from other kinds of families.

The phenomenon just discussed is quite common in the material I have been examining, and it raises interesting questions about the process of occupational socialization and selection, questions that cannot be pursued here. A possible explanation of the phenomenon is that boys who enter business without a family business tradition may espouse the ideology of business more enthusiastically than those who are merely inheriting an occupation. But to propose such an explanation is not to deny the importance of family influences in economic values and socialization. There is still strong support in the data for the hypothesis that family socialization affects economic values. Moreover, the apparent finding that family socialization is more strongly felt among those who do not plan to enter business occupations than among those who do must be evaluated in the light of evidence concerning inter- and intra-generational social mobility. Perhaps it should be evaluated also in the light of the actual occupations the respondents enter as opposed to those they intend to enter when they are students, although this may reveal as much about the relative number of employment opportunities in business occupations as about the effectiveness of family socialization.

Universalism. The various comparisons made in the course of analyzing the results of this study (see especially Table 8) indicated that there is a slight differential emphasis on particularistic values in Taipei business culture, contrary to the pattern imputed to American businessmen. Particularism as a value, an ideal norm for behavior, is often cited as characteristic of traditional Chinese society (Parsons 1951: 195–98; cf. DeGlopper's paper in this volume), and especially as an impediment to effective business activity (Levy and Shih 1949) and thus to industrialization (Levy 1949: 355–59). A corollary often derived from this view is that businessmen, reacting to the strain put on them in their business activities by particularistic norms, will tend to have more universalistic values than others in Chinese society. In fact, there is some empirical support for this view from as late as the mid-1930's (Lang 1946: 351–52).

In view of this latter evidence and of the weakness of the relationships demonstrated in this study between business contact and particularistic values, one might be inclined to dismiss the relationships. I believe this may be a case where a value exists but the method selected to measure it was ineffective. (The four items designed to measure universalism as an economic value include only a few aspects of a very complex concept; moreover, cognitive and evaluative aspects are confounded in several of them.)[*] However, the most that can be said with certainty in either direction is "Not proven."

Competition. To complete the discussion of patterns that were in some way unexpected, we may look at competition (*ching-cheng*), which was negatively valued by students in the commercial school. Five items were used that bear on valuation of competition in business life and in general, including one that in effect asks the respondent to choose between competition as a value and small business as a value: "Small business should be protected from the competition of large corporations." Although students with business connections appear to favor small enterprise on this question, this may be because they reject competition as a general value. For example, 72.8 percent of the commercial-school students agreed with the statement, "Business firms should get

---

[*] The four items designed to measure universalism were (1) Loyalty to friends is more important than personal ambition; (2) The only way to get ahead in the business world is to have the "right connections"; (3) I expect my friends to help me if I am in trouble, even if it means getting around rules or regulations; (4) A businessman should build a new factory to replace an inefficient one, even if it means putting people out of work. The most pronounced differences between the sons of businessmen and other boys were observed on the fourth item, 52.9 percent of the businessmen's sons agreeing as against 63.5 percent of the other boys ($p < .01$).

together to stop 'cutthroat' competition," as against 62.3 percent of the academic-school students ($p = .01$).* The major connotations of competition in Taipei business culture seem to be those of excess and harm rather than those of vitality and progress.

Progress. Table 8 showed that progress as a concept and as a value was characteristic of boys from business backgrounds only when they had themselves chosen business as a career. It is one of the values on which the commercial students scored significantly higher than the academic students. However, boys from business backgrounds did not score significantly higher on it than other boys. Thus we cannot say that progress is a part of the business culture transmitted through the family. This negative finding can be explained by postulating, as Ryan did from his Indonesian data (1954: 49–52), that progress is an emergent concept and the business value-system is therefore partially differentiated along generational lines. A conception of material well-being as an overriding standard by which to evaluate progress, and a certain amount of optimism in the sense of a belief in the possibility of progress, is characteristic of the new business value-system of the younger generation.†

Practicality. The content of the five items measuring the degree to which practicality is valued and the pattern of its relationships with various aspects of business contact suggest that this value has much in common with the preceding one of progress, although the two can be separated logically.‡ As measured in this study, both practicality and progress might be subsumed under a more general value of "materialism," and there is evidence to suggest that materialism is part of the business value-system that is transmitted through the family.

Tables 5 (first two columns) and 8 together show such a transmission as a definite possibility, as do the responses to certain individual items on the questionnaire. Responses to the frank statement, "The only purpose of work is to make money," for example, show clearly that a ma-

---

* The other three items were (1) Competition is not really necessary if businesses are well run; (4) Competition leads to one's gain, but to another's loss; (5) Competition is needed to encourage people to do their best.

† The four statements were (1) New things are better than old things; (2) In the long run, all progress can be measured by the standard of living a people enjoys; (3) The future is sure to be a better place to live in; (4) Life is better now than it was in any previous period of time.

‡ (1) I most admire a person who is practical; (2) The main purpose of a college education is to get training for a better job; (3) Scientists should concentrate on finding things of practical value and use; (4) The only purpose of working is to earn money; (5) The final result is more important than the way in which things are done.

terialistic view of things is more characteristic of boys from business backgrounds (23.8 percent agree) than of other boys (12.7 percent agree) in the sample, and more characteristic of the commercial-school students (23.66 percent agree) than of the academic-school students (12.4 percent agree).*

Work. The relatively more instrumental orientation implied by the somewhat higher evaluation of practicality and progress (or of a combined value of materialism) by the boys with more business contact leads to a difficulty in interpreting the value of work, a value that was among those found to be transmitted through family socialization. The items designed to measure the degree to which work is valued seem more likely to elicit an intrinsic rather than an instrumental orientation to the importance of work; for example, "I feel sorry for rich people who never learn how good it is to have a steady job.† Surprisingly enough, this statement is endorsed by three-quarters of the commercial students but by only half of the academic students. The apparent contradiction in these results is not unique to this study. Ryan's results, using a concept of work identified with the Chinese term *ch'in-hsin*, contain the same ambiguity. It cannot be determined from Ryan's discussion whether work when contrasted with, for example, unearned wealth still remains a valued concept. The fact that Ryan concludes his discussion by saying that only independent entrepreneurial work is really valued suggests an instrumental qualification to the otherwise purely intrinsic value placed on work by respondents in his study. Further empirical research is indispensable to the solution of this problem, but the form of the solution may well follow Ryan's suggestion of a dominant value and another compensating, "contrapuntal" value.

Risk-taking. The boys in the middle-school sample were asked to respond to four statements concerning the taking of risks, both in business endeavor and in a more general sense (cf. Ryan's characteristic of "nerve" [*kan*]).‡ Table 8 indicates that the general orientation toward risks originates in family socialization, in that boys from business fami-

---

* The differences between the two kinds of school and between business and non-business backgrounds in the academic school were significant by t-test ($p < .01$).

† The other four items related to work as an intrinsic value were (1) Hard work and devotion to a job are often not rewarded; (3) Those who take life easy are happier than those who work hard; (4) People work hard only for money and security; (5) Everyone should take pride in his work, no matter what his job.

‡ The four items were (1) People who are not willing to "gamble" in life are rarely successful; (2) A secure job is better than a challenging (exciting) yet relatively insecure job; (3) When I am forty, I would be willing to invest everything I own in a "once-in-a-lifetime" business opportunity; (4) The tried and proven way is the best way to succeed.

lies are more inclined than the other boys to endorse statements favoring risk-taking, particularly in an investment situation.

Individualism. The material analyzed in this paper offers some support for the conclusion that individualism is one of the values differentiating the business culture from the non-business culture in Taipei. For example, the statement, "Success depends mostly on learning to rely on and work with others," is endorsed least by students in the commercial school (59.8%), next least by students from business families in academic schools (66.1%), and most by students with no business background in the academic schools (76.1%).* This finding seems indirectly to contradict the indication that boys from business backgrounds favor particularistic relationships somewhat more strongly than do boys from non-business backgrounds, a contradiction that may reveal a strain in the integration of the value-system. In any case, the same contradiction appears in Ryan's study, where both self-reliance and interdependence (especially in the particularistic relations called *hou-pi-shan*) are considered integral to the value-system of Chinese businessmen in Java.

Generally positive attitude toward business and belief in the social utility of business. Many of the items in the survey instrument can be interpreted as relevant, to one degree or another, to two closely related values: the attitude toward business and businessmen, and toward a conception of business activity as beneficial to all members of society.† A relatively favorable perception of business is in this study most closely

---

* The other four statements were (2) Most people do their best work when part of a group; (3) If a man can't better himself, it is his own fault; (4) A man who is his own boss usually does more work than any boss could get him to do; (5) It is best for everyone in the long run if each person looks after his own interests.

† The statements designed to measure attitudes toward business and businessmen were as follows: (1) Businessmen are rarely dishonest in their dealings with the public; (2) Public and private enterprise are equally efficient; (3) Businessmen usually look out for the public welfare; (4) Most businessmen are people of initiative and foresight; (5) Most employers are deeply interested in the welfare of their workers; (6) Owners and managers of business firms don't usually work as hard as their employees.

The statements designed to test a belief in the social utility of business were (1) Business activities serve the people, and everyone benefits from them; (2) Wealthy people are necessary since they are the ones who start up new business to supply our wants; (3) What is good for business in the long run is good for the country in general; (4) A higher standard of living for everyone is inevitable under the free-enterprise system of business; (5) Democracy depends on the existence of free business enterprise; (6) In the free-enterprise system everyone benefits if each business seeks to make the highest possible profit.

The first principal component in an unrotated principal-axes factor analysis of these data is dominated by items from these two value areas. Since components are extracted in the order of the amount of variance they can "explain," the attitude toward business must be considered a basic part of the Taiwan Business Ethic.

related to choice of business as a career, and understandably so, but it is also related to a business background. For example, to the statement, "Businessmen usually look out for the public welfare," the proportion agreeing goes from 4.5 percent for boys from a non-business background who do not themselves choose business as a career, to 22.1 percent for sons of business families who do choose business (both background and choice significant; $p < .01$). One might also note from the absolute percentages in this example the generally low level of confidence Taiwanese seem to have in businessmen, a survival, perhaps, of the low value placed on commercial activity in traditional China. Even where the degree of business contact is high, at least three-fourths of middle-school boys are distrustful of businessmen in general.

Attitudes toward investment and toward labor. These two values do not show a consistent relationship with business or non-business background. They do, however, show strong relationships with choice of business as a career, and with type of school attended. They should, therefore, be considered as part of the Taiwan Business Ethic, though not as transmitted through family socialization.*

Profit-sharing and government regulation. Among the fifteen value areas dealt with in the study, two stand out as being particularly strongly related to a family business tradition. These are opposition to government regulation and activity of any sort, and a conviction that the profits of business ought not to be shared—whether by government, workers, or the general public.

---

* One caution must be noted concerning the method used here to measure attitudes toward labor. Whereas all of the other fourteen value measures are operationally if not conceptually independent, this measure is not. Since so few of the original items bearing directly on the respondent's view of labor could be used in Taiwan (for example, those concerning labor unions were useless because the government-controlled Taiwanese unions bear so little resemblance to the powerful independent American unions), some items designed to measure other values but bearing indirectly on labor were employed. This means that there is the possibility of redundancy in the postulated relationships, although different directions of the relationships between these several summary scores and antecedent variables should prevent this from becoming a problem.

The actual items used to measure the attitude toward labor were (1) Workers should be given a voice in running the company; (2) Besides their wages, workers have a right to a share of their company's profits; (3) Most employers are deeply interested in the welfare of their workers; (4) A businessman should build a new factory to replace an inefficient one, even if it means putting people out of work.

Those used to measure the attitude toward investment were (1) The main purpose of saving money is to provide for emergencies; (2) In the long run, everyone benefits if lower taxes encourage people to invest money in business; (3) People should be encouraged to invest their money in business rather than just saving it; (4) Business profits should be put into expansion instead of higher wages or dividends.

Opposition to government regulation is couched in extremely *laissez-faire* terms, such as "The best government engages in the fewest activities," and extends even to welfare activities of the government, few as they are in Taiwan. Consistent differences between the sons of businessmen and the other boys in the sample on individual items such as these demonstrate that a generalized value exists in this area, but it is also clear that the primary reference of the value is government regulation of commercial activities. For example, as might be expected from the generally low opinion of the trustworthiness of businessmen, most students in the sample agree that "Business needs constant watching and regulation or the public will be cheated."* However, the sons of businessmen in our sample were much less likely to agree with this statement than were boys from non-business backgrounds (72.4 percent *vs.* 81.7 percent; $p < .01$).

The concept of profit-sharing as measured in the questionnaire is a general one, not limited to taxation or other government action; but this narrower interpretation is clearly the most important category in the questions and in the concept. Thus, for example, sons of business families were much less likely than others to agree that "Workers have a right to share in their company's profits" (67.1 percent *vs.* 79.5 percent; $p < .01$). They were also less willing to agree that "Government should tax the 'excess' profits of a company" (62.4 percent *vs.* 77.1 percent; $p < .001$).†

It seems that, of the economic values that are transmitted through family socialization, those concerning government and its relation to business activity and profit are the most salient. This has probably always been the case in Chinese society. The competition and accommodation between entrepreneurial and bureaucratic subcultures is certainly one of the most significant aspects of traditional Chinese society. The material analyzed in this paper suggests that it is still so in Taiwan today, and the paragraph translated below gives some of the flavor of

---

* Besides the two statements already dealt with, five others in the survey instrument were designed to determine a respondent's view of government regulation: (1) Government planning results in the loss of essential liberties and freedom; (2) Sometimes it is best if government agencies limit business profits; (3) Public relief hurts the free-enterprise system; (5) The government should provide *only* those things which private business cannot provide; (7) Government intervention is necessary for progress.

† The other three statements related to profit-sharing were (1) Business profits should be taxed heavily to obtain money for roads, libraries, hospitals, schools, etc.; (3) Businesses should pass their profits on to the public in the form of lower prices, rather than continuing to make huge profits; (4) If they had to share their profits with workers, businessmen wouldn't be willing to work as hard as they do.

the conflict. In the midst of a discussion on commercial prosperity in Taiwan, particularly Taipei, the editors of a directory of Taiwan inserted a plea entitled "The Distress and Hope of Businessmen" (*Ta hua wan pao* 1960: 232):

Speaking of the distresses of businessmen, no matter in what place or in what line of business, there is a common feeling that the complexity of taxation procedures, the plethora of tax laws and their arbitrary change, the excessively heavy rates and lack of timely adjustment, as well as the so-called price control that disrupts normal supply and demand—all these things not only cause businessmen distress, but moreover cause breaking of the law, leading to the misery of punishment. Therefore, what businessmen earnestly wish of those in government is that they simplify tax procedures and revise the tax rates according to the businessman's ability to pay and to the business situation, which is to say, to move toward a compassionate, reasonable, and law-abiding solution.

Conclusion

Evidence has been presented to indicate that there exists in urban Taiwan a differentiated business value-system, and that a significant part of this value-system is transmitted from one generation to the next within business families. This is the process I call economic socialization, though my approach to the data gathered in this study by no means exhausts the kinds of influences that should be considered part of the process. Differentiation of the business value-system is on a fairly high level of generality; the evidence suggests that it is shared in large measure by business families representing the whole range of entrepreneurial activities. It is probable that the Taipei business community is also internally differentiated in its value-system, as was indicated in the discussion of small size as a value in itself in business. It is unlikely, however, that for very many of the values discussed internal differentiation would be great enough to make any two segments of the business community more like the non-business community than like one another.

The choice of values to be examined in this paper and, to some degree, my approach to the data were influenced by the availability of substantial previous research on the American business value-system and the lack of corresponding resources for the study of Chinese value-systems. However, some connections have been established with Ryan's work on overseas Chinese businessmen and their values, most notably where two positively valued concepts come into conflict. It is here, especially, that further empirical and conceptual analysis is required.

In Ryan's work we have the beginnings of a systematic description of a Chinese business value-system. Since this work was done in Indonesia, however, the question arises how applicable its results—or indeed those of any study done among overseas Chinese—will be to Chinese economic society in general. In other words, to the extent that the values of an immigrant people are adapted to the conditions of its adopted land, and to the extent that provincial Java, traditional mainland China, and present-day Taiwan, for instance, differ socially and economically, formulating a "Chinese" business value-system will be complicated and perhaps impossible by the methods used thus far. However, there does exist a small body of literature on traditional Chinese business culture. Although less systematic than Ryan's work, it could still provide the basis for a comprehensive treatment of Chinese business values (e.g. Eberhard 1962). At the very least, it could tell us what questions to ask and how to ask them. Thus armed, we might determine and compare the business values of many types of Chinese communities, noting which values remained constant. Another approach would be to compare the values of the overseas Chinese business community in a culture with those of the native business community. I hope that this paper will be useful in such an undertaking.

Doing Business in Lukang

DONALD R. DE GLOPPER

Today the old port of Lukang lies like a beached whale three kilometers inland from the west coast of Taiwan. During the Ch'ing dynasty it was the second largest city of the island, the economic center for a large region of central Taiwan. In the latter part of the nineteenth century the harbor silted up and the city began a slow decline. In the fifteen years after the Japanese occupation of Taiwan in 1895, the economy of Lukang declined precipitously. This decline was due primarily to the construction of the railroad and the reorientation of central Taiwan's trade away from Fukien, via Lukang, and toward Japan, via Keelung. As Lukang slipped down the central-place hierarchy, thousands of its people left to seek their fortunes in Taipei and the growing cities along the railroad. Throughout the Japanese Period (1895–1945), Lukang remained a backwater while other cities boomed.

Lukang is now a placid town of about twenty-eight thousand people. It is regarded by its inhabitants and by outsiders as quaint, old-fashioned, dull and bereft of opportunity, a place where the best way to get on is to get out. Seen from the outside, in an ahistorical perspective, it differs but little from the scores of other country towns that dot the Taiwanese landscape. There is no trace of the old harbor, and the town serves as a market center for the surrounding farmers. It is also a minor center of handicraft and small-scale light industry.

Many of the town's businessmen subsist by providing goods and services to the people of the villages that surround the town. The land around Lukang is intensively cultivated and densely populated, with a rural population density of about twenty-one hundred people per square mile. Most of the surplus agricultural produce of the area is not marketed through Lukang, but goes directly to the cities or to processing factories. This obviates any substantial brokerage role for the businessmen of the town. Farmers sell their crops for cash, some of which is spent in Lukang; they do not rely to any great extent on credit from Lukang shops.

Farmers can bypass Lukang and send their crops directly to the cities or to large wholesale markets some distance from their homes because of the highly efficient transport available in Taiwan today. Most villages have access to an all-weather road, and major cities are linked by paved roads and railroads. It is only twelve kilometers by paved road from Lukang to the city of Changhua, the regional economic center, and from there it is easy to reach the rest of Taiwan. Today it is possible for inhabitants of Lukang or of the surrounding villages to take a bus, a taxi, a motorcycle, or a motorized cart to Changhua, or to go another thirty kilometers to the metropolis of Taichung. Both Changhua and Taichung offer a wider selection of shops, cinemas, restaurants, and medical facilities than does Lukang. The retail shops and service enterprises of Lukang must compete with those of the larger cities. They must also compete with smaller establishments in the countryside. Population growth and the rural prosperity following land reform and technical improvements in agriculture have led to a great increase in the number of rural shops and to the growth of small new commercial centers in the countryside. The settlement of Ts'ao Kang, some seven kilometers north of Lukang, was as late as 1958 simply a large village with a police station, a primary school, and a bus stop for Lukang and Changhua. Two rows of concrete shop houses that have risen from the rice fields now supply the local farmers with their daily necessities.

Lukang's central-place functions and role as market town have been undercut, then, both by improved transportation facilities and by commercial growth in the countryside itself. On the other hand, population growth and a vastly improved standard of living have generated a much greater total volume of business, as well as a mass demand for many products and services that simply did not exist twenty years ago. There are now far more businesses in Lukang than twenty years before, and the town remains one of the major commercial centers of Changhua Hsien. Furthermore, the improvement of transport and the growing use of trucks rather than the railroad, along with the rapid growth of Taiwan's total economy, has made it possible for Lukang to become a center of light industry.

The city is now the site of some five hundred small factories and handicraft enterprises. Some of them produce things like plows, bricks, or coffins, which are consumed within the town or its marketing area. Others produce articles for the island-wide or the international market.

Small factories turn out hinges, twine, motorcycle reflectors, and phonograph cabinets for sale in Taipei or anywhere else in Taiwan. Others manufacture such things as scissors, toy parasols, and screwdrivers, which are shipped off to Thailand, Zambia, and the United States. This sector of the town's economy is firmly integrated with national and international markets. It is also the sector that has grown most rapidly in the past twenty years, and the one in which the largest profits can be made.

Today the population of Lukang is only slightly larger than it was in 1900, and many of its natives have emigrated to the booming cities of Taipei, Taichung, and Kaohsiung. Lukang has not experienced the sort of explosive growth that many of the towns in the area have, and it is no longer the regional commercial center that it was a hundred or fifty years ago. Natives of the town complain that there are no opportunities there, that business is not especially good. But many new enterprises have been founded, and some local businessmen have done quite well for themselves. It is true that if one wants to become really rich, to succeed in a big way, one must leave Lukang and try one's luck in the speculative, highly competitive business world of Taipei or Kaohsiung. But it is still possible to make a fair living in Lukang, to become moderately wealthy, and many people have chosen to stay at home rather than join the migrants. They are the subjects of this account, businessmen of small or medium scale in a quiet provincial town.*

In September 1968 the administrative units that make up urban Lukang had a registered population of 28,464 people. The none-too-accurate business registration statistics of the Changhua Hsien government listed 1,083 businesses in the city. A count of shops and street sellers in November 1967 showed 711 shops, 234 market and street stalls, and 129 street peddlers. Roughly, then, Lukang has one retailer of goods or services for every fourteen adults, a shop or stall for every five households, and one registered business for every seven males above the age of fifteen. Almost all the retail shops are family businesses, employing only the owner and his household, or are run by the wife to supplement family income. Few manufacturing or craft firms have more than ten employees. Such small-scale factories or workshops are of course not peculiar to Lukang; they are typical of Taiwan (Chen Cheng-hsiang 1963: 537–39).

One's first impression of business in Lukang is that there is so much of it on so small a scale. The town has no large factories, nor is its econ-

* My fieldwork in Lukang from 1967 to 1968 was supported by the Foreign Area Fellowship Program, whose support I gratefully acknowledge.

omy dominated by a single product. Woodworking is one of the most common local crafts, but it is carried out by scores of small enterprises, each producing one particular item, from night-soil buckets to carved altar tables. The economic structure of the town is best summed up as one of a large number of very small-scale enterprises with extreme functional differentiation and diversity. One small shop makes and sells bicycle seat covers, nothing else. On the streets of Lukang one can buy dried fish, teapots, a single needle, shirts of the latest gaudy fashion, electric pumps, hormone-enriched chicken feed, cabinets for ancestral tablets, and deep-fried oyster cakes. It is possible to have one's watch, motorcycle, thermos bottle, or insecticide-sprayer repaired, to have one's teeth capped with gold, or to hire a specialist to extricate one's grandmother's soul from the Buddhist hell. The natives of the town manufacture everything from bean curd, to the huge vats used by pickle makers, to the fake aborigine artifacts that will eventually be sold to Japanese tourists in Taipei.

There are no large factories or wholesalers. The streets are lined with many small and totally independent businesses, often selling or manufacturing the same thing. There are, for example, twenty-nine grocery stores, each selling canned goods, seasonings, flour, sugar, and the like. There are twenty-one Chinese drug stores, nineteen furniture shops, and nine photographers. One finds the same multiplicity of apparently identical small shops that Barbara E. Ward discussed in her article on cash and credit crops (Ward 1960: 148). It follows from this that there is no hierarchy of business in Lukang; that is, no pattern of relations between large and small firms, or between wholesaler and retailer.

Nor are the businesses of Lukang joined in any common formal association. There is no chamber of commerce. All trades in Taiwan are organized by the government into quasi-official trade associations (t'ung-yeh kung-hui). The territorial base of such associations is the county (hsien) rather than the town or city. There is no Lukang branch of the druggists' association; the local druggists are simply members of the Changhua Hsien druggists' association. In Lukang such trade associations are almost universally regarded as otiose, as something imposed from the outside by the government for its own ends. The usual response to questions about the functions of trade associations is a laugh, and the comment that they don't do anything. With the exceptions of the barbers' and butchers' associations, trade associations in Lukang do not regulate prices, control entry to the trade, or settle disputes between members. To a large degree, then, the small businesses of the town function as autonomous units, with few formal constraints on their operation or on the relations they establish with customers or suppliers.

At this point it is useful to raise the general question of business relations, and of the forces that shape or constrain such relations. Economic relations in Chinese society have been described as highly particularistic and functionally diffuse (Levy 1949: 352–58). Studies of Chinese business have demonstrated the importance of such things as kinship, common place of origin or schooling, and particularistic personal relations (see Fried 1953; Ryan 1961; Silin 1964; T'ien 1953; Ward 1960). To understand why economic relations take the form they do, it is necessary to understand the categories of personal relations and the solidarities that are thought to exist between persons whose relations are described in certain terms (Fried 1953; Silin 1964). It is also necessary to consider the conditions under which relations of trust can be established (Silin 1964) and the way credit is established and granted (T'ien 1953; Ward 1960), as well as hiring practices and the reasons given for trading with one firm rather than another (Levy 1949; Fried 1953).

Here I want to discuss the pattern of business relations in Lukang in 1967–68. I am interested in the sorts of things that shape, influence, and constrain such relations. I am also interested in the way the businessmen of Lukang describe their economic relations, in what they see as important or necessary for the establishment of some degree of mutual confidence. To discuss these matters it is necessary to say a bit about the social structure of Lukang, the matrix within which business relations are established, as well as about the sorts of businesses the description is based on.

It is important to point out that the population of Lukang is homogeneous, in the sense that nearly everyone who lives there was born there, as were their fathers and grandfathers. Many people have left Lukang, but hardly any have moved in. The few resident outsiders work as schoolteachers, police, or functionaries in public administration. They do not engage in business. All of the businessmen in town are natives, and, as far as I know, all the businesses are owned by local men. Everyone therefore shares a common place of origin; everyone is *t'ung-hsiang*. Furthermore, the people of Lukang share a strong sense of local identity and pride. The social boundaries between Lukang and the outside world are well defined. It is a very parochial place. Its inhabitants are given to frequent assertions of their solidarity and community, and claim that "in Lukang everyone knows everyone else, and people get along well." Since there are some twenty-eight thousand people, everyone does not in fact know everyone else, but people talk as if they did or could if they wanted to. The stress on parochial identity and solidarity goes along with a certain coolness toward those outsiders resident in the town. The manager of one of the two banks, a man from Taichung, described society in Lukang as extraordinarily self-contained, turned in on itself. This strong sense of local solidarity has consequences for business relations, for everyone I talked with agreed that it would be impossible, or at best very difficult, for an outsider, even a Taiwanese from Changhua city, to open a business in Lukang and make a success of it. "Maybe if he had lived here for ten years or so and knew a lot of people fairly well, or if he had a monopoly in something people had to have, then he could do it. But otherwise he'd fail."

If the people of Lukang stress the distinctions between themselves and everyone else, they minimize distinctions among themselves. They recognize certain obvious differences—some are rich, some poor; some live in one neighborhood, others in another; some have one surname, others another; some earn their living in one way, some in another. But each distinction cuts a different way. There are no highly visible or corporate subgroups within the population of the city. Lukang consists of a number of named neighborhoods, each with its own temple. But every neighborhood contains rich and poor, people of various surnames, and men who earn their living in many different ways. One can speak of the people of a neighborhood as a unit, a group, only when they are contrasted with the people of another neighborhood, as they may be on certain ritual occasions. Lukang's population bears three major surnames and a host of less common ones. But those of one surname have little in common besides that name. A man's surname is important if he is worshipping his ancestors or considering a marriage, but in other situations its significance is less certain. In short, within the general category of "Lukang men," every individual is a potential member of many subgroups, each defined by different criteria and important in certain specific contexts. There are no bounded and corporate groups between the town itself and individual households.

Businessmen I talked with were unanimous in asserting that such categories as surname or neighborhood, in and of themselves, were of no importance in doing business. Membership in such categories was acknowledged as important for some purposes, but not for business. The field of potential partners to a business relation extended to all natives of Lukang, and was not limited to fellow members of a defined segment of the town's populace. The autonomy and the freedom of the individual businessman were stressed, and I was assured that one was free to establish business relations with anyone one wanted to.

This does not mean, however, that business relations within Lukang are established at random, or that they consist only of relations of exchange, based on pure economic rationality in a free market. There are certain constraints on business relations, and pure economic rationality is not the sole determinant of the structure of economic relations. It is simply that some of the factors that influence business relations in overseas Chinese communities or in large urban centers do not operate in Lukang. After all, if all of one's potential partners in a business relation are one's *t'ung-hsiang*, and every third one bears the same surname, one cannot use such criteria to narrow down the field of possible partners, as one could perhaps in a large city or an overseas community. Other criteria will be used.

The very first thing to say about the structure of business relations in Lukang is that one does not do business with people one does not know. No one deals with strangers. Business relations are always, to some degree, personal relations. They need not be very close, but both participants in a business relation should be acquainted, familiar, "siek-sai" as the Taiwanese say (cf. Mandarin *shu-ssu*).

At this point it is appropriate to make clear just what sorts of business I am talking about, for the pattern of business and credit relations will vary from one trade to another. A vegetable retailer does not have the same sorts of relations as the owner of a factory that produces for the international market, and the owner of a rice mill deals with different sorts of people than a man who makes furniture. In some sorts of business, access to supplies or markets is restricted. In Lukang this is true of the trade in rice and fertilizer, for these commodities are controlled by local governmental and administrative bodies. It is also true of some building suppliers and contractors, most of whose business is devoted to public works. The owners of such businesses must establish and cultivate very close relations with those local officials who control their supplies and constitute their market. Since such relations depend to a large extent on favors and favoritism, they contravene the official regulations that, in theory, govern the allocation of scarce supplies and of contracts. They are technically illegal and are therefore shrouded in secrecy, and I do not intend my remarks to apply to them.

The businesses with which I am most familiar—like most of the businesses in Lukang—are those in which access to supplies, labor, and markets is relatively unrestricted. The owners of such businesses have a choice of many people with whom they can establish business relations, and potential customers have a choice of many establishments to buy from. The businesses are small and are managed directly by the owner or owners. Most businesses in Lukang fall into this category rather than the previous one. The ones I know best are the cloth retailers, the furniture manufacturers, the wood-carvers, the sawmills, the hardware stores and the vegetable retailers. A common vocabulary is used among them to discuss business relations, although the precise meaning of the terms varies somewhat from one trade to another.

In every case the most important concept, the term most often used in discussing business and its problems, is *hsin-yung*. This is a fairly complex concept, and can be translated in several ways, depending on its context. The dictionary definition is "credit," and it is used in this way in the term for a credit cooperative. Colloquially it means "to credit, to have confidence in; to be worthy of confidence and credit." One speaks of a man's *hsin-yung*, meaning his trustworthiness, his willingness and ability to meet his business and financial obligations. A man who can't pay his debts, who for whatever reason fails to meet his obligations, immediately loses his *hsin-yung*. Business relations of mutual confidence are described as having *hsin-yung*. The word also refers to the quality and reliability of goods. One may ask of a piece of cloth or a radio, "How's its *hsin-yung*?" Is it sturdy, does it work well, will it fall apart in a month?

Hsin-yung refers to an individual's or a firm's reputation, reliability, credit rating. It is the most important thing in business, a firm's most valuable asset. People say that to start a business one needs capital, but capital isn't enough. One must have *hsin-yung*, and to have *hsin-yung* one must know people, have a good reputation with some set of people, such as the other members of one's trade. Similarly, when a business fails, as often happens, the failure is described as the result of a loss of *hsin-yung*: "If someone, for whatever reason, can't pay his bills when they are due, he immediately loses his *hsin-yung*. No one will advance him any more money or goods, and his creditors start demanding immediate repayment. That's the end—he goes bust."

Hsin-yung is predicated on performance in business. It is not given or ascribed. Nobody has good *hsin-yung* just because his surname is Lin or Chen. It has no direct relation to an individual's moral character or general popularity. An unpleasant man who pays all his bills on time will have better *hsin-yung* than a good fellow who can't meet his obligations. In at least one sense *hsin-yung*, like a credit rating, is a scalar quantity, of which one can have more or less. And one can gain or lose it by increments, or, in the case of losing it at least, all at once.

Hsin-yung in the restricted sense of credit and *hsin-yung* in the more general sense of reputation and trustworthiness meet in the nearly universal practice of doing business with postdated checks. Retail transactions are usually in cash, but those between businesses almost always involve payment with a check dated anywhere from ten days to a year later. Thirty days seems to be the most common period, followed by ten and then by ninety days. The use of postdated checks is explained as being the "custom" of businessmen, "the way you do business. If you are a serious businessman, then you use checks." It is claimed that even marginal retailers and petty traders will open an account with the credit bureau of the farmers' association or the credit cooperative, simply so that they can write checks and thus be proper businessmen.

At one point the Ministry of Finance ruled that postdated checks are illegal and may be cashed immediately. Since anyone who refuses to accept postdated checks will have great difficulty doing business at all, the ruling has had little effect (Tenenbaum 1963: 73). Certainly no one I talked with in Lukang seemed aware that postdated checks were illegal, for everyone said that one great advantage of checks was that they were legal documents, admissible in court. If someone failed to pay his check when it was due, he could be taken to court. Even if he formally declared bankruptcy, one could at least get a settlement of 30 percent of what he owed. In fact very few people actually resort to the courts, but it is claimed that since everyone knows what would happen if they did, they simply settle for 30 percent of the debt.

People say that in the past, before 1945, there were no checks, or that they were used only by big businessmen. Business then was said to be based solely on verbal agreements, which made *hsin-yung* and mutual confidence far more important than they are now. The stress on *hsin-yung* and verbal agreements is said to have restricted the number of people one could deal with, since they had to be very well known to be trusted. The present system of checks is said to be better because it permits greater flexibility, and allows dealing between businessmen in the absence of very close personal ties.

The acceptance of postdated checks is of course a form of credit extended by the payee, and in this sense almost all business except retail sales operates on credit. The credit is not free. Businessmen claim that there is no interest on a postdated check—and indeed they charge no interest as such. But if they expect that most payments for what they are selling will be by postdated check, they simply allow for that factor in the quoted price and give a discount for immediate cash payment. Timber, for example, is sold by a cubic measure called a *ts'ai*. The price of timber fluctuates, but it is always cheaper by five *mao* (half a New Taiwan dollar, U.S. 1.25 cents) per *ts'ai* if the customer pays with cash instead of a thirty-day check. This amounts to an interest charge for credit.

It is impossible to determine the exact interest rate for postdated checks in general, for the cash discount varies both with the amount of the purchase and with the relation between buyer and seller. The precise wholesale price of commodities varies for different customers according to their informal credit rating, their *hsin-yung*. A large, well-established firm whose continued custom is desirable will usually get things at a lower unit price than a small, more marginal shop, even when both pay with a thirty-day check. Such variation can be regarded either as a price concession to the larger firm in the interest of higher volume and long-term sales, or as a higher interest rate on the credit extended to the poorer risk.

In general, however, interest charges on postdated checks appear to be equivalent to or slightly higher than those for unsecured personal loans. The following table represents the informed opinion of a bank official in Lukang, with interest calculated, as it so often is in Taiwan, as simple interest on a per diem basis.

INTEREST RATES IN LUKANG, MARCH 1968

Category	Interest Rate (New Taiwan dollars)
Secured mortgage loan	$3.9/10,000/day = 1.17%/month = 14.24%/year
Bank credit loan	5/10,000/day = 1.5%/month = 18.25%/year
Private loan (est.)	6/10,000/day = 1.8%/month = 21.9%/year
Postdated check (est.)	7/10,000/day = 2.1%/month = 25.6%/year

The figures for private loans and postdated checks are, of course, estimates, and instances of both higher and lower rates could be found. Woodworkers said that it was about 2 percent cheaper to buy timber for cash than to pay with a thirty-day check. An old, well-established draper's shop received a discount of 1.8 percent per month if it paid cash rather than using the customary sixty-day check.

A postdated check, then, represents a fairly expensive form of credit. One wonders why the practice is as common as it is. People in Lukang claimed that it was partly a matter of status and emulation, men using checks to demonstrate their standing as proper merchants, and tending to extend the period of their checks in a spirit of keeping up with the Chens: "If you give me a thirty-day check, then I'll give you one for thirty days. Then you'll give me one for sixty days, and so on. Why, right now in the Western drug business they're using checks that run for as long as a year. There's no real reason for that; it's just this sort of competition." Nevertheless, one tends to feel that there is something more involved than simple status emulation. Many small businessmen clearly use checks because they do not have the ready cash, and other, cheaper, forms of credit are not available to them. It is almost impossible for a small businessman to get a loan from a bank or from the credit cooperative without collateral, "a house and fields" as people say. A formal loan involves a great deal of fuss and red tape. It often necessitates asking rich men to serve as guarantors, which obligates one to them, and it is sometimes necessary to provide gifts or entertainment for the bank or credit cooperative officials as well. It is too much bother (*ma-fan*), say small businessmen, and not a practical alternative.

In spite of high interest rates, postdated checks do have some advantages. Like any other form of credit, they permit the retailer to stock his shop with a wider selection of goods, which he need not pay for unless he sells. Such increased inventories in retail outlets are also to the advantage of the manufacturer or wholesaler, for they promote better distribution and more sales. They also permit a certain degree of flexibility in business arrangements, more than would be the case if all transactions were in cash. Cloth sellers, for example, can return a bolt of cloth if they have not sold any of it during the sixty-day period of their checks, or they can keep it for another sixty days at no increased cost. If they cut the bolt, it is theirs and they must pay for it. This practice, incidentally, gives rise to occasional dramas at the draper's, when a customer has her heart set on a certain kind of cloth, which is one of the unpopular, uncut bolts. The shopkeeper does not want to sell her a few feet, lest he have to pay for the whole bolt and be stuck with it. He therefore quotes a ridiculously high price and refuses to be bargained down, tries to catch her fancy with other sorts of cloth, and offers another, more expensive, pattern at an actual loss, all the while trying to weigh up the relative disadvantages of refusing to sell her what she wants—perhaps losing her custom and that of her friends and relatives—and of letting her have it and losing on the sale.

One furniture-manufacturing firm decided to install power tools and thus raise its production. The tools arrived, but the workmen, skilled craftsmen used to making everything by hand, refused to use them. They justified their Luddite position by saying they were not familiar with the machines, wouldn't be able to make such fine, high-quality furniture with them, and were afraid of losing their fingers and being unable to work at all. They may also have been aware that a machine which does the work of two men puts one of the men out of a job, as had happened that year when another furniture-maker in town installed a set of machines. After a series of meetings with the disgruntled workmen, the owner of the firm stopped payment on the postdated check he had used to pay for the machines and told the factory to come take the machines back.

Postdated checks also permit businessmen to get credit from many different sources and thus avoid becoming too dependent on any single supplier. People in Lukang often cited this as one of the primary reasons for the popularity of postdated checks. Most businessmen in Lukang pursue a conscious policy of spreading their patronage, of purchasing goods from several suppliers. Grocery stores get soy sauce or soft drinks from two or three distributors; cloth retailers deal with fifteen or twenty wholesalers; and woodworkers purchase timber, often the same kind, from several sawmills. Such a practice also permits the retailer or small manufacturer to play wholesalers off against each other, to shop for credit. Salesmen court shopkeepers with promises of special deals and token gifts. Soft-drink companies distribute T-shirts and baseball caps bearing the name of their product, and every grocer in Lukang seems to clothe his children in shirts proclaiming the virtue of some soft drink. Similarly, building suppliers' children glory in hats advertising paint, while druggists' children go about in shirts emblazoned with the names of aphrodisiac tonics. Such conditions obtain only when there are several competing suppliers. If something is in short supply or is monopolized by one distributor the situation is reversed, and the retailers do the courting.

When compared with the old system of business relations based on verbal agreements, under which close relations of mutual confidence were of the utmost importance, the use of postdated checks can be seen as a sign of a shift toward a more legal-rational, functionally specific foundation for business relations. But *hsin-yung*, if not as all-important as in the past, is still very much a part of the businessman's world. Accepting a postdated check, after all, involves the extension of credit and trust to the writer of the check, and indicates some degree of mutual confidence. One does not accept a check from just anyone. Some checks are inherently better than others. Businessmen prefer checks from the bank to those from the credit bureau of the farmers' association, for it takes less money to establish an account with the farmers' association than with the bank, and people with such accounts are considered more likely to default.

A check will not be accepted from a complete stranger. The first few transactions in any business relation require payment in cash. Only after a few mutually satisfactory exchanges, when the participants have become more "intimate" and better acquainted, will a check be accepted. One must first establish the reliability of the other. The trustworthiness of wholesalers and suppliers is as problematic as that of anyone else, and retailers test them carefully. A draper explained to me that when a new wholesaler is introduced to him, a lot depends on just who introduces him, and on how well he trusts that man. The introducer is in no narrow sense responsible for the wholesaler; he is definitely not a guarantor, but his recommendations do carry weight. Some wholesalers, salesmen in fact, come by without being introduced. In such cases the retailer never buys anything at the first visit. The salesman returns, showing samples of his wares and offering cigarettes and betel nut, the tokens of sociability; and after he has come at least three times, the retailer may buy a little and see whether he is honest and trustworthy. The retailer will also discuss the salesman or wholesaler with other retailers, and see what their experience with him has been, what they think of him. If he proves reliable, the retailer will eventually buy more and more from him.

The wholesaler is of course equally concerned with the *hsin-yung* of his customers. When he approaches a shop, with or without an introduction, he will ask all the other wholesalers he knows about its *hsin-yung*. He will also inquire of the other shopkeepers he knows how the potential customer's business is going. *Hsin-yung* is based on a series of mutually satisfactory transactions, and reports of the transactions of others are also taken into account when calculating the *hsin-yung* of a particular businessman. In this latter sense, *hsin-yung* is reputation, informal credit rating. Within the confines of Lukang, where it is claimed with some exaggeration that "everyone knows everyone else," the reputation of most businessmen is well if not too accurately known to others in the same line, the *nei-hang jen*. All transactions take place before a potential audience, or chorus, of *nei-hang jen*, who observe and comment on each other's doings. This is why it is so disastrous for an individual to fail to pay a check when it comes due. Everyone hears about it, and the unhappy defaulter loses the confidence, not only of the person holding the worthless check, but of everyone else who might accept a check from him. He loses his *hsin-yung* and is on the way to failure unless he can somehow come up with the money in a hurry and convince his skeptical creditors that such a lapse will not occur in the future.

This quasi-public sense of *hsin-yung* as credit-rating in the eyes of one's *nei-hang jen* is one reason that it would be hard for an outsider to do business in Lukang, for he would not be privy to the gossip and speculation about each other's financial affairs that occupies so much of the time and energy of the natives of the town. Such information is public in that it is a matter of public concern and interest, but not public in the sense of being freely available, for each businessman attempts to keep his own financial affairs a matter of the deepest secrecy, while eagerly speculating on those of his fellows. A missionary once noted that "all China is a whispering gallery," and the statement certainly applies to Lukang. The extension of credit and trust depends on information, and, given the habit of extreme secrecy about financial affairs, one's fellow townsmen and those in the same line have more information, imperfect though it may be, than do strangers. One is more likely to obtain credit from fellow townsmen or relatives than from strangers, not because of the prescriptive solidarities of co-residence or common kinship, for such credit is in most cases paid for at fairly high rates, but because one's intimates have more information and are in a better position to judge their chances of being paid back.

Thus, in the furniture trade there is a fairly common pattern of buying timber from sawmills in Lukang with a check but paying cash for that purchased in the big timber centers of Chiayi and Fengyuan, where the mills are in no position to judge the reliability of a small firm in Lukang. Besides deciding whether or not to accept a check, one must also agree on when it will be paid. Since time is money, and interest is calculated by the day, it seemed reasonable to me that the time a check ran before payment was due would be associated with the *hsin-yung* of the writer. I assumed that long-term credit would be extended only to well-established firms, which would be less likely to default and more able to pay the presumably higher interest on a long-term check. However, those businessmen with whom I discussed the question were unanimous in asserting that the length of time a check ran had nothing to do with *hsin-yung*, attributing the period of a check either to established custom in certain trades or to status emulation. One explained, "Look, if I'm afraid you won't be able to pay your check, it won't make me any happier if it's for ten days instead of two months. And if I know you can pay it, then it's not too important when it comes due, because I know I can count on it." I remain dubious that the matter is quite so simple, but since it was not possible to get precise information on just how much different firms were paying for checks of varying length, I cannot flatly contradict what everyone told me. However, my material on the furniture trade, which is both fairly complete and fairly reliable, suggests that long-term checks are, in fact, used only by those firms with good *hsin-yung*. Old, well-established furniture-making concerns tend either to pay cash for their timber or to buy it with exceptionally long-running checks, up to three months. Smaller firms almost always pay with a thirty-day or occasionally a ten-day check, while the most marginal usually pay cash, presumably because no one is willing to accept a check from them.

The businessmen of Lukang recognize a category of relations called "business relations." With the exception of retail sales, business relations can be described as those in which postdated checks are exchanged. In such relations *hsin-yung* and some degree of intimacy are important. But all the businesmen I talked with insisted quite firmly that business relations can be established with anyone at all, and that they are not influenced or constrained by such things as kinship, co-residence, sworn brotherhood, or relations that could be said to involve an element of sentiment, of *kan-ch'ing*. *Hsin-yung* is said to be determined entirely by a man's performance as a businessman, and to have nothing to do with the solidarities of common surname, schooling, or worship. Business relations are described as explicitly predicated on economic rationality and mutual self-interest. They are narrowly defined, functionally specific ties, based on the satisfactory performance of contractual obligations and sanctioned ultimately by the legal system. As one man said after I had been asking about the relation of such things as affinal kinship, co-residence, and common schooling to *hsin-yung*, "Look, *hsin-yung* is just a matter of whether or not someone pays his checks when they come due. That's all there is to it."

The owner of a furniture shop carefully explained that although he could be said to be "intimate" with the owners of the sawmills from which he bought his timber, and that he might occasionally go to a feast or wedding at their homes or invite them to his, such social relations were not necessary for the conduct of business and did not influence his decision to buy from one sawmill rather than another. "There are many kinds of wood, and the quality of each kind varies. I need several kinds of wood to make furniture, depending on just what I'm making. If this week I should need some cedar or *wu-t'ung* wood, I go out and see which sawmill has it and how good it is. I buy it from the place that best suits my particular needs. And the quality of the timber is very important. A lot of the quality is determined by the skill of the workers in the sawmill. I bought a lot of wood last week from Mr. Chen's mill, because his craftsmen are so skillful. The man who runs the planer is careful, so the planks are smooth and of uniform thickness. My workmen don't have to waste time planing them down by hand, and I don't have to pay for expensive wood like cedar that gets wasted as shavings and scrap. In this business it's the quality of the materials and the skill of the workmen that counts. That's the most important thing. It's not a matter of intimacy or sentiment (*kan-ch'ing*) at all."

The same man employs some twenty-five skilled cabinetmakers and apprentices. None of them are his kinsmen. When he wants more craftsmen he tells his workers, who recommend their "friends" or *nei-hang jen*, who are not their kinsmen either. He decides to hire or fire workers, and determines their wages, on the basis of their skill, on how well they perform their jobs as craftsmen. He sells his furniture to customers who walk in from the street. They come from all over central Taiwan, for Lukang furniture has a high reputation. He estimates that perhaps 30 percent of his customers come because other satisfied customers have recommended the shop to them. But, like all the owners of furniture firms with whom I talked, he insists that customers always visit a number of shops to compare quality and prices, and that recommendations do not determine where a customer will buy.

People in Lukang tend to deny that other sorts of social relationships or solidarities have any relation to business. One restaurant owner responded to my questions about the utility of sworn brotherhood in business by replying, "No, no, you don't understand. Business is an affair of money. Sworn brotherhood has nothing to do with money. It's just an affair of sentiment, of *kan-ch'ing*." People from the same neighborhood are described as "intimate" because they all know each other, and they form a group defined by their relation to their neighborhood temple and its annual festival. But this sort of relation or intimacy is said to be one of pure sociability, with no instrumental purpose.

In ideal terms, people in Lukang describe the sum of their social relations with a set of discrete categories. There are business relations; there are kinship relations; there are neighborly relations; and there are what are usually called "social" relations. Each of these has its own principles and purposes, its own satisfactions and problems. One expects different things from, and owes different things to, the people in each category. If one defines business relations narrowly as relations of buying and selling, then other sorts of relations can be seen to have little to do with business. Here, it is important to keep in mind the extensive structural differentiation and the degree of integration with the national economy that characterize Lukang's economy. It is unlikely that the owner of a factory that makes scissors, some of which are exported to Ghana, will have very many kinsmen or neighbors who are even potential participants in his business relations. Nor will a retailer who deals with a fairly large number of wholesalers, many of them residents of other communities, be able to call on presumed solidarities of common residence or schooling.

But business involves more than just buying and selling, and in practice the different categories of social relations tend to overlap somewhat. Simple economic rationality and functional specificity suffice to explain much of the pattern of economic relations in Lukang, but they are not the only forces at work. If one looks at other aspects of business life, one finds that, in certain situations, what may be loosely described as particularistic and functionally diffuse personal relations are of considerable significance. Their importance is most easily seen if one looks at problems of credit, of access to restricted or limited supplies or markets, and of partnership.

Most businesses operate partially on credit extended by suppliers through postdated checks, on the basis of some degree of "intimacy" and mutual confidence. But since a few satisfactory cash transactions must take place before a check will be accepted, it is impossible to start a business on credit. Nor is it assumed that a business will regularly yield such smooth profits that all checks can be paid when they come due. Difficulties and slack periods are to be expected. Yet if checks are not paid on time, *hsin-yung* is lost. Often it is necessary to borrow or somehow raise funds to pay a check and preserve one's reputation, or simply to meet operating expenses during slack periods. Neither the bank nor the credit cooperative is a practicable source of credit for most small businessmen. Given the norm of extreme reticence about financial affairs, the common practice of keeping two or more sets of books, and the absence of certified public accountants and of any reliable public system of credit ratings, the banks are in no position to make rational economic decisions about which businesses are good risks. They perforce fall back on making loans only with substantial collateral, a practice not very different from pawnbroking (see Tenenbaum 1963: 73). Small businessmen in Lukang often remark that the only people who can get loans from banks are those who don't need them. To start a business and to meet unexpected difficulties, businessmen must rely on credit obtained through informal, private channels.

The term used to describe such informal relations of credit and mutual assistance is *min-ch'ing*. Rotating credit societies, sworn brotherhoods and unsecured personal loans provide examples of *min-ch'ing*. People say that *min-ch'ing* depends on verbal agreements; nothing is written down. Obligations predicated on *min-ch'ing* are thus not legally enforceable, since there is no properly witnessed and sealed piece of paper to introduce as evidence in court. Such arrangements are sanctioned by reciprocity and appeal to community opinion. There is some risk in all such relations, and people are reluctant to participate unless they know and trust the others involved. It is assumed that people one has grown up with, who are committed to life in Lukang and bound up in its complex nexus of local social relations, are more worthy of trust than are strangers. People who have a family in Lukang, who have a general reputation for probity and have demonstrated a concern for community opinion are good candidates for an association or relation based on *min-ch'ing*.

Min-ch'ing is described as quite distinct from "business relations," and indeed it is. But *min-ch'ing* relations have an important, if somewhat indirect, effect on business. Relations with others in temple or festival committees, in rotating credit societies, in sworn brotherhoods, or in the informal groups that habitually sit in shops and exchange gossip are not described as "business relations." Rather, they are described as participation in "society," as "knowing people," or as affairs of generalized sociability, sentiment, or *kan-ch'ing*. By participating in such activities, by contributing time and money to temples, and by occasional acts of charity, a man defines himself as a responsible member of the community, a moral person concerned with the affairs of others and with their opinion of him. Such a person is likely to receive aid, including financial aid, when he needs it. It is possible to abstain from such activities and suffer no immediate injury to one's business. As long as checks are paid on time and the goods one purveys are of competitive price and quality, there is no loss of *hsin-yung*. But should troubles arise, the unsociable merchant is on his own; no one will go out of his way to help him.

In an emergency it is possible to borrow money from close kinsmen, or from such people as sworn brothers, if one has any. But such aid, even from brothers, may be given grudgingly, and it may be made clear that it represents a favor. The favor as well as the money will have to be returned. People dislike being under a special obligation to anyone else, even their own brothers. It is also possible to get a personal loan from one of several wealthy men in the city who act as moneylenders. This is to be avoided if at all possible. Not only is the interest high, but one is obligated to the wealthy man and perhaps to the person who acted as go-between in arranging the loan. The men who make such loans are in many cases local political figures who use moneylending as one way to extend their influence. Once indebted to such a man, in any way, a small businessman loses some of his autonomy, and his freedom to do business with whomever he pleases is curtailed. He may find himself under pressure to deal with associates of the moneylender, or to extend favors or support to them.

The best way to raise money and provide insurance against emergencies is through a rotating credit society. Such associations in Lukang resemble those described in other Chinese communities, and no extensive account is necessary (A. Smith 1900: 152–60; Gamble 1954: 260–70; Burton 1958). Credit associations in Lukang are fairly large, sometimes ranging up to twenty-five members, and they do not usually gather for monthly meetings or feasts. Members deal only with the organizer of the association, and may not even know who all the other participants are. It is claimed that almost every household in the town participates in at least one rotating credit association, and it is possible to take part in as many as one can afford. Many businessmen participate in several at a time, and some people speak of belonging to as many as twenty. It is usually possible to arrange one's monthly bids so as to get the principal from each association at the same time. This is a common way of raising at least some of the capital necessary to start a business, and it is the preferred method of meeting emergencies and getting over temporary periods of slack business. By using rotating credit societies businessmen obtain short-term credit from many sources. Just as they prefer, if possible, to deal with many suppliers rather than one, so they prefer to borrow money in small amounts from many people rather than ask one person for a large loan. The participants in a rotating credit society are defined as equals, and their rights and obligations are clearly understood. Obtaining money from such a source permits one to avoid having to ask a kinsman, a semi-professional moneylender, or a bank official for a loan, and so obligating one's self to one of them.

Of course there are risks in rotating credit associations, for if one member fails to make a payment when it is due, the association is likely to collapse, and those members who have not yet had the principal lose their entire investment. It is best to be cautious both in joining and in asking others to join one. I cannot say just how often credit associations do fail or what the exact risk of losing one's money is, but they fail often enough for people to be very well aware of the dangers involved. The first response of an acquaintance of mine, a young engineer, to a question about rotating credit associations was to warn me, "Don't join any. You don't know people well enough." It is felt that the possibility of losing one's investment can be minimized by joining only with people one knows very well, or has known for a long time. The actual decision of whom to ask or whose invitation to accept is said to depend on a careful estimate of one's relations with the other person involved, of his credibility and of the likelihood of his meeting his obligations. One of the many factors considered is his past record in credit associations. A man who has participated in several associations, and thereby both rendered aid to the organizer and demonstrated his reliability, will find it easier to organize one when he wants to than would an equally wealthy man who has never taken part.

Unlike "business relations," which are understood to consist of limited, well-defined exchanges of money or checks for goods and services, those relations described as based on *min-ch'ing* depend on an assessment of a man's total personality and his place in the social structure. One establishes the good character necessary for acceptance in the sphere of *min-ch'ing* only by participating in "society," by knowing a lot of people and interacting with them in the role of community member rather than in a narrowly defined occupational role. The life of a small businessman in Lukang is uncertain enough as it is, and the insurance provided by relations based on *min-ch'ing*, which permit him to extend his relations of debt and credit to a circle of people quite distinct from those he has "business relations" with, may make the difference between success and failure in business. The ideal businessman, therefore, should not confine himself to his shop and deal only with the others in his line. He should supplement "business relations" with "social relations." And since, in Lukang, participation in "social relations" and community affairs is restricted to natives of the town, any outsider who attempted to establish a business would lack the insurance provided by *min-ch'ing*, and would be more vulnerable than a native.

A businessman's personal, particularistic relations are also important in partnership. Partnerships are quite rare in Lukang, and it is said that the relation between partners, unlike that between men who exchange checks, should be close, intimate, and "thick." Partnership in business is described as an inherently fragile arrangement, easily disrupted and best avoided. The problems were explained to me as follows: "Say three men who are very intimate and whose *kan-ch'ing* is good decide to form a partnership and do business together. One contributes $2,000 N.T., one $1,800 N.T., and one $1,700 N.T. When some difficulty in the business arises, the one who put in 2,000 will say, 'I put in 2,000, and all I get for it is an equal share with you.' The one who put in 1,700 will reply, 'My investment was less, but I'm here all the time working for the sake of the business. If you'd pay more attention to the business instead of running around wasting time, we wouldn't have the trouble we have now.' Dissension arises and their relations get worse. So they break up." It seems to be expected that partnership entails absolute equality between partners, but that balancing each partner's interests, rights, duties, contributions, and rewards to insure perfect equity is ultimately impossible.

Most partners in Lukang businesses are brothers, or fathers and sons. Such partnerships do not represent large, complex families that have postponed the usual division of the family. Large, undivided households are rare in Lukang, and those few that exist are regarded more as curiosities than as status-generating realizations of a cultural ideal. In almost all cases, brothers who are business partners have separate households, each with its own budget, often dwelling in different houses. The business is described as "just like a corporation; we each have a share and get so much money a month, no matter how many people there are in each household."

Partnerships between brothers do not endure indefinitely, and there are no large, complex businesses run jointly by several brothers and their sons. Such enterprises do exist in Taiwan's major cities, and their absence in Lukang may simply reflect the fact that Lukang is not a terribly good place to do business, or that economies of scale are not very important in its retail shops and small factories. The family business that goes on for generations, on the European or Japanese model, is not found in Lukang, although one should keep in mind that most of the town's businesses, especially in the industrial sector, have been founded only in the last twenty years. The histories of some of the older firms, such as rice mills and furniture factories, reveal a pattern of ameboid fission. The oldest existing furniture shop, still one of the largest and most successful, was founded in 1908 by six brothers. Today it is managed by the fifth and only surviving brother, a man of seventy-two, and one of his middle-aged sons. Next door is another furniture shop, run by the son of the oldest brother and his two young married sons. Across the street the widow of another of the original six brothers runs yet another shop with her two adult sons. The two others split off from the original shop sometime in the mid-1930's, following the deaths of some of the founding brothers. The elderly survivors are vague about the reasons for the split, and members of the younger generation say they have no idea why the family and the business were divided. There are said to have been at least four other furniture shops in Lukang in the past thirty years run by descendants of the original six brothers. There are also said to be at least five furniture establishments in Taipei, Taichung, and Chiayi run by descendants of the six brothers, some of whom moved their business from Lukang. In Lukang, then, it is rare to find family firms run as a joint estate by several adult brothers. More commonly the brothers act as partners, much as would unrelated men. Over time, these arrangements, too, break down, resulting in fission of the business into small independent firms.

People describe brothers cooperating in business not in terms of maintaining an undivided family estate, or in terms of prescriptive fraternal solidarity, but in terms of the personal relations between particular brothers. Brothers are said to be better as business partners than unrelated men, not so much because they occupy the status of "brother," but because they know each other so very well, and are so "intimate." They are said to be well aware of their common interest, and less likely to be disturbed by relatively minor upsets and difficulties. Hence, each is willing to work hard for the sake of the business without worrying about exactly how much time and effort the other is devoting to it.

Some brothers cooperate in business, others do not. If they do, it is said to be because their personal relations are good, their *kan-ch'ing* is good. *Kan-ch'ing*, as the term is used in Lukang, refers to the affective component of all human relations. It does not necessarily vary with the closeness or structural importance of the tie. It applies to relations between brothers and close kinsmen as well as to all other persons. Girls hope to marry into a family where the *kan-ch'ing* is good, where there isn't a lot of quarreling and fighting. Some brothers have good *kan-ch'ing* and a lot of interaction (*lai-wang*), and others do not (Pasternak 1968; Wolf 1970). The quality of the affective bond between brothers does not, or should not, affect the axiomatic base of the relation. Brothers owe certain things to each other, simply because they are brothers, and fraternal duties and obligations exist whether brothers like each other or not. Brothers are one's ultimate security, the people one can rely on automatically in times of crisis, and the man who has no brothers is to be pitied. Should a man be injured, or struck down with a severe illness, his brother will look after him and his family for as long as necessary. Should he be killed, his brother will look after his family. The attitude toward fraternal obligations can be summed up as "Home is where, when you have to go there, they have to take you in."

The relations between brothers and between all close kinsmen can be described as consisting of a core of axiomatic obligations, upon which is superimposed an affective personal bond. In the long run, and in crises, one can depend on one's brothers. But no one wants to be dependent on his brothers, and an able-bodied man should not expect his brothers or kinsmen to make many sacrifices for his sake. And in Lukang cooperation or special help in business affairs is not considered one of a brother's axiomatic obligations. Any use of one's brothers in business is a function of the personal relation, the *kan-ch'ing*, that exists.

The same could be said of all kinship relations. One is not obliged to do business with or to hire another person simply because he is a kinsman. Most of the retail businesses in Lukang are so small that there is no question of hiring anyone at all, all work being done by the owner and his household. Most jobs in industry or handicraft either demand technical skill of a fairly high order or are so hard and so poorly paid that giving one to a kinsman would constitute no great favor. Most of the assistance or support a man gets from his kinsmen takes the form either of services, such as help with the cooking for a feast or a wedding, or of money, the universal medium of exchange. If the owner of a metal-working factory were to help his brother's son who had failed his middle-school entrance examination, he would be more likely to use his influence to get the boy admitted to a private school, or to help pay his tuition, than to give the boy a sweatshop job.

Retailers are expected to give close kinsmen a lower price, but the kinsman is also expected to buy without a lot of quibbling. An unusually candid cloth retailer told me that he gave his close relatives a more "honest" price. But they did not constitute any appreciable proportion of his clientele, and he did not make very much profit from selling to them. "So I don't really care if they buy here or not; I don't get that much out of it anyway." One old lady carefully avoided shopping at the mixed-goods shop run by her sister's son because she would feel obliged to buy once she went in. If she wanted a blue thing and all they had were red ones, she would have to take a red one. So she went to the shop of a non-kinsman where she could carefully look for something that exactly suited her taste, walk out if she didn't find it, and bargain fiercely if she did.

Had the old lady been sure she could get exactly what she wanted at her nephew's shop, she would have gone there and saved money. If there is a choice, and everything else is equal, one will indeed prefer to deal with a kinsman or a person with whom one has something in common, or with whom one is at least acquainted. It is better than dealing with strangers. Kinsmen or *t'ung-hsiang* are people with whom one has the potential of establishing closer relations, relations involving some degree of mutual confidence. But, such relations are potential, and mutual confidence cannot be taken for granted. To do someone a favor or to extend trust to him simply because he is of the same surname or attended the same school would be regarded as a bit simple-minded. Other things being equal, in the absence of any other criteria, business relations would be influenced by membership in such common categories as surname, schooling, or residence. But in Lukang, in business, other things are very seldom equal. As the owner of a furniture shop pointed out above, a great many things are taken into account when deciding just whom to do business with. Kinship, membership in some recognized social category, or the affective content of the relation is considered, but so are many other things. A friend of mine noticed that his wife patronized a shop in the market rather than the one across the street. He asked her why she went all the way to the market when the owner of the local shop was a neighbor (*t'ung-hsiang*) and of the same surname (*t'ung-hsing*) as well. She replied, "At the shop in the market the prices are lower and the selection is better."

In the absence of any other criteria, people will prefer to deal with kinsmen, fellow townsmen, or schoolmates because they "know them better." One has the impression that if a native of Lukang were suddenly dropped into the anonymous urban bustle of Taipei or Singapore, such categories as *t'ung-hsiang* and *t'ung-hsing* would become very important indeed, and that he would carefully cultivate close personal relations, described in terms of *kan-ch'ing*, with those who were in a position to affect his livelihood. But at home, in Lukang, such gross categories are rejected in favor of more complex and subtle criteria that operate beneath the bland surface of "friends and neighbors." People are quite reluctant to discriminate within the category of "friends and neighbors," to say who is more intimate, more trustworthy, more likely to be asked to join a rotating credit society. Unique personal relations, acquaintance, and mutual interaction are stressed, and people insist that one cannot talk about such general categories as "affinal kinsmen," for "it all depends on the person himself." Sentiment rather than structure is emphasized, and the vocabulary used to describe social relations beyond the narrow confines of immediate kinship consists largely of such imprecise expressions as "people you know," "people you've known a long time," "people with whom you have a lot of interaction (*lai-wang*)," or "those with whom your *kan-ch'ing* is good." Relations are described in what seems a deliberately vague terminology, one that blurs distinctions and avoids making any categorical statement of mutual obligations. Such social relations are thought of, or at least spoken of, in terms of natural human sociability rather than as positions in a social structure or as calculating, instrumental relations.

Relations with others in one's personal network, one's friends and neighbors, the people one invites to feasts or joins in a rotating credit society, are seen as rooted in affect. Associations of such people are referred to as based on *min-ch'ing*, which might be translated as "sentiments of sociability or community." But such relations are not necessarily or even ideally very close or intimate. The aim seems to be a lot of amiable, matey, but not too intimate ties with as many people as possible. People give the impression of being hesitant about getting too close, too deeply involved with or committed to anyone else. Amiable relations may break down if too much is expected of them. In business one should not expect others to do business or give concessions only because of affective, amiable feelings, which would be described in terms of "intimacy" or *kan-ch'ing*. Indeed one of the most common uses of the term *kan-ch'ing* is in a negative retroactive sense, to explain why two people don't get on so well any more. "Their *kan-ch'ing* used to be very good, but then something happened, and it broke up." Such usage is common in discussing business partnerships.

The rather diffuse, particularistic relations referred to as those of acquaintance or affective attachment are seen, then, as rather fragile, and not to be relied on in business. And in spite of the rhetoric of mutual support and affect, it is recognized that particularistic relations based on *min-ch'ing* can be exploited, one man profiting from the misplaced trust of another. Apparent concessions and special favors, allegedly based on particularistic bonds, may turn out to be no favors at all, or may be extended only to obligate the recipients. Cloth retailing is described as being largely a matter of salesmanship, since the cloth sold in all the shops comes from the same factories and wholesalers. One of the principles of successful cloth retailing is said to be the establishment of a personal relation with the customer, thus making the transaction something more than a pure encounter between strangers. A skillful retailer will chat with the customer, seeking something they have in common, and trying to persuade him that he is being granted a special concession because of the supposed relation. The retailer may point out that they are both graduates of the same primary school, or have a friend in common, or claim that because the customer has the same surname as the retailer's wife they are in some sense affinal kinsmen. The recognition of the relation will, ideally, make the customer feel more obliged to buy. One retailer explained as follows. "I take a common sort of cloth that most people know the price of and say, 'Usually this is ten dollars a foot, but since you are my affinal kinsman and are bringing me so much business, I'll let you have it for only nine a foot.'" The customer, pleased at such a bargain, does not realize that the wily draper is raising the price of another, less well-known sort of cloth by an equivalent amount. It is claimed that this sort of approach works best with rustics, who are reputed to take such things as kinship solidarity more seriously, and to be more socially naïve than the cynical townsmen. The same retailer told me that if he were to try the same sort of approach on a middle-class native of Lukang, the man would feel that he was being tricked and become even more suspicious than customers usually are.

In a similar vein, the woman who ran the very small and poorly stocked general store across the street from our house used to tell my wife that we should buy all our soap and toothpaste from her rather than the larger shops in the market "because we're neighbors."

Most people, and most businessmen, are perfectly aware that *min-ch'ing* relations can be exploited, and are therefore reluctant to appeal to them and rather suspicious of those who do. One man I knew ran a hardware shop, specializing in the sale and installation of pumps and pipes for irrigation. He spent a lot of time out in the countryside, and was often invited to rural weddings and village festivals, where he met a lot of people. Often someone he had met at such an affair would show up at the shop to buy something, which was all to the good. But the customer would demand credit or promise to pay after the harvest because, having eaten and drunk together, he and the shopkeeper were "friends." The shopkeeper claimed that such demands for credit or failures to pay bills on schedule were his greatest problem. He was confident that he would get his money eventually, but he himself had checks to pay and wanted his money as quickly as possible. He doubtless used the rather superficial relations of "friendship" existing between himself and the farmers to try to persuade them to buy from his shop rather than another, but suffered when they used the same superficial relation as an excuse for delaying payment. He claimed that he tried, as far as possible, to do all business on a cash basis, but that this was simply not possible when dealing with farmers who did not have a regular cash income.

When sources of supply or custom are limited, businessmen will try to cultivate close personal relations of a particularistic nature, but this is usually considered a second choice, something one does only when there is no alternative. During my stay in Lukang, cement was hard to get, since Taiwan was exporting vast quantities of it to Vietnam. The price of cement rose, and still there was none to be had. Building projects came to a halt or were delayed for months, and building suppliers in Lukang, at the end of the distribution network, were frantic. They sought out cement wholesalers and took them out to winehouses, entertaining them lavishly and pointing out what good customers they were. They stressed their *kan-ch'ing* with the suppliers, and tried to use any potential common category they could, begging for a few bags of cement, regardless of price, to satisfy their own customers and maintain their own *hsin-yung*. They did not enjoy doing this, and described the wholesalers as taking advantage of the situation in spite of protestations of fellowship and good feeling, but said that they had no choice.

Businessmen are wary of attempts to make use of particularistic relations, not only because such relations may be exploited, but because any special favor received puts one under obligation and thus reduces one's autonomy. The old man who ran the town's largest furniture enterprise asserted that he never accepted invitations to feasts or trips to winehouses, because if he ate someone else's food he was indebted to the host, which was a bad thing. He would, he said, go to weddings because there the guests contribute a red envelope with money and, in a sense, pay for their food. Factory workers and such skilled craftsmen as woodcarvers made a point of not asking their employers for loans or advances in pay, since that would obligate them too deeply to the boss. If they had troubles they turned to their "friends and neighbors," and to associations based on *min-ch'ing*. The organization of the numerous small factories and workshops was anything but paternalistic, and both owners and workers seemed content with a "business-is-business" approach to their relations.

To do business in Lukang one must know people and establish relations of mutual confidence, but one need not know people terribly well, and it is better to have limited relations with a lot of people than very close ties with only a few. Close, particularistic relations are important only in special circumstances. The small businessmen of Lukang desire to maximize their autonomy and freedom of choice, and prefer limited, functionally specific relations to diffuse ties, fused with personal relations. Such close personal relations are of less importance in Lukang's business relations than in those of Chinese communities described by other anthropologists (T'ien 1953; Ward 1960; Fried 1953; Ryan 1961; Silin 1964). The businessmen of Lukang, it must be recalled, operate on a small scale in their home community, one that is unusually homogeneous and that thinks of itself as perhaps even more homogeneous than it is. They do business in a booming national economy with a stable currency, and have access to fairly adequate if not ideal sources of capital, credit, and goods. Their customers have money to pay them, and they need not extend credit or ask any special favors to survive in business. T'ien explains the particular pattern of business relations in Sarawak by pointing out that "the characteristic features of business in Sarawak are lack of capital and emphasis on speculation; both of which provide ideal conditions for those who lend money to extend their influence" (T'ien 1953: 70). Such conditions simply do not apply in Lukang. The small businessmen of Lukang operate under a different set of economic and social conditions than the Chinese businessmen of Sarawak, Chu Hsien, or Modjokuto, and the particular pattern of business relations in Lukang is to be understood as a response to a particular situation.

The businessmen of Lukang are doubtless as devoted to success and the pursuit of wealth as their colleagues in Hong Kong or the Nanyang, but, when asked what they think is necessary for success, do not reply in terms of cultivating *kan-ch'ing* or of striving to "fuse business relations with personal relations" (Ryan 1961: 22). Nor do they put much emphasis on industry and frugality. These qualities are not denigrated, but are taken for granted. Everyone is industrious and frugal. Industry and perseverance do not bring a sure reward; they permit one to get by, to be a respected member of the community. A hard-working man will be able to support his family at a reasonable level, but no one expects him to become wealthy. Farmers and laborers are regarded as industrious and frugal, but they are not thought of as incipient tycoons.

To become rich one should of course be willing to work hard, but that is not the essential quality. What one needs is brains, cleverness. It is recognized that some people have a talent for doing business and making money, and others do not. Anyone can work hard and get by, or run a small shop, but only a few are clever enough to become wealthy. A Lukang proverb says: "It's difficult to raise a child who can do business." Another points out: "Without cleverness one will never become a merchant."

Cleverness is important, but success in business is not usually ascribed to sharp practice or low cunning alone. Success takes more than that. The essential quality of a good businessman could be summarized as the ability to look at a situation, interpret it in terms of business success, and adapt one's own behavior to the situation. The world is complex, and it is difficult to perceive just what a given situation holds in the way of business advantage, or how it is likely to change. The man who can best do this, and thinks of a way to turn a situation to his advantage, is the one who succeeds, who becomes rich.

A cloth retailer explained that in the cloth business one has to be smart and use one's head. "When a customer comes in you should be able to size him up, to know just what he wants and how much he's willing to pay for it. Cloth is very complex now; there are all sorts, colors, patterns, and degrees of quality." The retailer has to match up the customer's specific wants, which the customer himself may not be very well aware of or able to articulate, with one of the several hundred possible sorts or combinations of cloth. To sell cloth successfully one has to be able to think fast, to empathize with each unique customer and respond to him in the appropriate way. "You have to 'research,' to know all kinds of people and what is in people's hearts."

Rather than discussing competition with other businessmen in the same line, the merchants and craftsmen of Lukang prefer to speak more vaguely of an impersonal market or "conditions." To succeed, one must be able to meet the demands of the market. Business failures are usually described as the result of insufficient capitalization, getting too far in debt, and inability to satisfy the market, rather than as the result of the competition of other businessmen. Rather than recognizing an antagonistic relation between those in the same line, the *nei-hang jen*, people speak of an abstract "market" or "conditions," which everyone in a given sort of business must try to satisfy. Retailers stress the contest with the customer rather than that with the *nei-hang jen*. Cloth sellers ascribe success to their ability to size up customers and manipulate them, and celebrate the virtues of the salesman. "People say that a really skillful Lukang cloth seller can go up to a dead person and start talking with him, cajoling him, and gradually the dead person will rise up, bit by bit. In this business a clever tongue is what really counts." Craftsmen such as furniture makers or wood-carvers stress their skill and the quality of their products, the *hsin-yung* of these products as well-made objects. They say that one has to satisfy customers, give them what they want, but that customers can recognize quality, and will choose to buy from one firm rather than another because of the quality of the goods offered.

The emphasis is on fitting, matching up with what seem to be impersonal, given conditions. One merchant said that each person has his own way of looking at things, his own orientation to conditions and the market. Some ways of approaching things are better than others, for they accord with the demands of the market, and the man who is able to fit in with the conditions of the trade will prosper. A good cabinetmaker has to select the right kind of wood and decide the best use for each unique piece. A retailer must treat each customer differently, cater to him. He must know which customers like to look at a lot of things and bargain hard before they buy, and which prefer a simple transaction and will walk out if the merchant quotes his initial bargaining price instead of the one he is willing to sell for. Circumstances are constantly changing and one must keep up with them. Behavior that is appropriate in some circumstances will be inappropriate in others.

The qualities of a good businessman are summed up in the success story of Mr. Lin, a Lukang man who made a fortune in Taipei. As a young man Mr. Lin was very poor and could find no work in Lukang, so he went to Taipei to seek his fortune. There he worked at seal carving, a genteel but low-paying street trade. Somehow he managed to save or get his hands on a little money. With it he bought a small piece of land. The land was the least desirable in the city, the waste land where trash was dumped and burned. It was therefore quite cheap, and Mr. Lin gradually bought more and more until he owned two whole trash dumps. Taipei grew and the price of the land rose tremendously. Mr. Lin's two trash dumps, close to the center of the city, became very valuable and he sold them at an immense profit. He invested the money in an import-export business and so became very wealthy.

Like the protagonist of a Taoist parable, Mr. Lin succeeded because he was able to see the value of the useless and the unwanted. He saw an advantage that others did not, and was able to adapt his behavior to the demands of the situation, the market. And he succeeded because he was free to invest in trash dumps; he did not have to explain what he was up to, or get the approval of anyone else. He was clever and he maintained his autonomy. Many of the small businessmen in Lukang could be said to be trying, each in his own way, to emulate the legendary Mr. Lin. By insisting on their freedom to do business with whomever they choose, by maintaining strict secrecy about the details of their financial affairs and their intentions, and by spreading their debts and obligations as widely as they safely can, they are maximizing their autonomy and their ability to take advantage of any opportunity that comes their way.

Marketing and Credit in a Hong Kong Wholesale Market

ROBERT H. SILIN

Chinese economic relations have often been described as personalistic, although the criteria by which business associates are selected and the principles by which economic relations are maintained have not been extensively studied. In this paper I describe the organization of a Hong Kong wholesale vegetable market, the Kennedy Town Market, as I observed it.* By focusing on the dynamics of certain long-term trading relationships I was able to look closely at particularism. Specifically, I analyzed the relative influence of ascriptive ties and various criteria of performance on the organization of economic activity among small- and medium-scale Chinese traders. I also looked at the factors, both economic and non-economic, that maintain systems of reciprocity in economic relations and at the limits placed on these systems by Chinese society.

In 1963 Hong Kong imported 60 percent of the vegetables it consumed. All the imported vegetables as well as a significant portion of those produced domestically were distributed through the Kennedy Town Market, a walled compound containing six concrete sheds divided into stalls. The six sheds face on three streets, two of which are devoted to trading in fresh vegetables. The third street, not included in this study, is occupied by dealers in fresh-water fish. The market site is

* This paper is based on material gathered during six months (August 1963 through January 1964) of fieldwork in Hong Kong under a grant from the East-West Center at the University of Hawaii. A fuller account of the market is contained in an earlier paper (Silin 1965). All references to dollars are in Hong Kong dollars. At the time of the study one American dollar was equal to approximately HK $5.70. The romanization of Cantonese appearing in the text is according to Mayer and Wempe (1932). The unit measures used in the market were the catty, equal to 1.33 lbs., and the picul, equal to 100 catties.

owned by the Hong Kong government, which rents stalls to traders. There are now some five hundred people working on the two streets. The majority of these people come from vegetable-producing areas in three *hsien* neighboring Hong Kong (Hsin Hwei, Tung Kuan, and Chung Shan). Space is very scarce, and many traders sublet half or even a third of a stall.

The traders who occupy the market stalls are of two sorts: commission agents (hereafter called simply agents) and jobbers. Agents take produce on commission and sell it at auction to jobbers and wholesale customers. Agents sell only complete containers, which range in weight from 75 to 150 catties. Jobbers, individually or in groups, buy containers from agents and usually resell in smaller lots to wholesale customers.* The following background sections describe first the categories of wholesale customers who buy in the market and then the way the agents and jobbers operate. The bulk of the paper then analyzes relations between jobbers and agents, among jobbers, and between jobbers and their customers.

Wholesale Buyers

Buyers in the market include both large- and small-scale customers. Large-scale buyers are those who buy complete containers from either agencies or jobbers for re-export, for sale to large institutional buyers, or for processing in food factories. Small-scale buyers normally buy less than complete containers. They include retailers, managers of teahouses, and canteen operators.

Large-scale buyers. There is a steady flow of vegetables through the Kennedy Town Market to Malaysia and Singapore. Seven firms regularly export produce, and a number of others participate occasionally. These firms buy in Hong Kong when the price is significantly lower than in Singapore. Produce for export is obtained in one of three ways: exporters may negotiate with an agent who then has the produce shipped to Hong Kong; occasionally they may bid for produce at the auctions held by the agents in the market; and under conditions of dire necessity they may buy produce from jobbers.

Agents prefer to sell to exporters, for they buy in large quantities and only when there is a considerable difference between prices in Hong

---

* The Cantonese term for agent is *laan* (Mandarin *lan*). For background on the production and marketing of vegetables in Hong Kong and on domestic *laan* see Topley 1964. The term for jobber is *ch'aak-ka* (*ch'a-chia*). Both terms as used in the market refer both to the individuals who own the business and to the type of business.

Kong and Singapore. They consequently are able and willing to pay higher prices than domestic buyers. Exporters also have a reputation for paying bills rapidly (in eight days or less). One employee of an agent speaking about exporters remarked:

Having exporters bidding at an auction is good. We usually get higher prices, as the agent knows that exporters have orders on hand and they must fill them. Also, when one exporter has orders then many [exporters] have them. They will therefore compete to get produce and in that way force prices up.

There are several large provisions companies in Hong Kong that supply fresh vegetables as well as canned goods to large institutions (such as hospitals, schools, and prisons), to ships, and to wealthy European and Chinese families living in the Colony. These firms often buy directly from agents and usually have long-standing relationships with one or more firms in the market. The largest firm of this type, the Asia Company, deals almost exclusively with a single agency, which is reputedly owned by one of its major shareholders.

Preserved ginger is a very popular item in Hong Kong, and many of the food-processing firms in the Colony also buy quantities of ginger for processing into preserved ginger. Factory representatives usually have prearranged orders with agents for the delivery of specific types of ginger on certain dates. Occasionally such buyers will also bid against jobbers for ginger sold by agents.

Small-scale buyers. Retail vegetable sales are made primarily by retailers located either in areas provided by the government (government markets or supervised areas) or in any other site of sufficient population density to warrant the founding of a small "illegal market." The twenty-two-hundred-odd licensed vegetable retailers of Hong Kong Island* can be divided into three groups according to the volume of their business and their capital. The first group, comprising about 10 per cent of all vegetable retailers, have well-established retail trades and up to $1,000 in capital. Stall owners in the Central Market, the main retail market, who supply produce to large restaurants as well as to wealthy Europeans and Chinese, make up the core of this first group. They require large quantities of superior-quality produce. These retailers often purchase produce from agents, and invariably they maintain trading relationships with two or more jobbers.

A second group comprises the majority of retailers, those having between $300 and $500 in capital. They sell in densely populated areas

* Statistics supplied by the Department of Urban Services, Hong Kong Government.

and operate on narrow profit margins. Having more limited storage space than the first group, these retailers less frequently speculate. Members of this group rely on trading relationships with two or three jobbers and buy from agencies less frequently than do members of the first group.

The third group is composed of those who have little or no capital. These people lack a good selling location, often gathering with other small retailers to set up an "illegal" market. Many are handicapped or elderly and operate only with the help of one or more members of their families. They buy usually in small quantities and always from jobbers.

Most teahouses require small quantities (30 to 40 catties) of good-quality vegetables daily. Market people prefer not to deal with them, for they traditionally pay their bills monthly and are considered therefore to be more trouble than they are worth. Nevertheless, the teahouses, though small, provide a steady means for disposing of small quantities of goods.

Within the Colony there are also many small firms that specialize in supplying food for factory and office canteens. Such caterers daily require limited quantities of quality vegetables. Because they have contracts to fulfill, food caterers are often willing to buy vegetables even when prices are high. As a source of steady patronage, such customers are appreciated.

Agents

At the time of this study, there were nineteen agents, and three jobbers who occasionally acted as agents, in the market. Since 1955 a cleavage has existed between agents who sell produce from mainland China, whom I shall call mainland agents, and those who sell produce from other areas, whom I shall call foreign agents. Before 1955 any agent could sell mainland produce. In that year the People's Republic of China restricted the import and sale of vegetables by agents in Hong Kong. The government appointed thirteen agents (twelve in 1963) to act as its representatives. In turn each agent had to deposit between $30,000 and $60,000 as security with the Bank of China. Since 70 to 80 percent of all the fresh vegetables imported into Hong Kong come from mainland China, this action effectively created an oligopoly among agents.

Although I am primarily concerned here with foreign agents and jobbers, I will first describe briefly the operations of mainland agents as a background to the central discussion. The Communist government allows mainland agents to sell only the produce it supplies to them. In the allocation of produce among these agents a distinction is made between vegetables coming from North and from South China. Northern produce, shipped primarily from Tientsin and Shanghai, generally arrives in large quantities at scheduled intervals. Southern produce, shipped from the *hsien* neighboring Hong Kong, arrives in smaller quantities at unscheduled intervals. Nine agents deal in northern produce, which is sold to jobbers, who buy in stable groups, and to other customers once a day at an auction held at 8:00 A.M. The position of auctioneer rotates among the personnel of the nine firms.

Produce from South China is divided among all mainland agents and is sold at auctions conducted by individual agents. In the last two years, however, mainland agents have been increasingly willing to sell directly to wholesale customers at a price similar to that at which produce is sold to jobbers.

The disastrous harvests on the Mainland during the late 1950's and early 1960's resulted in a sharp decline in the volume of mainland produce reaching Hong Kong and opened the market to produce from other areas, and to the so-called foreign agents. Today they sell vegetables not cultivated on the Mainland, or not plentiful in the mainland shipments at a given time. The main varieties sold are celery, potatoes, certain kinds of ginger, tomatoes, cabbage, and melons. Japan and Taiwan are their major sources of supply, although produce also comes from the Philippines and America. There are now seven foreign agents, and three jobbers who occasionally act as agents, in the market. Foreign agents obtain bulk lots and sell them in the market. Produce is generally supplied on consignment by importers in Hong Kong or by exporters in other countries. As soon as the entire consignment has been sold, the agent returns to the supplier the value of the sale less his commission, which varies between 3 and 4 percent. Only rarely does a supplier have more than one agent acting as his representative in the market. All sales by agents are on credit. Therefore, to pay the supplier on time, agents must have large capital resources, which are used to extend credit to their customers. The term of such credit varies according to the amount of produce a customer normally buys, the agent's volume of sales, and the relationship between the agent and the customer, but all debts are cleared at the end of the year in which they are incurred. Although dire consequences are threatened if one fails to clear one's debts on time, I am not certain what actually happens in this event.

The owners of foreign agencies generally find that the volume of produce they receive as agents is insufficient to ensure continuous activity, and therefore they must supplement their stock by importing produce directly from non-Communist countries. At any given time, foreign agents may be acting both as agents and as importers. Since they assume the latter role only when the volume from their primary sources declines, the two roles do not seem to conflict.

Lacking the large and steady volume of produce received by the mainland agencies as well as the strength of an oligopoly, the owners of foreign agencies feel obliged to seek out customers more aggressively than their mainland counterparts. They also try harder to sell their produce rapidly, are more willing to negotiate with customers when the quality of produce is not in accordance with the original agreement, and extend more liberal credit terms. Significantly, foreign agents depend on developing and maintaining close personal bonds with their customers. The dynamics of these relationships will be discussed more fully in the next section.

The relationship between agents and jobbers is shaped largely by the terms on which agents grant credit to jobbers. In consultation with their bookkeepers, agents assign each customer a credit ceiling based on his reputation and his reliability in previous dealings. As long as the jobber's total indebtedness does not rise above his credit ceiling, he is free to buy from the agent. However, credit ceilings are kept fairly low relative to the sales volume jobbers could and do achieve, and in order to stay under their ceilings and still get enough produce for their customers, jobbers must repay part of their debts each week. Obviously, credit ceilings determine the volume of business jobbers can do. Along with actual supply of produce, they also determine to a certain extent the rate at which agents can expect to be repaid by jobbers, for jobbers also sell on credit and can continue to collect from their customers only if they always have more produce for the customers to sell. Only among retailers are most transactions on a cash basis. Thus the setting of credit ceilings can be a delicate matter, for it is in the interest of everyone in the market to ensure a steady flow of produce from large supplier to small supplier, and so on.

Agents sell produce to both wholesale buyers and jobbers, at a price set by private negotiation or by auction. Sale by private negotiation is rare and is normally limited to transactions with large-scale buyers, for auctions are the focal points of the internal distributive system. All customers who buy produce from a single consignment pay the price determined in the auction. Auctions are conducted by an employee of the agent whom I shall call the auctioneer or seller. The price-setter—the bidder who makes the offer accepted by the seller—takes the largest single portion of the consignment. The exact portion (between 40 and 70 percent) is determined during the course of the auction and is an important element in bargaining. The part not sold to the price-setter is divided among other jobbers who have requested produce prior to the commencement of the auction. The amount allocated to each of these subsidiary buyers depends on his relationship with the auctioning agency.

Participation in the auction is informally limited to larger jobbers, who buy individually or for groups of other jobbers. The agent informs the jobbers of the arrival of a consignment, and those interested come to the stall to inspect sample cases. The auction is conducted by means of an abacus in a series of discreet bargaining interchanges between the auctioneer and various bidders. The auctioneer indicates the desired price on his abacus and the bidder then counter-offers by moving the beads. In discreet tones, they discuss the portion of the produce to be accepted.

The auction is concluded when the seller accepts a bid or announces that he will not sell the consignment at the first auction. Such a withdrawal from sale occurs only rarely, as agents are under considerable pressure to repay their suppliers. In determining prices, the major factors taken into account are the quality and quantity of the produce already available in the market, the quality of the consignment, and weather conditions that might affect preservation. Auctioneers do not always accept the highest price offered. They attempt instead to obtain the highest price at which they can sell the entire consignment.

If the highest bid is acceptable to the agency and has been offered by more than one bidder, and if neither is willing to raise his offer, then the first person to offer the price is considered the price-setter. One seller explains:

I have some idea of what people will offer. I know the market. If you are in the market you know who has stock and who does not. When you ask $10 and a guy offers $8 and he has stock on hand, you know that it is his maximum. . . . You bargain with other guys and if they do not have stock on hand, you know that they will be willing to give you a higher price, because they must have something to sell. For instance, yesterday Mr. Chen paid $30 for the same kinds of vegetables he offered $48 for today. That is about the maximum he would give, considering that he got the bid yesterday and that he now has a lot of goods on hand. The final auction price was $55.

Of the ten firms acting as foreign agents, seven and possibly eight are individually owned, one is a partnership, and another is a joint-stock company.* As a group, agency owners have had extensive experience in the vegetable business both in Hong Kong and in China. When they work in the agency, owners normally concentrate their efforts on procuring produce to sell and on collecting debts. They also supervise the agency's overall activities. When the owner does not personally manage the agency's daily activities, he appoints a manager. Managers have extensive authority, consulting owners only about credit ceilings for larger customers and the hiring and firing of senior employees. In partnerships it is not unusual for one of the partners to act as manager. Of the four foreign agencies with managers, one is managed by a relative of the owner (his wife's brother) and another by a partner. Two are managed by employees of long standing with no other known connections to the owner.

As the person who conducts the sale of the agency's produce, the auctioneer is considered the most important employee. All auctioneers have worked in the market for at least ten years and have either owned or worked in a jobber's business. In addition to bargaining ability, the successful auctioneer has the confidence and the loyalty of jobbers.

Auctioneers receive a high salary, many earning $1,000 per month. They frequently own or have shares in jobbing firms, often ones closely associated with the agency they represent. An auctioneer so equipped has a ready avenue for the disposal of produce and thus a stronger position in an agency. Six of the seven foreign agencies have auctioneers or sellers, three of whom own shares in jobbing firms. The owners of such agencies have mixed feelings about this practice, which is becoming more and more common. They fear that other jobbers will accuse the agency of favoring the firms owned by their employees. Even when sellers do not own firms, it is clear that they are recruited from among those closely associated with large jobbers.

In addition to keeping books, agency bookkeepers are responsible for allocating those goods not assigned to the price-setter, following the credit ratings of customers, making out bills and receipts, and drawing up daily market reports that are given to the firms whose produce the agent sells. Large agencies often have several bookkeepers. The chief bookkeeper then handles the overall bookkeeping and the allocation of produce, while his assistants deal with daily billings and receipts. Bookkeepers have shares in other firms less frequently than do auctioneers. A good bookkeeper earns $650 a month.

---

* The following discussion of organization is based on observations of foreign agents; however, discussions with these people indicate that approximately similar conditions exist among the mainland agencies.

The weigher obtains sample cases from boats when they arrive and also weighs produce before it is delivered to buyers. When an agency expects to have trouble selling produce, the weigher is often sent out to solicit sales from jobbers. Weighers, like sellers, are outgoing. Their constant contact with jobbers provides them ample opportunity to develop friendships and connections. Weighers earn about $350 a month. Ambitious weighers often become independent jobbers and sellers.

Most agencies have one or more people of low status, generally earning $250 a month, who are used for running errands outside the market, sweeping, and doing chores. They also have one or more employees who do heavy work such as moving cases and making deliveries directly from the agent's stall to jobbers. These people are paid under $200 a month.

Jobbers

The ideal among people working in the market is ownership of their own business. Since most will never possess the resources to own an agency, they aim to become large jobbers. Even those who have long been employed by others conceive of their position as temporary and look forward to the time when they will have their own firm. There are now about two hundred jobbing firms, two-thirds of which are owned by individuals and operated with the help of two employees at most. The large jobbers, of whom there are some twenty, have up to $10,000 in capital. Most jobbers have between $3,000 and $7,000 in capital. Each jobber has a steady clientele who buy from him regularly and to whom he extends credit and offers other concessions.

Mainland produce was once shipped in wicker baskets holding 300 to 600 catties each. Jobbers bought these baskets, dividing their contents into smaller units for resale. In the last decade the size of wholesale containers has gradually been reduced. The reduction has made it easier for wholesale buyers to purchase directly from mainland agents. Jobbers continue to operate in the face of increasing competition from agents for several reasons. The number of customers a jobber can maintain is limited by his capital and by his ability to obtain credit. As a result, jobbers offer each customer better service—more complete market information, more personal and compliant treatment—than do agents. The agencies continue to sell only in full containers, and the jobbers usually get the best produce in any consignment. One retailer observed:

The advantages of buying from jobbers are that they usually have produce of high quality and you can select when buying from them. Retailers in this market must sell vegetables of high quality, so if an agent has goods for $20.50 and a jobber for $21 or $21.50, then I would rather spend the extra money and buy from the jobber.

Jobbers tend to specialize in certain types of produce. Half deal exclusively in highly perishable ("wet") green vegetables such as Chinese lettuce and watercress, much of which comes from Hong Kong itself, while the remainder deal in somewhat less perishable ("dry") produce such as potatoes, cabbages, tomatoes, ginger, and onions.* In a later section of the paper I will discuss the implications of specialization more fully. Foreign agents sell mostly dry vegetables, and those jobbers specializing in dry produce deal most often with foreign agents. The value of produce coming from non-Communist areas, however, is insufficient to maintain a jobber; therefore, no jobber deals exclusively with foreign agents. Many jobbers, however, sell mainland produce exclusively.

Interviews with jobbers indicate that they have usually worked in the market for at least five years before starting their own businesses. To be a successful jobber, a man needs steady customers, capital, and connections with agencies and with other jobbers. During the years of working for someone else, he gets all these, as well as certain specific skills, such as judging the quality of produce, handling customers, and managing credit. At the same time, others in the market observe his conduct and form an opinion of his worth.

Trading Relations

The marketing of a perishable product, like vegetables, is a risky operation at best, and doubly risky when the seller has only limited control over the quantity and the quality of produce entering the market. If agents and jobbers are to prosper or even to survive under such conditions, they must always be able to dispose of their produce quickly. They are for the most part able to do so, largely because of long-standing trading relationships with certain reliable customers. Such relationships enable firms at each level to minimize the effects of both scarcity and oversupply, and to ensure the rapid disposal of produce. Within the market, a majority of transactions occur between individuals linked in such long-term trading relationships and are based on credit. In this section, I examine in greater detail certain of these relations and attempt to show how long-term considerations affect economic decisions and behavior in general. Buying decisions are guided by the desire to pro-

---

* Domestic produce is sold in the market both by agents and by jobbers. Produce is obtained directly from farmers and sold on 10 percent commission. The cost of baskets and transport is absorbed by the agent.

tect existing alliances and by fear of sanctions in case of misconduct. Success in the market does not always come to him who buys at the lowest possible price and sells at the highest. After discussing the market as a community and the role of personal reputation and popularity as background against which people operate, I will review the criteria used in the selection of trading partners, the rights and obligations associated with such relations, and three specific types of relationships.

For those who work there, the market is more than a mere source of income: it is an important focus of social activity, a community to which each member owes support. There are no strangers within it, only those linked in relations of greater or lesser intimacy. All know one another and, although in competition, share a sense of physical safety and common attitudes toward participation in ritual and social relations. The sense of physical security is intangible yet real. People are secure inside the market in a way that they are not outside it. Although many are concerned about carrying large sums of money outside the market, they do so with no fear inside it.

Any employee who receives an invitation to a wedding or other ritual affair is obliged to accept. Those who fail to perform socially prescribed duties, both ritual and commercial, will be judged lacking in *jen-ch'ing*, or human feelings. A standard comment about attendance at weddings is, "I didn't want to go to the wedding, but I had to for the sake of human feelings."

To be judged lacking in human feelings by a group of peers is to be judged incapable of participating in society. The judgment carries with it strong moral overtones that delineate the environment in which interpersonal relations are conducted among people working in the market.

An individual's personal reputation, the degree to which others are willing to trust him, is the most important factor in business success. Fear of losing this trust is the major deterrent to commercial malpractice in the market. By maintaining a good name, one protects present relationships and makes future ones possible. People try to protect their reputations by fulfilling business obligations to others doing business in the market and by avoiding a reputation for habits that could lead to extravagances, such as excessive gambling, drinking, or attendance at dance halls.

The term *hsin-yung*, or "trust," expresses the Western concept of reputation. Speaking about the term, an informant notes, "A person's reputation is measured by his conduct and responsibility. If he is diligent and thrifty, fulfilling all his responsibilities, and is without bad habits, then he will have a good reputation."

When it was suggested to one man that the foreign agent he worked for could make a large sum of money by breaking an oral commitment to an exporter, the employee reacted with some surprise: "We have an agreement, and if we break the agreement, then the exporter will not continue to do business with us. We will lose our reputation, and other exporters will not buy from us any more." Similarly agents and jobbers fear potential loss of business if they give customers short weight. The importance of a good reputation was evident in all my interviews. When asked whether it was more important to be popular or to have a good reputation, one informant replied without hesitation, "A good reputation is more important. Without it you can't borrow and you can't get credit. You can't do business. Because of 'trust' we do not have to borrow from outsiders."

A good reputation does not by itself create business success, but it should definitely be considered a prerequisite for the formation of solid relationships. To succeed in the market, a man should also have personal popularity and the ability to maintain a wide range of contacts. The term conveying the equivalent of the English concept of "popularity," *jen-yuan*, connotes not only a large number of friends but a positive capacity for relating to others. People who have good *jen-yuan* are not just outgoing and gregarious, but sensitive to the interpersonal needs of others. The inter-connection between popularity, reputation, and financial success is noted by one jobber: "For a businessman to be a success he must have capital and connections. Connections means friends. This you get by treating other people fairly in business."

A good reputation gives one access to lines of credit that are fundamental, whereas popularity opens the way for personal contacts that are an important element in success. The person who has a good credit standing but who is not cordial to others, who holds himself apart, is considered too proud, or *ta-p'ai*. Such a person is unpopular and has trouble achieving significant business success, since no one is interested in cooperating with him. Generosity and restraint in competition are important elements in preserving one's popularity.

Selection of trading partners. Although everyone who works in the market strives to maintain a good reputation with all who work there, and to achieve a general popularity, agents and jobbers do have closer relations with some people than with others. These people are their trading partners. Trading partners are selected primarily on the basis of reliability. This emphasis on performance arises from the importance of credit in the operation of the market. One selects as partners people in whom one has the greatest personal confidence and who have proven their reliability in previous associations. All market people have an inclination to select first among those individuals with whom they have previously worked, or those who are bound to them by traditional bonds of solidarity. The role of traditional solidarities (similar place of origin and kinship or school ties) can be overemphasized. These relationships are more important in delineating categories from which partners may be selected than in the actual selection. People are more likely to initiate relationships with members of these categories; if they do not conform to standards, they will be dropped.

The relative homogeneity of the market population in terms of place of origin and dialect would suggest that people often have trading partners who share some ascriptive ties with them. More important is the fact that there are people sharing such bonds who are not commercially intimate, and this situation is taken for granted. Although statistical data on the subject were impossible to obtain, this impression was repeatedly reinforced by informants' replies. In relations among kinsmen, for example, apart from members of a man's nuclear family and perhaps his maternal uncles and cousins, there was no consistent evidence that kinsmen lent support to each other. The relationships between father and son were not necessarily intimate if the two did not work in the same business. In fact, there is evidence, not limited to this market (Ryan 1961), that in commercial relations kinsmen use criteria of reliability for one another similar to those they use for non-kinsmen, the difference being that kinsmen often have more information about one another and can therefore make keener evaluations. Prevailing conditions are well summarized by one man who was asked whether he thought his relatives were more important in his native village or in Hong Kong. "My personal feeling," he replied, "is that they are more intimate in Hong Kong than at home. Here there are fewer kinsmen than at home; there everyone is related." A little later he returned to this point, saying, "In my native village there were very few kinds of people, but in Hong Kong there are many kinds of people. The society was not so complex at home. Kinsmen in Hong Kong are more intimate with each other because they are far from their native village." Business relations, however, were another matter: "But in business, it [the relation between kinsmen] is about the same [in both places]. You judge the man by whether he is honest and can be trusted."

Trading relationships do develop between individuals not linked by particularistic bonds, although the initial growth of rapport preceding the firm establishment of such relations requires more time than when such bonds exist. Daily contact in the market and the repeated exchange of small favors can foster the mutual confidence between two unrelated people that provides the basis for more intimate association. Regardless of whether or not traditional solidarities were originally involved, the relationship will not develop beyond an initial exploratory phase unless the person in question demonstrates that he is reliable by fulfilling his business obligations. Although the majority of market people are linked to many others by relations involving obligations of support, they will select only a few from this group for closer, long-term relationships, and this crucial choice is based primarily on commercial integrity.

When trading relationships exist between two people not linked by traditionally sanctioned solidarities, the individuals concerned simply claim to share *kan-ch'ing*, or rapport.* This term is used in the market to describe the association of two individuals in a diffuse relationship involving mutual consideration and an expectation of continuity. Bonds of *kan-ch'ing* invest any association with flexibility and confidence. Such relationships are frequently established on the basis of mutual compatibility and often involve greater personal warmth than those among kinsmen. People rarely speak of having confidence in each other; instead they stress the degree of intimacy and warmth between them, the state of their *kan-ch'ing*. The level of confidence, if not emotional rapport, implicit in the concept of good *kan-ch'ing* also exists between those already sharing other bonds who have become close trading associates. Exactly when people speak of their relationships in terms of ascriptive ties and when in terms of *kan-ch'ing* is a point on which my data are too limited to allow me to speak.

Trading relationships are hierarchical—that is, usually between an agent and a jobber or between a jobber and a retailer—and consequently bear many resemblances to patron-client relationships. They are perpetuated and shaped by the ability of the "patron" to control the allocation of produce and the extension of credit. In each transaction the higher-ranking individual expects his trading partners to help him sell his consignments even when produce is plentiful and in turn is obligated to see that his "clients" are provided with produce on credit even when produce is scarce. Trading relationships thus involve reciprocity, but not equality. Nevertheless, once a trading relationship is formed, it is to the advantage of both parties to perpetuate it, since each receives concessions he would not otherwise obtain.

Economic aspects. The economic aspects of trading relationships can

---

* On *kan-ch'ing* relationships see Fried 1953 and DeGlopper's paper in this volume. In Cantonese the term is *kom-ts'ing*.

be reviewed under five headings: credit, volume of business, prices, market information, and labor recruitment.

The extension of credit is the element that shapes all other aspects of the relationship between trading partners. Credit of course allows both parties to increase the volume of their business beyond the limits that would otherwise be imposed by their capital, and is thus beneficial to both. However, since the amount of credit extended effectively determines the volume of business the lower-ranking partner can achieve, the question of what that amount shall be causes some tension even in well-established relationships (Geertz 1963: 37–38).

Trading relationships also influence the volume of business a lower-ranking partner may do in other ways. One jobber noted:

When produce is in oversupply, then *kan-ch'ing* becomes very important. The agent may ask you to take some of the goods and you will have to do so. But when produce is scarce and you ask the seller of an agent for 50 cases, then he may say, "I can't do that, but here, take 40 cases," while someone else may only get 4. In the same way the jobber may show favor by giving a customer more produce when it is short. But at the same time, the customer has to share the loss when goods are in oversupply.

Price concessions are not the primary objective of trading relationships. When given, price concessions are of two general types: reductions in the cost per standard unit measure (a direct price reduction), and the provision of more than the standard measure at the agreed price. According to informants, the former occurs only rarely. If the quality of a purchase is below the quality of the samples shown at the auction, then buyers may request that the price be lowered. But even then they will instead merely be billed for less weight than they actually purchased. The willingness of agencies to make such adjustments depends on the quality of their relations with the buyer.

One large jobber summarized prevailing opinion thus when he was asked what would happen if an agent had good *kan-ch'ing* with a certain jobber and sold him produce more cheaply than he sold it to others:

This would arouse criticism and as a result other jobbers might not buy from him. If an agent continued to sell goods to a jobber with whom he had good *kan-ch'ing* at a better price, then that would not be fair to the others, for they would have to pay a higher price. . . . If you have *kan-ch'ing* with someone then you expect to get more produce but not lower prices.

The same informant went on to summarize other elements of trading relationships:

Another advantage is that if you are friends, you will have tea together and spend time with each other during which you will glean information about the arrival of shipments and what is happening in the market. In this way you get to know about the market and how to act. But [even] if you know about the market and what to buy, if you go to an agent with whom you have no *kan-ch'ing* then . . . he will not sell you any more than usual, and your information about the market will be of no use. The owner of that agency will naturally reserve large quantities of produce for the jobbers with whom he has good relations. If the owner of an agency has too much produce, then he will go to the jobbers with whom he has good relations, and those people will take some of his produce. Each helps the other.

The preceding quotation delineates the limits within which relationships legitimately can be manipulated. A colloquial saying frequently heard in the market, "Business is business and *kan-ch'ing* is *kan-ch'ing*," supports the commonly held opinion that individuals who often invoke personal ties in business are obtaining advantages unfairly and are bad businessmen. During business transactions, even during bargaining, no direct invocation of a relationship to obtain concessions is normally evident. When someone does invoke *kan-ch'ing*, the other party feels obliged to make greater concessions than would be normal. Consequently, people refrain from speaking of special bonds unless they expect losses in a transaction. Another jobber expresses the prevailing attitude:

People who use too much *kan-ch'ing* in the market are not good businessmen. It is a kind of favoritism, and using it too much would be unfair. If someone is losing money, then he can call on the good will of others, but not if he is doing well.

Open reciprocity legitimizes certain types of assistance within the market:

Mr. Ch'en is the seller of an agent and people do not grumble about the favors he does for his cousins because they feel that he and his cousins are relatives and that they help one another. When there are goods that Mr. Ch'en has difficulty getting rid of, his cousins will help him sell them. . . . People are not angry because they are using each other and helping each other.

But personal influence can go only so far before it becomes bribery. Visible reciprocity is an important factor distinguishing particularism from bribery. The use of bribery (the offer of personal gain for a non-reciprocal favor) is universally condemned. Although such condemnation does not mean that bribery does not occur, the frequency and intensity with which it is condemned leaves little doubt that it is at least considered unethical and is probably rare. One is free to take others to tea or to dinner and thereby strengthen a relationship, but the giving of money or other rewards is unacceptable:

Q. When produce is scarce, do people ever give the employees of agencies money to try to get more produce?
A. No (emphatic).
Q. Don't you think that money is just a more efficient form of *kan-ch'ing* or rather that they are both about the same?
A. No. Taking money would be accepting a bribe. If we give a person gifts on his birthday, that is one thing, but if we give gifts when times are hard, then that is bribery. . . . If you give money that would be bribery, but to build *kan-ch'ing* by going out to tea is not bribery.

Market information is generally concerned with the condition of vegetables in a given shipment, the size of various shipments, and the "market price" of vegetables at a given time. Trading partners exchange mutually beneficial information. One incident may suggest the quality of such exchanges. Mr. Wang (a jobber) and I were talking when an employee of an agent dropped in. The conversation seemed very general for about twenty minutes, and, since this employee frequently visited, everything seemed normal to me. Then word arrived that this agent was about to hold an auction. As he was leaving, the employee casually said: "The seller feels that $12 (per picul) is a good price for the cabbages, and if you bid $13 you will win."

Labor recruitment is limited to kinsmen and friends of market people. Jobbers, for example, often find relatives and villagemates their first jobs in agencies. Similarly, sellers frequently secure employment with jobbers for people they know.

Trading partners are also expected to support each other in other aspects of market activity, especially when both partners work in the market. Two important areas of support are granting short-term loans and serving as go-between. Informants, particularly jobbers, claimed to prefer to borrow from trading partners when they needed short-term loans. They may either ask one or more associates for the money directly, or form a revolving credit society (Freedman 1961: 11).* Market informants conceive of loan associations as simply individuals sharing *kan-ch'ing*. The owner of a large agency who did not approve of loan associations claimed that "people generally join loan associations to stay on good terms with their friends and to have dinner once a month."

* See Topley (1964: 178–79) on loan associations and sources of credit in Hong Kong.

The role of the go-between is often crucial in the market. The go-between not only introduces people who have not dealt with each other before, but also stands as a guarantor of their reliability each to the other, thereby staking his reputation on the relationship. Individuals are reluctant to be called on to act as go-betweens, but trading partners feel obliged to support each other in this capacity. If a jobber, for example, needs stall space but does not know anyone willing to rent to him, he will ask an agent or another jobber with whom he is on good terms to intercede for him.

The relationship between trading partners includes many non-economic obligations, especially if both work within the market. Partners often spend their non-working time together. The hierarchical aspect of such relationships is particularly visible at these times in the greater frequency with which the higher-ranking partners pay for entertainment. Associates in trading relationships are also obliged to support each other by participating in weddings, funerals, and birth ceremonies in each other's families. Close business associates of the groom or his father play especially important roles in wedding dinners, both by the conspicuousness of their gifts and by their attendance at the side of the groom.

Specific Relationships

All transactions among firms take place as part of what has been termed a "trading relationship," but the intensity of these relationships varies. Limitations on capital and, to a lesser extent, on produce force agents to make distinctions in the treatment of customers. Each foreign agent likes to have several large jobbers closely associated with him. These firms are the agent's *chu-lik* or "main forces."* These superior businessmen serve as the *chu-lik* of only one agent, and naturally become quite intimate with him and with his auctioneer. They daily buy large quantities of produce for themselves and for smaller firms from the agent they represent, and they receive higher credit ceilings than other customers of the agent. In one agency with approximately $100,000 outstanding in credit, the five largest customers, the agency's main forces, each had upwards of $7,000 in credit, whereas the majority of other customers had under $2,300 in credit. If a *chu-lik* begins to reduce his volume of purchases without repaying a proportionate part of his debt, the agent will naturally press for collection. By allowing proven

---

* I have not translated the Cantonese term *chu-lik* (Mandarin *chu-li*) literally; there was no appropriate English term that could be used. Mainland agents do not use the *chu-lik* system.

businessmen to buy large quantities of produce, the owners of foreign agencies try to maintain a high volume of sales.

The process by which *chu-lik* are selected is complex. In one agency, for example, there are four. One is owned by a partner, though run by a manager; a second is a partnership composed of the agent's seller, the seller's maternal first cousin, and two others from their native village; the third is owned by the seller's cousin (the exact relationship is unclear); and the fourth is owned by a friend of the seller. Among the twenty largest jobbing firms at the time of the study, thirteen were owned by individuals, five were partnerships, and in two instances ownership was unclear. Each of the five partnerships involved people who either worked for or had invested in an agency, whereas of the thirteen individually owned firms, two and possibly three were owned by someone associated with an agency, either foreign or mainland. Not all agencies owned their own jobbing firms, and when they did, the firms were not necessarily large. However, ties of kinship and direct ownership between large jobbers and agency owners were too numerous to be dismissed.

The data just given suggest the importance of sellers. They are hired not simply for their technical ability but also for the business they bring in through their connections. It was my impression that at least two agencies hired sellers primarily for the amount of patronage they could bring. Neither appears to have done sufficient business otherwise to warrant hiring a person specifically to handle selling.

Medium-sized jobbers tend to have their closest relations with large jobbers. While medium-sized jobbers depend on credit from agents, just as large jobbers do, their smaller trade makes them less desirable customers, and therefore they are not always able to obtain produce in quantity. The large jobbers, therefore, in addition to buying their own produce, often act as buyers for medium-sized jobbers in a group-buying arrangement. Under this system a jobber participating in an auction buys produce for one or more other jobbers. If his bid is successful he informs the agency how his share is to be divided. If he fails to win the auction but obtains a quantity of produce, then he is free to dispose of it at will, as there is no established rule as to how produce obtained in this manner is to be divided. The agent then bills each group member independently. Once a group is formed, its participants are obliged to accept the produce the buyer obtains. Otherwise, they would not only lose business standing, but find it difficult to participate in subsequent groups. Group buying developed, informants stated, because the consignments received by the agencies were so large that no single buyer could take enough of a given lot to please the agency owners. The owners, it will be remembered, want the price-setter to take a large part, at least 40 percent, of the lot.

Buying groups may be permanent, or a group may be formed for a single transaction. The sale of North-China produce, which arrives in large lots, has traditionally involved buying groups of fixed membership. All large and medium-sized jobbers selling dry vegetables belong to one of four standing groups. The stability of these groups is attributed to the single daily auction of northern produce.

Produce coming from South China and that sold by foreign agents arrives in smaller lots and is sold by individual firms. Accordingly, buying groups tend to be smaller. Membership in them is not strictly fixed. The smaller size of these groups and the more numerous sources of supply have both influenced the development of specialization among jobbers. There are now four types of specialists: those dealing in potatoes and onions, in ginger, in cabbages and cauliflower, and in tomatoes and green peppers. The largest traders specializing in a particular type of produce act as the leaders of these buying groups.

Although groups buying produce from South China and from foreign agents are not closed, people normally buy with the same people. There is also a high correlation between membership in these groups and membership in groups buying North-China produce. A review of the membership in the four North-China buying groups and the types of produce in which jobbers specialize suggests prevailing conditions.

Although the volume of business of the four North-China groups is not significantly different, their composition varies. The oldest group consists of seven large jobbers. One man directs the buying and the division of the group's produce, which runs heavily to potatoes and onions. The owner of one of the jobbing firms in this group is also a partner in a mainland agency that stands in a special position among mainland agencies as a specialist in potatoes; approximately half the mainland potatoes arriving in the market go through this agency. This man's brother also owns a jobber that participates in this group.

The second group comprises seven jobbers. Although the average size of these firms is smaller than that of those in the first group, the leader of the second group is the largest jobber in the market. The members of this group buy a larger share of South-China produce than do others. Both the leader and the members of these first two groups buy almost exclusively from mainland agents.

The leaders and members of the third and fourth groups, by contrast, often deal with foreign agents. The third group is composed of many smaller jobbers, numbering eighteen in all. The owners of the three largest firms in this group share the buying and receive the largest portion of the produce. The fourth group is a relatively small group that has recently separated from the third, comprising two large and six small jobbers.

Comments by the leader of the second group, although perhaps over-idealistic, suggest the flavor of the relationship among members of a buying group. This man stated that it is natural for people to seek help from friends when they need a lot of capital as they do when dealing in North-China produce. When produce is good and his friends want to buy some vegetables, he feels he should let them do so, but when it is bad, he will not force them to buy, although that is the general rule among groups. In general, the members of a group will always try to help each other. If someone bought produce and then did not give any to another person who asked for it, he might still remain a part of the group, but people would not trust him in the same way as they had previously done.

The relationship between standing groups and the less rigid groups buying produce from foreign agencies and South China is further illustrated in an exchange with the same person:

Q. Mr. Chen just bought carrots. Will he share them?
A. Before someone buys [produce] on his own, he will ask others if they want to buy some of it, saying if he makes money on it and they have not bought then it will be their own fault. If all the others say that they do not want to buy, then he can go ahead and buy for himself. . . . If you do not want to buy, then it is your own fault if you do not make money. But later if someone of your group asks you to sell him some goods, then you really should do it. If you do not, then you will lose *kan-ch'ing* with him.

Group-buying arrangements are felt to benefit all parties. Agency owners gain because they can dispose of larger quantities of produce more rapidly than they might otherwise be able to do. Large jobbers not only have more produce to sell than they might otherwise have, but they gain influence over the disposal of increased quantities of produce and thereby increase their utility to agents. At the same time, they obviously strengthen their position in their dealings with agents. The smaller jobbers gain by being able to get more produce than if they were simply assigned goods after the auction. Those jobbers who frequently buy together spend considerable free time together. The social support these groups of jobbers extend to each other is an important element in market life.

The relationship between jobbers and their customers resembles that between agents and their trading partners. Jobbers attempt to develop as many steady customers, preferably large buyers, as they can within the limits of their capital and their credit ceilings. Large wholesale buyers are referred to as *hao pang-shou*, or "good helping hands," a term equivalent to the "main force" applied to the large jobbers that deal with certain agents. To regular customers, jobbers sell produce on credit (ranging in term from six days to several weeks), provide market information, and make other concessions.

The majority of wholesale buyers are retailers who lack space in the market and are highly mobile. They can and do vanish into the general population, leaving unpaid debts in the Kennedy Town Market. More so than between agent and jobber, therefore, the extension of credit by jobbers to their customers is an expression of confidence. This is a confidence based on criteria of performance, as market people claim there are few kinship or other connections between themselves and retailers.

Among a jobber's customers, there will be some whom he has known since they were employees in other firms and whose reliability has been proven over time. In seeking new customers, jobbers favor, when possible, those with established businesses, and failing this they prefer to deal with people having several children, assuming that the obligation to support large families reduces the likelihood of absconding.

The process by which a jobber develops his customers is described by one jobber thus:

> Retailers do not put up security and therefore you must be very careful about whom you give credit. There are no guarantees that you will get your money back. When you get a new customer you sell to him only for cash during the first two or three months. During this time you look him over.
>
> Q. What do you mean, look him over?
>
> A. You try to see if he always has cash, and then you also try to check up on him. When you go out to collect bills you may stop by his stall and see how he does business. You also see how often he buys goods and in what quantity.

The importance of personal relationships is reflected in the attitude of jobbers toward their employees. Within a firm, the relationships between customers and employees are personal. Buyers owe allegiance not so much to the firm as to the individual with whom they regularly trade. Employees are free to handle all aspects of selling except for the setting of the total amount of credit the customer may obtain. Jobbers prefer to hire workers with considerable experience. The preferred employee is an experienced worker of good reputation; especially desirable is someone with whom an employer has previously worked. The dilemma of jobbers is neatly summarized by one owner:

> It is difficult to get a good employee today, for if you offer him $200 a month, that won't be enough for him. If you offer him more, then you can't make

ends meet. Further, if you train him for three years, he will have good rapport with some of your customers. . . . Because you want to have good business you must teach him everything. Once this happens, he will want to establish his own business.

One expression of the trust between jobbers and their steady customers is the absence of prolonged bargaining. Steady customers inquire about price and either accept or reject it. The customer knows that the jobber will offer a good price on the first offer. Normally when dealing with occasional customers, there is more extensive bargaining.

I witnessed a typical example of dealings with old customers one day. A man came up to a stall to buy tomatoes, offering $.50 a catty. The employee countered with $.60 a catty and the man then offered $.55. The employee again refused him, and the man walked away. I then asked, "Do you ever make the price higher than you expect to receive so that you have room to bargain?"

"No," he replied. "Most of our customers are old customers, and when we give a price it is the best price we can give." After a few minutes, the man returned and bought the tomatoes at $.60 a catty.

In determining the price at which produce is sold to old customers, jobbers take their own costs and add to that between $1 and $3 per picul. For a given customer, the markup, although influenced somewhat by market conditions, remains about the same. The difference between customers charged $1 and those charged $3 is primarily a matter of credit standing. The normal period of debt-repayment is five to eight days. Those customers who consistently buy small quantities and take longer than the average periods to pay for them, are made to pay for this service. In addition to higher prices, poor credit risks frequently are required to buy all their produce from the jobber who is willing to grant them credit.

Relationships between jobbers are not characterized by a great deal of competition in prices. The long-term nature of trading relationships requires that the majority of traders do business with regular customers. Jobbers are limited in the number of customers they can maintain by the amount of capital they possess and the total amount of credit they can obtain. Under these conditions, they seek new customers, assuming that their resources are fully employed, only when they can increase their capitalization. The occasional customer, one with whom a jobber lacks a trading relationship, rather than receiving a lower price, frequently is quoted one higher than that quoted to steady customers. The reasoning of one jobber was common: "I know that they must have tried somewhere else and that I am the only jobber who has the goods they want to buy. That is why I raise the price on strangers." Another important reason is the existence of a permissible area of malpractice that provides even reputable traders with room to maneuver. Acts normally considered improper, such as sending produce of lower quality than bargained for, supplying less produce than agreed on, or charging prices well above the market price, are accepted when a firm is losing money. The occasional customer, a person to whom one is not bound by established bonds and preferably one without space in the market, is the one most often exploited. A jobber comments:

Sometimes you have to be cunning because you do not want to lose a profit. If the price of something stays at a certain level, say $10, and people know that you are making a profit of $2 per picul, that is right. But if you then try and use cunning methods to sell that produce for $11, then it would be unfair. You should only use cunning if the price of something drops and you want to cover your investment. For instance, if the price of oranges dropped from $20 to $18 then it would be right for you to use cunning to try and pressure the irregular customer into buying at $20 from you rather than from someone else.

When trying to obtain long-term customers, a jobber must be quite circumspect, both because of the possibility of default and because retailers also specialize in produce and therefore it is not unlikely that he will be selling to the customer of someone in a buying group with which he is associated. To jeopardize his position within that group and the unity of the group over a single customer is deemed imprudent.

The market is a moral community, one in which economic and social relations are interconnected. A hierarchy exists with agency owners at the top, jobbers in the middle, and wholesale customers at the bottom. Allocation of credit and of produce are the points of control that bind traders together. There exists a clear distinction between relations among those working in the market and relations between market people and outsiders. In the former instance, economic transactions are imbedded in social relations. At stake is one's peers' evaluation of one's moral worth. To be found morally wanting by the group excludes one not only from operating a business but from the prestige and social support normally extended to associates. These conditions suggest the origins of the live-and-let-live attitude toward competition and business in general that was summarized by one jobber:

You can say that there are certain limits to which business people will go and not beyond. . . . One should not be too ruthless in business, for a good impression is necessary to jobbers who have to move around in the market all the time. Sometimes even a certain amount of friendliness is required. One should do business without being so ruthless as to create a bad impression and without being so friendly as to suffer a loss.

Although direct competition existed, there were strong pressures to deny it. Like the Javanese traders described by Geertz (1963: 33) the traders in the Kennedy Town Market tended to reduce the aggressive element in competition by emphasizing the entrepreneur's ability to fill the demands of the customer rather than his ability to meet offers among his competitors selling the same goods.*

Dealings with people who do not have space in the market are less deeply imbedded in social relationships than those with market people and lack the weight of sanctions to maintain social control. Pressure for fulfillment of obligations is less strongly felt. The occasional customer, for example, lacking sustained contacts with a trader, is most likely to be treated sharply.

Conclusion

I believe behavior in the Kennedy Town Market to be typical of Chinese economic activity. There are striking similarities between Hong Kong market people as I observed them and the Chinese merchants living in Java as Ryan described them (1961). My own research serves to illustrate how the ideals or norms for behavior described by Ryan are translated into actual behavior in a specific context—the market. T'ien's (1953) analysis of Chinese economic organization in Sarawak and De-Glopper's discussion in this volume of merchants in Lukang, Taiwan, strongly suggest that the same principles of organization are operative.

Freedman's suggestion (1957: 88) that much of Chinese economic organization in Singapore rests on solidarities constructed on a non-kin basis is certainly valid in the market. Non-kin play a role equal to if not more important than that of kinsmen. The solidarities that bind non-kinsmen as well as kinsmen, while they may originate in prescriptive loyalties, are maintained on the basis of successful interaction in business. The essential distinction is not between kin and non-kin but between those who continually validate their relationships and those who do not. The significance of universalistic criteria for the maintenance of trading relationships is little understood and yet is an important aspect of Chinese economic activity, one that gives traders considerable flexibility.

Writers who have emphasized the importance of kinship and other prescriptive ties as major factors influencing Chinese economic activity have been in the majority. These authors have observed people linked by bonds such as kinship and territoriality dealing with each other and

---

* On both negative evaluations of competition and the relative importance of ascriptive and universalistic ties in Chinese society see also Olsen's paper in this volume.

have not considered the range of candidates or the alternatives open to merchants and how selections of business associates are actually made.

There is little concrete evidence to support the argument that kinship and other prescriptive ties impair economic activity. I have no specific data suggesting that among market people, for example, demands of kinsmen for funds prevent traders from accumulating capital. Similarly the necessity of trading with those linked to one by prescriptive ties was not supported. Both my own data and Ryan's (personal communication) make it clear that merchants enter into business relationships only with people they consider reliable, regardless of their kinship ties. Superior knowledge about kinsmen causes people to be especially judicious in selecting business associates among them. Previous accounts of economic activity have stressed the importance of nepotism as a factor in recruitment (cf. Lang 1946: 181–89; Levy 1949: 535–65). There was little concern about this in the Kennedy Town Market.

Some writers also claim that Chinese businessmen attempt to maximize immediate gains and are little concerned with business reputation (Topley 1969: 203). These statements must be viewed in context and with caution. Market people among themselves were clearly concerned with long-term trading relationships and reputation. Only when one moves outside the field of people one knows well, where social sanctions are less binding, does short-term maximization at the potential expense of business reputation occur. These differences between generalized accounts of Chinese business activity and market activity as I observed it are due not simply to differences in the scale of market activity and the risks involved in marketing, but rather to the failure to examine the operation of economic institutions in detail.

Although great stress has been placed on the importance of performance, it should not be assumed that market people are visibly preoccupied with whether associates can be trusted, nor do they attempt minutely to balance debts and favors. Confidence-creating behavior is largely cultural behavior. Jobbers normally worry about the price of cabbage and about weather conditions, not about the state of their trading relationships. There are manipulative individuals in all societies. Chinese society in Hong Kong is no exception. Prevailing attitudes were well summarized by the leader of a North-China buying group: "All human beings are emotional animals, and you can say that *kan-ch'ing* is really a business tactic. But it is also true that we are all dependent on each other and cannot live isolated from each other."

A Small Factory in Hong Kong:
Some Aspects of Its Internal Organization

BARBARA E. WARD

The past twenty years have seen an industrial revolution in Hong Kong. Dependent largely upon the huge influx of capital, management, and labor that began around 1949, it has involved a complete change in the pattern of trade as the Colony's economy switched over from an entre-pôt to an industrial basis. Already by 1965 more than 50 percent of the employed population was engaged in industrial and construction work, and well over 90 percent of the total exports consisted of industrial products, of which the large majority were taken by North America and Western Europe (Chou 1966).

Two of the most striking features of Hong Kong's prodigiously rapid industrialization have been the remarkable diversification of its products and its dependence upon private enterprise. Cotton textiles and garment manufacturing, completely dominant in the early days, have now been joined by an ever-increasing range of export goods the very nature of which was unknown in the Colony a few years ago. They include plastic products, wigs, steel cutlery, beach wear, sports gear, optical and scientific instruments, and electronic equipment of all kinds. It is worth noting that these are all products requiring a high degree of skill at least at certain stages of their production. As for private enterprise, all manufacturing industry in Hong Kong is essentially capitalistic. It is true that the public sector has regularly contributed about 30 percent of the total annual domestic investment (Chou 1966: 74), but this contribution has customarily gone into administration and such traditional public works as roads, water supplies, and public building. In addition to this valuable contribution to the infrastructure, the government has also provided certain minimum controls over factory sites and the employment of labor, and has developed a number of advisory services, but beyond this it has explicitly and consistently refused to "interfere" in either commerce or industry.

The typical factory in Hong Kong probably does not exist. The range from squatter huts housing outworkers for the plastic flower industry to air-conditioned, electrically powered cotton mills is too great. In any case, the factory described in the following paragraphs was chosen not because it was typical but simply because it was available.* Further investigations may well show it to be unusual in many ways, but I do not expect it to prove unique. It certainly shared most of the characteristics mentioned above: it was privately owned, it turned out a modern product, and it depended largely upon immigrant capital and management.

The fieldwork on which this paper is based was intended to be part of a pilot study for what I hope to develop into a comprehensive investigation of industrialization in Hong Kong. Informing my approach to the whole topic was a wish to discern what, if anything, was specifically "Chinese" about the socioeconomic relationships involved. This is the aspect of the study that is followed up here. Broadly speaking, my conclusion is that in this factory the primary factors determining the structure and organization of relationships were the restraints imposed by the technical requirements of the process of production as such. These were straightforward, "rational" requirements that left hardly any room for culturally differentiated *nuances* in performance. Only in those areas where the demands of the technology itself were not overriding was there room for variations in what I later call the "style" of organization. Such areas were to be found in the relationships between the management and the workers, in some aspects of the relationships between workers, and, most significantly for the development of the business, in relationships at the level of the directorate. In this last set of relationships, however, other—probably universal—factors also came into play; notably a tendency, once the technological structure of the firm was assured, for leadership to move increasingly out of the hands of the technologists and into the hands of the managers and market men. These findings may give rise to a number of hypotheses concerning the

* The information on which this paper is based was obtained during six weeks' fieldwork in the spring of 1968. I wish to thank the Directors of the Ford Foundation and the Southeast China Program at Cornell University for the great generosity which made it possible for a foreign scholar to travel to Hong Kong for this fieldwork; the Director of the School of Oriental and African Studies, University of London, for giving me leave of absence during the Easter Vacation; and, most of all, the directors, staff, and workers of the Kau Fung Glass Factory for their kindness and cooperation.

process of industrialization in general. They may be particularly relevant to the question whether the kind of technological process carried on in a factory is related to its socio-politico-economic environment, specifically the degree of freedom that exists for the development of differences in "style." The relative efficiency of such stylistic differences, the possible concomitants of change, and so on, could also be examined on the basis of the kind of data reported here. Much of this is conjecture for future exploration, however. The paper remains essentially an ethnographic account of a single Hong Kong factory as it existed in 1968.

The progress of the firm has certainly been dramatic. Starting from scratch in March 1967, it received its first overseas inquiries (from Germany) after five months. During the few weeks of my fieldwork in April 1968, further inquiries came in from South Africa, South America, Canada, India, Indonesia, and Australia.

Factory Layout and Organization of Work

The factory makes glass. It is a special kind of heat-resistant glass, very clear and strong. You can fill a flask of it with cold water, put it over a naked flame until the water boils, then take it off the flame and plunge it straight into a bucket of cold water, and it does not crack. Unlike the majority of goods manufactured in Hong Kong, this glass makes use of one locally available raw material, namely sand. All the rest are imported.

The process of manufacture is relatively simple. The various raw materials are weighed out, mixed in an electrically operated tumbler, and fed at regular intervals into one or the other of two large furnaces. Fed in as a kind of coarse powder, the mixture quickly melts and attains temperatures as high as 1,600° Fahrenheit. The liquid glass passes gradually through the furnaces—which are about forty feet long—to be drawn out at the far end like large blobs of colorless treacle on the ends of long brass and steel tubes. Skilled blowers grasp the tubes, spin them rapidly, and blow the blobs into the required balloon-like shapes. These are then quickly molded in a two-sided, hinged metal mold and splashed with cold water before being taken by another worker to the annealing furnaces where they are stacked, at precisely controlled temperatures, and allowed to cool gradually over a period of twenty-four hours. Removed from the (now cold) annealing furnaces next day, the glass globes or funnels (or whatever) are finally cut with coal-gas flame cutters to the right size, polished, finished, and packed ready for export. At the time of my study, the whole process, from weighing the raw materials to sending out the finished product, employed just forty-eight men and women, of whom two were managing directors, two were paid white-collar managerial and secretarial staff, and forty-four were classed as workers.

In the process of production outlined above, each stage follows necessarily in order upon the last, the order of events being set by the very nature of the process. It follows that there is little room for argument and decision-making about the work flow. With enough space, a rational layout is almost unavoidable. By no means do all kinds of industrial production share this characteristic. Where the final product is not, as here, the result of a single, straightforwardly cumulative process, but rather of collecting and putting together a number of different components each of which is made separately, the work can be organized in many different ways. In such circumstances, an outside investigator might find that differences in the culture or the personality (or both) of management and labor were reflected in differences in organization. In glass-making the central process imposes its own ineluctable rationality, a fact of which the managers of the factory under discussion were very well aware. The problem they had to solve was to find enough space for this central process to be carried out and, having done that, to organize the flow of preliminary and final processes with as nearly the same rationality as possible. Culture or personality could make little or no difference at this level.

In diagrammatic form the flow of production comprised the ten stages, pictured in Figure 1, of which Numbers 4–7 comprise the central process and Numbers 1–3 and 8–10 the preliminary and final processes respectively. It will be noted that without sufficient storage space for the ready-mixed batches of raw material and for the cooled but not yet cut and finished glass products there could be no pauses between the successive stages. The diagram also makes the key position of the delivery stage (10) quite evident: the limited storage space made rapid clearance of the finished and packed goods essential. In this connection it must be remembered that space is one of the scarcest resources in Hong Kong; even if adequate space were available, it would not normally be economical to rent it merely for storing finished products.

Finding any space for the factory had, indeed, been one of the major problems at the beginning. During the second half of 1966 the items of capital equipment being accumulated had to be stored for several months in a garage belonging to the brother-in-law of one of the directors. The only site available at first, the one still being used at the time of my fieldwork, was relatively cramped and not particularly convenient. It was an irregular rectangle, measuring 160 feet by 67 feet and situ-

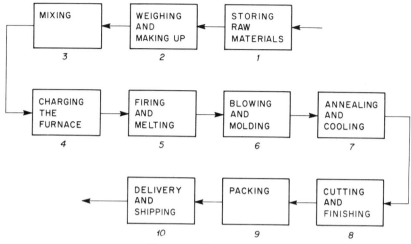

FIGURE 1. WORK FLOW

ated about 300 yards from the main road. Access to this road was difficult because the side streets were narrow and steep. The problem of space was complicated by the Fire Brigade regulations, because stages 4 to 8 of the production process obviously required very high temperatures and the use of naked flames.

When I studied the factory, the layout was according to the plan shown in Figure 2. This plan shows clearly the "natural" rationality of the locations chosen for the central stages of production—charging the tank (4), smelting (5), blowing and molding (6), and annealing (7)—and the way in which the management placed the preliminary and final stages in relation to them. Stages 1–3 (storing the raw materials, weighing and making up, mixing) were arranged to take place close together and closely under the supervision of the managing director (A) in his office. The raw materials were stored at some distance from the main entrance through which they had to be brought in, but this was because it was even more important for the offices to be adjacent to the main entrance, and for them and the rest room next to them (in fact the sleeping quarters of Office Worker a) to be on an outer wall with windows for light and air, than it was for the raw materials to be stored near their point of entry. The position of the offices being fixed in this manner, the placing of the first three stages followed almost automatically from the managing director's need to oversee and participate in them. (Certain ingredients were kept under lock and key in his office, weighed by him on a delicate spring balance of his own design, and added only

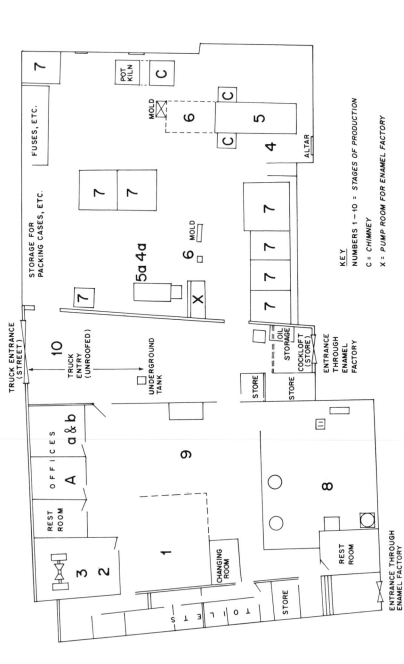

FIGURE 2. FLOOR PLAN OF THE KAU FUNG GLASS FACTORY, HONG KONG (1968)

by his own hand.) The result was, however, that two workers had to carry each heavy batch of made-up raw material almost the full length of the building and through the packing section (9) to the tanks (4, 4a, 5, 5a).

Two other major defects of this layout were obvious to all. First, the clumsy trolleys that carried the glass pieces from the annealing furnaces to the cutting and finishing room had to be pushed too great a distance. Part of their route lay across the open-air passage, which was often obstructed, and where they sometimes bumped into either the batch carriers or those who were trying to load the outgoing truck. Second, the space available for packing was inefficiently small, and storage places were both inadequate and inappropriate for stacking the boxed finished products. This layout was, however, expected to be temporary: by June or July of 1968 at the latest the large tank (5) would have to be replaced, thus providing an opportunity for replanning, and it was hoped that it would be possible at the same time to acquire more space. (After I had left the field, this did happen.)

The layout of the factory was, of course, only one aspect of the process of production. The other was the organization of the work. Here one of the most significant factors was the small size of the labor force and the consequent opportunity for face-to-face relationships at all levels.

During the period under review the formal structure of the factory underwent certain changes that will be described in a later section. Fundamental though they were and potentially of great significance for worker-management relationships, they did not alter the organization on the factory floor. This remained throughout essentially the same as when I observed it in April 1968. Figure 3 summarizes the simple, essentially rational, formal internal organization of the process of production.

Buying, storing, weighing, and mixing the raw materials were under the personal control of the managing director (A) who alone had full knowledge of the chemical processes involved (and claimed that certain essential ingredients were his personal secret). Making up and mixing took place in a room next door to his own office (see Figure 2), and were performed under his eye by a woman whose full-time job it was, assisted by a man who worked part-time in the packing section (stages 9 and 10). When not actually engaged in weighing and mixing, the woman swept, made tea, and so on.

Stages 4–7 all took place in the largest room, which housed the two

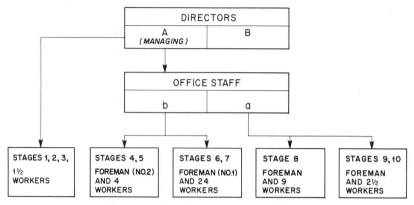

FIGURE 3. THE ORGANIZATION OF WORK

smelting furnaces (tanks) and the annealing furnaces. The workers here were all under the general supervision of Office Worker *b*, but the work was actually directed by two foremen (known sometimes as "Number One" and "Number Two" in the factory) who were in charge of the shaping and cooling of the glass products and the smelting tanks, respectively. Superficially these two men could hardly have been more different: Number Two (the furnace man) was over fifty years of age, a well-educated man with a military background (he had held a commission in the Kuomintang army, and his brother was still an army officer in Taiwan); Number One, also a refugee, but only twenty-nine, was the nearly illiterate son of a tannery worker. Both were excellent and reliable craftsmen, with a quiet, confident manner, respected by workers and management alike.

The furnace foreman's responsibility was the more limitedly technical. He had constantly to watch the temperature, keep an eye on the level of molten glass, decide when to feed in more "batch" and how much. (He was also skilled in the highly technical craft of building furnaces, of which more below.) At the very high temperatures reached in the main tank, mistakes could be dangerous as well as costly. Tanks used at these temperatures have a life of a year or less, and the last few months of this period are times of justifiable anxiety. On one wall over the furnace, Number Two had installed a small shelf surmounted by a red paper poster carrying the name of the God of Furnaces, and night and morning he saw to it that this small altar was duly furnished with incense sticks. This was the only evidence of religious activity that I saw within the factory.

The uneducated but highly intelligent Number One was the most skilled glass blower in the factory. Moreover, he organized the work of about two dozen other men. He it was who, in consultation with *b*, made up the work schedules, vetted the consistency of the molten glass, supervised the quality of the others' work, helped train new workers, and also kept an eye on the workers at the annealing furnaces. Stacking and unloading these furnaces were also skilled jobs. The workers concerned kept records of the number of completed pieces in each chamber and the dates and times each was sealed, writing this information on small blackboards fixed at the side of each furnace. These records were frequently checked by the office worker (*b*) in charge. It is important to appreciate the informal and generally friendly nature of these relationships. Neither Number One nor Number Two used an authoritarian approach, and *b* was forever strolling in and out of the furnace room, joking and chatting with the foremen and the workers in a quiet way.

On removal from the annealing furnaces the glass pieces were stacked on crate-like wooden trolleys to be trundled somewhat laboriously on small, metal-shod wheels across to the cutting and finishing room. This transfer and the final packaging were under the general supervision of the other member of the office staff (*a*), who also supervised the loading of the boxed glassware into the firm's truck and then delivered it to the purchasers or to the docks at Kowloon. The other part of his job was to handle all the consignments of raw materials, fuel, etc., as they came into the factory. Cutting and finishing the glass globes and vessels was done by nine workers (including a girl whose sole job was to stencil the appropriate trademarks on the pieces) under the supervision of a short, stout foreman who never seemed to stop working (or smiling). In this step of production, the workers used a series of coal-gas burners mounted on rotating stands. The foreman inspected each finished piece for cracks or flaws.

From the cutting and finishing room (8), the finished products were once more pushed laboriously by hand in the same clumsy trolleys, this time only to the packing room (9). Here, in much too cramped a space, they were individually wrapped in a single layer of tissue paper and packed into collapsible cardboard cartons. Finally, the trademarks, the descriptions of contents, and the addresses of the consignees were stenciled on the boxes, which were then ready to be sent out. This work, under the general supervision of the "outside" office man (*a*), was directly under the control of one male worker (dignified with the status "foreman" in Figure 3) with full-time help from one woman and part-time assistance from the man otherwise engaged in weighing and mixing in the "batch" room. As a matter of fact, however, the packing section, small though it was, was often occupied by a much larger number of people. Anyone not working at his regular task, including the office staff or even the directors' wives, could be seen from time to time helping out with wrapping and boxing. This stage (9) was, indeed, the least efficiently organized of the whole process—largely because of the lack of adequate space either for the packing operations themselves or for the bulky parcels once they were made up. A day's backlog in outward delivery (stage 10) meant near chaos in the packing department, which, being at the end of the production line, was in constant danger of being crowded out with finished products. I have already suggested that the high cost of space and the problem of finding it in the first place probably made this difficulty unavoidable.

For, and this was an important aspect of the built-in rationality of the work-flow, the nature of glass-making in this factory gave to the process of production not only a regular order but also a steady pace. There were two reasons for this, both of them connected with the tanks. On the one hand, it was, of course, necessary for the molten glass once drawn from the tank to be blown or molded immediately, while it was still viscid, and for the shaped products then to be stacked at once in the annealing chambers so that the glass should be cooled at the correct rate. The significance of speed and accurate timing is obvious here. But time was also important at the other end of the tank, where it was necessary to keep the temperature and level of the molten material within fairly narrow limits for the sake of safety as well as efficiency. Level and temperature were checked once every hour, and both heat and the flow of raw materials adjusted accordingly. Thus the central production process created a kind of push-pull effect that regulated the tempo of the whole factory. As temperatures and levels dropped, more "batch" had to be ready to feed into the tank, more weighing and mixing had to be done, and—ultimately—a steady supply of raw materials had to be maintained. (A temporary shortage of one particular ingredient during the winter of 1967–68 caused great anxiety and nearly led to a complete shutdown.) On the other side of the tank, in turn, the raising of the temperature and level meant that the blowers and molders had to be ready to remove the molten glass, which once drawn out had to be dealt with immediately. The process once started, the tanks themselves acted as regulators to keep production going at a steady pace.

It follows that, as long as raw materials were steadily available, the tanks and other equipment were sound, and the chemical formula produced the desired results, there was as little room for decision-making in the strategy of organizing the work as in the planning of the factory layout. Moreover, with such small numbers of workers in face-to-face relationship, the daily tactical decisions about such matters as work schedules were in general arrived at by amicable mutual consent under the leadership of the three major foremen and the office staff. As far as the organization of work went, only two important matters fell outside the automatic control provided by the central process of production: namely, the recruitment and stabilization of an appropriate labor force and the development of adequate marketing outlets.

Recruitment and Stabilization of Labor

Up to this point my argument has been that the organization of production in the glass factory was essentially rational in the sense that the layout of the factory floor, the order in which the stages of production took place, and the tempo of production were all ultimately regulated by the requirements of the process itself. Another way of putting this would be to say that the basic structure of the activities necessary for turning out the completed glass products was unaffected by cultural factors. From an anthropological standpoint the term "universal" might be more illuminating than "rational": there has been nothing specifically "Chinese" about the organization as described so far—unless a strong tendency to use economic common sense is to be regarded as a peculiarly Chinese quality.

When we turn from the techniques of production to the problems of the recruitment and management of labor, however, we may find ourselves forced to consider local culture-linked factors. In other words, we may expect to be asked whether or not the methods used and the relationships set up reflect values and practices that can be described, however loosely, as "characteristically Chinese."

Before considering precisely what this phrase may mean, let us examine first the factory's stated policy about recruitment and the history of that policy, and then the general principles and practice of reward and management.

From discussions about recruitment policy with the two directors and both members of the office staff, three main points emerged. First, skilled workers such as glassblowers, stackers, and furnace men were scarce in Hong Kong. It was therefore essential to attract and hold them by offering higher wages, better promotion prospects and conditions, and more fringe benefits than other firms. The number of glassworks in Hong Kong was quite small, with the result that anybody employed in the industry for any length of time knew a great deal about the conditions and the personnel in all the other glass factories. Managing Director A, who had had previous experience in managing a glassworks and was known to be a brillant technical man, was therefore able to do a certain amount of personal recruiting before the factory first opened. Nearly half the skilled men, including both leading foremen, came in this way. About a quarter came a little later, through personal contacts either with A or with the skilled craftsmen already employed. The rest appeared in response to advertisements posted at the factory entrance (see Table 1).

Now it is important to notice that in using his personal contacts and the glass industry's grapevine to recruit skilled workers, A was in fact employing the most efficient method available. In circumstances of absolute shortage of and high competition for particular skills, personal contact is often the best (if not the only) source of information and channel of communication. Although A used personal methods, his criterion for recruitment was nonetheless universalistic: he wanted skill and knew how to assess it. None of the men who came from the factories in which he himself had previously been employed was linked to him by any of the usual Chinese particularistic ties, such as kinship, or school, being classmates, or having a common place of origin or dialect. Yet all the skilled men who had worked in glass factories before were recruited either by A's personal invitation or through the glass industry's grapevine. Such men could be found only in existing factories: without them a new glass business could not even begin.

The second point the management stressed was a general one regarding the state of the Hong Kong labor market at the time. The shortage of skilled labor (by no means confined to glass manufactories) existed alongside a superabundance of unskilled labor. It was, they told me, the practice of unskilled workers to shop around, trying out this firm and that in order to find the best pay and conditions, for there was a sense in which unskilled workers could afford to be more choosy than the skilled men, whose opportunities were limited by the relatively small number of firms requiring their particular competence. As a result, they said, there was no problem of recruiting unskilled labor; an advertisement on the factory wall outside the main entrance would bring in plenty of inquirers. The problem was to keep them. This argument that the existence of a large, mobile pool of labor inevitably forces wages up was repeated to me several times by the management. It formed the basis of their policy of recruitment and reward for unskilled workers,

TABLE 1. CHANNELS OF RECRUITMENT, ALL RECRUITS, KAU FUNG GLASS
FACTORY, HONG KONG, MARCH 1967 TO APRIL 1968

Channel of recruitment	Permanent (Primarily skilled)	Temporary (Primarily unskilled)
I Personal contact		
(a) By managing director	8	1
(b) Glass-industry grapevine	9	5
(c) Friend or neighbor	1	10
(d) Relative in factory	1	7
II Advertisement	8	41
III Unknown	1	6
Total	28	70

NOTE: See text for full distinction between the two categories of workers.

the large majority of whom did in fact come in response to written advertisements posted outside the main entrance of the factory. Most of them were, therefore, not previously known to the management (directors or office staff), to the other workers, or to each other.

Table 1 sets out the different channels of recruitment for the ninety-eight workers who were on the factory's books at one time or another during the year March 1967 to April 1968.

A few comments on this table are necessary. First, the category "friend or neighbor" may well overlap the category "grapevine." The entries here have been transcribed from my questionnaire replies as follows: if the worker said he had been introduced by a friend or neighbor the entry is under I(c); if he said he had worked in a glass factory before, it is under I(b) unless a specific statement was added mentioning the managing director as his "introducer." (None said both.) Second, several of the large number in the "unskilled" category who said they came in answer to an advertisement may well have had their attention drawn to the advertisement by friends or acquaintances already employed in the factory. I did not check this possibility in the factory. I was, however, repeatedly assured by the office staff that "most" of their unskilled recruits were in fact obtained by advertisement, and I myself witnessed about a dozen inquiries from casual passersby. Third, the categories "skilled" and "unskilled" themselves need some reconsideration. This appears in the immediately following paragraphs.

One striking feature of the first year's operation of the factory was the high turnover in labor, particularly in "unskilled" labor. Whereas 22 of 28 "skilled" recruits were still employed in the factory at the end of the year (i.e. in April 1968), only 22 of 70 "unskilled" workers recruited during the same period remained. This difference, which bore out the directors' expectations expressed above, was probably closely connected with differences in the systems of rewards offered to the two categories. Before describing these, however, it is necessary to draw attention to the fact that the two categories were not in fact distinguished purely in terms of skill. As indicated in Table 1, the terms actually used in the factory, as elsewhere in Hong Kong, were not "skilled" and "unskilled" but "permanent" and "temporary." It happened that all the fully skilled workers fell into the permanent category, but a number of the semi-skilled and one or two unskilled were also included there, whereas by no means all the temporary workers were completely unskilled. Allocation to the permanent category was made on the basis of a combination of criteria of which skill was the most important; but hard work, long service, and responsibility also counted. In addition to all the skilled blowers, for example, the permanent category also included the woman who worked full time at weighing and mixing the raw materials (stages 1–3) and the full-time male assistant in the packing section (stage 9).

The formal difference between permanent and temporary workers was that the latter were engaged on a daily basis, the former by the month. In addition, there were a number of fringe benefits for which only permanent workers were eligible. These included a meals allowance of $2 a day, a bonus scheme, sickness pay, eligibility (for single men) to reside rent-free in the firm's own hostel, and the opportunity to attend the firm's annual dinner and receive gifts of new clothing at Chinese New Year. A similar division between permanent and temporary workers obtains in nearly all Hong Kong's industries, although the benefits available to the former vary both in detail and monetary value. These "extras" are widely regarded as an important part of the system of rewards, their explicit object being to encourage good workers to stay. It is for this reason that promotion to permanent status is open to semi-skilled and even unskilled workers. The management of the glass factory claimed that the difference in the rate of turnover between the two categories was closely connected with this incentive scheme. Temporary employees were having to be replaced every month, but permanent workers left only infrequently. There were at least four months in the year prior to my fieldwork in which temporary workers were lost faster than they could be replaced.

Conversations with permanent workers left me in no doubt that they very much liked the scheme, and consciously valued the increased security as well as the fringe benefits that their status commanded. It seems likely that in Hong Kong at the present time the system contributes to a greater stability of valuable labor than would otherwise be found in such a highly fluid situation. However, insofar as the skilled men were concerned specifically, their stability is as likely to be ascribable to two other mutually linked factors: the specific nature of their skills (which meant that there were very few other factories in which they could find equivalent employment), and their relatively high wages (they were the highest-paid glassblowers and furnace men in the Colony).

Wage differentials, always with the chance of an increase, existed within each category. Wages were calculated at daily rates, but paid out at sixteen-day intervals. There were two methods of calculating a day's work, both in effect a time rate, although the second was described to me in piece-rate terms. For most workers, a day's work was reckoned as ten hours; anything over that was paid at double rates. For the glassblowers and stackers, however, the idea was that a day's work consisted of the performance of a certain stint; once that was completed any additional work was payable at double rates. Since their stint had been calculated as requiring eight hours of work, theoretically they had the choice of working a shorter day than any of the other workers, or of earning more overtime pay than any of the other workers. In practice, they almost always chose to work more than eight hours.

Additional piece rates, in the strict sense, were paid to the two leading blowers, the foreman cutter, the foreman packer, and the two men responsible for taking the cooled glass products out of the annealing furnaces. These piecework payments, acting as a kind of foreman's reward, were shared out by the recipients among the members of their work gangs. For example, on April 28, 1968, the number-one glassblower received in addition to his fortnight's total of $407.75, a further sum of $62.15 for blowing especially big glass globes (used for fishermen's lamps) at $.55 each; it was then his responsibility to share this sum with the four or five other blowers who were skilled enough to assist him in this job.*

Permanent workers were eligible for three other regular monetary payments, some of which have already been mentioned briefly. These were as follows: $2 a day for food, a bonus of twenty-four extra days' pay a year, and the special overtime rate of two-and-a-half times the

---

* The currency referred to in every case is the Hong Kong dollar, worth approximately eighteen cents in United States currency.

TABLE 2. TAKE-HOME PAY OF SELECTED WORKERS, KAU FUNG GLASS FACTORY, HONG KONG, APRIL 1968

Category and job, age and sex	Daily rate	Days worked (max. 16)	Overtime (days' pay)	Bonus days	Total days counted for pay	Meals money	Repayment of advance	Take-home pay	Remarks
Permanent									
No. 1 blower M/29	$18.00	16	2.875	2	20.875	$32	—	$407.75	Plus $62.75 in shared piece rates
Mixer F/44	7.00	15.5	7.5	2	25	32	—	207.00	Only female permanent worker
No. 1 furnace man M/51	15.00	16	4.5	2	22.5	32	$40	329.50	No. 2 on factory floor
Cutter and finisher M/16	6.80	15	5.1	2	22.1	30	—	180.20	Recently promoted
Temporary									
Cutter and finisher M/17	8.50	15.5	5.6	—	21.1	—	—	179.35	
Helper (carrying, molding) F/47	7.00	14	—	—	14	—	—	98.00	
Glass smasher M/26	10.00	12.5	—	—	12.5	—	$20	105.00	
Cutter and finisher F/21	8.00	11.8	1.75	—	13.55	—	—	108.40	

NOTE: The workers included in this table were selected not so much to typify the temporary and permanent categories as to represent certain other categories such as age, sex, skill, and status. The cutter and finisher appearing last in the permanent category should by my calculations have earned $180.30, but the figure shown was his actual pay.

ordinary pay for work done on any one of nine annual public holidays; namely, four days at Chinese New Year, Ch'ing Ming (April 5), the Dragon Boat Festival (fifth day of the fifth lunar month), May 1, the Mid-Autumn Festival (ninth day of the ninth lunar month), and the day of the winter solstice. (It is perhaps worth noting that with the exception of May 1 these are all traditional Chinese festival dates.)

Daily rates of pay fell within the range $7.00 to $11.00 for temporary workers and $6.50 to $18.00 for permanent workers. (Because of the increase obtainable from the fringe benefits available to permanent workers, promotion from the temporary category normally involved an initial drop in the daily rate received.)

On one payday I observed (April 28, 1968) the average size of the fortnight's pay packet actually taken home was $122.00 for temporary workers and $230.00 for permanent workers. The actual pay of most temporary workers nearly approximated the average, but for permanent workers the range was much wider: the number-one blower, for example, received, as we have already seen, $407.75 (before piece-work money); the most recently promoted permanent workers, $136.90 and $149.00, respectively. But it is worth noting that, although the last two mentioned were on daily rates of only $6.50, only two of the temporary workers (on rates of $8.00 and $8.50, respectively) took home more. It is also worth noting for comparison that very many white-collar workers in Hong Kong at the time received monthly salaries of between $500 and $600.

Table 2 presents a breakdown of the fortnightly pay packets taken home by eight selected workers on April 28, 1968.

The system of rewards included quite frequent reviews of wages and the possibility of increases, especially for the permanent workers. There was no regular rule about this, but the system was operated on the basis of the personal knowledge and judgment of the office worker (*b*) in charge of the accounts, in consultation with the appropriate foreman and the managing director. The same applied to questions of promotion from temporary to permanent status. Table 3 sets out the daily wage patterns as they were in operation in April 1968. It shows at a glance the greater use of flexibility and pay increases for the permanent workers and the overall differentials between the categories and between males and females.

There is some evidence that permanent workers worked longer hours than temporary workers. My records of the payday calculations for April 28, 1968, indicate that the permanent workers worked an average of approximately 15.5 regular days out of a maximum of 16, and earned

TABLE 3. DAILY RATES OF PAY FOR WORKERS BY CATEGORY AND SEX,
KAU FUNG GLASS FACTORY, HONG KONG, APRIL 1968

Daily rate	Permanent		Temporary	
	Male	Female	Male	Female
$18.00	1	—	—	—
16.00	2	—	—	—
15.00	3	—	—	—
12.00	2	—	—	—
11.00	1	—	1	—
10.50	2	—	—	—
10.00	1	—	2	—
9.00	1	—	—	—
8.50	—	—	3	—
8.00	—	—	6	—
7.50	—	—	—	2
7.30	1	—	—	—
7.00	3	1	—	7
6.80	1	—	—	—
6.50	2	—	—	—
Total	20	1	12	9

NOTE: Two female temporary workers were paid piece rates only for taking products out of the annealing furnaces. Here and throughout the remaining tables, these two workers are omitted from consideration, leaving a total of 42.

an average of about 2.5 days' pay in overtime work, whereas the temporary workers worked an average of approximately 14 regular days and earned an average of only about 1.2 days' pay in overtime work.

It is not easy to deduce from these data the extent to which the stability and industriousness of the labor force in this glass factory are to be connected with peculiarly Chinese patterns of reward and recruitment. The findings could also be explained by reference to universal economic considerations. The shortage of skilled workers made it inevitable that there would be competition for their services, and this in turn made for higher wages. The wages of the skilled workers were indeed relatively high, and made even higher by their fringe benefits as permanent workers. One wonders why it should have been considered more useful to cast these additional rewards in the form of bonuses and benefits rather than simply increasing the money wage. Two possible reasons come to mind, both of them at least partially culture-linked. The first is that workers in the Chinese context in Hong Kong today may value improvement in status almost as much as increase in income. This is a culture in which prestige still goes in the traditional way to scholars and white-collar workers. I have already stated that a skilled glassblower can earn more in a month than a typist—and this without including the monetary value of the fringe benefits. In Hong Kong today this is by no means an unusual state of affairs. Yet parents continue to demand the exclusively literary education that most Hong Kong schools provide, and unemployment and underemployment among white-collar workers and shop assistants continue to increase. Is it not possible to see the creation of a higher ("permanent") division of industrial workers as an attempt to provide some of the prestige normally denied the wage-earner?

The second possibility is that the attempt to draw certain (good) workers into closer connection, as it were, with the firm by providing fringe benefits may be an example of the often-remarked Chinese preference for multiplex rather than single-stranded relationships. There is a constant endeavor in Hong Kong to bind one's economic collaborators to one by whatever other ties one can activate: kinship, fictive kinship, friendship, *kan-ch'ing*, and so on. Almost any economic transaction except the most casual purchase tends to attract other, social, attributes; and where, as here, the transactions are between employers and employees, it is felt appropriate by both sides that these should be paternalistic. Such arrangements, regarded by the employees as a guarantee of security (as well as increased income) and by the employers as insurance against the loss of valuable workers, are typical in present-day Hong Kong. To that extent they may certainly be described as "Chinese." Paternalism of a similar general kind has, however, appeared at certain times in the industrial development of most societies, and it is possible that in part at least it may be a characteristic of a certain scale and stage of economic development rather than a specifically culture-linked phenomenon.

The Workers: Background and Attitudes

In any social analysis of the early stages of industrialization, the background of the workers and their attitudes regarding employment may well be crucial factors. During the last few days of my six weeks in the glass factory, I was able to interview every worker. In addition to data (about kind of job, rate of pay, length of employment, etc.), I obtained information as to age, marital status, language, and provenance; how long each had been in Hong Kong, how much education he had, and what had been the occupations of his father and other close relatives. I also discussed with each one the number of relatives he or she still had in China, if any, and tried to assess attitudes about factory work in general and this factory in particular. My formal questionnaire, however, included only factual questions. I used no attitude tests. The individual interviews were supplemented by more or less daily observations, conversations, and eavesdropping during the whole fieldwork period. The following tables and paragraphs summarize my findings. I am of course very well aware that the sample is far too small to allow any significant generalizations from the findings, even if it were possible— as it is not—to argue that this factory was "typical." The figures are given here primarily as a convenient method of presenting description; it is possible, too, that they may give rise to some hypotheses for testing in the future.

There is little need for comment on Tables 4 and 5. The age structure of Hong Kong's population, of which about 50% is nineteen years old or younger, was not closely represented in the factory. As might be expected, however, skilled workers were congregated in the younger classes; the unskilled were scattered more generally throughout the age range. The youngest employee was sixteen years old. There were no consistent sex-related differences in the ages of employees. If one includes

TABLE 4. AGE OF KAU FUNG GLASS FACTORY WORKERS BY SEX AND
CATEGORY, APRIL 1968

	Permanent		Temporary	
Age	Male	Female	Male	Female
Under 20	3	—	3	4
20–29	9	—	4	1
30–39	3	—	1	2
40–49	3	1	3	2
50 and over	1	—	1	—
Unknown	1	—	—	—
Total	20	1	12	9

TABLE 5. MARITAL STATUS OF KAU FUNG GLASS FACTORY WORKERS BY
SEX AND CATEGORY, APRIL 1968

	Permanent		Temporary	
Marital status	Male	Female	Male	Female
Single, including divorced and widowed	10	—	7	4
Married, spouse in Hong Kong	6	1	3	4
Married, spouse elsewhere	3	—	—	1
Unknown	1	—	2	—
Total	20	1	12	9

those whose spouses were not residing in Hong Kong (three in China, one in Indonesia), a little over half the workers were living singly. One of these was a widow with four children. Most of the single men in the permanent category were living in the firm's hostel.

The mother tongue of all but five of the workers was Cantonese. Of these five, one was from Kiangsi; one, whose first language was Bahasa Indonesia, was from Java; and one was a Teochiu-speaking immigrant recently from Vietnam (Cholon). All the others had been born either in Hong Kong or in Kwangtung Province; two of the latter said they were Hakkas. There was no discernible tendency for people to have originated from the same native place in Kwangtung. All the workers spoke Cantonese to each other. It should be added that none of the management was a native Cantonese speaker, and that the managing director spoke that language hardly at all, though he understood it perfectly well.

An analysis of the length of time each worker claimed to have lived in Hong Kong gives the results shown in Table 6.

If we assume that only those neither born in Hong Kong nor living there before 1949 can be meaningfully classed as "refugees," it is clear that just under half the workers fell into that category. It is interesting that they accounted for just under half the permanent workers, too. In other words, this factory depended for its workers, both skilled and unskilled, as much upon natives of the Colony and long-term residents as upon recent immigrants. This is partly to be linked with the connec-

TABLE 6. LENGTH OF STAY IN HONG KONG BY CATEGORY, KAU FUNG
GLASS FACTORY WORKERS, APRIL 1968

Residence history	Permanent	Temporary	Total
Born in Hong Kong	5	8	13
Came as a child pre-war[a]	2	1	3
Came about 1947[b]	4	2	6
Arrived 1950	3	1	4
Arrived 1951	—	1	1
Arrived 1954	2	—	2
Arrived 1955	1	—	1
Arrived 1960	—	1	1
Arrived 1961	—	2	2
Arrived 1962	2	1	3
Arrived 1963	2	2	4
No information	—	2	2
Total	21	21	42

[a] I.e. before the Japanese occupation in December–January 1941–42.
[b] I.e. at the end of World War II when many previous residents returned.

tion between skill and youth already mentioned. Of the thirteen workers born in Hong Kong, ten gave their ages as 21 years or less. Only one of these was the child of a truly local family, his father having farmed ancestral land in the New Territories. All but one of the others, including the two (aged 28 and 46 respectively) who were born some years before 1949, stated that their fathers had been immigrants. There is, however, nothing unusual or new about this for Hong Kong's urban population, and it does not follow that the fathers referred to were all "refugees." On the contrary, in addition to the one youngster whose ancestors were all New Territories people, six stated that their fathers had come to Hong Kong before the Japanese occupation; the other five did not know when their fathers had arrived.

Because a history of recent immigration is normal for Hong Kong's urban population, it is probably not very useful to try to relate individual differences to date of arrival. These differences are more likely to be connected with such factors as level of education and degree of previous acquaintance with factory employment. This likelihood is explored in the following paragraphs and in Tables 7–9.

Table 7 shows that there was some degree of correlation between level of education and permanent or temporary status, in that rather more workers in the permanent category claimed to have received rather more education than those in the temporary category. The correlation may have been largely coincidental—or if causative, only in the sense that

TABLE 7. LEVEL OF EDUCATION BY CATEGORY AND SEX, KAU FUNG
GLASS FACTORY WORKERS, APRIL 1968

Educational level	Permanent		Temporary	
	Male	Female	Male	Female
Post-secondary education	—	—	—	—
Secondary school completed				
3 years	3	—	1	—
2 years	3	—	—	1
1 year	1	—	—	—
Primary school completed				
6 years	2	—	3	2
5 years	3	—	—	—
4 years	1	—	1	—
3 years	4	—	3	2
2 years	—	—	—	—
1 year	1	—	—	2
No education	1	1	3	2
No information	1	—	1	—
Total	20	1	12	9

the same qualities that would lead a person to seek further education might make him both more able and more willing to meet the criteria for promotion to permanent status. In any case, there are indications that the workers themselves saw very little causality in the relationship. None of the temporary workers whose ultimate ambition apparently was to become permanent workers reported that they intended further education. And the four workers who reported attending or intending to take classes—although three of the four were temporary workers who would have welcomed permanent status while at the factory—all aspired ultimately to become white-collar workers and leave factory work altogether. (These four were the youngest employee, who had just completed four years of primary schooling, and three others, one of them a woman, who had reached or completed middle school.) In this, they reflect the prevalent patterns of upward mobility in Hong Kong that were discussed briefly above.

It should be added here that all four of the managers (directors and salaried staff) had received at least some post-secondary education. Managing Director A had a Ph.D. from a European university.

Among workers under thirty there was little or no evidence of sex-linked differences in level of education attained.

With regard to father's occupation (see Table 8), there are few differences between the permanent and temporary categories, though a surprising number of the temporary workers were unable to give any information about their father's work. In most cases this was because the fathers had died many years before.

In the light of the previous paragraphs it is at first sight surprising to find two permanent workers, apparently uninterested in further educa-

TABLE 8. FATHERS' OCCUPATIONS BY CATEGORY, KAU FUNG GLASS FACTORY WORKERS, APRIL 1968

Father's occupation	Permanent	Temporary
Profession or management	2	—
Farming[a]	7	6
Glass factory	1	1
Shop or small trade	4	2
Other[b]	2	5
"Retired"	3	—
No information	2	7
Total	21	21

[a] Includes one described as a "gardener" and employed by the Urban District Council.
[b] Includes two factory- or office-cleaners, a beach lifeguard, a sailor, a tailor, a hairdresser, and a matshed-maker.

tion, with fathers in professional and managerial positions (teacher and agent in an import-export firm). This is explained by the refugee situation: both these workers were older men (they included the already well-educated furnace foreman, aged fifty-one) who had come down in the world.

It is worth remarking, also, the very small number (two) of factory workers and the relatively large number of farmers among the workers' fathers. Both factory workers happen to have been employed in the making of glass. Small, rather primitive, factories for melting down old glass bottles to make new ones have existed in Canton, Macao, and Hong Kong for at least several decades. It may or may not be a simple coincidence that in the only cases where fathers were in factory employment children have, in fact, entered work in the same kind of factory. Workers with farming fathers are not, as might perhaps have been postulated, all older people, but rather equally scattered through the age groups. The relatively large number of farming fathers probably reflects simply the fact that the industrial revolution in Hong Kong began less than a generation ago.

All but two of the workers in this factory were thus first-generation factory employees. More than half of them were also the only factory employees in their respective kin sets, probably a further reflection of the recency of industrialization in Hong Kong. As with father's occupation, there is no significant difference between permanent and temporary workers, or even between the sexes, on this variable. Only in examining the previous experience of employees do any such clear differences emerge (see Table 9).

Here are no farmers, only one non-urban type of employment, and a strong tendency for factory workers to remain in factory employment. The tendency is so striking (particularly for the women) that one can

TABLE 9. PREVIOUS EMPLOYMENT BY CATEGORY AND SEX, KAU FUNG GLASS FACTORY WORKERS, APRIL 1968

| | Permanent | | Temporary | | |
Previous employment	Male	Female	Male	Female	Totals
Factory work—not glass	11	1	6	8[a]	26
Glass factory	7	—	1	—	8
Construction	—	—	1	—	1
Forestry	—	—	1	—	1
None	1	—	1	1	3
No information	1	—	2	—	3

[a] Includes one previously an outworker.

state firmly that this factory has not drawn its workers from a general pool of totally "raw" recruits. On the contrary, with only one exception and despite the fact that Hong Kong's industrial revolution is so new that only two workers had fathers with industrial experience, every worker on the books in April 1968 had previously been employed in industry (if we include the one in construction). This finding gives some credence to the view that, despite all appearances to the contrary, Hong Kong's industry may be facing the possibility of a shortage even of unskilled labor. At the very least, Table 9 raises the question whether or not the prejudice against non-white-collar employment, which has been mentioned above (pp. 370–71), may be creating a kind of artificial labor shortage.

Management: The Salaried Staff

There were only two salaried managing staff employees at the factory in 1968 (see Figure 3 above). Both had arrived in Hong Kong since 1949, and neither was Cantonese. Both were college-educated, and one spoke fair English. Both in their late twenties and unmarried, previously unknown to each other, they had each been recruited personally by one or other of the two directors.

Managing Director A had brought Managing Clerk *a* with him from the glass factory where they had both been employed. This man, who held a truck and car driver's license, was well acquainted with most aspects of importing raw materials and exporting finished products, and well known to most of the agents of the firms concerned. His job was mainly with these outside contacts. He was also charged with the general overseeing of the packing section in the factory, and the preparations for delivery. He was in no way related to A, nor did he even come from the same province or language group. Their original acquaintance was purely a business one. Both were, of course, aware that *a* owed his new position entirely to A.

Office Worker *b* was in charge of the accounts and records, and, under A's direction, kept a watching eye over all the internal management of the factory not overseen by *a*. I have already described the pleasant, cheerful, friendly manner in which he discharged this duty. He also handled the petty cash, and presided over payday when, having worked out the wages due, he checked each sum with each worker individually and handed over the pay packets. He lived with his mother only a few hundred yards away, and except at night was almost constantly in the factory. As a result he was responsible for a large number of the more or less routine decisions, coping with minor crises, etc. At night, *a*, who had sleeping quarters in the factory, took this responsibility, but as work was not normally continued beyond 10:00 P.M., his position in this respect was less important.

Office Worker *b* had been offered his post by Director *B*, under whom he had already worked for about five years in the office of the publishing firm by which *B* was still employed at the time of my fieldwork. There was no previous relationship between the two men, nor did they come from the same province in China. (They did, however, both have "gentry" backgrounds, as did also Managing Director *A*, Staff Member *a*, and the furnace foreman (Number Two). *B* had selected *b* for his abilities: accuracy, conscientiousness, good humor, intelligence, reliability, and complete loyalty.

Nominally *a* and *b* each received $600.00 a month, but, as for this purpose a convention that there were fourteen months in a year was accepted, the actual sum each received was almost $700.00 a month. In addition, *a* had free lodging in the factory. Each received a free mid-day meal, taken with the directors if they were present (see below) and paid for out of petty cash.

In general status there was no doubt at all about the superiority of the managing staff. This distinction was both expressed and reinforced in many small ways. The office staff always wore collars and ties, and spoke Mandarin together, normally using Cantonese only when speaking to the workers, and then with a strong accent. The office staff and directors ate with the workers only on ceremonial occasions; normally the workers took their lunch at a nearby café, while the office staff and the directors lunched together at one or other of the excellent local restaurants. With the one exception of the furnace foreman, whose special case has already been discussed, the managers were very much better educated than the workers—a fact that was apparent in dozens of small unconscious mannerisms and in their overall bearing. Social distance thus evidenced appeared to be accepted by both sides as right and proper. Its impact was greatly modified by marked and, I believe, genuine friendliness in conversation, by paternalism coupled normally with great care over giving "face," and by an explicit belief, held by both the managers and at least those workers who had attained or aspired to permanent status, that as far as the firm was concerned their interests were the same.

Management: The Directors

Basically simple though the process of glass manufacture is, it nevertheless requires a number of technological skills. One of these, the skill (and physical strength) required by the glassblowers, has already been commented upon. I have also mentioned the skill required for stoking the tanks and maintaining the proper loads and temperatures in them. A further very valuable skill, that of actually making the tanks, is closely linked with a fourth and most important skill; namely, a sophisticated knowledge of industrial chemistry and, in particular, of refraction. With the exception of glassblowing, these skills were all in the command of one man, Director A.

As the sole technical expert, A appeared to be indispensable to the glass factory. As noted above, he supervised the mixing of the raw materials, to which he added certain ingredients that he weighed behind the locked door of his private office. The formula was his own. The layout of the factory followed his plan. He allocated work tasks and devised schedules. Present almost every day, he took a minute interest in every aspect of the practical work, and he brought his two wives and their respective children with him to help in certain of the secret jobs. Both women also lent a hand with packing the finished glassware, as did anybody else who had a spare moment and felt so inclined.

The second director, B, knew virtually nothing about the technology of making glass. He was the public-relations man, the maker of outside contacts, searcher-out of markets, negotiator of credit; his was the task of arranging advertising and coping with licenses, fire regulations, relationships with buyers, and so on. He had interests in a number of other business enterprises of various kinds.

At this point it is necessary to go back about three years to the time when A first considered setting up a separate glass factory and B was looking for fresh fields for the investment of his financial and personal talents. At that stage (1964–65) A was certainly the key man. Without his skill, no glass factory could have appeared. At that stage, too, his personal contacts and credit in the glass business were also crucial. Through them he was able to borrow money, secure advance orders, acquire some of the necessary equipment cheaply, and recruit skilled laborers, some of whom he had previously trained himself. He also had a small amount of financial capital and personal contacts in the business community that made it easy for him to borrow money from the banks. He still needed more capital, however, and he also needed a kind of "contact man" with drive and initiative to help find a factory site, organize advertising, and so on. A's own assets were unique: he, and only he, could found and run a specialized glass factory. The skills required of the partner he needed were entirely generalized: B could have gone into any kind of business. It was in a sense purely by accident that B found himself engaged in manufacturing glass, and not plastic flowers or cotton vests or wigs or transistor radios. It should be added that both men were refugees, one from Central and one from North China, arriving in Hong Kong in 1949 and 1950 respectively.

Once the two men had agreed to enter into informal partnership (this was in 1965) the dominance of A's role was complete. B helped find the site, negotiated a loan, borrowed trucks for transporting equipment, badgered the authorities for licenses, and so on, but all this was under the direction of A, who alone knew what was required technically, could put it into operation, recruit labor, and direct commercial contacts in the glass trade. Indeed, at this stage, and for more than the first year of the factory's operation (including the whole period of my fieldwork) B's employment in the firm remained on a part-time basis. He did not take on full-time responsibilities until July of 1968.

Already after about six months' operation, however, once the factory was in steady working order, the locus of leadership began to shift. The change was accelerated when an advertising campaign was developed and foreign inquiries began to flow in. In their turn, B's professional expertise and contacts now came into their own. In February 1968 a full-scale article on the glass factory appeared in *Hong Kong Enterprise*, a journal put out monthly by the Hong Kong Trade Development Council. It was a superb piece of commercial writing, with first-class photographs. Within two months it had stimulated inquiries and orders from every continent in the world. When I arrived in April 1968, the leadership statuses of the two men were more or less in balance.

Both men were fairly clearly aware of their competitive situation. So were the two members of the office staff and at least some of the workers, in particular the two foremen. It was here that B's personality and social conscience, as well as his special structural position, became important. A, a reserved man without local ties, commanded little sympathy among the predominantly Cantonese workers. His necessarily strict day-to-day technological supervision of the delicate operations of his specialized process (preparation and weighing of formula, temperature control, prevention of breakage, etc.) inevitably led to direct confrontations with careless individuals. His high technical standards, his "foreign" upper-class manner, and his structural position as overseer tended to alienate even the key skilled workers he himself had brought to the factory at the beginning.

B, by contrast, had a Cantonese wife and spoke the language well. He had a disarmingly gay, friendly manner and a genuine concern for other people and their problems. He had also a much less intimate connection with the day-to-day running of the factory, no responsibility for the standards of work, and virtually no disciplinary function. With a joke for everybody, and a proven willingness to help anyone in personal trouble, he evoked a generally warm response all round. Moreover, the workers believed that *B* had obtained most of their increases in wages, and had succeeded in improving their fringe benefits, over *A*'s objections.

Probably the swing of worker allegiance from *A* to *B*, which was at its critical point at the time of my investigation, was structurally inevitable. In any complex technological system the role of the technical expert, thrown into day-to-day supervisory contact with the workers and compelled to maintain high standards, must have some disciplinary features. The organizer of the factory's outside contacts, on the other hand, can avoid this. Seeing the workers less regularly, controlling them hardly at all, he has no need to keep much social distance, and can afford warm friendliness. At the same time there is a constant tendency for the outside contact man, like *B*, to be seen to be active in the more popular aspects of worker management, such as recruitment and the initiative for improvement in working conditions and wages, for these are the two major functions that are assimilated to the "outside" part of the factory's overall organization. When *A* fired a bad worker, it was *B* who found a replacement; whereas *A* was concerned with the maintenance of his furnaces, *B* knew that other factories had better lavatories, more valuable lunch vouchers, or bigger pay packets, and that his must be improved accordingly if his workers were to remain. It seems likely that the way in which *B* was beginning to take over the leadership from *A*, once the major technical problems had been solved, exemplifies a universal tendency in the second stage of a factory's development. In a small concern the two stages and tendencies are likely to be very clearly distinguishable, and when, as here, the "outside man" has far the more winning personality, the outcome is not hard to predict: other things being equal, the technical man is likely to lose out, whereupon the factory's development will enter a third stage.

Early in April 1968, *B* began to put into operation a plan he had long been considering. His own statement was that it sprang directly out of his personal experience as a down-and-out refugee in Hong Kong in the early fifties. From that experience he had gained a passionate determination to help improve social conditions and a firm conviction that neither state control nor capitalism provided the answers he was looking for. In brief, his scheme was to provide for a kind of joint control of the business by setting up a private limited company in which, though he and A were to be the main shareholders, there should also be a number of other members with equal voting rights. The entire month was spent arguing the case for registering the firm as a private limited company and including in its membership the two office staff workers, and five of the workers from the shop floor, the shares of all these employees to be acquired in the beginning by free gifts of $1,000 each from B. It was also to be made known that any permanent worker could look forward to becoming a shareholder in the future.

As far as I have been able to ascertain, this was a unique development in Hong Kong. Although the practice of setting up registered limited companies, never very popular in the past, has been catching on quite dramatically in the last few years, none had, so far as I could establish, included salaried staff, to say nothing of blue-collar workers. B was enthusiastically proud of his plan, constantly discussing it and reiterating his hope that it might become a model not only for Hong Kong but for industrializing countries in general. In spite of A's initial hostility, not only to the idea of worker membership, but also to the whole notion of forming a limited company, the company was registered early in May 1968 with a board of seven, consisting of A, one of his wives, B, the two white-collar staff members, and two foremen.

Such a radical restructuring of the legal framework of the factory's ownership raises a number of interesting questions, only two of which can be considered here: namely, the possible reasons behind it, and its effects upon the day-to-day organization of production.

The importance for economic development of an adequate framework of commercial and industrial law has often been remarked. In Hong Kong such a framework has existed for a very long time, but until fairly recently the particular aspect of it that enabled the creation of corporate and continuing legal entities (private limited companies) was seldom invoked. Very likely, so long as businesses remained family concerns, any possible advantages that might result from forming such a company were outweighed by the disadvantage of having to disclose shareholdings at the time of formation. The Kau Fung Glass Factory, however, like an increasing number of others today, was not a family business. We have already referred to the consistent tendency for Chinese businessmen in Hong Kong to prefer multiplex to single-stranded relationships. Confidence in Chinese business is so much a matter of multiplex relationships that, as I have said above, almost any transaction beyond the most casual purchase tends to take on social attributes.

It is possible that men who lack personal relationships (as in the refugee situation was often the case), or who for any reason have entered into non-family partnerships (these are increasing at what is likely to be an accelerating pace), and who may also be influenced by modern values in favor of universalistic rather than particularistic relationships, may be motivated to look for legally binding contractual ties instead. Hence (so runs the argument put to me by a number of well informed official and unofficial observers in Hong Kong in 1968) the increase in the number of limited companies registered in the past few years—the glass factory among them.

This seems a plausible hypothesis. It certainly fits the situation under discussion. The two directors had no mutually binding particularistic obligations with which to cement their mutual interest in the factory, and, given their different personalities and dissimilar backgrounds, little chance of developing any. Moreover, both had been exposed in different ways to modern, universalistic values, and at least to a certain extent both accepted them (we have seen this at work in the firm's policy and practice about recruiting workers and staff). At the same time, both were aware that their mutual relationship was a precarious one, and each may have seen the entry into a legal contract as a possible safeguard, A after some initial hostility to the whole idea.

But this explanation does not account for the unique element in the new situation; namely, the inclusion of the salaried staff and some workers in the articles of association. Here the personal influence of B was decisive. Questioned, he denied having read any of the literature on co-partnership in industry or allied topics: the idea appears to have been genuinely original. He saw it both as a method of distributing power and as a way of binding workers and management more firmly together through the actualization of the belief that their interests in the firm were the same. He was explicit about all this, and I have no doubt that he was sincere. Nevertheless I suggest that the move also held certain strategic advantages for himself.

We have seen how, lacking technical expertise of the kind that had made A indispensable in the early stages, B had nonetheless acquired a balancing position in the directorate. From his point of view the formation of the limited company was more than just an attempt to perpetuate this situation, for by forming it in such a way that he himself controlled a majority of the votes, B made it possible for the firm to continue as a legal entity no matter what steps A might take. As time went on, the factory's dependence upon A's technical expertise would probably grow less. It was possible to foresee a situation in which, if it came to confrontation (or the threat of confrontation), A might withdraw, leaving B in sole effective control.

Style and Organization: "the Chinese Way"

My period of fieldwork came to an end in early May of 1968, so all this is speculation.* What is quite clear, however, is that at the level of actual production the changes in the structure of ownership made little or no difference. This was partly because the layout and organization of the factory were already as rational and efficient as space would allow, and partly because the firm was still small enough for face-to-face relationships to exist throughout. This made it possible for workers and managers to be personally known to each other, and joint consultation had always been continuous and effective. This was no accident. B and b explained to me many times that personalized methods of management were much better than others because they permitted the giving of "face" and so ensured mutual respect and self-respect. They usually referred to this approach as "the Chinese way," and contrasted its economic effectiveness with what seemed to them to be the essential irrationality of the Western preference for impersonal, single-stranded relationships.

Until now the descriptive analysis contained in this paper has given little support to the notion that there was anything peculiarly Chinese about the internal organization of the glass factory. Layout, work flow, job allocation, labor recruitment, even most aspects of the workers' previous experience and background did not appear to be specifically culture-linked. Even among the managing staff and directors there were no particularistic ties of a traditional nature. Only the system of rewards by categories seemed to be somewhat unusual, and even that is quite common in other parts of the Orient. As a piece of organizational machinery, the glass factory may be said to conform more closely to a "universal" than to a culture-specific pattern.

Nevertheless, and making full allowance for the fact that smallness of scale anywhere allows a personalized flexibility in management and encourages acceptable paternalism, there remain some features to which, taken together, the phrase "Chinese way" can be meaningfully applied. They include beliefs about the value of education, the virtue of hard work, and the self-evident goal of economic self-betterment,

---

* I have since been informed that A did, indeed, leave the firm in December 1968. The salaried staff member a left at the same time.

shared by workers and management alike. This set of values was accompanied by an ingrained habit of giving "face," in my opinion closely linked with the strong preference for multiplex rather than single-stranded relationships that has been mentioned in a number of contexts. It is my present hypothesis that insofar as it may be possible to isolate any aspects of the internal organization of this factory as uniquely "Chinese," they will be found not in the structural framework or the organizational plan, but in intangibles such as these, none of which alone is specific to Chinese culture but all of which in sum constitute a peculiarly Chinese style of running economic institutions.

Economic Management of a Production Brigade in Post-Leap China

JOHN C. PELZEL

This is a case study of economic management in one brigade of a commune in southern Kwangtung Province during the early 1960s.* The brigade lies on the plain of a navigable river of moderate size, a few miles in from the coast, and is referred to as the "River Brigade."

The River Commune, of which this brigade is a part, comprised 16 brigades, and with a population of about 55,000 was of roughly average size for the region. Its relative productivity is unknown to me, but it had considerable resources at the time of my study. With only about 70 per cent of its 55,000 *mou* of paddy and none of its 26,000 *mou* of dry fields planted to rice, it could still count on two rice crops yielding about 32 million catties of grain, of which only 19 million were needed to meet the basic cereal ration of the population, most of the remainder going as public-grains taxes and surplus-grains forced sales to the State. In addition, it was able to produce such a variety of special crops, to carry on so flourishing an animal husbandry of hogs and fowl, and to collect so many forest products that it could fill sizable State procurement quotas, satisfy local needs, and still have something left over for trading on the State and free markets. Inland waterways permitted the maintenance of a considerable network of bulk water transport facilities, while reasonably good roads allowed most parts of the commune to be linked together by regular bicycle, bus, and truck transport.

Unlike many sections even of the same commune, the villages of the River Brigade had never been heavily dependent on migration to Hong Kong or other overseas areas. However, the internal industrialization

---

* This paper is condensed from a monograph on the same subject jointly authored by myself and Mr. K. K. Fung, who collaborated also on the fieldwork involved. This single-author presentation is offered with the kind permission of Mr. Fung.

and urbanization of the mid-1950's drained away a certain proportion of young workers, and in 1957, perhaps mid-stream of this drain, the population of the present brigade area stood at about 3,000, in somewhat fewer than 600 households. By 1964, population had risen to 3,400, for an increase of 13 percent in only seven years, but we are unable to determine what parts had been played in that change, respectively, by natural increase and by the reversal of migration that took place after the failure of the Great Leap.

The River Brigade's resources were perhaps even richer than was average for its commune, for it had only river-bottom paddy, with no dry fields, and its location out on the river plain gave it unusually good transport and commercial opportunities. It is also apparent that brigade farmers had for some time had a good sense of enterprise. For example, immediately subsequent to Land Reform nearly 90 percent of brigade households converted at least a part of their lands to tangerine orchards —a most profitable conversion if, as was reported, the production of a single *mou* could be sold for only JMP 96 if the crop was rice, but for JMP 1120 if the crop was tangerines.

By the time this study began, however, this enterprise had been harnessed to a State plan that called for concentration upon basic and staple foods. As early as 1954 the *hsien* forbade further conversions of paddy to orchards, and after 1955 tangerines had to be sold to the State at a price somewhat below the market rate, with 30 percent of the cash realized being given to the cooperative and another 25 percent being paid to the State as taxes. Local farmers remained quite well off, however, and in spite of the large amount of land in orchards even managed to produce a surplus of rice. Then, in 1958, villagers were forced to convert all of their orchards back into paddy, with tax and basic-cereal-ration burdens that theoretically required them to plant 70 percent of their lands in rice and a procurement quota that should have prescribed use of the rest of their lands for growing staple cash crops. The much lower normal yields of these crops, plus bad growing weather and the mismanagement of the Great Leap, resulted in so precipitous a decline in local income that informants believed residents were worse off than before Liberation.

In the early 1960's, regional large-scale water-conservancy projects resulted in the brigade's losing about 10 percent of its arable land to its neighbors. By 1964, therefore, the River Brigade had been reduced from 3,000 to 2,700 *mou*, planted to far less productive crops than before collectivization, at the same time that the population to be supported had risen markedly. From having had 1 *mou* per person in high-yield crops in 1957, it had been reduced to 0.8 *mou* per person in low-income crops, and informants reported that residents felt themselves to be no better off, even with the good harvest years through 1965, than they had been in 1949.

A Brief History of Collectivization

Before Liberation, almost no brigade residents had been identified with the new regime, and thus the first action of the imported cadre after pacification had been to select local people to serve as cadre trainees. As such, the latter manned the peasants' associations and the militia, and a few were enrolled in the Communist Youth League. It was not until 1954, however, that a League branch was formed, and not until 1956 that a Party branch was organized, branches that in 1964 had memberships, respectively, of 37 and about 50. During the early years, therefore, local cadres operated closely under the control, first, of the imported cadre, and, later, of higher-level cadres who came into the area with each innovation in the rural system, tutored the local people, and led them in implementing the change.

The first Mutual-Aid Teams were formed in 1954, well after Land Reform had been completed. Together, the teams included only 10–15 percent of local farmers, but this small membership seems to have reflected the deliberate decision of cadres to keep numbers small and procedures experimental. Local people at that time were reportedly still enthusiastic about almost everything the new regime proposed, and ex-landlord and middle-peasant elements at least quiet. Land Reform had not been accompanied by any bloodshed locally.

The Mutual-Aid Teams were favored by the State in many of the ways that were to become common later in the treatment of "Key Points." For example, they received substantial loans, and were permitted deficits against their obligations to pay taxes. However, certain managerial weaknesses at once became apparent. For one thing, new techniques such as multiple plowing were not yet refined and adapted to local conditions, and did not increase production enough to make up for the losses they caused. For another thing, the cadres had chosen as team members a high proportion of naturally deficit households (those with too few labor hands per consumer; those with few draft animals, etc.), so that available animals and workers were overtaxed. Similarly, no one was yet used to keeping even the simple records that were now required, and confusions, inequities—and so dissatisfactions—resulted.

Nevertheless, enthusiasm for collective farming seems to have remained high among the majority of poorer farmers. In the next year,

1955, the first lower-grade cooperative was formed from the former mutual-aid teams, somewhat enlarged. The cooperative cadre at once took over governmental functions for the entire geographical area of the present brigade, but as an economic organization the cooperative still included only a minority of farm households—the "four categories" being excluded, and middle peasants on the whole staying out voluntarily—and the teams were widely separated from one another in a territory still primarily farmed on an independent household basis.

After only a few months, however, local cadres began—for the first time—actively to encourage all except the "four categories" to join the cooperative. For the most part they seem to have been able to get farmers to join with nothing more than persuasion, and to keep their relations with local people on a friendly level. In only a few cases were they forced, it is reported, to use the extensive State economic and political powers they now controlled—e.g., the allocation to households of taxes and procurement quotas, of farm credits and rationed consumer and producer goods, etc.

By the beginning of 1956, almost all qualified households had joined, and the area was reorganized into several lower-level cooperatives. Most component teams were of course primarily agricultural, but specialized work—such as local industry, tool-repairing and -manufacture, animal-tending, etc.—was given to specialized teams, attached directly to the headquarters of the cooperatives. Because of the shortage of qualified cadres, agricultural teams were left individually larger than was even then considered desirable, and for a variety of reasons teams varied greatly in population, in the ratio of workers to consumers, in the quality of their lands and equipment, etc., and consequently in their potentialities for management and for economic well-being.

At the beginning of 1957 the several cooperatives were fused into a single higher-level cooperative organization, and almost at once a number of strains began to appear. No doubt a variety of forces were here at work—resentment felt by farmers who had contributed more than their share of the animals and tools of the unit but who now received no compensation for their capital, the pause in morale and the doubts now being expressed nationally in the "Hundred Flowers" movement, etc. But one important cause seems to have been that the cadres, having overworked for several years, now tended to sit back and rest on their achievements, at precisely the time when realization of a fully collectivized economy required the most strenuous management activity. Similarly, the procedures of collective economic management had neither been tested and perfected in theory nor made routine in practice. In any event, confusion and inefficiency were reportedly common at this time. Work morale fell, and many households spent more time on their private plots or on subsidiary occupations than on collective field work. In the collective summer harvest of 1957, production fell considerably, and thereafter many cadres began openly to be accused of, for example, the "five-same" ideology (nepotism, etc.). For a time, our informants report, the threat of violence hung in the air, and local cadres took to carrying knives for personal protection.

These difficulties were evidently general enough so that during the late summer and fall of 1957 the regime locally mounted its "Strike down buffalo, ghosts, snakes, and evil spirits" campaign, which resulted in public criticism of some cadres, and even in transportation to labor reform for a few others. Thereafter, undirected criticism of the cadres was discouraged. More important, 1957 saw the beginning of the formulation of a distinct local-cadre role. No longer volunteer activists in a charmed self-improvement movement, the cadres now had to learn to act as officials, occupying a permanent intermediary status between the farmers and workers below and higher-echelon cadres above. To both they were responsible not only for what they themselves did or did not do, but also for everything that happened in their geographical jurisdictions. They were given powers of coercion that they now must use when their authority failed, but they were themselves subject to protean power sanctions—ranging from envy, disrespect, passive disobedience, and promotion difficulties, to public humiliation, labor reform, and active rebellion.

The periods of communization and the Great Leap were locally much as they have been described from other sources. We may point out that the aims of these movements included a very rapid increase in and diversification of rural productivity, and a correction of the unequal potentialities of units. Equalization was to be achieved by creating large organizations within which resources could be re-allocated administratively—mess-hall feeding, the transfer of the surpluses and deficits of component units, etc. The catastrophic decline in productivity that in fact resulted no doubt had many other causes, including the de-motivation resulting from the success of earlier stages of equalization itself, but it appears to have been in part the result of a serious managerial failure.

Whether because of the speed with which extreme production and equalization goals were sought, or because of the primacy given political techniques, local management during this period acted primarily on *ad hoc* decisions made by higher-echelon cadres. Local cadres were left with virtually no freedom for initiative or action. The evolution of effective management procedures for even the basic requirements of what was after all still a new and untried collective economy was aborted. It was impossible to establish routines either in technique or in procedure, because both techniques and procedures were continually being altered by new *ad hoc* decisions from above. So long as the frenzy of the Great Leap lasted, there was neither a local managerial role, nor a local management culture.

New Directions

The reorientation that was to give the local situation its distinctive character during the early 1960's took a great variety of directions. Most can be traced to higher-level policy changes, but we shall here introduce them in the form of the institutional changes observable on the local scene.

1. *The economic framework.* For one thing, production goals were sharply revised. Deadlines were extended, quantities were reduced, and requirements as to how the goals were to be acheived were relaxed. No longer was rural productivity to be enormously increased and diversified overnight, and units were left to build slowly on the basis of the combined subsistence-commercial agricultural economy and the handicraft economy they already possessed.

The new economic goals were transmitted to units in the form of a written plan for 1961, a plan that was to remain in effect for the next ten years. The plan outlined carefully the factors of production of the unit, as established from numerous earlier surveys, went on to describe recommended technical and managerial procedures, and gave guidelines for the distribution of unit income, including the burden of State exactions (public-grains taxes, surplus-grains forced sales, and procurement-quota forced sales of non-cereal products) to be laid annually on the unit.

Production quotas were based on the unit's demonstrated productive capacity rather than, as during the Great Leap, on national needs or some ideal standard of local productivity. Exactions, production costs, and basic personal income were tied to so-called "normal" yields, calculated by averaging the actual yields of nine previous good, bad, and middling years. The State guaranteed to reduce the burden of exactions in any year in which natural disasters should reduce yields markedly (at least 30 percent) below "normal," and thus went a good deal of the way toward safeguarding a minimal level of unit income. It also promised to maintain the same absolute burden of exactions for ten years (though it might annually alter the proportions contributed thereto by given crops), and thus agreed that real increases in productivity should accrue to the unit itself. Economic management could thus be carried out within a framework that was economically both realistic and reasonably secure from political drain.

As another of its contributions to the "economizing" of local management, the State set about creating or expanding a huge array of higher-level economic institutions and facilities that could support the rural economy, and making them routinely available to local unit managers.

Roads were improved, and better transport facilities were provided both by land (bicycle, bus, and truck lines) and by water (junk fleets). The mail service was made more reliable, and regular telephone links were installed among all unit headquarters. An increasing volume of both producer and consumer goods needed in the country was turned out at all levels of industry, and distributional facilities were built up to improve the process of bringing goods to the village and removing its exports (warehouses and transport companies, specialized exchange companies, State stores and local supply and marketing cooperatives, etc.). Commercial institutions that increased the opportunities for exchange were created—a State purchasing network for non-tax and non-quota goods, and the free market for both individual and unit transactions.

To the same ends, agricultural experiment stations were opened within the commune, and local cadres were encouraged to visit them as a substitute for an extension service. State banking institutions were extended down to the brigade level, where agents of the People's and Agricultural Banks provided facilities for routine financial transfers, for collecting and paying interest on the savings of units and individuals, and for making loans for production purposes. Private plots were allowed again, not only as a means for using individualistic motivations, but also as a real aid to the collective economy. They shifted from that economy the burden of certain crucial production tasks—the raising of non-cereal subsistence foods for the rural population, and the supply of animal products—which experience had proved collective management could not yet handle effectively. Likewise, by taking plots from marginal lands, and reassigning them every few years to the collective, the system ensured that a heavier expenditure of labor would be put into improving them than collective management could yet guarantee.

Together, these measures provided a framework for the local economy that was economically a good deal more rational than any that had preceded it and in many ways more promising than the environment of the private economy before 1949.

2. *The conditions of local management.* At the same time that these economic changes were taking place, extensive alterations were made in the conditions under which local economic management was to be carried out. In general, we can of course say that politics was no longer in command of the process by which local economic goals were to be sought, but this shift toward an economic emphasis took several more specific directions.

In the first place, the ownership and control of all economic resources in rural areas was assigned officially to one or another level of local administration. Teams were to own lands and the tools for farming them, and were to control the agricultural labor of their own populations. Brigades were to own certain service, industrial, and specialized food-production facilities, and to control the labor (of full-time specialists and of part-time farm workers) to man them. Commune, *hsien*, and State agencies were to own and control still larger-scale or more highly specialized installations, even when physically located in the brigade areas.

Secondly, each unit was assigned "independent accounting" status, which meant that it was, with certain minor exceptions, forced to pay all the costs of the facilities it controlled out of the post-exaction income it was able to make from them. Producer and consumer goods, higher-echelon services, etc., were increasingly available from outside the unit, but only for sale, barter, or fees out of the unit's income, not as grants. State credits were increasingly provided for both short-term and investment needs, but only as loans to be repaid with interest from the income of the unit, not as subsidies. A unit could count on net outside aid only in the forms of a small rebate of the non-agricultural taxes it paid, a minor portion of the salaries of its Party cadre and of the costs of its health and educational facilities, welfare grants to indigent and politically reliable members after the unit's own welfare funds should be exhausted, and a reduction of its State exactions if it should be hit by a very serious natural disaster.

Independent accounting status thus tended to require that local cadres be economically responsible, just as the moratorium on changes in State exactions and the provision of a more supportive large-scale economic framework invited them to show enterprise. Equalization goals were not abandoned. At the team level they were attained perhaps better than ever before by redistricting, the teams of the River Brigade being made as nearly as possible equal not only in total population, but also in the ratio of workers to consumers, and in the proportion it held of each grade of land, with draft animals and farm tools to match.

At the brigade level and higher it was difficult to apply the same device so successfully, and equalization was there pursued more through economic mechanisms. Poorer units received proportionately more of the cheaper, rationed producer goods, for instance, and larger development credits. Such measures might have furthered equalization over a long period of time. During the years in question, however, the supply of rationed producer goods remained very short, and units had often to look for unrationed sources, while the prices of both were driven upward by the short supply so that only the wealthier units could afford to buy them. Likewise, banks seemed loath to make loans unless the borrower showed a good ability to repay, and the granting of a loan gave the bank legal authority to oversee the management of the unit, a function that all our informants believed was exercised more in the interest of fiscal responsibility than of welfare.

In any event, equalization was now stressed less than economic responsibility and enterprise. Likewise, since the local cadres now had legal control of unit resources and were required to make ends meet, they had considerably more economic autonomy than ever before. Several measures were taken to consolidate this independence.

Communization had created local units that were too large for the inexperienced cadres to handle and whose boundaries coincided poorly with the distribution of economic resources and the pattern of social relations with which both farmers and cadres had been familiar. When the unit boundaries were redrawn to correct these difficulties, care was taken simultaneously to equalize the economic potential of teams within a given brigade. This effort began almost as soon as the communization that had created the difficulties was completed, in 1958. By 1961, units already had virtually the form they retained throughout the period of this study.

The result of redistricting was to make all units smaller again, and to bring their boundaries into conformity with pre-collectivization ecological and social areas. Cadres redrew team boundaries so that member households were on good terms with one another, and in extreme cases families were assigned to teams other than those to which their neighbors belonged. Brigade boundaries were redrawn so as to include natural features historically used by brigade members, and to coincide with their customary trading, mutual aid, and intermarrage ties. The "bad" tendencies that might still inhere in traditional solidarities were considered less important than the greater ease of managing such a unit, the surer cooperation to be expected among its members, and the better knowledge they would have of local resources. Most brigade members tended to have effective contact primarily with people they had been reared with. By the early 1960's, many of the out-migrants of the previous years had returned to the brigade, and new out-migrations were severely curtailed, both by economic conditions and by administrative action. City cadres and students meant to help in production all but ceased to visit, as did higher-level cadres, at least without prior notice. Mail service was improved, official telephone links were installed among headquarters, and extensive record-keeping became routine. As these means for communication among cadres came to be more extensively used, personal contacts with extra-brigade cadres came increasingly to be confined to official occasions.

We were unable to learn enough of the details of the decision-making process to discover to what degree higher-level cadres were still able, even through these now impersonal and formal links, to impose their will upon local units. It was our informants' opinion that during these years unit cadres enjoyed a high degree of freedom. Decisions were always announced in the name of the formally appropriate post, and most economic decisions affecting the brigade as a whole were now made at some post in the brigade headquarters. Prior consultations and meetings, both between and within headquarters units, remained numerous and perhaps actually increased in frequency. Communications were better and the economic system was more complex. On the whole, however, informants felt these were only such as were appropriate to the formal chain of command, and were normally conducted in the spirit of democratic centralism. Thus, the Party Branch Secretary was reportedly the crucial figure in all decisions affecting his unit, but his behavior in consultations with his subordinate cadres consisted primarily of eliciting or giving information and opinions, galvanizing and persuading others, and bringing their views together to formulate the official decision.

The principle of local-cadre autonomy was thus greatly furthered both by the terms of the 1961 economic plan and by the manner in which it was administered. The plan must also have been a crucial educational device for the professionalization of local cadres. It was the first comprehensive and integrated statement of norms for the local collective economy that had been tested over any considerable period of time; earlier plans, from 1955 to 1957 locally, had been only partial statements of tentative norms, and had been superseded almost immediately by rapid changes occurring in the collective unit itself and finally by the planlessness of the Great Leap.

The 1961 plan, however, should be viewed less as an order to local cadres than as an argument. It undertook to show that each unit's lands, if farmed by recommended techniques, would be adequate to produce the State's exactions, and at the same time feed its population and pay for the producer goods it would need to import. In the case of the River Brigade this argument held that, at normal yields, approximately 48 percent of the unit's land and farm labor would produce enough to cover public- and surplus-grains requirements and procurement quotas, while another 35 percent would provide the basic ration of cereals and edible oils for its own members and fill the various "funds" to pay the non-wage costs of production, welfare, and administration.

Thus, after assignment of up to 5 percent of lands to private plots, some 12 percent of agricultural resources could be managed as the local cadre wished, and the income from that portion be used for additional investment capital or to pay wages beyond the bare subsistence level provided by the ration and the private plots, or both. The unit's side-line operations were also left virtually unplanned, except for a rather heavy tax on actual transactions. Since the sideline sector in the River Brigade provided some full- or part-time work paying higher wages than came from farming to perhaps 20 percent of brigade workers, it, together with the unplanned agricultural resources, constituted an economically significant area of local freedom.

Moreover, even with respect to the 83 percent of agricultural resources covered by the plan, that document was in intent and practice largely a textbook and reference guide rather than a strict mandate. The parts of the plan that seemed most inflexible were those stipulating that the unit pay its State exactions in prescribed amounts of prescribed crops and that it disburse rice rations averaging 30 catties per brigade member per month; and those illustrating how given fields, amounts of fertilizer, inputs of labor, etc., could be used to produce these crops. In fact, however, the River Brigade was able, year after year, to gain permission to commute some of the burden of exactions into goods of different kinds and even into money payments. In the same spirit it grew a non-prescribed third crop of sweet potatoes on the paddy and, arguing from local dietary practice, used it to pay part of the basic cereal ration. Thus, part of the more valuable rice crop was freed to be used as the brigade wished. Given these freedoms, and having a free market available, the cadres turned many of the brigade's resources to growing unstipulated crops, crops that they believed would yield more or would be easier or more efficient for them to grow, and either substituting them for crops exacted in the plan or selling or bartering them in the market for money or for the necessary quantities of the exacted crops.

Thus the brigade, using its resources somewhat differently than the plan had envisaged, substantially reduced the 83 percent of agricultural production the plan saw as needed for exactions, basic rations, administration, and non-wage costs of production. In the process, the cadres also modified recommended techniques considerably—for example, multiple plowing and close planting. Moreover, by motivating farmers to turn out the more intensive labor that higher-yield crops normally require, and by creating employment—both in specialized agriculture and in the sideline industries—for the unbudgeted free time that always exists in an underdeveloped farm economy, the brigade must have been able to mobilize a larger effective labor supply than the plan credited it with having, and to use that labor in more productive ways. Likewise, it is clear that during these years the cadres of the River Brigade were able to persuade their members to place the good of the unit above the good of the household, at least temporarily, since they invested a considerably larger amount than the plan foresaw in agricultural producer goods and in equipment for sideline operations, and could do so only by using goods or money that would otherwise have gone as wages.

It seems clear, therefore, that during these years the cadres of the River Brigade and its component units were in effective charge of the local collective economy, and managed it with a fair degree of autonomy. They were reasonably successful economically, not only maintaining solvency but showing a good deal of enterprise and increasing capital resources. Although nothing should be allowed to detract from this conclusion, the degree of local autonomy enjoyed in collectivized areas at this time should not be overemphasized. It was certainly not absolute; and indeed had the brigade been really autonomous it could scarcely have been so successful: it certainly could not have built a local economy capable of forming the foundation of a national system suited to development.

The cadres' autonomy was restricted in the first instance, of course, by the general doctrinal requirement that approximately 95 percent of a unit's non-labor agricultural resources—and an indeterminate but more or less equal proportion of its other resources—be devoted to a collective rather than a private economy. This was a highly sensitive issue even in these years, and the rural Socialist Re-Education Campaign, beginning locally in 1962, kept all eyes on the problem. The dividing line between "collective" and "private" economic procedures, difficult to distinguish at many points in any case, shifted with time and with the local and regional climate of cadre opinion. Near our research site (though not in the River Brigade itself), certain local cadres went so far as to parcel out all farm resources to individual households, requiring them only to turn in enough of their crops to pay the cost of unit exactions, production, and administration. This degree of deviation was condignly punished, however, and the situation was rectified by higher-level political and administrative action. These were in fact the only instances we observed during these years in which higher echelons took a strong initiative or resorted to clearly political action with respect to the local economy. The River Brigade did not go nearly so far, as we shall note later.

A much more immediate source of constraint upon local cadres was the requirement that a high proportion of resources be devoted to the production of staple crops. This section of China had long enjoyed a highly diversified farm economy, raising both staple and specialized crops for subsistence and for sale, and the River Brigade had been firmly within this tradition until about 1958, as has been suggested. After that date, however, it was forced to return to a simpler economy devoted primarily to staples apt for subsistence, whether its own or that of the cities and deficit areas to which its exactions were exported. Even though it might, as we have suggested, deviate widely from the written plan, it could do so only within the limits of the market, and the State still controlled the market in such a way that only goods for subsistence or for export could be grown in any quantity. Whether or not this policy was justified in the short run to overcome the failures of the Great Leap, or in the long run by the need to create a base for ultimate urbanization and industrialization, or even by the cyclical worsening of the population-resources ratio, it must be acknowledged that the policy imposed great restraints upon the enterprise of local economic managers.

Equally important, as a source both of constraints on and prescriptive guidance for the cadres during this period were the many kinds of higher-level supportive facilities outlined earlier. The economic institutions that impinged upon the local unit from outside were becoming not only more numerous and more varied, but also better integrated into something approaching a national economic system. As such, they created a host of requirements and opportunities, and in either case of rules, to which local cadres must increasingly relate. Dicta were handed down in an increasingly impersonal and regularized manner, and political considerations became less important, but the dicta were no less binding for being governed by certain rules and routines, or for being limited to economics. The autonomy of the brigade in this context was real, but only as part of an equally real larger system of economic roles and institutions.

Organization and Certain Management Functions

The headquarters organization at both the commune and the brigade level (but not at the team level) was formally divided into two parallel agencies—one pertaining to the Party, the other considered the organ of local government. In spite of the formal separation of Party and government, both agencies operated throughout the entire range of governmental activity, the Party organ having more to do with policy and local government having more to do with implementation. The Party group, in addition, had sole purview of whatever were considered purely "Party matters."

The Party executive at each level consisted of a committee, chaired at commune level by the Party secretary and at brigade level by the Party branch secretary. Each committee comprised a number of formal posts, some of which (propaganda and organization members, the league tutor) had duties related to specifically Party affairs, while others (e.g., production, culture and education, public security members) were concerned primarily with local governmental functions.

At both commune and brigade levels the parallel local government agency was a standing executive committee, the so-called Management Committee of the periodic Representative Congress. Chaired by the commune or brigade chief, this committee comprised posts for deputy chief(s), and for supervisors of the several recognized sectors of local government—in the River Brigade a political member, a public-security supervisor, a cashier, a credit-cooperative member, and an economic-management member—plus a certain number of lower-ranking clerical and technical positions.

The holders of posts at brigade level were responsible with respect to their specific functions to the holders of similar posts at commune level—the Party branch secretary to the commune Party secretary, the brigade chief to the commune chief, the brigade cashier to the commune finance member, etc. At the same time, within a given headquarters, the Management Committee was subordinate to the Party Committee, and this doctrinal hierarchy was reinforced by two organizational features: the responsibility of a specific post in the Management Committee to a corresponding post in the Party counterpart, and an interlocking directorate of individuals filling these positions. Thus in the River Brigade the Party political member had authority over the posts of political member and public-security supervisor on the Management Committee, and all three posts were in fact held by the same man. In the same manner, the brigade chief was subordinate to the Party branch secretary, and the individual who was Party organization member also held the post of brigade chief. Only the Party branch secretary, in this and other brigades known to us, typically held no formal post on the Management Committee at all; most other major Party cadres concurrently occupied most of the principal positions in local government.

It is of course possible that during the years in question a few individuals held a great many posts in part because of a shortage of persons qualified to act as cadres. But our informants considered it to be a matter of doctrine rather than of convenience that there should be a double set of organizations, manned in an interlocking manner, as well as functional links between posts at adjacent levels. Moreover, though they were relatively critical of the present regime, our informants were unanimous and decided in their view that this complex leadership organization was in practice highly effective, producing no significant conflicts. Posts of similar function but at different echelons, in their opinion, normally cooperated well with one another even while, within a single headquarters, local governmental posts were fully responsive to Party positions. As one informant volunteered, "Loyalty to the higher echelon and to the Party is quite compatible with loyalty to the brigade." This compatibility must of course be judged in terms of the situation of the early 1960's, and of the local levels for which it was alleged.

Our informants maintained that within the River Brigade the Party branch secretary during this period came to be seen as, and in their opinion was, responsible for everything that happened within his geographical jurisdiction. They did not rate him an unusually able or enterprising man, but they did uniformly see him as serious, hard-working, quite incorrupt, and completely loyal to both the Party and the welfare of his brigade.

If the branch secretary was involved in everything that happened in the unit, the brigade chief was during these years said to have been concerned primarily with economic matters. In this work he had to coordinate and supervise coordination with higher-echelon agencies, and to supervise the brigade cadres specializing in economic functions, the heads of the sideline organizations attached directly to brigade headquarters, and the leaders of the several agricultural teams.

Brigade Cadre Operations

We shall delay for a moment considering the basic operations having to do with agricultural production and with distribution in order to discuss some of the principal contacts of the brigade with the larger economic system.

Many higher-level facilities were manned by their own personnel rather than by brigade members, even when operating in the lower unit's territory, and the brigade made use of them only on occasion. Thus, commune and *hsien* organizations maintained junk, bus, truck, horse-cart, and bicycle fleets, each with its own terminals in or near brigade territory. Small mail was delivered to and taken from the office of the brigade's credit cooperative by State postal employees, and except on official business, brigade members had to go to the post office at commune headquarters to handle large parcels or to use telecommunications. Farmers and local cadres went from time to time to the commune-run agricultural research laboratory to learn about new farming techniques. Brigade cadres had to coordinate with the commune water-utilization department to receive water from commune-controlled reservoirs, as well as on plans for reservoirs controlled by the brigade itself, the physical supervision of waters once inside brigade territory being in the hands of the brigade public-security supervisor and his subordinate militia. Team work-parties transported rice taxes and edible oil quotas to commune food-control company warehouses scattered throughout the commune area, and other quotas to the warehouses of the commune forestry and animal husbandry department, or the commerce department at commune headquarters, on schedules and in amounts negotiated by the respective cadres. The *hsien*-level federation of industry and commerce provided, at its branch at commune headquarters, certain recreational and welfare services to non-agricultural personnel of the brigade. If the brigade's own welfare funds would not cover its needs, it might negotiate additional aid from the commune's civil affairs committee, which also in theory (no occasions arose during the period of the study) might have provided mass relief in the event of a natural disaster with which even the scheduled reduction of unit quotas and taxes could not cope.

Other higher-level facilities, however, were so central to the brigade's operations that their provision or supervision was assigned to regular brigade cadres. Thus, the brigade cashier, with his assistant the brigade accountant, was in charge of drawing up and keeping all budgets, accounts, and records, and with forwarding at least digests of them up the line, according to the rules and under the supervision of the commune. Sideline organizations and the agricultural teams had their own recorders, who submitted their reports to the cashier monthly, and all accounts were audited once a year by a recorder or cashier from another brigade at a general session attended by all such officers at commune headquarters. Whether or not this arrangement led to more accurate reporting to the State Council than during the Great Leap years, in the opinion of our informants it did lead to reasonably accurate and comprehensive records of all kinds, at least within the commune. Moreover, during this period workers no longer seemed dissatisfied with the recording of their work points, etc., as they had often been in the early years of collectivization.

In the same way, the brigade credit cooperative member—in the River Brigade he was also the cashier—managed the State postal system within brigade territory and, more importantly, was the brigade banker, keeping all unit and individual clearance and savings accounts and making and supervising all loans. In the latter role, he was of course subject to the rather demanding rules of the People's and Agricultural Banks, and he was responsible to the commune finance member for seeing that these rules were kept both by his peers and by his superiors in the brigade.

The brigade branch of the commune's supply and marketing cooperative handled State purchases of non-quota brigade products, as well as sales to brigade units and members of producer and consumer goods. This store was managed by the deputy brigade chief, who was also responsible for supervising all transactions carried on at the free market by brigade units. In this latter duty he was in turn supervised by the commune's market management committee, which controlled the local free-market enclosure. Likewise, the deputy brigade chief was responsible for all large-scale commercial exchanges between units of which at least one was under brigade control, but was normally supervised by the commune's food-control company. All such unit sales or exchanges, moreover, had first to be specifically approved by the commune headquarters, which during this period was extremely wary of authorizing any sale in which purely middleman profits might be realized. Likewise, brigade members were discouraged from being regular vendors in the free-market enclosure (most such vendors were commune headquarters personnel licensed by the commune police station), but they could buy or sell at the free market on a single occasion with a written permit from the brigade clerk, the assistant to the deputy chief.

In these and similar roles, brigade cadres were, if not the representatives of a higher echelon, at least subject to norms and rules that could conflict with brigade interests or place them in awkward situations within their brigades. As a banker supervising a loan to his brigade, for example, the cashier often had to stipulate what the local Party secretary might and might not do. Under the commune's rules, the deputy brigade chief must often prescribe or limit the commercial dealings of his chief. We can, however, only echo the opinion of our informants that during the period in question these potential conflicts seem to have been resolved without any great strains.

Once the River Brigade had attained the basic economic security and responsibility envisaged by the 1961 plan—as it seems to have done fairly easily—the most important task of its cadres during these years was to maximize its profits within legal limits. Although all cadres were to work in this direction, the office most directly responsible was that of the economic management member, and our informants were of the opinion that the River Brigade succeeded as it did because of the ability of the individual who filled this post. His duties were to draw up all brigade and team plans for production and investment, and to determine, as these plans were put into practice, whether they were making the greatest possible contribution to the income of the unit. He had to be shrewd in using the several avenues open—tax commutations, higher-yield crops, better investments, commercial opportunities—and he had to consider both present and future markets. The economic management member of the River Brigade was not a Party member, came from rich-peasant origins, and had at least tenuous connections with the KMT before Liberation. During the period of the study he was often in ideological trouble, not only because of his background, but because he helped déclassé kinsmen, made deals that benefitted the brigade but that cut ideological corners, and otherwise made it clear that he was incapable of understanding or abiding by Party principles. Nevertheless, he received his post because before Liberation he had made a success of the tile kiln that was now the brigade's outstanding industrial property, and he was kept on, informants believed, because he was obviously not especially self-seeking, and he had unique planning and entrepreneurial abilities that were in fact being used for the welfare of the brigade.

Sidelines

The River Brigade at this time directly controlled five sideline operations. A waste-collection station, amalgamating the former part-time businesses of several farmers, licensed individual waste collectors who bought usable metal, etc., and sold it to the station, which in turn sold it to a similar station at commune headquarters. A yarn-making workshop, operating on sub-contract to a yarn factory owned by commune headquarters, was busy enough throughout this period to give full-time employment to sixty or seventy brigade women. The brick and tile kiln mentioned above, collectivized and expanded from the kiln once owned by the economic management member, employed a number of full- and part-time artisans. During the early 1960's the kiln made so much profit that it enabled the brigade to set up a modern electrically powered sugarcane processing plant. The brigade thereafter delivered its sugar procurement quota to the State in the form of sugar rather than raw cane, being enabled thereby to retain a sugar-processing fee that amounted to about JMP 0.90 per 100 catties of cane. The cadres of the brigade estimated that this margin would permit them to amortize the investment, pay good wages to a number of brigade members, and hopefully still make a small net profit.

A tool and building repair station gave full-time employment to a number of men who had been at least part-time specialists in these trades before Liberation, at rates of pay sufficiently higher than those for agricultural labor to continue to attract new apprentices. After several abortive organizational experiments, the present station was formed in 1960 as a distinct sideline operation directly responsible to brigade headquarters. Its members worked for about half of each year on detached duty to the agricultural teams, repairing their tools and public buildings; and the rest of the year in or out of the station, making simple tools for units, or doing repair and construction work for individual brigade members. In all cases, contracts were drawn between the station and the unit or individual in question, who paid the station. Workers received piecework wages.

Agricultural Teams

By the early 1960's, redistricting had increased the number of the River Brigade's agricultural teams from 10 to 20, each of about 35 households and 170 members. Each had about the same ratio of workers to consumers, the same number of draft animals and tools, and lands of the same productivity, at least initially, though any differences among teams in the reproductive capacity of families, in luck, or in enterprise could of course be expected to restore inequality in all these factors within a few years.

The cadre of a team comprised a leader, one or more deputy leader(s), a recorder, a storekeeper, and normally two so-called "field-management members." All were elected at an annual meeting of team members, and could normally expect to be re-elected year after year. Though they clearly had to be acceptable to brigade cadres, who attended elections, few in the River Brigade's teams were either Party or

League members, and our informants stated that during this period political activism was not an important criterion for their selection. The tendency was for them to be individuals of "maturity" and local practical experience, who had the personal confidence of team members.

Correspondingly, although the team leader, like the brigade branch secretary, was in theory responsible for everything that happened in his team, these years saw him relatively uninvolved in political matters and busy primarily with the economy of his unit. Routine governmental functions, such as issuing various permits, tended to be handled directly between individuals and brigade cadres, while Party matters within the team were usually taken care of by whatever individuals happened to be Party or League members, in direct negotiations with Party cadres at brigade headquarters. Unlike the brigade cadres, the team leadership included no posts of specifically Party status, and none of the teams of the River Brigade had enough members for a distinct Party or League organization.

The increasingly complex economic organization of these years demanded that team cadres coordinate their activities closely with those of brigade leaders. Production, investment, and distribution plans had to be worked out as integral parts of brigade plans that, as we have seen, were frequently altered in the attempt to take maximum advantage of the changing economic situation. Credits could be obtained only through the brigade, and on its terms. The team received water and delivered taxes and quotas according to schedules given it by its brigade, and could get producer goods or engage in trades only as arranged by, and under the supervision of, brigade cadres. A host of records had to be kept and forwarded, and tools and animals had to be handled as brigade regulations required. Even real wages could be paid only as the brigade distribution plan allowed. For these reasons, more paperwork and more *ad hoc* consultations and formal meetings with brigade cadres were undoubtedly demanded of team leaders than ever before.

At the same time, the team leaders we talked to maintained that team cadres operated a great deal more independently during these years than ever before. So long as higher-level stipulations were observed, or once fairly mutualistic negotiations had produced a decision on principle that was at least minimally agreeable to the team leader, he was left pretty much alone to apply this principle in his own way.

Within what may appear to have been a surprisingly short time, team roles seem to have become specialized and stabilized. The leader himself came to take over most of the work of liaison with the brigade cadres and otherwise confined himself to supervision of his own cadre.

Field-management members, uniformly elected from among veteran farmers, acted as technical advisors both to the leader and, in constant inspections in the field, to farmers. Deputy leaders or field-management members came to supervise particular work-group sections of the farmers, on given fields, over a long period of time. The storekeeper controlled all large tools, considered to belong to the team as a whole, and kept records of all small tools owned by individual farmers; he repaired or arranged for the repair and replacement of all equipment, although farmers had to pay for this service in the case of tools they themselves owned. The recorder handled paperwork in the team office, and kept all records required by higher echelons, as well as the records—individual work points, etc.—needed within the organization, and, as we have noted, in a way that apparently obviated the many confusions and dissatisfactions that had been so prominent a feature of the early years of collectivization.

As the special skills and the amount of time required to be a cadre member came to be recognized, team cadres no longer spent much time—even if they were assigned as work-group leaders—in actual field labor, although in theory they should still have spent most of their time there. They continued to be paid in work points, mostly assigned for their cadre duties in such a manner that the team leader received a real income slightly above that of the highest-earning worker in his unit during the year, whereas the real income of other cadres would fall within the range received by other high-earning farmers. Thus, administration was in effect being rewarded as among the most valuable of the types of work available.

Team Labor Management

What crops were to be grown, what special techniques and imported producer goods were to be used, what work points were to be paid for each piece of labor, and the like were of course determined by team plans for production, investment, and other aspects of team endeavor, themselves coordinated with brigade plans. In the teams of the River Brigade, collective farming retained certain features of the traditional private economy while adopting a framework of collective supervision and reward or punishment.

The labor force of the team was divided into work groups of eight to ten households each, under a deputy team leader or an economic management member, whose own household normally belonged to the group. Each work group was given responsibility for certain fields, which it could expect to continue farming for an indefinite period.

Moreover, of these fields, certain ones were assigned for at least an entire growing season to a consortium that usually consisted of two friendly and cooperative households. Ideally, one of the two would have a deficiency and the other a surplus of labor. The consortium was responsible for all work on these fields except during the busy seasons of transplantation and harvest. Then the work group as a whole, under the personal direction of its leader, worked in rotation on the lands assigned to it. Otherwise, the consortium of households managed its own work, subject only to frequent inspection by the leader.

This system provided the reliable supply of group labor at busy seasons that farmers had never been able to count on in the old private economy, but under collective direction to ensure efficiency and proper credit in work points for actual work done. At the same time, for most of the round of field work, household independence and responsibility were retained, but within a collective framework of supervision and reward, including of course the supervision supplied informally by at least one other household in each consortium. It was argued locally that this system gave each household a considerable stake in good performance, since its effectiveness could be judged not simply by the hours put in or by such conditional criteria as the amount of land plowed, but by the success of the crop in that household's control, a criterion of accomplishment that would affect the work points assigned it by the group leader or its reassignment to better or worse fields in the future. It was also argued that, by giving the household control of its own labor force, this system allowed it to make use of young or old part-time labor that could not otherwise be tapped for either collective or private tasks, and to work at the times and speed most convenient to it without requiring the wasteful and often demeaning consultations with cadres, trips to the work-point recorder, and the like that full collective direction had necessitated. We should also note that there should be certain other results: skills, including low-level managerial skills, should become more important to the individual farmer's own self-image; and the solidarity and authority structure of the household should be reinforced.

Self-responsibility, within a framework of collective planning and supervision, was also substituted for the previous collective responsibility in other crucial tasks of the farming team. Procurement quotas for pork, fowl, and eggs, once assigned to the team as a whole, were now assigned directly to individual households. In fact, most consortiums tended animals jointly, and used a certain part of the produce of private plots, augmented by rations such as sweet-potato vines from the collective, to feed them.

Likewise, draft animals, still considered to belong to the team as a whole, were now assigned individually to given handlers, who might in consultation with the team cadre veto their use at a given time or in a given way, and who were responsible for the efficient use, the overall health, and the timely reproduction of the animals. Good handlers could earn a great many work points. Just as the production of pork and fowl increased markedly under the new system during this period, so too the numbers of healthy draft animals, which during the late 1950's had fallen into a serious decline, became adequate again.

It is conventional to say, and native critics have argued, that the system of the early 1960's contained greater opportunities for individual or household profits than had the previous system. Some of these opportunities were of course outside the collective economy—in the private plots, the free market as used by individuals, etc. Others, however, if the River Brigade was typical, were present now in the core of the collective economy. Higher-paying jobs could be had as cadres, as specialists with animals or in a brigade sideline. And the new field system that assigned to the household a wide measure of labor responsibility, with rewards and punishments to match, unquestionably worked to a degree in the same direction. Collective planning, allocation of productive resources, and control of work was still exercised—and, one might argue, more efficiently than under earlier, more thoroughly collective, systems. Furthermore, the free market and other higher-echelon facilities were used overwhelmingly more often by the collective unit than by the individual. Finally, the distribution of collective income was handled in a thoroughly collective manner.

Distribution

Since both teams and brigades were independently accountable during these years, and since there was also a small private economy, it will be useful to treat distribution separately for the three levels of unit normally involved—team, brigade, and household. The team was of course the principal unit of distribution. In this agricultural economy, the majority of all income accrued to the teams, and all residents of the commune, including sideline workers and brigade cadres other than the branch secretary, were attached to one or another team for the purpose of sharing in collective income.

A team's gross income comprised (1) the goods produced by some 96 or 97 percent of its lands (teams normally assigned only 3 to 4 percent, rather than the legal maximum of 5 percent, as private plots), which during these years consisted mainly of starch crops (rice and sweet potatoes, with some wheat and maize), sugarcane, peanuts, soybeans, and jute; (2) its share of the net profit of brigade sidelines; (3) its share of 5 percent of all non-agricultural taxes paid by brigade units and members, rebated by the State; and (4) a part of the wages paid to individual team members working as brigade cadres or in brigade sidelines.

From this income, it had theoretically to disburse 48 percent of its crops in payment of State exactions, but the State paid cash for that part of the exaction represented by surplus grains and non-starch procurement quotas. On the one hand, this payment was at rates somewhat below those paid on the free market for the same products, but, on the other hand, non-rice quota crops were normally of higher value than the rice that was called for in the unreimbursed public-grains quotas. In trying to estimate the real burden of exactions, one should also keep in mind that every year the State could change the relative quotas of the exacted crops, and could even alter the ratio between the unreimbursed public grains and the reimbursed surplus grains and thus alter the team's cash income. In general, the State reportedly tended to raise public-grains quotas in good years, and thus reduce team income from this source.

In consequence, after taxes a team theoretically had roughly 50 percent of the goods it had produced, plus cash equivalent to the value of perhaps another 25 percent of its production, plus the non-agricultural incomes already noted. In practice, it might also during the years in question augment its after-tax income by raising higher-yield crops than those called for in the plan, and by selling and bartering on the State or free markets, on which transactions, however, it had to pay an appreciable transactions tax.

From whatever its after-tax income might be, it was first required by the written plan to deposit certain sums—in kind (seed grains) or cash —in funds controlled by either itself or the brigade, to pay for its own non-wage costs of production, to provide some of the investment capital for brigade sidelines, and to contribute to welfare and higher-level administrative and social services. It must also, after each harvest, set aside enough starch and edible-oil crops to pay the basic population ration until the next harvest. As already noted, these disbursements together theoretically accounted for 35 percent of total crop production. The remainder of the unit's income was then available for distribution as the wages of labor.

Real wages were paid against work points, the monetary value of a work point being computed by dividing all work points earned by team members during the year into the monetary value of the income remaining after the disbursements noted above less the disbursement for basic rations. That is, rations were now treated as a part of wages, and must be earned. Thus, the value of all rations paid to all members of a household had to be paid for by work points earned by the laboring members of that household. Income still remaining after that debit was to be paid in cash to workers, corresponding to work points remaining to their credit at the year's end.

In the lean years after the failure of the Great Leap and until 1962, most teams had little more retained income than enough to pay the basic ration, which thus constituted the entire wages of labor. Even in good years, cadres are said to have been concerned by the numbers of households that, because of a labor deficiency or some kind of emergency, earned only enough work points to pay for the ration, if that. Welfare funds were of course used to tide such households over, but welfare grants reportedly seldom covered more than the barest subsistence needs. Moreover, welfare was invariably treated during these years as a loan, not a gift, to be repaid whenever the household should again be making enough work points to be able to do so.

After 1962, however, residual team income was said to have averaged enough to cover both rations and a minimally satisfactory living standard, if it were paid out entirely in wages as the plan of 1961 had prescribed. Naturally, there was considerable pressure from the farmers for this course of action. On the other hand, particularly in view of the availability of relatively more household income from private sources, there was considerable feeling among the cadres, and pressure from higher echelons, to use a good part of residual team income for more capital investment and more producer goods than had been envisaged by the written plan.

What resulted in the River Brigade, and apparently widely throughout South China, was a compromise. Most of the residual collective income was indeed treated as wages. However, these wages were never actually paid out, but were deposited in the households' savings accounts in the People's Bank, there to draw interest. The team then borrowed an amount equal to these deposits from the bank, at interest, and used it as development capital. The banking system would of course have been in difficulties if all the farmers had withdrawn their savings at once, but this possibility was effectively prevented by freezing individual savings for long periods (many uncharitable people said in perpetuity). A depositor could not withdraw any savings without written permission from the team leader and the brigade cashier. This permission was apparently granted only in cases of extreme household emergency, and even then only a certain proportion of the savings on record could be withdrawn.

Income at the disposition of brigade headquarters consisted in (1) the primarily cash income it received from its sidelines—after payment of a transactions tax to the State; (2) the rebate by the State of 5 percent of the non-agricultural taxes paid by all brigade units and members; and (3) the sums contributed by teams to brigade-controlled funds for welfare, administration, social services, and brigade sideline investment.

Out of this income, the brigade had to pay the costs of brigade side-lines, including both wages transferred to teams to which sideline workers belonged and sums invested in capital improvements; a further rebate to the several teams of most of the 5 percent of non-agricultural taxes received from the State; brigade cadre salaries and the other costs of brigade-level administrative and social services; a part of the welfare needs of team members; and a distribution to the teams of a part of the net profit of brigade sidelines. In this connection it should be noted that the sums received from the teams for brigade administration, social service, welfare, and sideline investment funds did not equal the amounts budgeted therefor by the brigade, so that it in effect also contributed a share to each of these costs out of its other sources of income, primarily the sidelines.

The brigade also seems to have been able to realize value, and in some cases real income, from its role as middleman between the teams and higher echelons, and, in connection with welfare, between the teams and their own members. Sums contributed by the teams to brigade-controlled funds were not necessarily disbursed immediately, and could on occasion be used by the brigade to draw interest, or to cover its own short-term operating deficits and save it the necessity of paying interest. Likewise, since the teams normally owed large operating debts to outside agencies or higher echelons that were settled through the brigade, brigade headquarters rarely in fact disbursed any goods or cash at all to the teams in settlement of its own debts to them, instead merely transferring accounts.

Our data are inadequate to determine whether the brigade made or lost money on such transfer operations. It is clear, however, that during the years in question the brigade adopted the same device with respect to sharing the net profits of the sidelines with the teams that the teams had used with respect to paying marginal wages to workers.

Team accounts were credited with the proper amounts, but the teams were rarely permitted to draw against them, the money instead being used for still further investment in sideline expansion.

As has been noted, during the years of the study a great majority of brigade households theoretically earned enough from their wages in the collective farm economy to provide at least a minimally decent standard of living. However, since part of these earnings was put into blocked savings accounts, it seems probable that the real income received from collective work did not quite support even such a standard, let alone the higher standard that the average household almost inevitably wished to have.

The private plots undoubtedly went far toward assuaging these desires. They contributed certain goods that could be sold in the free market for cash and a large part of the vegetables with which the farmer complemented his basic ration. In the River Brigade a marginal income that was very considerable, and perhaps as important for many households as that contributed by the private plots, came from other sources, most of them collective. Most important was the much higher wage paid for work in the brigade sideline operations than for an equal amount of work on the land. As we have noted, perhaps 20 percent of all workers in the brigade worked at least part time at these sideline jobs, and perhaps the majority of them were members of households that normally also worked the land. A part of the wages earned at sidelines was paid to teams, and no doubt was subject to the same forced-savings scheme as were agricultural wages. But a part of such wages was paid directly to the worker in cash, even though for accounting purposes it was credited to his team. What does seem clear is that such jobs were eagerly sought, and every sideline was said to have had a long waiting list for every opening.

Likewise, as already noted, procurement quotas for hogs and fowl were during this period assigned to individual households, which were paid what was considered a high price for pork, fowl, and eggs turned in to the State on quota, and an even higher price for amounts produced above quota. One result was a rapid improvement in the national supply of animal food products, and although this in turn produced a decline in prices, farmers did not, during the period of the study, reduce production. Instead, they themselves began to eat small amounts of these foods for a clear improvement in their living standard. The private plots of course produced an important part of the fodder used to raise these animals, but much of the fodder also came from scrap from the collective fields, and the major cost of production was simply the more productive use of the otherwise unbudgeted household labor of old people and children.

We were unable to collect exact budgets for any households. But it was apparent that simple processed foods and other manufactured household necessities were regularly available at the brigade supply and marketing cooperative and that during the latter part of the period of study farmers had begun to repair homes that had gone without repair for almost fifteen years. A primary school at brigade headquarters now took most of the children of the unit at a small cost to the parents, and a middle school at commune headquarters was available, although it attracted very few children from the River Brigade. A five-bed clinic was now available at brigade headquarters with a permanent corpsman and midwife, and doctors who came on duty tours from commune headquarters, where a larger hospital was available for serious illnesses. Radio provided some entertainment and much propaganda for anyone who wished to go to the brigade headquarters area to hear it, and traveling troupes from time to time brought the same mixture into the brigade area; at commune headquarters, there were recreational facilities for non-agricultural workers of the brigade, and some permanent exhibitions, movies, and the like for all. Travel outside the brigade was still difficult, and travel beyond commune headquarters almost impossible; and the local supply of newspapers and books was small and largely in the hands of Party or League members. But the living standard of the average farmer was once again perhaps supportable.

References

References

Introduction

Childe, V. Gordon. 1951. *Man Makes Himself*. New York: New American Library.

Elvin, Mark. 1970. "The Last Thousand Years of Chinese History: Changing Patterns in Land Tenure," *Modern Asian Studies* 4, 2: 97–114.

Geertz, Clifford. 1966. *Agricultural Involution, the Process of Ecological Change in Indonesia*. Berkeley: University of California Press (for the Association of Asian Studies).

Ho, Ping-ti, 1959. *Studies on the Population of China, 1368–1953*. Cambridge Mass.: Harvard University Press.

Ryan, Edward. 1961. The Value System of a Chinese Community in Java. Unpublished Ph.D. dissertation, Harvard University.

Skinner, G. William. 1964. "Marketing and Social Structure in Rural China," Part I, *Journal of Asian Studies* 24, 1 (November): 3–43.

Smelser, Neil J. 1963. *The Sociology of Economic Life*. Englewood Cliffs, N.J.: Prentice-Hall (Foundations of Modern Sociology Series, ed. Alex Inkeles).

Steward, Julian H. 1955. *Theory of Culture Change: The Methodology of Multilinear Evolution*. Urbana: University of Illinois Press.

The Organizational Capabilities of the Ch'ing State in the Field of Commerce: The Liang-huai Salt Monopoly, 1740–1840

Adshead, S. A. M. 1970. *The Modernization of the Chinese Salt Administration, 1900–1920*. Cambridge, Mass.: Harvard University Press.

Almond, Gabriel A., and G. Bingham Powell, Jr. 1966. *Comparative Politics*. Boston: Little, Brown.

Chou Tao-chi. 1964. *Han-T'ang tsai-hsiang chih-tu* (The institution of the prime office in the Han and T'ang dynasties). Taipei: Cultural Foundation of the Chia-hsin Cement Co.

Chou Wei-liang. 1963. "T'ao Wen-i kung kai-ko Liang-huai yen-wu k'ao-lüeh" (An outline of the master T'ao Chu's reform of Liang-huai salt affairs). *Yen-yeh t'ung-hsün*, 142: 9–11, 144: 13–15, 145: 11–12.

CSL: *Ta-Ch'ing li-ch'ao shih-lu* (The veritable records of the successive reigns of the great Ch'ing dynasty). Dai Manshū teikoku kokumu-in, 1937–38.

CTHPTL: *Ch'in-ting hu-pu tse-li* (Imperially endorsed regulations of the Board of Revenue). 1851.

Etzioni, Amitai. 1961. *A Comparative Analysis of Complex Organizations.* New York: Free Press of Glencoe.

Fu Tsung-mao. 1967. *Ch'ing-tai chün-chi-ch'u tsu-chih chi chih-chang chih yen-chiu* (A study of the functions and organization of the Grand Council of the Ch'ing dynasty). Taipei: Cultural Foundation of the Chia-hsin Cement Co.

Fujii Hiroshi. 1941. "Kaichū no imi oyobi kigen" (The meaning and origin of kaichū), in *Katō Hakuse kanreki kinen Tōyōshi shūsetsu* (Collected articles on oriental history in honor of Dr. Katō's sixty-first birthday). Tokyo: Tomiyama.

———. 1943. "Mindai enshō no ikkōsatsu" (A study of the salt merchants of the Ming dynasty), *Shigaku zasshi* 54, 5: 506–55, 6: 627–66, 7: 693–735.

———. 1952 and 1954. "Mindai enjō no kenkyū" (A study of the salt fields of the Ming dynasty). *Hokkaidō daigaku bungakubu kiyō*, 1: 65–100 (part 1); 3: 89–132 (part 2).

Hatano Yoshihiro. 1950. "Shindai Ryōwai seien ni okeru seisan soshiki" (The organization of production in the Liang-huai manufacture of salt during the Ch'ing period), *Tōyōshi kenkyū* 11, 1: 17–31.

HMCSWP: *Huang-Ming ching-shih wen-pien* (The august Ming dynasty's writings on statecraft), 30 vols. Compiled by Ch'en Tzu-lung *et al.* Taipei: Kuo-lien t'u-shu ch'u-pan yu-hsien kung-ssu (1964 reprint of an edition printed *c.* 1630–40).

Ho, Ping-ti. 1954. "The Salt Merchants of Yang-chou: A Study of Commercial Capitalism in Eighteenth-Century China," *Harvard Journal of Asiatic Studies* 17: 130–68.

Ho, Ping-ti. 1959. *Studies on the Population of China, 1368–1953.* Cambridge, Mass.: Harvard University Press.

Ho Wei-ning. 1966. *Chung-kuo yen-cheng-shih* (A history of China's salt administration). Taipei: Ho Lung Li-fen.

Hummel, Arthur W., ed. 1944. *Eminent Chinese of the Ch'ing Period,* 2 vols. Washington, D.C.: United States Government Printing Office.

King, F. H. H. 1965. *Money and Monetary Policy in China, 1845–1895.* Cambridge, Mass.: Harvard University Press.

LCYFC 1729: *Liang-che yen-fa-chih* (Salt laws gazetteer of the Liang-che zone). Taipei: Hsüeh-sheng shu-chü (1966 reprint of a 1792 reprint of an edition with preface dated winter of 1728–29).

LHYFC 1693: *Liang-huai yen-fa-chih* (Salt laws gazetteer of the Liang-huai zone). Taipei: Hsüeh-sheng shu-chü (1966 reprint of edition with preface of 1693).

LHYFC 1806: *Liang-huai yen-fa-chih* (Salt laws gazetteer of the Liang-huai zone). Yangchow (1870 reprint of a work completed in 1806).

LHYFC 1904: *Liang-huai yen-fa-chih* (Salt laws gazetteer of the Liang-huai zone).

Li Ch'eng. *Huai-ts'o pei-yao* (Essentials of Liang-huai salt affairs). Preface of 1823.

Metzger, T. A. 1962. "T'ao Chu's Reform of the Huaipei Salt Monopoly (1831–1833)," *Papers on China,* 16: 1–39.

———. 1970. "The State and Commerce in Imperial China," *Asian and African Studies* 6: 23–46.

———. In press. *The Internal Organization of Ch'ing Bureaucracy.* Cambridge, Mass.: Harvard University Press.

Pao Shih-ch'en. 1846. *An-wu ssu-chung.*

Pye, Lucian W. 1968. *The Spirit of Chinese Politics.* Cambridge, Mass.: M.I.T. Press.

Sa Meng-wu. 1965–66. *Chung-kuo she-hui cheng-chih-shih* (A social and political history of China), 4 vols. Taipei: Sa Meng-wu.

Saeki Tomi. 1962. *Shindai ensei no kenkyū* (A study of the salt administration of the Ch'ing dynasty). Kyoto: The Society of Oriental Researches, Kyoto University.

Salt: Production and Taxation. 1906. In *China. Imperial Maritime Customs.* V. (Office Series): *Customs Papers No. 81.* Shanghai: published by order of the Inspector General of Customs.

Selznick, Philip. 1949. *TVA and the Grass Roots.* Berkeley: University of California Press.

TCHTSL: *Ch'in-ting ta-Ch'ing hui-tien shih-li* (Imperially endorsed precedents and regulations supplementary to the collected statutes of the great Ch'ing dynasty). Taipei: Ch'i-wen ch'u-pan-she (1963 reprint of the 1899 edition).

Tseng Yang-feng. 1966. *Chung-kuo yen-cheng-shih* (A history of China's salt administration). Taipei: Taiwan Commercial Press.

TWI: *T'ao Wen-i kung ch'üan-chi* (The complete writings of the master T'ao Chu). Preface of 1840. Harvard-Yenching Library.

TYT: *T'ao Yün-ting hsien-sheng tsou-shu* (The memorials of the master T'ao Chu). Printed sometime after 1833. Harvard-Yenching Library.

Wang Shou-chi. 1872. "Yen-fa i-lüeh" (An outline of the salt system), in *P'ang-hsi-chai ts'ung-shu.*

Wei Yüan. 1839. *Ku-wei-t'ang nei-wai-chi.* Taipei district: Wen-hai ch'u-pan-she, 1964. (Wei Yüan's essay on Liang-huai, pp. 711–28, was mostly written *c.* 1839.)

Yamamura Jirō. 1942. "Shindai Ryōwai no sōko ippan" (An outline of the Liang-huai salt makers in the Ch'ing dynasty). *Shigaku zasshi,* 53, 7: 827–59 (part 1).

Yen Ken-wang. 1961. *Chung-kuo ti-fang hsing-cheng chih-tu-shih: chüan shang: Ch'in Han ti-fang hsing-cheng chih-tu* (A history of regional and local administration in China; Part 1: The Ch'in and Han periods). Taipei: Academia Sinica, Institute of History and Philology.

Finance in Ningpo: The 'Ch'ien Chuang,' 1750–1880

Arimoto Kunizō. 1931a. "Nimpō kachō seido no kenkyū" (A study of the Ningpo transfer-tael system), *Tōa keizai kenkyū* 15, 1–2 (April): 111–37.

————. 1931b. "Nimpō ni okeru kin'yū seido" (The monetary system at Ningpo), *Tōa keizai kenkyū* 15, 4 (October): 579–96.

Ashton, T. S. 1955. *An Economic History of England: The Eighteenth Century*. London: Methuen and Company.

Bergère, Marie-Claire. 1964. *Une crise financière à Shanghai à la fin de l'ancien régime*. Paris: Mouton.

Cameron, Rondo. 1967. *Banking in the Early Stages of Industrialization: A Study in Comparative Economic History*. New York: Oxford University Press.

Chang Chung-li. 1962. *The Income of the Chinese Gentry*. Seattle: University of Washington Press.

Chang, George H. 1938a. "A Brief Survey of Chinese Native Banks," *The Central Bank of China Bulletin* 4, 1: 25–32.

————. 1938b and 1939. "The Practices of Shanghai Native Banks," *The Central Bank of China Bulletin* 4, 4 (1938): 310–19; 5, 2 (1939): 134–42.

Chang Kuo-hui. 1963. "Shih chiu shih chi hou pan ch'i Chung-kuo ch'ien chuang ti mai pan hua" (The Chinese native banks as compradores in the latter half of the nineteenth century), *Li shih yen chiu* 6: 85–98.

Ch'en Ch'i-t'ien. 1937. *Shan-hsi p'iao chuang k'ao lüeh* (A brief historical study of the Shansi banks). Shanghai: Shang wu yin shu kuan.

Ch'in Jun-ch'ing. 1926. "Shang-hai chih ch'ien chuang shih yeh" (Banking in Shanghai) (as told to Han Tsu-te), *Ch'ien yeh yüeh pao* 6, 10 (November 19): 22–40.

Crawcour, Sydney. 1961. "The Development of a Credit System in Seventeenth-Century Japan," *Journal of Economic History* 21, 3 (September): 342–60.

Crissman, Lawrence W. 1967. "The Segmentary Structure of Urban Overseas Chinese Communities," *Man* n.s. 2, 2 (June): 185–204.

Elvin, Mark. 1969. "The Gentry Democracy in Chinese Shanghai, 1905–14," in Jack Gray, ed., *Modern China's Search for Political Form*. London: Oxford University Press.

Fairbank, John King. 1953. *Trade and Diplomacy on the China Coast: The Opening of the Treaty Ports, 1842–1854*. Cambridge, Mass.: Harvard University Press.

Ferguson, J. C. 1906. "Notes on the Chinese Banking System in Shanghai," *Journal of the North China Branch of the Royal Asiatic Society* 37: 55–82.

Feuerwerker, Albert. 1958. *China's Early Industrialization: Sheng Hsüan-huai and Mandarin Enterprise*. Cambridge, Mass.: Harvard University Press.

Freedman, Maurice. 1959. "The Handling of Money: A Note on the Background to the Economic Sophistication of the Overseas Chinese," *Man* 59, 89: 64–65.

Fu Lo-shu. 1966. *A Documentary Chronicle of Sino-Western Relations (1644–1820)*, 2 vols. Tucson: University of Arizona Press.

Fujita Toyohachi. 1917. "Sodai no shihakushi oyobi shihaku jorei" (The Superintendency of Merchant Shipping and regulations concerning it under the Sung dynasty), *Tōyō gakuhō* 7, 2: 159–246.

GBSP vols. 53 (1865), 71 (1866), 75 (1880), 91 (1881), 82 (1884), 80 (1884–85). Great Britain, Sessional papers, Commons.

Hall, John. 1949. "Notes on the early Ch'ing copper trade with Japan," *Harvard Journal of Asiatic Studies* 12: 441–61.

Hammond, Bray. 1957. *Banks and politics in America from the Revolution to the Civil War.* Princeton, N.J.: Princeton University Press.

Himeda Mitsuyoshi. 1957. "Chūgoku kindai gyogyōshi no hito koma—Kanpō hachi nen Kin ken no gyomin tōsō o megutte" (An incident in the recent history of the Chinese fishing industry: the fishermen's riot in Yin Hsien in 1858), in *Kindai Chūgoku nōson shakai shi kenkyū* (Studies in the recent history of rural Chinese society). Tokyo: Daian.

Hirohata Shigeru. 1933. *Shina kahei shi sensō kō* (A history of money in China, with an investigation of Chinese native banks). Tokyo: Kensetsu sha.

Ho, Ping-ti. 1954. "The salt merchants of Yang-chou," *Harvard Journal of Asiatic Studies* 17 (June): 130–68.

———. 1959. *Studies in the Population of China, 1368–1953.* Cambridge, Mass.: Harvard University Press.

———. 1964. *The Ladder of Success in Imperial China.* New York: Wiley, Science Editions.

———. 1967. "The significance of the Ch'ing period in Chinese history," *Journal of Asian Studies* 26, 2 (February): 189–95.

IMC: China, Imperial Maritime Customs, Decennial reports, 1882–1891; 1892–1901.

Ishihara Michihiro. 1964. *Wakō* (Pirates). Tokyo: Yoshikawa kōbunkan.

Kagawa Shun'ichirō. 1948. *Sensō shihon ron* (An essay on Chinese native banking capital). Tokyo: Jitsugyō no Nihon sha.

Katō Shigeshi. 1936. "Shindai ni okeru sonchin no teiki ichi" (Periodic marketing during the Ch'ing dynasty), *Tōyō gakuhō* 23, 2 (February): 153–204.

———. 1952–53. "Shindai ni okeru sempō sensō no hattatsu ni tsuite" (On the development of money shops and native banks during the Ch'ing dynasty), in Wada Sei *et al.*, *Shina keizai shi kōshō* (Studies in Chinese economic history) 2: 463–77. Tokyo: Toyo bunko.

Kimiya Yasuhiko. 1931. "Nisshi no kōtsūro" (Routes for the Sino-Japanese trade), *Rekishi chiri* 57, 4: 409–28.

King, Frank H. H. 1965. *Money and monetary policy in China, 1845–1895.* Cambridge, Mass.: Harvard University Press.

Kuo Hsiao-hsien. 1933. "Shang-hai ti ch'ien chuang" (Native banking in Shanghai), *Shang-hai shih t'ung chih kuan ch'i k'an* 3: 803–57.

Lo Jung-pang. 1954–55. "The emergence of China as a sea power during the late Sung and early Yüan periods," *Far Eastern Quarterly* 14: 489–503.

Lou Tsu-i. 1958. *Chung-kuo yu i shih liao* (Materials on the history of the Chinese postal service). Peking: Jen min yu tien ch'u pan she.

Matsuyoshi Sadao. 1932. *Nihon ryōgae kinyū shiron* (Historical essays on money-changing and banking in Japan). Tokyo: Bungei shunjusha.

Ming shih (A history of the Ming dynasty). Comp. by Chang T'ing-yü (1672–1755) *et al.*, 332 chüan. K'ai-ming edition.

Miyazaki Ichisada. 1950. "Chūgoku kinsei ni okeru seigyō shihon no taishaku ni tsuite" (The loan of funds for small trades in recent Chinese history), *Tōyōshi kenkyū* 11, 1 (September): 1–16.

Morse, H. B. 1890. "Abstract of information on currency and measures in China," *Journal of the North China Branch of the Royal Asiatic Society* 24: 46–135.

————. 1909. *The Guilds of China*. London: Longmans, Green, and Company.

Murphey, Rhoads. 1953. *Shanghai: Key to Modern China*. Cambridge, Mass.: Harvard University Press.

————. 1970. *The Treaty Ports and China's Modernization: What Went Wrong?* Ann Arbor: Michigan Papers in Chinese Studies, 7.

Negishi Tadashi. 1951. *Shanhai no girudo* (The guilds of Shanghai). Tokyo: Nippon hyoronsha.

Nishizato Yoshiyuki. 1967. "Shinmatsu no Nimpō shōnin ni tsuite" (On the Ningpo merchants at the end of the Ch'ing dynasty), *Tōyōshi kenkyū* 26, 1 (June): 1–29; 26, 2 (September): 71–89.

P'eng Hsin-wei. 1958. *Chung-kuo huo pi shih* (A history of money in China). Shanghai: Shang-hai jen min ch'u pan she.

Reischauer, Edwin O. 1940. "Notes on T'ang dynasty sea routes," *Harvard Journal of Asiatic Studies* 5, 2: 142–64.

SHCCSL. 1961. *Shang-hai ch'ien chuang shih liao* (Materials on the history of native banking in Shanghai). Shanghai: Shang-hai jen-min ch'u pan she.

Shiba Yoshinobu. In press. "Markets and the urban economic system: the case of Ningpo," in G. W. Skinner, ed., *The City in Late Imperial China*. Stanford: Stanford University Press.

Skinner, G. William. In press. "The City in Chinese Society," in G. W. Skinner, *The City in Late Imperial China*. Stanford: Stanford University Press.

SKZS. *Shina keizai zensho* (The Chinese economy: a compendium). Tokyo: Tōa dōbunkai, 1907–1908.

SSZ. 1919. *Shina shōbetsu zenshi* (A comprehensive gazetteer of the provinces of China), 13. Tokyo: Tōa dōbun shoin, 1919.

Smith, Thomas C. 1955. *Political Change and Industrial Development in Japan: Government Enterprise, 1868–1880* (Stanford: Stanford University Press.

Soyeda, Juichi. 1896. "A History of Banking in Japan," in *A History of Banking in All the Leading Nations*. New York: The Journal of Commerce and Commercial Bulletin 4: 407–544.

Spence, Jonathan. 1969. *To Change China: Western Advisers in China, 1620–1960*. Boston: Little, Brown.

Stanley, C. John. 1961. *Late Ch'ing Finance: Hu Kuang-yung As an Innovator*. Cambridge, Mass.: Harvard University Press.

Suzuki Chūsei. 1952. *Shinchō chūki shi kenkyū* (A study of the mid-Ch'ing period). Toyohashi: Aichi Daigaku kokusai mondai kenkyū jō.

Tamagna, Frank M. 1942. *Banking and finance in China*. New York: Institute of Pacific Relations.

Tomita Shigeaki. n.d. The Land Tax Revolt of Chinese Peasants in Yin Hsien, Chekiang, in 1852 and an Analysis of Its Causes. Unpublished master's essay, Columbia University.

Toyama Gunji. 1945. "Shanhai no shinshō Yan Bō" (Yang Fang, a merchant-official of Shanghai), *Tōyōshi kenkyū*, 9, 4 (November): 17–34.

Tsunoda Ryusaku, tr. 1951. *Japan in the Chinese dynastic histories: Later*

Han through Ming dynasties, ed. L. C. Goodrich. South Pasadena: P. D. and Ione Perkins.

Tuan Kuang-ch'ing (1798–1878). 1968. *Ching-hu tzu hsüan nien p'u* (An autobiography by Tuan Kuang-ch'ing). Tokyo: Daian.

Usher, Abbott Payson. 1943. *The Early History of Deposit Banking in Mediterranean Europe*, vol. 1. Cambridge: Harvard University Press.

Wang Erh-min. 1969. The History and Impact of the Practice of Borrowing Foreign Troops in the Yangtze Valley, 1860–1864: The Key to the Critical Changes in the Early Stages of the Opening of Shanghai as a Trade Port. Unpublished paper presented at the East Asian Research Center, Harvard University, March 1969.

Wang Hsiao-t'ung. 1933. *Chung-kuo shang-yeh shih* (A history of commerce in China). Shanghai: Shang-wu yin shu kuan.

Wang Yi-t'ung. 1953. *Official Relations Between China and Japan, 1368–1549*. Cambridge, Mass.: Harvard University Press.

Wagel, Srinivas R. 1915. *Chinese Currency and Banking*. Shanghai: *North China Daily News and Herald*.

Ward, Barbara E. 1967. "Cash or Credit Crops? An Examination of Some Implications of Peasant Commercial Production with Special Reference to the Multiplicity of Traders and Middlemen," in Jack M. Potter *et al.*, eds., *Peasant Society: A Reader*. Boston: Little, Brown.

"Why Chinese native banks are more powerful than modern banks," *Chinese Economic Bulletin*, 8, 264 (March 13, 1926): pp. 134–35.

Wright, Mary C. 1966. *The Last Stand of Chinese Conservatism: The T'ung-chih Restoration, 1862–1874*. Atheneum reprint: Stanford University Press.

Yamawaki Teijiro. 1960. *Kinsei Nitchū bōeki shi no kenkyū* (A study of the history of modern Sino-Japanese trade). Tokyo: Yoshi kawa kōbunkan.

Yang Lien-sheng. 1952. *Money and Credit in China: A Short History*. Cambridge, Mass.: Harvard University Press.

Yang Tuan-liu. 1962. *Ch'ing tai huo pi chin jung shih kao* (A draft history of currency and money in China). Peking: Sheng huo tu shu hsin chih san lien shu tien.

YHTC. 1936. *Yin hsien t'ung chih* (A comprehensive gazetteer of Yin Hsien) comp. by Ch'en Hsün-cheng *et al.*, *Shih huo chih* (Monograph on trades and livelihood), vol. 3, *ts'e* 10, *ts'e* 13.

Sericulture and Silk Textile Production in Ch'ing China

Allen, G. C., and Audrey G. Donnithorne. 1954. *Western Enterprise in Far Eastern Economic Development: China and Japan*. London: Allen and Unwin.

CCTL: *Ch'ing Shih lu ching chi tzu liao chi yao.* (Economic information selected from the *Ch'ing Shih lu*). 1958. Edited by Department of History, Nankai University. Shanghai: Chung hua shu chü.

Chang Hsing-fu. 1774. *Ch'an shih yao lueh* (Essentials of sericulture), vol. 361. Ssu pu pei yao edition (Taipei edition, 1965).

Ch'en Heng-li. 1958. *Pu Nung shu yen chiu* (A study of Shen's *Book of Agriculture*, Amended). Peking: Chung hua shu chü.

Chin Yu-li, ed. n.d. *T'ai-hu pei k'ao* (The Lake T'ai Region). n.p., edition published in the Ch'ien-lung period.

Chu Kuo-chen. n.d. *Yung chuang hsiao p'in* (Notes from the Yung-chuang Pavilion). n.p., edition from the T'ien-ch'i period, 1621–27.

Ch'ü Tui-chih. 1945. *Jen wu feng su chih tu ts'ung t'an* (Miscellany on persons, customs, and institutions). Hong Kong: Lung men shu tien (reprint of Shanghai 1945 edition).

Ch'üan Han-sheng. 1957. "Mei chou pai yin yü shih pa shih chi Chung kuo wu chia ko ming ti kuan hsi" (American silver and the price revolution in China during the eighteenth century). *Bulletin of the Institute of History and Philology*, Academia Sinica, 28 (May): 517–50.

Ch'üan Han-sheng and Y. C. Wang. 1961. "Ch'ing tai jen k'ou ti pien tung" (Population changes in China during the Ch'ing dynasty). *Bulletin of the Institute of History and Philology*, Academia Sinica, 32: 139–80.

CR: *The Chinese Repository*. 1832–51. Canton (Tokyo reprint edition, 1967).

Cranmer-Byng, J. L., ed. 1962. *An Embassy to China: Being the Journal Kept by Lord Macartney During His Embassy to the Emperor Ch'ien-lung, 1793–1794*. London: Longmans.

Fortune, Robert. 1852. *A Journey to the Tea Countries of China*. London: John Murray.

Fu I-ling. 1956. *Ming Ch'ing shih tai shang jen chi shang yeh tzu pen* (Merchants and commercial capital during the Ming and Ch'ing periods). Peking: Jen min ch'u pan she.

HCCTLT: *Huang ch'ao cheng tien lei tsuan* (Records on the public policies of the Ch'ing dynasty). 1903. Edited by Hsi Yü-fu. Shanghai (Taipei reprint edition, 1969).

Hedde, Isidore. 1845. "An Excursion to the City of Suchau in the Autumn of 1845." *Chinese Repository*, vol. 14, pp. 36–37.

————. 1848. "A Passage Along the Broadway River from Canton to Macao —[A] Description of the Silk Industry of Shunte," *Chinese Repository*, 17: pp. 427–28.

Ho, Ping-ti. 1959. *Studies on the Population of China, 1368–1953*. Cambridge, Mass.: Harvard University Press.

Hou, Chi-min. 1965. *Foreign Investment and Economic Development in China 1840–1937*. Cambridge, Mass.: Harvard University Press.

IMC: Imperial Maritime Customs. 1906. *Decennial Reports 1892–1901*. Shanghai: Inspectorate General of Customs.

KCTSCC: *Ku chin t'u shu chi ch'eng* (The great compendium of published works in China since ancient times). 1964. Taipei: Wen Hsing shu tien reprint.

Kuang-chou fu chih (Gazetteer of Canton Prefecture). 1879. Compiled by Jui-lin *et al.* Taipei reprint, 1967.

Li Chien-nung. 1957. *Sung Yüan Ming ching chi shih kao* (Draft economic history of the Sung, Yuan, and Ming dynasties). Peking: San lien shu tien.

LSTL: Shih Chang-ju *et al.* 1961. *Chung Kuo li shih ti li* (An historical geography of China). Taipei: Chung hua wen hua ch'u pan shih yeh she.

Lu-an fu chih (Gazetteer of Lu-an Prefecture). 1770. Compiled by O-pao *et al.*

Morse, H. B. 1925. *The Chronicles of the East India Company Trading to China 1635–1834*. Oxford: Oxford University Press (Taipei reprint edition, 1966).

Nung sang chi yao (Essential information on agriculture and sericulture). n.d. Compiled by Yuan Dynasty Bureau of Agriculture. Ssu pu pei yao edition (Taipei reprint edition, 1965, vol. 361).

NYS: *Chung Kuo chin tai nung yeh shih tzu liao* (Source material on the history of agriculture in modern China). 1957. Edited by Li Wen-chih. Peking: Research Institute of Economics, Chinese Academy of Sciences.

P'eng Hsin-wei. 1958. *Chung kuo huo pi shih* (A history of money and currency in China). Second Edition. Shanghai: Jen min ch'u pan she.

P'eng Tse-i, ed. 1957. *Chung kuo chin tai shou kung yeh shih tzu liao* (Source materials on the history of handicraft industries of modern China), vol. 1. Peking: San lien shu tien.

P'eng Tse-i. 1963. "Ch'ing tai ch'ien ch'i Chiang nan chih tsao ti yen chiu" (A study of the Imperial Silkworks in the early Ch'ing). *Li shih yen chiu*, 4: 91–116.

PKTL: *Chiang su sheng Ming Ch'ing i lai pei k'o tzu liao hsuan chi* (Selected stone-inscription source materials in Kiangsu since Ming and Ch'ing times). 1959. Edited by Kiangsu Provincial Museum. Peking: San lien shu tien.

Shih Min-hsiung. 1968. *Ch'ing tai ssu chih kung yeh ti fa chan* (The development of the silk textile industry in the Ch'ing period). Taipei: Commercial Press.

Shun-te hsien chih (Gazetteer of Shun-te District). 1929. Compiled by Ho Tsao-hsiang *et al.* Taipei reprint edition, 1966.

Spence, Jonathan D. 1966. *Ts'ao Yin and the K'ang-hsi Emperor: Bondservant and Master.* New Haven: Yale University Press.

Sun Yü-t'ang, ed. 1957. *Chung kuo chin tai kung yeh shih tzu liao* (Source materials on the history of modern industries in China). First series: 1840–1895, vol. 1. Shanghai: K'o hsueh ch'u pan she.

Sung Hsi-hsiang. 1947. *Chung kuo li tai ch'üan nung k'ao* (An enquiry into the promotion of agriculture in Chinese history). Shanghai: Cheng chung shu chü.

Ta Ch'ing hui tien shih li (Precedents of the Statutes of Ch'ing). 1886. Taipei reprint edition, 1963.

TPCIMY: *Chung Kuo tzu pen chu i meng ya wen t'i t'ao lun chi* (Essays on the question of incipient capitalism in China). 1957 (second collection, 1960). Compiled by Department of Chinese History, People's University of China. Peking: San lien shu tien.

Wang Chung-min, ed. 1963. *Hsü Kuang-ch'i chi* (Collected writings of Hsü Kuang-ch'i). Shanghai: Chung hua shu chü.

Yabuuchi Kyoshi [Yabuuti], ed. 1967. *Sō Gen jidai no kagaku gijutsu shi* (History of science and technology in the Sung and Yuan periods). Kyoto: Kyoto University.

Yü chih keng chih t'u (Pictorial descriptions of agriculture and sericulture). 1879. By Imperial Commission; original preface 1696. Shanghai: Tien chih tsai.

Cotton Culture and Manufacture in Early Ch'ing China

Amano Motonosuke. 1954a, b, and c. "*Nō sō shū yō* to monsaku no tenkai" (The *Summary of agriculture and sericulture* and the development of cotton culture), *Tōyō gakuhō* 37: (June) 1–45, (Sept.) 61–94, (Dec.) 52–84.

Buck, John Lossing. 1937. *Land Utilization in China*, vol. I. Nanking: University of Nanking.

Ch'i-hsia hsien chih. 1754. (Ch'i-hsia *hsien* gazetteer).

Chia-ting hsien chih. 1882. (Chia-ting *hsien* gazetteer).

Chu-ching chih. 1802. (Gazetteer for Chu-ching).

Ch'u Hua. 1937. *Mu mien p'u* (Treatise on cotton), in *Ts'ung shu chi ch'eng.* Changsha: Shang wu yin shu kuan.

Ch'üan Han-sheng. 1958. "Ya p'ien chan cheng ch'ien Chiang-su ti mien fang chih yeh" (The pre–Opium War Kiangsu cotton textile industry), *Tsing Hua Journal of Chinese Studies*, N.S. 1 (Sept.): 25–32.

Cook, J. Gordon. 1964. *Handbook of Textile Fibers*. Watford, England: Merrow Publishing Company.

Dietrich, Craig. 1970. Cotton Manufacture and Trade in China (*ca.* 1500–1800). Unpublished Ph.D. dissertation, University of Chicago.

Fang Kuan-ch'eng. 1809. *Mien hua t'u* (Illustrations of cotton), in *Shou i kuang hsün*, in *Hsi yung hsuan ts'ung shu*, block-print edition.

Fu I-ling. 1963. *Ming tai Chiang-nan shih min ching chi shih t'an* (Essay on the economy of urban dwellers in Kiangnan in the Ming). Shanghai: Jen min ch'u pan she.

Gamble, Sidney D. 1954. *Ting Hsien: A North China Rural Community*. New York: Institute for Pacific Relations. (Reissued in 1968 by Stanford University Press.)

Ho Ch'ang-ling. 1963. *Huang ch'ao ching shih wen pien* (Collected documents of Ch'ing administration). Taipei: Kuo feng ch'u pan she.

Hommel, Rudolf P. 1937. *China at Work*. New York: John Day.

Hsing-t'ang hsien chih. 1763. (Hsing-t'ang *hsien* gazetteer).

Hsü Kuang-ch'i. 1837. *Nung cheng ch'üan shu* (Complete book of agricultural management), block-print edition.

Hua-t'ing hsien chih. 1521. (Hua-t'ing *hsien* gazetteer).

Huang Ang. 1896. *Hsi Chin shih hsiao lu* (Record of miscellany in Wu-hsi and Wu-chin counties), block-print edition.

Jui-an hsien chih. 1809. (Jui-an *hsien* gazetteer).

Kissel, Mary L. 1918. *Yarn and Cloth Making*. New York: Macmillan.

Lu Jung. 1936. *Shu yuan tsa chi* (Vegetable garden miscellany), in *Ts'ung shu chi ch'eng*. Shanghai: Shang wu yin shu kuan.

Nash, Manning. 1964. "The Organization of Economic Life," in Sol Tax, *Horizons of Anthropology*. Chicago: Aldine.

Needham, Joseph. 1965. *Science and Civilization in China*, vol. 4, part 2. Cambridge: Cambridge University Press.

Nishijima Sadao. 1966. *Chūgoku keizaishi kenkyū* (A study of Chinese economic history). Tokyo: Tōkyō daigaku shuppan kai.

Schafer, Edward H. 1963. *The Golden Peaches of Samarkand*. Berkeley: University of California Press.

Shih Hung-ta. 1957. "Shih lun Sung Yuan Ming san tai mien fang chih sheng ch'an kung chü fa chan ti li shih kuo ch'eng" (A discussion of the historical stages in the development of cotton textile technology in the Sung, Yuan, and Ming dynasties), *Li shih yen chiu* no. 4: 19, 35–42.

Ssu-ma Kuang. 1927. *Tzu chih t'ung chien* (Comprehensive mirror for aiding government), in *Ssu pu pei yao*. Shanghai: Chung hua shu chü.

Sun, E-tu Zen. 1966. *T'ien-kung k'ai-wu; Chinese Technology in the Seventeenth Century*. University Park: Pennsylvania State University Press.

Sung-chiang fu chih. 1663. (Sung-chiang prefectural gazetteer).

Sung Po-yin. 1962. "Ts'ung Han hua hsiang shih t'an so Han tai chih chi kou tsao" (The looms of the Han period as revealed by Han stone reliefs). *Wen wu* 3: 26–27.

Sung Ying-hsing. 1955. *T'ien kung k'ai wu* (The natural and artificial origins of things). Taipei: Chung hua shu chü.

Te-p'ing hsien chih. 1796. (Te-p'ing *hsien* gazetteer).

Teng-chou fu chih. 1674. (Teng-chou prefectural gazetteer).

Terada Takanobu. 1958. "So Shō chihō ni okeru toshi no mengyō shōnin ni tsuite" (Merchants in the urban cotton industry in Soochow and Sung-chiang prefectures), *Shirin* 41, 6: 56–68.

Ubukata Naokichi. 1939. "Nankin momen kōbōshi" (History of the rise and decline of nankeens), *Tōa ronsō* 1 (July).

Wang Chen. 1956. *Nung shu* (Book of agriculture). Peking: Chung hua shu chü.

Wu Ch'eng-lo. 1957. *Chung-kuo t'u liang heng shih* (A history of Chinese weights and measures). Shanghai: Shang-wu yin shu kuan.

Yabuuchi Kiyoshi *et al.* 1959. '*T'ien kung k'ai wu*' *yen chiu lun wen chi* (Collected studies on *The natural and artificial origins of things*), trans. Chang T'ai and Wu Hsien. Peking: Shang-wu yin shu kuan.

Yen Chung-p'ing. 1963. *Chung-kuo mien fang chih shih kao* (Draft history of cotton manufacture in China). Peking: K'o hsueh ch'u pan she.

Yokoyama Suguru. 1960; 1961. "Shindai ni okeru tambugyō no keiei keitai" (Structure of the cotton calendering industry in the Ch'ing period). *Tōyōshi Kenkyū* 19: (Dec. 1960) 23–36; (Mar. 1961) 19–36.

Yü Ching-jang. 1954a, b, and c. "Ming Li Shih-chen Pen ts'ao kang mu mu mien hsiang chien shih" (Comments and explanation concerning the "cotton" entry in the *Materia Medica and Commentary* by Li Shih-chen of the Ming period), *Ta lu tsa chih*, 9: (Sept. 15) 1–4; (Sept. 30) 26–29; (Oct. 15) 14–20.

The High-Level Equilibrium Trap: The Causes of the Decline of Invention in the Traditional Chinese Textile Industries

Amano Motonosuke. 1967. "Gen no Ō Jō 'Nōsho' no kenkyū" (The *Treatise on Agriculture* by Wang Chen of the Yuan Dynasty), in Yabuuchi 1967a: 341–468.

Baines, Edward. 1835. *A History of the Cotton Manufacture of Great Britain*. London: Fisher, Fisher and Jackson.

Carter, Thomas F. 1925. *The Invention of Printing in China and Its Spread Westward*. New York: Columbia University Press.

Chang Ch'un-hua. 1839. *Hu ch'eng sui shih ch'ü ko* (Street songs on the year's activities in Shanghai), in Shang-hai t'ung she, ed., *Shang-hai chang ku ts'ung shu* (Collected historical materials relating to Shang-hai). 1936. Shanghai: Chung hua shu chü.

Chu Hua. (Mid-eighteenth century). *Mu mien p'u* (Cotton Manual), in *Shang-hai chang ku ts'ung shu* (see preceding entry).

Ch'üan Han-sheng. 1958. "Ya p'ien chan cheng ch'ien Chiang-su ti men fang chih yeh" (The cotton textile industry in Kiangsu before the Opium War), *Tsinghua Journal of Chinese Studies* 1, 3: 25–32.

Defoe, Daniel, and S. Richardson. 1753. *A Tour Thro' the Whole Island of Great Britain* . . . , 4 vols. London (first edition 1727).

Diderot, Denis, ed. 1765. *Encyclopédie ou dictionnaire raisonné des Sciences, des Arts et des Métiers* . . . , t. vi. Neufchastel: S. Faulche.

Elvin, Mark. 1970. "The Last Thousand Years of Chinese History. Changing Patterns in Land Tenure," *Modern Asian Studies* 4, 2: 97–114.

———. Forthcoming. "Market Towns and Waterways. The County of Shang-hai from 1480–1910," in G. W. Skinner, ed., *The City in Late Imperial China*. Stanford: Stanford University Press.

Franke, Herbert. 1949. *Geld und Wirtschaft in China unter der Mongolen-Herrschaft*. Leipzig: Otto Harrassowitz.

Fu I-ling. 1956. *Ming Ch'ing shih tai shang jen chi shang yeh tzu pen* (Merchants and mercantile capital in the Ming and Ch'ing periods). Peking: Jen min ch'u pan she.

———. 1963. *Ming tai Chiang-nan shih min ching chi shih t'an* (The economy of the urban population of Kiangnan during the Ming Dynasty). Shanghai: Shang-hai jen min ch'u pan she.

Fujii Hiroshi. 1953. "Shin-an shōnin no kenkyū" (The merchants of Hsin-an), part 1, *Tōyō gakuhō* 6, 1.

Hartwell, Robert. 1962. "A Revolution in the Chinese Iron and Coal Industries during the Northern Sung, 960–1126 A.D.," *Journal of Asian Studies* 21, 2.

———. 1966. "Markets, Technology, and the Structure of Enterprise in the Development of the Eleventh-Century Chinese Iron and Steel Industry," *Journal of Economic History* 26, 1.

———. 1967. "A Cycle of Economic Change in Imperial China: Coal and Iron in Northeast China, 750–1350," *Journal of the Economic and Social History of the Orient*, 10.

Hatano Yoshihiro. 1961. *Chūgoku kindai kōgyō shi no kenkyū* (Studies on early modern industry in China). Kyoto: Tōyōshi kenkyū kai.

Ho, Ping-ti. 1959. *Studies on the Population of China, 1368–1953*. Cambridge, Mass.: Harvard University Press.

Hsu Kuang-ch'i. 1639. *Nung cheng ch'üan shu* (Complete treatise on agriculture). Citations from Shanghai edition of 1843 or Chung hua shu chü reprint of 1956.

Imura Kōzen. 1936–37. "Chihō-shi ni kisaiseraretaru Chūgoku ekirei ryakkō" (A summary of Chinese epidemics as recorded in local gazetteers), *Chūgai i ji shimpō* (1936) 6–12, (1937) 1.

Iwama Kazuo. 1968. *Chūgoku seiji shisō shi kenkyū* (Studies in the history of Chinese political thought). Tokyo: Miraisha.

Katō Shigeshi. 1953. *Shina keizai shi kōshō* (Studies in Chinese economic history), 2 vols. Tokyo: Tōyō bunko.

Koizumi Teizō. 1943. "Shina minsen no keiei ni tsuite" (The management of junks in China), *Keizai ronsō* 57.

Li Chien-nung. 1957. *Sung Yuan Ming ching chi shih kao* (A draft economic history of the Sung, Yuan and Ming Dynasties). Peking: San-lien shu-tien.

Li Ch'ung-chou. 1959. "Shih chieh shang tsui tsao ti shui li fang chi ch'e— shui chuan ta fang ch'e" (The world's first water-powered spinning machine), *Wen wu ts'an k'ao liao*, 12.

Li Wen-yao, ed. 1750. *Shang-hai hsien chih* (Shang-hai *hsien* gazetteer). Shanghai.

Loehr, Max. 1964. "Some Fundamental Issues in the History of Chinese Painting," *Journal of Asian Studies* 23, 2.

Miyazaki Ichisada. 1943. *Gōdai sōshu no tsūka mondai* (The currency problem during the Five Dynasties and the early Sung). Tokyo: Hoshino shoten.

———. 1957. "Sōdai ni okeru sekitan to tetsu" (Coal and iron in the Sung Dynasty), *Tōhōgaku* 13.

Nakahara Teruo. 1959. "Shindai sōsen ni yoru shōhin ryūtsū ni tsuite" (The flow of commodities on the grain transport ships during the Ch'ing dynasty), *Shigaku kenkyū* 72.

Needham, Joseph, and L. Wang. 1959. *Science and Civilisation in China*, vol. 3. Cambridge: Cambridge University Press.

———. 1965. *Science and Civilisation in China*, vol. 4, part 2. Cambridge: Cambridge University Press.

Nishijima Sadao. 1947. "Shina shoki mengyō shijō no kōsatsu" (The early Chinese cotton market), *Tōyō gakuhō* 31, 2.

———. 1948. "Mindai ni okeru kiwata no fukyū ni tsuite" (The spread of the cotton plant during the Ming Dynasty), *Shigaku zasshi* 57, 4 and 5.

———. 1966. *Chūgoku keizai shi kenkyū* (Studies in the economic history of China). Tokyo: Tōkyō daigaku shuppan kai.

Schmookler, Jacob. 1966. *Invention and Economic Growth*. Cambridge, Mass.: Harvard University Press.

Shen Kua. 1086–91. *Meng ch'i pi t'an* (Dream pool essays). Taiwan: Shang wu yin shu kuan reprint of 1965.

Shiba Yoshinobu. 1968. *Sōdai shōgyō shi kenkyū* (Commerce in the Sung Dynasty). Tokyo: Kazama shobō.

Smith, D. E., and Y. Mikami. 1914. *A History of Japanese Mathematics*. Chicago: Open Court.

Sudō Yoshiyuki. 1954. *Chūgoku tochi seido shi kenkyū* (Studies in the history of land tenure systems in China). Tokyo: Tōkyō daigaku shuppan kai.

———. 1962. *Sōdai keizai shi kenkyū* (Studies in the economic history of the Sung dynasty). Tokyo: Tōkyō daigaku shuppan kai.

Sung Ying-hsing. 1637. *T'ien-kung k'ai-wu: Chinese Technology in the Seventeenth Century*. Translated by E-tu Zen and S. C. Sun. 1966. University Park: Pennsylvania State University Press.

Terada Takanobu. 1958. "Sō-Shō chihō ni okeru toshi no mengyō shōnin ni tsuite" (The cotton merchants of the cities of the Soochow and Sungchiang region), *Shirin* 41, 6.

Twitchett, Denis. 1963. *Financial Administration under the T'ang Dynasty*. Cambridge: Cambridge University Press.

Wang Chen. 1313. *Nung shu*. (Treatise on agriculture).

Wang Ch'i. 1609. *San ts'ai t'u hui* (Universal encyclopedia).

Yabuuchi Kiyoshi. 1967a. "Sō-Gen jidai no sūgaku" (Mathematics in the Sung and Yuan period), in Yabuuchi 1967b: 53–88.

Yabuuchi Kiyoshi, ed. 1967b. *Sō-Gen jidai no kagaku gijutsu shi* (Science and technology in the Sung and Yuan period). Kyoto: Kyōto daigaku jimbun kagaku kenkyūjo.

Yamaguchi Michiko. 1958. "Shindai no sōun to senshō" (The transport of the tribute grain and shipping merchants under the Ch'ing), *Tōyōshi kenkyū* 17, 2.

Yang, Lien-sheng. 1952. *Money and Credit in China.* Cambridge, Mass.: Harvard University Press.

Yeh Meng-chu. (Late seventeenth century). *Yueh shih pien* (A survey of the age), in *Shang-hai chang ku ts'ung shu.* (See Chang Ch'un-hua.)

Yokoyama Suguru. 1960–61. "Shindai ni okeru tambugyō no keiei keitai" (The management structure of the calendering industry during the Ch'ing), *Tōyōshi kenkyū* 19, 3 (1960) and 4 (1961).

Yoshida Mitsukuni. 1966. "Sōdai no tetsu ni tsuite" (Iron in the Sung Dynasty), *Tōyōshi kenkyū* 24, 4.

―――. 1967. "Sōdai no seisan gijutsu" (Techniques of production in the Sung dynasty), in Yabuuchi 1967b: 235–78.

The Commercialization of Agriculture in Modern China

Amano, Motonosuke. 1962. *Chūgoku nōgyōshi kenkyū* (Studies of Chinese agricultural history). Tokyo: Nōgyō sōgō kenkyū.

Blyth, Conrad A. 1969. "Primitive South Pacific Economies: Their Consumption Pattern and Propensity To Save Out of Cash Income," *The Economic Record* 45, 111 (September): 352–65.

Boserup, Ester. 1965. *The Conditions of Agricultural Growth.* Chicago: Aldine.

Buck, John L. 1930. *The Chinese Farm Economy.* Chicago: University of Chicago Press.

―――. 1937a. *Land Utilization in China.* Chicago: University of Chicago Press.

―――. 1937b. *Land Utilization in China: Statistics.* Chicago: University of Chicago Press.

Ch'en Pai-chuang. 1936. *P'ing Han yen hsien nung ts'un ching chi tiao ch'a.* (A survey of the village economy along the Peking–Hankow railroad). Shanghai: Chung hua shu chü.

Cheng, Yu-kwei. 1956. *Foreign Trade and Industrial Development of China.* Washington, D.C.: The University Press of Washington, D.C.

Chiao, Chi-ming, and Buck, John L. 1928. "The Composition and Growth of Rural Population Groups in China," *Chinese Economic Journal* 2, 3 (March): 219–35.

Chūgoku nōson kankō chōsa kankōkai. 1957. *Chūgoku nōson kankō chōsa* (An investigation of Chinese village customs), vol. 5. Tokyo: Iwanami Shoten.

Department of Agriculture and Forestry, Taiwan Provincial Government. 1952. *Nung chia ching chi tiao ch'a pao kao* (Report on the investigation of the farm economy for rice- and miscellaneous-cropping farm families). Taipei: Taiwan Provincial Government.

Department of Agriculture and Forestry, Taiwan Provincial Government.

1962. *Taiwan nung chia chi chang pao kao* (A report of farm-record-keeping families in Taiwan). Taipei: Taiwan Provincial Government.

Feng Ho-fa, ed. 1936. *Chung kuo nung ts'un ching chi tzu liao* (Materials on the Chinese farm economy), vols. 1 and 2. Shanghai: Li ming shu chü.

Gamble, Sidney, D. 1945. "Four Hundred Chinese Farms," *The Far Eastern Quarterly*, 14, 4 (August 1945): 341–66.

Hoku-Shi jimmukyoku chōsabu. 1939. *Shōwa jūni nendō nōka keizai chōsa hōkoku* (A survey report of the farm household economy for 1937). Peking: South Manchurian Railway Company.

————. 1941. *Shōwa jūyon nendō nōka keizai chōsa hōkoku* (A survey report of the farm household economy for 1939). Peking: South Manchurian Railway Company.

Hsieh, S. C., and Lee, T. C. 1958. *An Analytical Review of Agricultural Development in Taiwan, An Input-Output and Productivity Approach.* Taipei: Joint Commission on Rural Reconstruction.

Inspector General of Customs. 1934–40. *Report on the Trade of China, 1930–40.* Shanghai: Inspector General of Chinese Customs.

Ka-Hoku sangyō kagaku kenkyūjo (The north China industrial scientific research institute). 1937. *Kokumin seifu no nōgyō seisaku* (The agricultural policy of the nationalist government). Publication place unknown: Ka-Hoku sangyō kagaku kenkyūjo.

Kokumuin jitsugyōbu rinji sangyō chōsakyoku (Provisional industrial research bureau in the state enterprise division). 1936. [*Kōtoku gannendo*] *nōson jittai chōsa* (An investigation of rural [village] conditions, 1934), 3 vols. Hsinkyō.

K'ung Tz'u-an. 1965. "Chung kuo liu ta tu shih ti jen k'ou chi ch'i tseng chien" (Population fluctuations of six large Chinese cities), in Hsiang kang Ya tung hsüeh she, ed., *Chung kuo li tai jen k'ou wen t'i lun chi* (Collected essays on China's dynastic population problem), pp. 209–29. Hong Kong: Lung men shu tien.

Mantetsu Hoku-Shi jimmukyoku chōsabu. 1939. *Shintō kinkō ni okeru nōson jittai chōsa hōkoku* (An investigation report of village conditions in the suburbs of Tsingtao). Tsingtao: South Manchurian Railway Company.

Mantetsu Shanhai jimusho chōsashitsu (Shanghai branch of the South Manchurian Railway Company), comp. 1940. *Kōsoshō Taisōken nōson jittai chōsa hōkokusho* (A report of agrarian field investigation in T'ai ts'ang Hsien, Kiangsu). Shanghai: South Manchurian Railway Company.

Mantetsu Shanhai chōsabu. 1941. *Kōsoshō Nantsūken nōson jittai chōsa hōkokusho* (An investigation report of rural conditions in Nan-t'ung Hsien, Kiangsu). Shanghai: South Manchurian Railway Company.

Mantetsu taiheiyō mondai chōsa jumbikai (The survey and preparatory committee on Pacific problems of the South Manchurian Railway Company). 1931. *Nōka no keiei narabi ni keizai jōtai yori mitaru Manshū nōka o chūbu Shina nōka no taisho* (A comparison of Manchurian and central Chinese farms as seen from the economic and managerial aspects of the family farm). Dairen: South Manchurian Railway Company.

Minami Manshū tetsudō kabushiki kaisha. 1938. *Kitō nōson jittai chōsa hōkokusho daiyonpan, Shōreiken* (An investigation of agrarian conditions in northeast Hopei: no. 4, Ch'ang-li Hsien). Darien: South Manchurian Railway Company.

Minami Manshū tetsudō kabushiki kaisha, Shanhai jimusho chōsashitsu (Shanghai branch of the South Manchurian Railway Company), comp. 1941. *Kōsoshō Nantsūken nōson jittai chōsa hōkokusho* (A report of agrarian field investigation in Nan-t'ung Hsien, Kiangsu Province). Shanghai: South Manchurian Railway Company.

Miracle, Marvin P. 1968. " 'Subsistence Agriculture': Analytical Problems and Alternative Concepts," *American Journal of Agricultural Economics*, 50, 2 (May): 292–310.

Murakami, Sutemi. 1941. "Hoku-Shi nōgyō keiei ni okeru sakubutsu hensei to sono shōhinka" (The process of commercialization and changes in crop cultivation in farm management of North China), *Mantetsu Chōsa Geppō* 21, 6 (June): 1–44.

Myers, Ramon H. 1969a. "Taiwan," in Shang, R. T., ed., *Agricultural Development in Asia*, pp. 25–52. Canberra: Australian National University Press.

———. 1969b. "Rural Institutions and Their Influence Upon Agricultural Development in Modern China and Taiwan," *The Journal of the Institute of Chinese Studies*, 2, 2 (September): 349–70.

———. 1970. *The Chinese Peasant Economy: Agricultural Development in Hopei and Shantung, 1890–1949*. Cambridge: Harvard University Press.

———. n.d. The Chinese Peasant Economy: A Comparative Study of Mainland China and Taiwan, 1890–1937. Unpublished manuscript.

Myers, Ramon H. and Ching, Adrienne. 1964. "Agricultural Development in Taiwan under Japanese Colonial Rule," *The Journal of Asian Studies*, 23, 4 (August): 555–70.

Nichi-Man nōsei kenkyūkai (The research committee for Japanese-Manchurian agricultural policy). 1940. *Manshū nōgyō yōran* (A survey of Manchurian agriculture). Hsinkyo: Hsinkyō jimmukyoku.

Nishijima, Sadao. 1966. *Chūgoku keizaishi kenkyū* (Studies in Chinese economic history). Tokyo: Tōkyō daigaku shuppankai.

Otte, Friedrich. 1928. "Sketch of Chinese Agricultural Policy," *Chinese Economic Journal*, 2, 5 (May): 361–72.

Ou Pao-san, 1934. *Chung kuo liang shih tui wai mao i: ch'i ti wei ch'u shih chi pien ch'ien chih yuan yin (1912–1931)* (China's foreign grain trade: its role in foreign trade, general trends, and the reasons for trade changes 1912–31). Shanghai: publisher unknown.

Perkins, Dwight H. 1969. *Agricultural Development in China, 1368–1968*. Chicago: Aldine.

Sarai, Rokurō. 1937. "Chū-Man nōson no okeru kokunai shijō hatten no ichi kōsatsu" (A study of the development of rural markets in central Manchuria), *Mantetsu Chōsa Geppō*, 17, 1 (January): 69–152.

Shand, R. 1965. "The Development of Trade and Specialization in a Primitive Economy," *The Economic Record*, 41, 94 (June): 193–206.

Suzuki, Kohei. 1936. "Kantōshū ni okeru ichi nōson no nōka shūnyū" (Farm-household income in a village of the Kwantung peninsula), *Mantetsu Chōsa Geppō*, 16, 4 (April): 175–202.

Taiwan shokusankyoku nōmuka (Agricultural affairs section of the bureau to promote enterprise in Taiwan). 1933. *Taiwan nōkai yōran* (A survey of farmer associations in Taiwan). Taipei: Taiwan sōtokufu shokusankyoku.

Taiwan sōtokufu shokusankyoku. 1921. *Taiwan nōka shokuryō shōhi chōsa* (Investigation of food consumption of Taiwanese family farms). Taipei: Taiwan sōtokufu shokusankyoku.

Taiwan sōtokufu shokusankyoku. 1923. *Taiwan nōka keizai chōsa* (An economic survey of Taiwanese family farms). Taipei: Taiwan sōtokufu shokusankyoku.

Taiwan sōtokufu shokusankyoku. 1924. *Nōsanbutsu jukyū oyobi nōgyō kinyū chōsa* (A survey of the supply and demand for farm products and agricultural finance). Taipei: Taiwan sōtokufu shokusankyoku.

Tōa keizai chōsakyoku. 1936. *Anjiken Hakkamuson kyūjukyūko no kakei chōsa hōkokusho* (A survey report on the household economy of 99 families in Pai chia wu village of Antzu Hsien, Shansi). Tokyo: Tōa kenkyūjo.

Wharton, Clifton R., Jr. 1969. "Subsistence Agriculture: Concepts and Scope," in Clifton R. Wharton, ed., *Subsistence Agriculture and Economic Development*. Chicago: Aldine.

The Sociology of Irrigation: Two Taiwanese Villages

Brief Introduction of Chia-nan Irrigation Association. 1967. Tainan: Chia-nan Irrigation Association.

Chen Cheng-siang. 1963. *Taiwan: An Economic and Social Geography*, vol. I, Research Report no. 96. Taipei: Fu-min Geographical Institute of Economic Development.

Chia-nan ta-chün hsin-she shih-yeh kai-yao (Principles of recent canal construction in Chia-nan). 1930. Tai-wan Jih-jih Hsin-pao She [in Japanese].

Cohen, Myron L. 1967. "Variations in Complexity Among Chinese Family Groups: The Impact of Modernization," *Transactions of the New York Academy of Sciences*, ser. II, vol. 29, no. 5: 638–44.

Eisenstadt, S. N. 1958. "The Study of Oriental Despotisms as Systems of Total Power," *Journal of Asian Studies*, 17: 435–46.

Gallin, Bernard. 1966. *Hsin Hsing, Taiwan: A Chinese Village in Change*. Berkeley: University of California Press.

Geertz, Clifford. 1970. *Agricultural Involution*. Berkeley: University of California Press.

Hsieh Chiao-min. 1964. *Taiwan—Ilha Formosa*. Washington, D.C.: Butterworth.

Leach, E. R. 1959. "Hydraulic Society in Ceylon," *Past and Present*, 15: 2–25.

Lijphart, Arend. 1968. *The Politics of Accommodation*. Berkeley: University of California Press.

Orenstein, Henry. 1956. "Irrigation, Settlement Pattern, and Social Organization," in Anthony F. C. Wallace, ed., *Selected Papers of the Fifth International Congress of Anthropological and Ethnological Sciences*. Philadelphia: University of Pennsylvania Press.

———. 1965. "Notes on the Ecology of Irrigation Agriculture in Contemporary Peasant Societies," *American Anthropologist*, 67: 15–31.

Pan-American Union. 1955. *Irrigation Civilization: A Comparative Study*. Washington, D.C.

Pasternak, Burton. 1968. "Social Consequences of Equalizing Irrigation Access," *Human Organization*, 27, 4: 332–43.

Report on the 1964 Irrigated Land Survey of Irrigation Associations in Taiwan, The Republic of China. 1965. Taiwan Provincial Water Conservancy Bureau.

Steward, Julian. 1955. *Theory of Culture Change*. Urbana: University of Illinois Press.

Tai-nan Hsien-chih kao tzu-jan chih (Gazetteer of Tainan Hsien, Natural History), vol. 1, no. 1. 1960. Tainan Hsien Wen-hsien Wei-yüan Hui.

Tai-wan Sheng t'ung-chih kao (Taiwan Province Encyclopedia of Geographical and Topical Matters), vol. 4, no. 1. 1955. Taipei: Tai-wan Sheng Wen-hsien Wei-yüan Hui.

Wittfogel, Karl A. 1935. "The Foundations and Stages of Chinese Economic History," *Zeitschrift für Sozialforschung*, 4: 26–60.

———. 1938. *New Light on Chinese Society: An Investigation of China's Socio-Economic Structure*. International Secretariat, Institute of Pacific Relations.

———. 1957. *Oriental Despotism*. New Haven: Yale University Press.

Marketing on the Changhua Plain, Taiwan

Amano Motonosuke. 1953. "Nōson no Kenshi shijō" (Traditional rural markets); "Nōson shijō no Koeki" (Rural Marketing), *Chūgoku nōgyō no shomondai (Problems of Chinese agriculture)* 2: 69–174. Tokyo.

Berry, Brian J. L. 1967. *Geography of Market Centers and Retail Distribution*. Englewood Cliffs, N.J.: Prentice-Hall.

Christaller, Walter. 1966. *Central Places in Southern Germany*. Translated by Carlisle W. Baskin. Englewood Cliffs, N.J.: Prentice-Hall.

Guttman, Louis. 1950. "The Basis for Scalogram Analysis," in S. A. Stouffer *et al.*, *Measurement and Prediction*. Princeton, N.J.: Princeton University Press.

Katō Shigeshi. 1936. "Shindai ni okeru sonchin no teiki ichi" (Rural periodic markets of the Ch'ing dynasty), *Tōyō gakuhō* 23: 153–204.

Marshall, John U. 1969. *The Location of Service Towns*. Toronto: University of Toronto Press.

Menzel, Herbert. 1953. "A New Coefficient for Scalogram Analysis," *Public Opinion Quarterly* 17: 268–80.

Siegal, Sidney. 1956. *Nonparametric Statistics for the Behavioral Sciences*. New York: McGraw-Hill.

Skinner, G. William. 1964. "Marketing and Social Structure in Rural China," Part I, *Journal of Asian Studies* 24, 1: 3–43.

———. 1965. "Marketing and Social Structure in Rural China," Part II, *Journal of Asian Studies* 24, 2: 195–228.

Smith, Arthur H. 1900. *Village Life in China*. London: Oliphant, Anderson, and Ferrier (1970 reprint by Little, Brown, Boston).

Ward, Barbara E. 1967. "Chinese Fishermen in Hong Kong; Their Post-Peasant Economy," in Maurice Freedman, ed., *Social Organization, Essays Presented to Raymond Firth*. Chicago: Aldine.

Yang, Ching-kun. 1944. *A North China Local Market Economy*. New York: Institute of Pacific Relations, International Secretariat.

The Inculcation of Economic Values in Taipei Business Families

Aberle, David F. 1961. "Culture and Socialization," in F. L. K. Hsu, ed., *Psychological Anthropology.* Homewood, Ill.: Dorsey Press.

Albert, Ethel M. 1956. "The Classification of Values: A Method and Illustration," *American Anthropologist* 58: 221–45.

Barber, Bernard. 1957. *Social Stratification: A Comparative Analysis of Structure and Process.* New York: Harcourt, Brace.

Brim, Orville G., Jr. 1959. *Socialization for Child Rearing.* Glencoe: Free Press.

Bronfenbrenner, Urie. 1958. "Socialization and Social Class Through Time and Space," in Eleanor Maccoby *et al.*, eds., *Readings in Social Psychology.* New York: Henry Holt.

Clausen, John A., ed. 1968. *Socialization and Society.* Boston: Little, Brown.

Danziger, Kurt. 1960a. "Independence Training and Social Class in Java," *Journal of Social Psychology* 51: 65–74.

———. 1960b. "Parental Demands and Social Class in Java," *Journal of Social Psychology* 51: 75–86.

Eberhard, Wolfram. 1962. *Social Mobility in Traditional China.* Leiden: E. J. Brill.

Goode, William J. 1959. "The Sociology of the Family," in Robert K. Merton *et al.*, eds., *Sociology Today.* New York: Basic Books.

Hodges, Harold M., Jr. 1964. *Social Stratification: Class in America.* Cambridge, Mass.: Schenkman.

Johnson, Ronald C., Carol Johnson, and Lea Martin. 1961. "Authoritarianism, Occupation, and Sex Role Differentiation of Children," *Child Development* 32: 271–76.

Kluckhohn, Clyde. 1951. "Values and Value-Orientations in the Theory of Action: An Exploration in Definition and Classification," in T. Parsons and E. Shils, eds., *Toward a General Theory of Action.* Cambridge, Mass.: Harvard University Press.

Kohn, Melvin L. 1969. *Class, Occupation and Values.* Homewood, Ill.: Dorsey Press.

Lang, Olga. 1946. *Chinese Family and Society.* New Haven: Yale University Press.

Levy, Marion J., Jr. 1949. *The Family Revolution in Modern China.* Cambridge: Harvard University Press.

Levy, Marion J., Jr., and Shih Kuo-heng. 1949. *The Rise of the Modern Chinese Business Class.* New York: Institute of Pacific Relations.

Maccoby, Eleanor E., ed. 1966. *The Development of Sex Differences.* Stanford: Stanford University Press.

Marsh, Robert M. 1962. "The Venality of Provincial Office in China and in Comparative Perspective," *Comparative Studies in Society and History* 4 (July): 454–66.

Merton, Robert K. 1957. *Social Theory and Social Structure,* revised edition. Glencoe: Free Press.

Miller, Daniel R., and Guy E. Swanson. 1958. *The Changing American Parent.* New York: Wiley.

Olsen, Nancy J. 1971. The Effect of Household Composition on the Child-

Rearing Practices of Taiwanese Families. Unpublished Ph.D. dissertation, Cornell University.

Olsen, Stephen M. 1965. Occupational Values and Choice among High School Boys in Three Communities in Djakarta, Indonesia. Unpublished M.A. thesis, Cornell University.

——. 1971. Family, Occupation, and Values in a Chinese Urban Community. Unpublished Ph.D. dissertation, Cornell University.

Parsons, Talcott. 1937. *The Structure of Social Action*. New York: McGraw-Hill.

——. 1951. *The Social System*. Glencoe: The Free Press.

Pearlin, Leonard I., and Melvin L. Kohn. 1966. "Social Class, Occupation, and Parental Values: A Cross-National Study," *American Sociological Review* 31 (August): 466–79.

Prothro, Edwin T. 1966. "Socialization and Social Class in a Transitional Society," *Child Development* 37: 219–28.

Rosenberg, Morris. 1957. *Occupations and Values*. Glencoe: Free Press.

Ryan, Edward J. 1961. The Value System of a Chinese Community in Java. Unpublished Ph.D. dissertation, Harvard University.

Sigal, Roberta, ed. 1965. *Political socialization*, issue of *Annals of American Academy of Political and Social Science*, September 1965.

Skinner, G. William. 1966. "Filial Sons and Their Sisters: Configuration and Culture in Chinese Families," a paper prepared for the conference on Kinship in Chinese Society, September 15–18, 1966, Greyston House, Riverdale, New York; sponsored by the Subcommittee on Research on Chinese Society of the Joint Committee on Contemporary China of the SSRC and the ACLS (mimeographed).

Statistical Abstract of the Republic of China. 1968. Taipei: Republic of China, Administrative Yüan, Department of Accounts and Statistics.

Statistical Abstract of Taipei Municipality, Number 19. 1965. Taipei Municipal Government, Office of Accounting and Statistics.

Straus, Murray A., and Cecelia E. Sudia. 1965. "Entrepreneurial Orientation of farm, working-class, and middle-class boys," *Rural Sociology* 30: 291–98b.

Sutton, Francis X., et al. 1956. *The American Business Creed*. Cambridge, Mass.: Harvard University Press.

Sutton-Smith, Brian, John M. Roberts, and B. G. Rosenberg. 1964. "Sibling Associations and Role Involvement," *Merrill-Palmer Quarterly of Behavior and Development* 10: 25–38.

Ta Hua wan pao (Chinese News, Taipei). 1961. *T'ai-wan T'ung-lan*. Taipei: Ta hua wan pao she.

Taiwan Demographic Factbook. 1966. Taipei: Taiwan Provincial Government, Department of Civil Affairs.

Thomas, J. L. 1952. "Religious Training in the Roman Catholic Family," *American Journal of Sociology* 57: 178–83.

Williams, Robin M., Jr. 1951. *American Society: A Sociological Interpretation*. New York: Knopf.

Wilson, Richard W. 1967. Childhood Political Socialization in Taiwan. Unpublished Ph.D. dissertation, Princeton University. (Published in 1971 as

Learning to Be Chinese: The Political Socialization of Children in Taiwan.
Cambridge, Mass.: MIT Press.)

Wittfogel, Karl. 1957. *Oriental Despotism.* New Haven: Yale University Press.

Doing Business in Lukang

Burton, Robert A. 1958. "Self-Help, Chinese Style," *American Universities Field Service Reports,* East Asia Series 6, 9 (July).

Chen Cheng-hsiang. 1963. *Taiwan: An Economic and Social Geography.* Taipei: Fu-Min Institute of Economic Development.

Fried, Morton H. 1953. *The Fabric of Chinese Society: A Study of the Social Life of a Chinese County Seat.* New York: Praeger.

Gamble, Sidney D. 1954. *Ting Hsien: A North China Rural Community.* New York: Institute of Pacific Relations (reissued in 1968 by Stanford University Press).

Levy, Marion J., Jr. 1949. *The Family Revolution in Modern China.* Cambridge, Mass.: Harvard University Press.

Pasternak, Burton. 1968. "Atrophy of Patrilineal Bonds in a Chinese Village in Historical Perspective," *Ethnohistory* 15, 3 (Summer).

Ryan, Edward. 1961. The Value System of a Chinese Community in Java. Unpublished Ph.D. dissertation, Harvard University.

Silin, Robert. 1964. Trust and Confidence in a Hong Kong Wholesale Vegetable Market. Unpublished M.A. thesis, University of Hawaii.

Smith, Arthur H. 1900. *Village Life in China.* London: Oliphant, Anderson, and Ferrier.

Tenenbaum, Edward A. 1963. *Taiwan's Turning Point.* Washington, D.C.: Continental-Allied.

T'ien Ju-k'ang. 1953. *The Chinese of Sarawak: A Study of Social Structure.* London: London School of Economics Monographs on Social Anthropology, 12.

Ward, Barbara E. 1960. "Cash or Credit Crops? An Examination of Some Implications of Peasant Commercial Production with Special Reference to the Multiplicity of Traders and Middlemen," *Economic Development and Cultural Change* 8, 2 (Jan.).

Wolf, Margery. 1970. "Child Training and the Chinese Family," in Maurice Freedman, ed., *Family and Kinship in Chinese Society.* Stanford: Stanford University Press.

Marketing and Credit in a Hong Kong Wholesale Market

Freedman, Maurice. 1957. *Chinese Family and Marriage in Singapore.* London: Her Majesty's Stationery Office.

———. 1961. "The Handling of Money: A Note on the Background of the Economic Sophistication of Overseas Chinese," in T. H. Silcock, ed., *Readings in Malayan Economics.* Singapore: Eastern Universities Press.

Fried, Morton H. 1953. *The Fabric of Chinese Society.* New York: Praeger.

Geertz, Clifford. 1963. *Peddlers and Princes.* Chicago: University of Chicago Press.

Lang, Olga. 1946. *Chinese Family and Society*. New Haven: Yale University Press.

Levy, Marion J., Jr. 1949. *The Family Revolution in Modern China*. Cambridge, Mass.: Harvard University Press.

Mayer, Bernard F. and Theodore F. Wempe. 1932. *The Student's Cantonese-English Dictionary*. New York: Field Afar Press.

Ryan, Edward. 1961. The Value System of a Chinese Community in Java. Unpublished Ph.D. dissertation, Harvard University.

Silin, Robert H. 1965. Trust and Confidence in a Hong Kong Wholesale Vegetable Market. Unpublished M.A. thesis, University of Hawaii.

T'ien Ju-K'ang. 1953. *The Chinese of Sarawak*. London: London School of Economics Monographs on Social Anthropology, 12.

Topley, Marjorie. 1964. "Capital, Savings and Credit among Indigenous Rice Farmers and Immigrant Vegetable Farmers in Hong Kong's New Territories," in Raymond Firth and B. S. Yamey, eds., *Capital Savings and Credit in Peasant Societies*. London: Allen and Unwin.

———. 1969. "The Role of Savings and Wealth Among Hong Kong Chinese," in Ian C. Jarvie and Joseph Agassi, eds., *Hong Kong: A Society in Transition*. New York: Praeger.

A Small Factory in Hong Kong:
Some Aspects of Its Internal Organization

Chou, K. R. 1966. *The Hong Kong Economy: A Miracle of Growth*. Hong Kong: Academic Publications.

Character List

Character List

Amano Motonosuke 天野元之助
An-ning 安寧

ch'a-chia 拆家
chan ssu 棧司
Ch'an shih yao lueh 蠶事要略
Chang Ch'un-hua 張春華
chang fang 帳房
Chang Han 張瀚
Changhua 彰化
Chang Lü-hsiang 張履祥
chang pu kuo-chang 帳簿過帳
chang t'ou 長頭
ch'ang 場
Ch'ang-chou Hsien 長州縣
ch'ang-shang 場商
che-chia 折價
chen 鎮
Chen-hai 鎮海
Chen-tse 震澤
Ch'en 陳
Ch'en Ch'i-yuan 陳啓沅
Ch'en Hung-Mou 陳宏謀
Ch'en Kan 陳淦
cheng 正
cheng-chia 正價

Cheng-ting fu 正定府
Cheng-yang Hsien 正陽縣
cheng-yin chih chia 正引之價
ch'eng 承
chi-ch'a 稽查
chi-hu 機戶
chi-t'ien 基田
chi-yin 積引
Ch'i-chiang Hsien 綦江縣
Ch'i-ch'iao 憩橋
Ch'i-hsia Hsien 捿霞縣
ch'i-ssu 緝私
chia 甲 (unit of land)
chia 家 (family; specialist)
Chia-nan 嘉南
Chia-nan Ta-chün Hsin-she Shih-yeh Kai-yao 嘉南大均新設事業概要
Chia-ting Hsien 嘉定縣
Chiang p'ing 江平
Chiang-su sheng Ming Ch'ing i lai pei k'o tzu liao hsuan chi 江蘇省明清以來碑刻資料選集
chien-chia ti-ssu 減價敵私
ch'ien chuang 錢莊
ch'ien p'iao 錢票
ch'ien p'u 錢鋪

ch'ien tien　錢店
chih fang tien　職方典
Chih tsao chü　織造局
chin　斤 (catty)
chin　錦 (brocade)
Chin-kuei　金匱
chin lung chi　進籠雞
ch'in-hsin　勤心
Ch'in Jun-ch'ing　秦潤卿
ching che kuo-chang　經摺過帳
ching-cheng　競爭
ching chuang　京莊
ching hang　經行
ching shou　經手
Ch'ing-yang Hsien　青陽縣
ch'ing yeh hang　青葉行
Chiu-chiang　九江
Chiu Ta　久大
Ch'o-shui　濁水
ch'ou　綢
ch'ou ling t'ou　綢領頭
Chu-ching chen　洙涇鎮
Chu Hua　褚華
Chu Kuo-chen　朱國楨
chu-li　主力
Chu Shih　朱軾
chu-tan　硃單
chü jen　舉人
Ch'ü Ta-chün　屈大均
chüan　卷 (section of a book)
chüan　絹 (gauze; silk fabric used
　to pay summer tax)
chuang-hu　庄戶
chuang p'iao　莊票
Chung Hua-min　鍾化民
chung-pao　中飽
Chung-she　中社
ch'ung-hsiao　統銷

daifukuchō　大福帳

Fan-ch'ang fu　繁昌府

Fan Lien　范濂
fang　坊
fang chang chu jen　放帳主任
fang chang fang k'uan yüan　放帳
　放款員
Fang Chieh-t'ang　方介堂
Fang Jun-chai　方潤齋
Feng-hua Hsien　奉化縣
Feng Ping　馮幷
Feng Wang-ch'ing　馮望鄉
fu shou　副手
Fujii Hiroshi　藤井宏

hang p'iao　行票
hao pang-shou　好擘手
Hatano Yoshihiro　波多野善大
Ho Ch'ang-ling　賀長齡
hou-pi-shan　後壁山
Hsi She-Jen　席舍人
hsia-shui　夏稅
hsiao-ch'ü　小區
hsiao ling t'ou　小領頭
hsiao-p'iao　小票
hsiao-tsu　小組
hsiang　鄉
hsiang ssu hang　鄉絲行
Hsieh　謝
hsin fang　信房
hsin-yung　信用
Hsing-t'ang Hsien　行唐縣
Hsiung Chien-ku　熊澗谷
Hsü　徐
Hsü Hsien-chung　徐獻忠
Hsü Kuang-ch'i　徐光啓
hsün　旬
Hu　胡
Hu-chou　湖州
Hu Kuang-yung　胡光墉
hu-t'u　胡塗
hua chuang　划莊
Hua-t'ing Hsien　華亭縣
huai　槐

Huai-nan 淮南
Huai-pei 淮北
Huang Ch'ao 黃巢
Huang Tso-ch'ing 黃佐鄉
hui-hua tsung-hui 匯劃總會
Hun 焜
Hung 洪

i 易 (to exchange)
i 議 (advice)
Imura Kozen 井村哮全

jen-ch'ing 人情
jen-yuan 人緣
ju-chui 入贅
Ju-kao Hsien 如皋縣
Jui-an Hsien 瑞安縣
Jui-chin Hsien 瑞金縣
jung-hsiao 融銷

kai yin kuo-chang 蓋印過帳
k'ai chung fa 開中法
kan 敢
kan-ch'ing 感情
k'an-ho 勘合
k'an-pu 看布
k'an-t'ien t'ien 看天田
kang 綱
kang-an 綱岸
kang-fa 綱法
k'ao-ch'eng 考成
Katō Shigeshi 加藤繁
ko 箇
k'o-hang 客行
Koizumi Teizō 小泉貞三
k'u p'ing 庫平
k'u-p'ing wen-yin 庫平紋銀
kuan-li 管理
Kuang hang 廣行
kuang yen-ch'an 廣鹽產
kuei yin kuo-chang 規銀過帳
kung tuan 貢緞

kuo-chang 過帳

lai-wang 來往
lan 欄
li 力 (exert oneself fully)
li 里 (unit of distance)
Li Chung-shun 李衷純
Li Pa 李拔
li-shang pien-min 利商便民
li-shao fa-yen 利少法嚴
Li Yeh-t'ing 李也亭
liang 兩
Liang-huai 兩淮
lieh-ssu 列肆
lien 職
Lin-ch'ing Hsien 臨清縣
Lin-feng-ying 林鳳營
Lin-pien 林邊
lin-ssu 隣私
ling 綾
ling kung ssu liang pien 令公私兩
　便
Liu-chia 六甲
Liu Yen 劉晏
Lou 樓
Lu-an Prefecture 潞安府
Lukang 鹿港
Jü Jo 呂若

ma-fan 蔴繁
mai-pu yen-hang 買補鹽行
mao 毛
Mao K'un 茅坤
miao yeh 秒葉
min 民
min chien 民間
min-ch'ing 民情
min hsin chü 民信局
Ming-chou 明州
Miyashita Saburō 宮下三郎
Miyazaki Ichisada 宮崎市定
mou 畝

mu-yu　幕友

Nakahara Teruo　中原晃雄
Nan-hsün　南潯
Nan-hui Hsien　南匯縣
nan keng nü chih　男耕女織
Nan-kung Hsien　南宮縣
nan p'ai　南派
nan pang　南幫
nan shih　南市
nei chang fang　內帳房
nei-hang jen　內行人
nei-shang　內商
Nei Yüan　內園
Nishijima Sadao　西嶋定生
Nung sang chi yao　農桑輯要
Nung shu　農書

p'ai　派
pang　幫
pao　包
pao-chia　保甲
Pao Shih-ch'en　包世臣
pao-t'ou　包頭
p'ao chieh　跑街
pei p'ai　北派
pei pang　北幫
pei shih　北市
P'eng Tse-i　彭澤益
pi　弊
P'i　匹
piao　標
pien-ch'ao　邊鈔
pien-shang　邊商
pien-yin　邊引
p'ing-tung　屏東
pu-chuang　布庄
pu i ting　不一定
Pu Nung shu　補農書
P'u-yuan　濮園

san chien　三肩

sang chi　桑基
sha　紗
shang-ssu　商私
Shang-yü　上虞
shao chih wei fa　稍知畏法
Shao-hsing　紹興
Sheng-tse　盛澤
Shiba Yoshinobu　斯波義信
shih　石
Shih　世
shih-an　食岸
shih chang　市丈
shih chin　市斤
shih huo tien　食貨典
shih-lien　石蓮
Shih Min-hsiung　施敏雄
shih-yen　食鹽
shih-yen-ti　食鹽地
Shou Shih t'ung k'ao　授時通考
Shu chin　蜀錦
shu-ssu　熟似
Shuang-lin　雙林
shui-shang　水商
Shun-te Hsien　順德縣
so-pu　梭布
Ssu-ming Kung So　四明公所
Su-ning Hsien　肅寧縣
Su Tung-p'o　蘇東坡
Sudo Yoshiyuki　周藤吉之
Sui　歲
Sung-chiang Prefecture　松江府

ta chi　大祭
Ta hua wan pao　大華晚報
ta-p'ai　大牌
Ta-t'ieh　打鐵
ta t'ung hang　大同行
tai-yün　帶運
T'ai hu　太湖
T'ai-nan Hsien-chih kao　臺南縣志稿
T'ai-nan Hsien Wen-hsien Wei-yüan Hui　臺南縣文獻委員會

t'ai shang huang　太上皇

T'ai-wan Jih-jih Hsin-pao She　臺灣
日日新報社

T'ai-wan Sheng T'ung-chih Kao　臺
灣省通志稿

T'ai-wan Sheng Wen-hsien Wei-yüan
Hui　臺灣省文献委員會

tan　單 (set, group)

tan　擔 (picul, unit of account for
the picul)

t'ang-li　帑利

T'ao Chu　陶澍

t'ao-ta yu-cheng　套搭預徵

Te-p'ing Hsien　德平縣

Teng-chou Prefecture　登州府

Terada Takanobu　寺田隆信

t'i-yin　提引

ting　丁

Ting-hai Hsien　定海縣

Ting Hsien　定縣

t'ing　亭, 墩

t'ing-ch'ang　墩場

Tsai-hsiang　宰相

tsai-lai　在來

ts'ai　才

ts'ang-k'an　倉勘

tsao-chia　阜莢

tsao-chiao　阜角

tsao-ti　竈地

tsao-ting　竈丁

Ts'ao Shih-p'in　曹時聘

ts'ao-tang　草蕩

tseng-wen　曾文

Tsou Hsi-ch'un　鄒錫淳

tsou-hsiao-ts'e　奏銷冊

tsu-chih　祖制

tsung-shang　總商

tu　督

Tu Ch'i-t'u　席啟圖

t'u ssu　土絲

tuan　緞

Tuan Kuang-ch'ing　段光清

tui fang　兌房

t'ui-hsieh　推卸

t'un-hu　囤戶

Tung　董

Tung Hsien-Liang　董憲良

Tung Hung-tu　董宏度

Tung Li-chou　董蠡舟

Tung-t'ing　洞庭

t'ung-hsia　統轄

t'ung-hsiang　同鄉

t'ung-hsing　同姓

t'ung-hsueh　同學

t'ung-yeh kung-hui　同業公會

t'ung-yeh t'uan-t'i　同業團体

tzu-hao　字號

Tz'u-ch'i　慈谿

wai chang fang　外帳房

wai-chih wai-hsiao　外支外銷

Wang Chen　王禎

Wang Ch'i　王圻

Wang Yang-ming　王陽明

Wang Yuan　汪琬

wei　圍

wei-yüan　委員

Wei Yüan　魏源

Wei-yüan Hsien　威遠縣

Wu-chiang Hsien　吳江縣

Wu-chin Hsien　武進縣

Wu-hsi Hsien　無錫縣

Wu-ni ching　烏泥涇

Wu San-kuei　吳三桂

Wu-shan-t'ou　烏山頭

wu-tung　梧桐

ya tzu kuo-chang　軋字過帳

Yabuuchi Kiyoshi　藪內清

Yamaguchi Michiko　山口廸子

Yeh　葉

Yeh Meng-chu　葉夢珠

yeh sang che　業桑者

yen　元

Yen　嚴
Yen-fa-k'ao　鹽法考
yen-k'o　鹽課
yin　引
yin-ch'ao　引鈔
yin-chia　引價
yin fang　銀房
Yin Hsien　鄞縣
Yokoyama Suguru　橫山英
Yoshida Mitsukuni　吉田光邦
yu-tun　尤墩
Yü Ch'ang　豫昌
yü-k'o　餘課

Yü-tz'u Hsien　榆次縣
Yü-yao　餘姚
yü-yen chia-yin　餘鹽價銀
yü-yen chih chia　餘鹽之價
yü-yen chih yin　餘鹽之銀
yü-yin　餘銀
yüan　垣　(salt depots)
yüan　圓　(monetary unit)
Yüan　袁
Yüan Chüeh　袁桷
Yüan-ho Hsien　元和縣
Yung chiang　甬江

Index

Index